T0338286

Principles of Sequencing
and Scheduling

Wiley Series in Operations Research and Management Science

Operations Research and Management Science (ORMS) is a broad, interdisciplinary branch of applied mathematics concerned with improving the quality of decisions and processes and is a major component of the global modern movement towards the use of advanced analytics in industry and scientific research. The *Wiley Series in Operations Research and Management Science* features a broad collection of books that meet the varied needs of researchers, practitioners, policy makers, and students who use or need to improve their use of analytics. Reflecting the wide range of current research within the ORMS community, the Series encompasses application, methodology, and theory and provides coverage of both classical and cutting edge ORMS concepts and developments. Written by recognized international experts in the field, this collection is appropriate for students as well as professionals from private and public sectors including industry, government, and nonprofit organization who are interested in ORMS at a technical level. The Series is comprised of four sections: Analytics; Decision and Risk Analysis; Optimization Models; and Stochastic Models.

Advisory Editors • Optimization Models
Lawrence V. Snyder, *Lehigh University*
Ya-xiang Yuan, Chinese Academy of Sciences

Founding Series Editor
James J. Cochran, University of Alabama

Analytics
Yang and Lee • *Healthcare Analytics: From Data to Knowledge to Healthcare Improvement*
Attoh-Okine • *Big Data and Differential Privacy: Analysis Strategies for Railway Track Engineering*
Kong and Zhang • *Decision Analytics and Optimization in Disease Prevention and Treatment*

Forthcoming Titles
Dai • *Handbook of Healthcare Analytics: Theoretical Minimum for Conducting 21st Century Research on Healthcare Operations*

Decision and Risk Analysis
Barron • *Game Theory: An Introduction*, Second Edition
Brailsford, Churilov, and Dangerfield • *Discrete-Event Simulation and System Dynamics for Management Decision Making*
Johnson, Keisler, Solak, Turcotte, Bayram, and Drew • *Decision Science for Housing and Community Development: Localized and Evidence-Based Responses to Distressed Housing and Blighted Communities*
Mislick and Nussbaum • *Cost Estimation: Methods and Tools*

Forthcoming Titles
Aleman and Carter • *Healthcare Engineering*

Optimization Models
Ghiani, Laporte, and Musmanno • *Introduction to Logistics Systems Management*, Second Edition
Bozorg-Haddad • *Meta-heuristic and Evolutionary Algorithms for Engineering Optimization*
Baker and Trietsch • *Principles of Sequencing and Scheduling*, Second Edition

Forthcoming Titles
Smith • *Learning Operations Research Through Puzzles and Games*
Tone • *Advances in DEA Theory and Applications: With Examples in Forecasting Models*

Stochastic Models
Ibe • *Random Walk and Diffusion Processes*

Forthcoming Titles
Donohue, Katok, and Leider • *The Handbook of Behavioral Operations*
Matis • *Applied Markov Based Modelling of Random Processes*

Principles of Sequencing and Scheduling

Second Edition

Kenneth R. Baker and Dan Trietsch

Registered Office
John Wiley & Sons, Inc., 111 River Street, Hoboken, NJ 07030, USA

Editorial Office
111 River Street, Hoboken, NJ 07030, USA

For details of our global editorial offices, customer services, and more information about Wiley products visit us at www.wiley.com.

Wiley also publishes its books in a variety of electronic formats and by print-on-demand. Some content that appears in standard print versions of this book may not be available in other formats.

Library of Congress Cataloging-in-Publication Data

Names: Baker, Kenneth R., 1943– author. | Trietsch, Dan, author.
Title: Principles of sequencing and scheduling / Kenneth R Baker, Dan Trietsch.
Description: Second edition. | Hoboken, NJ, USA : John Wiley & Sons, Inc., [2019] | Series: Wiley series in operations research and management science | Includes bibliographical references and index. |
Identifiers: LCCN 2018019714 (print) | LCCN 2018021976 (ebook) | ISBN 9781119262589 (Adobe PDF) | ISBN 9781119262596 (ePub) | ISBN 9781119262565 (hardcover)
Subjects: LCSH: Production scheduling.
Classification: LCC TS157.5 (ebook) | LCC TS157.5 .B35 2019 (print) | DDC 658.5/3–dc23
LC record available at https://lccn.loc.gov/2018019714

Cover design: Wiley
Cover image: © Slavica/iStockphoto

Set in 10/12pt Warnock by SPi Global, Pondicherry, India

Printed in the United States of America

V10014126_091919

Contents

Preface

This textbook provides an introduction to the concepts, methods, and results of scheduling theory. It is written for graduate students and advanced undergraduates who are studying scheduling, as well as for practitioners who are interested in the knowledge base on which modern scheduling applications have been built. The coverage assumes no background in scheduling, and for stochastic scheduling topics, we assume only a familiarity with basic probability concepts. Among other things, our first appendix summarizes the important properties of the probability distributions we use.

We view scheduling theory as practical theory, and we have made sure to emphasize the practical aspects of our topic coverage. Thus, we provide algorithms that implement some of the solution concepts we describe, and we use spreadsheet models where appropriate to calculate solutions to scheduling problems. Especially when tackling stochastic scheduling problems, we must balance the need for tractability and the need for realism. Thus, we stress heuristics and simulation-based approaches when optimization methods and analytic tools fall short. We also provide many examples in the text along with computational exercises among our end-of-chapter problems.

Coverage of the Text

The material in this book can support a variety of course designs. An introductory-level course covering only deterministic scheduling can draw from Chapters 1–5, 8–10, 12–14, and 16–17. A one-quarter course that covers both deterministic and stochastic topics can use Chapters 1–11 and possibly 15. Our own experience suggests that the entire book can support a two-quarter sequence, especially with supplementary material we provide online.

The book contains two appendices. The first reviews the salient properties of well-known probability distributions, as background for our coverage of stochastic models. It also covers selected topics on which some of our advanced coverage is based. The second appendix includes background derivations related to the "critical ratio rule," which arises frequently in safe scheduling models.

Our coverage is substantial compared with that in other scheduling textbooks, but it is not encyclopedic. Our goal is to enable the reader to delve into the research literature (or in some cases, the practice literature) with enough background to appreciate the contributions of state-of-the-art papers.

For the reader who is interested in a more comprehensive link to the research literature than our text covers, we provide a set of online Research Notes. The Research Notes represent unique material that expands the book's coverage and builds an intellectual bridge to the research literature on sequencing and scheduling. In organizing the text, we wanted to proceed from simple to complex and to maintain technological order. As much as possible, each new result is based only on previous coverage. As a secondary guiding principle, the text minimizes any discussion of connections between models, thus keeping the structure simple. Scheduling theory did not develop along these same lines, however, so research-oriented readers may wish to look at the bigger picture without adhering to these principles with the same fidelity. One purpose of our Research Notes is to offer such a picture. Another purpose is to provide some historical background. We also mention open research questions that we believe should be addressed by future research. Occasionally, we provide more depth on topics that are not sufficiently central to justify inclusion in the text itself. Finally, for readers who will be reading research papers directly from the source, we occasionally need to discuss topics that are not crucial to the text but arise frequently in the literature.

Historical Background

This book is an updated version of Baker's text, so some historical background is appropriate at the outset. *Introduction to Sequencing and Scheduling* (ISS) was published by John Wiley & Sons in 1973 and became the dominant textbook in scheduling theory. A generation of instructors and graduate students relied on this book as the key source of information for advanced work in sequencing and scheduling. Later books stayed abreast of developments in the field, but as references in journal articles would indicate, most of those books were never treated as fundamental to the study of scheduling.

Sales of ISS slowed by 1980, and Wiley eventually gave up the copyright. Although they found a publishing house interested in buying the title, Baker took back the copyright. For several years, he provided generous photocopying privileges to instructors who were still interested in using the material, even though some of it had become outdated. Finally, in the early 1990s, Baker revised the book. The sequel was *Elements of Sequencing and Scheduling*

(ESS), self-published in 1992 and expanded in 1995. Less encyclopedic than its predecessor, ESS was rewritten to be readable and accessible to the student while still providing an intellectual springboard to the field of scheduling theory. Without advertising or sales reps, and without any association with a textbook publishing house, ESS sold several hundred copies in paperback through 2007. Another generation of advanced undergraduate and graduate students used the book in courses, while other graduate students were simply assigned the book as a required reading for independent studies or qualifying exams. Current research articles in scheduling continue to cite ISS and/or ESS as the source of basic knowledge on which today's research is being built.

Perhaps the most important topic not covered in ESS was stochastic scheduling. With the exception of the chapter on job shop simulations, almost all the coverage in ESS dealt with deterministic models. In the last 15 years, research has focused as much on stochastic models as on deterministic models, and stochastic scheduling has become a significant part of the field. But traditional approaches to stochastic scheduling have their limitations, and new approaches are currently being developed. One important line of work introduces the notion of safe scheduling, an approach pioneered by Trietsch and others, and more recently extended in joint work by Baker and Trietsch. This book updates the coverage of ESS and adds coverage of safe scheduling as well as traditional stochastic scheduling. Because the new material comes from active researchers, the book surpasses competing texts in terms of its timeliness. And because the book retains the readability of its earlier versions, it should be the textbook of choice for instructors of scheduling courses. Finally, its title reinforces the experiences of two generations of students and scholars, providing a thread that establishes this volume, now in its second edition, as the latest update of a classic text.

New in the Second Edition

The second edition adds coverage of two major advances in stochastic scheduling and also addresses a few other new topics. One major development involves the application of branch and bound techniques and mathematical programming models to some safe scheduling problems. That new work, incorporated in Chapters 7 and 8 shows that the toolkit developed for deterministic scheduling can be applied to safe scheduling as well. The second major development builds on the validation of lognormal distributions for various empirical data sets. That new work implies that we can implement the full spectrum of analytics and modeling to scheduling, most importantly in project scheduling. Accordingly, Chapter 18 is a new chapter devoted to project analytics. The previous Chapter 18 is now Chapter 19, with an expanded coverage of hierarchical safe scheduling for projects. We also expanded Appendix A to include project analytics background material, including coverage of mixtures, which occur often, especially in projects. We also added a section on the lognormal tail distribution to Appendix B. Chapter 6 now includes a section on fuzzy scheduling and on robust scheduling. These approaches have been promoted as alternatives to stochastic scheduling that ostensibly avoid the need to fit stochastic distributions to observed processing times, but we argue that the distribution-based approach remains the most useful one. That argument is especially valid now that stochastic scheduling models in general, and safe scheduling models in particular, can rely on validated distribution models.

Acknowledgments

We wish to acknowledge Lilit Mazmanyan of the American University of Armenia for her assistance with many detailed aspects of the first-edition's preparation. We also wish to acknowledge a set of first-edition reviewers who provided guidance to our editors as well as anonymous comments and suggestions to us. This set includes Edwin Cheng (The Hong Kong Polytechnic University), Zhi-Long Chen (University of Maryland), Chung-Yee Lee (Hong Kong University of Science and Technology), Michael Magazine (University of Cincinnati), Stephen Powell (Dartmouth College), and Scott Webster (Syracuse University).

1

Introduction

1.1 Introduction to Sequencing and Scheduling

Scheduling is a term in our everyday vocabulary, although we may not always have a good definition of it in mind. Actually, it's not scheduling that is a common concept in our everyday life; rather it is *schedules*. A schedule is a tangible plan or document, such as a bus schedule or a class schedule. A schedule usually tells us when things are supposed to happen; it shows us a plan for the timing of certain activities and answers the question, "If all goes well, when will a particular event take place?" Suppose we are interested in when dinner will be served or when a bus will depart. In these instances, the event we are interested in is the completion of a particular activity, such as preparing dinner, or the start of a particular activity such as a bus trip. Answers to the "when" question usually come to us with information about timing. Dinner is scheduled to be served at 6:00 p.m., the bus is scheduled to depart at 8:00 a.m., and so on. However, an equally useful answer might be in terms of sequence rather than timing: That is, dinner will be served as soon as the main course is baked, or the bus will depart right after cleaning and maintenance are finished. Thus, the "when" question can be answered by timing or by sequence information obtained from the schedule.

If we take into account that some events are unpredictable, then changes may occur in a schedule. Thus, we may say that the bus leaves at 8:00 a.m. unless it is delayed for cleaning and maintenance, or we may leave the condition implicit and just say that the bus is scheduled to leave at 8:00 a.m. If we make allowances for uncertainty when we schedule cleaning and maintenance, then passengers can trust that the bus will leave at 8:00 a.m. with some confidence. Using a time buffer (or *safety time*) helps us cope with uncertainty.

Principles of Sequencing and Scheduling, Second Edition. Kenneth R. Baker and Dan Trietsch.
© 2019 John Wiley & Sons, Inc. Published 2019 by John Wiley & Sons, Inc.

Intuitively, we think of scheduling as the process of generating the schedule, although we seldom stop to consider what the details of that process might be. In fact, although we think of a schedule as something tangible, the process of scheduling seems intangible, at least until we consider it in some depth. For example, we often approach the problem in two steps: sequencing and scheduling. In the first step, we plan a sequence or decide how to select the next task. In the second step, we plan the start time, and perhaps the completion time, of each task. The determination of safety time is part of the second step.

Preparing a dinner and doing the laundry are good examples of everyday scheduling problems. They involve tasks to be carried out, the tasks are well specified, and particular resources are required – a cook and an oven for dinner preparation and a washer and a dryer for laundry. Scheduling problems in industry have similar elements: they contain a set of tasks to be carried out and a set of resources available to perform those tasks. Given tasks and resources, together with some information about uncertainties, the general problem is to determine the timing of the tasks while recognizing the capability of the resources. This scheduling problem usually arises within a decision-making hierarchy in which it follows some earlier, more basic decisions. Dinner preparation, for example, typically requires a specification of the menu items, recipes for those items, and information on how many portions are needed. In industry, analogous decisions are usually part of the *planning* function. Among other things, the planning function might describe the design of a company's products, the technology available for making and testing the required components, and the volumes that are required. In short, the planning function determines the resources available for production and the tasks to be scheduled.

In the scheduling process, we need to know the type and the amount of each resource so that we can determine when the tasks can feasibly be accomplished. When we specify the tasks and resources, we effectively define the boundary of the scheduling problem. In addition, we describe each task in terms of such information as its resource requirement, its duration, the earliest time at which it may start, and the time at which it is due to complete. If the task duration is uncertain, we may want to suppress that uncertainty when stating the problem. We should also describe any logical constraints (precedence restrictions) that exist among the tasks. For example, in describing the scheduling problem for several loads of laundry, we should specify that each load requires washing to be completed before drying begins.

Along with resources and tasks, a scheduling problem contains an objective function. Ideally, the objective function should consist of all costs that depend on scheduling decisions. In practice, however, such costs are often difficult to measure or even to completely identify. The major operating costs – and the most readily identifiable – are determined by the planning function, while scheduling-related costs are difficult to isolate and often tend to appear fixed. Nevertheless, three types of decision-making goals seem to be prevalent in scheduling: *turnaround, timeliness,* and *throughput.* Turnaround measures the time required to complete a task. Timeliness measures the conformance of a particular task's completion to a given deadline. Throughput measures the amount of work completed during a fixed period of time. The first two goals need further elaboration, because although we can speak of turnaround or timeliness for a given task, scheduling problems require a performance measure for the entire set of tasks in a schedule. Throughput, in contrast, is already a measure that applies to the entire set. As we develop the subject of scheduling in the following chapters, we will elaborate on the specific objective functions that make these three goals operational.

We describe a scheduling problem by providing information about tasks, resources, and an objective function. However, finding a solution is often a fairly complex matter, and formal problem-solving approaches are helpful. Formal models help us first to understand the scheduling problem and then to find a good solution systematically. For example, one of the simplest and most widely used models is the *Gantt chart*, which is an analog representation of a schedule. In its basic form, the Gantt chart displays resource allocation over time, with specific resources shown along the vertical axis and a time scale shown along the horizontal axis. The basic Gantt chart assumes that processing times are known with certainty, as in Figure 1.1.

A chart such as Figure 1.1 helps us to visualize a schedule and its detailed elements because resources and tasks show up clearly. With a Gantt chart, we can discover information about a given schedule by analyzing geometric relationships. In addition, we can rearrange tasks on the chart to obtain comparative information about alternative schedules. In this way, the Gantt chart serves as an aid for measuring performance and comparing schedules as well as for visualizing the problem in the first place. In this book, we will examine graphical, algebraic, spreadsheet, and simulation models, in addition to the Gantt

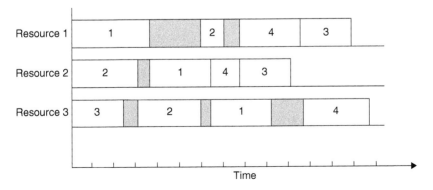

Figure 1.1 A Gantt chart.

chart, all of which help us analyze and compare schedules. In essence, models help us formalize the otherwise intangible process we call scheduling.

Many of the early developments in the field of scheduling were motivated by problems arising in manufacturing. Therefore, it was natural to employ the vocabulary of manufacturing when describing scheduling problems. Now, although scheduling work is of considerable significance in many nonmanufacturing areas, the terminology of manufacturing is still frequently used. Thus, resources are usually called *machines* and tasks are called *jobs*. Sometimes, jobs may consist of several elementary tasks called *operations*. The environment of the scheduling problem is called the *job shop*, or simply, the *shop*. For example, if we encounter a scheduling problem faced by underwriters processing insurance policies, we could describe the situation generically as an insurance "shop" that involves the processing of policy "jobs" by underwriter "machines."

1.2 Scheduling Theory

Scheduling theory is concerned primarily with mathematical models that relate to the process of scheduling. The development of useful models, which leads in turn to solution techniques and practical insights, has been the continuing interface between theory and practice. The theoretical perspective is also largely a quantitative approach, one that attempts to capture problem structure in mathematical form. In particular, this quantitative approach begins with a description of resources and tasks and translates decision-making goals into an explicit objective function.

We categorize the major scheduling models by specifying the resource configuration and the nature of the tasks. For instance, a model may contain one machine or several machines. If it contains one machine, jobs are likely to be single-stage activities, whereas multiple machine models usually involve jobs with multiple stages. In either case, machines may be available in unit amounts or in parallel. In addition, if the set of jobs available for scheduling does not change over time, the system is called *static*, in contrast to cases in which new jobs appear over time, where the system is called *dynamic*. Traditionally, static models have proven to be more tractable than dynamic models and have been studied more extensively. Although dynamic models would appear to be more important for practical application, static models often capture the essence of dynamic systems, and the analysis of static problems frequently uncovers valuable insights and sound heuristic principles that are useful in dynamic situations. Finally, when conditions are assumed to be known with certainty, the model is called *deterministic*. On the other hand, when we recognize uncertainty with explicit probability distributions, the model is called *stochastic*.

Two kinds of *feasibility* constraints are commonly found in scheduling problems. First, limits exist on the capacity of machines, and second, technological restrictions exist on the order in which some jobs can be performed. A *solution* to a scheduling problem is any feasible resolution of these two types of constraints, so that "solving" a scheduling problem amounts to answering two kinds of questions:

- Which resources should be allocated to perform each task?
- When should each task be performed?

In other words, a scheduling problem gives rise to allocation questions and sequencing questions. From the start, the scheduling literature has relied on mathematical models to help answer such questions. In more recent developments, referred to as *safe scheduling*, the models use safety time to mitigate disruptions due to uncertainty.

Traditionally, many scheduling problems have been viewed as problems in optimization subject to constraints – specifically, problems in allocation and sequencing. Sometimes, scheduling is purely allocation (e.g. choosing the product mix with limited resources), and in such cases mathematical programming models are usually appropriate for determining optimal decisions. These general techniques are described in many available textbooks and are not emphasized in our coverage. At other times, scheduling is purely sequencing. In these cases, the problems are unique to scheduling theory and account for much of our emphasis in the chapters that follow.

The theory of scheduling also includes a variety of methodologies. Indeed, the scheduling field has become a focal point for the development, application, and evaluation of combinatorial techniques, simulation procedures, and heuristic solution approaches. The selection of an appropriate method depends mainly on the nature of the model and the choice of objective function. In some cases, it makes sense to consider alternative methods. For this reason, it is important to study methodologies as well as models.

A useful perspective on the relation of scheduling problems and their solution techniques comes from developments in a branch of computer science known as *complexity theory*. The notion of complexity refers to the computing effort required by a solution algorithm. Computing effort is described by order-of-magnitude notation. For example, suppose we use a particular algorithm to solve a problem of size n. (Technically, n denotes the amount of information needed to specify the problem.) The number of computations required by the algorithm is typically bounded from above by a function of n. If the order of magnitude of this function is polynomial as n gets large, then we say the algorithm is *polynomial*. For instance, if the function has order of magnitude n^2, denoted $O(n^2)$, then the algorithm is polynomial. On the other hand, if the function is $O(2^n)$, then the algorithm is nonpolynomial (in this case, exponential). Other things being equal, we prefer to use a polynomial algorithm because as n grows large, polynomial algorithms are ultimately faster.

A class of problems called *NP-complete* problems includes many well-known and difficult combinatorial problems. These problems are equivalent in the sense that if one of them can be solved by a polynomial algorithm, then so can the others. However, many years of research by mathematicians and computer scientists have not yielded a polynomial algorithm for any problem in this class, and the conjecture is that no such algorithm exists. Optimization problems as difficult as these, or even more difficult, are called *NP-hard* problems. The usefulness of this concept, which applies to many scheduling problems, is that if we are faced with the need to solve large versions of an NP-hard problem, we know in advance that we may not be able to find optimal solutions with available techniques. We might be better off to use a *heuristic* solution procedure that has a more modest computational requirement but does not guarantee optimality. NP-hard instances exist for which it would take less time to actually perform the work in the shop (using any reasonable sequence) than to solve the problem optimally on the fastest available computer. Therefore, the reliance on heuristics is often the rule in practice, rather than the exception. Finally, some solution procedures involve simulation. Although simulation is inherently imprecise, it can produce nearly optimal solutions that are completely satisfactory for practical purposes. In that respect, simulation is conceptually similar to the use of heuristics.

We will have occasion to refer to the computational complexity of certain algorithms. We will also mention that certain problems are known to be NP-hard. This is relevant information for classifying many of the problems we introduce, but the details of complexity theory are beyond the scope of our main coverage. For a thorough introduction to the subject, see Garey and Johnson (1979).

1.3 Philosophy and Coverage of the Book

Scheduling now represents a body of knowledge about models, techniques, and insights related to actual systems. If we think of scheduling as including pure allocation problems, the formal development of models and optimization techniques for modern scheduling theory probably began in the years preceding World War II. Formal articles on properties of specialized sequencing problems gained recognition in the 1950s, and textbooks on the subject date from the 1960s. An early collection of relevant papers is Muth and Thompson (1963), and the seminal work in the field is Conway, Maxwell, and Miller (1967). Articles and textbooks, not to mention the demand for solving scheduling problems in government and industry, stimulated even more books in the field during the 1970s and 1980s. The better-known examples are Coffman (1976) and French (1982), in addition to the first precursor of this volume, Baker (1974). Eventually, additional perspectives were compiled by Morton and Pentico (1993), Blazewicz et al. (1993), Pinedo (1995), Brucker (1995), Leung (2002), and T'Kindt and Billaut (2002). Now the field of deterministic scheduling is well developed, and there is a growing literature on stochastic models, including safe scheduling. With this perspective as background, we can think of scheduling knowledge as a tree. Around 1970, it was possible to write a textbook on scheduling that would introduce a student to this body of knowledge and, in the process, examine nearly every leaf. In a reasonable length text, it was possible to tell the student "everything you always wanted to know" about scheduling. But over the last three decades, the tree has grown considerably. Writing a scheduling text and writing a scheduling encyclopedia are no longer similar tasks.

This material is a text. The philosophy here is that a broad introduction to scheduling knowledge is important, but it is no longer crucial to study every leaf on the tree. A student who prepares by examining the trunk and the major branches will be capable of studying relevant leaves thereafter. This book addresses the trunk and the major branches: it emphasizes basic knowledge that will prepare the reader to delve into more advanced sources with a firm sense of the scope of the field and the major findings within it. Thus, our first objective is to provide a sound basis in deterministic scheduling, because it is the foundation of all scheduling models. As such, the book can be thought of as a new edition of its precursors, Baker (1974) and (2005). But we also have a new objective: to present the emerging theory of safe scheduling (Baker and Trietsch 2007) and to anticipate the future directions in which it may develop. There are growing concerns after half a century of intensive development that scheduling theory has not yet delivered its full promise. One reason for this shortcoming could be the fact that most scheduling models do not address safety time. For this reason, we believe that our second objective is an important one.

Our pedagogical approach is to build from specific to general. In the early chapters, we begin with basic models and their analysis. That knowledge forms the foundation on which we can build a broader coverage in later chapters, without always repeating the details. The priority is on developing insight through the use of specific models and logical analyses. In the early chapters we concentrate on deterministic scheduling problems, along with a number of optimal and heuristic solution techniques. That foundation is followed by a chapter introducing stochastic scheduling and another chapter with our initial coverage of safe scheduling. Thereafter, we address safe scheduling issues as extensions of the deterministic models, in the spirit of building from the specific to the general.

We approach the topic of scheduling with a mathematical style. We rely on mathematics in order to be precise, but our coverage does not pursue the mathematics of scheduling as an end in itself. Some of the results are presented as theorems and justified with formal proofs. The idea of using theorems is not so much to emphasize mathematics as it is simply to draw attention to key results. The use of formal proofs is intended to reinforce the importance of logical analysis in solving scheduling problems. Similarly, certain results are presented in the form of algorithms. Here, again, the use of algorithms is not an end in itself but rather a way to reinforce the logic of the analysis. Scheduling is not mainly about mathematics nor is it mainly about algorithms, but we use such devices to develop systematic knowledge and understanding about the solution of scheduling problems.

The remainder of this book consists of 18 chapters. Chapter 2 introduces the basic single-machine model, deals with static sequencing problems under the most simplifying set of assumptions, and examines a variety of scheduling criteria. By the end of Chapter 2, we will have encountered some reasonably challenging sequencing problems, enough to motivate the study of general-purpose optimization methodologies in Chapter 3 and heuristic methods in Chapter 4. In Chapter 5, the discussion examines a variation of the single-machine model that has been the subject of intensive study and that also happens to be highly relevant for safe scheduling. Chapter 6 introduces stochastic models, and in Chapter 7, we introduce the most basic safe scheduling models. In Chapter 8, we relax several of the elementary assumptions and analyze the problem structures that result.

The second section of the book deals with models containing several machines. Chapter 9 examines the scheduling of single-stage jobs with parallel machines, and Chapters 10 and 11 examine the flow shop model, which involves multistage jobs and machines in series. Chapter 12 takes a look at the details of workflow in the flow shop. Chapter 13 treats the case where it is more economical to batch jobs into groups, or families, and sequence among groups and within groups in two separate steps. Chapter 14 is an overview of the most widely known scheduling model, the job shop, which also contains multistage jobs but which does not have the serial structure of the flow shop. Chapter 15 discusses simulation results for job shops. To a large extent, the understanding of models, techniques, and insights, which we develop in the preceding chapters, is integrated in the study of the job shop. Similarly, the knowledge developed in studying this material builds the integrative view necessary for success in further research and application in the field of scheduling.

In the third section of the book, we focus on nonmanufacturing applications of scheduling. Chapter 16 covers basic project scheduling, and Chapter 17 discusses the added complications of resource constraints. Chapter 18 shows how to obtain reliable data with which to feed project scheduling models. Finally, Chapter 19 extends project scheduling to include safe scheduling considerations. Two technical appendices support our coverage of stochastic models.

Bibliography

Baker, K.R. (1974). *Introduction to Sequencing and Scheduling*. Hoboken, NJ: Wiley.

Baker, K.R. (2005). *Elements of Sequencing and Scheduling*. Hanover, NH: Tuck School of Business.

Baker, K.R. and Trietsch, D. (2007). *Safe Scheduling, Chapter 5 in Tutorials in Operations Research* (ed. T. Klastorin), 79–101. INFORMS.

Blazewicz, J., Ecker, K., Schmidt, G., and Welgarz, J. (1993). *Scheduling in Computer and Manufacturing Systems*. Berlin: Springer.

Brucker, P. (1995). *Scheduling Algorithms*. Berlin: Springer.

Coffman, E.G. (1976). *Computer and Job-Shop Scheduling Theory*. Hoboken, NJ: Wiley.

Conway, R.W., Maxwell, W.L., and Miller, L.W. (1967). *Theory of Scheduling*. Reading, MA: Addison-Wesley.

French, S. (1982). *Sequencing and Scheduling*. Chichester: Ellis Horwood, Ltd.

Garey, M.R. and Johnson, D.S. (1979). *Computers and Intractability: A Guide to the Theory of NP-Completeness*. San Francisco: Freeman.

Leung, J.-T. (2002). *Handbook of Scheduling*. Boca Raton, FL: Chapman and Hall/CRC.

Morton, T.E. and Pentico, D.W. (1993). *Heuristic Scheduling Systems*. Hoboken, NJ: Wiley.

Muth, J.F. and Thompson, G.L. (1963). *Industrial Scheduling*. Englewood Cliffs, NJ: Prentice Hall.

Pinedo, M. (2016). *Scheduling: Theory, Algorithms, and Systems*, 5e. Upper Saddle River, NJ: Prentice Hall.

T'Kindt, V. and Billaut, J.-C. (2002). *Multicriteria Scheduling: Theory, Models, and Algorithms*. Berlin: Springer.

2

Single-machine Sequencing

2.1 Introduction

The pure sequencing problem is a specialized scheduling problem in which an ordering of the jobs completely determines a schedule. Moreover, the simplest pure sequencing problem is one in which there is a single resource, or machine, and all processing times are deterministic. As simple as it is, however, the one-machine case is still very important. The single-machine problem illustrates a variety of scheduling topics in a tractable model. It provides a context in which to investigate many different performance measures and several solution techniques. It is therefore a building block in the development of a comprehensive understanding of scheduling concepts. In order to completely understand the behavior of a complex system, it is vital to understand its parts, and quite often the single-machine problem appears as a part of a larger scheduling problem. Sometimes, it may even be possible to solve the imbedded single-machine problem independently and then to incorporate the result into the larger problem. For example, in multiple-operation processes, a bottleneck stage may exist, and the treatment of the bottleneck by itself with single-machine analysis may determine the properties of the entire schedule. At other times, the level at which decisions must be made may dictate that resources should be treated in the aggregate, as if jobs were coming to a single facility.

In addition to the limitation to a single machine, the basic problem is characterized by these conditions:

C1. There are n single-operation jobs simultaneously available for processing (at time zero).
C2. Machines can process at most one job at a time.
C3. Setup times for the jobs are independent of job sequence and are included in processing times.
C4. Job descriptors are deterministic and known in advance.

Principles of Sequencing and Scheduling, Second Edition. Kenneth R. Baker and Dan Trietsch.
© 2019 John Wiley & Sons, Inc. Published 2019 by John Wiley & Sons, Inc.

C5. Machines are continuously available (no breakdowns occur).

C6. Machines are never kept idle while work is waiting.

C7. Once an operation begins, it proceeds without interruption.

Under these conditions there is a one-to-one correspondence between a sequence of the n jobs and a permutation of the job indices 1, 2, ..., n. The total number of distinct solutions to the basic single-machine problem is therefore $n!$, which is the number of different sequences of n elements. Whenever a schedule can be completely characterized by a permutation of integers, it is called a *permutation schedule*, which is a classification that extends beyond single-machine cases. In describing permutation schedules, it is helpful to use brackets to indicate position in sequence. Thus [5] = 2 means that the fifth job in sequence is job 2. Similarly, $d_{[1]}$ refers to the due date of the first job in sequence.

After covering some preliminaries in Section 2.2, we review the elementary sequencing results in Section 2.3 for problems containing no due dates and in Section 2.4 for problems involving due dates. Section 2.5 introduces two ways in which decision-making flexibility is sometimes added to the basic model. The chapter is organized to show how differences in the choice of a criterion often lead to differences in the optimal schedule. In the next chapter, we examine several general-purpose methodologies that can be applied to single-machine problems.

2.2 Preliminaries

In dealing with job attributes for the single-machine model, it is useful to distinguish between information that is known in advance and information that is generated as the result of scheduling decisions. Information that is known in advance serves as *input* to the scheduling process, and we usually use lowercase letters to denote this type of data. Three basic pieces of information that help to describe jobs in the single-machine case are:

Processing time (p_j): The amount of processing required by job j.

Release date (r_j): The time at which job j is available for processing.

Due date (d_j): The time at which the processing of job j is due to be completed.

Under condition C3 the processing time p_j generally includes both direct processing time and facility setup time. The release date can be thought of as an arrival time – the time when job j appears at the processing facility – and in the basic model, the assumption in condition C1 is that $r_j = 0$ for all jobs. Due dates may not be pertinent in certain problems, but meeting them is a common scheduling concern, and the basic model can shed some light on objectives oriented to due dates.

Information that is generated as a result of scheduling decisions represents *output* from the scheduling function, and we usually use capital letters to denote this type of data. Scheduling decisions determine the most fundamental piece of data to be used in evaluating schedules:

Completion time (C_j):   The time at which the processing of job j is finished.

Quantitative measures for evaluating schedules are usually functions of job completion times. Two important quantities are:

Flowtime (F_j):   The time job j spends in the system: $F_j = C_j - r_j$.

Lateness (L_j):   The amount of time by which the completion time of job j exceeds its due date: $L_j = C_j - d_j$.

These two quantities reflect two kinds of service. Flowtime measures the response of the system to individual demands for service and represents the interval a job waits between its arrival and its departure. (This interval is sometimes called the *turnaround* time.) Lateness measures the conformity of the schedule to a given due date and takes on negative values whenever a job is completed early. Negative lateness represents earlier service than requested; positive lateness represents later service than requested. In many situations, distinct penalties are associated with positive lateness, but no benefits are associated with negative lateness. Therefore, it is often helpful to work with a quantity that measures only positive lateness:

Tardiness (T_j):   The lateness of job j if it fails to meet its due date or zero otherwise: $T_j = \max\{0, L_j\}$.

Schedules are generally evaluated by aggregate quantities that involve information about all jobs, resulting in one-dimensional *performance measures*. Measures of schedule performance are usually functions of the set of completion times in a schedule. For example, suppose that n jobs are to be scheduled. Aggregate performance measures that might be defined include the following:

Total flowtime:	$F = \sum_{j=1}^{n} F_j$
Total tardiness:	$T = \sum_{j=1}^{n} T_j$
Maximum flowtime:	$F_{\max} = \max_{1 \le j \le n} \{F_j\}$
Maximum tardiness:	$T_{\max} = \max_{1 \le j \le n} \{T_j\}$
Number of tardy jobs or the total unit penalty:	$U = \sum_{j=1}^{n} \delta(T_j),$ where $\delta(x) = 1$ if $x > 0$ and $\delta(x) = 0$ otherwise
Maximum completion time:	$C_{\max} = \max_{1 \le j \le n} \{C_j\}$

Under our basic assumptions, $C_{max} = F_{max} = \sum p_j$, and this quantity is also known as the *makespan*. (These three performance measures may not be identical, however, under a different set of assumptions.)

With this notation, it is convenient to refer to the minimization of total flowtime as the *F*-problem and similarly for the *T*-problem, the C_{max}-problem, and so on. Total flowtime, for example, is simply the sum of each of the job flowtimes. In this type of function, each job makes a direct contribution to the performance measure, because each individual flowtime time is part of the sum. On the other hand, for the F_{max}-problem, some jobs may make only an indirect contribution to the performance measure. That is, job *j* may not be scheduled so that it attains the largest flowtime, but its scheduling may cause the delay of the job that does.

Instead of total flowtime, we could just as easily take mean flowtime as a performance measure. The mean value is simply the total value divided by the number of jobs, or F/n. Similarly, total tardiness could be scaled by $1/n$ to yield mean tardiness, and U could be scaled to yield the proportion of jobs tardy.

Each of these measures is a function of the set of job completion times, so that their general form is

$$Z = f(C_1, C_2, ..., C_n)$$

Furthermore, these quantities belong to an important class of performance measures called regular measures. A performance measure Z is *regular* if:

a) The scheduling objective is to minimize Z.
b) Z can increase only if at least one of the completion times in the schedule increases.

More formally, suppose that $Z = f(C_1, C_2, ..., C_n)$ is the value of the measure that characterizes schedule S and that $Z' = f(C_1', C_2', ..., C_n')$ represents the value of the same measure under some different schedule S'. Then Z is regular as long as the following condition holds:

$Z' > Z$ implies that $C_j' > C_j$ for some job j.

The aggregate measures introduced above are all regular measures, as are many important scheduling criteria, and we will deal mainly with regular measures. The definition is significant because it is usually desirable to restrict attention to a limited set of schedules called a *dominant set*. To verify that a set D is a dominant set of schedules for regular measures of performance, we can use the following reasoning:

1) Consider an arbitrary schedule S (which contains completion times C_j) that is excluded from D.
2) Show that there exists a schedule S' in D, in which $C_j' \leq C_j$ for all j.
3) Therefore $Z' \leq Z$ for any regular measure, and so S' is at least as good as S.

4) Hence, in searching for an optimal schedule, it is sufficient to consider only schedules in D.

For example, assumption C6 could be relaxed to allow idle time, but inserted idle time would never lead to a schedule that is better than the best permutation schedule. We prove this property to illustrate the four-step reasoning given above.

■ **Theorem 2.1** In the basic single-machine problem with a regular performance measure, schedules without inserted idle time constitute a dominant set.

Proof. Let S represent a schedule containing inserted idle time. In particular, suppose that under S the machine is idle for some interval (a, b).

Let S' represent a schedule that is identical to S through time a and in which all the processing that occurs in S after time b is moved forward in time by an amount $b - a > 0$. Then any job j for which $C_j \leq a$ under schedule S will have $C'_j = C_j$ under S'. Also, any job j for which $C_j > a$ under S will have $C'_j = C_j - (b - a)$ under S'. Hence, $C'_j \leq C_j$ for all j.

It follows that $Z' \leq Z$ for any regular measure of performance, so that removing inserted idle time can never lead to poorer performance. Therefore, schedules without idle time constitute a dominant set. □

Similarly, it is possible to show that in the basic single-machine problem, the set of permutation schedules is a dominant set for any regular measure of performance. In other words, assumption C7 could be relaxed, allowing jobs to be preempted, but preemption would never lead to a schedule that is better than the best permutation schedule. The proof of this claim – reiterated below as Theorem 2.2 – also follows the four-step argument of Theorem 2.1.

■ **Theorem 2.2** In the basic single-machine problem with a regular performance measure, schedules without preemption constitute a dominant set.

As a consequence of these two theorems, it follows that conditions C6 and C7 need not be stated as explicit assumptions in the single-machine problem with regular performance measures, because they characterize dominant sets of schedules under assumptions C1–C5.

2.3 Problems Without Due Dates: Elementary Results

2.3.1 Flowtime and Inventory

Sometimes, the costs associated with scheduling decisions involve service to customers, as reflected by their time spent in the system, and the scheduling objective is rapid turnaround. In other situations, the costs involve investment in system resources, as reflected by the behavior of in-process inventories, and the scheduling objective is to maintain low inventory levels. The intimate relation between these two objectives can be illustrated in the basic single-machine model.

The time spent by a job in the system is its flowtime, and the "rapid turnaround" objective can be interpreted as minimizing total flowtime. The "low inventory" objective can be interpreted as minimizing the average number of jobs in the system. Let $J(t)$ denote the number of jobs in the system at time t, and let J be the time average of the $J(t)$ function. For the basic single-machine model, the behavior of $J(t)$ is easy to visualize. At time zero, n jobs are in the system, so $J(0) = n$. There is no change in $J(t)$ until the completion of the first job, which occurs at time $F_{[1]} = p_{[1]}$. Then $J(t)$ drops to $(n - 1)$ and remains there until the completion of the second job, which occurs at time $F_{[2]} = p_{[1]} + p_{[2]}$. Continuing in this manner, we can see that $J(t)$ is a decreasing step function over the entire length of the schedule, as shown in Figure 2.1. Also, the length of the schedule is equal to $F_{max} = p_1 + p_2 + \cdots + p_n$, which is independent of the sequence in which the jobs are processed. For the interval $[0, F_{max}]$, consider the sum

$$A = np_{[1]} + (n-1)p_{[2]} + \cdots + 2p_{[n-1]} + p_{[n]}$$

This sum is just the area under the $J(t)$ function, expressed as the sum of the vertical strips in Figure 2.1. Thus $J = A/F_{max}$.

Now recall that

$$F = F_{[1]} + F_{[2]} + \cdots + F_{[n]}$$

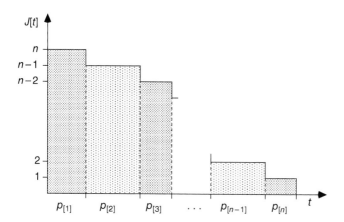

Figure 2.1 The $J(t)$ function.

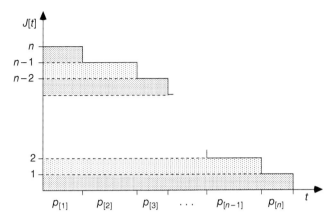

Figure 2.2 An alternative view of the $J(t)$ function.

This sum is also equal to A, expressed as the sum of the horizontal strips shown in Figure 2.2. Thus $F = A$. Combining and rearranging these two relations, the algebraic result is

$$A = F = JF_{max}$$

Since F_{max} is a given constant, J is directly proportional to F. As a result, the job sequence that minimizes F (total flowtime) simultaneously minimizes J (average in-process inventory). Whether the vantage point is one of optimizing customer service or minimizing in-process inventory levels, the problem is the same: Find the sequence that minimizes F.

This relation between flowtime and inventory extends well beyond the single-machine sequencing problem. It arises in the dynamic environment (where jobs arrive over time), in infinite-horizon models (where new work arrives continually), in probabilistic systems (where processing times are uncertain), and in situations where the inventory costs may vary among jobs. Much of the theoretical work in scheduling has been directed to the total flowtime problem and its generalizations. What might at first seem to be undue emphasis on the turn-around criterion is not really so restrictive, in light of this relation between flowtime and inventory, because total flowtime actually encompasses a broader range of scheduling-related costs.

2.3.2 Minimizing Total Flowtime

Consider the $J(t)$ graph and the problem of minimizing total flowtime, F. An equivalent problem is that of minimizing the area under the $J(t)$ function. The selection of a sequence can be interpreted as the construction of a path on the $J(t)$ graph from the point $(0, n)$ to the point $(F_{max}, 0)$. The path consists

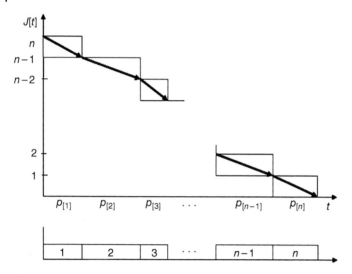

Figure 2.3 The $J(t)$ function for a schedule and its Gantt chart.

of n vectors with given slopes, $-1/p_j$. Figure 2.3 shows the $J(t)$ graph for one such sequence, along with the corresponding Gantt chart.

Clearly, the area can be minimized by placing the steepest slope to the left, then the next steepest slope, and so on. This configuration amounts to sequencing the processing times in nondecreasing order. Sequencing the jobs in nondecreasing order of processing times is known as *shortest processing time* (SPT) sequencing, for obvious reasons, but it is also known by a variety of other names, such as shortest operation time and shortest imminent operation. Theorem 2.3 formalizes the optimality of SPT, and its proof illustrates a useful technique, called the method of *adjacent pairwise interchange*.

■ **Theorem 2.3** Total flowtime is minimized by shortest processing time (SPT) sequencing $(p_{[1]} \leq p_{[2]} \leq \cdots \leq p_{[n]})$.

Proof. Consider a sequence S that is not the SPT sequence. That is, somewhere in S there must exist a pair of adjacent jobs, i and j, with j following i, such that $p_i > p_j$. Now construct a new sequence, S', in which jobs i and j are interchanged in sequence and all other jobs finish at the same time as in S. The situation is depicted in Figure 2.4, where B denotes the set of jobs preceding jobs i and j in both schedules and A denotes the set of jobs following i and j in both schedules. We use the notation $k \in A$ when job k is a member of set A. In addition, $p(B)$ denotes the total processing time for the jobs in set B, that is, the point in time at which job i begins in S and at which job j begins in S'. Also, we temporarily adopt the notation $F_k(S)$ to represent the flowtime of job k under schedule S.

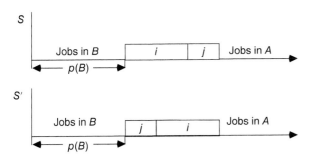

Figure 2.4 A pairwise interchange of adjacent jobs.

We first show that $\sum_{j=1}^{n} F_k$ is smaller under S' than under S:

$$\sum_{j=1}^{n} F_k(S) = \sum_{k \in B} F_k(S) + F_i(S) + F_j(S) + \sum_{k \in A} F_k(S)$$

$$= \sum_{k \in B} F_k(S) + \left(p(B) + p_i\right) + \left(p(B) + p_i + p_j\right) + \sum_{k \in A} F_k(S)$$

$$\sum_{j=1}^{n} F_k(S') = \sum_{k \in B} F_k(S') + F_j(S') + F_i(S') + \sum_{k \in A} F_k(S')$$

$$= \sum_{k \in B} F_k(S') + \left(p(B) + p_j\right) + \left(p(B) + p_j + p_i\right) + \sum_{k \in A} F_k(S')$$

By construction,

$$\sum_{k \in B} F_k(S) + \sum_{k \in A} F_k(S) = \sum_{k \in B} F_k(S') + \sum_{k \in A} F_k(S')$$

Therefore,

$$\sum_{k=1}^{n} F_k(S) - \sum_{k=1}^{n} F_k(S') = p_i - p_j > 0. \qquad \square$$

In words, the interchange of jobs i and j reduces the value of F. Therefore, any sequence that is not an SPT sequence can be improved with respect to F by interchanging an adjacent pair of jobs. It follows that the SPT sequence itself must be optimal.

The essence of this argument is a proof by contradiction. First, we assume that some non-SPT sequence is "optimal." Then we show with a pairwise interchange of an adjacent pair of jobs that a strict improvement can be made in this "optimal" sequence. Therefore, we conclude that it is impossible for a non-SPT sequence to be optimal.

It is also instructive to interpret the logic as a proof by construction:

1) Begin with any non-SPT sequence.
2) Find a pair of adjacent jobs i and j, with j following i, such that $p_i > p_j$.
3) Interchange jobs i and j in sequence, thereby improving the performance measure.
4) Return to Step 2 iteratively, improving the performance measure each time, until eventually the SPT sequence is constructed.

The validity of either argument is not affected by ties – that is, by the existence of a pair of jobs with $p_i = p_j$. Moreover, the method of adjacent pairwise interchange is useful in other situations, as we shall see later on.

Another perspective on Theorem 2.3 may be helpful. We can express the sum of the flowtimes as

$$\sum_{j=1}^{n} F_j = \sum_{j=1}^{n}\sum_{i=1}^{j} p_{[i]} = \sum_{j=1}^{n} (n-j+1)p_{[j]} \tag{2.1}$$

This last sum can be viewed as the scalar product of two vectors with given elements – one containing the integers $1, 2, …, n$ in descending order and the other containing the processing times in order of sequence. It is well known that in order to minimize such a scalar product, one sequence should be decreasing (or at least nonincreasing) and the other should be increasing (or at least nondecreasing). Since the terms $(n - j + 1)$ are already decreasing, the minimum is achieved by taking the p_j in nondecreasing order.

Associated with Theorem 2.3 are several related properties. First, by virtue of the relationship between flowtime and inventory, SPT sequencing minimizes J as well as F. Second, if the waiting time of job j is defined as the time it spends in the system prior to the start of its processing, then SPT minimizes total waiting time. Third, SPT minimizes the maximum waiting time. Finally, SPT also minimizes total completion time.

2.3.3 Minimizing Total Weighted Flowtime

In a common variation of the F-problem, jobs do not have equal importance. One way of distinguishing the jobs is to assign a value or weight, w_j, to each job and to incorporate these weights into the performance measure. The weighted version of total flowtime is *total weighted flowtime*, defined by

$$F_w = \sum_{j=1}^{n} w_j F_j$$

where we can think of weights as unit delay costs. We shall specifically examine the extensions of the flowtime–inventory relation and the optimality of SPT.

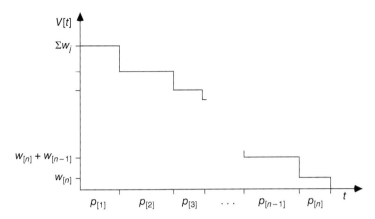

Figure 2.5 The $V(t)$ function.

In the presence of weights, it is natural to define holding costs to be proportional to the value of in-process inventory. Job j contributes w_j to the value of total in-process inventory while it awaits completion, and we can define a function $V(t)$ to be the total value of inventory in the system at time t. The $V(t)$ function is a step function, but unlike $J(t)$, this step function decreases in steps of w_j rather than steps of 1. Figure 2.5 depicts $V(t)$. If V denotes the time average of $V(t)$ over the processing interval, we can again derive two expressions for the area under the $V(t)$ graph. Summing vertical strips, as shown in Figure 2.5, we obtain

$$A = \sum_{j=1}^{n} p_{[j]} \sum_{i=j}^{n} w_{[i]} = VF_{\max}$$

Summing horizontal strips in a manner similar to that of Figure 2.2, we obtain

$$A = \sum_{j=1}^{n} w_j F_j = F_w$$

If we now equate the two expressions for A, we obtain the generalized flowtime–inventory relation:

$$F_w = VF_{\max}$$

Observing that $F_{\max}$ is a constant, we conclude that V is directly proportional to F_w and that the sequence that minimizes one minimizes the other.

Having seen that the optimal rule for minimizing total flowtime is shortest-first sequencing, we should expect that the optimal rule for the total weighted flowtime should be a weighted version of SPT. As before, the nature of the optimal rule can be deduced from the graphical model. In this case, we seek a path on the $V(t)$ graph that connects the point $(0, \sum_{j=1}^{n} w_j)$ with the point $(F_{\max}, 0)$.

This time, the vectors that make up the path have slopes of $-w_j/p_j$, and to minimize the area under $V(t)$, we again place the steepest slope first. In effect, the optimal rule is *shortest weighted processing time* (SWPT) sequencing, stated formally below.

■ **Theorem 2.4** Total weighted flowtime is minimized by SWPT sequencing $(p_{[1]}/w_{[1]} \leq p_{[2]}/w_{[2]} \leq \cdots \leq p_{[n]}/w_{[n]})$.

A proof by the method of adjacent pairwise interchange is analogous to the proof of Theorem 2.3.

The optimality of SWPT for the F_w problem may seem at first to be a specialized scheduling result. However, an examination of the vast literature on industrial engineering, operations research, information systems, and related fields will reveal that the sequencing model with a weighted flowtime objective is a rich model indeed. A specialized bibliography on the model has been compiled by Rau (1973).

Lastly, note that SPT and SWPT represent different sequences in general, so when the job set contains unequal weights, SWPT minimizes F_w and V but not necessarily the mean number of jobs in the system or the total flowtime.

2.4 Problems with Due Dates: Elementary Results

2.4.1 Lateness Criteria

Recall that job lateness is defined as $L_j = C_j - d_j$, or the discrepancy between the due date of a job and its completion time. A somewhat remarkable result is that minimum total lateness is achieved by SPT.

■ **Theorem 2.5** Total lateness is minimized by SPT sequencing.
Proof. By definition,

$$L = \sum_{j=1}^{n} L_j = \sum_{j=1}^{n} (C_j - d_j) = \sum_{j=1}^{n} (F_j - d_j) = \sum_{j=1}^{n} F_j - \sum_{j=1}^{n} d_j = F - \sum_{j=1}^{n} d_j$$

The last term is the sum of the given due dates and is therefore a constant. Because L differs from F by a constant that is independent of sequence, the sequence that minimizes L must be the sequence that minimizes F, and this sequence is given by SPT. □

This result is somewhat remarkable because a sequencing rule that ignores due date information is optimal for a due date-oriented criterion. However, another interpretation of the result might be that L is only superficially a due date-oriented performance measure.

Instead of using SPT, an intuitive approach to meeting due dates might well be to sequence the jobs according to some measure of due date urgency. One obvious measure of urgency for a given job is the time until its due date. Sequencing the jobs by *earliest due date* (EDD) cannot guarantee, however, that L will be minimized, because only SPT guarantees that. Instead we can show that EDD sequencing minimizes the maximum lateness in the schedule.

■ **Theorem 2.6** Maximum lateness and maximum tardiness are minimized by earliest due date (EDD) sequencing $(d_{[1]} \leq d_{[2]} \leq \cdots \leq d_{[n]})$.

Proof. We again employ the method of adjacent pairwise interchange (see Figure 2.4). Consider a sequence S that is not the EDD sequence. That is, somewhere in S there must exist a pair of adjacent jobs, i and j, with j following i, such that $d_i > d_j$. Now construct a new sequence, S', in which jobs i and j are interchanged and all other jobs complete at the same time as in S. Then

$$L_i(S) = p(B) + p_i - d_i \qquad L_j(S') = p(B) + p_j - d_j$$
$$L_j(S) = p(B) + p_i + p_j - d_j \qquad L_i(S') = p(B) + p_j + p_i - d_i$$

from which it follows that $L_j(S) > L_i(S')$ and $L_j(S) > L_j(S')$. Hence,

$$L_j(S) > \max\{L_i(S'), L_j(S')\}$$

Let $L_{AB} = \max\{L_k | k \in A \text{ or } k \in B\}$, and notice that L_{AB} is the same under both S and S'. Then

$$L_{max}(S) = \max\{L_{AB}, L_i(S), L_j(S)\} \geq \max\{L_{AB}, L_i(S'), L_j(S')\} = L_{max}(S')$$

In other words, the interchange of jobs i and j does not increase the value of L_{max} and may actually reduce (improve) it. Therefore, an optimal sequence can be constructed as follows:

1) Begin with an arbitrary non-EDD sequence.
2) Find a pair of adjacent jobs i and j, with j following i, such that $d_i > d_j$.
3) Interchange jobs i and j.
4) Return to Step 2 iteratively until an EDD sequence is constructed. At each iteration, L_{max} either remains the same or is reduced. Because an EDD sequence can be reached from any other sequence in this manner, there can be no other sequence with a value of L_{max} lower than that corresponding to EDD sequencing.

Again, ties do not disturb the logic. A similar argument establishes that EDD minimizes T_{max}, beginning with the inequality

$$T_{max}(S) = \max\{0, L_{max}(S)\} \geq \max\{0, L_{max}(S')\} = T_{max}(S'). \qquad \square$$

A second measure of urgency for a given job is the time until its due date less the time required to process it. This urgency measure is called *slack time*, and, at time t, the slack time of job j is represented as $(d_j - t - p_j)$. In particular, among jobs with identical due dates, the longest is most urgent. Slack time may appear to be a more sophisticated quantification of urgency than the due date alone. Nevertheless, there is little to be said for optimality of *minimum slack time* (MST) sequencing in the single-machine problem. Its only general property involves a mirror image of Theorem 2.6, which is of questionable usefulness in this situation.

■ **Theorem 2.7**   Among schedules with no idle time, the minimum job lateness is maximized by minimum slack time (MST) sequencing ($d_{[1]} - p_{[1]} \leq d_{[2]} - p_{[2]} \leq \cdots \leq d_{[n]} - p_{[n]}$).

Proof. The proof is a mirror image of the proof of Theorem 2.6 and utilizes an adjacent pairwise interchange argument. Observe that $L_{\min}$ is not a regular measure of performance – hence the need, in Theorem 2.7, to restrict consideration to schedules without inserted idle time.   □

An important variation of the basic model involves the designation of both a primary and a secondary measure of performance. The primary measure is the dominant criterion, but if there are alternative optima with respect to the primary measure, we then want to identify the best sequence among those alternatives with respect to a secondary measure.

For example, suppose that a tardiness-based measure (such as $T_{\max}$) is the primary measure and that several sequences are considered "perfect" because they contain no tardy jobs. Furthermore, suppose that F is the secondary measure. Then, to construct a perfect sequence that minimizes F, we can employ a result known as *Smith's rule*:

Job i may be assigned the last position in sequence only if

(S1) $d_i \geq \sum_{j=1}^{n} p_j$ and

(S2) $p_i \geq p_k$ among all jobs k such that $d_k \geq \sum_{j=1}^{n} p_j$

This rule should seem quite logical, for if some other job were to come last in sequence, then there would be room for improvement. If (S1) is violated, then total tardiness can be reduced by shifting some job that satisfies (S1) to the last position. If (S1) holds but (S2) is violated, then F can be reduced, without increasing tardiness, by interchanging the last job with a job that satisfies (S2). Once Smith's rule has identified the last among n jobs, there remain $(n - 1)$ jobs to which the rule can be applied. If we continue in this fashion, the rule eventually constructs an optimal sequence, working backward.

■ **Example 2.1**   Consider a problem containing $n = 5$ jobs, as described in the table.

Job j	1	2	3	4	5
p_j	1	2	3	4	5
d_j	9	13	11	15	10

It is not hard to verify (using EDD) that a perfect sequence exists. The only job that satisfies (S1) is job 4, which is placed last. At the next stage, jobs 2 and 3 both satisfy (S1), and job 3 is chosen to be fourth, according to (S2). Next, jobs 1, 2, and 5 all satisfy (S1), and job 5 is chosen to be third. Finally, job 2 is chosen to be second, leaving job 1 to be first. In this manner, Smith's rule generates a perfect sequence with $F = 38$. In contrast, EDD yields $F = 42$.

2.4.2   Minimizing the Number of Tardy Jobs

If the EDD sequence should yield zero tardy jobs, or should it yield exactly one tardy job, then it is an optimal sequence for U. If it yields more than one tardy job, however, the EDD sequence may not be optimal. An efficient algorithm for the general case is given below. The solution method assumes a particular form for an optimal sequence, shown in Figure 2.6.
The form is as follows:

- First, a set (B) of early jobs, in EDD order.
- Then, a set (A) of late jobs, in any order.

The early jobs are assumed to be in EDD order without loss of generality because if any sequence (or subsequence) of jobs has no tardiness, then by Theorem 2.6 we know that the EDD sequence for those jobs must have no tardiness.

Algorithm 2.1   *Minimizing U*

Step 1. Index the jobs using EDD order and place all jobs in B. Let set A be empty.
Step 2. Calculate the completion times of jobs in B. If no job in B is late, stop: B must be optimal. Otherwise, identify the first late job in B. Suppose that turns out to be the kth job in sequence.
Step 3. Identify the longest job among the first k jobs in sequence. Remove that job from B and place it in A. Return to Step 2.

Next, we illustrate the implementation of the algorithm with an example.

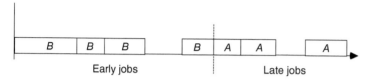

Figure 2.6 The form of a sequence that minimizes U.

■ **Example 2.2** Consider a problem containing $n = 5$ jobs, as described in the table.

Job j	1	2	3	4	5
p_j	1	7	6	4	3
d_j	2	8	9	10	12

In the example, the jobs are already indexed by EDD, as required in Step 1 of the algorithm. In Step 2, job 3 is found to be the first late job. In Step 3, the longest job in the sequence up to and including job 3 is job 2; thus job 2 is removed from B and placed in A. In the next pass at Steps 2 and 3, job 3 is removed from B and placed in A. Thereafter, no tardy jobs remain in B. The algorithm therefore yields two optimal sequences, 1-4-5-2-3 and 1-4-5-3-2, corresponding to the two different ways of sequencing the late jobs.

The weighted version of the U-problem, in which the objective is to minimize $U_w = \sum_{j=1}^{n} w_j \delta(T_j)$, is NP-hard and requires a general solution method such as we describe in Chapter 3.

2.4.3 Minimizing Total Tardiness

The performance objective of "meeting job due dates" is one of the scheduling criteria most frequently encountered in practical problems. While meeting due dates is only a qualitative goal, it usually implies that time-dependent penalties are assessed on late jobs but that no benefits derive from completing jobs early. This interpretation leads naturally to the tardiness measure as a quantification of the scheduling objective, and a fundamental sequencing problem is the minimization of total tardiness. The difficulty of dealing with this measure, and with most other tardiness-based performance measures, arises from the fact that tardiness is not a linear function of completion time. This means that finding optimal solutions often requires that we draw on general techniques of combinatorial optimization. Furthermore, because of the complexities of combinatorial methods, there is apt to be more attention paid to efficient heuristic techniques. In the next chapter, we shall discuss general-purpose combinatorial optimization techniques and demonstrate their application to the total tardiness criterion. Here, we examine how much progress we can make with simpler techniques.

A logical first approach to the tardiness problem is to analyze an adjacent pairwise interchange. Consider a schedule S, in which jobs i and j are adjacent in sequence, and the schedule S' that is identical to S except that jobs i and j are interchanged (see Figure 2.4). We seek conditions that will tell us which job should appear earlier in the sequence. Rather than comparing T for both sequences, it suffices to compare the contributions to T that come from jobs i and j, because the total contributions of the other jobs are the same in both sequences. Thus let

$$T_{ij} = T_i(S) + T_j(S) = \max\{p(B) + p_i - d_i, 0\} + \max\{p(B) + p_i + p_j - d_j, 0\}$$

and

$$T_{ji} = T_j(S') + T_i(S') = \max\{p(B) + p_j - d_j, 0\} + \max\{p(B) + p_i + p_j - d_i, 0\}$$

where, as before, $p(B)$ denotes the time at which job i or job j can be started. To begin, let us assume that $p_i \geq p_j$ and $d_i \geq d_j$. When the processing times and due dates of jobs i and j are ordered similarly, as in this assumption, we say that the processing time and due date parameters are *agreeable*. (Formally, two sets of parameters, u_j and v_j, are agreeable if $u_i < u_j$ implies $v_i \leq v_j$.) For the time being, we shall refer to the case of agreeable processing times and due dates as Case 1.

Case 1.1 $p(B) + p_i \leq d_i$

$$T_{ij} = \max\{p(B) + p_i + p_j - d_j, 0\}$$

$$T_{ji} = \max\{p(B) + p_j - d_j, 0\} + \max\{p(B) + p_j + p_i - d_i, 0\}$$

Notice that T_{ij} is at least as large as the first maximum in T_{ji} (because $p_i \geq 0$) and at least as large as the second (because $d_i \geq d_j$). Therefore, if one or both of the maxima in T_{ji} are zero, we will have $T_{ij} \geq T_{ji}$. Now suppose that neither term in T_{ji} is zero. Then

$$T_{ij} - T_{ji} = \left(p(B) + p_i + p_j - d_j\right) - \left(p(B) + p_j - d_j\right) - \left(p(B) + p_j + p_i - d_i\right)$$

$$T_{ij} - T_{ji} = -p(B) - p_j + d_i \geq -p(B) - p_i + d_i \geq 0$$

Therefore, Case 1.1 yields $T_{ij} \geq T_{ji}$, so it is preferable to have job j precede job i.

Case 1.2 $d_i < p(B) + p_i$

$$T_{ij} = p(B) + p_i - d_i + p(B) + p_i + p_j - d_j$$

$$T_{ji} = \max\{p(B) + p_j - d_j, 0\} + p(B) + p_j + p_i - d_i$$

$$T_{ij} - T_{ji} = p(B) + p_i - d_j - \max\{p(B) + p_j - d_j, 0\}$$

If the maximum in the last term is zero, then the condition specifying Case 1.2 implies that $T_{ij} \geq T_{ji}$; and if the maximum in the last term is positive,

$$T_{ij} - T_{ji} = p(B) + p_i - d_j - \left(p(B) + p_j - d_j\right) = p_i - p_j \geq 0$$

Therefore, Case 1.2 yields $T_{ij} \geq T_{ji}$, so it is preferable to have job j precede job i.

These two cases reveal that when the processing times and the due dates are agreeable, the shorter job (or, equivalently, the job with the earlier due date) should come first. We state this partial result more formally as follows.

■ **Theorem 2.8**   If processing times and due dates are agreeable for all pairs of jobs, then total tardiness (T) is minimized by SPT sequencing with ties broken by EDD (or, equivalently, by EDD with ties broken by SPT).

Proof. The proof follows directly from adjacent pairwise interchange analysis, with the same interpretation as in the proof of Theorem 2.6.   □

Furthermore, although Theorem 2.8 assumes that *all* pairs of jobs have agreeable parameters, it can be shown that if any *two* jobs are agreeable, then they should be sequenced by EDD/SPT even if some other jobs are sequenced between them. Now we turn to the more complicated situation, where the parameters are not agreeable. Let $p_i \geq p_j$ and $d_i < d_j$.

Case 2.1 $p(B) + p_i \leq d_i$

$$T_{ij} = \max\{p(B) + p_i + p_j - d_j, 0\}$$
$$T_{ji} = \max\{p(B) + p_i + p_j - d_i, 0\} \geq T_{ij}$$

Therefore, Case 2.1 yields $T_{ji} \geq T_{ij}$, so it is preferable to have job i (the job with the earlier due date) precede job j.

Case 2.2 $d_i < p(B) + p_i$

Case 2.2.1 $p(B) + p_i + p_j \leq d_j$

$$T_{ij} = p(B) + p_i - d_i$$
$$T_{ji} = p(B) + p_j + p_i - d_i \geq T_{ij}$$

Therefore, Case 2.2.1 yields $T_{ji} \geq T_{ij}$, so it is preferable to have job i (the job with the earlier due date) precede job j.

Case 2.2.2 $p(B) + p_j \leq d_j < p(B) + p_i + p_j$

$$T_{ij} = p(B) + p_i - d_i + p(B) + p_i + p_j - d_j$$
$$T_{ji} = p(B) + p_j + p_i - d_i$$
$$T_{ij} - T_{ji} = p(B) + p_i - d_j$$

Therefore, Case 2.2.2 yields the result that it is preferable to have job i (the job with the earlier due date) precede job j unless $p(B) + p_i > d_j$, in which case job j (the shorter job) may precede job i.

Case 2.2.3 $d_j < p(B) + p_j$

$$T_{ij} = p(B) + p_i - d_i + p(B) + p_i + p_j - d_j$$

$$T_{ji} = p(B) + p_j - d_j + p(B) + p_j + p_i - d_i$$

$$T_{ij} - T_{ji} = p_i - p_j \geq 0$$

Therefore, Case 2.2.3 yields $T_{ij} \geq T_{ji}$, so it is preferable to have job j (the shorter job) precede job i.

We can now combine the various subcases and conclude that, for Case 2, job i may come first except when

$$p(B) + p_i > d_j$$

in which case job j should come first. In fact, we can combine Case 2 with Case 1 and restate the result as follows.

■ **Theorem 2.9**   If jobs i and j are the candidates to begin at time t, then the job with the earlier due date should come first, except if

$$t + \max \{p_i, p_j\} > \max \{d_i, d_j\},$$

in which case the shorter job should come first.

This decision rule is specific – it provides a choice between any pair of candidate jobs – but the outcome may depend on t. That is, the rule could choose job i in favor of job j early in the schedule but job j in favor of job i late in the schedule. More importantly, the rule does not tell us whether jobs i and j *should* come early in the schedule or late in the schedule. Thus, the decision rule is a weaker result than those in Theorems 2.3–2.7 because it does not sequence the jobs unambiguously.

We can look at this result from another perspective. Suppose we define the *modified due date* (MDD) of job j at time t to be

$$d_j' = \max\{d_j, t + p_j\}$$

In words, MDD is either the original due date or else the earliest time at which the job could possibly be completed, whichever is later. It is a dynamic quantity, because it may change as time passes. Therefore, if we give priority to the job with the earliest MDD, then the choice between jobs i and j may be different early in the schedule than it is late in the schedule. The MDD priority rule is consistent with the prescriptions of Cases 1 and 2: if jobs i and j are the candidates to begin at time t, then the job with the earlier MDD should come first.

Again, the MDD rule is weaker than such rules as SPT and SWPT. It tells us that if we examined an optimal sequence, we would find that each pair of jobs is sequenced consistently with MDD; however, starting at time zero and sequencing the jobs by MDD may not produce an optimal schedule. To put it another way, the MDD rule represents a necessary condition for optimality, but it is not a sufficient condition.

We conclude our treatment of the T-problem with some specialized results concerning optimal sequences:

- If the EDD sequence produces no more than one tardy job, it yields the minimum value of T.
- If all jobs have the same due date, then T is minimized by SPT sequencing.
- If it is impossible for any job to be on time in any sequence, then T is minimized by SPT sequencing.
- If SPT sequencing yields no jobs on time, then it minimizes T.

The weighted version of the total tardiness problem is even more difficult to solve than the T-problem, which itself is NP-hard, and we postpone its discussion until we examine more general methods of solution in Chapter 3.

2.5 Flexibility in the Basic Model

The most basic version of the single-machine model is restricted to conditions C1–C7, as listed at the outset of this chapter; but this characterization did not include the specification of an objective function. Once we specified a class of objective functions (regular measures of performance), two of the conditions became superfluous, but the alternative possibilities for an objective function led to a variety of sequencing insights, as covered in Sections 2.3 and 2.4. In this section, we highlight two ways in which decision-making flexibility can be added to the basic model: (i) allowing due dates to be treated as decisions and (ii) allowing job selection as a possible decision.

2.5.1 Due Dates as Decisions

Normally, we treat due dates as given parameters. This approach reflects the premise that in many realistic circumstances, the due date is determined by the customer – or by a higher planning level in the hierarchy – and becomes part of the specification of the job to be carried out, just like the processing time. Often, however, the producer can set the due date or at least influence it. We might appropriately think of the due date as a matter of negotiation between the producer and the customer. Nevertheless, a reasonable model of the due date as a negotiated parameter would introduce much more complexity. A simple step in this direction is to treat the due date as a decision variable, possibly subject to some constraint that represents a proxy for the negotiation process.

Suppose that the due date can be selected at the job's release date (r_j). The selection of the due date represents a target for the *flow allowance* or the amount of time that the job will spend in the system. We might select due dates according to one of the following rules:

CON: *constant* flow allowance: $d_j = r_j + \gamma$

SLK: *equal slack* flow allowance: $d_j = r_j + p_j + \beta$

TWK: *total work* flow allowance: $d_j = r_j + \alpha p_j$

where each rule contains a single tightness parameter (γ, β, or α) that must be specified. For equal release dates, however, any one of these due date rules will result in agreeable due dates and processing times. By Theorem 2.8, it follows that SPT (which will be equivalent to EDD) minimizes total tardiness.

When due dates are completely discretionary, it is not difficult to minimize total tardiness: for any schedule we could select the due dates to be loose enough that no job would be late. However, in an environment where due dates can be selected, it seems reasonable to seek the tightest due dates possible. Tight due dates correspond to short flow allowances and thus represent commitments to customers that orders will be filled promptly. Of course, such commitments would be meaningless if there were no hope that they could be met. Therefore, we impose the constraint that no job is allowed to be tardy, and we examine how to set the due dates so they are as tight as possible.

To measure the tightness of a set of due dates, we use the sum of the due dates or

$$D = \sum_{j=1}^{n} d_j$$

The problem becomes one of minimizing D, subject to the requirement that $C_j \le d_j$.

In principle, we can easily find an optimal solution to this problem. For any schedule, the tightest possible set of due dates is obviously given by $d_j = C_j$. Therefore, D can be minimized by minimizing the sum of the completion times or, equivalently, total flowtime. Since we know by Theorem 2.3 that this is accomplished by SPT, our solution can be found by constructing an SPT schedule of the jobs, computing the completion time of each job in this schedule, and setting the due date of each job equal to its completion time. This optimal solution requires that the due date of each job depends on specific information about every other job in the schedule, which we refer to as a comprehensive information base. A more practical approach is to rely on such rules as CON, SLK, and TWK, in which the selection of a due date depends only on information about the job itself (its release date and its processing time) and on a tightness parameter. Next, we might ask whether one of those three limited information rules is best.

It is possible to show that for any set of n jobs, CON due dates are dominated by either SLK or TWK due dates. That is, D will never be larger under SLK or TWK than it is under CON.

■ **Example 2.3**   Consider a problem containing $n = 3$ jobs, as described in the table below, with $r_j = 0$ for all jobs.

Job j	1	2	3
p_j	1	2	16

Suppose our problem consisted of just the first two jobs. Then the tightness parameters would be selected as follows:

CON:	$\gamma = 3$	For which $D = 6$
SLK:	$\beta = 1$	For which $D = 5$
TWK:	$\alpha = 1.5$	For which $D = 4.5$

In this case, the optimal (full information) value is $D = 4$. When our problem consists of all three jobs, the results are as follows:

CON:	$\gamma = 19$	For which $D = 57$
SLK:	$\beta = 3$	For which $D = 28$
TWK:	$\alpha = 1.5$	For which $D = 28.5$

Here, the optimal (full information) value is $D = 23$. Our two examples demonstrate that either TWK or SLK can be the best of the three rules. The examples also illustrate the fact that CON is always dominated. A computational study (see Baker and Bertrand, 1981) suggests that TWK tends to be the best rule most of the time and that its advantage grows with larger problem sizes and with variability among processing times. Therefore, in practice, a good approach is to use TWK and adjust α by trial and error to maintain the shop due date performance on target.

2.5.2   Job Selection Decisions

In the basic sequencing model, the workload is given, and due dates are given, and the scheduling task is to find the best sequence. When due dates are decisions, as in the previous section, we face a variation of the basic sequencing model that allows for additional flexibility. When, instead, the workload is a decision, we face a different kind of flexibility. Specifically, in the *job selection model*, we must decide which of the available jobs to accept (and which to reject). As in the basic model, processing times and other parameters are given, along with a penalty (or opportunity cost) for each job rejected. For the jobs selected, the scheduling task remains one of finding the best sequence.

In the job selection model, the objective thus has two components: a time-based performance measure, such as total flowtime, and an economic measure, the total penalty. Because rejected jobs are simply removed from the scheduling problem, a suitable representation for the economic measure is a lump-sum penalty $e_j > 0$, incurred if job j is rejected. This penalty could represent a contractual payment or an opportunity cost, such as lost profit or the inefficiency cost of assigning the job to some other resource. A more direct way of representing the economic measure, however, is to associate revenue with each job that is processed.

Consider the performance measure for accepted jobs. Standard scheduling objectives, such as makespan (C_{max}), weighted flowtime (F_w), and maximum tardiness (T_{max}), are not intrinsically economic criteria. In addition, they measure time intervals, whereas the rejection penalty is a lump sum. Therefore, the most consistent scheduling objectives are also lump-sum measures, such as the maximum number of on-time jobs or the minimum weighted number of tardy jobs. Nevertheless, the scheduling and economic components may not be commensurable, so in some cases we may prefer to adopt a weighting factor to combine them into a single objective function.

Perhaps the simplest nontrivial model involves lump-sum revenues and costs. Suppose job j is characterized by a processing time p_j, a due date d_j, and a tardiness penalty w_j, which is incurred if the job is accepted and completed after its due date. If job j is accepted, then it generates revenue of v_j; otherwise, it is rejected. No direct cost is associated with a job's rejection. (All parameters are assumed to be positive.) For the solution, we define the following sets:

A = the set of accepted jobs
R = the set of rejected jobs
Z = the set of late jobs
Y = the set of on-time jobs

We use lowercase to denote the number of jobs in each set: a = the number of accepted jobs, etc. Thus $n = a + r$ and $a = y + z = n - r$. Finally, for a given job set S, we can write the objective function as follows:

$$F(S) = \sum_A v_j - \sum_Z w_j$$

The expression $F(S)$ is meant to convey that, conceptually, the first step is to select the jobs in A, after which the next step is to sequence them optimally. Suppose the revenues and costs are identical: $v_j = v$ and $w_j = w$. That means the net revenue for an accepted job completed late is $v - w$. If $v - w > 0$, then acceptance is preferred to rejection, even if tardiness occurs; it is optimal to accept all jobs and then maximize the net benefit, $vn - wz(S)$. This criterion corresponds to minimizing the number of tardy jobs $z(S)$, which is achieved with

Algorithm 2.1. Thus, this particular case reduces to a well-known scheduling problem without rejection that can be solved in polynomial time.

If $v - w \leq 0$, then rejection is no worse than acceptance with tardy completion. In this case, it is optimal to complete all accepted jobs on time and reject the rest. The objective function becomes $av = vy(S)$. We can maximize this quantity by maximizing the number of on-time jobs, which is also accomplished by Algorithm 2.1.

In the identical parameter case, the problem reduces to finding two sets – an on-time set and its complement. Furthermore, the impact on the objective function of completing a job on time versus placing it in the complementary set is the same for all jobs. However, when the parameters are job dependent, we cannot rely on Algorithm 2.1 to provide an optimal solution. Moreover, the general form of the problem involves finding three sets – an on-time set of accepted jobs, a tardy set of accepted jobs, and the set of rejected jobs. Given that a job will not be accepted and completed on time, the choice between rejecting the job and accepting it but completing it late is dictated by the value of $v_j - w_j$. Moreover, that preference can be determined at the outset. Thus, let $c_j = \max\{0, v_j - w_j\}$. When $c_j = 0$, if job j is not completed on time, it should be rejected. Similarly, when $c_j > 0$, if job j is not completed on time, it should still be accepted. Even when these observations are applied, the general problem remains challenging. To obtain optimal solutions, we would need to implement more powerful techniques, such as those described in Chapter 3.

2.6 Summary

The single-machine model is fundamental in the study of sequencing and scheduling. It is considered a rather simple scheduling problem because it does not have distinct sequencing and resource allocation dimensions. Nevertheless, as the T-problem begins to illustrate, the sequencing problem itself may sometimes be fairly complicated. Even in this fundamental type of problem, the set of feasible solutions can be quite large, and the determination of an optimum can be a formidable task. In some special cases, optima can be found readily, most notably in the minimization of F_w, T_{max}, and U; but in general, it may be necessary to resort to general-purpose methodologies, such as those described in the next chapter.

Several important scheduling objectives can be illustrated in the single-machine model, and these often give rise to a variety of solution strategies. Graphical and algebraic methods have been used to prove the optimality of SWPT for total weighted flowtime and the optimality of EDD for maximum tardiness, respectively. In those cases, knowledge of an optimal pairwise job ordering allows the optimal sequence to be constructed with a simple sorting mechanism. A more intricate construction is required to minimize the number of tardy jobs. For more complicated criteria, including total tardiness, we need to use general-purpose methodologies, although in cases where the parameters are agreeable, the solution may be found more easily.

These observations underscore the significance of the single-machine model in our understanding of scheduling decisions. Also, as we noted at the beginning of this chapter, the solution of practical scheduling problems can make direct use of these results in certain situations or at least build on this basic understanding in approaching more complicated situations.

Exercises

2.1 Prove that in the basic single-machine problem, schedules without preemption constitute a dominant set (Theorem 2.2).

2.2 An obvious definition of longest processing time (LPT) sequencing is

$$p_{[1]} \geq p_{[2]} \geq \cdots \geq p_{[n]}$$

In general, LPT exhibits properties that are antithetical to those of SPT. In particular, assuming a schedule with no idle time, prove:
a) LPT maximizes F.
b) LPT maximizes J.
c) LPT maximizes L.
d) LPT maximizes total waiting time.

2.3 Use an adjacent pairwise interchange argument to prove that SWPT minimizes F_w; i.e. prove Theorem 2.4.

2.4 A single-machine facility operates around the clock and faces the problem of sequencing the production work for the six customer orders described in the table below.

Order	1	2	3	4	5	6
Hours	20	27	16	6	15	24

a) What production sequence will minimize the total flowtime of these orders, assuming all six arrived at the same time? What is the total flowtime in this schedule?
b) Suppose that customer orders 2 and 6 are considered three times as important as the rest. What production sequence would you propose?

c) Now suppose you wish to use a due date setting rule to assign due dates to the various orders. Find the sum of the due dates under the CON, SLK, and TWK rules. Compute how close each result is to the optimal sum of due dates.

2.5 The following problem involves the sequencing of one machine.

Operation j	A	B	C	D	E	F
Processing time p_j	12	2	6	14	8	13
Due date d_j	41	4	44	16	35	30

The manager mainly wants to minimize the maximum lateness but also wants to reduce the number of late operations.
a) What sequence do you suggest? Justify your choice.
b) Calculate L_{max} and U for your solution.
Is this result optimal for one of these measures? For both? Explain.

2.6 *The least cost testing sequence problem.* An item is subjected to a series of n tests (e.g. hardness, weight, and length). Associated with the ith test are two known constants: K_i, the cost per item of carrying out the ith test, and R_i, the probability of rejecting the item on the ith test. The tests are independent in the sense that they may be run in any order, and the constants K_i and R_i are independent of test order. For a given sequence of tests, an item is subjected to each test in the sequence in turn as long as the tests accept the item; if an item is rejected by any test, no further tests are performed. Determine the test sequence that minimizes the total expected cost of testing an item.

2.7 The following sequence might be called the VIP sequence:

$$w_{[1]} \geq w_{[2]} \geq \cdots \geq w_{[n]}$$

Suppose that a scheduling objective is to minimize F_w and that weighting factors are assigned according to processing times. Show that:
a) If $w_j = \alpha p_j$ (weighting factors are directly proportional to processing times), then all sequences are equivalent.
b) If $w_j = \alpha p_j^{\beta}$ where $\beta > 0$, then VIP is optimal when $\beta > 1$, but it is the worst sequence when $0 < \beta < 1$. Discuss specifically the case when $\beta = 0$.
c) If $p_j = p$ (all processing times are equal), then VIP is optimal.

2.8 Prove the following:
   a) If the EDD sequence produces no more than one tardy job, then it yields the optimal value of T.
   b) If all jobs have the same due date, then T is minimized by SPT sequencing.
   c) If all jobs have the same processing time, then T is minimized by EDD sequencing.
   d) If it is impossible for any job to be on time in any sequence, then T is minimized by SPT sequencing.
   e) If SPT yields no jobs on time, then it minimizes T. How would you break ties in this case?
   f) An optimal solution to the T-problem must satisfy the MDD rule.
   g) To minimize T, any two jobs with agreeable processing times and due dates must be in SPT/EDD sequence (as prescribed by Theorem 2.8) even if some other jobs are inserted between them.

Bibliography

Baker, K.R. and Bertrand, J.W.M. (1981). A comparison of due date selection rules. *AIIE Transactions* 13: 123–131.

Maxwell, W.L. (1970). On the generality of the equation $L = \lambda W$. *Operations Research* 18: 172–174.

Moore, J.M. (1968). An n job, one machine sequencing algorithm for minimizing the number of late jobs. *Management Science* 15: 102–109.

Rau, J.G. (1973). Selected comments concerning optimization theory for functions of permutations. In: *Symposium on the Theory of Scheduling and its Applications* (ed. S.E. Elmaghraby). New York: Springer-Verlag.

Shabtay, D., Gaspar, N., and Kaspi, M. (2013). A survey on offline scheduling with rejection. *Journal of Scheduling* 16: 3–28.

Slotnick, S. (2011). Order acceptance and scheduling: a taxonomy and review. *European Journal of Operational Research* 212: 1–11.

Smith, W.E. (1956). Various optimizers for single stage production. *Naval Research Logistics Quarterly* 3: 59–66.

3

Optimization Methods for the Single-machine Problem

3.1 Introduction

In the previous chapter, we explored fundamental performance measures for the single-machine problem and observed that different scheduling procedures were appropriate for different measures. In the T-problem, we encountered a relatively simple problem statement for which the determination of an optimal sequence was not a simple matter. Although we made some progress toward the solution of the T-problem with adjacent pairwise interchange methods, we deferred discussion of a complete solution until we could examine more powerful optimization techniques. In this chapter we introduce some general-purpose optimization methods for sequencing and scheduling problems and illustrate their application to the T-problem.

As a general setting, suppose that a cost function, denoted $g_j(t)$, is incurred when job j completes at time t. We assume only that $g_j(t)$ is nondecreasing. Typical scheduling problems involve minimizing the maximum $g_j(t)$ value (the maximum cost problem) or minimizing the sum of $g_j(t)$ values (the total cost problem). We first examine the solution of the maximum cost problem.

Let P represent the total processing time of the jobs to be scheduled. Obviously, P is equal to the completion time of the last job. The following result identifies the job that should be placed last.

■ **Theorem 3.1** When the objective is to minimize the maximum cost, job i may be assigned the last position in sequence if $g_i(P) \leq g_k(P)$ for all jobs $k \neq i$.

Proof. Suppose S is an optimal schedule that does not conform to the theorem, as depicted in Figure 3.1, and adapt the notation so that $g_i(S)$ denotes the cost for

Principles of Sequencing and Scheduling, Second Edition. Kenneth R. Baker and Dan Trietsch.
© 2019 John Wiley & Sons, Inc. Published 2019 by John Wiley & Sons, Inc.

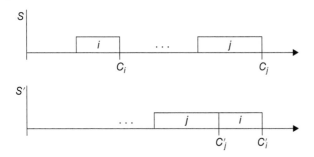

Figure 3.1 Inserting job i into the last position.

job i in schedule S. Let j denote the last job in sequence, and let $G(S)$ denote the maximum cost among jobs other than i and j. Then, for schedule S,

$$g_i(S) \leq g_j(S)$$

$$g_{\max}(S) = \max\{g_j(S), G(S)\}$$

Construct schedule S' by inserting job i into the last position. Let $G(S')$ be defined analogously to $G(S)$. As a result,

$$g_i(S') \leq g_j(S) \quad g_j(S') \leq g_j(S) \quad G(S') \leq G(S)$$

Hence, $g_{\max}(S') = \max\{g_i(S'), g_j(S'), G(S')\} \leq \max\{g_j(S), G(S)\} = g_{\max}(S)$, and schedule S' is no worse than schedule S. □

The solution algorithm implied by Theorem 3.1 is straightforward. We compute P and find the job with minimum cost at time P. This job is assigned the last position in sequence. Removing this job from consideration, we reapply the procedure to the remaining $(n-1)$ jobs, and we continue until all jobs have been sequenced.

As a familiar example, suppose the cost function takes the special form $g_j(t) = \max\{0, t - d_j\}$. This special case corresponds to the $T_{\max}$ problem. The algorithm proceeds by computing P and finding the minimum value of $g_j(P) = \max\{0, P - d_j\}$. Clearly, the job with the largest d_j will attain the minimum value, so it may be placed last. Continuing in this fashion, we construct the EDD sequence, from the end of the schedule to the beginning.

Theorem 3.1, along with the accompanying algorithm, provides a straightforward means of finding a solution to the maximum cost problem. For each position in sequence, the algorithm must find the minimum value of $g_j(P)$; thus, the computational effort is $O(n^2)$ to construct an optimal sequence.

The rest of this chapter is mainly devoted to the total cost problem. Although the techniques we cover are general, we shall use the T-problem to illustrate their application.

3.2 Adjacent Pairwise Interchange Methods

We have seen that an adjacent pairwise interchange argument can prove the optimality of certain sequencing rules (e.g. SWPT minimizes F_w or EDD minimizes T_{max}). The thrust of the adjacent pairwise interchange argument may be stated as follows: A sequence is sought for which all adjacent pairwise interchanges lead to poorer performance – this will be an optimal sequence. It is important to recognize, however, that there are limitations to this approach.

Suppose that the single-machine problem is concerned with minimizing Z and that a sequence S is found for which all adjacent pairwise interchanges lead to an increase in Z. Does this information imply that S is the optimal sequence? The answer, as we have seen, is certainly yes when Z is F and S corresponds to SPT sequencing, but the answer is not always yes.

■ **Example 3.1**   Consider the following three-job problem, with the criterion of minimizing total tardiness.

Job j	1	2	3
p_j	1	2	3
d_j	4	2	3

The optimal sequence is 2-1-3, with $T = 3$. However, if all six sequences are examined, the complete set of solutions can be depicted as in Figure 3.2, where each sequence is linked to those sequences that can be obtained from it by an adjacent pairwise interchange.

Note that for sequence 3-1-2, all (two) adjacent pairwise interchanges lead to an increase in T, yet 3-1-2 is not an optimal sequence. This example shows that the adjacent pairwise interchange property will not be sufficient to identify optimal sequences in the T-problem, but might lead only to identification of a local optimum. In the previous chapter we observed a clue as to why this local

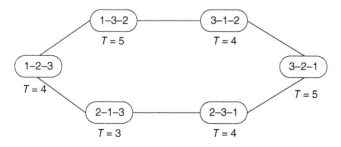

Figure 3.2 Feasible sequences for the three-job example.

optimality might arise: In general, the result of an adjacent pairwise interchange between a given pair of jobs may depend on where in the sequence the interchange occurs. In particular, the decision rule that emerges involves the time at which the interchange occurs. By contrast, the decision rule that emerges from an adjacent pairwise interchange in the F-problem involves only a comparison of the processing times of the jobs being interchanged.

The adjacent pairwise interchange method is sufficient to prove optimality for only a limited class of sequencing rules. For sequencing rules that employ only information about individual jobs in constructing a sequence, a crucial property involves the transitivity of the optimal job ordering. (An ordering relation R between two jobs is *transitive* whenever iRj and jRk imply iRk.) For such rules as SWPT, EDD, and MST, the optimal sequence is characterized by a transitive pairwise ordering of the jobs. In the case of the measure T, however, we can conclude only that the optimal sequencing rule (whatever it might be) is not transitive.

These observations point to a simple way of using adjacent pairwise interchange methods in solving new sequencing problems. We first analyze an interchange and derive a condition that specifies how two jobs should be ordered. If this condition turns out to be transitive, the ordering will indeed be optimal. Otherwise, a more complicated approach will be needed to locate an optimum.

3.3 A Dynamic Programming Approach

A regular measure of performance, Z, is a function of job completion times, and when the function is additive, we can write

$$Z = \sum_{j=1}^{n} g_j\left(C_j\right)$$

For example, if Z is total tardiness, then

$$g_j\left(C_j\right) = \max\left\{0, C_j - d_j\right\}$$

As another example, if Z is weighted number of late jobs, then

$$g_j\left(C_j\right) = w_j\delta\left(\max\left\{0, C_j - d_j\right\}\right)$$

When Z has an additive form, as in these examples, we can find an optimal sequence with a dynamic programming approach. *Dynamic programming* is a general optimization technique for making sequential decisions. Here, for example, we have to decide which job comes first, which comes second, and so on. Dynamic programming applies to problems that can be partitioned into subproblems, each involving a subset of the decisions, in such a way that the following *optimality principle* holds: Suppose we have already made the first

k decisions (optimally or not), then the remaining $(n - k)$ decisions can be optimized by considering only the subproblem that involves them. For example, suppose we wish to find the shortest driving route from San Francisco to New York. If we are contemplating a route that goes through Chicago, then regardless of how we get there, we will have to follow the shortest path from Chicago to New York if the route we are contemplating is to achieve the optimal distance. The optimality principle is satisfied in sequencing (in other words, a sequencing problem can be partitioned appropriately) whenever the objective function is additive.

To apply dynamic programming for our sequencing problem, let J denote some subset of the jobs, and let $p(J)$ denote the total time required to process the jobs in set J. For convenience, we use $(J - j)$ to denote the set J with the element j removed. Suppose that a sequence has been constructed in which the jobs in set J precede all other jobs. Let

$G(J)$ = the minimum cost for the subproblem consisting of the jobs in set J

Next, suppose that job j is assigned the last position in this subset, so that it completes at time $p(J)$, as shown in Figure 3.3.

Given that job j comes last, the value of $G(J)$ is the sum of two terms, the cost incurred by job j and the minimum cost incurred by the remaining jobs. This latter term, which we can write as $G(J - j)$, is the optimal value obtained by solving the subproblem involving only the jobs in set $(J - j)$. If we compare all possible jobs j that could come last in set J and select the best one, we shall find the minimum cost for the set J. In symbols,

$$G(j) = \min_{j \in J} \left\{ g_j[p(J)] + G(J - j) \right\} \tag{3.1}$$

where

$$G(\phi) = 0 \tag{3.2}$$

and ϕ denotes the empty subset.

Finally, let X denote the set of all jobs. Because the cost function G is defined on subsets of jobs, the minimum total cost can be written $G(X)$, where

$$G(X) = \min_{j \in X} \left\{ g_j[p(X)] + G(X - j) \right\} \tag{3.3}$$

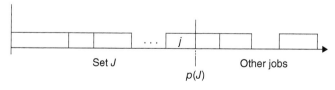

Figure 3.3 The form of a sequence in dynamic programming.

At each stage, the function $G(J)$ measures the total cost contributed by the jobs in set J, when set J occurs at the beginning of the schedule and is sequenced optimally. The recursion relation (3.1) indicates that in order to calculate the value of G for any particular subset of size k, we first have to know the value of G for subsets of size $(k - 1)$. Therefore, the procedure begins with the value of G for a subset of size zero, from Eq. (3.2). Then, using Eq. (3.1), we can calculate the value of G for all subsets of size 1, then the value of G for all subsets of size 2, and so on. In this manner, the procedure considers ever larger sets J, ultimately using Eq. (3.3) to determine which job should be scheduled last. The optimal value of Z is $G(X)$. If we keep track of where minima in Eq. (3.1) occur at each stage, then, after finding $G(X)$, we can reconstruct the optimal sequence.

■ **Example 3.2**   Consider the following four-job problem, with the criterion of minimizing total tardiness.

Job j	1	2	3	4
p_j	5	6	9	8
d_j	9	7	11	13

The essential dynamic programming calculations are displayed in Table 3.1. To illustrate these calculations, consider the set $J = \{1, 2, 4\}$ that is encountered at Stage 3. For this set $p(J) = 19$, the total processing time for the jobs in this set. If job 1 comes last in the set, then its tardiness is $g_1(19) = 10$, and for the remaining jobs, $G(\{2, 4\}) = 1$ from Stage 2. Thus, the total contribution from this set, when job 1 comes last, is 11. An adjacent column indicates that if job 2 comes last, then $g_2(19) = 12$ and $G(\{1, 4\}) = 0$, totaling 12; and if job 4 comes last, $g_4(19) = 6$ and $G(\{1, 2\}) = 2$, totaling 8. The minimum of these three totals is 8, which is designated as $G(J)$ in the table; this is achieved when job 4 comes last, as indicated by the column in which $G(J)$ is shown.

To reconstruct the optimal sequence in the example, note that at Stage 4 the lowest tardiness is achieved when job 3 comes last. Since this leaves jobs 1, 2, and 4 to be sequenced, we examine the set $\{1, 2, 4\}$ that was evaluated at Stage 3. Here, as we have seen in detail, the calculations show that job 4 should come last in this set; thus job 4 should occupy the next to last position in the optimal sequence. Continuing in this fashion, we construct the optimal sequence 2-1-4-3 for which the total tardiness is $G(X) = 25$.

The number of subsets considered by the dynamic programming procedure is 2^n, since that is the total number of subsets of n elements. Finding $G(J)$ for each subset J involves a minimization over all possible jobs that could come last, so the computational effort required for dynamic programming grows in proportion to $n2^n$. In this respect, dynamic programming is typical of many

Table 3.1

Stage 1

J	{1}	{2}	{3}	{4}
$p(J)$	5	6	9	8
$j \in J$	1	2	3	4
$g_j[p(J)]$	0	0	0	0
$G(J-j)$	0	0	0	0
$G(J)$	0	0	0	0

Stage 2

J	{1, 2}		{1, 3}		{1, 4}		{2, 3}		{2, 4}		{3, 4}	
$p(J)$	11		14		13		15		14		17	
$j \in J$	1	2	1	3	1	4	2	3	2	4	3	4
$g_j[p(J)]$	2	4	5	3	4	0	8	4	7	1	6	4
$G(J-j)$	0	0	0	0	0	0	0	0	0	0	0	0
$G(J)$	2		3		0		4		1		4	

Stage 3

J	{1, 2, 3}			{1, 2, 4}			{1, 3, 4}			{2, 3, 4}		
$p(J)$	20			19			22			23		
$j \in J$	1	2	3	1	2	4	1	3	4	2	3	4
$g_j[p(J)]$	11	13	9	10	12	6	13	11	9	16	12	10
$G(J-j)$	4	3	2	1	0	2	4	0	3	4	1	4
$G(J)$	11			8			11			13		

Stage 4

J		{1, 2, 3, 4}		
$p(J)$		28		
$j \in J$	1	2	3	4
$g_j[p(J)]$	19	21	17	15
$G(J-j)$	13	11	8	11
$G(J)$		25		

Optimal sequence: 2-1-4-3 $\sum T_j = 25$

general-purpose procedures for combinatorial optimization, in that the effort required to solve the problem grows at an exponential rate with increasing problem size. This trait makes dynamic programming an inefficient procedure for finding optimal sequences in some of the simple problems we have examined. For example, when F_w is the criterion, we could employ dynamic programming with

$$g_j(t) = w_j t$$

Also, when U is the criterion, we could employ dynamic programming with

$$g_j(t) = 1 \quad \text{if } t > d_j$$
$$= 0 \quad \text{if } t \leq d_j$$

But in both instances it is computationally more efficient to use the specialized results developed in Chapter 2. In particular, the F_w-problem and the U-problem can be solved by algorithms that require no more computational effort than is required to sort n numbers. (The most efficient procedure for sorting has a computational requirement that grows at a rate that is asymptotically proportional to $n\log n$.) On the other hand, for problems in which efficient optimizing procedures have not been developed, such as minimizing total weighted tardiness or weighted number of tardy jobs, dynamic programming may be a reasonable approach.

Although the computational demands of dynamic programming grow at an exponential rate with increasing problem size, the approach is still more efficient than complete enumeration of all feasible sequences, for the computational effort of complete enumeration grows with the factorial of the problem size. Because dynamic programming considers certain sequences only indirectly, without actually evaluating them explicitly, the technique is sometimes called an *implicit enumeration* technique. Although it is more efficient than complete enumeration, the fact that its computational requirement exhibits exponential growth places a premium on the ability to curtail the dynamic programming calculations whenever possible. Such a strategy is described in the next section.

In the exposition above, we organized the dynamic programming calculations by treating the subsets in the order of their size: computing $G(J)$ for all subsets of size k, then all subsets of size $(k + 1)$, and so on until reaching the subset of size n. Although this might be the most natural way to organize the calculations, other schemes are also possible. In fact, the most convenient way to implement dynamic programming on a computer uses an alternative scheme. The only requirement is that at the time we treat set J, we should already have treated all the subsets of J.

For computer implementation, we assign each subset a label. We can think of this label as the sum of the labels of all jobs in the subset, where each job has its own label. To ensure that the label of a subset will tell us unambiguously which

Table 3.2

Subset	Label	Binary
ϕ	0	0000
{1}	1	0001
{2}	2	0010
{1, 2}	3	0011
{3}	4	0100
{1, 3}	5	0101
{2, 3}	6	0110
{1, 2, 3}	7	0111
{4}	8	1000
{1, 4}	9	1001
{2, 4}	10	1010
{1, 2, 4}	11	1011
{3, 4}	12	1100
{1, 3, 4}	13	1101
{2, 3, 4}	14	1110
{1, 2, 3, 4}	15	1111

jobs are contained in the subset, we use binary notation. Specifically, the label for job k is 2^{k-1}. For example, a 4-job problem contains 16 subsets, including the empty subset, as listed in Table 3.2.

Note that the binary representation allows us to translate sets into labels and labels into sets. For the set {1, 2, 4}, for example, the label is just the sum of the individual job labels 2^0, 2^1, 2^3, or 11. The label 11, when converted to binary notation (1011), reveals that jobs 1, 2, and 4 are members of the subset.

In a computer program, we store the value of $G(J)$ at a location with an address equal to the label of J. In the basic recursion (3.1), we want quick access to the value of $G(J - j)$. Knowing the label of J, we can obtain the label of $(J - j)$ simply by subtracting the label of job j, or 2^{j-1}. This quick-access lookup for the value of $G(J - j)$ lies at the heart of the calculations. It is imbedded in a minimization loop that determines the choice of j that yields $G(J)$.

An outer loop provides a scheme for generating all the subsets. Let $b(i)$ take on the value 1 or 0 to reflect that job i is in or out of the subset. Start with $b(i) = 0$ for all i. To generate the next set, the loop proceeds as follows:

- Find the smallest integer j for which $b(j) = 0$. (If all $b(i) = 1$, then stop: All subsets have been generated.)
- Set $b(j) = 1$.
- For all $i < j$, set $b(i) = 0$.

In effect, the b-vector contains the binary representation of the label of set J, and we could add the labels of the jobs in J to compute the label for J. However, it is simpler to maintain the label of the set being treated by simply adding 2^{i-1} whenever $b(i)$ is switched from 0 to 1 and subtracting 2^{i-1} whenever $b(i)$ is switched from 1 to 0.

In summary, the computer implementation of dynamic programming requires two efficient devices, a scheme for labeling subsets and an algorithm for generating subsets. The labeling scheme provides efficient access to the value for a previously treated subset, while the generating algorithm ensures that all subsets are treated in a suitable order.

3.4 Dominance Properties

In the previous chapter, we encountered dominance properties involving *schedules*. We saw that schedules without preemption and without inserted idle time constitute a dominant set. Restricting attention to the dominant set reduces the number of alternatives – and therefore the computational effort – involved in searching for an optimal solution.

Now, we examine dominance properties involving *jobs*. For the T_w-problem, a simple dominance property is illustrated by the following result.

■ **Theorem 3.2**   Suppose that T_w is the measure of performance and that for some job k, the condition $d_k \geq p(X)$ holds. Then there exists an optimal schedule in which job k is assigned the last position in sequence.

Proof. Let S represent a schedule in which job k is not the last job. Construct schedule S' by removing job k and inserting it in the last position in sequence. Under the condition in the theorem, the shift does not increase the tardiness of job k. Moreover, all other jobs complete as early or earlier after the shift, so the tardiness of all jobs is no greater in schedule S than in schedule S'. Thus, the total weighted tardiness in any schedule will not become larger as a result of assigning job k to the last position. □

Theorem 3.2 states that it is sufficient for job k to follow all other jobs. This result defines a dominant set of sequences, in which k is the last job. In effect, the problem is reduced in size, for it remains only to determine how to assign the first $(n-1)$ positions to the remaining $(n-1)$ jobs. If we were enumerating sequences, this result would cut the search effort by a factor of n.

Another type of dominance property involves a relationship between a specific pair of jobs. Such a result states that it is sufficient for job i to follow job j or, equivalently, for job j to precede job i. If we were enumerating sequences, this result would cut the search effort by a factor of 2, and in combination, several such results could have a major impact. Some useful dominance properties of this type have been developed for the T-problem. Recall from the previous section that $p(J)$ represents the sum of processing times in set J and that X denotes the set of all jobs. Let

A_i = the set of jobs that have been shown to follow job i in an optimal sequence, sometimes called the *after* set.

A_i' = the complement of set A_i, defined as $A_i' = X - A_i$.

B_i = the set of jobs that have been shown to precede job i in an optimal sequence, sometimes called the *before* set.

The next result gives conditions under which job i precedes job j in an optimal sequence.

■ **Theorem 3.3** In the T-problem, an optimal schedule exists in which job j follows job i if one of the following conditions is satisfied:

a) $p_i \leq p_j$ and $d_i \leq \max\{d_j, p(B_j) + p_j\}$
b) $d_i \leq d_j$ and $d_j \geq p(A_i') - p_j$
c) $d_j \geq p(A_i')$

Condition (a) generalizes Theorem 2.8. Condition (c) generalizes Theorem 3.2 and holds for the T_w-problem as well. Conditions (a) and (b) extend to the T_w-problem if we also require $w_i \geq w_j$. We can prove condition (a) by interchanging jobs i and j. Also, we can prove conditions (b) and (c) by shifting job j to a position immediately after job i.

When we encounter a pair of jobs i and j that satisfies one of the conditions of Theorem 3.3, we can add job i to B_j and add job j to A_i. Each condition is based in part on information about the sets B_j or A_i. Initially, these sets may be taken to be empty. If one of the conditions holds for the pair of jobs i and j, then the sizes of B_j and A_i increase. This increase, in turn, may make it possible to satisfy the conditions for additional job pairs and thus for the size of the original problem to be reduced even further.

We collect the dominance information systematically in a dominance matrix D. The generic element of D is $d_{ij} = 1$ if job j follows job i, and $d_{ij} = 0$ otherwise. Two quantities that appear in Theorem 3.3 are denoted as follows:

$$Q_i = p\left(A_i'\right) \text{ and } R_j = p_j + p\left(B_j\right)$$

Also, let $|A_j|$ and $|B_j|$ denote the sizes of the sets A_j and B_j, respectively. Then a computational display for collecting the dominance information is shown in Table 3.3 as an expanded D-matrix. The matrix is filled in by testing pairs of jobs to determine whether one of the conditions in Theorem 3.3 holds. Each time one of the conditions succeeds, A_i and B_j are updated.

Once the matrix is filled in, it may be possible to reduce the size of the problem. If $|B_j| = n - 1$, then job j may be assigned the last position in sequence, and n

Table 3.3

	Job j					
Job i	d_{11}	d_{12}	...	d_{1n}	Q_1	$|A_1|$
	d_{21}	d_{22}	...	d_{2n}	Q_2	$|A_2|$
	$\vdots$	$\vdots$		$\vdots$	$\vdots$	$\vdots$
	d_{n1}	d_{n2}	...	d_{nn}	Q_n	$|A_n|$
	R_1	R_2	...	R_n		
	$|B_1|$	$|B_2|$	...	$|B_n|$		

can effectively be reduced by 1. If $|A_j| = n - 1$, then job j may be assigned the first position in sequence, and n can similarly be reduced by 1. (In this case, the problem that remains is reformulated by subtracting p_j from each due date.) When no more of these reductions are possible, we invoke an optimization procedure.

As it happens, dynamic programming is well suited to finding an optimal sequence in the presence of dominance properties. Thus, we assume that a dominance matrix has been determined, and we next wish to exploit that information in dynamic programming. Basically, this means that we want to carry out the dynamic programming calculations, but instead of examining all 2^n subsets, we want to limit consideration to undominated subsets. As we saw in the previous section, the key elements for computer implementation are a labeling scheme and a generation procedure.

The labeling scheme consists of a mechanism for assigning labels to jobs; then the label for a particular subset is simply the sum of the labels for the jobs contained in the subset. Suppose we renumber the jobs so that $i < j$ whenever $d_{ij} = 1$; that is, whenever job i dominates job j. Let N_j denote the set of jobs with a lower number than job j:

$$N_j = \{i \mid i < j\}$$

Let L_j denote the label for job j, and let $L(S)$ denote the sum of labels for the jobs contained in set S. Then

$$L_j = L(N_j) - L(B_j \cap N_j) + 1$$

In words, we sum the labels of all jobs numbered lower than j. Then we subtract the labels of all jobs in this set that dominate j. Then we add one. (If we had no dominance properties available, this scheme would reduce to the binary labeling scheme described in the previous section.)

The generation algorithm is only slightly modified from the one introduced for the basic form of dynamic programming. Recall that we renumber the jobs so that $i < j$ whenever job i dominates job j. The main loop proceeds as follows:

- Find the smallest integer j for which $b(j) = 0$. (If all $b(i) = 1$, then stop: All subsets have been generated.)
- Set $b(j) = 1$.
- For $i < j$, if $b(i) = 1$ and $J \cap A_i = \phi$, set $b(i) = 0$.

Here the only difference from the basic form of dynamic programming lies in the condition $J \cap A_i = \phi$. As we examine set J, we normally compute $G(J)$ from Eq. (3.1) by considering all subsets in which one job is removed from J. In the presence of dominance properties, however, we can limit ourselves to removing only those jobs that do not dominate other jobs in J.

■ **Example 3.3**   Consider a five-job problem with the criterion of minimizing total tardiness, in which we encounter the following dominance matrix:

$$D = \begin{bmatrix} --- & 0 & 1 & 0 & 0 \\ 0 & --- & 0 & 0 & 1 \\ 0 & 0 & --- & 0 & 0 \\ 0 & 0 & 0 & --- & 1 \\ 0 & 0 & 0 & 0 & --- \end{bmatrix}$$

Specifically, the matrix shows three dominance relations: Job 3 follows job 1 and job 5 follows job 2 and job 4. The labeling scheme yields the labels shown in order below:

Job j	1	2	3	4	5
L_j	1	2	3	7	5

Then the generation algorithm produces the subsets J in the following order:

Subset	Label	Indicator
ϕ	0	00000
{1}	1	00001
{2}	2	00010
{1, 2}	3	00011
{1, 3}	4	00101
{1, 2, 3}	6	00111

(Continued)

(Continued)

Subset	Label	Indicator
{4}	7	01000
{1, 4}	8	01001
{2, 4}	9	01010
{1, 2, 4}	10	01011
{1, 3, 4}	11	01101
{1, 2, 3, 4}	13	01111
{2, 4, 5}	14	11010
{1, 2, 4, 5}	15	11011
{1, 2, 3, 4, 5}	18	11111

This list contains 15 feasible subsets, including the empty set. Without dominance properties, the list would contain 2^5 or 32 subsets. In addition, the labels are not all consecutive: In particular, labels 5, 12, 16, and 17 are missing. (We say that such a labeling is not *compact*.) In a computer implementation, this means that space would have to be reserved for 19 values of $G(J)$, even though only 15 of them would ever be used. Although the gaps in this example do not present much of a difficulty, larger problems may have several wide gaps.

Once the labeling scheme is carried out, the size of the maximum label predicts how much computer storage capacity will be needed in order to find the optimal solution by dynamic programming. The computational effort required to solve the problem is, however, driven mainly by the number of feasible subsets. The advantage of using the dominance conditions is therefore to reduce the computational requirement, but there is usually a substantial reduction in storage capacity as well.

3.5   A Branch-and-bound Approach

A useful method for solving many combinatorial problems is a general-purpose strategy known as *branch and bound*. As its name implies, the approach consists of two fundamental procedures. *Branching* is the process of partitioning a large problem into two or more subproblems, and *bounding* is the process of calculating a lower bound on the optimal solution of a given subproblem.

The branching procedure replaces an original problem by a set of new problems that are:

a) Mutually exclusive and exhaustive subproblems of the original.
b) Partially solved versions of the original.
c) Smaller problems than the original.

Furthermore, the subproblems can themselves be partitioned in a similar fashion. As an example of a branching procedure, let $P(0)$ denote a single-machine sequencing problem containing n jobs. The problem $P(0)$ can be partitioned into n subproblems, $P(1)$, $P(2)$, ..., $P(n)$, by assigning the last position in sequence. Thus, $P(1)$ is the same problem, but with job 1 fixed in the last position; $P(2)$ is similar, but with job 2 fixed in the last position; and so on. Clearly, these subproblems are smaller than $P(0)$ because only $(n - 1)$ positions remain to be assigned, and obviously each $P(i)$ is a partially solved version of $P(0)$. In addition, the set of subproblems $P(i)$ is a mutually exclusive and exhaustive partition of $P(0)$ in the sense that if each $P(i)$ is solved, the best of these n solutions will represent an optimal solution to $P(0)$. Therefore, the $P(i)$ satisfy conditions (a), (b), and (c) above.

Next, each of the subproblems can be partitioned (see Figure 3.4). For instance, $P(2)$ can be partitioned into $P(12)$, $P(32)$, ..., $P(n2)$. In $P(12)$, jobs 1 and 2 occupy the last two positions of the sequence in that order; and in $P(32)$, jobs 3 and 2 occupy the last two positions. Therefore, the second-level partition $P(i2)$ bears the same relation to $P(2)$ as the first-level partition $P(i)$ bears to $P(0)$. That is, the partitions at each level satisfy conditions (a), (b), and (c). At level k, then, each subproblem contains k-fixed positions and can be further partitioned into $(n - k)$ subproblems, which form part of level $(k + 1)$. If this branching procedure were to be carried out completely, there would be $n!$

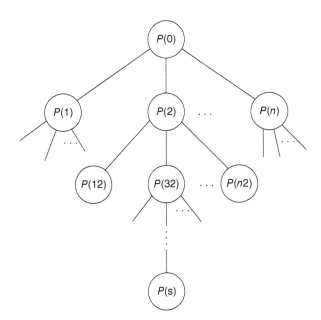

Figure 3.4 A branching scheme for single-machine problems.

subproblems at level n, each corresponding to a distinct feasible solution to the original problem. In other words, exhaustive pursuit of the branching tree would be equivalent to complete enumeration of all sequences. The function of the bounding process is to provide a means for curtailing this enumeration.

The bounding procedure calculates a lower bound on the solution to each subproblem generated in the branching process. Suppose that at some intermediate stage, a complete solution has been obtained that has an associated performance measure Z. Suppose also that a subproblem encountered in the branching process has an associated lower bound $b > Z$. Then the subproblem need not be considered any further in the search for an optimum. That is, no matter how the subproblem is resolved, the resulting solution can never have a value better than Z. When such a subproblem is found, its branch is said to be *fathomed*. By not branching any further from fathomed branches, the enumeration process is curtailed because feasible solutions of a fathomed subproblem are evaluated implicitly rather than being constructed explicitly.

A complete solution that allows branches to be fathomed is called a *trial solution*. It may be obtained at the very outset by applying a heuristic procedure (i.e. a suboptimal method capable of obtaining good solutions with limited computational effort); or it can be obtained in the course of the tree search, perhaps by pursuing the tree directly to the bottom as rapidly as possible.

We can now illustrate how these concepts are applied in the T-problem, once we introduce some convenient notation. Let s denote a partial sequence of jobs from among the n jobs originally in the problem. Also, let js denote the partial sequence in which s is immediately preceded by job j. We can treat s as an ordered set of jobs, so that

$$s' = \text{the complement of } s$$

$$p(s') = \sum_{j \in s'} p_j$$

Let $P(s)$ represent a subproblem at level k in the branching tree, where $k \leq n$. This subproblem will be the original problem $P(0)$ with the last k positions in sequence assigned, where s specifies the positions. Associated with $P(s)$ is a value, v_s, which is the contribution of assigned jobs to total tardiness. That is,

$$v_s = \sum_{j \in s} T_j$$

The T_j values in this sum can be calculated because the completion time of each job in the partial sequence s is known even though the complete sequence has not yet been determined.

Normally, the branching process partitions $P(s)$ into $(n - k)$ subproblems. Each subproblem, $P(js)$, is constructed by selecting some job j to be last in s', where j can be chosen $(n - k)$ distinct ways. Because the completion time of job j in the partial sequence js is $p(s')$, the value associated with $P(js)$ is

$$v_{js} = \max\{0, p(s') - d_j\} + v_s$$

Subproblem $P(s)$ may be treated as a single-machine sequencing problem containing $(n - k)$ jobs. This means, in particular, that Theorem 3.2 may be invoked: If there exists a job i in s' such that $d_i \geq p(s')$, then it is sufficient in solving $P(s)$ to place job i last. In this situation, we need not partition $P(s)$ into $(n - k)$ subproblems. Instead, we can partition $P(s)$ into just one subproblem, $P(is)$. Thus, it may be possible to exploit dominance properties within the branching tree so that some branches are avoided. Curtailing the branching process with dominance properties is sometimes called *elimination*.

In the bounding process, we seek a means of calculating a lower bound b_s on the total tardiness cost associated with any completion of the partial sequence s. One way of calculating a bound is obvious:

$$b_s = v_s \tag{3.4}$$

A slightly stronger bound can be obtained by pursuing the fact that some job in s' must be completed at $p(s')$. We may use

$$b_s = v_s + \min_{j \in s'}\left\{ \max\left[0, p(s') - d_j\right] \right\} \tag{3.5}$$

More complicated procedures may be employed for calculating even stronger lower bounds. In fact, the most successful computational advances for solving the T-problem involve a careful analysis of the computational costs and benefits of using complex lower bounds.

Once b_s is calculated, it may be possible to determine whether a completion of the subproblem $P(s)$ might lead to an optimum. Suppose a trial solution is available with a total cost of Z. When we compare Z and b_s, if $b_s < Z$, then a completion of s could possibly be optimal. Therefore, the subproblems $P(js)$ must be constructed and examined. On the other hand, if $b_s \geq Z$, then no completion of the partial sequence s could ever achieve a total tardiness less than Z, so its completions need not be enumerated in the search for an optimum. In this case, the branch corresponding to s is fathomed, and the search is somewhat shortened.

The branch-and-bound algorithm maintains a list of all subproblems that have not been eliminated by dominance properties and whose own subproblems have not yet been generated. These are called *active* subproblems. At any stage of the algorithm, it is sufficient to solve all active subproblems to determine an optimal solution to $P(0)$. In the following version of the algorithm, the active list is ranked by lower bound, smallest first. At each stage, the first subproblem on the active list is replaced by its own subproblems. This strategy is equivalent to continuing the branching process from the subproblem with the lowest bound, wherever that may be in the branching tree. The algorithm terminates when a trial solution appears at the head of the active list, because then no other subproblem could lead to a better solution. Also, in this form of the algorithm, no trial solution is obtained until the branching process itself reaches the bottom of the branching tree at some stage.

Algorithm 3.1 *Branch and Bound*

Step 1. (Initialization) Place $P(0)$ on the active list. The value associated with this node is $v_0 = 0$ and $p(\phi) = \sum_{j=1}^{n} p_j$.

Step 2. Remove the first subproblem, $P(s)$, from the active list. Let k denote the number of jobs in the partial sequence s. If $k = n$, stop: The complete sequence s is optimal. Otherwise, test Theorem 3.2 for $P(s)$. If the property holds, go to Step 3; otherwise, go to Step 4.

Step 3. Let job j be the job with the latest due date in s'. Create the subproblem $P(js)$ with

$$p(js) = p(s') - p_j, \ v_{js} = v_s, \text{ and } b_{js} = v_s$$

Place $P(js)$ on the active list, ranked by its lower bound. Return to Step 2.

Step 4. Create $(n - k)$ subproblems $P(js)$, one for each j in set s'. For $P(js)$, let

$$p(js) = p(s') - p_j, \ v_{js} = v_s + p(s') - d_j, \text{ and } b_{js} = v_{js}$$

Now place each $P(js)$ on the active list, ranked by its lower bound. Return to Step 2.

Algorithm 3.1 invokes three important options, all of which are open to some scrutiny. First, the algorithm employs the lower bounds given in Eq. (3.4). An obvious alternative is to use Eq. (3.5).

A second option involves the use of a trial solution. At any stage, the best trial solution yet found can be used in reducing the list of active subproblems. First, no subproblem need ever be placed below the trial solution on the active list, for such a subproblem can never lead to an optimum. Second, whenever a complete sequence is placed on the active list, all subproblems with greater bounds can be discarded. However, no trial solution can be encountered until the branching process has reached level n. An obvious alternative is to obtain a trial solution in Step 1. For instance, if the branch-and-bound approach is used in the T-problem, then an initial trial solution can be obtained using the MDD decision rule, as described in Chapter 2.

A third option involves the branching tactic itself – that is, the selection of the subproblem with the smallest bound as the candidate for further branching. This tactic is known as *jumptracking*, because the branching process tends to jump from one part of the branching tree to another at successive stages in the algorithm. An alternative is a tactic known as *backtracking*, in which the branching process first proceeds directly to level n along some path to obtain a trial solution. Then the algorithm retraces that path upward until it reaches a level on which unsolved subproblems remain. It selects one of these and again proceeds toward level n along a single path. The process may actually reach another trial solution, or it may fathom the branch it pursues by utilizing the value of the on-hand trial solution. In either case, the algorithm again backtracks up to the first level at which an unfathomed branch remains and then proceeds toward level n.

The characteristics of jumptracking and backtracking are considerably different. Backtracking maintains relatively few subproblems on the active list at any one time, while jumptracking tends to construct a fairly large active list. This is a disadvantage for jumptracking, mainly because each time it places a subproblem on the ranked list, it must search the list to determine exactly where on the list to place the subproblem. This searching may become quite time consuming in problems of moderate size. (This disadvantage may be remedied somewhat by clearing the list below any trial solution that is placed on it.) In addition, the list size requirement may restrict computerized versions of the algorithm when storage capacity does not readily accommodate a large list. On the other hand, an advantage in jumptracking is that the trial solutions it encounters tend to be very close to optimal, while the early trial solutions obtained by backtracking may be relatively poor. Thus, jumptracking usually does less branching in total, and this feature may compensate for its larger time per branch. Jumptracking branches from every subproblem that has a bound less than the value of an optimal sequence, and it may also generate some nonoptimal trial solutions. Backtracking may, in addition, branch from several subproblems that have bounds greater than the optimal value and may also generate very many nonoptimal trial solutions.

In addition to the trade-offs associated with the choice of branching tactics, trade-offs arise with other choices. For example, the lower bound in Eq. (3.5) is stronger than the bound in Eq. (3.4) and would be more effective in curtailing the branching process, yet more calculations are involved in computing the stronger bounds. Similarly, we can eliminate branches that violate the conditions of Theorem 3.3, again at the expense of additional computations. Also, starting the algorithm initially with a good trial solution can curtail the branching process considerably, yet more effort must be invested to obtain a better initial trial solution. In many respects, Algorithm 3.1 is a general prototype for a whole array of branch-and-bound methods, and the specific choice of tactics might be described as something of an art.

■ **Example 3.4**   Consider the following five-job problem, with the criterion of minimizing total tardiness.

Job j	1	2	3	4	5
p_j	4	3	7	2	2
d_j	5	6	8	8	17

The branching tree for this example problem is displayed in Figure 3.5. The lower bound v_s for each subproblem is entered just below the corresponding node in the figure. The order of branching is indicated by the number that appears just above the corresponding node. Initially, the tree consists of $P(0)$, with $v_0 = 0$ and $p(\phi) = 18$. At Step 2, the initial problem is removed from the active list and subsequently replaced by $P(1), P(2), P(3), P(4)$, and $P(5)$. As shown in the figure, $v_1 = 13$, $v_2 = 12$, $v_3 = 10$, $v_4 = 10$, and $v_5 = 1$. The jumptracking strategy calls for branching next from $P(5)$, since it is first on the active list. At the next stage, $P(35)$ and $P(45)$ both have the lowest bound on the active list, and the tie between them is broken arbitrarily in favor of the latter, so that the

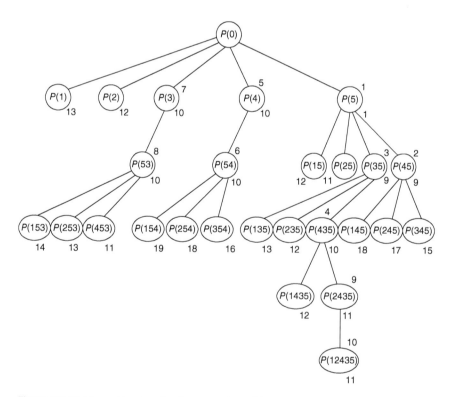

Figure 3.5 The branching tree for the example problem.

Table 3.4

Subproblem	Bound
$P(12435)$	11 trial solution
$P(453)$	11
$P(25)$	11
$P(1435)$	12
$P(235)$	12
$P(15)$	12
$P(2)$	12
$P(135)$	13
$P(253)$	13
$P(1)$	13
$P(153)$	14
$P(345)$	15
$P(354)$	16
$P(245)$	17
$P(254)$	18
$P(145)$	18
$P(154)$	19

subproblems of $P(45)$ are created. At this point, $P(35)$ is alone at the head of the active list and so its subproblems are generated next. Thereafter, the active list contains three subproblems with lower bounds of 10: $P(3)$, $P(4)$, and $P(435)$. In this type of situation, it is a good idea to break ties by branching from the problem that is closest to being completely solved, in this case, $P(435)$. In other words, priority is given to the subproblem with the largest k. Eventually, at the 10th branching iteration, the tree reaches the trial solution $P(12435)$ for which $v_{12435} = 11$. At this point, the trial solution is first on the active list, since k is being used as a tiebreaker; therefore, the algorithm terminates in Step 2. In effect, all branches have been fathomed at this stage, for the active list contains the 17 subproblems shown in Table 3.4. The optimal sequence 1-2-4-3-5 has a total tardiness equal to 11.

3.6 Integer Programming

The two main general-purpose approaches to finding optimal solutions in sequencing problems are dynamic programming and branch and bound, as described in previous sections. Although these descriptions (and the research articles from which those descriptions are taken) provide a road map for implementation, both approaches require some adaptation to the particular objective function of interest. Moreover, both require computer code to make the necessary calculations in all but the smallest problems, and the coding phase can be a challenge. Because the details of implementation are usually problem dependent, no general software exists for solving sequencing problems by dynamic programming or branch and bound. To find solutions using these methods, it is necessary to write computer code and tailor it to the type of problem being addressed.

On the other hand, general optimization software is widely available (and familiar to a broad audience) in the form of mathematical programming packages. An example would be Excel's Solver, which can be used on a spreadsheet platform without formal computer code. To use such a tool, we need only formulate the sequencing problem, and the software can then perform the desired optimization using an integer programming (IP) algorithm. Nevertheless, some alternative approaches exist, as we illustrate with the U_w-problem and the T-problem.

3.6.1 Minimizing the Weighted Number of Tardy Jobs

As discussed in Chapter 2, the U-problem can be solved using Algorithm 2.1. However, no simple extension of that algorithm exists for the U_w-problem. One possibility is to attack the U_w-problem with an IP approach.

The given parameters are processing times p_j, due dates d_j, and weights w_j that apply as lump-sum penalties to the tardy jobs. To formulate the problem, renumber the jobs so they conform to EDD ordering. (Recall that any set of on-time jobs can be sequenced in EDD order without causing tardiness.) Then let $x_j = 1$ if job j completes on time and $x_j = 0$ otherwise. The problem can then be expressed as follows:

$$\text{Maximize } \sum_{j=1}^{n} w_j x_j \tag{3.6}$$

$$\text{Subject to } \sum_{i=1}^{j} p_i x_i \le d_j, \quad \text{for } j = 1, 2, \ldots, n \tag{3.7}$$

$$x_j = 0 \text{ or } 1, \quad \text{for } j = 1, 2, \ldots, n \tag{3.8}$$

This is a rather simple formulation, which actually maximizes the weighted number of on-time jobs, a criterion that is equivalent to minimizing U_w. The constraints ensure that each on-time job is completed by its due date. The optimization model contains n binary variables and n constraints, and it can be built conveniently on a spreadsheet for the purposes of implementing Solver to find a solution.

■ **Example 3.5** Consider the following six-job problem, with the criterion of minimizing the weighted number of tardy jobs.

Job	1	2	3	4	5	6
Process time	64	79	19	27	6	27
Due date	82	83	106	118	142	155
Weight	9	8	5	10	7	7

A spreadsheet formulation of the integer program is displayed in Figure 3.6. To specify the model for Solver, we provide the following information:

- Maximize the objective function, B5.
- Take C4:H4 as the decision variables, all of which are binary variables.
- Satisfy the constraints I7:I12 ≤ K7:K12.

The model contains 6 decision variables and 6 constraints, and the optimal solution shown in Figure 3.6 provides for completing jobs 3 and 4 late, for a total tardiness penalty of 12. Equivalently, the total weight for on-time jobs is 32 when the remaining 4 jobs are positioned at the start of the sequence.

The spreadsheet platform affords the user considerable flexibility in model layout; the configuration shown in Figure 3.6 is just one of many possible ways to display the model on a spreadsheet.

The problem of minimizing the weighted number of tardy jobs can be solved effectively using the IP model in Eqs. (3.6)–(3.8). In fact, problems containing as many as 100 jobs can be solved in a few seconds using an IP approach and a

	A	B	C	D	E	F	G	H	I	J	K
1											
2					Decisions						
3			Job 1	Job 2	Job 3	Job 4	Job 5	Job 6			
4		Objective	1	1	0	0	1	1			
5		32	8	11	7	5	7	6			
6									LHS		RHS
7		Constraints	19						19 <=		60
8			19	29					48 <=		75
9			19	29	61				48 <=		78
10			19	29	61	72			48 <=		101
11			19	29	61	72	6		54 <=		102
12			19	29	61	72	6	13	67 <=		127
13											

Figure 3.6 Spreadsheet layout for the IP solution to Example 3.5.

spreadsheet platform. To provide some perspective on this result, consider two alternative approaches to finding a solution: (i) enumerating all possible sequences and choosing the best one and (ii) applying the dynamic programming algorithm in Eqs. (3.1)–(3.3). The enumeration code requires the systematic generation of all $n!$ job sequences. For each sequence, the code must calculate the value of the objective function, compare that value with the best value previously encountered, and save the better of the two. Such a code is relatively straightforward, but the number of sequences to be examined requires more and more time as the problem size increases. The dynamic programming code requires the systematic generation of subsets of jobs, which amounts to a smaller number than the number of sequences in enumeration. To get a sense of the computational requirements, these methods were compared with the requirements of an Excel-based IP approach. In each case, they were implemented with a computer that is representative of the hardware and software in current use.

Although the example problem can be solved in a fraction of a second by complete enumeration, a 10-job problem would take a few seconds. A 12-job problem would take a few minutes, and we can expect that the time required would grow roughly in proportion to $n!$ if we tested larger problem sizes. We can estimate that a 25-job problem would take around two weeks to solve. In practice, then, we would not expect to see problems larger than a dozen jobs solved by this method.

Dynamic programming solutions can be obtained more rapidly – in less than a second for problems as large as 15 jobs. However, we can anticipate that the time required increases roughly in proportion to $n2^n$, so that 30-job problems would take an hour or two. For larger sizes, we might begin to find that memory capacity may be inadequate to support the calculations.

By comparison, IP methods work quite well. To test solution times for IP, a set of randomly generated but nontrivial test problems was created, and the average solution time was recorded. (Complete enumeration and dynamic programming have time requirements that depend on the number of jobs but not on the details of other problem parameters. In contrast, the time requirements of IP vary somewhat with the configuration of processing times, due dates, and weights, so these experiments involved a sample of problems, based on which an average solution time was calculated.) Thus 30-job problems were solved in less than a second, and 100-job problems in just a few seconds. Such a quick solution of problems containing 100 jobs means that IP is a viable methodology for practical use, at least for the U_w-problem. More powerful branch-and-bound solutions have been presented in the research literature, but the ability to solve problems containing as many as 100 jobs with standard software in a matter of seconds renders the U_w-problem "solved" in practical terms.

However, the performance measure in the U_w-problem does not have to distinguish how late the tardy jobs are in the schedule, so in that respect it tends to be an easier problem to solve than most other sequencing problems. We look next at a different problem and an alternative IP approach.

3.6.2 Minimizing Total Tardiness

The T-problem is a challenging problem to solve, and we can use it to illustrate a different IP approach than the method for the U_w-problem. The given parameters are processing times p_j and due dates d_j. To formulate the problem, we can assign job numbers arbitrarily. The key binary variables are $x_{ik} = 1$ if job i is assigned to the kth position in sequence and $x_{ik} = 0$ otherwise. We refer to x_{ik} as the *sequence-position variable*. Another set of variables is the tardiness of kth job in sequence, denoted by t_k. With these variables, a mixed-integer program for the single-machine tardiness problem can be expressed as follows:

$$\text{Minimize} \quad \sum_{k=1}^{n} t_k \tag{3.9}$$

$$\text{Subject to} \quad \sum_{i=1}^{n} x_{ik} = 1 \quad \text{for all positions } k \tag{3.10}$$

$$\sum_{k=1}^{n} x_{ik} = 1 \quad \text{for all jobs } i \tag{3.11}$$

$$\sum_{i=1}^{n} p_i \left(\sum_{u=1}^{k} x_{iu} \right) - \sum_{i=1}^{n} d_i x_{ik} \leq t_k \tag{3.12}$$

$$x_{ik} = 0 \text{ or } 1; \quad t_k \geq 0 \tag{3.13}$$

The objective function in Eq. (3.9) is the sum of the tardiness values, which need not be integer valued. The sequence-position variables, on the other hand, must be binary. Thus, the model contains $(n^2 + n)$ variables, of which n^2 are binary. Constraints (3.10) and (3.11) describe a feasible job sequence, with one job assigned to each sequence position and one position occupied by each job. These are sometimes called *assignment constraints* because they occur in the classical assignment model. Constraint (3.12) calculates the lateness of the job in position k (on the left-hand side of the inequality) and compares it with the tardiness assigned to the job in position k. Because the tardiness variables are nonnegative by Eq. (3.13), minimization of the objective function will drive the value of t_k in Eq. (3.12) to equal the lateness of the job in position k if that job is tardy, and the value will be zero if the lateness of that job is negative or zero.

■ **Example 3.6** Consider the following five-job problem, with the criterion of minimizing total tardiness.

Job	1	2	3	4	5
Process time	40	78	73	11	22
Due date	54	66	143	145	149

A spreadsheet formulation of the integer program is displayed in Figure 3.7. The sequence-position variables appear in rows 9–13, with rows corresponding to jobs and columns to positions in sequence, as indicated by the labels. The tardiness values appear in row 8 and again in row 21, and the objective function appears in cell B8. To specify the model for Solver, we provide the following information:

• Minimize the objective function, B8.
• Take C8:G13 as the decision variables with C9:G13 as binary variables.
• Satisfy the row sum constraints H9:H13 = 1.

	A	B	C	D	E	F	G	H	I
1									
2		Data							
3		job	1	2	3	4	5		
4		process time	40	78	73	11	22		
5		due date	54	66	143	145	149		
6									
7		Objective (Min)	pos 1	pos 2	pos 3	pos 4	pos 5		
8		135	0	52	0	2	81	Row sum	
9		job 1	1	0	0	0	0	1	
10		job 2	0	1	0	0	0	1	
11		job 3	0	0	0	1	0	1	
12		job 4	0	0	0	0	1	1	
13		job 5	0	0	1	0	0	1	
14		Column sum	1	1	1	1	1		
15									
16		process	40	78	11	22	73		
17		complete	40	118	129	151	224		
18		due	54	66	145	149	143		
19		lateness	-14	52	-16	2	81		
20			<=	<=	<=	<=	<=		
21		tardiness	0	52	0	2	81		
22									

Figure 3.7 Spreadsheet layout for the IP solution to Example 3.6.

- Satisfy the column sum constraints C14:G14 = 1.
- Satisfy the tardiness definitions in constraints C19:G19 ≤ C21:G21.

The model contains 30 decision variables and 15 constraints, and the optimal solution shown in Figure 3.7 corresponds to the sequence 1-2-5-3-4, in which jobs 2, 4, and 5 are tardy, with a total tardiness of 135.

Again, the layout shown in Figure 3.7 is just one of many possible ways to display the model on a spreadsheet. For example, users more comfortable with integer programs in "standard form" might prefer a layout containing 30 columns, one for each variable. In any case, a software package such as Excel's Solver accommodates a variety of layouts and displays its solution directly on the spreadsheet. Moreover, the use of sequence-position variables, which is well suited to the T-problem, may not be the most efficient way to attack other sequencing problems with an IP approach.

The IP model for the T-problem has more variables and constraints than the model for the U_w-problem of the previous section. We might also expect that the computational properties are different as well. Again, a brief test of the IP model on a sample of randomly generated but nontrivial tardiness problems suggests the possibilities. In this case, 20-job problems can be solved in a few seconds by either dynamic programming or IP. However, 30-job problems might take an hour or two with dynamic programming, whereas the median solution time is around five minutes with IP. Beyond about 40 jobs, the time requirements for the IP approach may become prohibitive.

Other IP approaches to sequencing problems are available. For the T-problem, the evidence indicates that the sequence-position formulation is the most effective, but a small amount of research suggests that different formulations might work better for other performance measures. Nevertheless, if we were faced with the need to solve a 25-job problem, the IP approach is a practical way to obtain a solution. On the other hand, if we were faced with a 100-job problem, we would have to investigate the research literature to find a sophisticated procedure that was up to the task.

3.7 Summary

Challenging combinatorial optimization problems are encountered even in the simplest of scheduling problems. The previous chapter and Theorem 3.1 dealt with the relatively few situations in which we can easily characterize or construct the optimal solution. However, for most tardiness-based criteria, we must call on general-purpose techniques. Nevertheless, the methodologies described in this chapter contain many optional features that can determine their effectiveness in a given implementation. Some of these options are reviewed below.

The dynamic programming approach (Section 3.3) is a highly flexible implicit enumeration strategy that can be applied directly to many single-machine sequencing problems. Although no important design options arise in applying the technique to a given class of problems, an intriguing question is how to develop an efficient computer code for the algorithm. Because the computational demands of dynamic programming grow exponentially with problem size, it is particularly crucial to use an efficient code, even for moderate-sized problems. We discussed a strategy based on a labeling scheme and a set generation algorithm, but other strategies exist. We left open the question of how to identify alternative optima when they occur.

Dominance properties (Section 3.4) provide conditions under which certain potential solutions can be ignored. By exploiting dominance properties, the extensive calculations required by dynamic programming can be curtailed substantially. Based on this strategy, solution algorithms for the T_w-problem have been successful on problems of up to 30 jobs (Schrage and Baker 1978). Considering the improvements in CPU performance since these results were obtained, a speedup matched by memory and storage capacity improvements, we might expect dynamic programming to handle about up to roughly 40 jobs on a modern personal computer.

The branch-and-bound approach (Section 3.5) illustrates how implementing an optimization technique can require a good deal of judgment. This judgment must be exercised in the choice of a lower bound calculation, the potential use of an initial trial solution, the incorporation of complicated dominance checks, and the specification of a branching mechanism. In spite of the existence of these options, and the fact that they cannot be evaluated independently, branch-and-bound approaches have met with success in the solution of a wide variety of problems. For example, the T-problem has been attacked with branch-and-bound techniques that have been successful on problems as large as 500 jobs (Szwarc et al. 2001).

No comparable results are available for the T_w-problem, however. As it turns out, NP-hard problems belong to two broad classes: NP-hard *in the strong sense* (or the *strict* sense) and NP-hard *in the ordinary sense*. (Usually, the qualifier is used only for the former.) For the latter category, optimal solutions can be obtained by algorithms that are *pseudopolynomial*. As the term suggests, pseudopolynomial algorithms perform as efficiently as polynomial ones in practice but fail to meet the strict formal definition of a polynomial algorithm. For example, a pseudopolynomial algorithm may be polynomial in the total processing time but not in the number of processing times, which is typically the relevant measure of problem size. If that total processing time is small enough, the pseudopolynomial algorithm will perform efficiently. The existence of a pseudopolynomial solution usually implies that we can solve practical instances of the problem without prohibitive computational demands. Conversely, problems for which we can efficiently solve large instances – say, hundreds of jobs – are typically pseudopolynomial. This is the case for the T-problem, which has been shown to be pseudopolynomial by Lawler (1977). The T_w-problem, in contrast, is known to be NP-hard in the strong sense.

One complication with both dynamic programming and branch and bound is that no generic solvers exist. Instead, solutions are typically obtained from specially tailored code. In many situations, however, it is also possible to use an IP approach. The advantage of IP is that generic solvers are available and can even be implemented in spreadsheets.

Now, armed with some general optimization capabilities, we can investigate more complex problems in sequencing and scheduling. Ideally, we try to analyze the special structure of the problem and deduce the form of an optimal solution. However, sequencing and scheduling problems are notoriously difficult, and although we can make some progress with this type of analysis, we will often find its power is limited. When our analysis does not completely solve the problem, we can rely on such general techniques as dynamic programming, branch and bound, or IP.

Exercises

3.1 Consider the problem of minimizing the maximum weighted tardiness. Describe the optimal sequence in the following special cases.
a) All jobs have the same due date.
b) Weights and due dates are agreeable. In other words, $w_i > w_j$ implies $d_i \leq d_j$.

3.2 The following six jobs await sequencing on one machine.

Job j	1	2	3	4	5	6
Processing time p_j	12	2	6	14	8	13
Due date d_j	41	4	44	16	35	30
Cost factor c_j	3	5	2	4	3	5

When job j completes at time t, the cost function takes the following form:

$$f_j(t) = c_j \left[\max\{0, t - d_j\} \right]^2$$

Find the optimal sequence for minimizing the maximum value of $f_j(t)$.

3.3 Use dynamic programming to minimize U in the following example.

Job j	1	2	3	4	5
p_j	1	6	4	7	3
d_j	2	7	8	13	15

3.4 Formulate the problem of minimizing $T_{\max}$ as a dynamic programming problem by writing the appropriate recursion relations.

3.5 Describe how to identify multiple optima (assuming they exist) when using dynamic programming to solve the T-problem.

3.6 Solve the following T-problem by branch and bound.

Job j	1	2	3	4
p_j	5	6	9	8
d_j	9	7	11	13

a) Use Eq. (3.5) to compute bounds.
b) Use Eq. (3.4) to compute bounds.

3.7 Consider the example T-problem from Section 3.5.

Job j	1	2	3	4	5
p_j	4	3	7	2	2
d_j	5	6	8	8	17

Show which branches of the tree can be fathomed by using condition (a) of Theorem 3.3. Discuss the pros and cons of including this condition in the analysis.

3.8 Prove Theorem 3.3.

Bibliography

Baker, K.R. and Keller, B. (2010). Solving the single-machine tardiness problem using integer programming. *Computers & Industrial Engineering* 59: 730–735.

Elmaghraby, S.E. (1968). The one-machine sequencing problem with delay costs. *Journal of Industrial Engineering* 19: 105–108.

Emmons, H. (1969). One-machine sequencing to minimize certain functions of job tardiness. *Operations Research* 17: 701–715.

Kanet, J.J. (2007). New precedence theorems for one-machine weighted tardiness. *Mathematics of Operations Research* 32: 579–588.

Lawler, E.L. (1973). Optimal sequencing of a single machine subject to precedence constraints. *Management Science* 19: 544–546.

Lawler, E.L. (1977). A "pseudopolynomial" algorithm for sequencing jobs to minimize total tardiness. *Annals of Discrete Mathematics* 1: 331–342.

Mitten, L.G. (1970). Branch and bound methods: general formulation and properties. *Operations Research* 18: 24–34.

Rau, J.G. (1971). Minimizing a function of permutations of *n* integers. *Operations Research* 19: 237–239.

Rinnooy Kan, A.H.G., Lenstra, J.K., and Lageweg, B.J. (1975). Minimizing total costs in one machine scheduling. *Operations Research* 23: 908–927.

Schrage, L.E. and Baker, K.R. (1978). Dynamic programming solution of sequencing problems with precedence constraints. *Operations Research* 26: 444–449.

Shwimer, J. (1972). On the *n*-job, one-machine, sequence-independent scheduling problem with tardiness penalties: a branch and bound solution. *Management Science* 18: 301–313.

Szwarc, W., Grosso, A., and Della Croce, F. (2001). Algorithmic paradoxes of the single machine total tardiness problem. *Journal of Scheduling* 4: 93–104.

4

Heuristic Methods for the Single-machine Problem

4.1 Introduction

In earlier chapters, we studied the basic single-machine sequencing model, paying particular attention to the variations that arise for different objective functions. For some objective functions, such as total flowtime, we saw that an optimal solution can be obtained by a procedure as simple as sorting the jobs. For other objective functions, such as total weighted tardiness, no simple solution procedure is available, and we have to resort to more general techniques of combinatorial optimization.

As mentioned earlier, the computational effort required to solve problems using combinatorial procedures grows remarkably fast as the size of the problem increases. Suppose, for instance, that a computer application for the dynamic programming algorithm allows us to generate and evaluate 1 000 000 subsets per second. Then the solution of a 25-job problem would consume roughly half a minute of computer time, but a 35-job problem would take roughly 9 hours to solve, and a 45-job problem would take over a year. If we need a quick answer to a 45-job problem, the dynamic programming approach will hardly be suitable. In the case of branch-and-bound algorithms, we cannot guarantee a better performance because it is impossible to predict the computational effort precisely: It depends on the parameters in each specific problem.

Although it would be difficult to designate any one problem size as typical of practical problems, we believe that the ability to solve problems containing 30–50 jobs is usually sufficient for most practical needs. (Additional jobs are likely to be scheduled at a later time.) But we may also encounter the single-machine model as a component of more complex problems involving such features as precedence constraints, multiple machines, or multiple operations

Principles of Sequencing and Scheduling, Second Edition. Kenneth R. Baker and Dan Trietsch.
© 2019 John Wiley & Sons, Inc. Published 2019 by John Wiley & Sons, Inc.

per job. The ability to solve 30-job single-machine problems does not imply that we can solve optimally for 30 jobs in more complex problems. In multimachine models, single-machine submodels may have to be solved repeatedly, perhaps as many as 2^n times. Therefore, it is important to assess the computational demands of an optimizing technique whenever its use is contemplated. When those demands are substantial, we may want to consider suboptimal methods, or *heuristic procedures*, which are capable of obtaining good solutions with limited computational effort. In contrast to such methodologies as dynamic programming or branch and bound, these techniques do not guarantee that an optimum will be found, yet they are relatively simple and effective.

In this chapter, we introduce some generic heuristic procedures that have proven useful in solving scheduling problems. We describe their application to deterministic single-machine problems but mainly for illustration: The same procedures can be adapted to stochastic single-machine problems, as well as a variety of other scheduling problems. In later chapters, when we deal with more complicated models, we will refer to these techniques.

Because heuristic procedures do not reliably produce optimal schedules, it is logical to ask just how suboptimal they might be. In an experimental setting, a researcher might attempt to answer this question by solving several problems using a heuristic procedure and then estimating either the frequency with which optimal solutions are produced or the average deviation from optimality. Such performance measures give us some insight into the reliability of a particular procedure. In this chapter, we illustrate how heuristic procedures can be evaluated taking that approach.

4.2 Dispatching and Construction Procedures

As we noted earlier, some of the simplest solution methods require only the sorting of jobs. For example, in the *F*-problem, sorting the jobs according to SPT produces an optimal sequence. Actually, at the time the machine becomes idle, it is not really necessary to sort all of the waiting jobs – we need only identify the shortest waiting job and schedule that one to be next. More specifically, we use the term *sorting* to describe the use of a ranking scheme with the property that the relative ranking of two jobs does not change with time. In other words, sorting involves static priorities. In addition, if a new job is added to a sorted set, the relative ranking of the original jobs does not change. To determine whether the new job should be the next one scheduled, we do not have to resort the entire set of jobs – we need only compare the new job to the current job with highest priority.

More generally, we use the term *dispatching* to describe a procedure that uses a decision rule to select the next job each time the machine becomes free. Dispatching includes dynamic as well as static sorting rules. To illustrate a dynamic version, consider the T-problem. A simple yet effective heuristic rule ranks jobs by the MDD criterion. Recall from Chapter 2 that the modified due date of job j at time t is defined by

$$d'_j(t) = \max\{d_j, t + p_j\} \tag{4.1}$$

We also saw there that if jobs i and j are the candidates to begin at time t, then the job with the earlier modified due date should come first. We then noted that if we use the rule as a dispatching procedure, we may not obtain the optimal solution.

■ **Example 4.1** Consider a problem containing $n = 3$ jobs with known processing times and due dates.

Job j	1	2	3
p_j	8	9	12
d_j	15	13	10
$d'_j(0)$	15	13	12

Suppose that MDD is implemented as a dispatching procedure for the three-job problem in Example 4.1. At time $t = 0$, the modified due dates are given by $d'_j(0)$, so the ranking of the jobs at time zero is 3-2-1. Therefore, job 3 is selected to be first and completes at time 12. The next decision takes place at time $t = 12$, and the scheduling problem appears as follows:

Job j	1	2
p_j	8	9
d_j	15	13
$d'_j(12)$	20	21

Here, the modified due dates are given by $d'_j(12)$, and the rule selects job 1 before job 2, which reverses the ranking of the two jobs at time zero. The final sequence is 3-1-2, with $T = 23$, which happens to be suboptimal.

As the example illustrates, a dispatching procedure ranks all the unscheduled jobs each time a decision arises because the ranking may change over time. The result is a selection of the most urgent job when the machine becomes available. A sorting rule is easier to implement when it is static, because the jobs need to be ranked only once. A dynamic rule, such as MDD, requires repeated reranking of the jobs, but the computations are modest. In actual practice, a static sorting rule typically permits the use of a physical label for each job, displaying a number, which represents a relatively simple way to convey scheduling priorities. A dynamic rule does not lend itself easily to physical labels, but a computerized decision support system can update the priorities easily.

For another dynamic dispatching example, we turn to the more complex T_w-problem. A heuristic approach is to generalize MDD to the *weighted modified due date* (WMDD) rule, defined as nondecreasing order of the quantity $\max\{d_j - t, p_j\}/w_j$. Dispatching by this rule involves sorting the jobs and selecting the job with the smallest WMDD as the next job. The sequence is dynamic, because the dispatching criterion depends on t.

One useful way to judge heuristics is to trace their behavior in special cases and to check that they reduce to good decision rules. For example, if all weights are equal, then WMDD reduces to the MDD rule. Also, if all due dates are zero, WMDD reduces to SWPT, which is optimal when all jobs must be late. However, unlike MDD, WMDD is not guaranteed to sequence even two jobs optimally.

■ **Example 4.2**   Consider a problem containing $n = 2$ jobs with known processing times, due dates, and weights.

Job j	1	2
p_j	2	5
d_j	8	6
w_j	3	2

For job 1, the MWDD is calculated as $8/3 = 2.7$. For job 2 the calculation is $6/2 = 3$. Thus, by the WMDD heuristic, job 1 should precede job 2, leading to a total weighted tardiness of 2. The opposite sequence, by contrast, has no tardiness.

The desired sequencing can be detected in two ways. One is by trial and error. The other is by invoking a test based on an exact generalization of MDD. Suppose that jobs i and j are considered for the next two positions (without any other job inserted between them), and let $s_j^+ = \max\{d_j - p_j - t, 0\}$. If

$$\frac{p_i}{w_i}\left(1 - \frac{s_j^+}{p_i}\right) \le \frac{p_j}{w_j}\left(1 - \frac{s_i^+}{p_j}\right) \tag{4.2}$$

then i can precede j with at most the same total weighted tardiness. When we apply this test for the sequence 1-2 in Example 4.2, the test fails:

$$\frac{2}{3}\left(1 - \frac{1}{2}\right) > \frac{5}{2}\left(1 - \frac{6}{5}\right)$$

This result indicates that job 2 should precede job 1 if both of them are to be scheduled in the next two positions. In particular, the test can be applied to the first two jobs in any proposed sequence, taking $t = 0$. For later pairs of jobs, however, we need to know the value of t.

A *construction* procedure, like a dispatching procedure, builds a schedule from scratch, normally adding jobs to the schedule one at a time, but it does not necessarily add the jobs in order from earliest to latest. For example, one logical way to construct a schedule in the T-problem is to choose a job to be last in sequence. Because we know what time the last job will complete, we can select the job that will incur the least amount of tardiness when it finishes last. What remains is a problem consisting of $(n - 1)$ jobs, which we can resolve the same way. This approach is sometimes called a *greedy* procedure, in that it makes the next selection in the most favorable way, without regard to the consequences that might arise later in the algorithm. (A greedy algorithm could also focus on choosing the *first* job in sequence, but in tardiness-related problems, the last-to-first structure is often more productive.)

In this particular application of a greedy procedure, we make k comparisons when there are k jobs left to be scheduled. Thus, the computational effort is $O(n^2)$. An illustration follows.

■ **Example 4.3** Consider a problem containing $n = 5$ jobs with known processing times and due dates.

Job j	1	2	3	4	5
p_j	2	3	1	6	4
d_j	12	4	7	10	6

In this example, we know that the last job in sequence will complete at time 16. The job that would have the smallest tardiness if it were to complete at 16 is job 1. Once we assign job 1 to be last, we know that the fourth job will complete at time 14. Among the unscheduled jobs, the smallest tardiness at time 14 would occur for job 4, so we assign it to be fourth. Continuing in this fashion, the algorithm constructs the sequence 2-5-3-4-1, with a total tardiness of $T = 10$.

In the special case of the T-problem, the greedy algorithm reduces to a familiar device for static dispatching, namely, the EDD rule. In more complicated problems, greedy algorithms may not be as recognizable, but they tend to provide at least adequate results and are sometimes surprisingly effective. (For example, in this case, MDD – which is also greedy – yields $T = 8$, which happens to be optimal.)

Another widely used construction procedure is the *insertion* procedure, which works as follows. Consider the subproblem consisting of just jobs 1 and 2. Optimize their sequence (by comparing the alternatives 1-2 and 2-1). Next, keeping the relative order of the first two jobs fixed, find the best location in which to insert job 3. In other words, if 1-2 is the better of the two-job alternatives, consider the three alternatives 3-1-2, 1-3-2, and 1-2-3. If 2-1 is the better of the two-job alternatives, consider the three alternatives 3-2-1, 2-3-1, and 2-1-3. At stage k, we obtain a solution to the k-job subproblem consisting of the first k jobs. Then at stage $(k + 1)$, we keep the relative order of the first k jobs fixed in that sequence and consider inserting job $(k + 1)$ into each of the $(k + 1)$ possible positions. We select the best of these $(k + 1)$ alternatives for consideration at the next stage, and we stop when we have generated the best n-job alternative. The insertion procedure usually requires a computational effort of $O(n^3)$.

As an illustration, we use the data in Example 4.3. At the initial stage, we compare the two-job sequences 1-2 and 2-1:

Job j	1	2		Job j	2	1
T_j	0	1		T_j	0	0

Based on this comparison, we retain the partial sequence 2-1 and next consider where to insert job 3:

$$3\text{-}2\text{-}1\,(T = 0) \quad 2\text{-}3\text{-}1\,(T = 0) \quad 2\text{-}1\text{-}3\,(T = 0)$$

Here, we arbitrarily break the tie in favor of the first sequence encountered, 3-2-1. At the next stage, we have four partial sequences to consider:

$$4\text{-}3\text{-}2\text{-}1\,(T = 6) \quad 3\text{-}4\text{-}2\text{-}1\,(T = 6) \quad 3\text{-}2\text{-}4\text{-}1\,(T = 0) \quad 3\text{-}2\text{-}1\text{-}4\,(T = 2)$$

Here, we retain the partial sequence 3-2-4-1 and examine five ways to convert it to a complete sequence:

$$5\text{-}3\text{-}2\text{-}4\text{-}1\,(12) \quad 3\text{-}5\text{-}2\text{-}4\text{-}1\,(12) \quad 3\text{-}2\text{-}5\text{-}4\text{-}1\,(10) \quad 3\text{-}2\text{-}4\text{-}5\text{-}1\,(12) \quad 3\text{-}2\text{-}4\text{-}1\text{-}5\,(10)$$

Thus, the insertion procedure generates a solution with $T = 10$, producing two sequences that achieve this value. (As mentioned earlier, however, this value is not optimal.)

We turn now to the question of how well these procedures perform. One approach to answering this question involves a comparison of heuristic procedures using a common set of test problems. For the purposes of illustration, we use a set of twelve 20-job T_w-problems selected from a testbed developed by Rinnooy Kan et al. (1975). These test problems, reproduced in Table 4.8 at the end of the chapter, are known to be relatively difficult to optimize.

These test problems were solved with a variety of dispatching procedures, including a random dispatching mechanism. The same problems were also solved using the greedy and insertion procedures. For the WMDD dispatching rule, we also tested the improvement available by meeting the condition of Eq. (4.2). For each problem, the experiment recorded the ratio of the heuristic

Table 4.1

Algorithm	Optimizing frequency	Average ratio	Maximum ratio
Random	0 of 12	1.86	2.51
SPT	0 of 12	1.67	2.90
MST	0 of 12	1.49	1.79
EDD	0 of 12	1.46	1.77
SWPT	0 of 12	1.35	1.96
Greedy	0 of 12	1.22	1.39
Insertion	0 of 12	1.20	1.44
WMDD	4 of 12	1.02	1.10
WMDD + correction	5 of 12	1.02	1.10

solution to the optimal solution. Three performance measures were tallied: a count of the number of times the optimum was found, the average ratio of the heuristic solution to the optimal solution, and the maximum solution ratio. The results are summarized in Table 4.1. As the table clearly shows, most basic dispatching procedures were not especially effective in solving the T_w-problem. WMDD was the clear winner, followed by the greedy and insertion techniques. A decent heuristic usually gets within 10% of the optimum, and a really good one reliably gets within 1–2%. So WMDD is a decent heuristic, but there is still room for testing other kinds of heuristic approaches. In addition, WMDD applies only to the T_w-problem, so we must study additional heuristics if we want to tackle other objective functions.

The combination of WMDD and the correction of Eq. (4.2) is not a pure dispatching or construction procedure because it involves revisiting earlier decisions after later ones reveal they could be improved. Indeed, the correction step is a rudimentary example of a *search technique*. Search techniques, such as those we describe in later sections, are fundamentally different than construction procedures. Whereas construction methods start from scratch and build one schedule, search procedures assume that a solution has already been built, and they examine a series of alternative solutions in an effort to find improvements.

4.3 Random Sampling

It may seem surprising to speak of random sampling methods in connection with deterministic scheduling problems. However, random sampling has been employed directly in other combinatorial settings and may provide a viable solution strategy for many scheduling problems.

The essence of a sampling procedure is easy enough to describe. Using some random device, construct and evaluate N sequences, and identify the best sequence in the sample. We can view random sampling as a solution method that lies on a continuum between a specialized heuristic procedure and an optimizing procedure. Many heuristic procedures, such as the greedy algorithm described earlier, generate one sequence, while an optimizing procedure, such as branch and bound, enumerates all $n!$ sequences, at least implicitly. A random sampling procedure constructs some intermediate number of sequences and selects the best one. The design of a sampling scheme must resolve two tactical questions:

1) How to specify a particular device for carrying out sampling?
2) How to draw conclusions about the best sequence in the sample?

Much of the literature on sampling techniques has attempted to provide some insight into the answers to these questions, which we next explore in more detail.

It is not easy to draw substantive conclusions about the best sequence found in the sample. The ideal information is the likelihood that a sample contains an optimum or the distance from optimality. Unfortunately, these relationships are generally known only qualitatively: A larger sample is more likely than a smaller sample to contain an optimum, and the best sequence in a larger sample also tends to be closer to the optimal value. But without quantitative information about these relationships, there is virtually no logical way to select a sample size. In principle, there is a certain probability p that on a particular trial, a specified sampling procedure will construct an optimum for a given problem. Therefore, because sampling is essentially done with replacement, the probability that an optimum will be found in a sample of size N is $[1 - (1 - p)^N]$. The difficulty is to estimate p.

In the basic single-machine problem, there is perhaps one situation in which we can draw a quantitative conclusion. Suppose that a sequence is constructed by assigning the first position in sequence, then the second, and so on. In order to assign the first sequence position, suppose that a random device is used and that each job is assigned to this position with probability $1/n$. After this assignment, suppose that each remaining job is assigned to second position with probability $1/(n-1)$. If we continue in this manner, then we will assign each position by an equally likely selection device. In this structure, all of the $n!$ sequences are equally likely to be included in the sample. If the optimum is unique, then $p = 1/n!$, so in this procedure we can conclude that the best sequence in a sample of size N is an optimum with probability $[1 - (1 - 1/n!)^N]$. On the subject of how close to optimal the best sequence in the sample may be, it is still not possible to provide quantitative conclusions. In order to suggest the kind of behavior that might occur, a set of random sampling experiments was conducted with the 20-job test problems. Three different sample sizes were tested, and the results are shown in Table 4.2 and compared with the random dispatching and the greedy algorithm from Table 4.1. (The

Table 4.2

Algorithm	Optimizing frequency	Average ratio	Maximum ratio
Random	0 of 12	1.86	2.51
Sampling (N = 20)	0 of 12	1.59	2.08
Sampling (N = 100)	0 of 12	1.51	1.90
Sampling (N = 500)	0 of 12	1.41	1.72
Greedy	0 of 12	1.22	1.39

random dispatching procedure is equivalent to random sampling with a sample size of N = 1.)

Table 4.2 shows that solution efficiency improves with sample size, which we should have expected. We also observe that the sampling procedure is not nearly as effective as the greedy heuristic even for a sample size of 500, which involves a computational effort much greater than that of the greedy heuristic.

More generally, we should think in terms of selection devices that are not equally likely, and we should recognize that such mechanisms might yield a value of p much larger than $1/n!$. The following is an example of a simple method for performing *biased random sampling*. We begin by ordering the jobs according to some ranking rule. To assign the first position in sequence, we select the job in jth position on the ordered list with probability p_{1j} (j = 1, 2, ..., n). These probabilities are "biased" in the sense that they favor the first job on the list to the second, the second to the third, and so on. Next, we remove the assigned job from the list, and we assign the second position by selecting the job in jth position on the updated ordered list with probability p_{2j} (j = 1, 2, ..., n − 1). In this approach, we use a discrete distribution p_{kj} at the kth stage. A typical approach would use a set of p_{kj} values that follow a truncated geometric distribution. In this case the selection device corresponds to

$$p_{kj} = \pi^j Q_k, \quad j = 1, 2, ..., n + 1 - k$$

where Q_k is a normalizing constant. With this structure, the first job on the ordered list has the highest probability of being selected, the second job has the second highest probability, and so on. In addition, the probabilities decrease in a geometric manner, but the nature of the decrease can be controlled by selecting the parameter π. For example, if there are eight jobs and we set π = 0.6, then the probabilities are as follows:

j	1	2	3	4	5
p_{kj}	0.297	0.238	0.190	0.152	0.122

Table 4.3

Algorithm	Optimizing frequency	Average ratio	Maximum ratio
Sampling (N = 500)	0 of 12	1.41	1.72
Sampling (π = 0.8, N = 20; MST)	0 of 12	1.46	1.76
Sampling (π = 0.8, N = 20; EDD)	0 of 12	1.42	1.62
Sampling (π = 0.8, N = 20; SWPT)	0 of 12	1.30	1.82
Sampling (π = 0.8, N = 100; SWPT)	0 of 12	1.25	1.60
Sampling (π = 0.8, N = 500; SWPT)	0 of 12	1.21	1.53
Greedy	0 of 12	1.22	1.39

A larger value of π would make the jobs early on the list more likely to be selected, while a smaller π would distribute the selection probabilities more equally. Thus, we can bias the random selection process of the basic sampling method toward a given job ordering and thereby improve the efficiency of the sampling. For the 20-job test problems, Table 4.3 compares some biased sampling plans with the equally likely plan described in Table 4.2.

The results suggest that biased random sampling improves on pure random sampling. In other words, the intelligent choice of a job ordering and a bias in the randomization are worth more than a large amount of sampling. In Table 4.3, the performance of random sampling with a sample size of 500 was virtually matched by the performance of biased sampling with a sample size of only 20. In fact, with SWPT as the initial ordering, the biased sampling procedure was even better on average.

In short, random sampling is a procedure for obtaining good solutions to combinatorial problems with simple, straightforward logic and limited computational effort. In more complicated problems, both in and out of the scheduling field, sampling techniques have provided effective heuristic procedures. However, as the results in our next computational experiments suggest, sampling is not always competitive with other general-purpose heuristic procedures. Its virtues are ease of implementation and flexibility. The flexibility derives from many tactical options. These options include the initial ordering of the jobs for biased sampling, the selection of a probability distribution for assigning probabilities to positions, and the determination of sample size. The art of applying random sampling lies in specifying these tactics in order to arrive at an effective sampling procedure. Different tactics may perform well in different types of problems, so it may take some experimentation to determine the tactics that are best suited to any particular application. Finally, random sampling is potentially useful in combination with other heuristics. For example, each random sample could be subjected to the insertion heuristic; this combination is very likely to improve on the basic sampling procedure.

4.4 Neighborhood Search Techniques

The basic elements in the neighborhood search approach are the concept of a neighborhood of a solution and a mechanism for generating neighborhoods. The generating mechanism is a method of taking one sequence as a *seed* and systematically creating a collection of related sequences. For example, the adjacent pairwise interchange (API) operation might serve as a generating mechanism. If the seed sequence were $1, 2, 3, \ldots, n$, then any of the following sequences could be formed by a single API:

$$2,1,3,4, \quad \cdots, \quad n-2, n-1, n$$
$$1,3,2,4, \quad \cdots, \quad n-2, n-1, n$$
$$\vdots$$
$$1,2,3,4, \quad \cdots, \quad n-1, n-2, n$$
$$1,2,3,4, \quad \cdots, \quad n-2, n, n-1$$

This is a list of $(n - 1)$ distinct sequences, called the *neighborhood* of the seed sequence, for this particular generating mechanism.

It is not difficult to envision other methods of generating neighborhoods. The last-insertion (LI) mechanism inserts the last job of the seed into other positions. In this case, if the seed sequence were $1, 2, 3, \ldots, n$, the neighborhood of the seed would be

$$n,1,2, \quad \ldots, \quad n-1$$
$$1,n,2, \quad \ldots, \quad n-1$$
$$\vdots$$
$$1,2,3, \quad \ldots, \quad n,n-1$$

which is again a list of $(n - 1)$ sequences.

The choice of a generating mechanism determines the size of the neighborhood. For example, a neighborhood could be generated by all pairwise interchanges, not just the adjacent ones. This PI neighborhood contains a list of $n(n - 1)/2$ sequences. A generalization of the LI neighborhood described above is to insert the job in sequence position i into position j, where $j \neq i$. In this insertion neighborhood, there are $n(n - 1)$ sequences. In general, given a seed and a generating mechanism, any sequence that can be formed from the seed by a single application of the generating mechanism is defined to be in the neighborhood of the seed. In this context, a search algorithm requires the specification of a generating mechanism. A general description of a neighborhood search algorithm is given below.

Algorithm 4.1 *Neighborhood Search*

Step 1. Obtain a sequence to be an initial seed and evaluate it with respect to the performance measure.

Step 2. Generate and evaluate all the sequences in the neighborhood of the seed. If none of the sequences is better than the seed with respect to the performance measure, stop. Otherwise proceed.

Step 3. Select one of the sequences in the neighborhood that improved the performance measure. Let this sequence be the new seed. Return to Step 2.

Within this general framework, we must specify certain tactical options:

1) A method of obtaining the initial seed.
2) A generating mechanism.
3) A method of selecting a particular sequence to be the new seed.

■ **Example 4.4** Consider a problem containing $n = 5$ jobs with known processing times and due dates.

Job j	1	2	3	4	5
p_j	2	3	1	6	4
d_j	12	7	4	10	6

Suppose again that the objective is to minimize T and that the tactical options are handled as follows:

1) The initial seed is the sequence 1-2-3-4-5.
2) The generating mechanism is API.
3) The first improvement in the neighborhood becomes the new seed.

Table 4.4 traces the implementation of Algorithm 4.1 on the five-job example. The initial sequence, 1-2-3-4-5, attains the value $T = 14$. An improvement occurs in the first neighborhood, and the sequence 1-3-2-4-5 (with $T = 12$) becomes the new seed by virtue of being the first improvement in the neighborhood. Again, an improvement is found in the search of the new neighborhood, and the new seed is the sequence 1-3-2-5-4, with $T = 10$. Next, a search of the new neighborhood produces no improvement, and the search procedure terminates.

Table 4.4

Stage 1			
Seed	1-2-3-4-5	$T = 14$	
Neighborhood	2-1-3-4-5	$T = 14$	
	1-3-2-4-5	$T = 12$	*Selection
	1-2-4-3-5	$T = 19$	
	1-2-3-5-4	$T = 12$	
Stage 2			
New seed	1-3-2-4-5	$T = 12$	
Neighborhood	3-1-2-4-5	$T = 12$	
	1-2-3-4-5	$T = 12$	
	1-3-4-2-5	$T = 15$	
	1-3-2-5-4	$T = 10$	*Selection
Stage 3			
New seed	1-3-2-5-4	$T = 10$	
Neighborhood	3-1-2-5-4	$T = 10$	
	1-2-3-5-4	$T = 12$	
	1-3-5-2-4	$T = 10$	
	1-3-2-4-5	$T = 12$	
Search terminates with $T = 10$			

The search procedure of Algorithm 4.2 always terminates with a solution that is a *local* optimum with respect to the given neighborhood structure. Unfortunately, there is no general way to know whether the terminal sequence is also a *global* optimum. For example, in the T-problem, sorting by MDD can reveal whether a solution is locally optimal with respect to the API neighborhood, but not whether the solution is globally optimal. Similarly, in the T_w-problem, satisfying Eq. (4.2) is equivalent to local optimality but not global optimality. As in other kinds of search procedures, it is possible to augment the basic algorithm and improve its chances of finding a global optimum in a number of ways, for example:

1) Generate several sequences to serve as initial seed. Employ the full search procedure for each initial seed, and take the best terminal sequence found.
2) In each neighborhood, keep track of all sequences that improve on the seed. Use each of these as a seed for a new neighborhood.
3) Choose a generating mechanism that creates large neighborhoods.

Table 4.5

Algorithm	Optimizing frequency	Average ratio	Maximum ratio
Greedy	0 of 12	1.22	1.39
NS(API, greedy)	0 of 12	1.089	1.26
NS(PI, greedy)	10 of 12	1.003	1.04
NS(LI, greedy)	0 of 12	1.21	1.39
NS(AI, greedy)	9 of 12	1.0004	1.004
Insertion	0 of 12	1.20	1.44
NS(API, insertion)	2 of 12	1.078	1.22
NS(PI, insertion)	9 of 12	1.001	1.007
NS(LI, insertion)	0 of 12	1.20	1.44
NS(AI, insertion)	3 of 12	1.009	1.04

Although these and other augmentation methods are eminently logical, they still cannot offer a guarantee that a global optimum will be found. Nevertheless, a few experimental studies have indicated that even the fundamental version of the neighborhood search algorithm is fairly reliable as a general-purpose heuristic procedure. As an illustration, Algorithm 4.2 was applied to the 20-job test problems, with API neighborhoods and then with all PI neighborhoods. It was also tested with LI neighborhoods and all-insertion (AI) neighborhoods. Finally, the algorithm was initialized with two procedures, the greedy algorithm and the insertion algorithm. In Table 4.5, the neighborhood and the initial seed are indicated in parentheses, along with a summary of results. In each case, the first improvement in the neighborhood identified the new neighborhood.

The neighborhood search procedure was especially effective when it invoked the larger neighborhoods. As the table shows, the LI neighborhood had little impact, and the API neighborhood achieved modest gains. The PI and AI neighborhoods, which are $O(n^2)$ in size, provided more effective performance. No single combination dominated the others in this experiment, although the best value for each of the three tabulated performance criteria was obtained by starting with the greedy algorithm.

The neighborhood search technique generally appears to be a promising heuristic procedure for solving sequencing problems. Several options exist, however, including efficient methods of finding an initial seed, selecting a generating mechanism, and proceeding to a new seed. In the context of these open issues, the implementation of a neighborhood search procedure remains very much an art.

4.5   Tabu Search

The basic neighborhood search procedure is sometimes called a *descent* technique, because each new seed represents a lower value of the objective function (assuming that the objective is to minimize). If we were to graph the value of the objective function for the seed as a function of the seed number, the graph would be a decreasing function. In a large problem, the decrease might be rapid in the early stages of the search but much slower toward the end of the search, as in Figure 4.1.

One of the problems of neighborhood search procedures is their tendency to become "trapped" at local optima. It is eminently sensible, of course, to follow a path of ever-improving solutions, but such a path may not lead to a global optimum. At times it might be desirable to try a new seed that is worse than the old seed, as a means of escaping the trap and finding a path to an optimal solution. The flexibility to occasionally move to a worse solution is a feature of *tabu search* procedures.

In its basic form, a tabu search procedure can be viewed as a modified form of neighborhood search. Each time a neighborhood is generated and a new seed selected, we call the change from one seed to the next a *move*. A move is defined by the mechanism that generates neighborhoods and by the rule for selecting a solution in the neighborhood. In tabu search, the custom is to select the best value of the objective function in the neighborhood.

At the outset, a tabu search procedure operates much like a neighborhood search. Instead of stopping when a local optimum is encountered, however, a tabu search strategy accepts a new seed, even if its solution value is worse than that of the current seed. Of course, when the new seed is worse than the previous seed, the procedure could cycle indefinitely. To avoid this type of cycling, we designate a move back to the previous seed as tabu. In the same spirit, we might also designate a move back to the second or third previous seeds as tabu. In other words, we keep a list of tabu moves, a list that may be longer in length

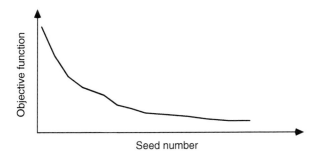

Figure 4.1 Improvement of the objective function in neighborhood search.

than one move. At each stage, the procedure selects the best solution from those in the neighborhood that are not on the tabu list.

Different possibilities exist for designating a move as tabu. Conceptually, the most straightforward is to keep sequences on the tabu list and thus prohibit a return to a previously encountered sequence. The tabu list is finite and generally fairly small. In some applications, a list size of one has been reasonably effective, but the original expositions of tabu search tended to recommend lists as long as seven moves. More recently, researchers have been experimenting with dynamic list sizes.

Whereas the neighborhood search procedure contains a built-in device for termination – the discovery of a local optimum – tabu search must have a termination rule imposed. Usually, the number of moves is fixed at the outset to ensure a certain level of computational effort. An alternative stopping rule is to limit the number of consecutive moves at which no improvement occurs. For purposes of comparison, the tabu search procedure was applied to the 20-job test problems with the neighborhoods and initial solutions illustrated earlier. The length of the tabu list was set at seven. The termination conditions were either (i) three consecutive seeds in which the tardiness increased or (ii) seven consecutive seeds without an improvement in the best solution yet found. The results are compared with neighborhood search in Table 4.6.

As the table shows, tabu search performed about as well as neighborhood search in each case. In fact, for the large neighborhoods, the solutions obtained by tabu search matched those obtained by the neighborhood search exactly.

Table 4.6

Algorithm	Optimizing frequency	Average ratio	Maximum ratio
Tabu (API, greedy)	0 of 12	1.087	1.26
NS(API, greedy)	0 of 12	1.089	1.26
Tabu (PI, greedy)	10 of 12	1.003	1.04
NS(PI, greedy)	10 of 12	1.003	1.04
Tabu (LI, greedy)	0 of 12	1.21	1.38
NS(LI, greedy)	0 of 12	1.21	1.39
Tabu (AI, greedy)	9 of 12	1.0004	1.004
NS(AI, greedy)	9 of 12	1.0004	1.004
Tabu (PI, insertion)	9 of 12	1.001	1.007
NS(PI, insertion)	9 of 12	1.001	1.007
Tabu (AI, insertion)	3 of 12	1.0087	1.04
NS(AI, insertion)	3 of 12	1.0087	1.04

The size of the neighborhood again seemed to have a major influence on the quality of the heuristic solution, with the PI neighborhoods leading to optimal solutions in a majority of cases.

4.6 Simulated Annealing

Tabu search overcomes one of the problems of neighborhood search – the local optimum trap. Advocates of tabu search usually recommend an aggressive philosophy in the selection of a new seed. According to this philosophy, the best non-tabu solution in the neighborhood should always be selected. In terms of the graph in Figure 4.1, this tactic tends to bring the curve down as steeply as possible at each stage. An alternative philosophy is to bring the curve down slowly. This approach is characteristic of *simulated annealing* procedures.

Annealing is a term borrowed from the physical sciences. The term refers to a process of cooling material slowly until the material reaches a stable (frozen) state. Early in this process, at high temperatures, particles in the material will sometimes change to higher-energy states, but at low temperatures such behavior is much less likely. At very low temperatures, particles virtually always move to lower-energy states whenever the opportunity arises. Eventually, the movement toward low-energy states leads to freezing.

In simulated annealing, we can think of each stage of the search as being carried out under a lower temperature than that which occurred at the previous stage. The value of the objective function is analogous to the temperature of the material being cooled. Early in the search (at high temperatures), there is some flexibility to move to a worse solution, but later in the search (at lower temperatures), less of this flexibility exists. Thus, the value of the objective function tends to fluctuate widely at the start of the search but hardly at all toward the end of the search, as in Figure 4.2.

To make this procedure more precise, suppose we are interested in minimizing the value of an objective function Z, and we employ the logic of a neighborhood search. At stage i the objective function is Z_i, corresponding to the Z-value for the ith seed. The procedure selects randomly from the solutions in the neighborhood of the ith seed. When the jth neighbor is generated, with objective function value Z_j, it may or may not become the next seed. If $Z_j < Z_i$, then, as in the standard descent method, the jth neighbor becomes the next seed. On the other hand, if $Z_j \geq Z_i$, there is still some chance that the jth neighbor will become the next seed, even though it is worse than the current seed. Let $\Delta Z = Z_j - Z_i$. Then the probability that the jth neighbor at stage i becomes the next seed is

$$q_{ij} = \min\{1, \exp(-\Delta Z / T(i))\}$$

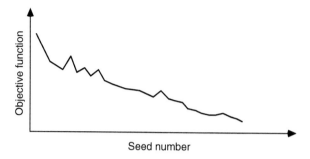

Figure 4.2 Improvement of the objective function with simulated annealing.

where $T(i)$ denotes the temperature at stage i. Two features of this probability function are important. First, the probability decreases as temperature decreases, other things being equal. Thus, as the search proceeds, there is a decreasing probability of moving to a worse solution. Second, the probability that a candidate will be selected to be the next seed is always 1 if there is improvement in the objective function, but if the objective function increases, then the probability varies inversely with the increase.

Finally, the search procedure requires a temperature schedule. After sampling from the neighborhood of the seed a specified number of times, we reduce the temperature and continue the search. For example, the temperature schedule may follow a geometric pattern, with $T(i + 1) = \pi T(i)$, where $0 < \pi < 1$ and $T(1)$ equal to the mean processing time.

For purposes of illustration, simulated annealing was used to solve the 20-job test problems, with the two larger neighborhoods (PI and AI). The temperature schedule followed a geometric pattern with $\pi = 0.9$ and 40 stages. At this computational effort, the performance of simulated annealing was roughly comparable with the other heuristic solutions. (By comparison, the neighborhood search procedure with PI neighborhoods converges after an average of 16 stages on these test problems.) Then additional runs were made with 80 stages. The results are reported in Table 4.7.

Clearly, the performance of simulated annealing is sensitive to the planned computational effort, as measured here by the number of stages in the temperature schedule. In addition, simulated annealing seemed to work more effectively in conjunction with PI neighborhoods than with AI neighborhoods.

This experiment was based on a very simple version of the simulated annealing procedure. Obviously, there are alternative parametric designs with different values of π and different numbers of stages. Alternative structural designs exist as well. In some implementations, several new seeds are generated at each

Table 4.7

Algorithm	Optimizing frequency	Average ratio	Maximum ratio
NS(AI, greedy)	9 of 12	1.0004	1.004
NS(PI, greedy)	10 of 12	1.003	1.04
Annealing (40; PI, greedy)	1 of 12	1.018	1.06
Annealing (40; AI, greedy)	1 of 12	1.016	1.08
Annealing (80; PI, greedy)	9 of 12	1.004	1.04
Annealing (80; AI, greedy)	3 of 12	1.010	1.06
NS(PI, insertion)	9 of 12	1.001	1.007
NS(AI, insertion)	3 of 12	1.009	1.04
Annealing (80; PI, insertion)	8 of 12	1.001	1.01
Annealing (80; AI, insertion)	4 of 12	1.008	1.02

temperature, with a certain "equilibrium" condition dictating when to proceed to a lower temperature.

4.7 Genetic Algorithms

A genetic algorithm (GA) may be viewed as a neighborhood search procedure that has similarities to several heuristics we have covered but also a radically different logic. Normally, a GA maintains a list of b promising solutions at each stage, and algorithmic iterations aim to generate better ones by searching a special type of neighborhood. Rather than define a neighbor by changing a single sequence, a GA combines two existing sequences, selecting some features from one and the remainder from the other. (In principle, a GA can combine more than two existing sequences, but here we illustrate the concept using exactly two.) Because new candidates can be viewed as offspring of the existing ones, the terminology is borrowed from evolution and genetics. Thus, in each generation, we start with b parents (sequences), which are the fittest (best-performing) survivors of former generations (iterations). Pairs of parents are selected – typically at random – to produce offspring. Each parent contributes genes (subsequences) to the offspring, and mutations (random changes) may also occur. The algorithm usually terminates after a prespecified number of generations, but other stopping rules can be imposed. The fittest of all survivors in the last generation is selected as the solution.

Algorithm 4.2 *Genetic Algorithm*

Step 1. Choose the population size $b > 2$ and the number of generations, K. Select b initial schedules by other heuristics (such as random search). Let $k = 0$.

Step 2. Increase k by 1. Generate at least $b/2$ offspring of pairs of individuals. (Offspring may be subject to random mutations.)

Step 3. Evaluate the offspring. If $k < K$, select the best b schedules out of all parents and offspring and return to Step 2. If $k = K$, stop (the best schedule found so far is the solution).

Within this general framework, we must answer certain tactical questions:

1) How to obtain the first generation of schedules?
2) How do parents generate offspring?
3) How to match parents for breeding?

The first generation of schedules can be generated randomly or by implementing one of the heuristic procedures described earlier in Section 4.2. For example, we could create b schedules by implementing b different dispatching procedures

In sequencing problems, the simplest mechanism for generating offspring follows one parent for the first few jobs and takes the remaining jobs in the same order as in the other parent. The last few jobs cannot simply be copied from the other parent, however, because that could cause duplications of jobs in the new sequence and omissions of other jobs. Therefore, a complementary offspring can be constructed in which the last few jobs are copied from one parent and the first jobs appear in the same sequence as in the other parent. Some schemes use both offspring, which may then be referred to as a son and a daughter. The number of jobs to select from each parent is a secondary design choice. We can set this parameter randomly, or we can generate all possible offspring based on this mechanism. In addition, following the analog of evolution, a GA allows random mutations, which are created by performing a small number of random insertions in the creation of an offspring.

The matching of parents can be random, or some systematic procedure can be adopted. For example, the best parent can be matched with the bth best parent, the second best with the $(b - 1)$st best parent, and so on. Alternatively, the best and second best parents can be matched, then the third and fourth best, and so on. In nature, the very best survivors may have more than their proportional share of matches, and this feature can also be emulated.

GA implementations used for research are usually described openly, but commercial codes are often proprietary. In the next section, we introduce a proprietary variation on the GA approach that happens to be conveniently available to users of Excel.

4.8 The Evolutionary Solver

Most of the algorithms we discuss, both optimization algorithms and heuristic algorithms, require specialized computer code for implementation. As yet, there are very few "off-the-shelf" codes available for sequencing, although the Internet may become a source in the future. Nevertheless, one widely used platform for calculations and algorithms is the electronic spreadsheet, Excel in particular. In this section, we describe an Excel-based approach to heuristic solution of sequencing problems.

For the purposes of illustration, we work with Example 4.4, introduced earlier, which is a *T*-problem containing five jobs.

Job j	1	2	3	4	5
p_j	2	3	1	6	4
d_j	12	7	4	10	6

In a spreadsheet implementation, we create modules for the problem data, the job sequence, the measure of performance, and the relevant calculations. Figure 4.3 shows a typical layout for the model. Borrowing from the terminology of optimization, the key parts of the model are:

- The problem data (cells C4:G6).
- The objective function (cell C8).
- The decision variables (the sequence in the range C12:G12).
- The relevant constraints (to be specified later).

The decisions in this model appear as the highlighted cells in row 12, and any permutation of the integers 1–5 can be entered there. Based on that sequence, we find the processing times in row 13 using a lookup procedure, referencing

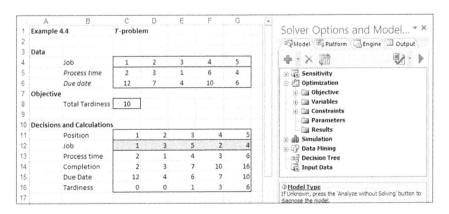

Figure 4.3 Spreadsheet layout for the *T*-problem example.

the data cells. In our example, the formula in cell C13 is INDEX (C5 : G5, C12), and this formula is copied to the right. Then the completion times in row 14 are calculated as we would by hand, by adding the current processing time to the completion time of the previous job in sequence.

The due dates in row 15 are obtained by referencing the data cells. In our example, the formula in cell C15 is INDEX (C6 : G6, C12), and this formula is copied to the right. In row 16, we calculate the tardiness of each job. For example, the formula in cell C16 is MAX (0, C14 - C15), and this formula is copied to the right. The objective function in cell C8 calculates the sum of the tardiness values, using the formula SUM (C16 : G16). With this layout, we could enter any job sequence in row 12, and the value of the objective function would appear in cell C8.

The optimization problem corresponding to our example is to choose the sequence in row 12 to minimize the value of the performance measure in cell C8. The software is Analytic Solver Platform (ASP). Briefly, ASP contains an upgraded version of the solver that comes with Excel. ASP actually contains four different optimization-type algorithms, one of which uses its Evolutionary Engine, an advanced GA that applies to many other types of problems but is specifically well suited to sequencing problems. Here, we refer to the *Evolutionary Solver* as a shorthand reference to the Evolutionary Engine in ASP software. In what follows, we assume that ASP has already been installed as an Excel add-in.

When ASP opens, it superimposes its task pane on the right-hand side of the spreadsheet, as shown in Figure 4.3. If the task pane is hidden, we can click on the Model icon (on the left-hand side of the ASP ribbon) to make it visible.

In anticipation of using the Evolutionary Solver, the first step is to select the Platform tab in the task pane, and in the Transformation section, proceed to the first entry, *Nonsmooth Model Transformation*. The drop-down menu that accompanies it offers three choices, and we should choose *Never*. (This choice prevents ASP from making an inefficient transformation of the optimization problem we're about to specify.)

Next we select the Model tab, where we specify the optimization problem with the following steps:

1) With cell C8 selected, specify the objective using the ASP ribbon (Optimization Model > Objective > Min > Normal). Alternatively, with cell C8 selected, select the folder icon for Objective in the task pane and click on the green cross in the header of the task pane. This step assumes that the objective is to be maximized, so we double-click the icon for C8. The Change Objective window appears, in which we select the radio button for Min, as shown in Figure 4.4.
2) With the range C12:G12 selected, specify the decisions (Optimization Model > Decisions > Normal). Alternatively, with the range C12:G12 selected, select the folder icon for Variables in the task pane and click on the green cross.

Figure 4.4 Specifying the objective and direction of optimization.

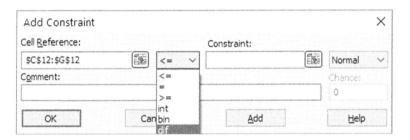

Figure 4.5 Specifying the alldifferent constraint.

3) With the range C12:G12 still selected, specify the constraints (Optimization Model > Constraints > Variable Type/Bound > AllDifferent). Alternatively, with the range C12:G12 still selected, select the folder icon for Constraints in the task pane and click on the green cross. The Add Constraint window then appears, in which we select *dif* from the drop-down menu, as shown in Figure 4.5.

The *AllDifferent constraint* ensures that the decision variable cells will comprise a legitimate permutation (in this case, a permutation of the integers 1–5.) In other words, the decision cells must correspond to a feasible sequence. The task pane captures the problem specification, as shown in Figure 4.6.

Next we select the Engine tab, specify the *Standard Evolutionary Engine* from the drop-down menu, and uncheck the box for Automatically Select Engine, as shown in Figure 4.7. The General section of the task pane lists a number of options, most of which can be left at their default values. The Evolutionary Solver will search for the best solution it can find, and its effectiveness is influenced by several user-determined parameters that are specified on this list. The most important of these parameters set the stopping conditions that control the termination of the search. A good generic set of parameters would be the following:

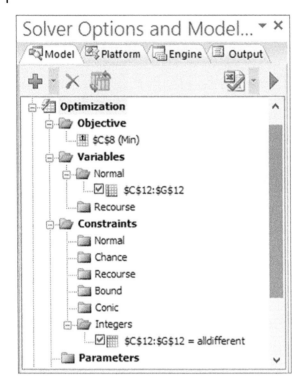

Figure 4.6 The problem specification.

Max time = 15 seconds (no default value is given initially)

Population size = 25 (no default value is given initially)

Mutation rate = 7.5%(default value)

Convergence = 0.01%(default value)

Global search = Genetic Algorithm (default value)

The Convergence option tells the Evolutionary Solver to stop its search if 99% of the 25 best solutions found lie within 0.01% of each other. If that configuration occurs, the search terminates before reaching the specified Max Time.

In the Limits section of the task pane, the following choices are suitable:

Max subproblems = leave blank

Max feasible solutions = leave blank

Tolerance = 0

Maximum time without improvement = 10 s

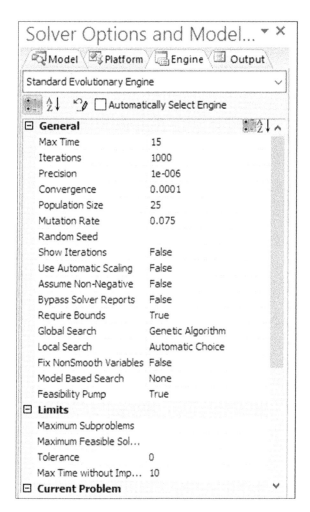

Figure 4.7 Information on the Engine tab.

As a result, ceilings on the number of subproblems or the number of feasible sequences do not impede the search. In addition, the search terminates if no improvement in the objective has been found in the last 10 seconds of searching.

To invoke the algorithm, we can use the ribbon (Solve Action > Optimize > Solve Complete Problem), or we can click on the green triangle near the top of the Output tab. If the Max Time option takes effect, the search will stop after running for 15 seconds with an offer to continue. When we choose Stop, a message appears in the task pane reporting that Solver stopped at the user's request. If the Max Time without Improvement takes effect, a message appears in the task pane reporting that Solver cannot improve the current solution. If the Convergence condition prevails, the message in the task pane reports that Solver has converged.

In general, the time limits can be adjusted according to the user's patience, but we have found that runs of roughly 15–30 seconds produce good results for sequencing problems up to 20 jobs. In fact, optimal or near-optimal solutions are usually found in far less time. In our five-job example, the Evolutionary Solver converges rapidly to a total tardiness value of 7, obtained by the sequence 3-5-2-1-4. For the set of 20-job problems in Table 4.8, the Evolutionary Solver (running with a 30-second time limit) produced optimal solutions in 10 out of the 12 problems, with an average ratio of 1.00008 and a maximum ratio of 1.0006. These results do not take advantage of the fact that the user can always rerun the Evolutionary Solver starting with the best solution found in the previous run. The user can also repeat the run after enlarging the population size or increasing the mutation rate if a run terminates with convergence or lack of improvement. Because the Evolutionary Solver contains random elements, it is usually desirable to make several runs under the same parametric settings to see whether improvements can be made.

4.9 Summary

Challenging combinatorial optimization problems are encountered even in the simple single-machine scheduling problem. Earlier, we discussed the relatively few cases in which general optimal solutions are known. For other cases, including most tardiness-based criteria, general-purpose optimization techniques must be brought to bear on the problem. Nevertheless, such techniques require a great deal of computational effort for even medium-sized problems, and in stochastic problems, the computational demands can be an order of magnitude greater. In situations where this effort is prohibitive, heuristic methods are appropriate.

For scheduling problems with straightforward structure, dispatching and construction procedures offer a way to build good schedules quickly. Dispatching procedures are sometimes effective, but it is often difficult to devise a logical dispatching rule for any given objective. For example, the U_w-problem offers a simple yet challenging single-machine problem for which there does not seem to be a reliable dispatching rule. The greedy and insertion algorithms, which do not have to be tailored to a particular objective function, tend to be more robust than dispatching procedures, yet they still require modest computational effort.

Random sampling, particularly biased random sampling, is an alternative approach to solving combinatorial scheduling problems. Although their performance in most sequencing problems is unremarkable, they can be adapted to many different types of problems, and their tactical choices can be refined for the situation at hand.

The neighborhood search procedure embodies a simple but effective concept for solving sequencing problems. Its primary tactical options include the initializing phase (to obtain the first seed), the choice of a mechanism for generating neighborhoods, and a rule for determining the new seed. With a certain amount of "fine-tuning" for these options, neighborhood search procedures can be reasonably effective at finding near-optimal solutions, as our brief experiments with the T_w-problem suggest. In addition, the neighborhood search approach is flexible and can be adapted to a variety of problem structures.

The neighborhood search procedure also provides a framework for more sophisticated search algorithms – such as tabu search, simulated annealing, and GAs – that overcome the local optimality trap. These other heuristic procedures have their own tactical options, and much remains to be learned about how those options should be chosen.

In general, implementing neighborhood search procedures requires specialized code. However, the Evolutionary Solver is a more recent innovation that provides an off-the-shelf implementation of a GA. That is, without having to write specialized code, we can invoke a sophisticated heuristic procedure that happens to be especially well suited to the problem of finding the best sequence. As a result, it provides users with an accessible and practical tool for finding solutions to the single-machine sequencing problem.

We draw attention to the options in each of these techniques for two reasons. First, in the gap between the concept of a solution methodology and its implementation, many important details need to be specified, even for the basic single-machine problem. Moreover, these details can influence performance in a significant way. Second, the treatment of more complicated models often includes a suggestion that a particular optimization technique or a particular heuristic strategy is suitable for a given scheduling problem. On these occasions, we should be sensitive to the fact that implementation itself may involve a host of tactical questions, even after the general methodology is selected, and resolving those questions is a computational art.

Various combinations of procedures sometimes work effectively. For example, when we studied the insertion procedure, we assumed the jobs were ordered arbitrarily, but they might as well have been ordered by a sorting or dispatching heuristic, such as MDD. The result is a combined heuristic that usually works better than the insertion heuristic alone. The idea of running several heuristics and selecting the best outcome is also used frequently and becomes especially attractive in a parallel-processor computing environment.

Now, armed with a variety of both heuristic and optimizing capabilities, we can proceed to more complex problems in sequencing and scheduling.

Table 4.8 Twelve test problems for the T_w-problem.

p_i	90	91	92	94	95	95	96	97	98	99
	99	99	100	101	102	103	104	104	104	105
d_i	657	754	940	289	204	941	686	509	621	103
	356	462	909	790	290	26	7	540	680	0
w_i	8	13	15	8	5	7	12	15	8	8
	11	5	14	13	15	6	7	14	12	13
	90	94	94	94	96	97	97	98	99	100
	101	102	102	103	103	104	104	105	106	107
	107	195	673	921	0	298	430	500	697	256
	513	478	644	0	0	267	622	859	60	271
	7	11	15	14	15	9	12	15	10	14
	8	12	12	6	14	8	12	13	10	11
	89	91	93	94	94	95	95	96	97	97
	97	98	98	99	99	100	100	101	101	112
	40	171	9	368	464	68	441	867	0	521
	978	639	740	14	976	730	959	811	908	20
	9	9	7	6	10	6	10	13	8	5
	14	6	8	15	14	6	10	10	5	8
	87	90	92	93	98	98	98	98	99	99
	99	100	100	101	101	102	102	103	106	113
	969	1041	363	258	415	494	1340	1366	242	986
	1139	215	736	270	714	593	1350	619	1263	976
	10	13	6	6	6	12	13	6	5	5
	10	12	12	6	9	7	14	12	5	12
	93	96	98	98	99	101	101	101	102	102
	102	104	104	104	105	105	106	107	109	109
	1365	1076	1269	1324	1334	387	496	1100	279	351
	755	376	1068	1349	444	1380	457	380	871	1138
	13	5	5	12	10	6	8	12	10	8
	15	8	6	8	11	10	14	11	9	10
	86	93	93	94	96	97	98	99	100	100
	101	101	102	102	103	103	104	104	110	113
	544	1193	1304	940	1207	407	721	318	220	873
	223	889	236	1185	465	1392	691	932	364	774
	14	11	8	6	12	14	12	13	13	15

Table 4.8 (Continued)

7	12	14	10	10	5	8	11	10	8
55	68	70	73	77	78	85	86	89	89
92	93	94	94	98	108	126	138	143	170
109	169	1039	1158	1107	0	767	993	643	667
75	612	780	816	721	555	1166	529	0	1237
10	9	7	6	13	9	12	15	14	10
6	8	12	13	12	5	13	8	8	6
51	71	71	76	81	81	81	90	94	98
107	107	110	112	115	116	117	119	142	148
0	0	365	646	516	873	932	326	87	0
254	613	783	0	0	1169	326	0	382	1150
15	11	7	11	9	10	14	6	10	8
6	10	9	6	14	14	9	11	9	13
74	74	82	85	86	96	99	103	108	110
112	115	119	123	124	126	127	129	139	142
290	595	415	0	0	555	894	1183	80	362
229	0	232	0	231	864	785	0	0	1001
7	5	10	14	11	8	13	6	9	13
12	6	5	9	13	10	9	5	10	11
60	71	71	76	81	82	93	104	108	108
108	109	113	115	116	118	118	120	122	145
404	394	534	308	778	917	482	472	702	803
1142	1115	811	1191	672	1139	1329	710	534	591
7	13	15	11	15	7	13	10	15	8
5	7	15	7	5	5	11	8	12	13
53	58	69	75	75	83	89	91	93	97
97	99	105	114	117	123	123	133	137	138
508	740	663	1097	1194	764	663	711	831	543
815	511	1032	424	786	816	823	489	587	521
9	7	8	12	9	7	14	9	15	14
10	15	14	10	14	14	8	7	5	8
68	79	80	86	89	94	96	97	100	105
106	109	109	112	118	119	120	124	127	135

(Continued)

Table 4.8 (Continued)

437	521	678	841	746	520	610	1112	772	566
928	472	910	499	498	1084	617	1153	1120	974
7	5	13	7	6	7	12	12	12	8
8	8	12	9	15	6	12	5	14	10

Exercises

4.1 Solve the following 10-job T-problem using heuristic procedures.

Job j	1	2	3	4	5	6	7	8	9	10
p_j	32	26	7	55	98	80	41	23	24	100
d_j	162	168	153	234	230	184	212	172	156	164

a) Find a solution using the best dispatching rule among SPT, EDD, and MDD.
b) Find a solution using the greedy heuristic procedure.
c) Find a solution using the insertion procedure.
d) Find a solution using a neighborhood search procedure (adjacent pairwise interchanges), initialized by a sequence that takes the jobs in EDD order.
e) Find a solution using a neighborhood search procedure (last-insertion neighborhoods), initialized by a sequence that takes the jobs in EDD order.

4.2 *Computer-based approach to Problem 4.1.* Solve the following 10-job T-problem using heuristic procedures.

Job j	1	2	3	4	5	6	7	8	9	10
p_j	32	26	7	55	98	80	41	23	24	100
d_j	162	168	153	234	230	184	212	172	156	164

a) Find a solution using a neighborhood search procedure (adjacent pairwise interchanges), initialized by a sequence that takes the jobs in EDD order.

b) Find a solution using a neighborhood search procedure (all-insertion neighborhoods), initialized by a sequence that takes the jobs in EDD order.

c) Find a solution using a neighborhood search procedure (all pairwise interchanges), initialized by a sequence that takes the jobs in EDD order.

d) Find a solution using a tabu search procedure, initialized by a sequence that takes the jobs in EDD order.

e) Find a solution using a simulated annealing procedure, initialized by a sequence that takes the jobs in EDD order.

f) Find a solution using random sampling, initialized by a sequence that takes the jobs in EDD order and terminated so that the computational effort is roughly equal to the average computational effort in part (c).

4.3 *Software-based approach to Problem 4.1.* Solve the following 10-job T-problem using the Evolutionary Solver.

Job j	1	2	3	4	5	6	7	8	9	10
p_j	32	26	7	55	98	80	41	23	24	100
d_j	162	168	153	234	230	184	212	172	156	164

4.4 Solve the following 10-job U_w-problem using heuristic procedures.

Job j	1	2	3	4	5	6	7	8	9	10
p_j	58	49	90	38	44	42	68	61	10	4
d_j	88	175	197	115	109	152	128	135	155	105
w_j	3	7	9	4	5	6	7	1	3	8

a) Find a solution using the best dispatching rule among SWPT, EDD, and WMDD.

b) Find a solution using the greedy heuristic procedure.

c) Find a solution using the insertion procedure.

d) Find a solution using a neighborhood search procedure (adjacent pairwise interchanges), initialized by a sequence that takes the jobs in EDD order.

4.5 *Software-based approach to Problem 4.4.* Solve the following 10-job U_w-problem using the Evolutionary Solver.

Job j	1	2	3	4	5	6	7	8	9	10
p_j	58	49	90	38	44	42	68	61	10	4
d_j	88	175	197	115	109	152	128	135	155	105
w_j	3	7	9	4	5	6	7	1	3	8

4.6 Solve the following 10-job T_w-problem using heuristic procedures.

Job j	1	2	3	4	5	6	7	8	9	10
p_j	58	49	90	38	44	42	68	61	10	4
d_j	88	175	197	115	109	152	128	135	155	105
w_j	3	7	9	4	5	6	7	1	3	8

a) Find a solution using the best dispatching rule among SWPT, EDD, and WMDD.
b) Find a solution using the greedy heuristic procedure.
c) Find a solution using the insertion procedure.
d) Find a solution using a neighborhood search procedure (adjacent pairwise interchanges), initialized by a sequence that takes the jobs in EDD order.

4.7 *Software-based approach to Problem 4.4.* Solve the following 10-job T_w-problem using the Evolutionary Solver.

Job j	1	2	3	4	5	6	7	8	9	10
p_j	58	49	90	38	44	42	68	61	10	4
d_j	88	175	197	115	109	152	128	135	155	105
w_j	3	7	9	4	5	6	7	1	3	8

4.8 Suppose that an equally likely mechanism is used for generating a random sample of sequences when there are eight jobs. How many sequences must be evaluated in order to yield a probability of 1/2 that an optimum will be found in the sample (assuming that a unique optimum exists)? How many sequences must be evaluated in complete enumeration?

Bibliography

Baker, K.R. (2011). Solving sequencing problems in spreadsheets. *International Journal of Planning and Scheduling* 1: 3–18.

Baker, K.R. and Bertrand, J.W.M. (1982). A dynamic priority rule for scheduling against due-dates. *Journal of Operations Management* 3: 37–42.

Glover, F. (1989). Tabu search: Part I. *ORSA Journal on Computing* 1: 190–203.

Kanet, J.J. and Li, X. (2004). A weighted modified due date rule for sequencing to minimize weighted tardiness. *Journal of Scheduling* 7: 261–276.

Kirkpatrick, S., Gelatt, C.D., and Vecchi, M.P. (1983). Optimization by simulated annealing. *Science* 220: 671–680.

Morton, T.E. and Pentico, D.W. (1993). *Heuristic Scheduling Systems*. New York: Wiley.

Potts, C.N. and Van Wassenhove, L.N. (1991). Single machine tardiness sequencing heuristics. *IIE Transactions* 23: 346–354.

Rachamadugu, R.M.V. (1987). A note on the weighted tardiness problem. *Operations Research* 35: 450–452.

Rinnooy Kan, A.H.G., Lenstra, J.K., and Lageweg, B.J. (1975). Minimizing total costs in one machine scheduling. *Operations Research* 23: 908–927.

Van Laarhoven, P.J.M. and Aarts, E.H.L. (1987). *Simulated Annealing: Theory and Applications*. Dordrecht: Reidel.

5

Earliness and Tardiness Costs

5.1 Introduction

In earlier chapters, we examined the basic single-machine model with regular measures of performance, which are nondecreasing in job completion times. Most of the literature on scheduling theory, and therefore much of our understanding of scheduling problems, relates to such regular measures as total flowtime, number of tardy jobs, and total tardiness. The total tardiness criterion, in particular, has been a standard way of measuring conformance to due dates, although it ignores the consequences of jobs completing early and penalizes only those jobs that finish late. However, this emphasis began to change with the growing interest in *just-in-time* (JIT) production, which espouses the notion that earliness – as well as tardiness – should be discouraged. In a JIT scheduling environment, a job that completes early must be held in inventory until its due date, whereas a job that completes after its due date may disrupt a customer's operations. Therefore, an ideal schedule is one in which all jobs finish exactly on their assigned due dates. Of course, JIT encompasses a much broader set of principles than those relating to due dates, but scheduling models with both earliness and tardiness (E/T) costs address a fundamental scheduling dimension of the JIT approach.

In this chapter, we examine the implications of the E/T criterion in the basic single-machine model. The goal of finishing all jobs exactly on their due dates can be translated into a scheduling objective in which a job incurs a cost related to the deviation between its completion time and its due date. Let E_j and T_j represent the earliness and tardiness, respectively, of job j. These quantities are defined as

$$E_j = \max\left\{0, d_j - C_j\right\} = \left(d_j - C_j\right)^+$$

$$T_j = \max\left\{0, C_j - d_j\right\} = \left(C_j - d_j\right)^+$$

Principles of Sequencing and Scheduling, Second Edition. Kenneth R. Baker and Dan Trietsch.
© 2019 John Wiley & Sons, Inc. Published 2019 by John Wiley & Sons, Inc.

Assuming that the cost functions are linear, we associate with each job a unit earliness cost $\alpha_j > 0$ and a unit tardiness cost $\beta_j > 0$. The basic E/T objective function for a schedule S can then be written as $f(S)$, where

$$f(S) = \sum_{j=1}^{n} \left[\alpha_j \left(d_j - C_j \right)^+ + \beta_j \left(C_j - d_j \right)^+ \right]$$

or, in light of the definitions given above,

$$f(S) = \sum_{j=1}^{n} \left(\alpha_j E_j + \beta_j T_j \right)$$

In some formulations of the E/T problem, due dates are given, whereas in others, the problem is to optimize the due dates and the job sequence simultaneously. Some of the simplest results for E/T problems have been derived for models in which all jobs have a common due date. A more general model allows distinct due dates, but as we shall see, solutions to problems with distinct due dates appear to be intrinsically different from solutions to problems with a common due date. In a similar vein, some models prescribe identical costs, but others permit differences among jobs or differences between the earliness cost and the tardiness cost.

With so many variations of the E/T problem, it is sometimes difficult to sort out exactly which results apply to which variations. However, a useful organizing principle is to think in terms of two main models: one with a common due date and one with distinct due dates. In these initial models, earliness and tardiness costs are symmetric, and they are the same for all jobs. Each of the two main models supports more elaborate assumptions, such as the following:

- Treating due dates as decisions may capture the practice in some shops of setting due dates internally, as targets to guide the progress of shop floor activities.
- Allowing asymmetric earliness and tardiness costs allows us to reflect different economic consequences for earliness than for tardiness.
- Imposing different costs for different jobs allows us to distinguish among jobs and/or customers.

The primary role of earliness and tardiness cost functions is to guide solutions toward the target of meeting all due dates exactly. A *perfect* schedule – one in which all due dates are exactly met – is not difficult to recognize, but it may be difficult to achieve. However, it may not be obvious how to compare *imperfect* schedules. Different cost functions can be seen as suggestions for measuring suboptimal performance when only the ideal has been well specified. In principle, modeling the economic implications more accurately can provide us with more realistic models, but typically the price is reduced tractability.

5.2 Minimizing Deviations from a Common Due Date

5.2.1 Four Basic Results

An important special case in the family of E/T problems involves minimizing the sum of absolute deviations of the job completion times from a common due date. In particular, the objective function can be written as

$$f(S) = \sum_{j=1}^{n} \left| C_j - d \right| = \sum_{j=1}^{n} \left(E_j + T_j \right) \tag{5.1}$$

where, in the latter form, it is understood that the due dates are identical. With the objective function in that form, it is clear that earliness and tardiness are penalized at the same rate for all jobs. We refer to this case, where $d_j = d$ and $\alpha_j = \beta_j = 1$, as the *basic* E/T problem.

At the outset, we give a somewhat simplified characterization of the optimal solution. Ideally, we would like to construct the schedule so that the due date is, in some sense, in the middle of the jobs. If d is too tight, then it is not possible to fit enough jobs in front of d, because no job can start before time zero. Thus, for a given set of jobs, we might discover that d is too tight; this gives rise to the *restricted* version of the problem. Otherwise, d is not too tight, giving rise to the *unrestricted* version. For example, if the due date is larger than the time required to process all jobs, then we have the flexibility to place any of the jobs in front of d, so the problem is unrestricted. Later, we shall see how to determine a more precise boundary between the restricted and unrestricted versions.

We first consider the unrestricted version of the problem. As an initial step, we look for dominance properties. For the unrestricted version, three important properties hold, and we can establish each one using a proof by contradiction.

■ **Theorem 5.1** In the basic E/T problem, schedules without inserted idle time between successive jobs constitute a dominant set.

Proof. Suppose that there exists an optimal schedule S with an idle interval of length t between consecutive jobs i and j, with j following i. Suppose that job i is early ($C_i < d$). Then total cost can be reduced if we shift job i (and any jobs that precede it) later by an amount Δt, where $\Delta t \leq \min\{t, d - C_i\}$. If primes denote values after the shift, then for all jobs k, we have $T'_k = T_k$ and $E'_k \leq E_k$ (with a strict inequality for at least one job). Similarly, suppose job j is tardy ($C_j > d$). Then total cost can be reduced if we shift job j (and any jobs that follow it) earlier by an amount Δt, where $\Delta t \leq \min\{t, C_j - d\}$. Because of the common due date, any schedule must have either job i early or job j tardy, so we have shown how to improve schedule S. Therefore, S cannot be an optimal schedule. □

Theorem 5.1 allows us to consider only schedules in which jobs are contiguous, but it does not allow us to assume that the first job starts at time zero. We can describe a schedule by specifying a sequence of the jobs and a start time for the first job in sequence, after which processing will be continuous. In principle, this means that the search for an optimum must consider $n!$ different sequences and for each sequence, the best start time.

■ **Theorem 5.2**   In the basic E/T problem, jobs that complete on or before the due date can be sequenced in LPT order, and jobs that start on or after the due date can be sequenced in SPT order.

Proof. Suppose S denotes an optimal schedule in which some adjacent pair of early jobs is not in LPT order. Then a pairwise interchange of these two jobs will reduce the total earliness cost and leave the total tardiness cost unchanged. Likewise, if S is an optimal schedule containing an adjacent pair of jobs that starts late and that violates SPT order, then an adjacent pairwise interchange will reduce the total tardiness cost and leave the total earliness cost unchanged. In either case, S cannot be an optimal schedule.   □

Theorem 5.2 specifies how to sequence the jobs that complete early and how to sequence the jobs that start late. In principle, there could also be a single job that starts before the due date and completes after the due date – that is, a *straddling* job. The following result, however, shows that schedules with a straddling job need not be considered.

■ **Theorem 5.3**   In the basic E/T problem, an optimal schedule exists in which some job completes exactly at the due date.

Proof. Suppose S is an optimal schedule in which job i starts before the due date and completes after it. In symbols,

$$C_i - p_i < d < C_i$$

Let b denote the number of early jobs in sequence, and let a denote the number of tardy jobs. Suppose that $a > b$. Consider shifting the entire schedule earlier so that job i completes exactly at time d. In other words, all jobs will complete earlier by an amount $\Delta t = C_i - d > 0$. Then the increase in earliness cost is $b\Delta t$, while the decrease in tardiness cost is $a\Delta t$. The net impact on total cost is $(b - a)\Delta t$, which is negative. On the other hand, suppose that $b \geq a$. In this case, shift the entire schedule later so that job i starts exactly at time d. In other words, $\Delta t = d - (C_i - p_i) > 0$. This time the impact on total cost is $(a - b)\Delta t$, which is nonpositive. In either case, therefore, we can find a schedule with the property of the theorem that is at least as good as S.   □

As a consequence of Theorem 5.3, we may schedule each job either entirely before the due date or entirely after it. This means that a solution can be partitioned into two sets of jobs, an early set, which includes the one job precisely on time, and a tardy set. Once the membership in the two sets is known, the sequence of the jobs within each set can be determined by Theorem 5.2. The resulting schedule is sometimes called a *V-shaped sequence*, because except for ties, the first set is sequenced in decreasing order of processing times, and the second is processed in increasing order of processing times. We can also refer to it as an *LPT/SPT sequence*. Once we know how jobs are assigned to the early set and the tardy set, sequencing the jobs is straightforward. Therefore, the search for an optimum need only consider the 2^n ways of forming sets, instead of all $n!$ sequences. Even if we know the optimal job sequence, Theorem 5.3 is critical. Without it, we would have a potentially infinite number of schedules to evaluate because the starting time of the first job in sequence would remain unresolved. Theorem 5.3 allows us to limit our attention to those schedules in which some job's completion time falls precisely at the due date – that is, to a finite set of possible schedules. As we shall see, these three properties generalize when we examine problems that are more complicated.

The detailed analysis of this problem demonstrates that many optimal solutions may exist. Let B represent the set of jobs completing on or before the due date, and let b denote the number of jobs in B, or the *cardinality* of B, denoted by $|B|$. Similarly, let A represent the set of jobs completing after the due date, and let $a = |A|$. Furthermore, let Bi denote the index of the ith job in B, and let Ai denote the index of the ith job in A. The earliness cost for job Bi is the sum of the processing times of all jobs in B that complete later. In symbols,

$$E_{Bi} = p_{B(i+1)} + p_{B(i+2)} + \cdots + p_{Bb}$$

where $E_{Bb} = 0$. The total cost for the jobs in B then becomes

$$C_B = \sum_{i=1}^{b} E_{Bi} = \sum_{i=1}^{b} \left[p_{B(i+1)} + p_{B(i+2)} + \cdots + p_{Bb} \right]$$

With some algebraic manipulation, this sum can be rewritten as

$$C_B = 0p_{B1} + 1p_{B2} + \cdots + (b-2)p_{B(b-1)} + (b-1)p_{Bb} \tag{5.2}$$

Similarly, the total cost for the jobs in A is

$$C_A = ap_{A1} + (a-1)p_{A2} + \cdots + 2p_{A(a-1)} + 1p_{Aa} \tag{5.3}$$

The objective function is the sum of C_B and C_A, and the processing times are given. When a and b are known, this sum of products is minimized by matching the smallest coefficient in the sum with the largest processing time, the next smallest coefficient with the next largest processing time, and so on, with ties broken arbitrarily. Thus, the smallest coefficient is zero and appears only in C_B. Therefore, the longest job is assigned to B and, in light of Theorem 5.2, appears first in sequence. The next smallest coefficient is 1, appearing in both

C_B and C_A. This means that one of the next two longest jobs can be assigned to A, as its last job, and the other to B, as its second job. Continuing in this fashion, we ultimately find that the shortest job is either the last job in B or the first job in A. At intermediate stages, there are two ways to assign each pair of jobs that must be split between the sets A and B. (If n is even, we can create a fictitious additional job with zero processing time to complete the last pair.) Thus, the total number of potentially optimal schedules is 2^r, where

$$r = \frac{n-1}{2} \quad \text{if } n \text{ is odd}$$

$$= \frac{n}{2} \quad \text{if } n \text{ is even}$$

(Actually, this observation assumes that the processing times are unique. If there are ties, the number of optimal schedules is even greater.) The implied procedure for constructing optimal schedules is as follows.

Algorithm 5.1 *Solving the Basic E/T Problem*

Step 1. Assign the longest job to set B.

Step 2. Find the next two longest jobs. Assign one to B and one to A.

Step 3. Repeat Step 2 until there are no jobs left, or until there is one job left, in which case assign this job to either A or B. Finally, order the jobs in B by LPT and the jobs in A by SPT.

Next, we provide an example that illustrates the application of Algorithm 5.1.

■ **Example 5.1** Consider the jobs described in the following table, with a given common due date of $d = 24$.

Job j	1	2	3	4	5	6
p_j	1	3	4	6	7	9

Following the first step of Algorithm 5.1, we assign job 6 to B. Then we split jobs 4 and 5 between A and B, and we split jobs 2 and 3 between A and B. Lastly, we assign job 1 to either A or B. The eight resulting schedules, each with total cost of 30, are listed in Table 5.1. Only four distinct sequences appear in the list of optimal schedules. Those occur because of the choice in Step 3 to assign the last job either to the end of B or the beginning of A. In either case, the sequence is the same, but the schedule is different. (The total processing time in set B is affected by this choice.) Finally, the start time of the schedule is the difference between the due date and the total processing time in B.

Table 5.1

Jobs in set *B*	Jobs in set *A*	Sequence	Time for set *B*	Start time
6-5-3-1	2-4	6-5-3-1-2-4	21	3
6-5-3	1-2-4	6-5-3-1-2-4	20	4
6-5-2-1	3-4	6-5-2-1-3-4	20	4
6-5-2	1-3-4	6-5-2-1-3-4	19	5
6-4-3-1	2-5	6-4-3-1-2-5	20	4
6-4-3	1-2-5	6-4-3-1-2-5	19	5
6-4-2-1	3-5	6-4-2-1-3-5	19	5
6-4-2	1-3-5	6-4-2-1-3-5	18	6

In light of the fact that there can be many optimal schedules in the basic E/T problem, we might be interested in a secondary measure of performance. In particular, suppose the secondary objective is to minimize the total processing time in set *B*. In Algorithm 5.1, this is accomplished by assigning the shorter job to *B* each time Step 2 is executed and if *n* is even, by assigning the shortest job to *A* in Step 3. We refer to this implementation as Algorithm 5.1*, which can be implemented to run in $O(n \log n)$ time.

Two insights emerge from this discussion. First, the implementation of Algorithm 5.1* dictates the values of *a* and *b*. In particular, if *n* is even, we can minimize the sum of Eqs. (5.2) and (5.3) by taking *b* = *a*; if *n* is odd, we take *b* = *a* + 1. A more formal statement follows.

■ **Theorem 5.4** In the basic E/T problem, an optimal schedule exists in which job [b] completes at time *d*, where $b = \lceil n/2 \rceil$, and $\lceil x \rceil$ denotes the smallest integer greater than or equal to *x*.

This result has another application. Suppose that the sequence of jobs is given and not necessarily optimal. Then Theorems 5.1 and 5.3 hold for schedules containing the given job sequence, and we can use Theorem 5.4 to determine which job should complete exactly at the due date.

Assume for convenience that the jobs are indexed in SPT order, with p_n as the longest processing time. When we implement Algorithm 5.1*, the total processing time in set *B* can be written as

$$\Delta = p_n + p_{n-2} + p_{n-4} + \cdots \tag{5.4}$$

In other words, we calculate Δ by taking the jobs in longest-first order and summing every other processing time.

The significance of Δ relates to the definition of the restricted and unrestricted versions of the problem. The definition of the unrestricted version given earlier was vague in that it was based on the notion that the due date should not be too tight. Now that we have developed Eq. (5.4), we can be more precise. The value of Δ in Eq. (5.4) is the smallest value of d consistent with an unrestricted version of the problem. In other words, the problem is unrestricted for $d \geq \Delta$ and restricted for $d < \Delta$. When the problem is restricted, Algorithm 5.1 may not produce an optimal schedule. When the problem is unrestricted, Algorithm 5.1* guarantees an optimal schedule.

We can see from Table 5.1 that in our example, $\Delta = 18$. Given the job set in this example, if the common due date were $d = 18$, the problem would still be unrestricted, and Algorithm 5.1* would produce an optimal schedule. For $d < 18$, the problem would be restricted.

Algorithm 5.1* thus achieves a feasible unrestricted solution whenever one exists. But this variation of Algorithm 5.1 maximizes the idle time before starting the first job and thus maximizes the makespan, $C_{\max}$. To prepare the machine for the next set of jobs, however, it may be safer as a secondary objective to *minimize* the makespan. Let Algorithm 5.1** be defined by reversing all the optional choices of Algorithm 5.1* – that is, we select the longer job for B in Step 2 and assign the shortest job to B in Step 3 if n is even (yielding $b = a + 2$ rather than $b = a$). Instead of Eq. (5.4), Algorithm 5.1** yields

$$\Delta^{**} = p_n + p_{n-1} + p_{n-3} + \cdots$$

If $d \geq \Delta^{**}$, Algorithm 5.1** yields an unrestricted solution and achieves the minimal makespan as a secondary objective. If $\Delta < d < \Delta^{**}$, then the E/T problem is unrestricted, but minimizing the secondary objective becomes NP-hard (in the ordinary sense). In Example 5.1, as long as the due date is 21 or more, Algorithm 5.1** solves the E/T problem optimally. In Table 5.1, the solution of Algorithm 5.1** is in the first row and that of Algorithm 5.1* in the last. For $d = 24$, the former yields $C_{\max} = 33$ and the latter $C_{\max} = 36$. Finally, when n is even, Algorithms 5.1* and 5.1** yield two distinct b values, $n/2$ and $1 + n/2$. This implies that for any sequence (optimal or not), it does not matter if job $[1 + n/2]$ completes exactly on the due date or starts exactly on the due date. Indeed, this job can even straddle the due date without compromising optimality.

5.2.2 Due Dates as Decisions

One variation of the basic E/T problem treats the due date as a decision variable. As we discussed in conjunction with the T-problem in Section 2.4.3, this formulation involves the objective of choosing the due date to be as tight as possible. Treating the due date as a decision in the E/T problem is equivalent to solving the unrestricted version of the basic problem by Algorithm 5.1*. Suppose we solve a particular unrestricted version with given due date d_1. Consider the problem consisting of the same set of jobs but a due date of $d_2 > d_1$. We can solve this second problem simply by taking the solution for d_1 and shifting the entire schedule later by $(d_2 - d_1)$. As long as d_1 and d_2 give rise to unrestricted versions of the problem, then the optimal values of their E/T objective functions must be the same. In other words, the optimal total cost in an unrestricted instance of the basic problem is constant as the due date is varied.

As for the restricted version, which we shall examine in the next section, it is very similar to the unrestricted version. Every feasible solution to the restricted version is also a feasible solution to the unrestricted version consisting of the same jobs and a sufficiently later due date. (The reverse is not true, however.) In fact, if we start with a restricted version and increase the value of the due date d, we find that the optimal total cost is nonincreasing in d. Furthermore, as we noted earlier, the optimal total cost eventually levels off when d is large enough to give rise to the unrestricted version. In short, we can think of the relationship between the optimal total cost and the due date as depicted by the graph in Figure 5.1. As the graph shows, Δ is the smallest value of d at which the optimal total cost attains its minimum.

If d is a decision variable, then one way to find an optimal solution is to set $d = \Delta$ and then utilize Algorithm 5.1*. Thus, faced with a problem in which d is a decision, we find a solution by solving the unrestricted version of the basic E/T problem.

5.3 The Restricted Version

The restricted version of the problem occurs when $d < \Delta$. In that case, Theorems 5.1 and 5.2 still hold, but Theorem 5.3 does not: The optimal solution may contain a straddling job. It turns out that V-shaped schedules still constitute a dominant set. (This is not as obvious as it was in the unrestricted version.

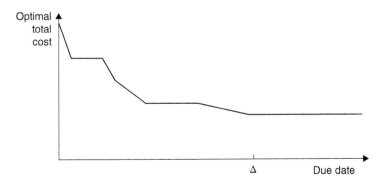

Figure 5.1 Optimal total cost as a function of the due date.

In a V-shaped schedule, the shortest job may be the last job to complete on or before the due date, the first job to start on or after the due date, or a straddling job.) Finally, Theorem 5.4 does not hold either, because it requires Theorem 5.3.

In the restricted version of the problem, it is tempting to assume that the schedule should start at time zero. This seems logical at first because the restricted version arises when the due date is too tight. We would prefer to place b selected jobs in set B, but sufficient time is not available prior to the due date. It makes sense that the schedule would then be compressed toward time zero. Nevertheless, this intuitive argument fails.

■ **Example 5.2** Consider a problem containing $n = 3$ jobs with known processing times and a given due date of $d = 5$.

Job j	1	2	3
p_j	1	1	10

There are six schedules with zero start time, and the minimum cost is 14, achieved by the sequences 1-2-3 and 2-1-3. However, if the start time of either schedule is delayed until time 3, then the cost drops to 11. As this example shows, it may be optimal to have a delay at the start of the schedule. It can be shown that an optimal schedule always exists in which either (i) the schedule starts at time zero, or (ii) some job completes exactly at the due date.

No simple way exists, comparable with the matching procedure in Algorithm 5.1, to find an optimal solution to the restricted version of the basic E/T problem. Indeed, the restricted version is NP-hard. Nevertheless, a pseudopolynomial solution algorithm based on dynamic programming is capable of solving problems containing several hundred jobs in modest amounts of computer time.

Although no simple technique exists for finding an optimum, a remarkably effective heuristic is available. The procedure builds a V-shaped schedule that starts at time zero. This means that the maximum completion time equals the sum of the job processing times. At each stage of the procedure, let L denote the amount of time available before the due date, and let R denote the amount of time available after the due date. As shown in Figure 5.2, we initially have

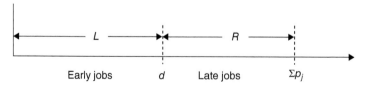

Figure 5.2 Layout for the heuristic procedure.

$$L = d \text{ and } R = \sum_{j=1}^{n} p_j - d$$

From this starting point, we fill the positions in the job sequence from both ends toward the middle. Taking the jobs in longest-first order, we use the following decision rule:

If $L > R$, assign the next job to the first available position in sequence.
If $L \leq R$, assign the next job to the last available position in sequence.

When we assign job j to the first position in sequence, we subtract p_j from L; when we assign job j to the last position in sequence, we subtract p_j from R.

■ **Example 5.3**   Consider the following six-job example, with $d = 90$.

Job j	1	2	3	4	5	6
p_j	1	10	11	48	50	53

The step-by-step construction of the sequence is detailed in Table 5.2. The sequence constructed by the procedure, 6-4-1-2-3-5, yields a total cost of 198.

We can add a simple test to this procedure that will sometimes identify a situation where the total cost can be reduced by delaying the start of the schedule. Let e denote the number of jobs that finish before the due date. Equivalently, $(n - e)$ is the number of jobs that finish on or after the due date. Suppose we delay the start of the schedule by a small amount, Δt. Then e jobs will have their costs reduced by Δt, and $(n - e)$ jobs will have their costs increased by Δt. The delay leads to a reduction in the total cost if

$$e\Delta t > (n - e)\Delta t$$

Table 5.2

L	R	Assignment	Sequence
$L = 90$	$R = 83$	Place job 6 first	6-X-X-X-X-X
$L = 37$	$R = 83$	Place job 5 last	6-X-X-X-X-5
$L = 37$	$R = 33$	Place job 4 first	6-4-X-X-X-5
$L = -11$	$R = 33$	Place job 3 last	6-4-X-X-3-5
$L = -11$	$R = 22$	Place job 2 last	6-4-X-2-3-5
$L = -11$	$R = 12$	Place job 1 last	6-4-1-2-3-5

Algebraically, this is equivalent to the condition $e > n/2$. Thus, if more than half the jobs are early, then the start of the schedule should be delayed, at least long enough to make the last early job complete exactly at the due date.

Suppose we invoke this test in our example for the sequence 6-3-2-1-4-5, which is a V-shaped alternative to the heuristic solution in the example above, but with a total cost of 210. In this solution, four jobs complete before the due date of 90, so $e > n/2$. The fourth job in sequence, job 1, finishes at time 75 when the schedule starts at time zero. Therefore, a delay of 15 is desirable: It reduces the total cost to 180, which is optimal for this example.

5.4 Asymmetric Earliness and Tardiness Costs

A generalization of the basic model derives from the notion that earliness and tardiness should be penalized at different rates. As noted earlier, α may represent a holding cost, while β represents a tardiness cost. These costs are likely to be different, especially because α tends to be determined by endogenous factors, whereas β tends to be exogenous. In particular, let

$$f(S) = \sum_{j=1}^{n} \left(\alpha E_j + \beta T_j \right)$$

This problem is in many respects a straightforward generalization of the basic E/T problem. Again, it gives rise to a restricted version as well as an unrestricted version. In the unrestricted version, an optimal solution has the following properties, generalizing Theorems 5.1–5.3:

1) There is no inserted idle time.
2) Jobs that complete on or before the due date should be sequenced in LPT order, and jobs that start late should be sequenced in SPT order.
3) One job completes at time d.

These results are again straightforward to prove by contradiction. As a result of Theorem 5.3, it again follows that an optimal schedule is V-shaped.

Next, the components of the objective function, analogous to (5.2) and (5.3), are the total cost for B, and the total cost for A,

$$C_B = 0p_{B1} + \alpha p_{B2} + \cdots + (b-2)\alpha p_{B(b-1)} + (b-1)\alpha p_{Bb} \tag{5.5}$$

$$C_A = a\beta p_{A1} + (a-1)\beta p_{A2} + \cdots + 2\beta p_{A(a-1)} + \beta p_{Aa} \tag{5.6}$$

The objective function is the sum of C_B and C_A, and the processing times are given. This sum of products can be minimized by matching the smallest coefficient in the sum with the largest processing time, the next smallest coefficient with the next largest processing time, and so on, with ties broken arbitrarily. An alternative statement of the algorithm, with a precise tie-breaking mechanism, is given as Algorithm 5.2. This procedure finds an optimal schedule and minimizes the total processing time in set B. Thus, it is analogous to Algorithm 5.1*.

Algorithm 5.2 *Solving the E/T Problem with Different Earliness and Tardiness Costs*

Step 1. Initially, sets B and A are empty, and the jobs are in LPT order.

Step 2. If $\alpha|B| < \beta(1 + |A|)$ then assign the next job to B; otherwise, assign the next job to A.

Step 3. Repeat Step 2 until all jobs have been scheduled. Finally, order the jobs in B by LPT and the jobs in A by SPT.

If $\alpha|B| = \beta(1 + |A|)$, the algorithm allocates the next job to A. If we allocate such jobs to B instead, we obtain a version that is analogous to Algorithm 5.1**. As an illustration, consider Example 5.1, with $d = 24$, and suppose that $\alpha = 5$ and $\beta = 2$. Again, the SPT ordering is as follows:

Job j	1	2	3	4	5	6
p_j	1	3	4	6	7	9

The steps in Algorithm 5.2 are listed in Table 5.3.

As a result of applying the algorithm, jobs 6 and 3 are assigned to B, and jobs 1, 2, 4, and 5 are assigned to A. All processing times are distinct, and the decision rule in Step 2 of the algorithm encounters no equalities, so only one optimal schedule can be produced. The sequence 6-3-1-2-4-5, with a start time of 11, yields a total cost of 84.

As in the basic E/T problem, two additional results apply. First, we can restate Theorem 5.4 more generally.

Table 5.3

$|B|$	$|A|$	α	β	$\alpha|B|$	$\beta(1 + |A|)$	Outcome
0	0	5	2	0	2	Assign job 6 to B
1	0	5	2	5	2	Assign job 5 to A
1	1	5	2	5	4	Assign job 4 to A
1	2	5	2	5	6	Assign job 3 to B
2	2	5	2	10	6	Assign job 2 to A
2	3	5	2	10	8	Assign job 1 to A

■ **Theorem 5.4a** In the basic E/T problem with unit earliness cost α and unit tardiness cost β, an optimal schedule exists in which the bth job in sequence completes at time d, where $b = \lceil n\beta/(\alpha + \beta) \rceil$.

In our example, the theorem implies that $b = \lceil 12/7 \rceil = 2$, as we observe in Table 5.3. When $\lceil n\beta/(\alpha + \beta) \rceil = n\beta/(\alpha + \beta)$, the alternative version of the algorithm would produce $b = \lceil n\beta/(\alpha + \beta) \rceil + 1$, and job $[n\beta/(\alpha + \beta) + 1]$ can straddle the due date.

The second result involves the total processing time for set B in the optimal schedule. Let

$$\Delta = p_{B1} + p_{B2} + \cdots + p_{B(b-1)} + p_{Bb} \tag{5.7}$$

As before, the problem is unrestricted for $d \geq \Delta$. Recall that in the simpler problem with $\alpha = \beta$, we can calculate Δ in Eq. (5.4) directly from given parameters, before solving the problem. Here, in the case of different earliness and tardiness costs, we cannot compute Δ in advance. We must solve the problem in order to calculate Δ in Eq. (5.7). In our example, jobs 6 and 3 make up set B; therefore, $\Delta = 13$. For $d < 13$, this problem corresponds to the restricted version.

In the restricted version of the problem, Theorems 5.1 and 5.2 still hold, and V-shaped schedules constitute a dominant set. We can also generalize the decision rule described in the previous section: Instead of the condition $L > R$, we now use $\alpha L > \beta R$. In addition, we can generalize the condition that indicates delaying the start of the schedule to $e > n\beta/(\alpha + \beta)$.

To suggest how effective the heuristic might be, it was tested on two sets of randomly generated problems, one with $\alpha = \beta$ and the other with $\alpha \neq \beta$. First, job processing times were generated, and the solution to the unrestricted version was obtained, thus allowing Δ to be calculated. Next, a due date was randomly sampled between $\Delta/2$ and Δ. The resulting problem was solved optimally and by the heuristic method. This process was repeated for each of 20 problems for each problem size in both sets of test problems. Table 5.4 summarizes the computational results for the 160 problems, where average error represents the percent deviation of the heuristic method from the optimum, averaged over the 20 replications. The main observations are (i) that the average error is usually below 1%, and (ii) that the heuristic finds an optimal solution roughly one-third of the time.

5.5 Quadratic Costs

In some cases, large deviations from the due date are highly undesirable, and it might be more appropriate to use squared deviations from the common due date as the performance measure. Thus, consider the objective function:

Table 5.4

Problem size	$\alpha = \beta$		$\alpha \neq \beta$	
	Average error (%)	Number of optima	Average error (%)	Number of optima
$n = 8$	0.40	10	1.52	5
$n = 10$	0.24	9	0.84	5
$n = 12$	0.26	4	0.66	7
$n = 15$	0.32	4	0.07	10

$$f(S) = \sum_{j=1}^{n} \left(C_j - d \right)^2 = \sum_{j=1}^{n} \left(E_j^2 + T_j^2 \right) \tag{5.8}$$

This objective is the quadratic analog of the absolute deviation criterion in Eq. (5.1). Moreover, suppose that d is a decision variable. If the values of the completion times C_j were known, then the best choice of d for minimizing f (S) would be the mean completion time:

$$\mu = \frac{1}{n} \sum_{j=1}^{n} C_j$$

With this choice of the due date, we would rewrite the objective function as

$$f(S) = \sum_{j=1}^{n} \left(C_j - \mu \right)^2$$

which, except for a factor of n, is the definition of the completion time variance. When the due date is given, the reasoning of Section 5.2.2 applies. As long as the problem is unrestricted, the optimal schedule assigns completion times so that their mean is equal to the given due date. Therefore, the unrestricted version of the quadratic E/T problem is equivalent to minimizing the variance of completion times.

In spite of its equivalence to the completion time variance problem, the quadratic E/T problem is not easily solved. For the unrestricted problem with objective function (5.8), Theorems 5.1 and 5.2 hold, but μ need not coincide with any completion time, so Theorems 5.3 and 5.4 do not hold. Only enumerative approaches have been developed for this problem, and some progress has been made with heuristic procedures. In fact, the most successful heuristic solutions have been obtained using neighborhood search techniques, where the neighborhoods are generated by pairwise interchanges.

5.6 Job-dependent Costs

An obvious direction for generalization is to permit each job to have its own costs α_j and β_j. Specifically, the objective function takes the form

$$f(S) = \sum_{j=1}^{n} \left(\alpha_j E_j + \beta_j T_j \right)$$

When $\alpha_j = \beta_j$, the tardiness cost matches the earliness cost for any particular job, but the costs may differ among jobs. Even the unrestricted version of this case is NP-hard. However, a pseudopolynomial solution algorithm based on dynamic programming is capable of solving problems containing several hundred jobs in modest amounts of computer time.

In the more general case where $\alpha_j \neq \beta_j$, versions of Theorems 5.1–5.3 hold, so an optimal solution has the following properties:

1) There is no inserted idle time.
2) Jobs that complete on or before the due date can be sequenced in nonincreasing order of the ratio p_j/α_j, and jobs that start late can be sequenced in nondecreasing order of the ratio p_j/β_j, thus forming an LWPT/SWPT sequence.
3) One job completes at time d.

We can again restate Theorem 5.4 more generally, to specify a condition for b.

■ **Theorem 5.4b**   In the basic E/T problem with unit earliness costs α_j and unit tardiness costs β_j, an optimal schedule exists in which the bth job in sequence completes at time d, where b is the smallest integer satisfying the inequality

$$\sum_{i \in B} (\alpha_i + \beta_i) \geq \sum_{j=1}^{n} \beta_j$$

As in the unrestricted version of the basic E/T problem, the search for an optimal schedule must enumerate the set of schedules consistent with these properties. However, no property analogous to the matching property is available to speed up this search. In principle, all 2^n dominant sets must be examined.

5.7 Distinct Due Dates

The general E/T problem contains different due dates in the job set. This feature tends to make it more difficult to determine a minimum-cost schedule than in the problems discussed thus far. However, if the due dates are treated as decision variables, the problem turns out to be relatively easy to solve. When the due dates are completely flexible, we can select any sequence we wish (using a secondary objective) and set $d_j = C_j$. In addition, if we choose total flowtime F as the secondary objective, we can trade-off total E/T costs with total flowtime, using the following objective function:

$$f(S) = \sum_{j=1}^{n} \left(\alpha E_j + \beta T_j + \gamma F_j \right)$$

The solution is given by SPT, with the schedule starting at time zero. This solution also minimizes $D = \Sigma d_j$ (which is typically the objective when due dates are decisions, as in Section 2.4.3).

In the general case, we assume that due dates are given and distinct and that the objective function is

$$f(S) = \sum_{j=1}^{n} \left(\alpha_j E_j + \beta_j T_j \right)$$

This problem is NP-hard even in the symmetric case with identical costs. Moreover, Theorems 5.1 and 5.2 do not extend to this case. In particular, inserted idle time may be desirable. Although the best sequence without inserted idle time is not necessarily the best sequence after allowing idle time, the search for an optimal schedule can be decomposed into two subproblems: (i) finding a good job sequence and (ii) scheduling inserted idle time. The second step involves scheduling the start times of all jobs, and we next examine this problem in more detail.

Consider the scheduling problem for a given job sequence, and assume that the jobs are numbered by sequence position. A schedule can be partitioned into *blocks*, which are sets of contiguous jobs in the schedule. Idle time is inserted *between* blocks but not *within* blocks. We can think of the schedule as if jobs were made available (or *released*) to the shop intermittently, in groups. The groups correspond to the blocks, and the time at which a block is permitted to start is called its *release date*. In an optimal schedule, the last job in any block cannot be early, and the first job in a block cannot be tardy unless it starts at time zero (which can happen only in the first block).

The procedure begins by assigning the first job to the first block and scheduling it to complete at its due date or, if this is not feasible, to start at time zero. Jobs are then considered in the order in which they appear in the given sequence. If job j is early when appended to the existing block, then it is rescheduled to complete at its due date, thus starting a new block. Otherwise, job j is appended to the existing block, starting when job $(j - 1)$ completes. At this stage, if we can achieve a better total cost by shifting all jobs in the block earlier, we do so. This shift is possible only if we have inserted idleness, or a *gap*, between the previous block and the current block. (If the current block starts at time zero, then it has a gap of zero.) If the gap between the blocks is consumed (becomes zero) before the block's cost is minimized, we merge the blocks. Any further shift now applies to the merged block. We can characterize an optimal release date of a block by adapting Theorem 5.4b to apply only to the jobs inside the block. Because the due dates are distinct, instead of requiring the bth job to finish precisely on time, we now require at most $(b - 1)$ jobs to be strictly early and at most $(n - b)$ jobs to be strictly tardy. (To satisfy both conditions, at least one job would have to be precisely on time.) A block that cannot satisfy this adapted condition must start as soon as possible: It should be merged with the previous block – and the merged block must then satisfy the same condition – or start at time zero.

■ **Example 5.4**   Consider the following nine-job example, with unit earliness cost $\alpha = 1$ and unit tardiness cost $\beta = 3$.

Job j	1	2	3	4	5	6	7	8	9
p_j	1	4	3	6	2	7	6	2	5
d_j	4	6	7	10	28	31	35	38	40

We take the jobs in numbered order, which is also the EDD sequence. Job 1 is due at time 4, so it can avoid costs by starting at 3. Job 2 cannot follow job 1 and complete on time, so we schedule it immediately following job 1, leading to completion at time 8. The cost of jobs 1 and 2 is $1 \times 0 + 3 \times 2 = 6$.

We examine the possibility of starting job 1 earlier. If it starts at time 2, its earliness cost is 1, but job 2 starts at time 3, completes at 7, and incurs a cost of 3. The total cost for the two-job block is 4, an improvement. If the block starts at time 1, its cost drops to 2, and if the block starts at time zero, its total cost rises to 4. So we keep jobs 1 and 2 as a block starting at time 1.

Next, consider job 3. Added to the block, job 3 completes at time 9, and the three-job block incurs a cost of 8. If the block starts at time zero, its total cost drops to 7, so we start the schedule at time zero. No further shifting is possible.

Next, consider job 4, which can start at time 8 and complete at time 14, making it late by 4. No shifting is possible. Job 5 could start at time 14, but it would then be quite early, so we start a new block consisting of job 5 alone, starting at time 26.

Next, consider job 6. Added to the second block, job 6 completes at time 35. The total cost for the second block is then 12, and we probe for cost reduction by starting the block earlier. We can shift the block to start as early as time 22, in which case job 6 completes at its due date, and the block incurs total cost of 4.

Next, consider job 7. Added to the second block, job 7 completes at time 37. We can shift the block 2 time units earlier, starting at time 20, to minimize the total cost in the block.

Next, consider job 8, which would be early if appended to the second block. We start a third block at time 36, allowing job 8 to complete at its due date.

Finally, consider job 9. Added to the third block, job 9 completes at time 43. The third block can be shifted earlier to reduce the total cost incurred by its jobs, but when the block is shifted earlier by one time unit, the time gap between the second and third blocks disappears. Those two blocks become merged, and no shift to an earlier start can reduce total costs.

The full schedule consists of two blocks, one starting at time zero with job 1, and the second starting at time 20 with job 5. Jobs 1–4 constitute the first block, in which the jobs are processed without inserted idle time, so the block completes at time 14. Jobs 5–9 constitute the second block, in which the jobs are processed without inserted idle time, completing at time 42. In the second block, four of the five jobs are early or on time, satisfying the condition of Theorem 5.4a. This condition does not apply to the first block because it could not be shifted earlier than time zero.

For the special case of symmetric and identical costs ($\alpha_j = \alpha = \beta = \beta_j$), it is computationally easy to decide how far back to push a block. At each stage, the procedure tries to maintain $b > a$, where b denotes the number of nontardy jobs in the block, and a denotes the number of tardy jobs in the block. When job j is added at the end of the block, if $b > a$ or if the schedule starts at time zero, then no improvement is possible at this stage. Otherwise, job j, along with the preceding jobs in its block, should be shifted earlier until one of three possibilities occurs: (i) the start of the entire schedule is shifted back to time zero, (ii) some job in the block completes exactly at its due date, or (iii) the inserted idle time following the previous block is squeezed to zero and the blocks are merged. When one of these three conditions is encountered, we proceed to the scheduling of job ($j + 1$), and we stop when all jobs are scheduled. An algorithm for scheduling inserted idle time for a given sequence can be implemented in polynomial time, even when the costs are not symmetric and identical, although a slightly more efficient implementation is possible in the special case. The computational efficiency is relevant because such a procedure must be incorporated into a routine that searches for the optimal sequence.

Given that the idle time can easily be optimized for a specified job sequence, the task remaining is to locate the best sequence. Branch-and-bound approaches to finding the optimal sequence have demonstrated the capability to solve problems containing at least 20 jobs, but larger problems are sometimes difficult to handle. Computational tests on small problems indicate that a neighborhood search heuristic yields solutions that average within 2% of optimum.

5.8 Summary

The earliness/tardiness problem has received considerable attention as JIT concepts have become more prominent in practice. The E/T problem represents a departure from most basic single-machine models because it involves a performance measure that is not regular. In the major results we have covered, we can discern two classes of problems. One class involves a common due date for all jobs; the other class accommodates different due dates. Solutions to the model with common due dates involve certain key features, namely, V-shaped schedules and no idle time between jobs, as described by Theorems 5.1 and 5.2.

It is worth contemplating how these properties might provide guidance for scheduling in complex systems with E/T criteria. The desirability of avoiding inserted idle time suggests that dispatching procedures can be effective. (Dispatching procedures allow a scheduling decision to be made in real time when a machine becomes idle, rather than in advance.) The optimality of V-shaped sequences presents some difficulties, however, because it calls for a changeover from longest-first dispatching to shortest-first dispatching. Furthermore, during the first phase, we should skip some long jobs and allocate them to the second phase. The optimal dispatching rule can therefore be viewed as a dynamic priority scheme that changes dramatically during processing. In contrast, static sequencing rules such as SPT or EDD have unchanging relative priorities. Thus, the lesson we draw is that E/T criteria with common due dates are likely to require relatively sophisticated dispatching procedures.

In addition, it is important to distinguish between the restricted and unrestricted versions of the common due date problem. In the unrestricted version (or equivalently, the version in which the due date is a decision), the due date coincides with a job completion time, and a specific decision rule determines the optimal location of the due date in any job sequence, as described by Theorems 5.3 and 5.4. However, the restricted version of the problem does not have these properties and is therefore more difficult to solve. If this result has a practical lesson, it may point to the difficulty of finding a good schedule when the due date is relatively tight. In other words, costs will be lower – and finding an optimum will be easier – if we can operate in a situation where the due date is not restrictive. Although this principle is not surprising, it suggests that in setting a due date, a scheduler should consider where the boundary lies between a restrictive due date and a nonrestrictive one.

The second, more important class of problems has distinct due dates. Problems in this class are intrinsically more difficult to solve, and few effective techniques have been established. Solving these problems involves two steps: sequencing the jobs and determining inserted idle time, where the best allocation of idle time depends on the job sequence. In general, it appears that inserting idle time is not a complex problem for a given sequence, but only branch-and-bound techniques, or some form of enumerative search, can be effective at finding the optimal sequence. The lesson from this class of problems may be that dispatching procedures – even sophisticated ones – do not provide the best hope for effective solutions. This observation suggests that in the presence of due dates and nonregular measures of performance, we must either plan idle time explicitly or negotiate earlier deliveries with reduced costs.

Compared with regular performance measurements, the E/T problem may provide a more realistic modeling of the true economic implications of scheduling decisions. Similarly, stochastic models that are based on the E/T problem can include a more realistic accounting of the economic implications of randomness. Indeed, this analysis leads to the specification of safety time. In the next two chapters, we develop this idea further.

Exercises

5.1 Prove that V-shaped schedules comprise a dominant set for the restricted version of the basic E/T problem.

5.2 Consider the following 10-job E/T problem with a common due date that is also a decision variable.

Job j	1	2	3	4	5	6	7	8	9	10
p_j	32	26	7	55	98	80	41	23	24	100

a) Take $\alpha_j = \beta_j = 1$. Find an optimal sequence that makes the due date as small as possible.

b) Repeat (a) when $\alpha_j = 2$ and $\beta_j = 4$.

5.3 Consider the following five-job E/T problem with a due date as a decision.

Job j	1	2	3	4	5
p_j	1	6	4	7	3
α_j	5	7	2	4	3
β_j	1	2	8	6	5

Find an optimal solution by enumerating the nondominated schedules.

5.4 Generalize the E/T problem with a common due date by incorporating a unimodal loss function – that is, a function that attains a minimum at a point that we call the due date and is monotone nonincreasing (nondecreasing) before (after) the due date. For example, the quadratic loss model is a special case of this generalization. Prove that an optimal solution for this generalized model is V-shaped, both for the restricted and unrestricted versions. (*Hint*: If a sequence is not V-shaped, it must contain a consecutive subset of three jobs such that the longest one is between two shorter ones. Show that the existence of such a set leads to contradiction.)

5.5 Suppose that the due date is a decision and that there is a disincentive for choosing the due date to be loose. In particular, a due date penalty is added to the objective function of the basic E/T problem. The objective function to be minimized takes the following form:

$$f(S) = \sum_{j=1}^{n} (E_j + T_j + \gamma d)$$

where $0 < \gamma < 1$.
a) Show that Theorems 5.1–5.3 hold for this problem.
b) Find the analogy to Theorem 5.4 for this problem.

5.6 Consider the unrestricted version of basic E/T problem with job-dependent earliness and tardiness penalties and a common due date. Suppose that the penalties are all symmetric, $\alpha_j = \beta_j$. Construct a four-job example for which an optimal solution contains no job finishing late.

5.7 Consider the basic E/T problem with due dates as decisions, and suppose that the due dates follow the SLK rule. (See Chapter 2.) That is, each job has equal slack, so the form of the due date for job j is $d_j = p_j + k$.
a) Find an expression for the sum of earliness and tardiness in the form of a scalar product that can be minimized by matching the smallest coefficient with the largest processing time, the second smallest coefficient with the next largest processing time, and so on.
b) Find the optimal value of k.
c) Now suppose that the due dates follow the CON rule. That is, each job has the same flow allowance, or $d_j = k$. Repeat (a) and (b) for this case, and show that, for any given set of processing times, the optimal value of the objective function is the same for CON and SLK.

Bibliography

Bagchi, U., Chang, Y., and Sullivan, R. (1987). Minimizing absolute and squared deviations of completion times with different earliness and tardiness penalties and a common due date. *Naval Research Logistics Quarterly* 33: 227–240.

Baker, K.R. and Scudder, G.D. (1990). Sequencing with earliness and tardiness penalties: a review. *Operations Research* 38: 22–36.

Cheng, T.C.E. (1984). Optimal due date determination and sequencing of *n* jobs on a single machine. *Journal of the Operational Research Society* 35: 433–437.

De, P., Ghosh, J., and Wells, C. (1989). A note on the minimization of mean squared deviation of completion times about a common due date. *Management Science* 35: 1143–1147.

Fry, T., Armstrong, R., and Blackstone, J. (1987). Minimizing weighted absolute deviation in single machine scheduling. *IIE Transactions* 19: 445–450.

Hall, N. and Posner, M. (1991). Earliness–tardiness scheduling problems, I: weighted deviation of completion times about a common due date. *Operations Research* 39: 836–846.

Hall, N., Kubiak, W., and Sethi, S. (1991). Earliness–tardiness scheduling problems, II: deviation of completion times about a restrictive common due date. *Operations Research* 39: 847–856.

Hassin, R. and Shani, M. (2005). Machine scheduling with earliness, tardiness and non-execution penalties. *Computers & Operations Research* 32: 683–705.

Kanet, J. (1981a). Minimizing the average deviation of job completion times about a common due date. *Naval Research Logistics Quarterly* 28: 643–651.

Kanet, J. (1981b). Minimizing variation of flow time in single machine systems. *Management Science* 27: 1453–1459.

Raghavachari, M. (1986). A V-shape property of optimal schedule of jobs about a common due date. *European Journal of Operations Research* 23: 401–402.

Sundararaghavan, P. and Ahmed, M. (1984). Minimizing the sum of absolute lateness in single-machine and multimachine scheduling. *Naval Research Logistics Quarterly* 31: 325–333.

Szwarc, W. (1989). Single machine scheduling to minimize absolute deviation of completion times from a common due date. *Naval Research Logistics Quarterly* 36: 663–673.

Szwarc, W. and Mukhopadhyay, S.K. (1995). Optimal timing schedules in earliness–tardiness single machine sequencing. *Naval Research Logistics Quarterly* 42: 1109–1114.

6

Sequencing for Stochastic Scheduling

6.1 Introduction

As we discussed in Chapter 2, the basic single-machine sequencing model is characterized by seven conditions:

C1. There are n single-operation jobs simultaneously available for processing (at time zero).
C2. Machines can process at most one job at a time.
C3. Setup times for the jobs are independent of job sequence and are included in processing times.
C4. Job descriptors are deterministic and known in advance.
C5. Machines are continuously available (no breakdowns occur).
C6. Machines are never kept idle while work is waiting.
C7. Once an operation begins, it proceeds without interruption.

Such conditions, which help us analyze the problem, may also restrict the applicability of the model. Specifically, by adopting conditions C4 and C5, we limit ourselves to deterministic models, with all parameters assumed to be known. In this chapter, we explore a relaxation of condition C4, allowing processing times to be random. We assume that condition C5 remains unchanged. However, if we relax C5 and allow machine breakdowns, the effect is ultimately quite similar to relaxing C4 because the time required to process a job becomes uncertain. When processing times are random, the problem that results is called a *stochastic scheduling problem*.

As discussed in Chapter 2, conditions C6 and C7 are inconsequential for regular performance measures in the deterministic version of the basic model – that is, inserted idle time and job preemption provide no advantage. However,

Principles of Sequencing and Scheduling, Second Edition. Kenneth R. Baker and Dan Trietsch.
© 2019 John Wiley & Sons, Inc. Published 2019 by John Wiley & Sons, Inc.

preemption can sometimes be advantageous in the stochastic case, potentially making the stochastic problem more difficult to solve. For that reason, we continue to require C7 as we begin our analysis of stochastic scheduling problems.

If we relax condition C4, we permit due dates and job weights to be uncertain, as well as processing times, but such models have limited practical significance. Therefore, we treat due dates and weights as deterministic. As a consequence, the EDD sequence is well defined (except for ties). In contrast, the SPT sequence is not well defined, because processing times are not known in advance. However, it is still possible to order jobs by nondecreasing *expected* processing times. This sequence is known as shortest expected processing time (SEPT). Similarly, the shortest weighted expected processing time (SWEPT) sequence is also well defined.

Historically, stochastic scheduling analysis has focused on the same performance measures considered in deterministic scheduling (F, T, L_{max}, T_{max}, U, etc.) and has sought to minimize their expected values. Thus, typical stochastic models aim to minimize $E[F]$, $E[T]$, $E[L_{max}]$, $E[T_{max}]$, $E[U]$, etc. We refer to such models as *stochastic counterparts* of the corresponding deterministic problems. For example, the stochastic counterpart of the F-problem is a stochastic scheduling problem in which the objective function is the expected total flowtime, $E[F]$. More generally, for deterministic models that seek to minimize the total cost or the maximum cost, stochastic counterparts seek to minimize the expected total cost or the expected maximum cost.

In this chapter, we first discuss counterpart models and how to solve them. In addition to analyzing stochastic counterparts of deterministic problems, we also examine the potential usefulness of deterministic counterparts. In other words, we explore whether the deterministic representation can tell us something about the solution to a stochastic problem. Next, we turn our attention to sequencing rules for performance measures based on the maximum cost and the total cost. This discussion highlights the tendency of the deterministic counterpart to produce optimistic performance measures, and we address this bias in more detail. To support optimal sequencing decisions, we then introduce the concepts of stochastic dominance and association.

6.2 Basic Stochastic Counterpart Models

We begin our coverage of stochastic scheduling with an examination of stochastic counterpart problems. The objective in such problems is the expected value of a performance measure such as total flowtime, maximum tardiness, total cost, and the like. To help clarify the nature of stochastic counterpart models, we explore a numerical example.

■ **Example 6.1** Consider a problem containing $n = 5$ jobs with stochastic processing times. The due date and expected processing time for each job are shown in the following table.

Job j	1	2	3	4	5
$E[p_j]$	3	4	5	6	7
d_j	8	5	15	20	12

Suppose that two factors influence these processing times, the weather and the quality of raw materials. Each factor has two equally likely conditions (good and bad), so together they define four states of nature: GG (when both conditions are good), GB, BG, and BB. Each job has a different processing time under each state of nature as follows.

State	Job j	1	2	3	4	5
GG	p_j	2.6	3.5	3.8	3.2	6.4
GB	p_j	2.8	3.9	4.4	5.5	6.6
BG	p_j	3.2	4.1	5.6	6.5	7.4
BB	p_j	3.4	4.5	6.2	8.8	7.6

Assume that the four states are equally likely, or in other words, each combination of five processing times, or each *scenario*, occurs with probability 0.25, and we can interpret the table as a discrete probability distribution. Suppose also that we are interested in total tardiness as a measure of performance. We begin by examining the EDD sequence, 2-1-5-3-4. As a first step, we reorder the columns of the given data set to produce Table 6.1.

Next, we calculate the job completion times for each state, as shown in Table 6.2.

Table 6.1

Sequence	2	1	5	3	4
State		Processing times			
GG	3.5	2.6	6.4	3.8	3.2
GB	3.9	2.8	6.6	4.4	5.5
BG	4.1	3.2	7.4	5.6	6.5
BB	4.5	3.4	7.6	6.2	8.8

From these results, we can compute the tardiness of each job for each state, as shown in Table 6.3.

As Table 6.3 shows, the total tardiness in the sequence depends on which state occurs, and the value of total tardiness ranges from a low of 1.8 to a high of 20.7. Taking into account the fact that the four states are equally likely, we can calculate the mean tardiness as 11.1 by taking the average of the figures in the last column.

We could make similar calculations for several other expected-value performance measures, giving rise to the results shown in Table 6.4, all for the EDD sequence.

Table 6.2

State	Completion times				
GG	3.5	6.1	12.5	16.3	19.5
GB	3.9	6.7	13.3	17.7	23.2
BG	4.1	7.3	14.7	20.3	26.8
BB	4.5	7.9	15.5	21.7	30.5

Table 6.3

State	Tardiness					Total
GG	0.0	0.0	0.5	1.3	0.0	1.8
GB	0.0	0.0	1.3	2.7	3.2	7.2
BG	0.0	0.0	2.7	5.3	6.8	14.8
BB	0.0	0.0	3.5	6.7	10.5	20.7
Average						11.1

Table 6.4

Scenario	F	C_{max}	L	L_{max}	T	T_{max}	U
GG	57.9	19.5	−2.1	1.3	1.8	1.3	2.0
GB	64.8	23.2	4.8	3.2	7.2	3.2	3.0
BG	73.2	26.8	13.2	6.8	14.8	6.8	3.0
BB	80.1	30.5	20.1	10.5	20.7	10.5	3.0
Average	69.0	25.0	9.0	5.5	11.1	5.5	2.8

In Table 6.4, we can recognize the expected tardiness value of 11.1, and we can see the expected value of the other 6 listed performance measures. Of course, if a different sequence is selected, then all these results can change. Thus, the example gives rise to seven stochastic counterpart problems, each aiming to minimize the relevant value in the last row of the table.

In stochastic counterpart models, it is convenient to assume that processing times are probabilistically independent. In words, *independence* means that the processing time realized for one of the jobs does not depend on which processing time is realized for any of the other jobs. Without this assumption, it is seldom possible to find analytic solutions that hold in general. In our coverage, however, we want to develop practical and flexible approaches to stochastic scheduling, so we do not necessarily limit ourselves by requiring independent processing times. For instance, in Example 6.1, we assumed independent *factors* that influenced all processing times in the same direction, but the resulting processing times were not independent – they were correlated. Nevertheless, the small size of our example enabled us to enumerate the states of nature, treat the set of possible outcomes as a discrete probability distribution, and calculate the required expected values.

In relaxing condition C4, we assume that processing times are random variables with given distributions. The basic stochastic scheduling model contains n such random variables, and a small table such as the one in Example 6.1 may not be sufficient to fully capture the probability distributions involved. However, the approach illustrated in our analysis of the example can still be applied if we rely on a table that is drawn from a much larger data set describing the probability distributions. Technically, we generate an $r \times n$ table of processing times resembling Table 6.1, where r is the number of scenarios, or the sample size, and n is the number of jobs. Typically, the scenarios are equally likely, but they could also be assigned probabilities. Row i contains n sampled processing times, one for each job, while column j includes r samples for the processing times of job j. If the table is exhaustive, as was the case in Table 6.1, then the data represent an exhaustive sample, and the table is essentially a discrete probability model. On the other hand, if the distribution is very large (or infinite, which would be the case for a continuous distribution), then any $r \times n$ table drawn from that distribution would be a sample. A sampling approach could accommodate both probabilistically independent and probabilistically dependent cases.

In this chapter, we represent random processing times with the aid of an $r \times n$ table. As the foregoing discussion indicates, such a table may hold an exhaustive sample, which represents a discrete probability model, or it may hold a limited sample, which can represent a set of equally likely scenarios observed in historical records or produced by simulation. This interpretation leads to a general technique of *sample-based analysis*, in which we rely on discrete probability models or simulation outcomes in our analysis. In Chapter 7, we extend our purview to continuous distributions as well. (See Appendix A for background on generating samples.)

In our second example, processing times are independent, and we can illustrate the simulation interpretation of the sample-based approach.

■ **Example 6.2** Consider a problem containing $n = 5$ jobs with stochastic processing times. The expected processing time for each job is shown in the following table. These match the values in Example 6.1.

Job j	1	2	3	4	5
$E[p_j]$	3	4	5	6	7
d_j	8	5	15	20	12

Here, the processing times are randomly distributed with a range of 4. In other words, the processing time for job 1 occurs randomly between 1 and 5, the processing time for job 2 occurs randomly between 2 and 6, and so on.

For the purposes of illustration, we work with a sample of 10 scenarios corresponding to the realizations shown in Table 6.5.

At the top of the table, we calculate the average of the 10 processing time realizations for each of the jobs, mainly as a check on the accuracy of the sampling. For example, job 1 has an average processing time of 2.984 in the sample, very close to its expectation of 3. The other averages are also close to their expectations.

Table 6.5

Job	1	2	3	4	5
Average	2.984	3.891	5.122	6.195	7.280
Scenario					
1	3.710	4.086	3.152	4.689	6.589
2	2.390	2.197	6.395	5.965	7.699
3	4.317	4.263	6.232	5.616	8.468
4	1.138	4.117	5.879	7.325	5.566
5	2.836	2.564	6.144	7.793	8.124
6	2.686	3.734	3.439	7.770	6.325
7	2.533	4.915	5.287	4.745	8.160
8	2.610	2.850	4.546	4.833	8.683
9	3.394	5.721	5.591	6.741	5.102
10	4.229	4.460	4.557	6.477	8.081

The basic idea of sample-based analysis is to find scheduling decisions that are optimal for the sample. To the extent that the simulated sample mimics reality, the sample represents the range of possible realizations. By increasing the sample size r, we can approximate the true optimal solution as precisely as we may wish. (Normally, a sample of size 10 is too small for the precision we seek, but a sample of 1000 is reliable enough for many applications.) We can even view the data in Example 6.1 as a special case of a sample in which the scenarios happen to be exhaustive. With this interpretation, a sample is operationally equivalent to a list of equally likely scenarios that represent possible random outcomes.

Starting with the sample in Table 6.5, we can explore the problem numerically. For example, suppose we adopt total flowtime as a measure of performance and begin with the sequence 1-2-3-4-5, which orders the jobs by SEPT. For each of the ten scenarios, we fix this sequence and compute the flowtime of each job under each scenario, as shown in Table 6.6. From these values, we compute the resulting value of F, shown in the right-hand column of the table.

Next, we find the average value, 65.522, which is shown at the top of the right-hand column in Table 6.6. In this column, as in the previous table, we display an average at the top.

Having evaluated the objective function for the sequence 1-2-3-4-5, our task is now to examine other job sequences and find the one that minimizes F. That search may be tedious, but it is at least straightforward. It turns out that the value of 65.522 is the minimum possible value for this sample, indicating that the sequence 1-2-3-4-5 is optimal for F.

Table 6.6

Job	1	2	3	4	5	F
Scenario	Flowtimes					65.522
1	3.710	7.796	10.948	15.637	22.225	60.317
2	2.390	4.587	10.982	16.947	24.646	59.553
3	4.317	8.581	14.813	20.428	28.897	77.036
4	1.138	5.255	11.134	18.459	24.026	60.012
5	2.836	5.400	11.544	19.336	27.460	66.575
6	2.686	6.420	9.859	17.629	23.954	60.548
7	2.533	7.448	12.735	17.480	25.641	65.838
8	2.610	5.460	10.006	14.839	23.522	56.437
9	3.394	9.115	14.706	21.447	26.549	75.211
10	4.229	8.689	13.246	19.722	27.804	73.690

Our main point is that sample-based analysis (conveniently implemented, for example, in a spreadsheet) is an appropriate general tool for solving stochastic counterpart problems, even though it relies on numerical calculations rather than analytic results. Later in this chapter, we describe a software alternative for implementing this type of analysis. In some cases, however, analytic results are available, sparing us the need to use sample-based analysis at all.

Consider the stochastic counterpart of the *F*-problem. In other words, processing times are random, and the objective is to minimize the expected value of total flowtime. We can also consider the related problem of minimizing the expected value of total lateness, because of the algebraic relationship between flowtime and lateness.

■ **Theorem 6.1**   E[*F*] and E[*L*] are minimized by shortest expected processing time (SEPT) sequencing (E[$p_{[1]}$] ≤ E[$p_{[2]}$] ≤ ··· ≤ E[$p_{[n]}$]).

Proof. We first prove the theorem for E[*F*]. Repeating Eq. (2.1),

$$\sum_{j=1}^{n} F_j = \sum_{j=1}^{n}\sum_{i=1}^{j} p_{[i]} = \sum_{j=1}^{n}(n-j+1)p_{[j]}$$

If we interpret $p_{[j]}$ as a random variable, this equation remains valid. Thus, the total flowtime is a weighted sum of random processing times (with deterministic weights). Therefore,

$$\mathrm{E}[F] = \mathrm{E}\left[\sum_{j=1}^{n} F_j\right] = \sum_{j=1}^{n}\mathrm{E}[F_j] = \sum_{j=1}^{n}(n-j+1)\mathrm{E}[p_j]$$

By the same argument that we used as an alternative proof for Theorem 2.3, this sum is minimized by SEPT. To prove the result for E[*L*], note that Theorem 2.5 still holds – that is, *L* = *F* – *D* so E[*L*] = E[*F*] – E[*D*] (where $D = \sum d_j$).   □

Theorem 6.1 shows how to solve two particular stochastic counterpart models optimally, but it does not say that total flowtime and total lateness are minimized by SEPT in every scenario. Rather, we proved that SEPT minimizes them *on average*. In the 10 scenarios of Example 6.2, sequences other than SEPT are optimal. (In the first scenario, for example, *F* is minimized by the sequence 3-1-2-4-5.) But such an observation is made in hindsight, and we cannot rely on hindsight for sequencing decisions, so SEPT is the best we can do *ex ante*, before the realizations are revealed. Thus, the theorem tells us that in Example 6.1, the sequence 1-2-3-4-5 is optimal for minimizing E[*F*], and it is not necessary to resort to sample-based optimization.

Using the same approach, we can also solve the weighted versions of these two problems, as stated in Theorem 6.2. We emphasize that Theorems 6.1 and 6.2 do not require the processing times to be stochastically independent.

■ **Theorem 6.2** $E[F_w]$ and $E[L_w]$ are minimized by shortest weighted expected processing time (SWEPT) sequencing ($E[p_{[1]}]/w_{[1]} \leq E[p_{[2]}]/w_{[2]} \leq \cdots \leq E[p_{[n]}]/w_{[n]}$).

Now consider the stochastic counterpart of minimizing maximum lateness, as approached by sample-based analysis. For every row in the sample, EDD is an optimal sequence. But this is true for any processing time outcomes – that is, we could sequence the jobs by EDD irrespective of their processing time realizations. In fact, this would be true for an exhaustive sample.

■ **Theorem 6.3** $E[L_{max}]$ and $E[T_{max}]$ are minimized by earliest due date (EDD) sequencing ($d_{[1]} \leq d_{[2]} \leq \cdots \leq d_{[n]}$).

In other words, EDD sequencing remains optimal when our model contains stochastic processing times.

6.3 The Deterministic Counterpart

Consider how we might use a deterministic sequencing model in a stochastic environment. The most obvious way is to use the mean processing times, $E[p_j]$, in place of p_j. That is, we can approach the stochastic problem by substituting expected values for random variables and proceeding as if the problem were deterministic. We refer to the resulting model as the *deterministic counterpart*.

For instance, take the deterministic counterpart in Example 6.1. The first step is to suppress all randomness and treat processing times as if they were deterministic, with values equal to their expectations. This gives rise to the data set shown in the following table.

Job j	1	2	3	4	5
p_j	3	4	5	6	7
d_j	8	5	15	20	12

Suppose we construct the EDD sequence, 2-1-5-3-4, and calculate the deterministic values of the seven performance measures of interest. We obtain the values shown in Table 6.7.

Some of these values happen to match those in Table 6.4, but some do not. For example, the tardiness in the deterministic counterpart is $T = 11$, which does not quite match the expected tardiness of 11.1 that we obtained in Table 6.3. Thus, as the example shows, the deterministic counterpart may not generate a value equal to the expected performance measure in the original stochastic problem. This comparison raises an interesting question, however: When does the deterministic counterpart generate a correct expected value? And related to that, when is the optimal sequence for the deterministic counterpart also optimal for the stochastic problem? Although these are not always easy questions to answer, the deterministic counterpart is often used in practice because it simplifies the analysis.

In Examples 6.1 and 6.2, the solution to the deterministic counterpart of the total flowtime problem is $F = 65$ for the sequence 1-2-3-4-5. Here, the deterministic counterpart provides the optimal sequence, and the value of its objective is equivalent to that of the true expected value. In fact, this result is imbedded in the proof of Theorem 6.1, which tells us how to sequence optimally. Part of that proof used the following equality:

$$ E[F] = \sum_{j=1}^{n} (n - j + 1) E\left[p_j\right] $$

This formula states that the optimal expected total flowtime can be calculated as the objective function for the corresponding deterministic counterpart, which is $F = 65$ in the example. To reach this result using the sample-based analysis of Example 6.2, we would need a sample size much larger than 10. (When we repeated the analysis with a random sample of size 1000, the estimated value of the objective function was 64.982, which is within 0.03% of the theoretical value.)

With regard to Theorem 6.3 and the optimization of $E[L_{\max}]$ and $E[T_{\max}]$, the result is different. In these problems, the deterministic counterpart may not provide an optimal value of the objective function. Consider the results for Example 6.1 and compare Tables 6.4 and 6.7. As we noted, the EDD sequence yields $E[L_{\max}] = 5.5$, whereas in the deterministic counterpart, EDD yields $L_{\max} = 5$. Based on this comparison, it might intuitively seem as if the deterministic counterpart should yield an objective function no greater than that in the original stochastic problem, but that is not the case for all objectives. In Table 6.4, we found $E[U] = 2.8$, whereas Table 6.7 yields a deterministic counterpart with $U = 3.0$. These examples illustrate that we cannot always rely on the deterministic counterpart to produce solutions to stochastic scheduling problems, although it happens to be valid for the F-problem and the L-problem.

Table 6.7

Objective	F	$C_{\max}$	L	$L_{\max}$	T	$T_{\max}$	U
EDD	69	25	9	5	11	5	3

6.4   Minimizing the Maximum Cost

In this section, we examine the stochastic counterpart of the $T_{\max}$ problem, or its more general form, minimizing the expected maximum cost. (Recall the problem described in Section 3.1.) At the outset, keep in mind that the expected maximum cost is *not necessarily* identical to the maximum expected cost. However, minimizing the latter objective appears to be easier. For minimizing the maximum expected cost, $Z = \max\{E[g_1(C_1)], E[g_2(C_2)], \ldots, E[g_n(C_n)]\}$, the solution is given by a direct generalization of Theorem 3.1.

◼ **Theorem 6.4**   When the objective is to minimize the maximum expected cost, job i may be assigned the last position in sequence if $E[g_i(P)] \leq E[g_k(P)]$ for all jobs $k \neq i$, where P denotes the time to complete all jobs.

Proof. By assumption, processing times do not depend on the job sequence (condition C2), so the distribution of P does not depend on the sequence. Because g_i is nondecreasing, $E[g_i(t)]$ is also nondecreasing in t. Therefore, we can replace $g_i(P)$ by $E[g_i(P)]$ for all i and apply the reasoning in the proof of Theorem 3.1.   □

Now consider the following special case:

$$g_j\left[C_j\right] = 1 \quad C_j > d_j$$
$$= 0 \quad C_j \leq d_j$$

Here, we have

$$\Pr\left\{C_j > d_j\right\} = \Pr\{\text{job } j \text{ is tardy}\} = E\left[g_j\left(C_j\right)\right]$$

This set of relationships proves the following corollary of Theorem 6.4.

Corollary 6.1   The EDD sequence minimizes the maximum tardiness probability.

As another way of looking at this result, suppose we define the *service level* for job j as $\Pr\{C_j \leq d_j\}$, the probability that the job is on time. Then Corollary 6.1 also states that the EDD sequence maximizes the minimum service level.

To exploit Theorem 6.4, we still need a procedure to implement the result of the theorem as it applies to sequencing, and we can use the sample-based approach. To solve an instance with a given sample, we initially take P as the sum of the n elements in each row. If we calculate $g_i(P)$ for each job in each row, then the average of these results estimates $E[g_i(P)]$. At the first scheduling stage, we can select the job with the minimal average and schedule it last. At the next scheduling stage, P is reduced for each row by the processing time of the job that has just been scheduled. To illustrate this procedure in a numerical example, we introduce the following form of the cost function $g_j(t)$:

$$g_j(t) = \delta(t - d_j)\left(a_j + b_j(t - d_j)\right)$$

where a_j, $b_j \geq 0$ and $a_j + b_j > 0$; $\delta(x) = 1$ if $x > 0$, and $\delta(x) = 0$ otherwise. Equivalently, $g_j(T_j) = \delta(T_j)(a_j + b_j T_j)$. By selecting the parameters a_j and b_j appropriately, we can produce a variety of models. For example, if $a_j = 0$ and $b_j > 0$ for all j, then the cost is equal to a job's weighted tardiness. If $b_j = 0$ and $a_j > 0$ for all j, then the cost is equal to a job's weight if it is tardy. The special case $b_j = 0$ and $a_j = 1$ for all j corresponds to the U-problem.

■ **Example 6.3**   Consider a problem containing $n = 5$ jobs with stochastic processing times. The due date and expected processing time for each job are shown in the following table.

Job j	1	2	3	4	5
$E[p_j]$	3	4	5	6	7
d_j	8	5	15	20	12

Furthermore, the processing time distributions are the same as in Example 6.1, with four equally likely states of nature.

State	Job j	1	2	3	4	5
GG	p_j	2.6	3.5	3.8	3.2	6.4
GB	p_j	2.8	3.9	4.4	5.5	6.6
BG	p_j	3.2	4.1	5.6	6.5	7.4
BB	p_j	3.4	4.5	6.2	8.8	7.6

In addition, the parameters of the cost function $g_j(T_j) = \delta(T_j)(a_j + b_j T_j)$ are given in the following table.

Job j	1	2	3	4	5
a_j	2.0	3.0	4.0	5.0	1.0
b_j	0.8	0.4	0.1	0.2	0.3

The analysis for the stochastic data of Example 6.3 is summarized below. Each stage shows the cost for every relevant job and state combination. Once a job is placed in the sequence, it is no longer under consideration for subsequent stages.

The last of these stages is trivial, because only one job remains. The procedure is the same at each stage – only the set of jobs under consideration changes. As shown in Table 6.8, the optimal sequence is 2-1-3-5-4. At each stage (that is, in each table), the choice is based on the minimum expected cost in the bottom row, and this value is shown in bold. The maximum of these values (4.8) gives the optimal value of $\max\{E[g_i(P)]\}$. By way of comparison, the optimal sequence in the deterministic counterpart is different (2-1-3-4-5), and the maximum cost is 4.9. (For that sequence, the value of the maximum expected cost is also 4.9.) But we still don't know the optimal value of the expected maximum cost.

We can identify the optimal sequence for both expected maximum cost and maximum expected cost in one special case. This case occurs when all the cost functions are *ordered* such that for any two jobs, i and k, and for all $t \geq 0$, either $g_i(t) \geq g_k(t)$ or $g_k(t) \geq g_i(t)$. In other words, no two cost functions intersect each other. When the functions are ordered, their order dictates the optimal sequence. We have already encountered a special case of this result in the optimality of EDD for T_{max} and L_{max}. More generally, we have the following dominance property.

■ **Theorem 6.5** Consider two jobs, i and k. If $g_i(t) \geq g_k(t)$ for any $t \geq 0$ and the objective is to minimize the expected maximum cost, then there exists an optimal sequence in which job i precedes job k.

Proof. Assume an optimal solution exists in which job k precedes job i and other jobs are possibly sequenced between them. For any set of n non-negative processing time realizations, we obtain $g_i(C_i) \geq g_k(C_i) \geq g_k(C_k)$. The first inequality holds by the hypothesis of the theorem; the second inequality holds because job i completes after job k by assumption. If we insert job k after job i, letting C'_k and C'_i denote the completion times after this resequencing, then $C'_k = C_i$ and $C'_i < C_i$. It follows that $g_k(C'_k) \leq g_i(C_i)$ and $g_i(C'_i) \leq g_i(C_i)$, so the objective function cannot increase. Because that is true for any possible set of realizations, the result does not depend on the processing time distributions. □

Corollary 6.2 Consider two jobs, i and k. If $g_i(t) \geq g_k(t)$ for any $t \geq 0$ and the objective is to minimize the maximum expected cost, then there exists an optimal sequence in which job i precedes job k.

Corollary 6.2 holds because the proof of the theorem also implies that the maximum expected value cannot be larger in another sequence. But, unless *all* cost functions are ordered, it would be a mistake to assume that the same sequence minimizes both objective functions. An example helps to underscore this point.

Table 6.8

Stage 1 (select job 4 as [5])					
Job j	1	2	3	4	5
GG	11.2	8.8	4.5	0.0	3.3
GB	14.2	10.3	4.8	5.6	4.4
BG	17.0	11.7	5.2	6.4	5.4
BB	20.0	13.2	5.6	7.1	6.6
Expected	15.6	11.0	5.0	**4.8**	4.9
Stage 2 (select job 5 as [4])					
Job j	1	2	3	4	5
GG	8.6	7.5	4.1	N/A	2.3
GB	9.8	8.1	4.3	N/A	2.7
BG	11.8	9.1	4.5	N/A	3.5
BB	13.0	9.7	4.7	N/A	3.9
Expected	10.8	8.6	4.4	N/A	**3.1**
Stage 3 (select job 3 as [3])					
Job j	1	2	3	4	5
GG	3.5	5.0	0.0	N/A	N/A
GB	4.5	5.4	0.0	N/A	N/A
BG	5.9	6.2	0.0	N/A	N/A
BB	6.9	6.6	0.0	N/A	N/A
Expected	5.2	5.8	**0.0**	N/A	N/A
Stage 4 (select job 1 as [2])					
Job j	1	2	3	4	5
GG	0.0	3.4	N/A	N/A	N/A
GB	0.0	3.7	N/A	N/A	N/A
BG	0.0	3.9	N/A	N/A	N/A
BB	0.0	4.2	N/A	N/A	N/A
Expected	**0.0**	3.8	N/A	N/A	N/A
Stage 5 (select job 2 as [1])					
Job j	1	2	3	4	5
GG	N/A	0.0	N/A	N/A	N/A
GB	N/A	0.0	N/A	N/A	N/A
BG	N/A	0.0	N/A	N/A	N/A
BB	N/A	0.0	N/A	N/A	N/A
Expected	N/A	**0.0**	N/A	N/A	N/A

■ **Example 6.4**   Consider the scheduling of two jobs, 1 and 2, with random processing times and with the following generic cost function parameters.

Job j	1	2
d_j	0	2
a_j	0	0
b_j	0.7	2

The processing time distributions of the two jobs are independent and identically distributed as follows.

State	Job j	1	2	Probability
A	p_j	1	1	0.5
B	p_j	2	2	0.5

There are two possible sequences, 1-2 and 2-1. For each possible sequence, there are four equally likely configurations of the processing times for jobs 1 and 2: AA, AB, BA, and BB. If we make the required calculations, we find the following:

Sequence 1-2 has a maximum expected cost of 2.
Sequence 1-2 has an expected maximum cost of 2.175.
Sequence 2-1 has a maximum expected cost of 2.1.
Sequence 2-1 has an expected maximum cost of 2.1.

Thus, for minimizing the maximum expected cost, the optimal sequence is 1-2, and the optimal value is 2. However, for minimizing the expected maximum cost, the optimal sequence is 2-1, and the optimal value is 2.1. Example 6.4 demonstrates the following proposition.

Proposition 6.1   The sequences that minimize the maximum expected cost and the expected maximum cost are not necessarily identical.

Although the optimal sequences need not be identical, a useful relationship exists between them. We state it here but defer the proof until the next section.

■ **Theorem 6.6**   Suppose S_1 and S_2 are two sequences (not necessarily distinct) that minimize the maximum expected cost and the expected maximum cost, respectively. Let Z_L and Z_U denote the maximum expected cost and the expected maximum cost of S_1. Then Z_2, the objective function value of S_2, satisfies $Z_L \le Z_2 \le Z_U$.

For instance, in Example 6.4, $Z_L = 2.0 \le Z_2 = 2.1 \le Z_U = 2.175$. The problem of minimizing the expected maximum cost does not satisfy the optimality principle, and therefore we cannot solve it by dynamic programming. This is the case because the objective is neither additive nor can it be transformed into an additive objective. Theorem 6.6, however, allows us to use a branch-and-bound approach, with Z_L and Z_U providing lower and upper bounds for partial sequences.

6.5 The Jensen Gap

In Example 6.1, we saw that the expected value of a maximum is at least as large as the maximum of the component expected values. This is a special case of a general rule, known as *Jensen's inequality*. For convenience in notation, let

$$E[h(g)] = E[h(g_1(C_1), g_2(C_2),...,g_n(C_n))]$$

and let

$$h[E[g]] = h[E[g_1(C_1)], E[g_2(C_2)],...,E[g_n(C_n)]]$$

For now, let h denote the maximum function, and with this notation, the example indicates that $E[\max\{g\}] \geq \max\{E[g]\}$. Generally, Jensen's inequality states that for any random variable X and any convex function h, we always have $E[h(X)] \geq h(E[X])$. In words, for a convex function, the expected value of the function is at least as large as the function evaluated at the expected value. Thus, imagine that we estimate the expected value of a complicated convex function of some random variable by substituting the expected value of the random variable and then evaluating the function. The calculations may be simpler, but our estimate would be biased downward. The maximum function is convex, so the result discussed above is an instance of the convex case. Because T_j is defined by $\max\{0, C_j - d_j\}$, the same rule applies for the T-problem.

For any function h, convex or not, we refer to the difference $E[h(g)] - h(E[g])$ as the *Jensen gap*. In stochastic instances of the T_{max} problem and the L_{max} problem, the objective function value often exceeds the value in the deterministic counterpart and cannot fall below it, so it has a nonnegative Jensen gap. In the single-machine problem with C_{max}, L, or F objectives, the objective function of the stochastic problem and the objective function of the deterministic counterpart are always the same. This agreement corresponds to a zero Jensen gap, which occurs when h is linear.

In the $E[U]$ case of Example 6.1, we observed a negative Jensen gap under EDD: The stochastic objective function is $E[U] = 2.8$, whereas the deterministic counterpart is $U = 3.0$. This case illustrates that the Jensen gap does not have to be nonnegative in scheduling problems. (The sign of the Jensen gap can be positive or negative for the U-problem because the objective is associated with a step function, which is not convex.)

With this background, we are ready to prove Theorem 6.6.

Proof of Theorem 6.6. By Jensen's inequality, $Z_L \le Z_U$. For the same reason, Z_2 is at least equal to the maximum expected cost of S_2, which, in turn, is bounded from below by Z_L (due to the optimality of S_1). Therefore, $Z_L \le Z_2$. As for Z_U, it is a feasible expected maximum cost, so it must be an upper bound on the minimum expected maximum cost. □

6.6 Stochastic Dominance and Association

The expected value of a sum is equal to the sum of its component expected values. That is, $E[\Sigma g_j(C_j)] = \Sigma E[g_j(C_j)]$. Cast in terms of the previous section, the sum function is linear, so its Jensen gap must be zero. Its additive structure enables us to use dynamic programming to find solutions to stochastic problems when the objective function is a sum. A difficulty arises, however, in generalizing dominance conditions from the deterministic case to the stochastic case. Ideally, the most convenient generalization would be to adopt the deterministic counterpart – that is, we would like to use $E[p_j]$ instead of p_j in the various dominance conditions. However, this approach turns out to be unreliable.

■ **Example 6.5** Consider the problem of sequencing two jobs with stochastic processing times and the objective of minimizing expected total tardiness.

Job j	1	2
d_j	2.9	3
$E[p_j]$	1.9	2

The processing time distributions of the two jobs are distributed as follows.

State	Job j	1	2	Probability
A	p_j	1	2	0.9
B	p_j	10	2	0.1

If we replace p_j by $E[p_j]$, the two jobs have agreeable parameters. In the deterministic counterpart, therefore, we apply condition (a) of Theorem 3.3 and sequence job 1 first. This yields $T = 0$ with probability 0.9 and 16.1 otherwise, so that $E[T] = 1.61$. But if we reverse the sequence, T is 0.1 with probability 0.9 and 9.1 otherwise, so $E[T] = 1$. The example demonstrates the following.

Proposition 6.2 The stochastic T-problem and its deterministic counterpart may not be optimized by identical sequences, and dominance conditions that apply for the deterministic counterpart are not necessarily valid in the stochastic case.

To summarize, we can use general combinatorial optimization methods to solve for the optimal sum of expected values, and the result will also minimize the expected value of the sum. However, because deterministic dominance relationships may not apply, we should expect these methods to take longer in the stochastic case than in the deterministic case. For this reason, we would like to identify circumstances under which counterpart dominance rules would still hold.

When $E[p_1] \leq E[p_2]$, we say that p_1 is (weakly) smaller than p_2 *by expectation*. We also write $p_1 \leq_{ex} p_2$. Example 6.5 demonstrates that $p_1 \leq_{ex} p_2$ is not sufficient to generalize deterministic dominance rules requiring $p_1 \leq p_2$, because the worst-case realization of p_1 could be larger than that of p_2. However, stochastic ordering relationships exist that preclude a worst-case reversal. We say that one random variable, X, is *stochastically smaller* than another, Y (denoted $X \leq_{st} Y$), if $Pr\{X \leq t\} \geq Pr\{Y \leq t\}$ for any t. This implies that the cdf of X, $F_X(t)$, is at or above the cdf of Y, $F_Y(t)$. That is, $F_X \geq F_Y$ everywhere. We also refer to this relationship as *stochastic dominance*, and if it applies to several pairs of random variables, we say that they are *stochastically ordered* (because the dominance relationship is transitive). Stochastic dominance is a strong relationship in the sense that $\leq_{st}$ implies $\leq_{ex}$. A useful way to visualize this relationship is to recall that the expected value of a nonnegative random variable is given by the area above its cdf below 1 and to the right of the origin (see Figure 6.1). However, if $F_X \geq F_Y$, then the area above F_X cannot exceed the area above F_Y. Therefore, the expected value of X cannot exceed the expected value of Y.

The definition of $\leq_{st}$ does not require statistical independence. For example, let X and Y be two independent and identically distributed (*iid*) random variables, and let Z be any nonnegative random variable (including the degenerate case, in which $Z = 0$ with certainty). Then $X \leq_{st} Y + Z$ and $X \leq_{st} X + Z$. The first relationship holds between independent random variables. When $Z = 0$ with certainty, we have that iid random variables X and Y are each stochastically smaller than the other. But in the second relationship, X and $X + Z$ are statistically dependent because of a common element shared by the two random variables. When random variables are positively correlated as a result of common causes of variation affecting more than one of them in the same direction, they satisfy the definition of associated random variables. Random variables are *associated* if the correlation between any positive nondecreasing functions of each is nonnegative. Independent random variables are associated, but negatively

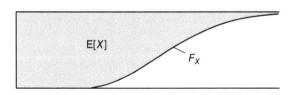

E[X]

F_X

Figure 6.1 Depicting the expected value as an area above the cdf.

correlated ones are not. Association may arise not only by adding the same random variable to two or more independent random variables but also by multiplying two or more positive random variables by the same positive element.

We introduce associated processing times because in practical settings, common causes of variation often affect more than one job in the same direction. For example, if a regular worker is faster than the replacement and the regular worker will be sick tomorrow with some positive probability, then for scheduling purposes, a positive dependence is introduced among all of tomorrow's processing times. As another example, if the quality of a particular tool deteriorates, then the jobs that require it may all take longer. In general, various causes are likely to introduce positive dependence among different subsets of jobs.

When processing times behave as associated random variables, the completion time variance is higher than for independent random variables, for all but the first job. For independent random variables, the variance of a sum equals the sum of the variances. But, by definition, two associated random variables have a nonnegative covariance, and the variance of a sum with positive covariance is higher than the sum of the variances. So, in effect, the independence assumption is optimistic for the variance of a completion time. Finally, if two jobs have processing times that are associated, then their costs are also associated because the cost functions are nondecreasing. This relation, in turn, implies that the variance of performance measures based on processing times that are associated random variables is also higher than the variance for independent processing times.

Two nonnegative random variables, X and Y, are *linearly* associated if there exist four independent nonnegative random variables, R, S, Z, and B, and two nonnegative parameters, α and β, such that $X = (R + \alpha Z)B$ and $Y = (S + \beta Z)B$. If we set $\alpha = \beta = 0$ and $B = 1$ with certainty, then $X = R$, $Y = S$, and they are independent by assumption (and thus associated). At the other extreme, if R and S are 0 with certainty, then X and Y are proportional (and thus associated). Here, B models a multiplicative bias shared by X and Y, whereas Z represents any additive element they may share. In what follows, we assume linear association. Furthermore, we treat the special case $\alpha = \beta = 1$. Less restrictive assumptions may suffice, but this one is simple to present yet still more realistic than the independence assumption.

■ **Theorem 6.7**   If X and Y are linearly associated, that is, $X = (R + Z)B$ and $Y = (S + Z)B$ where R, S, Z, and B are independent nonnegative random variables, then $X \leq_{st} Y$ if and only if $R \leq_{st} S$, and $X \leq_{ex} Y$ if and only if $R \leq_{ex} S$.

Theorem 6.7 allows us to generalize existing results based on statistical independence to the case of linearly associated random variables. For example, it can be shown that if $p_1 \leq_{st} p_2$, where p_1 and p_2 are independent, then $\Pr\{p_1 \leq p_2\} \geq 0.5$.

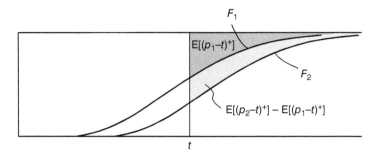

Figure 6.2 $E[(p_1 - t)^+]$ and $E[(p_2 - t)^+]$ as areas.

We can extend that result to stochastically ordered, linearly associated random variables. Furthermore, if $p_1 \leq_{st} p_2$, then $E[(p_1 - t)^+] \leq E[(p_2 - t)^+]$. To demonstrate this inequality, consider that $E[(p_j - t)^+]$ is the area above the cdf of job j and below 1 to the right of t (Figure 6.2). Because the cdf of the stochastically smaller random variable is above the other, the relevant area must be smaller. This argument, as stated, is correct for S and T, but it is inherited by X and Y through linear association. So, informally, it is a good bet to assume that $p_1 \leq p_2$ in this case. However, Example 6.5 demonstrates that it is not necessarily a good bet when all we know is that $p_1 \leq_{ex} p_2$. The relationship in that case was by expectation, but without stochastic dominance. Example 6.5 is predicated on the fact that the worst-case performance of p_1 was worse than the worst-case performance of p_2. But when the two processing times are stochastically ordered, such a worst-case reversal cannot happen.

■ **Theorem 6.8** In the T_w-problem, let jobs 1 and 2 satisfy $p_1 \leq_{st} p_2$, $d_1 \leq d_2$, and $w_1 \geq w_2$, then job 1 precedes job 2 in an optimal sequence. Furthermore, if we subject the jobs to linear association, the result remains true.

Proof. In Figure 6.3 (which elaborates on Figure 6.2), the expected tardiness of a job is depicted as a tail to the right of its due date, above the distribution that applies to it and below the upper horizontal line of 1. The relevant distributions

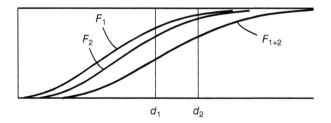

Figure 6.3 Comparing two sequences with stochastic dominance.

are either F_k if job k is scheduled first ($k = 1, 2$) or F_{1+2} if job k is scheduled second. These three distributions also reflect any preceding jobs that have already been scheduled or any jobs scheduled between jobs 1 and 2. As the figure shows, job 1 is stochastically smaller and has a lower due date, per the condition of the theorem. Let $T_{F,d}$ denote the area of the tail above distribution F (where $F = 1, 2$ or $1 + 2$) to the right of due date d (where $d = 1, 2$). $T_{F,d}$ measures an expected tardiness; for instance, $T_{1+2,1}$ is the expected tardiness of job 1 if it is sequenced second and is thus subject to the completion time distribution F_{1+2}. We start with the sequence 1-2, assuming the two jobs are adjacent. By an adjacent pair interchange, the tardiness cost of job 1 increases by $w_1(T_{1+2,1} - T_{1,1}) \geq w_1(T_{1+2,2} - T_{1,2})$, whereas the tardiness cost of job 2 decreases by $w_2(T_{1+2,2} - T_{2,2}) \leq w_2(T_{1+2,2} - T_{1,2})$. But because $w_2 \leq w_1$, $w_2(T_{1+2,2} - T_{1,2}) \leq w_1(T_{1+2,2} - T_{1,2})$, so the gain is bounded from above by a lower bound of the loss and the change cannot decrease but may increase the total weighted tardiness. Now allow additional jobs (which need not be stochastically ordered) between jobs 1 and 2. If we interchange the two jobs, all these intermediary jobs will follow a stochastically larger job so their expected tardiness cannot decrease. Hence, such jobs cannot provide incentive to perform the interchange either. To show that linear association will not change the result, invoke Theorem 6.7. □

Corollary 6.3 For linearly associated processing times that are stochastically ordered, if expected processing times and due dates are agreeable for all pairs of jobs, then the expected total tardiness E[T] is minimized by SEPT sequencing with ties broken by EDD (or, equivalently, by EDD with ties broken by SEPT).

Although Theorem 6.8 generalizes one dominance condition subject to a relatively strong assumption, even with this assumption in place, it remains difficult to generalize other deterministic dominance conditions. For example, generalizing Theorem 3.2 requires that a job will not be tardy with probability one. Hence, we are still left with the conclusion that the optimal solution to stochastic problems will always take significantly longer to find than the solution to their deterministic counterparts.

6.7 Using Analytic Solver Platform

In Chapter 4, we introduced an Excel-based approach for solving deterministic sequencing problems, using the Evolutionary Solver in Analytic Solver Platform (ASP). In Section 6.2, we introduced a sample-based approach for solving stochastic problems. In this section, we return to ASP and describe how its simulation capability can facilitate sample-based analysis.

Once ASP has been installed, it provides a specialized set of commands on the drop-down menus of its ribbon, as shown in Figure 6.4. We illustrate the use of these capabilities with an example.

■ **Example 6.6** Consider a problem containing $n = 5$ jobs with stochastic processing times and known due dates. For each job, the processing time follows a lognormal distribution with mean value and standard deviation as given in the table.

Job j	1	2	3	4	5
$E[p_j]$	2	3	1	6	4
σ_j	1.4	1.8	0.8	2.4	2.0
d_j	12	7	4	10	6

The first step in building a suitable Excel model is to construct the spreadsheet for the deterministic counterpart, as discussed in Section 4.8. The deterministic model is modified slightly, as shown in Figure 6.4, and contains two identical rows. Row 6 (Mean time) and row 8 (Outcome) initially contain the same data – mean processing times for the jobs. Row 7 contains the standard deviations, which would not apply in the deterministic case. However, when we convert to the stochastic model, row 8 holds probabilistic outcomes. In other words, we want the entries in row 8 to behave like lognormal random variables.

To incorporate probabilistic features into the model using ASP, we first place the cursor on cell C8 and select Simulation Model > Distributions > Common >

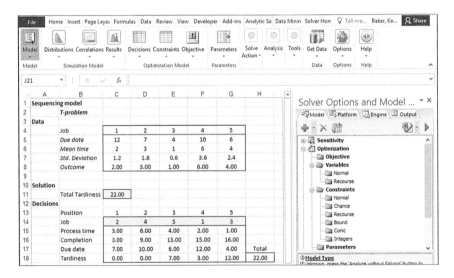

Figure 6.4 Spreadsheet layout for the deterministic counterpart.

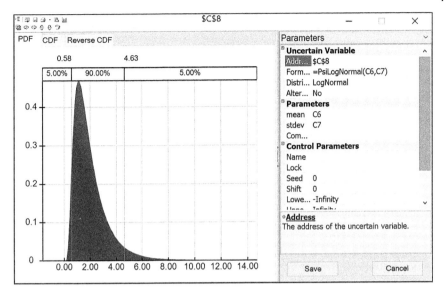

Figure 6.5 Lognormal probability distribution function.

LogNormal. ASP displays a probability distribution function (pdf), as shown in Figure 6.5, and in the Parameters window on the right, we can specify the mean and standard deviation by referencing cells C6 and C7, respectively. These are relative addresses, so when we copy cell C8 and paste the contents to D8:G8, each of those cells takes the mean and standard deviation from the two cells directly above it. At this stage, for example, cell D8 contains the formula PsiLogNormal(D6,D7). (We could equivalently enter this formula in cell D8 and avoid using the drop-down menu on the ribbon.) Furthermore, the cells in the range C8:G8 then contain the random samples drawn from the lognormal distributions; and from these values, the spreadsheet computes the resulting tardiness in cell H18.

Having incorporated probabilistic descriptions of the inputs, the next step is to define the model output so that ASP can save these values during a simulation run. In the spreadsheet model, we have just one output, the total tardiness, as calculated in cell H18. We place the cursor on H18 and from the ASP ribbon, we select Simulation Model > Results > Statistic > Mean. Then, we select the cell for which to compute the mean (H18) and then the cell where the statistic will be placed (C11). This selection adds the function =PsiMean(H18) in cell C11. (We could equivalently enter this formula directly in cell C11 and avoid using the drop-down menu on the ribbon.)

ASP allows the user to configure a simulation experiment by choosing several design parameters. The relevant options can be displayed by selecting Options > Options from the ribbon. (See Figure 6.6.) Most of these options can be left at

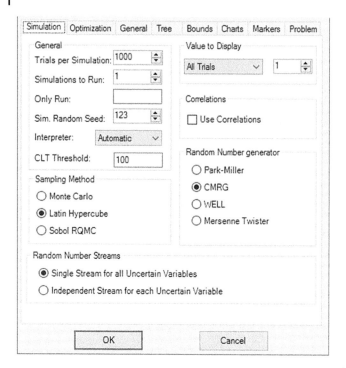

Figure 6.6 Simulation options in ASP.

their default values. We usually start by setting the Trials per Simulation parameter to 1000. The number of trials corresponds to the sample size in sample-based analysis. This figure is the number of times that the model output in cell H18 is recalculated for different random values of the inputs in cells C8:G8. We also usually select the Latin Hypercube method of sampling, as this represents a systematic method of sampling that provides more efficient results than if we used an uncoordinated method for drawing samples.

To execute the simulation run, we select Solve Action > Simulate > Run Once. This choice causes ASP to sample from each of the input probability distributions, calculate the resulting values for the output cell, and repeat for the number of trials. The status bar at the bottom of the task pane then displays the message, Simulation finished successfully. In this mode, ASP will not automatically run the simulation when we make another entry. However, if we select Solve Action > Simulate > Interactive, then ASP is placed in automatic mode, and a new simulation will be executed whenever the spreadsheet is recalculated. (Automatic mode is indicated when the light bulb in the Simulate icon appears in yellow.)

ASP stores the simulation results for the output cell in the cell itself. By double-clicking on the output cell, we can display the results in various formats.

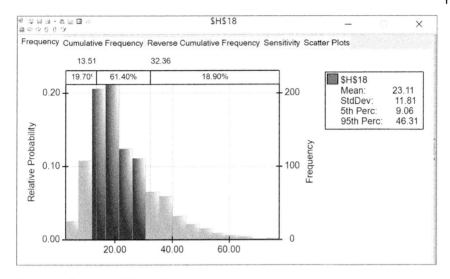

Figure 6.7 Summary of simulation results.

Figure 6.7 shows the frequency distribution, or *histogram*, for the tardiness calculated in cell H18.

When the simulation finishes, cells C8:G8 display the processing times drawn in the last of the 1000 simulated samples. Similarly, cell H18 displays the corresponding tardiness value. However, we are more interested in the mean value of tardiness because that is the objective function for the stochastic counterpart. We can obtain the simulated mean by placing the cursor on cell H18, selecting Simulation Model > Results > Statistic > Mean from the ribbon, and then selecting cell C11, leading to a display similar to that shown in Figure 6.8. (We can also record the mean value on the spreadsheet without using the ribbon by entering the formula =PsiMean(H18) in cell C11.)

The value 23.11 recorded in cell C11 is an estimate of the mean tardiness for the sequence 2-4-5-1-3. This estimate is subject to sampling error, which becomes smaller as the number of trials becomes larger. A standard measure of the precision in this estimate is the confidence interval for the mean. ASP allows this value to be computed along with the estimated mean, but in a different cell. To place this value in the spreadsheet, we first make sure that the cursor is on cell H18. Next, from the ribbon, we select Simulation Model > Results > Statistic > MeanCI and then select cell G11. The formula that appears in G11 is =PsiMeanCI(H18,0.95), meaning that this is half the width of a 95% confidence interval for the mean in cell H18.

As shown in Figure 6.8, the simulation run produces a value of 0.73 for this statistic, indicating that there is a 95% chance that the true mean lies within ±0.73 of the estimated value, 23.11. In this case, the confidence interval is about 3.2% of the estimate (on either side), which may or may not be sufficient

	A	B	C	D	E	F	G	H	
1	Example 6.6								
2									
3	Data								
4		Job	1	2	3	4	5		
5		Due date	12	7	4	10	6		
6		Mean time	2	3	1	6	4		
7		Std. Deviation	1.4	1.8	0.8	2.4	2.0		
8		Outcome	2.12	2.04	0.93	3.58	2.72		
9									
10	Solution								
11		Mean Tardiness	23.11			Mean C.I.	0.73		
12	Decisions								
13		Position	1	2	3	4	5		
14		Job	2	4	5	1	3		
15		Process time	2.04	3.58	2.72	2.12	0.93		
16		Completion	2.04	5.63	8.35	10.46	11.39		
17		Due date	7.00	10.00	6.00	12.00	4.00	Total	
18		Tardiness	0.00	0.00	2.35	0.00	7.39	9.74	
19									

Figure 6.8 Displaying the simulation results on the spreadsheet.

precision for our purposes. If we repeat the simulation with a sample size of 10 000, the confidence interval drops to 0.24 for an estimated mean of 23.21 (or about 1.0% on either side). If this level of precision is adequate for our purposes, we would keep the sample size set at 10 000.

Having fine-tuned the simulation parameters, we can search for a sequence that minimizes the expected tardiness. Our search tool is the Evolutionary Solver, which we introduced in Chapter 4 and for which we provided a default set of search parameters. In this example, we specify the objective function cell as C11 (the estimated mean tardiness), which we want to minimize. The decision variables appear in row 14, and we impose the requirement that they satisfy the alldifferent constraint. Running the Evolutionary Solver produces the sequence 3-5-2-1-4, with (estimated) mean tardiness of 8.66.

Integrating simulation with the Evolutionary Solver creates a powerful search tool for solving stochastic scheduling problems. We refer to the ASP User's Guide for additional detail.

6.8 Non-probabilistic Approaches: Fuzzy and Robust Scheduling

So far, we have restricted our attention to minimizing the expected value of an objective addressed by a counterpart deterministic model. In this section we discuss two noncounterpart approaches that have been studied in the literature, *fuzzy scheduling* and *robust scheduling*. However, these methods have not been widely applied; their main attraction lies in the mathematical challenges they pose.

Fuzzy logic is a practical and successful approach for controlling complex processes by the correct combination of possible adjustments that apply to multiple measurements. Suppose we need to control temperature and pressure, and we have several possible levers – or responses – with which to control them. Furthermore, using any single lever to adjust temperature may affect pressure in an undesirable way and vice versa. We want to find the right combination of levers. Before the advent of fuzzy logic, the solution would attempt to build a controller that could respond to any combination of temperature and pressure correctly, often a very challenging task. The basic idea of fuzzy logic is that the usefulness of a particular response depends on the distance from target as per a continuous function with values between 0 and 1. But similar functions – known as *membership functions* – apply to all possible responses. Using those membership values as weights (which usually requires normalization), one response is selected randomly and applied briefly; thus, a high weight response is more likely to be selected. A new measurement then induces new member- ship values, and a new brief response is selected accordingly. In effect, this creates a self-adjusting mixed response that has been shown by experience to work very well. It revolutionized the control of complex processes. That impres- sive practical success led to numerous attempts to apply fuzzy logic to other problems, including sequencing and scheduling decisions. However, selecting a sequence is not akin to the adjustment of a complex process by a mixture of responses: We cannot correct the choice very frequently based on new mea- surements. Nonetheless, when we wish to guide a random search with more than one objective, the fuzzy model may yet prove useful, as in each selection a different criterion may be selected based on membership weights.

Robust scheduling builds on the principles of decision theory. Decision theory models traditionally assume a finite set of possible actions and a finite set of out- come states, giving rise to a list of scenarios. Moreover, the models assume that the actual realization is included in these scenarios. We refer to this structure as a *scenario model*. This form is not appropriate when the number of possible actions or possible states is quite large or infinite, but in cases similar to Example 6.1, they are conceptually plausible.

A fundamental assumption in decision theory is that most decision makers are risk averse, which implies they are more concerned with avoiding excessive losses than with maximizing rewards, and in that respect they prefer conserv- ative choices. One way to capture this conservatism is to minimize the maxi- mum possible cost, often called the *minimax cost* criterion. The minimax cost criterion is especially attractive when we need protection against worst- case results and probabilities are not a major consideration. However, most of the literature on robust scheduling focuses on a relative measure of cost rather than an absolute measure – namely, *regret*. Regret is the difference between the result achieved by a particular decision in the random state that ultimately occurs and the best result that could have been achieved in that state. Decision makers facing uncertainty know that it is impossible to predict the future or to always select the best possible schedule; however, they might well assume that their decisions will subsequently be judged based on hindsight, after uncertainties are resolved. Therefore, the argument goes, risk-averse decision makers may choose to minimize regret.

But what does minimizing regret actually mean in the context of stochastic scheduling problems? One interpretation could be that the objective is to minimize expected regret, with the expectation taken over the distribution of random outcomes. However, minimizing expected regret is not really a distinct research area for scheduling, due to the following well-known property.

Property 6.1 For any performance measure, the minimum expected regret is achieved by minimizing the expected value of the performance measure.

Therefore, this interpretation of minimizing regret does not lead to new conceptual challenges because expected-value performance measures have been studied extensively, as the foregoing sections demonstrate. In addition, the notion of conservative decision-making usually focuses on worst cases, not probability distributions. Instead of minimizing expected regret, we can apply the minimax criterion to regret – that is, seek to minimize the maximum regret. It turns out that even scheduling problems that are easy to solve when the objective is an expected value become difficult when the objective is minimax cost or minimax regret. As an illustration, consider Example 6.7.

■ **Example 6.7** Consider a problem containing $n = 5$ jobs with stochastic processing times. The randomness in processing times is described by four equally likely states of nature: GG, GB, BG, and BB. Each job has a different processing time under each state of nature as follows.

State	Job j	1	2	3	4	5
GG	p_j	2.7	3.7	3.4	7.8	6.3
GB	p_j	2.5	4.9	5.3	4.7	8.2
BG	p_j	2.6	2.9	4.5	4.8	8.7
BB	p_j	3.4	5.7	5.6	6.7	5.1

What is the best sequence using a minimax criterion for total flowtime?

For instance, the GG state-specific solution is determined by shortest-first sequencing of the five processing times that occur in state GG, or 1-3-2-5-4. The corresponding total flowtime is 58.6 (listed under Best in Figure 6.9). When

Example 6.7

Sequence	1	3	2	4	5
Processing times					
GG	2.7	3.4	3.7	7.8	6.3
GB	2.5	5.3	4.9	4.7	8.2
BG	2.6	4.5	2.9	4.8	8.7
BB	3.4	5.6	5.7	6.7	5.1

						Total Flowtime	Best Flowtime	Regret
Completion times								
GG	2.7	6.1	9.8	17.6	23.9	60.1	58.6	1.5
GB	2.5	7.8	12.7	17.4	25.6	66.0	64.8	1.2
BG	2.6	7.1	10.0	14.8	23.5	58.0	56.4	1.6
BB	3.4	9.0	14.7	21.4	26.5	75.0	72.3	2.7
								2.7

						Regret Table			
Sequence	13254	14235	12345	15324	*Best*	13254	14235	12345	15324
GG	58.6	68.9	60.4	64.1	58.6	0.0	10.3	1.8	5.5
GB	69.5	64.8	65.6	75.7	64.8	4.7	0.0	0.8	10.9
BG	61.9	58.6	56.4	71.9	56.4	5.5	2.2	0.0	15.5
BB	73.4	77.2	75.1	72.3	72.3	1.1	4.9	2.8	0.0
							5.5	10.3	2.8	15.5

Figure 6.9 Calculations for Example 6.7, showing results for the sequence (1-3-2-4-5).

GB occurs, the best sequence is 1-4-2-3-5, with total flowtime of 64.8, and similarly for BG (1-2-3-4-5, with total flowtime 56.4) and BB (1-5-3-2-4, with total flowtime 72.3). These results give rise to the state-specific Regret Table shown at the bottom right of Figure 6.9.

In the state-specific Regret Table, each row corresponds to one of the four states, and each column corresponds to one of the sequences that produces minimum total flowtime in one of the states. The table entry is zero if the total flowtime for that sequence in that state is actually the minimum for that state. (For instance, in state BG, the sequence 1-2-3-4-5 produces the total flowtime of 56.4, and this is the minimum for BG.) The table entry is positive if the sequence does not produce the minimum; in that case, the entry is the difference between the total flowtime produced and the minimum value for the state. That difference is the quantitative representation of regret. (For instance, in state BG, the sequence 1-4-2-3-5 produces total flowtime of 58.6, whereas the minimum for that state is 56.4, so the regret is measured as the difference, 2.2.) Thus, the Regret Table shows that, of the four sequences identified so far, the minimax regret is 2.8, associated with 1-2-3-4-5, as determined by comparing the four values below the Regret Table. However, in this example, the minimax regret is actually produced by a sequence that is not one of the four identified so far. The optimal sequence is 1-3-2-4-5. Its maximum regret is computed by comparing its Total Flowtime in each state with the Best Flowtime in each state and recording the differences. The largest difference, 2.7, represents its maximum regret. As the example shows, it is possible that none of the four state-specific optimal sequences minimizes the maximum regret, and for that reason it may be necessary to expand the Regret Table and evaluate all possible sequences to find the optimum, perhaps using one of the optimization methods described in Chapter 3. Finding the minimax regret is known to be an NP-hard problem for the *F*-problem.

When minimax cost is the objective in Example 6.7, a similar analysis applies. Once again, in this example, the minimax cost is not attained by one of the state-specific minimax cost sequences. (Finding the minimax cost is also known to be NP-hard for the *F*-problem with scenarios.) Instead, an enumerative search is required to find the optimal sequence, which is 1-3-5-2-4, obtaining a maximum flowtime of 72.8. In brief, the sequence 1-3-5-2-4 achieves maximum flowtime of 72.8 and maximum regret of 11.3, whereas the sequence 1-3-2-4-5 achieves maximum flowtime of 75.0 and maximum regret of 2.7. Thus, we can see from this example that minimax cost and minimax regret are, in general, optimized by different sequences. To achieve optimal results on one measure may well require a sacrifice in the other measure. For this reason, it is not obvious which criterion to use, even when agreement exists that a risk-averse approach is desirable.

Our analysis so far essentially relies on the scenario model in which the set of scenarios must be finite and exhaustive. In practice, however, the assumption that we can list *all* possible scenarios is rarely applicable, and simulated scenarios are not usable for this purpose because they are not guaranteed to include the actual outcome. Instead, the *range model* is an alternative formulation that is suited to instances in which a finite set of exhaustive scenarios does not exist. In the range model, we specify a range for each realization. (These ranges represent intervals that are deemed likely to occur, but because probability distributions are not specified, no clear guidelines exist for determining them.) In this setting, given any regular performance measure representing a proxy for cost, solving for the minimax value simply requires substituting the longest possible processing times into a deterministic model. Furthermore, if those longest times are not finite, the minimax cost is unbounded, in which case minimax cost scheduling is neither challenging nor interesting. But the optimization of minimax regret remains challenging (and perhaps that is why the term *robust scheduling* is typically interpreted as driven by minimax regret rather than minimax cost). Nonetheless, the minimax regret solution can be found by limiting attention to extreme realizations in which each processing time lies at either the minimum or the maximum of its range. Thus, even if we allow for an infinite number of possible realizations, the range model allows us to consider only 2^n realizations to identify a minimax regret solution. That is, conceptually, we can treat extreme solutions as exhaustive scenarios. The following example illustrates the range model.

■ **Example 6.8** Consider a problem containing $n = 4$ jobs, with random processing times symmetrically distributed between the following minimum and maximum values.

Job j	1	2	3	4
Minimum	46	42	40	10
Maximum	48	54	58	90
Expected	47	48	49	50

In keeping with the philosophy of risk-averse decision-making, we don't need to know the probability distribution for each processing time, but knowledge of expected processing times allows us to compare the minimax regret solution to the SEPT sequence. Because it is sufficient in the range model to consider only extreme realizations, the example problem can be formulated as a scenario-based model with $2^n = 16$ scenarios. In the data set, the range maxima and the expected values appear in increasing order when we sequence the jobs 1-2-3-4. This sequence is therefore both the minimax cost sequence and the SEPT sequence, with $E[F_{max}] = 560$ and $E[F] = 480$. Because we use ranges, solving for $E[F_{max}]$ here is not more difficult than solving for SEPT, but the two optimal sequences need not agree in general.

Next consider minimax regret. First, we list the 16 extreme scenarios and for each one find the best possible total flowtime by taking the processing times in shortest-first order. Then, for each job sequence, we compare its total flowtime to the best possible value and record the largest difference for all 16 realizations – that is, the maximum regret. Finally, we search for the minimum value among the 4! possible job sequences to identify the minimax regret. In the example, the minimax regret is 104, achieved by the sequence 1-2-4-3. A comparison of the 16 extreme realizations for this sequence reveals a maximum flowtime of 592. The summary of these results in Table 6.9 reveals that the two minimax objectives are in conflict, optimized by different sequences. The minimax cost sequence (1-2-3-4) guarantees total flowtime of at most 560, but with maximum regret of 134. The minimax regret sequence (1-2-4-3) can reduce this value to 104, but only with exposure to a total flowtime of 592. In other words, the minimax regret sequence achieves an advantage (30) over the minimax cost sequence, but only by risking a larger disadvantage (32) in the worst case. In addition, the minimax regret sequence sacrifices a small amount (1) in the expected flowtime. However, because $E[F]$ is an average over all extreme states, it makes sense to give a reduction in expected flowtime more weight than a reduction in maximum regret. Furthermore, extensive numerical experience suggests that the minimax regret sequence can carry a much higher risk in terms of expected flowtime than in this example, as we discuss next.

Table 6.9

Sequence	Maximum cost	Maximum regret	Expected flowtime
1-2-3-4	560	134	480
1-2-4-3	592	104	481
Difference	32	30	1

We ran tests on problem instances containing $n = 7$ jobs, with ranges generated randomly. Table 6.10 summarizes the results. We observed, for example, that the same sequence is optimal for all three objectives in about 30% of the instances. In the remaining 70%, at least two of the objectives conflicted. In addition, expected flowtime and minimax regret were in conflict only 35% of the time, whereas minimax cost was in conflict with one of the other two objectives almost two-thirds of the time. When expected flowtime and minimax regret conflict, the sacrifice in one objective to optimize the other favors expected flowtime by almost an order of magnitude, if we value the measures as equivalent. The strong suggestion is that the SEPT sequence is the best choice for risk-neutral decision makers and can also serve as a decent heuristic for either minimax criterion, but the minimax cost sequence is preferred in risk-averse situations.

In summary, several major problems arise in the pursuit of minimax regret that make it impractical. First, in the scenario-based approach, practicability is significantly reduced by the requirement that all possible final outcomes must

Table 6.10

Conflicts	Percent (%)	
0	30	One sequence optimizes all three objectives
2	35	Expected flowtime and minimax regret are optimized by the same sequence
2	5	Expected flowtime and minimax cost are optimized by the same sequence
2	7	Minimax cost and minimax regret are optimized by the same sequence
3	<u>24</u>	Expected flowtime, minimax cost, and minimax regret are each optimized differently
	100	
	35	Expected flowtime and minimax regret are in conflict
	65	Expected flowtime and minimax cost are in conflict
	63	Minimax regret and minimax cost are in conflict

be listed among the scenarios. That requirement rules out sampling and simulation. Second, solving for either minimax cost or minimax regret under the scenario-based approach is also a challenging combinatorial problem. Third, when using ranges, there is no "robust" means of identifying minimum and maximum values for the ranges guaranteed to work, let alone work for the worst case. Finally, and most importantly, the minimax regret criterion is not an effective risk management tool. Instead of ameliorating potentially crippling risks, as proper risk management should, it provides expensive insurance against relatively affordable risks and often does so while increasing the risk of the worst-case scenario.

6.9 Summary

When we think about what makes a sequencing problem difficult to solve, we might conclude, in light of our coverage in previous chapters, that some problems are difficult because of variation in the data. Problems in which all jobs have the same weight and require the same processing time are easily solved. In those cases, either EDD or Algorithm 2.1 can solve all our basic problems (F, T, L_{max}, T_{max}, U). Difficulties in finding an optimal sequence arise when parameters are not identical – that is, when variation is present. Viewed from this perspective, stochastic problems compound solution difficulties by introducing another source of variation – that is, random variation – in addition to variation in due dates or in expected processing times. Consider the following objectives that are relatively easy to optimize in the deterministic case: F, F_w, L, L_{max}, T_{max}, and U.

- For F_w (and therefore also for F and L), we can use the deterministic counterpart to find an optimal solution in the stochastic case – that is, by replacing p_j by its expected value.
- For L_{max} and T_{max}, ideas developed for the deterministic models in Chapter 2 can be applied in the stochastic case, but we cannot rely on the deterministic counterpart to give us the objective function value.
- The U-problem resists simple generalization of the deterministic optimal approach.
- For problems such as T and T_w that are already NP-hard in the deterministic case, stochastic variation compounds the computational difficulty of finding optimal solutions by dynamic programming or branch and bound.

In this chapter, we developed several results that reveal the similarities and the differences between deterministic and stochastic models. In some instances, we saw that stochastic dominance is sufficient to retain some of the dominance properties characteristic of deterministic models, but in other cases, even stochastic dominance is insufficient. For this reason, we should not expect methods such as branch and bound and dynamic programming to solve stochastic problems of the same size that they can handle in the deterministic case.

We also showed that in some cases the deterministic approach may be less applicable. For example, dynamic programming cannot handle the maximum cost problem because $E[\max\{g_j\}]$ is not an additive performance measure. Given such difficulties in the stochastic environment, it is important to identify efficient solutions, or at least partial solutions, where they exist, and that has been the main thrust of the chapter. For problems that are beyond the reach of the methods we have introduced thus far, it remains important to develop practical heuristic approaches.

To handle general processing time distributions that are not necessarily statistically independent, we introduced sample-based analysis and showed how to compare sequences numerically. This approach is inherently more time consuming than the use of deterministic counterparts, but it remains practical and can be implemented in a spreadsheet. Nevertheless, sample-based analysis is intrinsically a heuristic approach, because a simulated sample cannot represent a model perfectly; it can identify solutions that are likely to be optimal, but it cannot guarantee optimality. Furthermore, the use of large samples is an additional computational burden. For instance, suppose we have a stochastic problem that we wish to solve by sample-based analysis with a sample of 1000 (roughly 2^{10}) using dynamic programming. Then, every function evaluation takes 1000 times longer than would be the case in the deterministic counterpart. If we assume the computational requirement in dynamic programming is roughly proportional to 2^n, then a given computational effort will solve for 10 fewer jobs in the stochastic case than in the deterministic counterpart. For example, if 25 deterministic jobs can be sequenced in half a minute of computation time, only 15 stochastic jobs can be sequenced in the same time. A similar reduction in tractable problem size occurs with branch-and-bound approaches.

The availability of user-friendly simulation software, such as ASP, expands the set of models that we can analyze with a sample-based approach. Thus, if we can determine an optimal sequence easily but encounter computational difficulty in evaluating the optimal value of the objective, we can enlist the help of ASP to make the evaluation easier. More importantly, we can integrate the Evolutionary Solver to produce a flexible and effective heuristic procedure for solving stochastic sequencing problems.

We also discussed two other approaches to scheduling under uncertainty, specifically fuzzy scheduling and minimizing maximum regret. These methods do not rely on probability distributions for processing times. Dubois et al. (2003) provide a widely cited survey on fuzzy scheduling, and the seminal paper on minimizing maximum regret in a scheduling context is due to Daniels and Kouvelis (1995). However, with respect to these two topics, the gap between research and practice remains substantial. The literature on minimizing the maximum cost – which we also discussed – is much more sparse. In addition, arguably, it emphasizes the importance of the worst case too much even when it is extremely unlikely. (Similar criticism applies to regret as well.)

In the next chapter we discuss a more practical approach designed to control the likelihood of a very bad outcome.

Exercises

6.1 Consider a problem containing $n = 5$ jobs with stochastic processing times. The randomness in the processing times can adequately be represented by three states of nature: good, normal, and bad, with probabilities of 0.2, 0.5, and 0.3, respectively.

State	Job j	1	2	3	4	5
Good	p_j	5	3	7	6	8
Normal	p_j	7	6	8	10	12
Bad	p_j	9	12	10	15	14
	d_j	10	22	40	31	25

a) Find the minimum value of the expected total flowtime, along with the sequence that achieves it. Compare the optimal value with that of the deterministic counterpart.

b) Find the minimum value of the expected maximum tardiness, along with the sequence that achieves it. Compare the optimal value with that of the deterministic counterpart.

c) Find the minimum value of the expected number of jobs tardy. Compare the optimal value with that of the deterministic counterpart.

6.2 Consider a problem containing $n = 5$ jobs with stochastic processing times, each of which follows a normal distribution with known mean and standard deviation.

Job j	1	2	3	4	5
μ_j	17	20	24	25	30
σ_j	3	4	2	5	3
d_j	60	80	70	50	90

a) Find the minimum value of the expected total flowtime, along with the sequence that achieves it. Compare the optimal value with that of the deterministic counterpart.

b) Find the minimum value of the expected maximum tardiness, along with the sequence that achieves it. Compare the optimal value with that of the deterministic counterpart.

6.3 Shown below is a sample of 10 observations for the processing times of $n =$ 5 jobs in a sequencing problem.

Job j	1	2	3	4	5
d_j	60	80	70	50	90

	Job 1	Job 2	Job 3	Job 4	Job 5
Sample 1	17.79	23.80	19.74	26.90	32.63
Sample 2	15.65	18.34	25.40	14.98	26.80
Sample 3	22.59	18.62	21.75	25.53	30.56
Sample 4	15.29	20.98	22.85	31.80	33.86
Sample 5	15.56	20.39	24.09	22.45	28.16
Sample 6	19.00	18.05	20.28	25.71	28.99
Sample 7	18.00	19.16	20.75	25.02	30.86
Sample 8	18.37	19.06	25.86	24.14	23.24
Sample 9	14.35	14.68	22.69	26.55	24.73
Sample 10	16.61	22.99	20.99	26.12	28.43

a) Find the minimum value of the expected maximum tardiness, along with the sequence that achieves it.

b) Find the minimum value of the maximum expected tardiness, along with the sequence that achieves it.

c) Find the minimum value of the expected number of jobs tardy.

6.4 Show that SWEPT is optimal for minimizing $E[F_w]$.

6.5 Consider a problem containing $n = 5$ jobs with stochastic processing times. The randomness in the processing times can adequately be represented by three states of nature: S1, S2, and S3, with probabilities of 0.3, 0.4, and 0.3, respectively.

State	Job j	1	2	3	4	5
S1	p_j	5	3	7	6	8
S2	p_j	7	6	8	10	12
S3	p_j	9	12	10	15	14
	d_j	10	22	40	31	25

In addition, the parameters of the cost function $g_j(T_j) = \delta(T_j)(a_j + b_j T_j)$ are given in the following table.

Job *j*	1	2	3	4	5
a_j	2.0	3.0	4.0	5.0	1.0
b_j	0.6	0.3	0.1	0.4	0.3

a) Find the minimum value of the expected maximum cost.
b) Compare the value in (a) with that of the deterministic counterpart.
   The proof of the new version of Theorem 6.8 already shows that. Furthermore, careful reading of the new version of the Theorem shows that there is no assumption the two jobs must be adjacent (which is why the proof includes the case of intermediate jobs).

6.6 Consider a problem containing $n = 5$ jobs with stochastic processing times, each of which follows a normal distribution with known mean and standard deviation.

Job *j*	1	2	3	4	5
μ_j	17	20	24	25	30
σ_j	3	4	2	5	3
d_j	60	80	70	50	90

a) Find the minimum value of the expected maximum tardiness, along with the sequence that achieves it. Use ASP and Evolutionary Solver to produce a solution.
b) Find the minimum value of the maximum expected tardiness, along with the sequence that achieves it. Does the sequence match the sequence in (a)?

6.7 Consider the range model with total flowtime criterion and minimax regret objective. We say that two ranges are *ordered* if the one with the smaller or equal lower limit also has a smaller or equal upper limit, with at least one inequality strict. It can be shown that jobs with ordered ranges should appear in that order in the optimal minimax regret sequence. (Note that two unequal ranges are *not* ordered only if one is strictly nested within the other, with no equal limit, as is the case for any two ranges in Example 6.8.)

a) Suppose all ranges have a lower limit of 0 (or any other equal value). Show that the minimax cost solution also attains the minimax regret.
b) Suppose processing times are stochastically ordered where the cdf of job j is $F_j(x)$. Let a and b be small positive numbers such that $a + b < 1$, and let the range limits for job j be $F_j^{-1}(a)$ and $F_j^{-1}(b)$ – where if $F_j^{-1}(x) = y$ then $F_j(y) = x$ – so each range has a confidence level of $1 - a - b$; for instance, for a 95% confidence interval, we may set $a = b = 2.5\%$. Show that SEPT minimizes expected flowtime, minimax cost, and minimax regret.
c) Suppose all processing times are lognormal with the same cv. Does the result of (b) apply?

6.8 It can be shown that any two lognormal random variables with the same cv are stochastically ordered by SEPT. Revisit Example 6.6 but now assume all jobs have $cv = 0.6$. Show that job 3 must be first. Are there any additional dominance conditions in the example that may apply by virtue of stochastic dominance?

Bibliography

Daniels, R.L. and Kouvelis, P. (1995). Robust scheduling to hedge against processing time uncertainty in single-stage production. *Management Science* 41: 363–376.

Dubois, D., Fargier, H., and Fortemps, P. (2003). Fuzzy scheduling: modeling flexible constraints vs. coping with incomplete knowledge. *European Journal of Operational Research* 147: 231–252.

Esary, J.D., Proschan, F., and Walkup, D.W. (1967). Association of random variables, with applications. *Annals of Mathematical Statistics* 38: 1466–1474.

Gutjahr, W.J., Hellmayr, A., and Pflug, G.C. (1999). Optimal stochastic single-machine-tardiness scheduling by stochastic branch-and-bound. *European Journal of Operational Research* 117: 396–413.

Hodgson, T.J. (1977). A note on single machine sequencing with random processing times. *Management Science* 23: 1144–1146.

Moore, J.M. (1968). An n job, one machine sequencing algorithm for minimizing the number of late jobs. *Management Science* 15: 102–109.

Ross, S.M. (1996). *Stochastic Processes*, 2e. Wiley.

Trietsch, D. (2005). The effect of systemic errors on optimal project buffers. *International Journal of Project Management* 23: 267–274.

Yang, J. and Yu, G. (2002). On the robust single machine scheduling problem. *Journal of Combinatorial Optimization* 6: 17–33.

7

Safe Scheduling

7.1 Introduction

In Chapter 6, our coverage of stochastic scheduling was confined to stochastic counterparts of models with regular performance measures. Indeed, those models are the most prominent subjects in the literature on stochastic scheduling. However, the typical stochastic model misses an important part of the problem: It fails to account for *safety time*. To use an analogy, imagine that we attempted to build stochastic inventory models by relying only on the analysis of average behavior and making no provisions for safety stock. Just as safety *stocks* are vital to practical inventory policies, safety *time* is vital to practical scheduling policies. However, the optimal determination of safety time has no counterpart in deterministic scheduling. *Safe scheduling* departs from the dominant paradigm in stochastic scheduling by considering safety time explicitly.

In stochastic inventory theory, safety stocks are usually determined in one of two ways – by meeting service-level targets explicitly or by minimizing the expected total cost due to overstocking and understocking and thereby deriving service-level constraints implicitly. We can use analogous approaches in safe scheduling, where, as in Chapter 6, processing times are random. To use service-level constraints, we replace the deterministic definition of "on time" by a stochastic one. Define the *service level* for job j as $SL_j = \Pr\{C_j \leq d_j\}$, the probability that job j completes by its due date.

Let b_j denote a given target for the service level. Then the form of a *service-level constraint* for job j is

$$SL_j = \Pr\{C_j \leq d_j\} \geq b_j.$$

We say that job j is *stochastically on time* if its service-level constraint is met; otherwise, the job is *stochastically tardy*. A complete sequence is called

Principles of Sequencing and Scheduling, Second Edition. Kenneth R. Baker and Dan Trietsch.
© 2019 John Wiley & Sons, Inc. Published 2019 by John Wiley & Sons, Inc.

stochastically feasible (or just *feasible*, when the context is clear) if all jobs are stochastically on time. The use of service-level constraints is simple and popular in practice. For example, to meet the 8:00 a.m. scheduled departure of the North bus, a prospective traveler might choose a service-level target of, say, 95% and then aim to leave home early enough to be stochastically on time. However, relying on arbitrary service levels may yield inferior economic results. For instance, depending on the costs involved and the distribution of the travel time to the station, the 95% target may be suboptimal; a target of 90% might be better, or perhaps 99% is better. In any event, we should reserve the service-level approach for cases where the relevant costs are unknown or difficult to estimate.

The alternative to arbitrary service-level constraints is to explicitly consider economic factors. If we can model the true economic costs of various decisions and outcomes, then we can look for a schedule that minimizes the expected total cost. Because a comprehensive economic objective function includes the cost of creating a buffer as well as the cost of failing to meet due dates, the solution automatically yields optimal safety. Often, however, we encounter practical problems of acquiring good cost data, especially when some cost elements are subjective. When costs are hard to identify, we fall back on the service-level approach.

Both alternatives allow us to incorporate considerations of safety, but they do not specify the overall scheduling problem. As in the deterministic case, two major formulations of the safe scheduling problem exist. One formulation treats due dates (and possibly release dates) as given and determines which jobs to accept and to reject and how to sequence the accepted jobs. The other formulation treats due dates and release dates as decisions and adjusts those choices in the process of minimizing expected total cost while accepting all jobs. In either case, optimal safety time is a by-product of the analysis.

In this chapter, we discuss several problems contained in this framework, starting with models that take due dates as decisions. We introduce the service-level approach in Section 7.2 and examine the trade-off between tardiness and due date tightness in Section 7.3. As an example of the economic approach, we study the stochastic version of the E/T problem in Section 7.4, again treating due dates as decisions. As in all the preceding chapters, we assume processing times do not depend on the sequence, so the completion time distribution of any subset of jobs depends only on which jobs are included. We demonstrate the usefulness of sample-based analysis, which requires no additional assumptions, but most of our coverage in those sections also assumes independent and normally distributed processing times. In Section 7.5 we consider lognormal processing times. We then turn to safe scheduling models with due dates as given parameters. In Section 7.6 we look at the possibility of release dates as decisions. In Section 7.7, we discuss the service-level approach to the stochastic counterpart of the U-problem, and we introduce the economic approach in Section 7.8.

7.2 Meeting Service Level Targets

7.2.1 Sample-based Analysis

In this section, we consider setting due dates to meet a given set of service-level targets. Recall from Chapter 2 (Section 2.5.1) that when we can set due dates, we generally want them to be as tight as possible – that is, we wish to minimize

$$D = \sum_{j=1}^{n} d_j \tag{7.1}$$

while maintaining stochastic feasibility. As an example, we consider a model with a discrete probability distribution for each of the processing times. We use the sample-based approach introduced in Chapter 6.

■ **Example 7.1** Consider a problem containing $n = 5$ jobs, each with its own service-level target. The stochastic nature of processing times is represented by 10 distinct states of nature, and for each state the processing time of each job is known. The given information is shown in the following table. The problem is to find due dates for the jobs that are as tight as possible while meeting each job's service-level target.

Job j	1	2	3	4	5
$E(p_j)$	3.00	4.00	4.02	4.04	5.00
Service level	90%	70%	60%	80%	60%
State 1	2.60	2.55	3.50	1.05	3.90
State 2	3.12	4.75	4.20	3.95	5.00
State 3	2.76	3.03	3.70	3.15	4.30
State 4	3.18	5.05	4.35	4.55	5.40
State 5	3.28	5.00	4.30	6.35	5.90
State 6	2.68	2.61	3.60	1.15	4.15
State 7	2.86	2.86	3.80	3.35	4.65
State 8	3.26	4.90	4.25	5.95	5.75
State 9	2.94	4.15	4.10	3.75	4.80
State 10	3.32	5.10	4.40	7.15	6.15

Suppose we fix the job sequence by taking the jobs in nondecreasing order of their expected processing times, or 1-2-3-4-5. (This is the SEPT sequence, as defined in Chapter 6.) Knowledge of the job sequence allows us to calculate the completion time for each job in sequence for each of the 10 states. For job j, and for any particular state, the sum of the first j processing times in the corresponding row of the sample yields C_j, as shown in Figure 7.1. In general, let $C_j(k)$ denote the value of the kth element in this list when it is sorted smallest to largest. For the purpose of exposition, we ignore the possibility of ties in the sorted list. Now suppose that we set $d_j = C_j(k)$, for some integer k. Then job j is early in $(k - 1)$ rows; it is exactly on time in one row (namely, row k); and it is tardy in the remaining $(r - k)$ rows. In general, even with ties, the service-level constraint is satisfied by setting

$$d_j = C_j\left(\lceil b_j r \rceil\right) \tag{7.2}$$

where $\lceil x \rceil$ denotes the smallest integer greater than or equal to x. In Eq. (7.2) this integer is the rank of the completion time among the sorted values for job j. Furthermore, any earlier due date violates stochastic feasibility, and any later due date is not as tight as possible.

The calculations are summarized in Figure 7.1, which shows the completion times for each state. For example, to calculate the due date for job 4, its required service level of 80% leads us to the eighth-ranked completion time (in ascending order) out of the 10 in the column of completion times corresponding to job 4. The eighth smallest value is 18.36. The due dates corresponding to the other service-level targets are shown in the table, leading to $D = 62.89$.

As this example illustrates, we can determine the tightest due dates that meet service-level targets provided we already know the job sequence. The sample-based approach allows us to handle cases in which the processing times are not

				Rows (r)	10	
Sequence	1	2	3	4	5	
SL	90%	70%	60%	80%	60%	
Completion times						
State 1	2.60	5.15	8.65	9.70	13.60	
State 2	3.12	7.87	12.07	16.02	21.02	
State 3	2.76	5.79	9.49	12.64	16.94	
State 4	3.18	8.23	12.58	17.13	22.53	
State 5	3.28	8.28	12.58	18.93	24.83	
State 6	2.68	5.29	8.89	10.04	14.19	
State 7	2.86	5.72	9.52	12.87	17.52	
State 8	3.26	8.16	12.41	18.36	24.11	
State 9	2.94	7.09	11.19	14.94	19.74	
State 10	3.32	8.42	12.82	19.97	26.12	
Rank	9	7	6	8	6	
Due Date	3.28	8.16	12.07	18.36	21.02	**62.89**

Figure 7.1 Detailed calculations for Example 7.1.

independent. (They are highly correlated in Example 7.1.) Furthermore, when the sample is produced by simulation, it can be drawn from any distribution, thus making the sample-based approach widely applicable. However, the more challenging problem is to find the optimal sequence, a problem that we discuss later. For the time being, we can easily imagine some logical heuristic rules for sequencing the jobs.

As noted, the sequence we evaluated corresponds to SEPT. This rule minimizes expected total flowtime (Theorem 6.1). We might observe, however, that SEPT uses information about means but ignores information about variability and service-level targets, so it omits some potentially relevant information. With a bit more calculation effort, we can sequence the jobs using a so-called *greedy algorithm* (see Chapter 2, Section 4.2) by augmenting a partial sequence with the job that produces the smallest increment to the objective function. For minimizing D subject to stochastic feasibility, this is equivalent to selecting the unscheduled job with the earliest due date (EDD) if it were to come next. We refer here to the optimal due date for the job, recognizing that this value depends on which jobs have previously been scheduled. For this reason, the EDD rule is a dynamic rule. In Example 7.1, EDD yields the sequence 1-3-5-2-4, which achieves $D = 65.01$.

A sequence is called *adjacent pairwise interchange (API) stable* if it is optimal in its API neighborhood. API stability is a necessary condition for optimality, but the SEPT sequence may not be API stable. In our example, the SEPT sequence, 1-2-3-4-5, is not API stable, but we can achieve an improvement by finding an API-stable sequence starting with SEPT. The best possible improvement is obtained by interchanging jobs 2 and 3, thus obtaining 1-3-2-4-5, with an objective function value of 62.39. With this sequence as the new seed, we achieve a further improvement by interchanging jobs 2 and 4, to obtain 1-3-4-2-5, with an objective function value of 62.21. Finally, interchanging jobs 3 and 4 yields the API-stable sequence 1-4-3-2-5, with an objective function value of 61.91. As it happens, this sequence is optimal.

As the example demonstrates, performing an API search starting with SEPT can outperform the greedy heuristic. But the simpler greedy heuristic yields good results in one important special case, as stated in the following property.

Property 7.1 When all service-level targets are equal ($b_j = b$), the greedy heuristic yields an API-stable sequence.

Proof. At any stage, let job i be the one selected next by the greedy heuristic (that is, d_i is the minimal possible due date in the first unscheduled position), and suppose job k follows directly. If we interchange *B-i-k* to *B-k-i* (where B is the set of all previously scheduled jobs), d_k is at least as large as the previous d_i, but the new d_i is equal to the former d_k (because the completion time distribution of the second job is the same and so is its service-level target). Hence, the sum of the two is minimized by keeping job i ahead of job k, for any k. This is true for all positions, so the greedy sequence is API stable. $\square$

7.2.2 The Normal Model

For the time being, we assume that the processing times are independent random variables and that, in particular, the processing time for job j follows a normal distribution with mean μ_j and standard deviation σ_j. (See Appendix A.1.3 for background on the normal distribution.) We use the normal because it is tractable, familiar, and plausible for many scheduling applications.

The assumption of normal processing times leads to a convenient result: In any sequence, the completion time of job j also follows a normal distribution because the sum of normal random variables is normally distributed. Using notation, let B_j denote the "before set" or the set of jobs preceding job j in the schedule. Then C_j follows a normal distribution with mean $E[C_j] = \sum_{i \in B_j} \mu_i + \mu_j$ and variance $V[C_j] = \sum_{i \in B_j} \sigma_i^2 + \sigma_j^2$. To simplify the notation, we write μ_{B_j} for $\sum_{i \in B_j} \mu_i$ and $\sigma_{B_j}^2$ for $\sum_{i \in B_j} \sigma_i^2$. Once we know the properties of the random variable C_j (which depends on the job sequence), we can determine the optimal choice of d_j.

To represent the service-level requirement in the normal case, let z_j represent the standard normal variate at which the cumulative distribution function (cdf) equals b_j. In standard notation, $\Phi(z_j) = b_j$. Then the appropriate choice for the due date of job j is

$$d_j = \mu_{B_j} + \mu_j + z_j \left(\sigma_{B_j}^2 + \sigma_j^2 \right)^{1/2} \tag{7.3}$$

In this expression, the optimal due date d_j depends on the previous jobs in sequence via the set B_j, and the objective function (7.1) can be expressed as

$$D = \sum_{j=1}^{n} \left[\mu_{B_j} + \mu_j + z_j \left(\sigma_{B_j}^2 + \sigma_j^2 \right)^{1/2} \right] \tag{7.4}$$

We can interpret this expression as the sum of two components: expected total flowtime and total safety time. This interpretation applies to any distribution, but Eq. (7.4) is specific to independent normal processing times.

■ **Example 7.2** Consider a problem containing $n = 5$ jobs with stochastic processing times. The processing times are independent, each drawn from a normal distribution with the mean and standard deviation shown in the table, and each job has been assigned a service level, also shown in the table.

Job j	1	2	3	4	5
$E(p_j)$	20	21	22	23	24
σ_j	4.0	2.0	3.5	4.5	4.0
b_j	90%	80%	75%	80%	70%

Example 7.2 contains five jobs with given service-level targets and illustrates the necessary calculations. Suppose we fix the job sequence as 1-2-3-4-5. Then the optimal due dates can be determined individually for each job. The relevant calculations are shown in Figure 7.2, as they might be calculated on a spreadsheet, and we elaborate on the details for job 4.

Job 4 has a mean completion time equal to the sum of the first four mean processing times, or 86. To find the variance of its completion time, we sum the variances of the first four jobs, obtaining 52.5. The corresponding standard deviation is the square root of this figure, or about 7.25. Job 4 has a service-level target of 80%, corresponding to a z-value of 0.842 in the standard normal distribution. Thus, using the formula in Eq. (7.3), we can meet the service level by setting $d_4 = 86 + 0.842 \, (7.25) = 92.1$. Similar calculations apply for the other jobs. As Figure 7.1 shows, the sum of the five optimally calculated due dates is $D = 343.2$.

Thus, we can make the calculations for the normal case using spreadsheet technology, provided we already know the job sequence. Once again, we can explore heuristic rules for finding a good job sequence.

By definition, if our current solution is not API stable, an API neighborhood search will improve the schedule. As shown in Figure 7.2, the SEPT rule, which corresponds to the sequence 1-2-3-4-5, achieves $D = 343.2$. The EDD rule – that is, the greedy heuristic – yields the sequence 2-3-5-1-4, which achieves

Example 7.2	SEPT				
Data	Job *j*	1	2	3	4	5
	E(pj)	20	21	22	23	24
	σj	4.0	2.0	3.5	4.5	4.0
	Target	90%	80%	75%	80%	70%
Schedule	Sequence	1	2	3	4	5
Calculations	Mean	20.00	21.00	22.00	23.00	24.00
	Cum. Mean	20.00	41.00	63.00	86.00	110.00
	St. Dev.	4.00	2.00	3.50	4.50	4.00
	Variance	16.00	4.00	12.25	20.25	16.00
	Cum. Var.	16.00	20.00	32.25	52.50	68.50
	Sq. Root	4.00	4.47	5.68	7.25	8.28
	S.L. Target	0.90	0.80	0.75	0.80	0.70
	z value	1.282	0.842	0.674	0.842	0.524
	Due date	25.1	44.8	66.8	92.1	114.3	343.2

Figure 7.2 Detailed calculations for Example 7.2.

D = 351.2. Accordingly, we select 1-2-3-4-5 as the seed for our API search. By interchanging jobs 1 and 2, we reduce the objective function value to 342.7. This sequence is API stable and turns out to be optimal as well.

In our example, SEPT was not optimal but much better than the greedy heuristic. For large n, a special property applies. A heuristic is *asymptotically optimal* if, as n grows large, the relative difference between the heuristic solution and the optimum becomes negligible. More formally, let $f(S^*)$ denote the objective function value with the optimal sequence, S^*, and let $f(S^H)$ be the value associated with a heuristic. We say that the heuristic is asymptotically optimal if $[f(S^H) - f(S^*)]/f(S^*)$ approaches 0 as n approaches ∞. That turns out to be the case for the SEPT heuristic, no matter which distribution applies, as long as processing times are independent. To understand why SEPT is asymptotically optimal, recall that D consists of the expected total flowtime and the sum of all safety times. Under the independence assumption, and if no single job can dominate too many other jobs combined, then as n grows large, expected total flowtime grows at a rate of $O(n^2)$, whereas total safety time grows a rate of $O(n^{3/2})$. Therefore, total safety time becomes negligible compared with expected total flowtime, which is minimized by SEPT.

We can conclude that, when combining SEPT with an API search, it is enough to perform the search on the first several jobs. Due to asymptotic optimality, we don't need to worry about the other jobs: As n grows large, SEPT is already an excellent sequence for the last jobs even without API. Extensive numerical experience shows that following SEPT by an API neighborhood search on the first few jobs yields the optimal solution more often than not. As an added touch, we recommend breaking ties by smallest variance and further ties by highest service-level target. Doing so is likely to impose the correct sequence between jobs with the same mean.

7.3 Trading Off Tightness and Tardiness

7.3.1 An Objective Function for the Trade-off

When due dates are decisions, an inherent trade-off arises. If due dates are chosen to be very loose, it may be possible to complete all required work on time, but the resulting schedule may also be inefficient. On the other hand, if due dates are chosen to be very tight, the schedule may be efficient, but due dates may be missed too often, and jobs may be excessively tardy. In the previous section, we avoided excessive tardiness by imposing service-level constraints that force sufficiently loose due dates. In this section, we seek a balance between tight due dates and job tardiness. The trade-off between due date tightness and job tardiness is captured by an objective function that combines a due date component with a tardiness component:

$$G(d) = D + \gamma \sum_{j=1}^{n} \max\{0, C_j - d_j\}$$

$$G(d) = \sum_{j=1}^{n} d_j + \gamma \sum_{j=1}^{n} T_j \tag{7.5}$$

We write $G(d)$ as shorthand for $G(d_1, d_2, \dots, d_n)$. We can also rewrite Eq. (7.5) as a total of job-by-job contributions to the overall objective:

$$G(d) = \sum_{j=1}^{n} G_j(d_j) = \sum_{j=1}^{n} (d_j + \gamma T_j) \tag{7.6}$$

In this expression, the term $G_j(d_j)$ represents the contribution of job j. The parameter γ arbitrarily determines the weight given to total tardiness relative to the sum of the due dates. As we shall see, the choice of γ determines the optimal service level for the jobs.

In the deterministic single-machine model, it is not difficult to minimize $G(d)$. In Eq. (7.6), we can write $d_j + \gamma T_j = \max\{d_j, (1 - \gamma)d_j + \gamma C_j\}$, so that for a fixed sequence, if $\gamma \le 1$ then $G(d)$ is minimized with $d_j = 0$ (assuming due dates are constrained to be nonnegative). On the other hand, if $\gamma > 1$ then $G(d)$ is minimized by setting $d_j = C_j$. In both cases $G(d)$ is proportional to the sum of the completion times (which equals total flowtime, F): For $\gamma > 1$, $G(d) = F$ (with zero tardiness), whereas for $\gamma \le 1$, $G(d) = \gamma F$ (because $d_j = 0$ so total tardiness is F). To minimize F, we sequence the jobs according to shortest processing time (SPT).

In the stochastic version of this problem, the objective is to minimize the expected value of the function in Eq. (7.6), which may be expressed as

$$H(d) = \mathrm{E}[G(d)] = \sum_{j=1}^{n} (d_j + \gamma E[T_j]) \tag{7.7}$$

In this form, each job contributes $H_j(d_j) = d_j + \gamma \mathrm{E}[T_j]$ to the total. The problem consists of finding a set of due dates and a sequence of the jobs that produces the minimum value of $H(d)$ in Eq. (7.7).

7.3.2 The Normal Model

As in the deterministic counterpart, we know that when $\gamma \le 1$, the due dates should be set to zero (and $H(d) = \gamma \mathrm{E}[F] \le \mathrm{E}[F]$, which is minimized by SEPT), so in what follows we assume $\gamma > 1$. As in Section 7.2.2, we assume that the processing times p_j are independent and follow a normal distribution with mean μ_j and standard deviation σ_j. This means that the completion time of job j follows a normal distribution and that the expressions for $\mathrm{E}[C_j]$ and $\mathrm{V}[C_j]$ apply as well. Once we know the properties of the random variable C_j, we can determine the optimal choice of d_j.

Let $z_j = (d_j - E[C_j])/(V[C_j])^{1/2}$ be the standardized due date, and use asterisks to denote optimal values. Because γ does not depend on j, the optimal standardized due date is the same for all jobs, so we may write it without an index.

■ **Theorem 7.1** Given the mean and standard deviation of the normal distribution for C_j, the optimal choice of the due date d_j is given by

$$\Phi(z^*) = \frac{\gamma - 1}{\gamma}$$

As before, $\Phi(\cdot)$ denotes the standard normal cdf or, equivalently, the probability (SL_j) that job j completes on or before its due date. In other words, the optimal service level for job j is given by the ratio $(\gamma - 1)/\gamma$. This result is a version of the well-known *critical fractile rule*, sometimes also called the *newsvendor property* of inventory theory. (See Appendix B for details on the critical fractile rule.)

Theorem 7.1 implies that the appropriate choice for the due date of job j is

$$d_j = \mu_{B_j} + \mu_j + z^* \left(\sigma_{B_j}^2 + \sigma_j^2 \right)^{1/2} \tag{7.8}$$

In this expression, as in Eq. (7.3), the due date d_j depends on the previous jobs in sequence[1] via the set B_j, and our objective is summarized in Eq. (7.7). From the algebra of critical fractile analysis with the normal distribution (see Appendix B), we can rewrite Eq. (7.7) by incorporating the optimal choice of d_j. The objective becomes

$$H(d^*) = \sum_{j=1}^{n} \left[\mu_{B_j} + \mu_j + \gamma \phi(z^*) \left(\sigma_{B_j}^2 + \sigma_j^2 \right)^{1/2} \right] \tag{7.9}$$

In this formula, $\phi(z^*)$ is the standard normal probability density function corresponding to the optimal service level of Theorem 7.1. As in Eq. (7.4), the objective function is composed of the expected total flowtime and a safety time component.

■ **Example 7.3** Consider a problem containing $n = 5$ jobs with stochastic processing times as described in the following table.

Job j	1	2	3	4	5
$E(p_j)$	24	25	26	28	30
σ_j	8	7	4	5	6

---

1 A small value of γ may theoretically lead to a negative due date, but such cases reflect the limitations of the normal probability model, so we ignore them.

The processing times are independent, each drawn from a normal distribution with the mean and standard deviation shown in the table. In addition, $\gamma = 10$.

In this model, the greedy heuristic yields an API-stable sequence. In effect, Property 7.1 extends to the tightness/tardiness trade-off and applies for any probability distribution. In this example, we have $(\gamma - 1)/\gamma = 0.9$, so the optimal service level is 90%, and the corresponding z-value is 1.282, for which $\gamma\phi(z^*) = 1.75$. Using this value in Eq. (7.9), we can calculate the potential contribution of all five jobs in the first position (with B_j empty); that is, we compare the values $\mu_j + 1.75\sigma_j$ of the five jobs and, in the spirit of the greedy algorithm, select the smallest. This means job 3 is scheduled first. For the second position, we have $\mu_B = 26$ and $\sigma_B^2 = 16$, so we consider the four unscheduled jobs and compare values of $26 + \mu_j + 1.75\left(16 + \sigma_j^2\right)^{1/2}$ from Eq. (7.9). Accordingly, we schedule job 2 next, update B_j, and continue in the same manner. The final greedy heuristic sequence is 3-2-1-4-5, with an objective value of 475.1. The detailed calculations are shown in Figure 7.3.

Although we have introduced the tightness/tardiness trade-off as a new model, its relation to the model of Section 7.2 is revealing. When we compare the objective functions, $H(d^*)$ in Eq. (7.9) with D in Eq. (7.4), we can see that the

Example 7.3						
Data	Job j	1	2	3	4	5
	$E(pj)$	24	25	26	28	30
	σj	8	7	4	5	6
	γ	10	10	10	10	10
Schedule	Sequence	3	2	1	4	5
Calculations	Mean	26	25	24	28	30
	Cum. Mean	26.00	51.00	75.00	103.00	133.00
	Stan.Dev.	4.00	7.00	8.00	5.00	6.00
	Variance	16.00	49.00	64.00	25.00	36.00
	Cum. Var	16.00	65.00	129.00	154.00	190.00
	Sq. Root	4.00	8.06	11.36	12.41	13.78
	γ	10.00	10.00	10.00	10.00	10.00
	cdf	0.90	0.90	0.90	0.90	0.90
	z value	1.282	1.282	1.282	1.282	1.282
	phi	0.175	0.175	0.175	0.175	0.175
	Due date	31.13	61.33	89.56	118.90	150.66
	$d + \gamma E(T)$	33.02	65.15	94.93	124.78	157.19	**475.1**

Figure 7.3 Detailed calculations for the jobs in Example 7.3.

two functions are structurally similar. We can express their common form as follows:

$$\text{Objective} = \sum_{j=1}^{n} \left[\mu_{B_j} + \mu_j + \theta \left(\sigma_{B_j}^2 + \sigma_j^2 \right)^{1/2} \right] \tag{7.10}$$

In this expression, which applies for the case of normal distributions, either $\theta = z$, as in Eq. (7.4), for minimizing the sum of stochastically feasible due dates, or $\theta = \gamma \phi(z^*)$, as in Eq. (7.9), in the optimal tightness/tardiness trade-off. For a given θ, the same sequence will be optimal for both models, but the service levels, and therefore the due dates, will *not* be the same for both models: The trade-off model requires lower service levels.

7.3.3 A Branch-and-bound Solution

As Examples 7.2 and 7.3 illustrate, we can determine the value of $H(d^*)$ in Eq. (7.9) provided we already know the job sequence. But the more challenging problem, which we examine next, is to find the optimal sequence.

We attack the sequencing problem with a branch-and-bound approach, although the details differ from the B&B approach of Chapter 3. In particular, we build a job sequence from the start of the problem (not from the end, as in Chapter 3). Thus, each partial sequence specifies the ordered subset of jobs at the beginning of the schedule. If we let π represent a partial sequence of jobs, and $P(\pi)$ represent the subproblem of optimally completing the partial sequence, then the forward-looking branching scheme takes the form of the tree shown in Figure 7.4, depicting each node as corresponding to a problem in which the initial partial sequence has been specified. (A comparison with Figure 3.4 reveals that the essential difference lies in the direction of augmenting partial sequences.)

The branching tree starts with the empty sequence and the corresponding problem $P(0)$ at Level 0. Level 1 of the tree contains n nodes $P(1)$, $P(2)$, ..., $P(n)$, according to the choice of the first job in sequence. At Level k of the tree, the first k positions in sequence have been assigned. With the partial sequence known, we can calculate the mean and variance of each completion time C_j in the partial sequence and evaluate contributions to the objective function in Eq. (7.9) made by the jobs in the partial sequence.

Finally, if we fill out the entire tree, Level n contains all $n!$ possible sequences. The best of those sequences is the optimal solution. However, the computational effort required to enumerate all those partial and full sequences can become prohibitive for large values of n, so the purpose of a B&B algorithm is to limit the enumerative task where possible by exploiting patterns in the parameters of the problem instance. Techniques for this purpose include

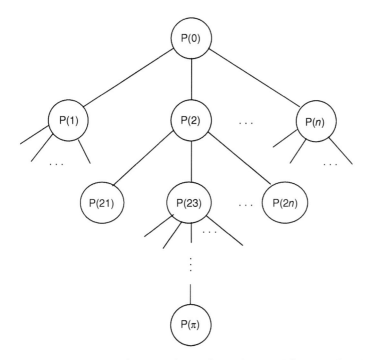

Figure 7.4 A portion of the branching scheme (B&B tree) for an *n*-job problem.

dominance properties, adjacent pairwise interchanges, lower bounds, and an initial solution.

Static Dominance. The basic dominance condition between two jobs, *i* and *j*, states that an optimal solution exists in which job *i* precedes job *j*. In other words, when searching for an optimal sequence, we need not consider any sequences in which job *j* appears in sequence before job *i*. A dominance property is *static* if it holds independently of the other jobs in the schedule. For example, a job dominates another if it has smaller mean and variance.

Property 7.2 If $\mu_i \leq \mu_j$ and $\sigma_i \leq \sigma_j$ then an optimal schedule exists in which job *i* precedes job *j*.

Even when one job does not have a smaller mean and variance, it may still dominate another based on the relative differences in the two means and variances.

Property 7.3 If $\mu_i < \mu_j$ and $\mu_j - \mu_i \geq \theta(\sigma_i - \sigma_j)$ then an optimal schedule exists in which job *i* precedes job *j*. (A sufficient condition is $\mu_j - \mu_i \geq \theta\sigma_i$.)

Properties 7.2 and 7.3 can be proven with pairwise interchange arguments. Satisfying Property 7.2 implies satisfying Property 7.3, but not the other way around, so it is efficient to check Property 7.2 first. These static dominance conditions can be evaluated once at the outset and then applied as needed during the generation and evaluation of partial sequences. Furthermore, if job j is dominated by job i by virtue of the sufficient condition of Property 7.3, then every job beyond job j in SEPT order is also dominated.

If we are augmenting a partial sequence and we find that job i dominates job j while neither appears in the partial sequence, then we need not consider the augmented partial sequence constructed by appending job j next. That is, only jobs that are not dominated by other unscheduled jobs have to be considered. Dominance conditions can reduce the search effort required to find an optimal schedule, but the extent to which dominance conditions apply may depend on the specific data in a given problem instance. For that reason, it is difficult to predict their effectiveness at curtailing the search effort.

Adjacent Pairwise Interchanges. We have already seen that requiring API stability can be helpful for heuristic applications. The same often applies to B&B as well. Suppose that job j appears immediately after job i somewhere in the sequence, and consider the conditions under which it would be better to interchange the two jobs. The completion times of jobs not involved in the interchange are unaffected by the swap, so the overall objective is improved if and only if the total contribution from jobs i and j is improved. The mean time to process the jobs preceding i and j can be denoted by μ_B and the variance of that time by σ_B^2.

For the sequence i-j, the contribution of the two jobs to the objective is

$$h(i,j) = \left(\mu_B + \mu_i\right) + \theta\left(\sigma_B^2 + \sigma_i^2\right)^{1/2} + \left(\mu_B + \mu_i + \mu_j\right) + \theta\left(\sigma_B^2 + \sigma_i^2 + \sigma_j^2\right)^{1/2}$$

The expression $h(j,i)$, for the reverse sequence j-i, is similar, and the change in the objective due to the interchange is

$$g_{ij}\left(\sigma_B^2\right) = h(j,i) - h(i,j) = \mu_j - \mu_i + \theta\left[\left(\sigma_B^2 + \sigma_j^2\right)^{1/2} - \left(\sigma_B^2 + \sigma_i^2\right)^{1/2}\right] \qquad (7.11)$$

Using Eq. (7.11), the interchange is undesirable (and the i-j order is at least as good as the reverse) as long as $g_{ij}(\sigma_B^2) \geq 0$, which we call the *API condition*.

■ **Theorem 7.2**   A necessary condition for a sequence to be optimal is that every pair of adjacent jobs i and j (with j following i) satisfies the API condition, $g_{ij}(\sigma_B^2) \geq 0$.

Unfortunately, the API condition does not lead to a universal rule for determining whether j should follow i because the condition depends on σ_B^2 and therefore on the jobs making up the partial sequence that precedes i and j. Nevertheless, the API condition can be used to eliminate some partial sequences and therefore curtail an enumerative search. Specifically, suppose that we are about to augment a partial sequence π by appending job i. Suppose further that the last job in π is job j. If the API condition holds, then the augmented sequence πi is dominated and can be eliminated.

For another perspective on the API condition, assume jobs i and j are in strict SEPT order ($\mu_i - \mu_j < 0$) but $\sigma_i^2 - \sigma_j^2 > 0$. In this case, Property 7.2 does not apply, and Property 7.3 may or may not hold, depending on θ. Under those conditions, Eq. (7.11) is monotone decreasing in σ_B^2, so there exists a threshold value $\sigma_B^2(i,j) \geq 0$ for which the optimal sequence of jobs i and j, if adjacent, switches from j–i to i–j. We can calculate this value in advance by,

$$\sigma_B^2(i,j) = \max\left\{ 0, \left(\frac{\theta}{2} \left(\frac{\sigma_i^2 - \sigma_j^2}{\mu_j - \mu_i} \right) + \frac{\mu_j - \mu_i}{2\theta} \right)^2 - \sigma_i^2 \right\} \tag{7.12}$$

As we add jobs to a partial sequence, the value of σ_B^2 increases. Once it reaches the threshold for (i, j), we never have to consider a partial sequence in which job i immediately follows job j.

Lower Bounds. Suppose that we have a partial sequence π and we wish to compute a lower bound on the value of the objective function that can be obtained by completing the sequence. The component of the objective function corresponding to the jobs j in π has already been determined from Eq. (7.10). Let π' denote the set of unscheduled jobs. In the set π', we take the set of means μ_j in smallest-first order and take the set of standard deviations σ_j in smallest-first order and treat these values as if they were paired. Then we calculate the values of $H_j(d_j)$ generated by these fictitious jobs and add them to the component for the partial sequence. This total is a lower bound on the value that could be achieved by completing the partial sequence in the best possible way. (A formal proof follows a pairwise interchange argument.)

Thus, if we ever encounter a partial sequence π for which the lower bound on the value of the objective function is greater than or equal to the value for a known sequence, we conclude that completing π can never lead to a full sequence with a better value than the known sequence. Such a condition, which amounts to fathoming $P(\pi)$, tells us that we do not need to solve $P(\pi)$, and we can thus eliminate it and curtail the tree search.

Initial Solution. Given that we are using a B&B algorithm, it makes sense to begin by finding a good initial solution that can be effective at fathoming partial sequences with relatively few jobs. That is, we can implement a heuristic procedure to construct a feasible solution before the tree search begins, on the chance that a good feasible solution may eliminate some partial sequences and reduce the search effort. For this purpose, we can implement a sorting rule, such as SEPT, or, with additional computational effort, the greedy heuristic.

As an example, we apply the B&B approach to Example 7.3 using these tools, starting with a heuristic initial solution. Suppose we implement SEPT, which corresponds to the sequence 1-2-3-4-5 and yields an objective function of 482.6.

Next, we investigate static dominance properties. In this example, Property 7.2 reveals that job 4 dominates job 5 and job 3 dominates both job 4 and job 5. Property 7.3 reveals that jobs 1 and 2 dominate job 5.

We begin the tree search starting with P(0), the empty sequence. The candidates for first position in sequence are only jobs 1, 2, and 3 because the other jobs are dominated. Thus, the first level of the tree contains P(1), P(2), and P(3). The detailed calculation of the lower bound for P(2) is shown in Figure 7.5. For this calculation, the initial partial sequence contains job 2 followed by four fictitious jobs (F1–F4) characterized by increasing means and variances. Similar calculations provide lower bounds for P(1) and P(3), as shown in the full search tree of Figure 7.6. These three lower bounds are well below the objective for the initial heuristic, so no fathoming is possible yet, and we proceed to Level 2.

Branching from P(1), we generate nodes for P(12) and P(13). (The static dominance properties eliminate the other two partial sequences that begin with job 1.) To evaluate P(12), we first apply the API condition and discover that P(21) dominates P(12). Similarly P(31) dominates P(13). Thus, P(12) and P(13) are eliminated. Branching from P(2) yields one undominated augmented sequence, P(21), and branching from P(3) yields three undominated augmented

Example 7.3	Lower bound calculation for P(2)					
Data	Job j	2	F1	F2	F3	F4
	$E(p_j)$	25	24	26	28	30
	s_j	7	4	5	6	8
	γ	10	10	10	10	10
Schedule	Sequence	1	2	3	4	5
Calculations	Mean	25	24	26	28	30
	Cum. Mean	25.00	49.00	75.00	103.00	133.00
	Stan.Dev.	7.00	4.00	5.00	6.00	8.00
	Variance	49.00	16.00	25.00	36.00	64.00
	Cum. Var	49.00	65.00	90.00	126.00	190.00
	Sq. Root	7.00	8.06	9.49	11.22	13.78
	γ	10.00	10.00	10.00	10.00	10.00
	cdf	0.90	0.90	0.90	0.90	0.90
	z value	1.282	1.282	1.282	1.282	1.282
	phi	0.175	0.175	0.175	0.175	0.175
	Due date	33.97	59.33	87.16	117.39	150.66
	$d + \gamma E(T)$	37.28	63.15	91.65	122.70	157.19	**472.0**

Figure 7.5 Lower bound calculation for partial sequence P(2).

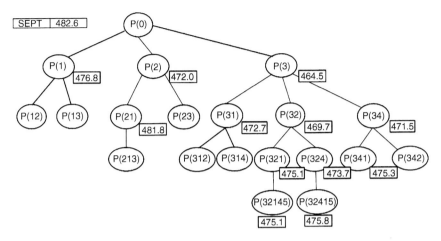

Figure 7.6 The B&B tree for Example 7.3.

sequences. The lower bounds for these four remaining partial sequences are shown in Figure 7.6.

At Level 3, the only undominated candidate to follow P(21) is job 3, but P(213) is dominated by P(231), so the P(213) branch can be fathomed. The partial sequences that survive the API condition are P(321), P(324), and P(341). Their lower bounds are shown in Figure 7.6.

At Level 4, we branch from P(321), yielding the full sequence 3-2-1-4-5 with objective 475.1, the best value thus far. This value allows us to fathom P(341) because its lower bound is larger than 475.1. The remaining node is P(324), which leads to the full sequence 3-2-4-1-5. Its value of 475.8 is larger than the best solution yet found, so the node is eliminated. Alternatively, we could check to see that 3-2-4-1 is not API stable, allowing its elimination one level earlier.

The full tree search is shown in Figure 7.6, demonstrating that only three complete sequences need to be evaluated during the B&B algorithm (as compared with 120 feasible permutations that would be evaluated by complete enumeration).

In summary, the B&B algorithm builds job sequences starting from time 0, augmenting partial sequences in all possible ways. For each partial sequence encountered, we first check dominance properties, allowing us to eliminate dominated partial sequences and to pursue only those that remain. If the dominance condition fails, we then compute the corresponding lower bound to see whether the partial sequence can be compared with the value of an existing solution and fathomed. If the lower bound does not permit fathoming, then the partial sequence remains active and is ultimately augmented by adding some unscheduled job to it. The augmented partial sequence is then examined for dominance or fathoming, and the process continues until the best job sequence is discovered.

The B&B approach has implications for finding optimal solutions to the problem of minimizing D subject to feasibility constraints. As we observed earlier, the objective functions $H(d^*)$ in Eq. (7.9) and D in Eq. (7.4) are structurally similar and can be expressed in a common form by defining θ appropriately. Thus, the B&B approach illustrated for the tightness/tardiness trade-off applies as well to minimizing the sum of stochastically feasible due dates.

Computational experiments with the B&B algorithm on random problem instances indicate that problems with well over 100 jobs can be solved in a matter of seconds, on average. Heuristic procedures such as the greedy algorithm can be used to solve very large instances quickly. In similar models with job-dependent θ values (for which Property 7.1 does not hold), another plausible heuristic rule would be to sequence the jobs in SEPT order followed by an API neighborhood search, which is asymptotically optimal for the case of common θ values.

7.4 The Stochastic E/T Problem

In the previous two sections, we examined the problem of finding the tightest due dates that satisfy given service-level constraints and the problem of trading off tightness and tardiness. We noted that both problems effectively seek to minimize an objective function composed of expected total flowtime and an adjustment for safety time or for the cost of failing to meet due dates. In this section, we examine an economic model that captures the costs of failing to meet due dates but without considering the flowtime. In particular, we consider the stochastic version of the E/T problem with due dates as decisions, adopting the notation introduced in Chapter 5 for job-dependent earliness and tardiness costs. The unit earliness cost α_j and the unit tardiness cost β_j apply to the difference between each job's completion time (C_j) and its due date (d_j). (We consider job-dependent parameters; otherwise, the sequencing problem could be solved by sorting according to smallest variance first.) Thus, the objective function takes the form

$$G(d) = G(d_1, d_2, \ldots, d_n) = \sum_{j=1}^{n} \left(\alpha_j \max\{0, d_j - C_j\} + \beta_j \max\{0, C_j - d_j\} \right)$$

$$= \sum_{j=1}^{n} \left(\alpha_j E_j + \beta_j T_j \right)$$

We still assume that the processing times p_j are independent and follow a normal distribution with mean μ_j and standard deviation σ_j. The expected value of

$G(d)$, or expected total E/T cost, becomes our objective function in the stochastic case, and we can express it as

$$H(d) = E[G(d)] = \sum_{j=1}^{n} \left(\alpha_j E[E_j] + \beta_j E[T_j] \right) \tag{7.13}$$

Setting due dates loosely, in such a way that idling occurs between jobs, can only reduce Eq. (7.13) because by ignoring flowtime the model does not account for the inefficiency that idling represents. Therefore, we assume that no idling is permitted. The optimal choice of due dates is again determined by a critical fractile rule, as stated in the following result.

■ **Theorem 7.3**   Assume all jobs are processed with no inserted idle time and the objective is to minimize the expected total E/T cost. Given the mean and the standard deviation of the normal distribution for C_j, the optimal choice of the due date d_j is given in standardized form by

$$\Phi\left(z_j^*\right) = \frac{\beta_j}{\alpha_j + \beta_j}$$

A derivation of this property appears in Appendix B. For a given job sequence, we calculate optimal due dates by applying Theorem 7.3 separately to each job, thereby minimizing expected total E/T cost. Recall that in the problem of determining the tightest feasible due dates, service levels are given. In the tightness/tardiness trade-off, service levels are determined by the critical fractile $(\gamma - 1)/\gamma$, where γ is given. In Theorem 7.3, service levels are also derived from a critical fractile property, but one in which job-dependent unit costs are given and jobs may therefore have different service levels.

From the result in Theorem 7.3, we can compute optimal due dates as we did in Eq. (7.8). In the stochastic E/T model, we obtain

$$d_j = \mu_{B_j} + \mu_j + z_j^* \left(\sigma_{B_j}^2 + \sigma_j^2 \right)^{1/2} \tag{7.14}$$

Then, as in Eq. (7.9) we can calculate the objective function:

$$H(d^*) = \sum_{j=1}^{n} \left(\alpha_j + \beta_j \right) \phi\left(z_j^*\right) \left(\sigma_B^2 + \sigma_j^2 \right)^{1/2} \tag{7.15}$$

For convenience, we define $c_j = \left(\alpha_j + \beta_j \right) \phi\left(z_j^*\right)$ and $s_j = \left(\sigma_B^2 + \sigma_j^2 \right)^{1/2}$ so that the contribution from job j to the objective function in Eq. (7.15) is simply $c_j s_j$.

In the spirit of the deterministic counterpart, suppose that we also consider setting due dates equal to expected completion times:

$$d_j = E(C_j) = \mu_{B_j} + \mu_j$$

These due dates amount to using safety times of zero, or equivalently, $z_j^* = 0$. The expected E/T cost for job j is then obtained by replacing z_j^* by 0 in Eq. (7.15). This cost must be at least as high as the optimal expected E/T cost associated with job j in Eq. (7.15) because $\phi(z)$ is maximized at $z = 0$.

As in the previous sections, we can get a feel for the calculations involved by examining a numerical example such as Example 7.4, which contains five jobs with nonidentical pairs of unit costs for earliness and tardiness. Suppose we fix the job sequence as 1-2-3-4-5. Then the critical fractiles and optimal due dates can be determined individually for each job. The relevant calculations are shown in Figure 7.7, and we elaborate on the details for job 3.

■ **Example 7.4** Consider a problem containing $n = 5$ jobs with stochastic processing times as described in the following table.

Job j	1	2	3	4	5
$E(p_j)$	21	24	30	32	36
σ_j	4	3	2	3	5
α_j	3	2	1	3	4
β_j	6	8	5	9	4
c_j	9	10	6	12	8

The processing times are independent, each drawn from a normal distribution with mean and standard deviation shown in the table.

Job 3 has a mean completion time equal to the sum of the first three mean processing times, or 75. To find the variance of its completion time, we sum the variances of the first three jobs, obtaining 29. The corresponding standard deviation is the square root of this figure, or about 5.39. Job 3 has a service-level target of 83.3%, corresponding to a z-value of 0.967 in the standard normal distribution. Thus, we can meet the service level by setting $d_3 = 75 + 0.967(5.39) = 80.2$. However, our objective function does not require the due date as such. Instead, we use the formula in Eq. (7.15) or $(\alpha_j + \beta_j)\phi(z_j^*)s_j = 6(0.25)(5.39)$ $= 8.073$. Similar calculations apply for the other jobs. As Figure 7.7 shows, the sum of the five optimally calculated costs is $H(d^*) = 84.00$.

Example 7.4

Data	Job j	1	2	3	4	5	
	$E[p_j]$	21	24	30	32	36	
	σ_j	4	3	2	3	5	
	α_j	3	2	1	3	4	
	β_j	6	8	5	9	4	
	$\alpha_j + \beta_j$	9	10	6	12	8	
Schedule	Sequence	1	2	3	4	5	
Calculations	β_j	6.00	8.00	5.00	9.00	4.00	
	$\alpha_j + \beta_j$	9.00	10.00	6.00	12.00	8.00	
	SL	0.667	0.800	0.833	0.750	0.500	
	z	0.4307	0.8416	0.9674	0.6745	0.0000	
	var	16.00	9.00	4.00	9.00	25.00	
	cum var	16.00	25.00	29.00	38.00	63.00	
	sq. root	4.00	5.00	5.39	6.16	7.94	
Optimal	phi	0.364	0.280	0.250	0.318	0.399	
	E/T cost	13.09	14.00	8.07	23.51	25.33	**84.00**
Expected	phi	0.399	0.399	0.399	0.399	0.399	
	E/T cost	14.362	19.947	12.890	29.511	25.332	**102.04**

Figure 7.7 Detailed calculations for the jobs in Example 7.4.

Also shown in Figure 7.7 is the calculation of expected costs obtained by setting each due date equal to the expected completion time. The key difference in the cost calculation lies in substituting $\phi(0)$ for $\phi\left(z_j^*\right)$ in Eq. (7.15). With this substitution, the cost becomes $H(d) = 102.04$. This figure is over 20% greater than the optimal value, a substantial difference that suggests the cost penalty that might be incurred when we use a deterministic counterpart as a proxy for a stochastic problem.

As these calculations illustrate, we can determine optimal due dates provided that we already know the job sequence. Again, however, the larger problem is to find the optimal sequence. Just as a B&B approach worked for the tightness/tardiness trade-off, we can attack the stochastic E/T problem in a similar fashion. The search tree is the same as the one in Figure 7.4. In addition, the components needed for a solution algorithm are (i) a dominance property to accelerate the search, (ii) a lower bound for partial sequences, and (iii) an effective heuristic procedure to use at the start. These components exist and resemble those encountered earlier when we addressed the problem of trading off tightness and tardiness. *Dominance.* In the stochastic E/T problem, a pairwise dominance condition holds, similar to that in Property 7.2.

Property 7.4   For two jobs i and j, if $c_i \geq c_j$ and $\sigma_i \leq \sigma_j$, then an optimal schedule exists in which job i precedes job j.

Again, this static dominance condition is determined at the outset and used during branching, when the B&B procedure augments a partial sequence. If we discover that job i dominates job j while neither appears in the partial sequence, then we need not consider the augmented partial sequence constructed by appending job j next. A version of the API condition applies as well.

Lower Bounds. Suppose we have a partial sequence of the jobs, denoted by π, so that π' denotes the set of unscheduled jobs. In the set π', we take the set of coefficients c_j in largest-first order and, separately, the set of standard deviations σ_j in smallest-first order, and we treat these values as if they were paired in the set of unscheduled jobs. These are fictitious jobs due to the rearrangement of coefficients and standard deviations. Next we calculate each fictitious job's contribution to the objective and add it to the portion for the partial sequence π. This total provides a lower bound on the value that could be achieved by completing the partial sequence in the best possible way. The justification is based on the following two properties.

Property 7.5   For any sequence of positive coefficients c_j, the expression $\sum_{j=1}^{n} c_j s_j$ is minimized by sequencing the jobs in nondecreasing order of σ_j.

Property 7.6   For any sequence of σ_j-values, the expression $\sum_{j=1}^{n} c_j s_j$ is minimized by sequencing the jobs in nonincreasing order of c_j.

Initial Solution. Once again, a simple sorting rule can be used to initiate the B&B search. In this case, a logical sorting rule takes the jobs in nondecreasing order of the ratio σ_j/c_j, yielding the sequence 4-2-1-3-5, with an expected cost of 76.97.

The B&B solution begins by testing dominance conditions and discovering that job 1 dominates job 5 and that job 4 dominates jobs 1, 2, and 5. Thus, our branching tree has only two nodes at Level 1 of the search tree, P(3) and P(4), as displayed in Figure 7.8.

At Level 2, the two-job partial sequences under consideration start with jobs 3 or 4 and contain ordered pairs consistent with the dominance conditions. As shown in Figure 7.8, this amounts to four nodes. We can also observe that P(34) and P(43) comprise the same jobs, but the value of the partial sequence is lower for P(34). Any completion of a full sequence starting with 3-4 will therefore have a lower cost than a full sequence starting with 4-3, so we can eliminate sequences that begin with 4-3. This elimination leaves only three partial sequences in the tree, P(34), P(41), and P(42).

At Level 3, the same "subset elimination" condition eliminates P(341) in favor of P(413), P(412) in favor of P(421), and P(423) in favor of P(342). P(415) is

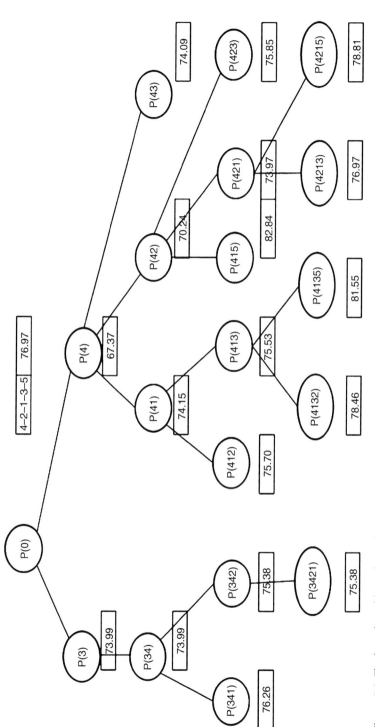

Figure 7.8 The branch-and-bound tree for Example 7.4.

fathomed based on its lower bound of 82.84, which exceeds the value of the initial solution. Pruning the tree in this way leaves only three partial sequences to be examined further. When these are followed all the way to the bottom of the tree, generating five complete sequences, we find that the optimal sequence is 3-4-2-1-5, with an objective function of 75.38.

The stochastic E/T problem can thus be solved by the same B&B approach described in the previous section, just as the approach can be adapted to minimizing the sum of stochastically feasible due dates. In each of these three cases, however, large problem sizes are likely to demand prohibitive amounts of computational effort. Fortunately, large versions of the problem can be solved very effectively by a sorting heuristic that gives priority to the smallest ratio of σ_j^2/c_j (4-3-2-1-5 in Example 7.4). This heuristic procedure is often optimal for small versions of the stochastic E/T problem, and for large n, it is asymptotically optimal. Among all possible sorting rules, only those consistent with this sorting rule are asymptotically optimal.

Because asymptotic optimality does not require normal processing times, the heuristic sorting rule is effective for any processing time distribution. Furthermore, we can use the sorting heuristic to find an initial seed and then perform neighborhood searches on the first several jobs (say, 5–10) to see whether an even better sequence can be found. For subsequent jobs, we can rely on the asymptotic optimality of the heuristic. We can use this sorting rule as a crude heuristic even when jobs are not statistically independent. To estimate job parameters for that purpose, we use their marginal distributions. After the sequence is determined, we can set the due dates using the critical fractile rule, which does not require statistical independence or normality. Although the use of marginal distributions is not theoretically precise, this method can at least generate a reasonable seed for a neighborhood search.

7.5 Using the Lognormal Distribution

The normal distribution as a model for processing times is convenient because it implies that completion times, which are sums of processing times, follow normal distributions as well. Among standard probability distributions that could be used to model realistic processing times, only the normal offers a straightforward characterization for sums of random variables. However, some features of the normal distribution are drawbacks: It is symmetric, it allows for negative outcomes, and when truncated at zero, its cv is relatively small. As we discuss in Appendix A, the lognormal distribution has much wider practical validity: It can approximate the normal very well for low variance processing times, and – unlike the normal – it is also applicable for high variance processing times. It may well be the most useful standard distribution for that purpose:

It is asymmetric (skewed to the right), its outcomes are positive, and its cv can be small or large, without limit. However, sums of lognormal distributions are not lognormal, implying that it would be difficult to model completion times exactly. Nevertheless, the lognormal also serves as a reasonable approximation for the sum of lognormal random variables, using the Fenton–Wilkinson approximation (FWA). We adopt this approximation as our default, because it is effective and computationally efficient, but it would also be possible to use simulated samples instead.

For the time being, we retain the assumption that processing times are independent random variables (with mean μ_j and standard deviation σ_j). If the distribution is lognormal, the processing time random variable has a logarithm described by a normal distribution with mean m_j and standard deviation s_j. The parameters of the two distributions are related as follows:

$$s_j^2 = \ln\left(1 + \sigma_j^2/\mu_j^2\right) \tag{7.16}$$

$$m_j = \ln\left(\mu_j\right) - s_j^2/2 \tag{7.17}$$

Let J denote the set consisting of the initial jobs in sequence, up to and including job j (that is, B_j and $\{j\}$). Given a job sequence, we know that the total processing time for the jobs in J (equal to C_j) follows a distribution with mean $\mu_J = \sum_{k \in J} \mu_k$ and variance $\sigma_J^2 = \sum_{k \in J} \sigma_k^2$. Using the FWA, we treat C_j as a lognormal random variable, so that its logarithm, Y_j, follows a normal distribution. The variance (s_J^2) and mean (m_J) corresponding to Y_j follow Eqs. (7.16) and (7.17):

$$s_J^2 = \ln\left(1 + \sigma_J^2/\mu_J^2\right) \tag{7.18}$$

$$m_J = \ln\left(\mu_J\right) - s_J^2/2 \tag{7.19}$$

Thus, the service level of job j can be calculated as follows:

$$\text{SL}_j = \Pr\left\{C_j \le d_j\right\} = \Pr\left\{Y_j \le \ln\left(d_j\right)\right\}$$

Suppose that we want to determine the minimum due date for which $\text{SL}_j \ge b_j$. Let z_j represent the value at which the cdf of the standard normal distribution equals b_j or $\Phi(z_j) = b_j$. Then the appropriate choice for the due date of job j is

$$\ln\left(d_j\right) = m_J + z_j s_J \tag{7.20}$$

Thus, $d_j = \exp(m_J + z_j s_J)$, and the objective function can be expressed as

$$D = \sum_{j=1}^{n} \exp\left(m_J + z_j s_J\right)$$

For some perspective, substitute m_J from Eq. (7.19) into Eq. (7.20), and rearrange terms to yield $d_j = \mu_J \exp(s_J(z_j - s_J/2))$. In general, s_J cannot be negative so $d_j > \mu_J$ only if $z_j > s_J/2$. Therefore, even for $z_j > 0$, the due date may be less than the mean completion time. In other words, safety time may not be positive even for service-level targets above 0.5.

To get a feel for the calculations involved, we return to Example 7.2 with the job sequence 1-2-3-4-5 but this time assuming that the lognormal distribution applies. The relevant calculations are shown in Figure 7.9, as they might be calculated on a spreadsheet, and we elaborate on the details for job 4.

The completion time for job 4 has the same mean and standard deviation as in the normal case: $\mu_J = 86.0$ and $\sigma_J = 7.25$. The corresponding normal parameters, from Eqs. (7.16) and (7.17), are $m = 4.45$ and $s = 0.0841$. Job 4 has a service-level target of 80%, corresponding to a z-value of 0.842 in the standard normal distribution. Thus, using the formula in Eq. (7.18), we can meet the service level by setting $\ln(d_4) = 4.45 + 0.842(0.0841) = 4.522$. Then $d_4 = \exp(4.522) = 91.98$. Similar calculations apply for the other jobs. Figure 7.9 shows the calculations for both the normal and lognormal cases. In the lognormal case, the sum of the five optimally calculated due dates is $D = 342.7$, which is within 0.2% of the value obtained using the normal distribution.

Example 7.2	SEPT	Lognormal				
Data	Job *j*	1	2	3	4	5
	E(pj)	20	21	22	23	24
	σj	4.0	2.0	3.5	4.5	4.0
	Target	90%	80%	75%	80%	70%
Schedule	Sequence	1	2	3	4	5
Calculations	Mean	20.00	21.00	22.00	23.00	24.00
	Cum. Mean	20.00	41.00	63.00	86.00	110.00
	St. Dev.	4.00	2.00	3.50	4.50	4.00
	Variance	16.00	4.00	12.25	20.25	16.00
	Cum. Var.	16.00	20.00	32.25	52.50	68.50
	Sq. Root	4.00	4.47	5.68	7.25	8.28
	S.L. Target	0.90	0.80	0.75	0.80	0.70
Normal	z value	1.282	0.842	0.674	0.842	0.524	
	Due date	25.1	44.8	66.8	92.1	114.3	**343.2**
Lognormal	Normal s	0.198	0.109	0.090	0.084	0.075	
	Normal m	2.976	3.708	4.139	4.451	4.698	
	z value	1.282	0.842	0.674	0.842	0.524	
	y value	3.230	3.799	4.200	4.522	4.737	
	Due date (x)	25.3	44.7	66.7	92.0	114.1	**342.7**

Figure 7.9 Detailed calculations for Example 7.2 with lognormal processing times.

As this example illustrates, we can make the calculations for the normal case or the lognormal case using spreadsheet technology, provided we already know the job sequence. The example also demonstrates that for low variation jobs, the normal and the lognormal models approximate each other closely.

Once again, we can explore heuristic rules for finding a good job sequence. For example, as shown in Figure 7.9, the SEPT rule achieves $D = 342.7$ using the FWA. If we perform an API search, we again obtain the sequence 2-1-3-4-5, which achieves $D = 342.3$ (an optimal value). We assume independent processing times, so as j grows large, C_j is approximately normal. Therefore, SEPT is asymptotically optimal in the lognormal model and so is its combination with API on the first few jobs.

To minimize $D + \gamma E(T)$ when processing times are lognormal using the FWA, optimal due dates are obtained by $d_j = \exp(m_J + z^* s_J)$, where z^* achieves a service level of $(\gamma - 1)/\gamma$. As shown in Appendix B, once due dates are optimized, the objective function is given by

$$D + \gamma E(T) = \sum_{j=1}^{n} \gamma \mu_J \Phi(s_J - z^*) = \sum_{j=1}^{n} \frac{\mu_J \Phi(s_J - z^*)}{\Phi(-z^*)}$$

In this expression, because we assume independent processing times, s_J tends to decrease when j grows large. This suggests that it is generally desirable to use SEPT, again, to associate large s with small μ, but because s depends on the sequence, this is still just a heuristic. An even better heuristic is to rely on Property 7.1 and select the next job as the one that increases the objective function the least.

Appendix B also develops the expression needed to solve the E/T model. With optimal due dates, the contribution of a job to the objective is $\mu[\alpha\Phi(z^* - s) + \beta\Phi(s - z^*)]$, for $z^* = \Phi^{-1}[\beta/(\alpha + \beta)]$, and the objective function is given by

$$\sum_{j=1}^{n} \mu_J \left[\alpha_j \Phi\left(z_j^* - s_J\right) + \beta_j \Phi\left(s_J - z_j^*\right) \right]$$

and, again, the same heuristics are useful.

No analytic solution has been developed for any of the above three lognormal models. One noteworthy special case arises in minimizing the sum of due dates with equal service-level targets or in minimizing the objective for the tightness/tardiness trade-off. It is predicated on the following theorem (which does not require stochastic independence).

■ **Theorem 7.4** For two jobs j and k, if $p_j \leq_{st} p_k$ then for minimizing D subject to a constant service-level constraint or for minimizing $D + \gamma E(T)$, job j dominates job k.

In other words, stochastically ordered jobs must appear in SEPT order even if separated by other jobs, as can be proven based on an adjacent pairwise interchange argument.

7.6 Setting Release Dates

Our safe scheduling models have so far treated due dates as decision variables. We turn next to a different set of problems, in which due dates are given. First, consider the stochastic E/T problem with a common due date, as it is a special case that can teach us something about the more general case with distinct due dates. This problem contains random processing times, but in other ways, it is identical to the deterministic version, which has been thoroughly analyzed. Thus, a logical first approach in the stochastic case might be to adopt the features of the deterministic counterpart wherever possible. The deterministic solution builds on Theorems 5.1, 5.2, and 5.3. These three results state: (i) Inserted idle time provides no benefit, (ii) a V-shaped schedule is optimal, and (iii) one job completes at the due date. In the stochastic case, of course, we would not expect the last condition to hold, but we might hope the other properties apply. However, as we might guess from examples with the normal distribution, V-shaped schedules may not be optimal because they do not account for variance. The remaining question is whether inserted idle time provides no potential benefit. Unfortunately, this feature does not carry over to the stochastic problem, either. To illustrate, we consider an example with a common due date and identical earliness and tardiness costs among the jobs.

■ **Example 7.5**   Consider the following three-job instance with a common due date and identical costs for earliness and tardiness.

Job j	1	2	3
$E(p_j)$	3.4	1	1
d_j	10	10	10
α_j	1	1	1
β_j	1	1	1

The processing times depend on which of two states of nature occur, as described in the following table.

State	Job j	1	2	3	Probability
S_1	p_j	1	1	1	0.2
S_2	p_j	4	1	1	0.8

In this instance, p_1 is a random variable, but the other two jobs have deterministic processing times. In the deterministic counterpart, job 1 comes first, and the other jobs follow in either order. The optimal schedule begins at time 5.6, so that the second job completes at time 10, and the total E/T cost is 2.

Now suppose we implement the sequence 1-2-3 in the stochastic case. If we start job 1 at time 5.6, the expected total cost is 3.52. If we explore other starting times, we find that starting job 1 at time 5.0 leads to an expected total cost of 3.4, which is the best objective for this sequence. If we schedule job 1 last, the best we can do is to start the schedule at time 8, leading to an expected total cost of 4.4.

Next, we explore the possibility of inserting idle time in the sequence 1-2-3. Suppose we start the schedule at time 5 but constrain the second job from starting earlier than time 9. In other words, when job 1 completes at time 6 (which occurs with probability 0.2), the machine is idle until time 9, when job 2 starts. This schedule achieves an expected total cost of 2.6, which is better than we could achieve with no inserted idle time.

This example reveals a complicating factor in stochastic problems with E/T criteria: It may be helpful to allow inserted idle time between jobs, even though (for the case of a common due date) such idle time would not be beneficial in the deterministic counterpart. Thus, we must pay attention to the general case in which inserted idle time is permitted.

In Example 7.5 the constraint on the start time for the second job is essentially a *release date*, r_j, for job j. If the machine is available before r_j, the machine must wait to start job j; but if the machine becomes free after r_j, the job can start immediately. It is not always necessary to assign an explicit release date to each job. We may start a search for optimal release dates under the assumption that each job has its own release date, but it is ultimately sufficient to describe a schedule by specifying only release dates that have a positive probability of actually delaying a job. We refer to such release dates as *active*. A release date that is not active is redundant because it never causes a machine to wait.

As discussed in Section 5.7, release dates define blocks. A *block* is a sequence of jobs processed without delay. If no release date is specified for a job, it is in the same block as the preceding job. (The only exception would be for the first job: If no release date is specified for the first job, then processing starts at time 0.) In the stochastic case, adjacent blocks may be processed with or without a gap between them, but the expected size of the gap is positive. In the optimal schedule for Example 7.5, we place job 1 first in sequence and take $r_2 = 9$. Job 1 thus belongs to block 1, whereas the other two jobs make up block 2, and the expected gap is $0.2 \times 3 = 0.6$.

Suppose we are given a set of jobs with distinct due dates and E/T costs, and suppose further that the job sequence is given. The task then is to set release dates that minimize the total expected E/T penalty. It is possible to show that the total expected E/T cost is a convex function of the release dates. Essentially, we need to search for the best combination of release dates to minimize this total expected penalty.

When we use a sample-based model, we can find the best combination of release dates by a numerical search, because the problem is convex and thus not difficult in practice.

■ **Example 7.6**   Consider a problem containing $n = 5$ jobs with stochastic processing times. The due date and expected processing time for each job are shown in the following table.

Job j	1	2	3	4	5
$E(p_j)$	3	4	5	6	7
d_j	8	5	17	20	12

The probability distributions are based on four equally likely states of nature.

State	Job j	1	2	3	4	5
GG	p_j	2.6	3.5	3.8	3.2	6.4
GB	p_j	2.8	3.9	4.4	5.5	6.6
BG	p_j	3.2	4.1	5.6	6.5	7.4
BB	p_j	3.4	4.5	6.2	8.8	7.6

The earliness and tardiness costs are given in the next table.

Job j	1	2	3	4	5
α_j	2	1	2	1	4
β_j	5	4	3	3	1

If the jobs are sequenced by EDD (2-1-5-3-4), the optimal release dates are given in the following table.

Job j	2	1	5	3	4
r_j	0	3.9	0	13.0	0

In this solution, release dates of zero allow the job to start as soon as the machine is available. Thus, jobs 2, 5, and 4 may start as soon as the machine completes their predecessors. Job 1 waits until job 2 is finished and follows immediately if job 2 completes at time 3.9 or later. (These completion times correspond to states GB, BG, and BB.) On the other hand, if job 2 completes at time 3.5 (state GG), then the machine remains idle – and job 1 must wait until time 3.9. In this situation, we say that job 1 has an *active* release date, meaning that the release date constrains the start of job 1 in at least one scenario. Similarly, job 3 is assigned an active release date, although it does not correspond to a possible completion time of job 5.

Our model determines optimal release dates for a given sequence, but we still do not have an efficient algorithm for finding the best sequence. For the time being, heuristic procedures such as neighborhood search represent the state of the art in searching for the optimal sequence.

As a footnote to our discussion of release dates, it is possible to show that inserted idle time is never beneficial for the tightness/tardiness trade-off when due dates are decisions. In general, inserted idle time cannot help when the delayed release is associated with a cost that exceeds the earliness penalty, and this is automatically the case for $D + \gamma E(T)$. In the stochastic E/T problem, however, inserted idle time could be valuable in separating the jobs into distinct one-job blocks and reducing the variance of each completion time to the smallest level possible. Such a tactic has little practical significance, so for that reason we assumed no inserted idle time in Theorem 7.3.

7.7 The Stochastic *U*-problem: A Service-level Approach

Thus far, we have studied safe scheduling models in which due dates (or release dates) are decisions. In this section, we turn to models in which due dates are given and release dates are all zero, but we continue to rely on service-level considerations, which are the distinguishing features of safe scheduling.

In Chapter 2, we stated the *U*-problem most simply as minimizing the number of late jobs. The solution algorithm constructed a "before" set B consisting of on-time jobs followed by an "after" set A containing late jobs. This structure can be interpreted as postponing the processing of late jobs so that the remaining jobs can be completed on time. In principle, the set of late jobs can be postponed indefinitely without altering the scheduling objective. Thus, we may equivalently consider the late jobs to be rejected, and Algorithm 2.1 can be viewed as a procedure for minimizing the number of rejected jobs (or maximizing the number of accepted jobs) in the deterministic version of the problem. Accordingly, we pose the stochastic version of the *U*-problem similarly, as a problem of accepting or rejecting jobs. Thus, for the stochastic *U*-problem with service-level constraints, we define set B as the set of jobs that satisfy their given service-level constraints and set A as the set of jobs that do not. The objective is to maximize the number of stochastically on-time jobs or, equivalently, to minimize the number of jobs in A.

To emphasize the parallels between the deterministic *U*-problem and the stochastic *U*-problem with service-level constraints, we look first at a basic special case in which processing ties are stochastically ordered and service-level targets are identical. In this formulation, each job is described by a stochastic processing time, p_j, and a deterministic due date, d_j. The objective is to maximize the number of jobs for which $SL_j = Pr\{C_j \leq d_j\} \geq b$.

The solution method assumes the same form for an optimal sequence that appears in the deterministic solution, as reproduced in Figure 7.10. The form is as follows:

- First, a set B of stochastically on-time jobs, in EDD order.
- Then, a set A of stochastically late jobs, in any order.

Recall that, in the deterministic version, we can assume jobs in set B appear in EDD order. (If any sequence of jobs has no tardiness, then by Theorem 2.6 we know that the EDD sequence for those jobs must have no tardiness.) Likewise, in the stochastic version, we can assume that the jobs in B appear in EDD order. This form is justified by Corollary 6.1 which states that the EDD sequence minimizes the maximum tardiness probability or equivalently maximizes the minimum service level. In other words, if any sequence of jobs is stochastically feasible for a given service level b, then the EDD sequence for those jobs is stochastically feasible. Building on this result, we can adapt the solution algorithm for the deterministic U-problem to the stochastic version, as specified in Algorithm 7.1.

Algorithm 7.1 *Minimizing U with Identical Service-level Targets and Stochastically-ordered Jobs*

Step 1. Index the jobs using EDD order and place all jobs in B. Let set A be empty.

Step 2. For each job in B, determine whether its service level is met. If all jobs in B meet the service level, stop: B must be optimal. Otherwise, identify the first stochastically tardy job in B. Suppose that turns out to be the kth job in sequence.

Step 3. Identify the job with the largest $E[p_j]$ among the first k jobs in sequence. Remove that job from B and place it in A. Return to Step 2.

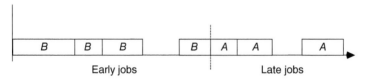

Figure 7.10 The form of a sequence that maximizes the number of stochastically feasible jobs.

The implementation of Step 2 requires that we analyze the probability distribution of C_j, the completion time of the jth job in sequence, to calculate the corresponding service level attained. This requirement raises the same challenge we confronted in other safe scheduling models – that is, the need to determine the properties of the random variable C_j. For a general solution, we would need to rely on a sample-based approach, but a direct approach is possible in special cases. One such case occurs when $b \geq 0.5$ and the processing times are independent and normally distributed with agreeable means and variances; that is, if $\mu_i < \mu_k$ then $\sigma_i \leq \sigma_k$.

■ **Example 7.7**   Consider a problem containing $n = 5$ jobs, as described in the table.

Job j	1	2	3	4	5
$E[p_j]$	10	70	60	40	30
σ_j	2	12	12	8	5
d_j	20	75	80	120	150

The processing times are independent, each drawn from a normal distribution with mean and standard deviation shown. $SL_j \geq b = 0.8$ is required.

The parameters are agreeable and $b > 0.5$, so Algorithm 7.1 is applicable. The structure for the necessary calculations is shown in Figure 7.11, in a spreadsheet format. The jobs are already indexed by EDD, as required in Step 1. In Step 2, the first stochastically tardy job is job 2, as summarized in Figure 7.11. In Step 3, the longest job among the first two in sequence is job 2; thus job 2 is removed from B and placed in A. In the next pass at Steps 2 and 3, job 3 is removed from B and placed in A. Thereafter, no stochastically tardy jobs remain in B. The algorithm yields two optimal sequences: 1-4-5-2-3 and 1-4-5-3-2, corresponding to the two different ways of sequencing the late jobs.

Even with stochastic ordering, the similarity in the solution procedures for the deterministic and stochastic versions does not completely generalize. The main complication relates to the sequencing of the stochastically on-time jobs – those in set B. In Algorithm 7.1, we relied on EDD sequencing in set B, but EDD is not necessarily optimal when we allow job-dependent service-level requirements b_j, as the following example demonstrates.

■ **Example 7.8**   Consider the problem of sequencing two jobs with stochastic processing times and the following parameters.

	A	B	C	D	E	F	G	H
1	Example 7.7							
2								
3	Data	Job j	1	2	3	4	5	
4		E(pj)	10	70	60	40	30	
5		σj	2	12	12	8	5	
6		dj	20	75	80	120	150	
7		Target	80%	80%	80%	80%	80%	
8								
9	Schedule	Sequence	1	2	3	4	5	
10								
11	Calculations	Mean	10.00	70.00	60.00	40.00	30.00	
12		Cum. Mean	10.00	80.00	140.00	180.00	210.00	
13		St. Dev.	2.00	12.00	12.00	8.00	5.00	
14		Variance	4.00	144.00	144.00	64.00	25.00	
15		Cum. Var.	4.00	148.00	292.00	356.00	381.00	
16		Sq. Root	2.00	12.17	17.09	18.87	19.52	
17		Due date	20.00	75.00	80.00	120.00	150.00	
18								
19		z value	5.000	-0.411	-3.511	-3.180	-3.074	
20		Service Level	100%	34%	0%	0%	0%	
21		Feasible	1	0	0	0	0	1
22								

First Pass	Sequence	1	2	3	4	5
	Service Level	100%	34%	0%	0%	0%

Second Pass	Sequence	1	3	4	5	2
	Service Level	100%	79%	75%	74%	0%

Third Pass	Sequence	1	4	5	2	3
	Service Level	100%	100%	100%	0%	0%

Figure 7.11 Summary of calculations for Example 7.7.

Job j	1	2
d_j	5.0	6.0
b_j	0.5	0.9
$E(p_j)$	1	3.5

Job 1 has a deterministic processing time, but job 2 has a processing time that follows a uniform distribution on the interval (1, 6).

Because $p_1 = 1 \leq p_2$, the processing times are stochastically ordered ($p_1 \leq_{st} p_2$). Figure 7.12a describes the situation for the EDD sequence. Two vertical segments with height 1, occurring at times 0 and 1, mark the start and finish of

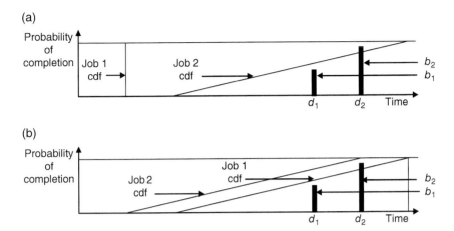

Figure 7.12 Graph for Example 7.8: (a) sequence 1-2 and (b) sequence 2-1.

job 1. The uncertainty in C_2 is represented by a linear cdf. Finally, the two service-level requirements are represented by vertical bars with heights b_j at the respective due dates d_j. Clearly, job 1 exceeds its service-level requirement because its cdf reaches a height of 1 prior to d_1. But job 2 fails to meet its requirement because by d_2, its cdf does not reach the height of b_2. Figure 7.12b demonstrates, however, that if we interchange the jobs and sequence against EDD order, then both service-level constraints are met.

Figure 7.12 illustrates a *stochastic Gantt chart*. In a regular Gantt chart, jobs are always depicted as rectangles, and job 1 is depicted this way in Figure 7.12a because its start and finish times are not uncertain. The height of its rectangle is equal to 1, and we can interpret the vertical line at time 1 as the cdf of C_1. The same job appears in Figure 7.12b, but in that case, its start time and finish time are uncertain and represented by cdfs. The area between the start cdf and the completion cdf of job 1 is the same in both figures and equals the expected processing time of the job. The horizontal line at the top of the figure can be interpreted as part of the cdf of the start time of the activity. As the figure demonstrates, a stochastic Gantt chart shows the probability of completion as a function of time (because it involves cdfs) and can also be used to check whether particular service levels are met.

Example 7.8 shows that the reliance on EDD sequencing for set B has its limitations. To make progress, we need a procedure for determining whether a feasible sequence exists for any given set of accepted jobs. As it happens, a relatively simple procedure is available. This *feasibility check* resembles the backward sequencing of Theorems 3.1 and 6.4. It starts by checking whether any job would satisfy its service-level constraint if scheduled last in set B. (The distribution of the last job's completion time does not depend on knowledge of the job sequence.) Any such job may be scheduled last in B and removed from further consideration. The procedure is then repeated for the remaining jobs in B. Because the procedure is constructive, it builds a sequence from back to front and yields a feasible sequence whenever the set of jobs is feasible.

Next, we must embed the feasibility check in the logic for accepting or rejecting jobs. If the jobs are stochastically ordered, we can adapt the logic of Algorithm 7.1, using the feasibility check in place of EDD sequencing.

Algorithm 7.2 *Minimizing U with Service-level Constraints and Stochastically Ordered Jobs*

Step 1. Sequence the jobs by SEPT (ties may be broken arbitrarily), and place all jobs in the unresolved set, so that sets A and B are empty.

Step 2. Tentatively add the first unresolved job to B and apply the feasibility check. If the result is feasible, record the sequence and add the job to B permanently. Otherwise add the job to A.

Step 3. If the unresolved set is not empty, return to Step 2. Otherwise, stop. The last recorded sequence of the jobs in B is optimal.

Algorithm 7.2 does not require stochastic independence: It applies for linearly associated processing times as well. To illustrate the application of the algorithm, we find the solution to Example 7.9 (which contains stochastically ordered and linearly associated processing times).

■ **Example 7.9** Consider a problem containing $n = 5$ jobs. The due date and expected processing time for each job are shown in the following table.

Job j	1	2	3	4	5
$E(p_j)$	6	8	10	12	14
d_j	17	16	34	40	25

Each job has a different processing time under four states of nature, as follows.

State	Job j	1	2	3	4	5
1	p_j	4.1	5.6	7.0	8.4	9.8
2	p_j	5.3	7.2	9.0	10.8	12.6
3	p_j	6.4	8.8	11.0	13.2	15.4
4	p_j	8.2	10.4	13.0	15.6	18.2

The service-level targets for the jobs are shown in the following table.

Job j	1	2	3	4	5
b_j	90%	60%	50%	80%	60%

In Step 1, all jobs are unresolved, and the SEPT order is 1-2-3-4-5. When we consider the set {1}, we find that job 1 meets its target service level because it is certain to complete by its due date ($d_1 = 17.0$), so in Step 2, we add job 1 to set B. When we consider the set {1, 2}, we find that job 1 cannot meet its target if it follows job 2 (as per EDD), but job 2 meets its target if it follows job 1. Therefore, in Step 2, we add job 2 to B and record the sequence 1-2. As we continue through the SEPT list, jobs 1, 2, 3, and 4 are each feasible, so they are added to B consecutively. After we add job 4, we record the sequence produced by the feasibility check, 1-2-4-3. But tentatively adding job 5 leads to infeasibility – no job can be feasibly scheduled in the last position. Therefore, job 5 is rejected, and the optimal solution is $|A| = 1$.

Suppose we use EDD (2-1-5-3-4) for the feasibility check of the jobs in set B. Because job 1 cannot feasibly follow job 2, it is rejected; jobs 5 and 3 are then accepted, but job 4 is rejected in the last position. Thus, $|A| = 2$, demonstrating again that EDD is suboptimal for general b_j. However, if $b_j > b_k$ implies $d_j \leq d_k$ then these parameters are called *agreeable*. It turns out that when due dates and service level targets are agreeable, then EDD is valid. In other words, we can extend Algorithm 7.1 for this case.

■ **Theorem 7.5** For stochastically ordered processing times, if the service-level constraints and the due dates are agreeable, then the number of jobs that must be rejected to meet all service-level constraints is minimized by Algorithm 7.1.

Proof. For the time being, assume that processing times are independent. If all jobs are stochastically feasible, the theorem holds, so assume at least one job is stochastically tardy. Therefore, during the execution of Algorithm 7.1, we encounter infeasibility at least once. Whenever this happens, consider two cases. In Case 1, the longest job by expectation in the infeasible set is the last one. Therefore, we know with certainty that to achieve feasibility for the other jobs in the subset, it is sufficient to reject this one. We also know, by an argument similar to that in the proof of Theorem 6.8, that it is the best choice for minimizing the necessary rejections among the jobs that follow the subset. In Case 2, the longest job by expectation is not last. To complete the proof for independent processing times, it remains to show that rejecting this job renders the last job feasible. We leave this part of the proof as an exercise. The final step is to remove the independence assumption and extend these results to linearly associated jobs by invoking Theorem 6.7. □

Here is a summary of the results known for the problem of maximizing the number of stochastically on-time jobs. The problem is NP-hard in general. However, if we know that the processing times are stochastically ordered, then we can find solutions with the general feasibility check and Algorithm 7.2. If we also know that due dates and service-level targets are agreeable, then we can find solutions with EDD as a basis for the feasibility check and Algorithm 7.1. In both cases, the result extends to linearly associated processing times.

7.8 The Stochastic *U*-problem: An Economic Approach

As discussed in the previous section, we can interpret the stochastic U-problem as constructing a schedule containing two sets – a set of stochastically on-time jobs and a set of stochastically tardy jobs – with the objective of minimizing the number in the latter set. Alternatively, we can interpret the problem as one of accepting or rejecting jobs – with the understanding that accepted jobs must be stochastically on time – and minimizing the number of rejected jobs. Rather than counting jobs, an economic approach to the U-problem involves specifying the revenues and costs for various outcomes and then maximizing an objective corresponding to expected net revenue. If we can capture the revenues and costs, then the economic objective function may reflect reality better than the traditional summary measure.

In the stochastic case, we can distinguish between a job that is rejected intentionally and a job that is tardy by chance. That is, we may accept a job with the intention of completing it on time, but the stochastic nature of its processing time (and the processing times of preceding jobs) may result in tardiness despite our intention. This structure leads to a more elaborate model: Every job that is completed early or on time represents a reward of R_E, a tardy job generates a reward of $R_T < R_E$, and the reward for rejecting a job is R_R. We require

$$R_E > R_R > R_T \tag{7.21}$$

Our objective is to maximize the expected total reward. The assumption in Eq. (7.21) is economically sound: If R_R were not strictly larger than R_T, we would have no incentive to reject a job – that is, we would actually process all jobs even if they were stochastically tardy because the reward would be greater than for rejecting them. Similarly, if R_R were not strictly smaller than R_E, we would reject all jobs right away. Thus the conditions of Eq. (7.21) allow for the most general schedule structure, given that the rewards are lump sums and not a function of earliness or tardiness.

By subtracting R_R from all rewards, we change the total expected reward by a constant, but the optimal sequence does not change. Therefore, without loss of generality, we may assume that $R_E > 0$, $R_R = 0$, and $R_T < 0$ when we search for an optimal schedule. After this adjustment, any optimal solution must be nonnegative because by rejecting all jobs, we can guarantee a total reward of zero.

To facilitate rejection decisions, we can use the service-level notion and derive a constraint that all accepted jobs must satisfy. As usual, let SL_j denote the probability that job j is on time. Then the expected reward $E[R_j]$ for job j when it is accepted becomes

$$E[R_j] = R_E SL_j + R_T (1 - SL_j)$$

This contribution is not positive unless

$$E[R_j] = R_E SL_j + R_T (1 - SL_j) > 0$$

implying that the service level is above breakeven when

$$SL_j > -\frac{R_T}{R_E - R_T} \tag{7.22}$$

The right-hand side of this inequality serves as a legitimate probability because $R_T < 0$. Furthermore, rejecting any job can only help reduce the tardiness of other jobs, so the optimal solution cannot call for accepting any job whose expected reward is negative. Therefore, if Eq. (7.22) is violated for any accepted job at any sequence position, that sequence cannot be optimal. The condition in Eq. (7.22) is necessary for each job, but not sufficient for optimality. For example, it may be suboptimal to accept an early job whose service level barely satisfies the service-level target given by Eq. (7.22). Although the direct result of accepting such a job would be a positive expected reward for the job, the consequence may be to reduce the service levels of later jobs and lead indirectly to a net loss.

■ **Example 7.10** Consider a problem containing $n = 5$ jobs, with accept/reject decisions possible. The processing times are independent, normally distributed random variables. The reward for completing a job on time is 20, and the penalty for completing a job late is 10. Our objective is to find the schedule with the maximum expected profit (net reward). The due date and expected processing time for each job are shown in the following table.

Job j	1	2	3	4	5
$E(p_j)$	30	40	50	60	70
σ_j	5	7	4	5	6
d_j	60	80	90	120	160

We illustrate the calculations needed to evaluate the sequence 1-2-3-4-5. In the layout shown, expected rewards that would literally display as negative in the last row of calculations are replaced by zero to signify rejection. The problem size in this example is small enough that we can enumerate the possible sequences, and we discover that the maximum total expected reward is 13.19, as shown in Figure 7.13. In this example, it is optimal to accept jobs 2 and 5 that are exposed to tardiness (as indicated by service levels of 88 and 97%, respectively) but for which the service level exceeds the break-even value of 58.3%.

It is possible to construct examples showing that the EDD sequence may not be optimal for the accepted jobs. In general, however, it is still necessary to search among all possible sequences for an optimal solution, although the break-even service-level target helps to curtail the search.

Although no optimization algorithm for this problem has been developed and tested, we can produce good solutions using the Evolutionary Solver (see Chapter 4) with a spreadsheet layout such as the one shown in Figure 7.14. The Evolutionary Solver can also be implemented with a sample-based model as demonstrated by Example 7.11.

Example 7.10								
Revenues	RE	20		RR	15	RT	8	
transformed	RE	5		B/E	0.583	RT	-7	
Data	Job *j*	1	2	3	4	5		
	E(pj)	30	40	50	60	70		
	σj	5	7	4	5	6		
	dj	60	80	90	120	160		
	RE	5	5	5	5	5		
	RT	-7	-7	-7	-7	-7		
Schedule	Sequence	1	2	5	3	4		
Calculations	Mean	30	40	70	50	60		
	Cum. Mean	30.00	70.00	140.00	190.00	250.00		
	Stan.Dev.	5.00	7.00	6.00	4.00	5.00		
	Variance	25.00	49.00	36.00	16.00	25.00		
	Cum. Var	25.00	74.00	110.00	126.00	151.00		
	Sq. Root	5.00	8.60	10.49	11.22	12.29		
	Due date	60.00	80.00	160.00	90.00	120.00		
	S.L.	1.00	0.88	0.97	0.00	0.00		
	E(Rj)	5.00	3.53	4.66	0.00	0.00	13.19

Figure 7.13 Spreadsheet model and calculations for Example 7.10.

Example 7.11		RE	20		B/E			
		RT	-10		0.333			
Data								
	Job j	1	2	3	4	5		
Scenario	dj	7.8	7.5	17	20	12		
GG	pj	2.6	3.5	3.8	3.2	6.4		
GB		2.8	3.9	4.4	5.5	6.6		
BG		3.2	4.1	5.6	6.5	7.4		
BB		3.4	4.5	6.2	8.8	7.6		
	Sequence	2	1	3	4	5		
	Due date	7.5	7.8	17	20	12		
	Processing times							
	GG	3.5	2.6	3.8	3.2	6.4		
	GB	3.9	2.8	4.4	5.5	6.6		
	BG	4.1	3.2	5.6	6.5	7.4		
	BB	4.5	3.4	6.2	8.8	7.6		
	Completion times							
	GG	3.5	6.1	9.9	13.1	19.5		
	GB	3.9	6.7	11.1	16.6	23.2		
	BG	4.1	7.3	12.9	19.4	26.8		
	BB	4.5	7.9	14.1	22.9	30.5		
	Rewards							
	GG	20.0	20.0	20.0	20.0	-10.0		
	GB	20.0	20.0	20.0	20.0	-10.0		
	BG	20.0	20.0	20.0	20.0	-10.0		
	BB	20.0	-10.0	20.0	-10.0	-10.0		
	Average	20.0	12.5	20.0	12.5	-10.0		
	Adjusted	20.0	12.5	20.0	12.5	0.0	65.0	

Figure 7.14 Spreadsheet model and calculations for Example 7.11.

■ **Example 7.11** Consider a problem containing $n = 5$ jobs, with accept/reject decisions possible. The reward for completing a job on time is $R_E = 20$, and the penalty for completing a job late is $R_T = -10$. Due dates and expected processing time for each job are shown in the following table.

Job j	1	2	3	4	5
$E(p_j)$	3.0	4.0	5.0	6.0	7.0
d_j	7.8	7.5	17.0	20.0	12.0

Each job has a different processing time under four states of nature, as follows.

State	Job *j*	1	2	3	4	5
1	p_j	2.6	3.5	3.8	3.2	6.4
2	p_j	2.8	3.9	4.4	5.5	6.6
3	p_j	3.2	4.1	5.6	6.5	7.4
4	p_j	3.4	4.5	6.2	8.8	7.6

In Figure 7.11 we show the calculations that are needed in a sample-based model such as Example 7.9. Here, again, we illustrate the EDD sequence, which turns out to produce the maximum expected total revenue of 65.

7.9 Summary

In this chapter, we introduced safe scheduling and discussed several problems that have a safe scheduling flavor – that is, problems in which safety time plays a key role. Using an analogy to stochastic inventory theory, we identified two main approaches to sizing time buffers: meeting service-level constraints or minimizing expected net revenue. We looked first at the problem of choosing due dates that are as tight as possible while maintaining stochastic feasibility.

Next we considered the tightness/tardiness trade-off. In that problem, due date tightness and job tardiness are balanced by a single arbitrary parameter, but its value ultimately determines the service-level target that characterizes the optimal solution. We examined a B&B algorithm for that problem, relying on three components: (i) an effective heuristic procedure that produces a good initial solution, (ii) dominance properties that limit the amount of branching needed, and (iii) a lower bound calculation that eliminates unproductive partial solutions. The algorithm could also be adapted to minimizing the sum of due dates while meeting given service levels.

Thirdly, we examined the stochastic E/T problem, in which the objective is to minimize the expected total cost due to earliness and tardiness. In that problem, the economics of earliness cost and tardiness cost lead individually to optimal service levels for the jobs, and, again, a B&B algorithm can provide optimal solutions to the sequencing problem. In Appendix B, we show that the optimal due dates for the tightness/tardiness problem are optimal for the stochastic E/T problem with a particular choice of unit earliness and tardiness costs. Furthermore, the tightness/tardiness objective can be viewed as the sum of total flowtime and the E/T objective.

In conjunction with the three problems, we studied different ways to model the stochastic behavior of processing times. The most general of these uses a table of realizations to represent a discrete probability distribution or a sample of equally likely outcomes. A sample-based approach is quite flexible and accommodates such traits as correlation and linear association. An alternative approach is to assume that processing times are independent and follow a standard distribution. Our examples focused mostly on the normal distribution. With that assumption, completion times are also normally distributed, providing tractability in the analysis. However, as long as we are willing to assume stochastic independence, even when the normal assumption does not apply, completion times are likely to be very close to normally distributed, meaning that the B&B algorithms should produce solutions that are at least very close to optimal. In Section 7.5, we also looked briefly at the use of the lognormal distribution, which exhibits several properties that make it an appealing choice for stochastic scheduling models. This is especially true if we replace the assumption of stochastic independence with linear association, where completion times are approximately lognormal. We demonstrated the types of calculations involved in using the lognormal and pointed out that under the independence assumption, it is closely approximated by the normal distribution in the context of safe scheduling models but that it also allows us to remove the independence assumption and replace it by linear association without sacrificing too much tractability.

No polynomial solution is known for any of the three safe scheduling problems with due dates as decisions. (We elaborate on their complexity in the Research Notes that accompany this book.) For each of the problems, we identified a sequencing heuristic that is asymptotically optimal, meaning that we can essentially find optimal schedules for problems with a very large number of jobs, while the B&B algorithm can be applied to small- or medium-size instances. An important lesson, however, is that the B&B approach, which has been refined through many applications to deterministic sequencing problems, provides viable solutions for some stochastic sequencing problems as well.

We then turned to problems in which due dates are given. We first explored the stochastic E/T problem with a common due date and found that release times and inserted idle times could play a key role. Those features make it difficult to find optimal solutions. We then studied two variations of the stochastic U-problem, summarizing what we know about the problem from a service-level perspective and an economic perspective.

Finally, we point out one important feature of the stochastic models in Chapters 6 and 7: The scheduling decisions are essentially made at the start of the problem, with potential randomness described by probability distributions. When the schedule is executed, and one or more of those random variables are realized, the model allows for no opportunity to revisit the scheduling decisions. In some applications, we can imagine the possibility of waiting until random variables are observed and then rescheduling in some way. Such dynamic models tend to be difficult to analyze and are beyond the scope of our coverage. Static models, however, can always serve as a heuristic basis for dynamic decisions, providing a base plan that we can update dynamically over time.

Exercises

7.1   Consider the problem of minimizing D subject to stochastic feasibility. For n independent stochastic jobs, we say that the service-level constraints b_j and the due dates d_j are *agreeable* if $b_j > b_k$ implies $d_j \leq d_k$.

a) Construct a counterexample to show that when service levels and processing times are agreeable, SEPT may not minimize D.

b) It has been conjectured that if service levels and processing times are agreeable, and the processing times are stochastically ordered, then SEPT minimizes D. Prove the conjecture for the special case where all service levels are equal.

7.2   Consider the problem of finding the minimum value of D with normally distributed processing times and a given service level corresponding to $z = 1$. Construct a three-job example to show that the EDD heuristic procedure does not always produce the minimum value of D.

7.3   Find the optimal solution to Example 7.2 using a branch-and-bound procedure.

7.4   Consider a problem containing $n = 5$ jobs. The expected processing time for each job is shown in the following table.

Job j	1	2	3	4	5
$E(p_j)$	6.0	8.0	10.0	12.0	14.0

Assume that four equally likely states of nature exist, with the processing time realizations shown below.

State	Job j	1	2	3	4	5
31	p_j	4.1	5.6	7.0	8.4	9.8
32	p_j	5.3	7.2	9.0	10.8	12.6
33	p_j	6.4	8.8	11.0	13.2	15.4
34	p_j	8.2	10.4	13.0	15.6	18.2

a) Suppose all service levels are 50%. Find the sequence and the individual due dates that minimize D.

b) Suppose all service levels are 75%. Find the sequence and the individual due dates that minimize D.

c) Suppose that jobs 1 and 4 have service levels of 75% and that the other service levels are 50%. Find the sequence and the individual due dates that minimize D.

7.5 Consider a problem containing $n = 6$ jobs with stochastic processing times. The processing times are independent, each drawn from a normal distribution with the mean and standard deviation shown in the table, and each job has been assigned a service level, also shown in the table.

Job j	1	2	3	4	5	6
$E(p_j)$	20	24	28	30	32	36
σ_j	3.0	2.5	2.0	3.5	4.0	2.0
b_j	90%	80%	85%	90%	85%	80%

a) Compare the performance of the SEPT, EDD, and SEPT followed by API search heuristics to discover which rule generates the minimum value of D.

b) Suppose instead that the processing times follow lognormal distributions. For each of the three rules in (a), calculate the difference between the lognormal approximation for D and the normal approximation for D.

7.6 Consider the lower bound calculation in the problem of finding optimal due dates when service-level targets are given. For the jobs in a partial sequence, the sum of their due dates can be computed precisely. For the set of unscheduled jobs, the lower bound calls for taking the corresponding set of means μ_j in smallest-first order and the standard deviations σ_j in smallest-first order and treating these values as if they were paired (i.e. as if both belonged to the same job). Then the sum of due dates generated by these fictitious unscheduled jobs is added to the component for the partial sequence. Prove that this total is a lower bound on the value that could be achieved by completing the partial sequence in the best possible way.

7.7 Consider the threshold of Eq. (7.12), where jobs i and j satisfy $\mu_i - \mu_j < 0$ and $\sigma_i^2 - \sigma_j^2 > 0$.

a) Show that Eq. (7.12) yields 0 if and only if Property 7.3 holds. In other words, if we check the simpler Property 7.3 first, we do not need the max structure in Eq. (7.12).

b) Given a partial sequence that does not include jobs i and j, with $\sigma_B^2 \geq \sigma_B^2(i,j)$, show that job i precedes job j in an optimal sequence of the remaining jobs, even if other jobs are scheduled between them.

In other words, for jobs in SEPT order that do not satisfy Property 7.3, we obtain a similar but dynamic dominance condition.

7.8 Consider a problem containing $n = 5$ jobs with stochastically independent processing times, each drawn from a lognormal distribution with the mean and coefficient of variation shown in the table.

Job j	1	2	3	4	5
$E(p_j)$	1.00	1.01	1.02	1.2	1.21
cv_j	0.4	0.4	0.4	2.0	2.0

The target service level, b, is 65% for each of the five jobs. (Recall that our default is to use the FWA for calculations.)
a) Find the EDD solution and show that it is optimal. (*Hint*: By Theorem 7.4 only 10 candidate sequences need be considered. But only two of them are API stable.)
b) What is the EDD solution for $b = 0.6$? Compare with SEPT in terms of API stability and objective function value. Starting with SEPT, perform an API neighborhood search and compare the result to the EDD sequence.
c) What is the EDD solution for $b = 0.7$? Compare with SEPT in terms of API stability and objective function value.
d) Observe that the jobs are indexed in SEPT order and their variances are also increasing. Explain why Property 7.2 does not necessarily hold.
e) Suppose now we wish to minimize $D + \gamma E(T)$ instead. For this particular example, show that SEPT is optimal for any γ level.

7.9 Consider a problem containing $n = 5$ jobs with stochastic processing times, each of which follows a normal distribution with known mean and standard deviation. In addition, job due dates are decision variables.

Job j	1	2	3	4	5
μ_j	17	20	24	25	30
σ_j	3	4	2	5	3

a) Find the optimal sequence and the optimal due dates for minimizing $D + \gamma E(T)$ when $\gamma = 2$.
b) Repeat (a) for $\gamma = 10$.

7.10 Consider a problem containing $n = 5$ jobs with stochastic processing times and due dates as decisions. The randomness in the processing times can be represented adequately by three states of nature: good, normal, and bad, with probabilities of 0.2, 0.5, and 0.3, respectively.

State	Job j	1	2	3	4	5
Good	p_j	5	3	7	6	8
Normal	p_j	7	6	8	10	12
Bad	p_j	9	12	10	15	14

The earliness and tardiness costs are given in the next table.

Job j	1	2	3	4	5
α_j	2	1	2	1	4
β_j	5	4	3	3	1

Find the optimal sequence and the optimal job due dates for minimizing the expected E/T cost.

7.11 The purpose of this exercise is to prove the proposition that no transitive sorting algorithm can solve the stochastic E/T problem optimally. Consider three jobs with $(\alpha_1 + \beta_1)\phi(z_1^*) = (\alpha_2 + \beta_2)\phi(z_2^*) = 1$, $(\alpha_3 + \beta_3)\phi(z_3^*) = 5$, $\sigma_1^2 = \sigma_2^2 = 1$, and $\sigma_3^2 = 2^2$. Any transitive sorting rule must sequence identical jobs consecutively, because they have the same values. To prove that no such rule exists, show that the optimal sequence places job 3 between the two identical jobs.

Bibliography

van den Akker, J.M. and Hoogeveen, J.A. (2008). Minimizing the number of late jobs in a stochastic setting using a chance constraint. *Journal of Scheduling* **11**: 59–69.

Arrow, K.J., Harris, T., and Marschak, J. (1951). Optimal inventory policy. *Econometrica* **19** (3): 250–272.

Baker, K.R. (2014a). Setting optimal due dates in a basic safe scheduling model. *Computers & Operations Research* **41**: 109–114.

Baker, K.R. (2014b). Minimizing earliness and tardiness costs in stochastic scheduling. *European Journal of Operational Research* **236**: 445–452.

Baker, K.R. and Trietsch, D. (2009). Safe scheduling: setting due dates in single-machine problems. *European Journal of Operational Research* **196**: 69–77.

Baker, K.R. and Trietsch, D. (2015). Trading off due-date tightness and job tardiness in a basic scheduling model. *Journal of Scheduling* **18**: 305–309.

Balut, S.J. (1973). Scheduling to minimize the number of late jobs when set-up and processing times are uncertain. *Management Science* **19**: 1283–1288.

Cai, X. and Zhou, S. (1996). Scheduling stochastic jobs with asymmetric earliness and tardiness penalties. *Naval Research Logistics* **44**: 531–557.

Dodin, B. (1996). Determining the optimal sequences and the distributional properties of their completion times in stochastic flow shops. *Computers and Operations Research* **23**: 829–843.

Kise, H. and Ibaraki, T. (1983). On Balut's algorithm and NP-completeness for a chance constrained scheduling problem. *Management Science* **29**: 384–388.

Lemos, R.F. and Roncini, D.P. (2015). Heuristics for the stochastic single-machine problem with E/T costs. *International Journal of Production Economics* **168**: 131–142.

Portougal, V. and Trietsch, D. (1998). Makespan-related criteria for comparing schedules in stochastic environments. *Journal of the Operational Research Society* **49**: 1188–1195.

Portougal, V. and Trietsch, D. (2006). Setting due dates in a stochastic single machine environment. *Computers & Operations Research* **33**: 1681–1694.

Soroush, H.M. (1999). Sequencing and due-date determination in the stochastic single machine problem with earliness and tardiness costs. *European Journal of Operational Research* **113**: 450–468.

Soroush, H.M. and Fredendall, L.D. (1994). The stochastic single machine scheduling problem with earliness and tardiness costs. *European Journal of Operational Research* **77**: 287–302.

Trietsch, D. (1993). Scheduling flights at hub airports. *Transportation Research Part B (Methodology)* **27B**: 133–150.

Trietsch, D. and Baker, K.R. (2008). Minimizing the number of tardy jobs with stochastically-ordered processing times. *Journal of Scheduling* **11**: 71–73.

Yano, C.A. (1987a). Setting planned leadtimes in serial production systems with tardiness costs. *Management Science* **33**: 95–106.

Yano, C.A. (1987b). Planned leadtimes for serial production systems. *IIE Transactions* **19**: 300–307.

8

Extensions of the Basic Model

8.1 Introduction

The basic single-machine model provides an opportunity to study a variety of scheduling criteria as well as a number of solution techniques. These themes have been central to the coverage in the preceding chapters. The assumptions of the basic model are highly specific, however, and for the results and insights to be of some general value, the assumptions must be extended to more complicated and realistic situations. We have already taken this route with respect to some assumptions. This chapter deals with additional models in which the assumptions of the basic model are relaxed.

We introduced the basic model with seven assumptions, two of which turned out to be derived conditions for regular measures. The assumptions were:

C1.   There are n single-operation jobs simultaneously available for processing (at time zero).
C2.   Machines can process at most one job at a time.
C3.   Setup times for the jobs are independent of job sequence and are included in processing times.
C4.   Job descriptors are deterministic and known in advance.
C5.   Machines are continuously available (no breakdowns occur).
C6.   Machines are never kept idle while work is waiting.
C7.   Once an operation begins, it proceeds without interruption.

In our coverage of stochastic models, we relaxed C4 and explored the implications of scheduling with uncertain information. We also encountered a situation in which it becomes desirable to violate C6. In this chapter, we examine variations of the basic model with a special focus on conditions C1, C3, C4, C6, and C7.

Principles of Sequencing and Scheduling, Second Edition. Kenneth R. Baker and Dan Trietsch.
© 2019 John Wiley & Sons, Inc. Published 2019 by John Wiley & Sons, Inc.

We can generalize condition C1 in several ways. For instance, the jobs to be scheduled may not all be available simultaneously. Instead, jobs may become available intermittently and therefore have different release dates. This pattern gives rise to a *dynamic* version of the single-machine model, in contrast to the *static* version prescribed by the original assumptions. Problems with nonsimultaneous arrivals are discussed in Section 8.2. Condition C6 – which we questioned in the previous chapter – and condition C7, which turned out to be implicit in the basic model, must both be revisited in the case of nonsimultaneous arrivals.

Another generalization of C1 occurs when precedence restrictions exist among sets of jobs. Such constraints express technological requirements or management policies and give rise to sets of *related* jobs. In this case, jobs with predecessors are not truly available for processing at time zero. Problems with related jobs are discussed in Section 8.3.

Condition C3 can be generalized by allowing sequence-dependent setup times. This situation arises when the setup time is not a constant for each job but depends on the previous job in sequence. Such a model relies on the "traveling salesperson problem," which is treated in detail in Section 8.4. In Section 8.5, we turn our attention to stochastic versions of the traveling salesperson problem, in which conditions C3 and C4 are relaxed together.

8.2 Nonsimultaneous Arrivals

The static version of a single-machine problem refers to the situation in which all jobs are simultaneously available for processing. Many sequencing problems, however, require models that accommodate different release dates. For example, jobs may occur in response to customer demands that appear over time. Alternatively, the single-machine model may represent a bottleneck facility, and the arrival of jobs to that facility may be staggered due to upstream operations.

When release dates are different, the set of available tasks changes over time, giving rise to a dynamic version of the single-machine model. An immediate consequence of allowing different release dates is the need to reexamine the questions of inserted idle time (condition C6) and job preemption (condition C7). To illustrate the role these two factors play, consider the two-job example shown below.

■ **Example 8.1**   Consider a problem containing $n = 2$ jobs, with a criterion of total job tardiness. In addition, let r_j denote the release date of job j.

Job j	1	2
r_j	0	1
p_j	5	2
d_j	7	4

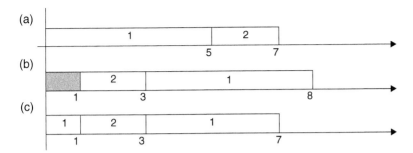

Figure 8.1 Three schedules for the two-job example.

Only one sequence satisfies conditions C6 and C7 by avoiding all inserted idle time and preemption, that is, the sequence 1-2 (see Figure 8.1a). That sequence has a total tardiness of 3.

When inserted idle time is permitted, the sequence 2-1 (Figure 8.1b) yields a total tardiness of 1. Furthermore, if a job can be preempted and later resumed from the point in its processing at which the interruption occurred, then a total tardiness of zero can be achieved, as shown in Figure 8.1c.

The type of preemption illustrated in Figure 8.1c is called the *preempt–resume* mode. In this mode, the total processing time required by job j is always p_j, and this amount is unaffected by the number of times the job is interrupted. When the preempt–resume mode applies, inserted idle time can never be beneficial in the static version of the problem. For that reason, in deterministic problems, schedules without inserted idle time constitute a dominant set for all regular measures.

The opposite extreme is the case in which a job must be restarted each time it is interrupted. This type of preemption is called the *preempt–repeat* mode. The difference between the two modes of processing is reflected in the way that scheduling decisions are made. In a preempt–repeat mode, no advantage exists in starting a job unless it can be completed. In deterministic situations, then, jobs might as well be scheduled as if no preemption is permitted, and schedules without preemption constitute a dominant set.

When the preempt–resume mode applies, properties associated with basic transitive rules are essentially unchanged. Consider, for example, the dynamic version of the T_{max}-problem. The optimal rule is *keep the machine assigned to the available job with the earliest due date*. The machine is assigned at completion times and at release dates as follows:

- At each job completion, examine the set of available jobs, and assign the machine to process the job with the earliest due date.
- At each job release, compare the due date of the newly available job with the due date of the job currently being processed. If the due date of the new job is tighter, allow the new job to preempt the job being processed; otherwise, simply add the new job to the set of waiting jobs.

In this case, the key information on which scheduling decisions are based – that is, the due date – does not change over time. By contrast, consider the dynamic version of the F-problem in preempt–resume mode. The optimal rule is, *keep the machine assigned to the available job with minimum remaining processing time.* The key information in this case is a job's remaining processing time, which changes while it is being processed. Thus, a job may enter the system with a large processing time (and correspondingly low priority), but after some partial processing, it will have a smaller remaining processing time (and higher priority). This dynamic sequencing rule is known as *shortest remaining processing time* (SRPT) sequencing. In preempt–resume mode, the dynamic adaptation of EDD or SPT requires no look-ahead features, even though jobs are released intermittently. At each decision point (a completion time or a release date), the necessary information is obtained from only the current set of available jobs. As a result, the actual scheduling decisions can be made at chronologically ordered points in time and each time on the basis of current status. Such a decision-making structure is called *dispatching,* and its significance lies in the fact that dispatching is easier to implement than decision-making based on look-ahead information.

A further consideration arises in the dynamic application of SPT to minimize F. Intuitively, one might think that the rule should apply for stochastic processing times as well. Indeed, it does apply when the remaining expected processing times are monotone decreasing as processing progresses, which is often the case. But processing time distributions exist for which the information that a job has been processed for a relatively long period implies that it is expected to take even longer from now on (see Appendix A). In such cases, we may have to preempt a job when its remaining expected processing time exceeds that of a waiting job. Thus, we obtain a more sophisticated form of dispatching where in addition to completions and releases, we have to add a new type of decision point to the rule and switch jobs when the remaining expected time of the current job exceeds the shortest expected time of a waiting job.

In short, a crucial feature of the dynamic single-machine model is the nature of job preemption. If processing can be carried out in preempt–resume mode, then some of the scheduling rules for optimal sequencing in the static problem can be extended. In particular, transitive job orderings can sometimes be adapted as optimal dispatching procedures, and inserted idle time is not a concern. On the other hand, if processing requires preempt–repeat mode, then inserted idle time can be helpful, but the comparison of permutation schedules to find an optimum becomes more difficult. Even problems that are relatively simple in the basic model require the use of general-purpose optimization techniques under preempt–repeat mode. In what follows, we assume that the preempt–repeat mode applies unless otherwise specified.

8.2.1 Minimizing the Makespan

In the basic single-machine model, the schedule length, or *makespan*, is always equal to the sum of the processing times. In the dynamic model, the makespan may include idle time. The objective of minimizing the makespan, C_{max}, also denoted M, is related to the *throughput* of the schedule. Because throughput is defined as the amount of work completed per unit time, and because the amount of work in the n-job model is fixed, we maximize throughput by minimizing the makespan.

In the dynamic version of the model, it is not difficult to show that M is minimized by a dispatching rule that always schedules the available job with the earliest release date (ERD), breaking ties arbitrarily. (The optimality of this rule extends to cases with stochastic processing times.) This type of rule belongs to the family of *nondelay* dispatching procedures, which never permit a delay (via inserted idle time) when the machine becomes available and work is waiting. In the dynamic model, any nondelay procedure will create a schedule consisting of one or more blocks (similar to the blocks discussed in Chapter 5). The first job in a block begins at its release date, but subsequent jobs in the block may be delayed past their own release dates. The first job also has the minimum release date in the block. The last job in a block completes before the release date of any job that appears later in the schedule.

An interesting generalization of the dynamic makespan problem involves the case in which each job has a given delivery time, q_j, in addition to a processing time and a release date. The delivery takes place immediately after the job completes, and deliveries can be done in parallel. The makespan is determined in this case by the latest delivery among the n jobs. Another interpretation of this model is possible. Think of all jobs as requiring three operations. The first and third operations are carried out in departments where the resources are plentiful, and no resource constraints apply. In effect, the jobs can be performed in parallel in these departments. The second operation occurs at a bottleneck facility, where the jobs must be processed one at a time. The problem is specified by a triplet (r_j, p_j, q_j) for each job j, where r_j denotes the processing time of the first operation, p_j the second operation, and q_j the third operation. (Sometimes, these parameters are called the *head*, *body*, and *tail* of each job.) The objective is to minimize the makespan of the three-department schedule.

The problem we have posed is NP-hard, but it is revealing to examine a simple heuristic solution method. Consider the nondelay dispatching procedure that always selects the available job with the largest tail (LT), q_j. (For the time being, we refer to this as the LT procedure.) The LT procedure is an intuitively appealing one. Obviously, we prefer to schedule jobs with large tails early and jobs with short tails later. The procedure follows this guideline in a nondelay mode, as described below.

Algorithm 8.1   *The Largest Tail (LT) Procedure*

Step 1. Initially, let $t = 0$.

Step 2. If there are no unscheduled jobs at time t, set t equal to the minimum release date among unscheduled jobs; otherwise, proceed.

Step 3. Find job j with the largest q_j among unscheduled jobs available at time t. Schedule job j to begin at time t.

Step 4. Increase t by p_j. If all n jobs are scheduled, stop; otherwise, return to Step 2.

The makespan generated by the LT procedure can be written as follows:

$$M = r_i + \sum_{j=i}^{k} p_j + q_k \tag{8.1}$$

for some job i that initiates a block and for some job k in the block called the *critical* job. (For convenience, we assume that the jobs are renumbered according to their sequence in the solution.) If it turns out that $q_k \leq q_j$ for all jobs j from i to k, then M is optimal. Otherwise, it is possible that M can be improved.

■ **Example 8.2**   Consider a five-job problem in which each job is characterized by a release date, a processing time, and a delivery time, as shown in the table.

Job j	1	2	3	4	5
r_j	0	2	3	0	6
p_j	2	1	2	3	2
q_j	5	2	6	3	1

At time $t = 0$, the LT procedure chooses between jobs 1 and 4 and selects 1. When job 1 completes at time $t = 2$, the procedure chooses between jobs 4 and 2 and selects 4. Continuing in this fashion, the procedure builds the sequence 1-4-3-2-5, with a makespan of $M = 13$. This schedule contains only one block, initiated by job 1. In addition, the maximum completion time of 13 occurs for job 3. Thus, in Eq. (8.1), we have $i = 1$ and $k = 3$. However, the optimality condition is not satisfied, because $q_3 > q_1$ and $q_3 > q_4$. This means that the optimal makespan may be less than 13, because the optimality condition is sufficient but not necessary.

This model is symmetric: We could just as easily solve the reversed problem (in which jobs enter the third department first and complete in the first department); the optimal makespan will be the same. The implication of symmetry is that the LT procedure should be executed twice: once for the original problem and once for the reversed problem. In our numerical example, the application of the LT procedure to the reversed problem yields a makespan of $M = 12$. (As it turns out, this is not an optimal solution either.)

Thus, Algorithm 8.1 uses an intuitive decision rule to construct a schedule, and in some cases it is possible to confirm the optimality of this schedule by means of a special condition. The condition fails if the critical job has a tail longer than some job that appears earlier in the same block. To find an optimal solution to the problem, a general optimization method is required. Existing computational evidence suggests that branch-and-bound methods work quite well.

8.2.2 Minimizing Maximum Tardiness

In the basic single-machine model, L_{max} (or T_{max}) is minimized by EDD sequencing. It is natural to ask whether a nondelay implementation of EDD is optimal in the dynamic model. It turns out that the dynamic version of the L_{max}-problem is NP-hard and the problem itself is essentially equivalent to the makespan problem studied in the previous section. To see this equivalence, suppose that we are given the release dates, processing times, and due dates for each of n jobs, with the objective of minimizing maximum lateness:

$$L_{max} = \max\{C_j - d_j\}$$

Next, denote by d_{max} the maximum of the due dates in the job set, and consider the makespan problem created by taking $q_j = d_{max} - d_j$. We can write

$$L_{max} = \max\{C_j - d_j\} = \max\{C_j - (d_{max} - q_j)\} = \max\{C_j + q_j\} - d_{max}$$

Clearly, in searching for an optimal schedule, we can ignore the constant d_{max}; what remains is the minimization of the makespan in the head–body–tail problem. Thus, the analysis of the optimal schedule for that problem carries over to the minimization of L_{max}. In fact, we can use any constant d in the role of d_{max}.

■ **Example 8.3** Consider a five-job L_{max}-problem in which we are given the release date, processing time, and due date for each job.

Job j	1	2	3	4	5
r_j	0	2	3	0	6
p_j	2	1	2	3	2
d_j	6	9	5	8	10

The transformation given by $q_j = 11 - d_j$ yields Example 8.2 in the previous section.

From this perspective, we can see that the LT procedure is equivalent to the nondelay implementation of EDD because the largest tail corresponds to the smallest due date. Furthermore, the sufficient condition for optimality applies. We state the result formally below.

■ **Theorem 8.1** In the dynamic L_{max}-problem, a nondelay implementation of the EDD rule yields

$$L_{max} = r_i + \sum_{j=i}^{k} p_j - d_k$$

for some job i that initiates a block and for some job k in the same block, where the jobs are numbered in order of appearance in the schedule. If $d_k \geq d_j$ for all jobs j from i to k, then L_{max} is optimal.

Proof. The formula for L_{max} is obvious, so we address the last sentence of the theorem. Consider the relaxed problem in which we eliminate all jobs except those from i to k in the final sequence. Next, set the release dates of the remaining jobs equal to r_i. This relaxed problem is essentially a basic single-machine problem, with r_i serving as time 0. Because it is a relaxation of the original problem, its optimal L_{max} is no larger than the optimal solution to the original problem. But its optimal L_{max} is attained by the EDD sequence, which will place job k last and result in no change to its lateness. Now, the original problem and the relaxed problem have equal objective function values, so the solution to the original must be optimal. □

The effectiveness of Algorithm 8.1 for minimizing L_{max} can sometimes be enhanced by exploiting symmetry, as mentioned earlier, and solving the reversed problem (where the tail comes first and the head follows the body). Specifically, the algorithm should be implemented twice, once for the original problem and once for the reversed problem. However, even with enhancements such as this, the nondelay implementation of EDD remains a heuristic procedure and does not guarantee optimality.

In general, locating an optimal schedule may require a branch-and-bound procedure. The standard approach would be to search in the tree of permutation schedules. Suppose that a partial sequence at level k corresponds to a specific assignment of the *first* k jobs in sequence. (This branching structure complements the structure introduced in Chapter 3, which focused on the last k jobs.) The associated subproblem requires the nonpreemptive sequencing of the remaining $(n - k)$ jobs, but an excellent lower bound for this problem is represented by the value obtained by using preempt–resume EDD scheduling (which can never do worse than preempt–repeat scheduling).

The preempt–resume solution is constructed by using a one-pass dispatching rule, and this calculation can be made quite efficiently. Finally, in the stochastic counterpart, any look-ahead approach would be difficult, but at least we can implement the nondelay EDD rule without any detailed information on the processing time distributions.

8.2.3 Other Measures of Performance

In general, whenever the preempt–resume version of the problem can be solved readily, the branch-and-bound approach should be considered seriously for the preempt–repeat version. However, it may be possible to make additional improvements by exploiting special structure. Indeed, it is possible to solve the L_{max}-problem for hundreds of jobs in this way. The dynamic U-problem and the dynamic T-problem represent another level of difficulty, however, because the corresponding preempt–resume solution is not obvious.

Turning now to heuristic solution procedures, the following property gives a sufficient condition for a certain nondelay schedule to be optimal.

■ **Theorem 8.2** In the dynamic L_{max}-problem, suppose that the nondelay implementation of EDD yields a sequence of the jobs in EDD order. Then this nondelay schedule is optimal.

Proof. Without loss of generality, we assume that the schedule contains just one block. Consider the relaxed problem generated by setting all release dates equal to zero. The optimal solution to the relaxed problem is given by the EDD sequence. Constraining the release dates to their original values does not disturb the feasibility of this sequence, so it must be optimal for the original problem, too. □

Theorem 8.2 is slightly weaker than Theorem 8.1 for the L_{max}-problem, but an analogous theorem applies for SPT in the F-problem and for SWPT in the F_w-problem. Two slightly more restrictive results, involving EDD and SPT, follow from corresponding versions of Theorem 8.2.

■ **Theorem 8.3** In the dynamic L_{max}-problem, if the release dates and due dates are agreeable, then the nondelay implementation of EDD is optimal.

■ **Theorem 8.4** In the dynamic F-problem, if the release dates and processing times are agreeable, then the nondelay implementation of SPT is optimal.

For the dynamic F-problem, we might expect that the nondelay adaptation of SPT performs quite well, even when the hypothesis of Theorem 8.4 does not hold. There are, however, alternative heuristic procedures available. One alternative is a rule that always chooses the job that will complete earliest. This is sometimes called the *first off first on* (FOFO) rule. Note that the FOFO rule may be considered an adaptation of the SPT principle to the dynamic model. Also, FOFO is not a dispatching procedure because it may use look-ahead information: The job that will complete earliest may not be available at the time the machine becomes free. An additional alternative is to give priority to the job with the smallest sum of earliest start time r_j and earliest finish time $r_j + p_j$. This rule, which amounts to choosing the job with minimal $(2r_j + p_j)$, seems to be the best of the three heuristic procedures, in limited testing.

For the dynamic T-problem, we can follow the logic behind Theorem 8.2 to the following result.

■ **Theorem 8.5**   In the dynamic T-problem, if the release dates, processing times, and due dates are all agreeable, then the nondelay implementation of MDD is optimal.

Again, we might expect the nondelay adaptation of MDD to perform quite well, even when the hypothesis of Theorem 8.5 does not hold. If we are interested in obtaining optimal solutions to the dynamic T-problem, a branch-and-bound approach is appropriate, although the computational effort might be greater than for the static version.

The dynamic U-problem is NP-hard but can be solved efficiently in the case of agreeable release dates and due dates. (In practice, due dates are often agreeable with release dates, as, for example, when due dates are set by the rules CON, SLK, or TWK.) The solution procedure generalizes Algorithm 2.1. Recall from that previous discussion that we can partition the optimal schedule into two sets, B (in which all jobs are on time) followed by A (in which all jobs are late).

Algorithm 8.2   *Minimizing U (Dynamic Version with Agreeable Parameters)*

Step 1. Order the jobs by ERD, and place all jobs in B. Let set A be empty.

Step 2. Compute the completion times of jobs in B. If no jobs in B are late, then stop: B must be optimal. Otherwise, identify the first late job in B. Suppose this job is the kth job in sequence.

Step 3. Remove one job from B so that the latest completion time among the first $(k - 1)$ jobs will be minimized. Place this job in A, and return to Step 2.

This description leaves Step 3 a little vague. In order to find the job indicated, two observations are helpful. First, we need to consider only the last block in the schedule. Second, if we were to remove the last job (say, job u) from the block, the reduction of the latest completion time for the jobs in B would be p_u. For any other job j in the block, the reduction would equal the smaller of p_j or the minimum waiting time (i.e. the difference between release date and start time) among jobs $(j + 1)$ through u. From this information we can identify the job creating the largest reduction as the one to remove in Step 3.

8.3   Related Jobs

In the basic single-machine model, the only type of constraint is the resource capacity constraint represented by a single processor. Another type of constraint in some scheduling problems is a technological restriction, which specifies the admissible sequence of two jobs. Such constraints create a set of *related* jobs and reduce the set of feasible solutions. However, that does not necessarily mean that optimal solutions can be found more readily.

Each technological restriction on the sequence of a job pair is called a *precedence* constraint. The notation $i \rightarrow j$ denotes the fact that job i precedes job j. In other words, job j is not permitted to begin until job i is complete. When $i \rightarrow j$, job i is said to be a *predecessor* of job j, and job j is a *successor* of job i. Job i is also called a *direct predecessor* of job j if no job k exists such that $i \rightarrow k \rightarrow j$. In words, if job i is a direct predecessor of job j, then it is permissible for jobs i and j to be adjacent, in that order, in the schedule.

As an example, consider the computer programs submitted for processing by a payroll department. Program A reads daily employee time cards, sorts the information, and updates the monthly records that are maintained in a database. Program B reads from the database and prints out paychecks. On the last day of the month, both programs are submitted, but B cannot be run until A is complete. Therefore, $A \rightarrow B$.

To illustrate the effect of adding precedence constraints to a sequencing problem, consider the F-problem with three jobs, a, b, and c, and suppose that $p_a < p_b < p_c$. Then, without precedence constraints, the optimal sequence is clearly a-b-c. Now suppose we impose one precedence constraint, $c \rightarrow a$. Although job b "ought" to follow job a and precede job c on the basis of its processing time, it is not immediately clear in this situation whether sequence c-a-b or sequence b-c-a is most desirable. (We can, however, rule out the sequence c-b-a with a simple adjacent pairwise interchange.) Thus, the existence of precedence constraints can complicate even the simplest scheduling problems. With more than three jobs and more than one precedence constraint, the problem is considerably more difficult to solve.

In the following sections, we examine the effects of adding precedence constraints in situations where the performance measure would normally lead us to sort the jobs but where precedence constraints may conflict with the order dictated by sorting. We illustrate the concepts for the T_{max}-problem and the F-problem, but further generalization of the concepts is possible.

8.3.1 Minimizing Maximum Tardiness

Suppose we are dealing with related jobs in a dynamic model, where we are given release dates, processing times, and due dates. If the objective is to minimize L_{max} (or T_{max}), then, on the basis of the precedence constraints, we can make some simple revisions in the given data that may help us find a solution.

Let i and j denote two related jobs, with $i \rightarrow j$. Suppose, in the given data, that we have $r_j < r_i + p_i$. In spite of this information, we know that in any feasible schedule job j cannot start any earlier than the completion time of job i because of the precedence constraint. Therefore, we can reset $r_j = r_i + p_i$. In a complementary fashion, suppose that we are given $d_i > d_j - p_j$. Then, we can reset $d_i = d_j - p_j$. This revision is allowable because even by making the due date of job i tighter, we will not directly affect the maximum lateness. Specifically, after the revision we obtain

$$L_i = C_i - d_i = C_i - \left(d_j - p_j\right) \leq \left(C_j - p_j\right) - \left(d_j - p_j\right) = C_j - d_j = L_j$$

Therefore, the lateness (or tardiness) of job i will still not be larger than the lateness (or tardiness) of job j.

The net effect of this revision is as follows. If job i is a predecessor of job j, then either the given information contains agreeable release dates and due dates consistent with the precedence constraint or else we can easily revise the parameters of jobs i and j so that agreeability occurs. We can then proceed as if there were no precedence constraint, although we may still need to call on a general-purpose solution procedure.

When all release dates are zero, it is sufficient to revise only the due dates. In fact, a consistent scheme is to reset the due date of job i equal to the minimum due date among its successors, if that minimum is lower than d_i. Thereafter, we can create an optimal schedule by applying the EDD rule with the revised due dates while respecting precedence constraints.

For the general criterion of minimizing the maximum cost with zero release dates, we based the solution algorithm for the single-machine model on Theorem 3.1. If precedence constraints exist, we amend the statement of the theorem slightly: When the objective is to minimize the maximum penalty, job i may be assigned the last position in sequence if job i has no unscheduled successors and $g_i(P) \leq g_j(P)$ for all jobs $j \neq i$ without unscheduled successors. Theorem 6.4, which adapts Theorem 3.1 to the stochastic case, can also be extended this way.

8.3.2 Minimizing Total Flowtime with Strings

For the F-problem, we begin with an observation that resolves the conflict between sorting and precedence constraints. Suppose that we have a single relevant precedence constraint $i \rightarrow j$ and that $p_j \leq p_i$. That is, job i precedes job j, but j is shorter than i and hence preferable to i for the F criterion. In this situation, an optimal sequence exists in which jobs i and j are adjacent, in that order. To see why this result holds, imagine that instead the optimal sequence had some job k between i and j. Job k would have to satisfy $p_k \leq p_i$ or $p_k \geq p_j$. In the first case, it would be at least as good to place k in front of i; in the second case, it would be at least as good to place k after j. Thus, it is not advantageous to have an intervening job between i and j.

We next consider the sequencing of job strings. A *string* is a set of jobs that must appear together (contiguously) and in a fixed order. The sequencing problem for job strings is one of sequencing these special job sets. Suppose the problem consists of s strings and that

n_k = number of jobs in string k ($1 \leq k \leq s$)
p_{kj} = processing time of job j in string k ($1 \leq j \leq n_k$)

From the given information we define

$$p_k = \sum_{j=1}^{n_k} p_{kj} = \text{total processing time in string } k$$

Also, let

$F(k,j)$ = flowtime of job j in string k
$F(k) = F(k,n_k)$ = flowtime of string k

First, if the objective is to minimize total *string* flowtime, that is, $\sum_{k=1}^{s} F(k)$, then the strings may each be treated as pseudojobs, yielding an optimal sequence characterized by a string-based version of SPT. In particular, the optimal string sequence is given by $p_{[1]} \leq p_{[2]} \leq \cdots \leq p_{[s]}$.

On the other hand, if the objective is to minimize total *job* flowtime, that is, $\sum_{k=1}^{s} \sum_{j=1}^{n_k} F(k,j)$, then in general a different sequence is optimal, as stated in the following theorem.

■ **Theorem 8.6** In the single-machine problem with job strings, total flowtime is minimized by sequencing the strings in the order

$$\frac{p_{[1]}}{n_{[1]}} \leq \frac{p_{[2]}}{n_{[2]}} \leq \cdots \leq \frac{p_{[s]}}{n_{[s]}}$$

Proof. Define a quantity q_{kj} to represent the processing time in string k that follows job j, that is, a *residual* processing time:

$$q_{kj} = \sum_{i=j+1}^{n_k} p_{ki}$$

where q_{kj} is understood to be zero when $j = n_k$. Note that q_{kj} is given. Hence,

$$F = \sum_{k=1}^{s}\sum_{j=1}^{n_k} F(k,j) = \sum_{k=1}^{s}\sum_{j=1}^{n_k}\left[F(k) - \sum_{i=j+1}^{n_k} p_{ki} \right]$$

$$= \sum_{k=1}^{s}\sum_{j=1}^{n_k}\left[F(k) - q_{kj} \right]$$

$$= \sum_{k=1}^{s}\sum_{j=1}^{n_k} F(k) - \sum_{k=1}^{s}\sum_{j=1}^{n_k} q_{kj}$$

Note that the last double sum is a constant, independent of sequence. Consequently, minimizing F is equivalent to minimizing the first double sum, which is

$$\sum_{k=1}^{s}\sum_{j=1}^{n_k} F(k) = \sum_{k=1}^{s} n_k F(k)$$

Minimizing this sum corresponds to minimizing total weighted flowtime for the strings, where the weighting factor associated with string k is just n_k. Hence, by Theorem 2.4, the optimal string sequence must be in nondecreasing order of the ratio p_k/n_k. ☐

The concept of a job string may seem restrictive because it requires a collection of jobs to be processed in a specific sequence. However, the concept helps structure situations where the string requirement is not strictly necessary. For example, recall the situation where sorting and precedence conflict. In particular, job i directly precedes job j and $p_j \leq p_i$. Then, as we saw earlier, we may assume that jobs i and j appear together in sequence, so we can treat (i, j) as a string for the purpose of constructing an optimal schedule.

As another example, there may be a *contiguity* constraint, under which a collection of jobs must be performed together but without specification of their sequence. This structure arises in scheduling groups of jobs, where each group represents a product family. Each family must be performed contiguously because they share a common major setup or perhaps a common resource. In this situation, the collection of jobs within a group can be ordered optimally (by SPT), and then the ordered set (augmented by the group setup time, if it applies) can be treated as a string for the purpose of sequencing all the groups, at which point Theorem 8.6 applies.

The significance of Theorem 8.6 extends even further. Define a *job module* to be a set S of jobs such that for each pair of jobs i and j in the set, no job k exists outside the set that satisfies $i \rightarrow k \rightarrow j$. In words, a job module is a set of jobs that *could* feasibly be sequenced contiguously. Furthermore, the notation $s \rightarrow t$, where s and t are strings, implies that each job in string s precedes every job in string t. Suppose that a job module consists of two strings, u and v, with $u \to v$ and $p_v/n_v \le p_u/n_u$. (This is a situation in which the precedence constraint between strings conflicts with the sorting of strings.) Then, for minimizing total flowtime, an optimal sequence exists in which strings u and v are adjacent, in that order. Furthermore, the two strings u and v can then be treated as a single string, and it may be possible to reapply the result to this new string and some other string.

For certain precedence structures, this modular approach to building a job sequence can lead us to an optimal schedule. In the next subsection, we examine the details of this approach.

8.3.3 Minimizing Total Flowtime with Parallel Chains

A *chain* is a special precedence structure in which each job has at most one direct predecessor and one direct successor. The jobs in a chain do not *necessarily* have to be sequenced contiguously, although it is permissible to do so; this flexibility distinguishes a chain from a string. Suppose that a job set consists of several chains in parallel. As a result of Theorem 8.6, this job structure can be sequenced by the following algorithm.

Algorithm 8.3 *Parallel-chains Algorithm for F*

Step 1. Initially, each job is a string.

Step 2. Find a pair of strings, u and v, such that u directly precedes v and $p_v/n_v \le p_u/n_u$. Replace the pair by the string (u, v). Then repeat this step. When no such pair can be found, proceed to Step 3.

Step 3. Sort the strings in nondecreasing order of p/n.

If no precedence constraints exist, then Step 2 produces no two-job strings, and Step 3 is equivalent to SPT. Otherwise, Step 2 identifies string pairs for which sorting and precedence conflict and also reconciles the conflict. Finally, when we reach Step 3, sorting and precedence are no longer in conflict, at least for the strings that exist at that stage, and the sort prescribed by Step 3 produces an optimal sequence.

■ **Example 8.4**   Consider the F-problem with $n = 9$ jobs shown in Figure 8.2a, where the processing time for each job is shown above the corresponding node in the network.

Five precedence constraints are shown as arcs in the network; these form parallel chains. Step 2 first combines jobs 1 and 2 into a string and then combines the string $(1, 2)$ and job 3 into a single string. Jobs 5 and 6 are similarly combined and so are jobs 7 and 8. When Step 2 is complete, we have five strings and one

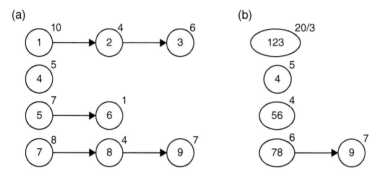

Figure 8.2 The example problem in (a) and after applying Step 2 in (b).

precedence constraint: String (7, 8) precedes job 9. This precedence constraint, however, is consistent with nondecreasing p/n order. The five strings are shown in Figure 8.2b, with the value of p_s/n_s shown above the node corresponding to string s. Step 3 sorts the five strings into the optimal sequence 5-6-4-7-8-1-2-3-9, with $F = 245$.

These concepts can most generally be extended to *series–parallel* precedence structures. A network N exhibits series–parallel structure if it consists of a single node or if N can be partitioned into two subnetworks N_1 and N_2 that are themselves series–parallel and where one of the following conditions is satisfied:

- N_1 is in series with N_2 (for every pair (i, j) with $i \in N_1$ and $j \in N_2$, we have $i \to j$).
- N_1 is in parallel with N_2 (for every pair (i, j) with $i \in N_1$ and $j \in N_2$, i and j are not related).

■ **Example 8.5** Consider the F-problem with $n = 8$ jobs and the network structure shown in Figure 8.3, where the processing time for each job is shown above the corresponding node in the network.

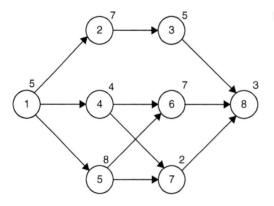

Figure 8.3 An eight-job example.

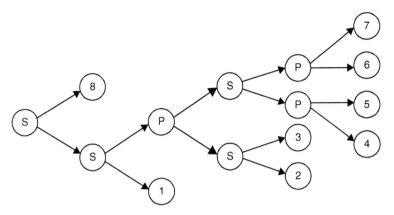

Figure 8.4 A decomposition tree for the example in Figure 8.3.

Series–parallel structures can be described by a *decomposition tree*. In this type of tree, there are two kinds of nodes. Nodes without successors correspond to individual jobs and are numbered accordingly. Other nodes have two successors and correspond to a partition of a network or a subnetwork. These decomposition nodes are designated S or P, depending on whether the appropriate partition is series or parallel. Figure 8.4 displays a decomposition tree for Example 8.5, thus demonstrating that it has a series–parallel precedence structure.

In order to find optimal sequences for series–parallel-structured job sets, the solution algorithm processes nodes N in the decomposition tree for which the subnetworks N_1 and N_2 have previously been processed. If the decomposition for N is of the series type, then N is processed by forming the string (N_1, N_2). If the decomposition is of the parallel type, then N is processed by applying Algorithm 8.3 to the parallel chains N_1 and N_2. In either case, the jobs contained in N are formed into an optimal sequence.

To demonstrate this procedure, we list the steps involved in sequencing the jobs in the example.

Subnetwork pair	Type	Resolution
4, 5	Parallel	(4, 5)
6, 7	Parallel	(7, 6)
2, 3	Series	(2-3)
(4, 5), (7, 6)	Series	(4, 5-7, 6)
(2, 3), (4, 5-7, 6)	Parallel	(4, 5-7, 2-3, 6)
1, (4, 5-7, 2-3, 6)	Series	(1-4, 5-7, 2-3, 6)
(1-4, 5-7, 2-3, 6), 8	Series	(1-4, 5-7, 2-3, 6-8)

The first two string pairs are resolved by SPT sequencing of the job pairs. The next two string pairs are resolved by their series structure: Job 3 must follow job 2, and job module (7, 6) must follow (4, 5). At this stage the p/n values are 6 for string (2-3), 4 for job 4, 5 for string (5-7), and 7 for job 6. Algorithm 8.3 then forms the sequence (4-5-7-2-3-6). Finally, jobs 1 and 8 are added according to their series relationships with the subnetwork already sequenced. The result is the optimal sequence 1-4-5-7-2-3-6-8 with $F = 186$.

Job sets in which series–parallel structures apply can thus be optimized efficiently by exploiting the parallel-chains algorithm in combination with the decomposition tree. Furthermore, no more general case of precedence structure is known that yields an efficient algorithm of the type described above. For general precedence structures, we would apparently need to employ a general-purpose solution procedure. For example, we could use dynamic programming but with precedence constraints in the role of dominance conditions.

8.4 Sequence-Dependent Setup Times

In many realistic problems, setup times depend on the type of job just completed as well as on the type about to be processed. In those situations, it is not valid to absorb the setup time for a job in its processing time, and explicit modifications must be made. The time interval in which job j occupies the machine is expressed $s_{ij} + p_j$, where i is the job that precedes j in sequence, s_{ij} is the setup time required for job j after job i is completed, and p_j is the amount of direct processing time required to complete job j.

Setup times that are *sequence dependent* are commonly found where a single facility produces several different kinds of items or where a multipurpose machine carries out an assortment of tasks. The use of a single system to produce different chemical compounds may require that some amount of cleansing be carried out between process runs on different compounds to ensure that tolerably low impurity levels are maintained. Sometimes, the extent of the cleansing depends on both the chemical most recently processed and the chemical about to be processed. Similar setup properties can be found in the production of different colors of paint, strengths of detergent, and blends of fuel. The same observations apply to certain assembly lines where retooling, inspection, or rearrangement of work stations could represent the setup activity.

In the basic single-machine problem, the makespan, M, is a constant. With sequence-dependent setups, however, the makespan depends on which sequence is chosen:

$$F_{[1]} = s_{0,[1]} + p_{[1]}$$

$$F_{[2]} = F_{[1]} + s_{[1],[2]} + p_{[2]}$$

$$\vdots$$

$$F_{[n-1]} = F_{[n-2]} + s_{[n-2],[n-1]} + p_{[n-1]}$$

$$F_{[n]} = F_{[n-1]} + s_{[n-1],[n]} + p_{[n]}$$

where state 0 corresponds to an initial state, usually an idle state. Also, if we define the state $(n + 1)$ as a terminal state (perhaps identical to state 0), then the schedule makespan becomes

$$M = F_{[n]} + s_{[n],[n+1]} = \sum_{j=1}^{n+1} s_{[j-1],[j]} + \sum_{j=1}^{n} p_j \qquad (8.2)$$

The second summation is a constant, so the problem of minimizing makespan is equivalent to minimizing the first summation. This sum represents the total nonproductive time in the full sequence, beginning and ending in the idle state.

The type of structure represented by this makespan problem is often interpreted as a *traveling salesperson problem* (TSP). In the classical formulation, a salesperson must visit clients in each of n cities. The salesperson wishes to choose a tour that goes to each city exactly once and returns to the point of origin. Given the distances between all pairs of cities, the salesperson's task is to find the tour with minimum total travel distance. An alternative formulation considers travel times in place of distances. In the sequencing problem, s_{ij} (the setup time for job j when it immediately follows job i) corresponds to the travel time between city i and city j. Although the classical version of the TSP usually involves a symmetric matrix ($s_{ij} = s_{ji}$), that need not be the case in the sequencing problem, so our default assumption is that travel times are asymmetric. In addition, our TSP formulation ignores the processing time of a job, although that could be easily modeled as the time the salesperson must spend in a city. This formulation demonstrates that the crux of the makespan problem is minimizing total setup times, regardless of processing times.

■ **Example 8.6** Consider scheduling a process line that manufactures four types of gasoline: racing fuel, premium, regular, and unleaded. The matrix of setup times, s_{ij}, is shown in Table 8.1. In a full production cycle, during which one batch is devoted to each product, the amount of nonproductive time (that is, setup time) depends on the sequence in which these fuels are produced.

The total amount of setup time differs in each of the six distinct sequences that include all four products, as listed below.

Table 8.1

Product		(1)	(2)	(3)	(4)
Racing	(1)	—	30	50	90
Premium	(2)	40	—	20	80
Regular	(3)	30	30	—	60
Unleaded	(4)	20	15	10	—

Sequence	Setup time
1-2-3-4-1	30 + 20 + 60 + 20 = 130
1-2-4-3-1	30 + 80 + 10 + 30 = 150
1-3-2-4-1	50 + 30 + 80 + 20 = 180
1-3-4-2-1	50 + 60 + 15 + 40 = 165
1-4-2-3-1	90 + 15 + 20 + 30 = 155
1-4-3-2-1	90 + 10 + 30 + 40 = 170

The TSP is NP-hard, but state-of-the-art algorithms are capable of solving very large problems, with thousands of cities. Although the solutions of really large instances rely on parallel processing and can consume years of CPU time, problems with hundreds of cities can be solved on personal computers. In the following subsections we limit our investigation to basic solution approaches for the TSP. To reinforce the concepts of Chapters 3 and 4, we examine two optimizing approaches – dynamic programming and branch and bound – as well as some simple heuristic procedures.

The following discussions assume that if an idle state is required in the formulation of the problem, it has already been included in the s_{ij} matrix. Also, for convenience, we use the terminology of the classical problem and refer to cities and distances or travel times rather than to jobs and setup times.

8.4.1 Dynamic Programming Solutions

With some slight modifications, the dynamic programming approach can be adapted to solve the TSP. The important structural modification is that a solution must correspond to a complete cycle, in which the tour returns to its starting point. Let J and S denote disjoint subsets of the n cities, choose a city i arbitrarily, and designate it as the origin of the tour. Now let X denote the set of all cities, excluding i. The optimal tour can be interpreted as consisting of the sets $\{i\}$, S, $\{k\}$, J, $\{i\}$. In other words, the tour begins at city i, proceeds to the cities in set *S*, visits a particular city *k*, then proceeds to the cities in set *J*, and finally returns to *i*. Sets *S* and *J* do not contain *k* or *i*. Also, if *J* contains *c* cities, then *S* must contain $(n - c - 2)$ cities. With this structure, an optimal tour can be described by the principle of optimality. Consider the portion of the tour that starts at city *k* and returns to *i*. This portion must be the shortest possible path from city *k* that passes through the cities in *J* and finishes at city *i*. (If this were not the case, the tour could not be optimal.) Now define

$f(k,J)$ = the length of the shortest path from city

k that passes through the cities in *J* and finishes at city *i*

Then the length of the optimal tour is given by

$$f(i,X) = \min_{j \in X} \left[s_{ij} + f(j, X - \{j\}) \right]$$

where, in general,

$$f(k,J) = \min_{j \in J} \left[s_{kj} + f(j, J - \{j\}) \right]$$

and where

$$f(k,\phi) = s_{ki}$$

By using these recursion relations, we can construct the optimal tour by first considering sets *J* of size 1, then sets *J* of size 2, and so on, until enough information has been accumulated to calculate *f*(*i*, *X*). Table 8.2 displays the calculations for the 4×4 matrix of Table 8.1, yielding an optimal processing sequence (as indicated in the original table) of 1-2-3-4-1.

This dynamic programming approach to the TSP is similar to the general dynamic programming approach presented in Chapter 3. The only major difference in the structure of this formulation is that the function at the heart of the recursion has two arguments instead of one.

8.4.2 Branch-And-Bound Solutions

An alternative optimization approach is the technique of branch and bound. In fact, one of the earliest research studies on branch and bound (Little et al. 1963) dealt with solving the TSP. This approach is worth examining in detail because it helps illustrate the flexibility inherent in branch-and-bound methods.

The branching scheme creates two subproblems at all levels: one subproblem containing a specific element of the s_{ij} matrix constrained to be part of the solution and the other subproblem prohibiting that same element. For example, a partition of the original problem might require the (1, 3) element to be in the tour of one subproblem and prohibit the (1, 3) element in the complementary subproblem.

Table 8.2

Let $i = 1$

Stage 1

$f(2, \phi) = 40$

$f(3, \phi) = 30$

$f(4, \phi) = 20$

Stage 2

$f(2, \{3\}) = 20 + 30 = 50$ $f(2, \{4\}) = 80 + 20 = 100$

$f(3, \{2\}) = 30 + 40 = 70$ $f(3, \{4\}) = 60 + 20 = 80$

$f(4, \{2\}) = 15 + 40 = 55$ $f(4, \{3\}) = 10 + 30 = 40$

Stage 3

$f(2, \{3, 4\}) = \min\{20 + 80, 80 + 40\} = 100$

$f(3, \{2, 4\}) = \min\{30 + 100, 60 + 55\} = 115$

$f(4, \{2, 3\}) = \min\{15 + 50, 10 + 70\} = 65$

Stage 4

$f(1, \{2, 3, 4\}) = \min\{30 + 100, 50 + 115, 90 + 65\} = 130$

Optimal tour: 1-2-3-4-1

Distance: 130

Lower bounds for a given s_{ij} matrix may be calculated by a method called *reduction*. Since any feasible solution contains exactly one element in each row, it is possible to subtract a constant from any row without altering the relative desirability of any feasible solution. In effect, this subtraction reduces the length of all tours by the same constant and, in particular, does not affect which of the feasible tours is optimal. In the reduction process, we subtract the minimum element from each row. Then, similarly, we can subtract the minimum element from each column. The matrix that emerges has at least one zero element in every row and in every column, and the sum of the subtraction constants serves as a lower bound on the optimal solution because this distance must be part of any feasible tour. To illustrate these steps specifically, consider the TSP (denoted P) associated with the matrix in Table 8.3a.

Reduction. By subtracting the minimum element in each row, the original matrix is reduced to the one shown in Table 8.3b. The sum of the elements subtracted is 20, which is a lower bound on the optimal solution. At this point, we have at least one zero in every column as well, as required.

Branching. The algorithm next partitions the problem by forcing one of the zero elements to be part of the tour on one branch and prohibiting the same

Table 8.3

(a)					(b)					(c)				
		P					P (reduced)					P (reduced)		
—	4	8	6	8	—	0	4	2	4	—	0^4	4	2	4
5	—	7	11	13	0	—	2	6	8	0^5	—	2	6	8
11	6	—	8	4	7	2	—	4	0	7	2	—	4	0^2
5	7	2	—	2	3	5	0	—	0	3	5	0^2	—	0^0
10	9	7	5	—	5	4	2	0	—	5	4	2	0^4	—

element on the other branch. To decide which zero element to choose, one logical method is to select the element that, when prohibited, would permit the largest possible reduction in the matrix. Therefore, we label each zero element with the sum of the minimum element remaining in its row and the minimum element remaining in its column, as shown in Table 8.3c. This rule selects element (2, 1). The original problem is partitioned into two subproblems: $P(21)$, which contains the (2, 1) element, and $P(^*21)$, which prohibits the (2, 1) element.

Bounding. The reduction procedure can now be applied to each subproblem. Since the (2, 1) element is part of the tour in $P(21)$, the (1, 2) element must be prohibited if the solution is to form a complete tour. In addition, we can also eliminate elements $(2, j)$ for $j \neq 1$ and elements $(i, 1)$ for $i \neq 2$. The matrix that results (Table 8.4a) can be reduced to the matrix shown in Table 8.4b (by subtracting 2 from the second column and 2 from the first row), leading to a bound of 24 (by adding 2 + 2 to the previous bound of 20). Meanwhile, $P(^*21)$ can be reduced to the matrix shown in Table 8.4c, which has a bound of 25 (20 plus the label on the (2, 1) element in the reduced matrix for P).

At the next stage, either subproblem could be partitioned further. Suppose the strategy is always to partition the subproblem that is closest to being fully solved. (In Chapter 3 we called this strategy backtracking.) Under this strategy, $P(21)$ is partitioned next. As indicated by Table 8.4b, several zero elements are equally desirable according to the selection rule. Such ties can be broken arbitrarily. Therefore, let element (5, 4) be the basis for the next partition. Thus we partition $P(21)$ into subproblems $P(21, 54)$ and $P(21, ^*54)$, which can both be reduced. These two subproblems (shown in Table 8.5a, b) have bounds of 26.

The list of unsolved problems and their lower bounds becomes

$P(21, 54)$	(26)
$P(21, ^*54)$	(26)
$P(^*21)$	(25)

Table 8.4

(a)					(b)					(c)				
		P(21)					P(21)					P(*21)		
—	—	4	2	4	—	—	2	0^2	2	—	0^4	4	2	4
0^*	—	—	—	—	0^*	—	—	—	—	—	—	0^4	4	6
—	2	—	4	0	—	0^2	—	4	0^0	4	2	—	4	0^2
—	5	0	—	0	—	3	0^2	—	0^0	0^2	5	0^0	—	0^0
—	4	2	0	—	—	2	2	0^2	—	2	4	2	0^4	—

Table 8.5

(a)					(b)				
		P(21, 54)					P(21, *54)		
—	—	0^0	—	0^0	—	—	2	0	2
0^*	—	—	—	—	0^*	—	—	—	—
—	0^0	—	—	0^0	—	—	—	4	0
—	3	0^3	—	—	—	3	0	—	0
—	—	—	0^*	—	—	0	0	—	—

Once again, we partition the problem that is closest to being fully solved. In P (21, 54), the desirable zero element is (4, 3). The list becomes

P(21, 54, 43)	(26)
P(21, 54, *43)	(29)
P(21, *54)	(26)
P(*21)	(25)

The problem $P(21, 54, 43)$ is essentially fully solved because only one feasible tour includes the elements (2, 1), (5, 4), and (4, 3). The complete tour must be 2-1-5-4-3-2, a solution with a value of 26. The fact that a trial solution has been found with a tour of length 26 allows two other branches of the tree to be fathomed. In particular, no completion of $P(21, 54, *43)$ or of $P(21, *54)$ can possibly improve on this trial solution, because their bounds are already at or above 26. The tree structure at this stage is shown in Figure 8.5. Below each node is the corresponding lower bound, designated "F" if the node has been fathomed.

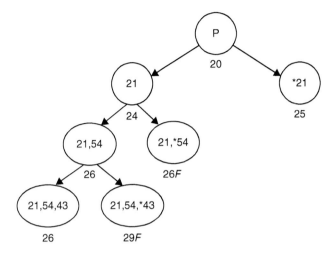

Figure 8.5 The partial tree for the example problem.

One subproblem, $P(^*21)$, remains. Proceeding from this subproblem, we can find a new trial solution (1-2-3-5-4-1) with a value of 25, and the solution tree that results is shown in Figure 8.6. Now, all unsolved subproblems have bounds of 26 or more, so no feasible solution can be better than the trial solution. The trial solution is therefore an optimum.

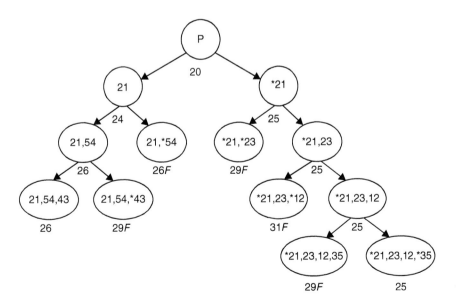

Figure 8.6 The final tree for the example problem.

Although the branching tree encountered in the TSP differs from the permutation tree illustrated in Chapter 3, it does illustrate the general characteristics: At each level, it replaces a problem with (two) mutually exclusive and exhaustive subproblems, and these subproblems are smaller, partially solved versions of the original. The calculation of lower bounds is accomplished in this tree via reduction, which identifies distances that are unavoidable in any feasible solution. The solution procedure could be enhanced with alternative methods of obtaining bounds. For example, an alternative is to solve the *assignment problem* associated with the matrix: That is, choose n elements from the matrix, with exactly one element in each row and exactly one in each column, such that their sum is a minimum. (The optimal solution to the assignment problem can be found with a polynomial algorithm, but that solution produces only a bound because it does not guarantee that the optimal assignment corresponds to a single tour.)

8.4.3 Heuristic Solutions

A fairly simple greedy procedure for the TSP is known as the "closest unvisited city" algorithm, in which the sequence is constructed by the greedy approach of always selecting the closest city not yet visited. (In terms of the sequencing model, this rule amounts to dispatching according to the shortest setup time.) In the problem of Table 8.3a, for example, suppose that city 5 is the origin. The closest city to the origin, corresponding to the minimum element in row 5, is city 4. Excluding city 5, the closest to 4 is city 3. The closest unvisited city to 3 is 2 and the closest to 2 is 1. The heuristic procedure thus constructs the sequence 5-4-3-2-1-5, which has a tour length of 26. Had this sequence been known at the outset of the backtracking scheme depicted in Figure 8.6, the branches corresponding to subproblems $P(21, 54)$ and $P(21, {}^*54)$ could have been fathomed as soon as they were created, improving the speed with which an optimum would have been located. The heuristic procedure need not be evaluated only in terms of its usefulness as part of a branch-and-bound scheme – it is important in its own right. Although the closest unvisited city algorithm cannot guarantee optimal solutions, its importance may lie in its ability to generate good solutions rapidly in problems where the cost of implementing an optimum-seeking method is prohibitive.

Several variations of this heuristic procedure have been developed that preserve the essence of the closest unvisited city approach. The first variation involves an interpretation of "closest." If the original s_{ij} matrix (Table 8.4a) is used in the calculations, then absolute distances are used to identify a closest city. Alternatively, if the reduced s_{ij} matrix (Table 8.4b) is used, then relative distances identify a closest city. A second variation involves a look-ahead feature that permits a closest unvisited *pair* of cities to be added to the tour. Under this variation, we again choose the origin arbitrarily. Then, instead of examining the paths from the origin to $(n - 1)$ other cities, we evaluate the paths from the origin to $(n - 1)(n - 2)$ ordered pairs of cities, and we add to the tour the pair associated with minimum distance. The third variation involves several applications of the algorithm: Instead of choosing the origin city once, arbitrarily, we apply the procedure n times, each time using a different city as the origin. Then we take the best of the n tours as the solution. This variation follows the principle that a heuristic procedure is often strengthened by the opportunity to choose among several solutions. These three variations in fact describe eight closest unvisited city algorithms, as listed in Table 8.6. Tests on randomly generated problems suggest that the closest unvisited city algorithm produces solutions within 10% of optimum for $n \leq 20$, but that performance of the algorithm deteriorates when considerable variability appears in the elements of the s_{ij} matrix.

The insertion procedure is an alternative heuristic approach. We begin with a randomly selected pair of cities, constituting a tour of length 2. Then a third city is inserted to minimize the resulting three-city tour; then a fourth city is inserted, and so on, until a complete tour has been constructed. Suppose, for example, that the method is applied to the problem in Table 8.3a, with the cities taken in numbered order. The "seed" pair 1-2 forms a two-city tour. A three-city tour is selected by evaluating the tours 3-1-2 and 1-3-2. (The latter has the shorter tour.) A four-city tour is formed by inserting job 4 somewhere in the three-city tour. In other words, a tour is selected from among 4-1-3-2, 1-4-3-2, and 1-3-4-2. At the last stage, a full tour is selected from among four candidates, producing a tour of length 26. Just as the closest unvisited city algorithm is sensitive to which city is designated as origin, the insertion procedure is sensitive to which pair of cities is designated as initial seed and to the order in which jobs are considered for insertion. Heuristic rules for these facets of the algorithm have not been thoroughly developed, but we could repeat the algorithm several times, each time beginning with a different seed pair.

The general-purpose search methods described in Chapter 3 can also be employed in the TSP. Indeed, search methods are often tested on the TSP in order to confirm their effectiveness.

Table 8.6

Algorithm		Variations	
1	Absolute distances	No look ahead	Arbitrary origin
2	Absolute distances	No look ahead	All origins
3	Absolute distances	Look ahead	Arbitrary origin
4	Absolute distances	Look ahead	All origins
5	Relative distances	No look ahead	Arbitrary origin
6	Relative distances	No look ahead	All origins
7	Relative distances	Look ahead	Arbitrary origin
8	Relative distances	Look ahead	All origins

8.5 Stochastic Traveling Salesperson Models

In this section, we explore stochastic counterparts and extensions of the TSP under the assumption of sequence-dependent, normally distributed, and stochastically independent travel times. For convenience, we ignore the fact that the normal distribution allows negative realizations. We also avoid models in which sequences with large variances – rather than small variances – provide better results. Usually, increasing variance is detrimental, but our Research Notes explore cases in which larger variances are beneficial.

Let the travel time between cities i and k have mean μ_{ik} and standard deviation σ_{ik}. For normally distributed travel times, two parameters suffice for the length of each tour: the mean μ (given by $\Sigma\mu_{ik}$ along the tour) and the standard deviation σ (given by $[\sum\sigma_{ik}^2]^{0.5}$). We briefly consider the stochastic counterpart of the makespan problem and then explore the stochastic counterpart of the tightness/tardiness trade-off.

In the stochastic counterpart of the makespan problem with sequence-dependent setup times, we seek the minimum value of the expected makespan. From Eq. (8.2), we have

$$E[M] = E\left[\sum_{j=1}^{n} s_{[j-1],[j]}\right] + E\left[\sum_{j=1}^{n} p_j\right] \tag{8.3}$$

In the first expectation, we assume that the idle state serves as the initial and final state and is included among the n setup states in the sum of setup times. In the second expectation, the expected value of a sum is the sum of its component expected values, so the second expectation is simply the sum of the mean processing times, which is a constant for any choice of sequence. To model stochastic travel times literally, we could calculate the sum of the setup time and the processing time for each pair of cities and use the result as travel time. The stochastic counterpart thus becomes the problem of finding a sequence that minimizes the sum of the expected travel times in a tour. This is equivalent to the deterministic counterpart, which is defined by an $n \times n$ matrix of mean setup times and which can be solved by the methods of Section 8.4.

A stochastic safe scheduling problem can be formulated based on the makespan in the case of the tightness/tardiness trade-off, under the assumption that the travel times each follow normal distributions. In particular, we use a single due date, denoted by d, and we define the tardiness in the schedule by $T = \max\{0, M - d\}$. Our criterion is $d + \gamma E[T]$ with $\gamma > 1$, as in Section 7.3, except that in this case only one due date applies and tardiness measures the difference between the makespan of the full tour and the due date. Because travel times are assumed to follow normal distributions, the makespan is also normally distributed. Drawing on the formula in Eq. (B.16), or on the reasoning in Section 7.3, we obtain the objective function

$$d + \gamma E[T] = \mu + \gamma\phi(z)\sigma \tag{8.4}$$

where z is the argument for which $\phi(z) = (\gamma - 1)/\gamma$ and the due date takes the form $d = \mu + z\sigma$.

If a particular tour minimizes both the mean and the standard deviation, then it is clearly optimal for Eq. (8.4). To discover whether such a tour exists, we solve two TSPs. The first uses a travel time matrix containing means μ_{ik}, so the solution minimizes the sum of the means along the tour, thus identifying the tour that minimizes the mean of the makespan. The second TSP uses a travel time matrix containing variances σ_{ik}^2, so the solution minimizes the sum of the variances along the tour, thus identifying the tour that minimizes the variance of the makespan. That tour also minimizes the standard deviation of the makespan, which could not have been accomplished except by working with a tour made up of variance terms.

If the optimal tour for both TSP matrices is the same, then it minimizes the objective in Eq. (8.4). In general, however, the tours that minimize mean and standard deviation will differ, creating a potential trade-off between the mean of the tour length and the standard deviation of the tour length. (For this reason the solution to the deterministic counterpart, which corresponds to minimizing only the mean, may not provide an optimal tour in the stochastic case.) In other words, if we characterize each possible tour by its mean and standard deviation, we must search for the combination that minimizes Eq. (8.4).

Imagine that we construct a graph in which points correspond to the μ–σ pairs for all possible tours, with the mean along the horizontal axis and the standard deviation along the vertical axis. If we connect all pairs of points by straight lines, the outside boundary forms a polygon called the *convex hull*, and the candidates for optimal tour correspond to points that appear on the lower left boundary of the convex hull, starting from the tour that minimizes the mean, moving counterclockwise, and ending with the tour that minimizes the standard deviation. No other tour can be optimal.

Unfortunately, no efficient procedure is available for searching directly among the candidate points in the convex hull of μ–σ points. However, we can search systematically on the boundary of the convex hull of μ–σ^2 points, where (it is possible to show) all candidate points lie. We illustrate the search procedure with an example.

◼ **Example 8.7** Consider the sequencing of $n = 7$ jobs with sequence-dependent stochastic travel times. The travel times follow independent normal distributions with known means and variances, and the objective is to optimize the tightness/tardiness trade-off when $\gamma = 6$ (for which $\gamma\phi(z) = 1.5$). The following two arrays list the parameters of the normal distributions, first for means μ_{ik} and then for variances σ_{ik}^2.

From\to	1	2	3	4	5	6	7
1	9 999	156.6	158.5	199.7	146.5	112.5	131.5
2	133.4	9 999	150.4	137.7	118.4	116.8	166.9
3	182.8	188.3	9 999	152.3	197.2	187	132.6
4	184.6	153.3	133.5	9 999	112.9	194.8	187.7
5	149.4	200.1	182.7	169.6	9 999	120.6	197.3
6	174.3	193.7	126.5	116.7	112.5	9 999	112.1
7	179	190.8	186.2	186.7	208.4	111.8	9 999

From\to	1	2	3	4	5	6	7
1	99 999	639.8	510.6	3402.5	0.5	1.4	316.1
2	204.6	99 999	900.1	3.8	2.6	5.7	165.5
3	2 516.1	2 544.3	99 999	393.3	379.4	177.7	1 19.6
4	846.3	95.2	161.3	99 999	0.8	2 925.5	3 458.6
5	98.9	245.4	1 459.9	287.6	99 999	13.8	19.5
6	648.9	1948	140.6	4.9	0.7	99 999	0.5
7	2 396.3	3 435.7	96.5	3907.9	1 626.4	0.1	99 999

Figure 8.7 shows the mean–variance pairs for all 720 possible tours feasible for these seven jobs. The candidate tours correspond to the following points.

Tour	Mean	Variance
0.00	930.4	1764.2
0.01	934.1	1024.2
0.14	940.7	831.9
0.44	984.2	688.4
1.00	1120.4	598.9

The first candidate on this list is the *minimum–mean tour*, (1-2-3-7-6-4-5-1), obtained by solving the deterministic counterpart; and the last candidate is the *minimum–variance tour*, (1-5-7-3-6-4-2-1), obtained by solving the TSP with variances as travel times. The other candidates are yet to be identified. Our basic solution procedure does not enumerate all possible tours or construct the full convex hull. Instead, it systematically identifies the tours on the lower left boundary of the convex hull. The procedure finds the optimal tour by solving a relatively small number of TSPs.

At any stage of the procedure, we focus on two candidate tours, starting with the two tours that minimize μ and σ^2. We connect these two points by a straight line or *search segment*. Let λ be the argument for which the *test function*

Figure 8.7 The complete set of mean–variance pairs for Example 8.7.

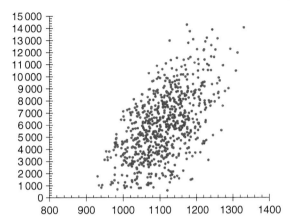

$(1 - \lambda)\mu + \lambda\sigma^2$ is constant along the search segment. At the first stage, $\lambda = 0$ corresponds to the minimum–mean tour, and $\lambda = 1$ corresponds to the minimum–variance tour. The constant can be found by equating the value of the test function at the endpoints of the search segment:

$$(1-\lambda)\mu_{0.00} + \lambda\sigma^2_{0.00} = (1-\lambda)\mu_{1.00} + \lambda\sigma^2_{1.00}$$

In this case, the values of the means and variances come from the minimum–mean and minimum–variance tours. Their means and variances are identified by the subscripts $\lambda = 0.00$ for the minimum–mean tour and $\lambda = 1.00$ for the minimum–variance tour. A general formula for the desired value of λ is

$$\lambda = \frac{(\mu_R - \mu_L)}{(\mu_R - \mu_L) - (\sigma^2_R - \sigma^2_L)} \tag{8.5}$$

where the subscripts R and L denote the right-hand and left-hand endpoints of the search segment. In our example, the calculation yields

$$\lambda = \frac{(1120.4 - 930.4)}{(1120.4 - 930.4) - (598.9 - 1764.2)} = 0.14$$

The tour corresponding to λ either identifies a new member of the candidate set or matches an endpoint. In this case, the value $\lambda = 0.14$ identifies a candidate point. We construct its travel time matrix with elements $(1-\lambda)\mu_{ik} + \lambda\sigma^2_{ik}$ and solve the resulting TSP, obtaining a tour with a mean of $\mu_{0.14} = 940.7$ and $\sigma^2_{0.14} = 831.9$.

Next, we create two search segments. The left-hand segment connects the points corresponding to $\lambda = 0.00$ and 0.14; the right-hand segment connects the points corresponding to $\lambda = 0.14$ and 1.00. On each segment, we calculate a value of λ that identifies a new candidate if possible and that establishes the next search segment. The procedure continues in this fashion as long as new candidates are identified.

In our example, searching between $\lambda = 0.00$ and 0.14 leads to a new candidate at $\lambda = 0.01$, but searching from that value toward $\lambda = 0.00$ or 0.14 does not lead to any new values. Similarly, searching between $\lambda = 0.14$ and 1.00 leads to a new candidate at $\lambda = 0.44$. Searching between $\lambda = 0.44$ and 1.00 does not produce a new value, and neither does searching between $\lambda = 0.14$ and 0.44. Thus, the search terminates with five candidates. When their μ_λ and σ_λ values are substituted in the expression for the objective function (8.4), we obtain the results below.

Tour	Mean	Variance	$d + \gamma E[T]$
0.00	930.4	1764.2	216.4
0.01	934.1	1024.2	205.1
0.14	940.7	831.9	206.9
0.44	984.2	688.4	246.5
1.00	1120.4	598.9	380.1

Thus, the optimal tour (1-2-3-7-6-4-5-1) corresponds to $\lambda = 0.01$, achieving an optimal value of the objective function equal to 205.1. In addition, the tour that corresponds to $\lambda = 0.14$ (that is, 1-3-7-6-4-2-5-1) is second best, and the last two tours are worse than the deterministic counterpart.

The following proposition summarizes the result at the heart of the solution procedure.

Proposition 8.1   For the stochastic version of the tightness/tardiness trade-off with normally distributed travel times, there exists a value of λ, with $0 \leq \lambda \leq 1$, such that the optimal solution of a deterministic TSP with travel times defined by $(1-\lambda)\mu_{ik} + \lambda\sigma_{ik}^2$ is optimal.

The value λ in Proposition 8.1 is not unique, but the procedure illustrated in the example finds a value that produces an optimal tour.

The solution procedure illustrated in Example 8.7 can be used in a variety of settings. For instance, close examination of Example 8.7 reveals that some individual travel times have high coefficients of variation but no tour in the candidate set has cv larger than 0.27. As a result, even if the distributions are not normal, the tour length will often be approximately normal, and the normal model will be valid. Furthermore, in the more practical case governed by lognormal distributions rather than normal distributions, the Fenton–Wilkinson approximation, introduced in Chapter 7, allows us to use essentially the same solution procedure, albeit without guarantee of optimality.

Computationally, the solution procedure depends on the ability to calculate the optimal tour length for a number of TSPs. Fortunately, a variety of computational approaches exist for the TSP. For the tightness/tardiness trade-off, modern solvers allow us to solve versions with hundreds of jobs, but TSPs of 25–30 jobs can be solved in a matter of seconds with spreadsheet-based integer programming software. Empirical studies also indicate that the number of TSPs that the procedure solves en route to an optimal solution is quite small and appears to grow roughly linearly with problem size. The same studies indicate that a heuristic method designed to avoid searching far from optimum and to terminate after two iterations tends to produce solutions that are within 1% of optimality.

Although we have illustrated the solution procedure for the tightness/tardiness trade-off, it applies as well to the solution of other models involving due dates and stochastic travel times. One example is minimizing the due date for which the service level, SL, satisfies a given target, b, where SL = Pr$\{M \leq d\}$, and we require $b \geq 0.5$. In both problems, the reasoning of Chapter 7 applies. For the tightness/tardiness problem, we set $\theta = \gamma\phi(z)$ as the price of a standard deviation unit, and we can express Eq. (8.4) as $d + \gamma E[T] = \mu + \theta\sigma$. In the service level problem, we set $\theta = z = \Phi^{-1}(b)$ and express the objective function in an identical form, $\mu + \theta\sigma$. It follows that the same candidate set applies for both models. Another example in which similar analysis applies is the complementary problem of maximizing the service level for a given due date, provided it is not smaller than the mean of the deterministic counterpart. Both problems are solved by selecting the best tour in the candidate set. In each case, the assumption of normality in setup and/or processing times leads to normality in tour lengths, but that would be approximately true for most practical probability distributions including the lognormal.

8.6 Summary

Generalizations of the basic single-machine model extend its applicability but lead to new difficulties in obtaining solutions. In some cases, the optimal solution to a problem involving the basic model can be directly adapted to the generalized model. At other times, however, a direct adaptation is not possible, and new solution approaches are required.

Dynamic models, in which jobs become available intermittently, require that assumptions regarding job preemption be carefully scrutinized. If jobs can be processed in a preempt–resume mode, no idle time need ever be inserted in a schedule, and dispatching procedures can be employed. On the other hand, if the preempt–repeat mode applies, or if preemption is prohibited, then inserted idle time can be justified, and look-ahead procedures become useful in determining schedules. Moreover, even simple sequencing problems in the latter model appear to require general-purpose techniques for finding optimal schedules, and the branch-and-bound approach appears to be quite effective whenever the corresponding preempt–resume problem is easily solved. Nevertheless, dispatching is especially useful in stochastic environments, and practitioners often prefer to avoid inserted idle time.

The generalization of SPT sequencing to strings and chains suggests that optimal rules may sometimes involve properties of job modules rather than the properties of individual jobs. In the F_w-problem with series–parallel precedence constraints, we also saw the need for a decomposition tree as a preliminary step in implementing the optimal sequencing procedure. When considering stochastic counterpart models without preemption, the F_w-problem is still simple to extend by replacing each processing time by its expectation.

Sequence-dependent setup times create complications even in the makespan problem, where they lead to TSPs with a city corresponding to each job. However, state-of-the-art algorithms can cope with TSPs containing thousands of cities. Nonetheless, progress with other performance measures has been limited. For practical purposes, solving for flowtime or tardiness, even for a single tour, can currently be addressed only by heuristics, except for relatively small problem sizes.

We introduced stochastic travel times into the TSP and explored the stochastic version of the makespan problem. We highlighted several related objectives that require small variances and not just small means, and we showed how to find solutions in the case of the normal distribution with stochastically independent but sequence-dependent travel times. These solutions rely on methods that have been successful in solving deterministic problems. In principle, they proceed by optimizing tour lengths based on a convex combination of the mean and the variance for each segment. The same approach has been shown to work as an effective heuristic for minimizing expected tardiness when given a due date and for lognormal travel times with linear association. We discuss those issues further, as well as models in which larger variances are beneficial, in our Research Notes.

Although the assumptions cited in Chapter 2 may have seemed somewhat restrictive, the array of extensions considered in this chapter enrich the basic model and demonstrate that its usefulness is actually quite broad. One aspect of condition C1 that was preserved throughout, however, was the availability of only a single machine. In the remaining chapters, we investigate more general models in which several machines are present.

Exercises

8.1 Construct an example to show each of the following properties for the dynamic single-machine model.

a) When no preemption is permitted, EDD sequencing does not guarantee minimum T_{max}.

b) When no preemption is permitted, SPT sequencing does not guarantee minimum *F*.

c) In preempt–resume mode, shortest weighted remaining processing time (the dynamic analogy of SWPT) does not guarantee minimum F_w.

8.2 Give a complete solution to the *F*-problem with jobs *a*, *b*, and *c* and a single precedence constraint.

8.3 Eight jobs are to be processed at a single machine. The processing times and due dates are given below.

Job *j*	1	2	3	4	5	6	7	8
p_j	2	3	2	1	4	3	2	2
d_j	5	4	13	6	12	10	15	19

Furthermore, the following precedence relationships must be satisfied:

$2 \rightarrow 6 \rightarrow 3$

$1 \rightarrow 4 \rightarrow 7 \rightarrow 8$

Determine the sequence that will minimize the maximum lateness subject to the given precedence restrictions.

8.4 Develop a sequencing rule that will minimize F_w for the single-machine problem with job strings.

8.5 Consider the set of nine jobs depicted in Figure 8.8. Prove that the precedence structure is series–parallel. (*Hint*: When partitioning to two sets N1 and N2, it is sufficient to find one partition that satisfies one of the conditions and then consider each of its parts in the same manner.)

Figure 8.8 Nine-job example.

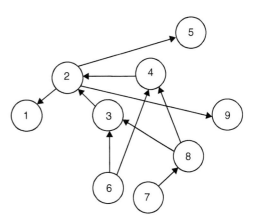

8.6 For n cities, suppose it is required to go from city i to city k and visit all other cities once each on the way. Show that the problem is identical to the TSP. Does your demonstration apply when the terminal city, k, is not specified?

8.7 In the optimal solution to the TSP for the matrix shown below (which includes the matrix in Table 8.3), does the optimal tour for the matrix in Table 8.3 appear intact as part of the larger optimum?

—	4	8	6	8	2
5	—	7	11	13	4
11	6	—	8	4	3
5	7	2	—	2	5
10	9	7	5	—	2
8	4	3	6	5	—

8.8 Find a solution to the TSP in the previous exercise using the closest unvisited city procedure with the following.
a) Absolute distances, no look ahead, and city 2 as the origin.
b) Relative distances, no look ahead, and city 2 as the origin.
c) Absolute distances, look ahead, and city 5 as the origin.

8.9 Consider a noncyclic problem of sequencing n jobs with sequence-dependent setup time such that the machine starts at some initial state and has to be left at some specified final state. Describe an equivalent TSP model. Similarly, show that any cyclic TSP model could be formulated as an instance of this noncyclic problem. (That is, show that the two problems are mathematically equivalent.)

8.10 Consider scheduling families of contiguous jobs when each family has a major family setup time. In other words, each family is scheduled once, as a batch of jobs processed in sequence and preceded by a single family setup. The family setup times are not sequence dependent.
a) Show how to minimize the total flowtime while taking the setup times into account.
b) Repeat (a) for the total weighted flowtime.

8.11 Consider the scheduling of $n = 3$ jobs with sequence-dependent stochastic setup times. The facility is already set up to process job 1 first. Then, after the other two jobs are completed, the facility will be in its desired final state. Processing times are deterministic, and each job takes 50 time units. In addition, each possible setup time follows a normal distribution. The task is to schedule jobs 2 and 3 and set their due dates to satisfy specified requirements (listed below) while taking into account both processing times and setup times. The following two arrays describe the distribution parameters.

Mean setup time from i to j				Standard deviation of setup time from i to j			
	To				*To*		
	1	2	3		1	2	3
1	—	40	45	1	—	6	9
From 2	0	—	60	*From* 2	0	—	8
3	0	50	—	3	0	12	—

a) Minimize the due date, d, for delivering all jobs (together) subject to a service level constraint, $SL \geq 0.75$. (*Hint*: To select the best sequence, processing times contribute a constant to d (because they are deterministic).)

b) Minimize $d + \gamma E[T]$ for $\gamma = 1.725$. Compare d with part (a). (*Hint*: Let z_a be the argument for which $\phi(z_a) = 0.75$ – that is, $z_a = 0.6745$ – and let z_b be the argument for which $\phi(z_b) = (\gamma - 1)/\gamma$ where $\gamma = 1.725$, then $z_a = \gamma\phi(z_b)$.)

c) Repeat (b) but for $\gamma = 4$ (for which $SL = 0.75$ is optimal).

d) Minimize the sum of individual job due dates, $D = d_1 + d_2 + d_3$, such that the service levels for each job will be at least 75%. (*Hint*: To select the best sequence, processing times do not matter (because they are equal for all jobs), and for the same reason, d_1 can also be ignored. However, they must be considered for the purpose of calculating D once the best sequence has been selected.)

e) Minimize $D + \gamma E[T_1] + \gamma E[T_2] + \gamma E[T_3]$ for $\gamma = 1.725$. Compare D with part (d).

f) Repeat (e) but for $\gamma = 4$ (for which $SL = 0.75$ is optimal).

Bibliography

Ahmadi, R. and Bagchi, U. (1990). Lower bounds for the single-machine scheduling problem. *Naval Research Logistics* 37: 967–979.

Applegate, D.L., Bixby, R.E., Chvatal, V., and Cook, W.J. (2007). *The Traveling Salesman Problem*. Princeton, NJ: Princeton University Press http://www.math.uwaterloo.ca/tsp/concorde/ (accessed 22 November 2017).

Baker, K.R. and Su, Z. (1974). Sequencing with due-dates and early start times to minimize maximum tardiness. *Naval Research Logistics Quarterly* 21: 171–176.

Carlier, J. (1982). The one machine sequencing problem. *European Journal of Operational Research* 11: 42–47.

Chandra, R. (1979). On $n/1/\bar{F}$ dynamic deterministic problems. *Naval Research Logistics Quarterly* 26: 537–544.

Chu, C. (1992a). A branch-and-bound algorithm to minimize total tardiness with different release dates. *Naval Research Logistics Quarterly* 39: 265–283.

Chu, C. (1992b). Efficient heuristics to minimize total flow time with release dates. *Operations Research Letters* 12: 321–330.

Chu, C. and Portmann, M.-C. (1992). Some new efficient methods to solve the $n/1/r_i/\sum T_i$ scheduling problem. *European Journal of Operational Research* 58: 404–413.

Emmons, H. and Vairaktarakis, G. (2013). *Flow Shop Scheduling: Theoretical Results, Algorithms, and Applications*. New York: Springer.

Gapp, W., Mankekar, D.S., and Mitten, L.G. (1965). Sequencing operations to minimize in-process inventory costs. *Management Science* 11: 476–484.

Gavett, J.W. (1965). Three heuristic rules for sequencing jobs to a single production facility. *Management Science* 11: B166–B176.

Hodgson, T.J. (1977). A note on single machine sequencing with random processing times. *Management Science* 23: 1144–1146.

Jaillet, P. (1988). A priori solution of a traveling salesman problem in which a random subset of the customers are visited. *Operations Research* 36: 929–936.

Jaillet, P., Qi, J., and Sim, M. (2016). Routing optimization under uncertainty. *Operations Research* 64: 186–200.

John, T.C. and Wu, Y.B. (1987). Minimum number of tardy jobs in single-machine scheduling with release dates—an improved algorithm. *Computers and Industrial Engineering* 12: 223–230.

Jonker, R. and Volgenant, T. (1983). Transforming asymmetric into symmetric traveling salesman problems. *Operations Research Letters* 2: 161–163.

Kao, H.P.C. (1978). A preference order dynamic program for a stochastic traveling salesman problem. *Operations Research* 26: 1035–1045. *See also Sniedovich* 1981.

Karg, R. and Thompson, G.L. (1964). A heuristic approach to solving travelling salesman problems. *Management Science* 10: 225–248.

Kenyon, A.S. and Morton, D.P. (2003). Stochastic vehicle routing with random travel times. *Transportation Science* 37: 69–82.

Kise, H., Ibaraki, T., and Mine, H. (1978). A solvable case of the one-machine scheduling problem with ready and due-times. *Operations Research* 26: 121–126.

Lageweg, B.J., Lenstra, J.K., and Rinnooy Kan, A.H.G. (1976). Minimizing maximum lateness on one machine: computational experience and some applications. *Statistica Neerlandica* 30: 25–41.

Laporte, G. (1992). The traveling salesman problem: an overview of exact and approximate algorithms. *European Journal of Operational Research* 59: 231–247.

Laporte, G., Louveaux, F.V., and Mercure, H. (1992). The vehicle routing problem with stochastic travel times. *Transportation Science* 26: 161–170.

Lawler, E.L. (1973). Optimal sequencing of a single machine subject to precedence constraints. *Management Science* 19: 544–546.

Lawler, E.L. (1978). Sequencing jobs to minimize total weighted completion time subject to precedence constraints. *Annals of Discrete Mathematics* 2: 75–90.

Little, J.D.C., Murty, K.G., Sweeny, D.W., and Karel, C. (1963). An algorithm for the traveling salesman problem. *Operations Research* 11: 972–989.

Mazmanyan, L. and D. Trietsch (2009). Stochastic traveling salesperson with safety time. Working paper. http://faculty.tuck.dartmouth.edu/images/uploads/faculty/principles-sequencing-scheduling/SafeTSP.pdf (accessed 20 October 2017).

Mazmanyan, L. and Trietsch, D. (2014). Stochastic traveling salesperson and shortest route models with safety time. *International Journal of Planning and Scheduling* 2(1): 53–76. http://faculty.tuck.dartmouth.edu/images/uploads/faculty/principles-sequencing-scheduling/StochasticTSP.pdf (accessed 20 October 2017).

McMahon, G. and Florian, M. (1975). On scheduling with release dates and due dates to minimize maximum lateness. *Operations Research* 23: 475–482.

Monma, C.L. and Sidney, J.B. (1979). Sequencing with series–parallel precedence constraints. *Mathematics of Operations Research* 4: 215–224.

Monma, C.L. (1981). Sequencing with general precedence constraints. *Discrete Applied Mathematics* 3: 137–150.

Morton, T.E. and Dharan, B.G. (1978). Algoristics for single-machine sequencing with precedence constraints. *Management Science* 24: 1011–1020.

Portougal, V. and Trietsch, D. (2001). Stochastic scheduling with optimal customer service. *Journal of the Operational Research Society* 52: 226–233.

Potts, C.N. (1980). Analysis of a heuristic for one machine sequencing with release dates and delivery times. *Operations Research* 28: 1436–1441.

Sidney, J.B. (1975). Decomposition algorithms for single machine sequencing with precedence relations and deferral costs. *Operations Research* 23: 283–298.

Sniedovich, M. (1981). Analysis of a preference order traveling salesman problem. *Operations Research* 29: 1234–1237.

9

Parallel-machine Models

9.1 Introduction

In general, scheduling requires both sequencing and resource allocation decisions. When there is only one resource, the allocation of that resource is completely determined by sequencing decisions. As a consequence, in the single-machine model, no distinction exists between sequencing and resource allocation. To appreciate that distinction we must examine models with more than one machine. Scheduling theory covers three basic types of multimachine models: parallel systems, serial (flow shop) systems, and hybrid (job shop) systems. In parallel systems, jobs consist of one operation, as in the single-machine model; but in flow shops and job shops, the structure of jobs is more complicated. This chapter treats the case of parallel machines, whereas the following chapters introduce the other multimachine models.

A simple setting in which we can investigate the effects of parallelism is the problem of scheduling single-operation jobs in the presence of several parallel machines. As in the basic model, n jobs are simultaneously available at time zero. We also have m parallel machines available for processing, and we assume that a job can be processed by at most one machine at a time. In the basic parallel-machine model, the machines are identical and the jobs are unrelated. When we address the fundamental performance measures in this setting, solutions reflect resource parallelism.

9.2 Minimizing the Makespan

In the basic single-machine model, the makespan is equal to a constant for any sequence of n given jobs, so the makespan problem needs no analysis. In the

Principles of Sequencing and Scheduling, Second Edition. Kenneth R. Baker and Dan Trietsch.
© 2019 John Wiley & Sons, Inc. Published 2019 by John Wiley & Sons, Inc.

static parallel-machine model, the sequence of jobs on any particular machine is immaterial; thus, the makespan problem is purely one of allocating jobs to machines. However, the makespan problem is still very challenging.

The simplest makespan problem arises when the jobs are unrelated and we permit preemption. With preemption allowed, the processing of a job may be interrupted, and the remaining processing can be completed subsequently, perhaps on a different machine. The formula for the minimum makespan, M^*, is given by

$$M^* = \max \left[\sum_{j=1}^{n} \frac{p_j}{m}, \; \max_j \{p_j\} \right] \tag{9.1}$$

It should not be hard to see why this result holds: The formula states that either the work is allocated evenly among the machines, or else the length of the longest job determines the makespan. A method of constructing an optimal schedule follows.

Algorithm 9.1   *Minimizing M with m Parallel, Identical Machines*

Step 1. Select some job to begin on machine 1 at time zero.

Step 2. Choose any unscheduled job and schedule it as early as possible on the same machine. Repeat this step until the machine is occupied beyond time M^* or until all jobs are scheduled.

Step 3. Reassign the processing scheduled beyond M^* to the next machine instead, starting at time zero. Return to Step 2.

This problem does not have a unique solution, and the construction method in Algorithm 9.1 produces only one of many optimal schedules. In particular, the method makes no attempt to minimize the number of preemptions.

■ **Example 9.1**   Consider a makespan problem with $m = 3$ machines in which we wish to schedule the following eight jobs.

Job j	1	2	3	4	5	6	7	8
p_j	1	2	3	4	5	6	7	8

From Eq. (9.1), $M^* = 12$. The schedule in Figure 9.1 results from the application of Algorithm 9.1 to this eight-job set (in numerical order). The schedule shown in Figure 9.1 achieves the optimal makespan of 12 and involves preemptions of jobs 5 and 7. Because the processing time of the longest job cannot

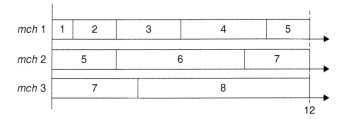

Figure 9.1 An optimal schedule for the eight-job example.

exceed M^*, preempted jobs are never scheduled on different machines at the same time (which would be infeasible), and it is also clear that they actually start on the machine on which they are scheduled at time 0. In this instance, it would not be difficult to construct a schedule that achieves the optimal makespan with no preemptions at all. In general, however, minimizing the number of preemptions in an optimal schedule is a challenging problem: It is NP-hard even for just two machines.

9.2.1 Nonpreemptable Jobs

If we prohibit job preemption, then the problem of minimizing the makespan is NP-hard in the strong sense. (The two-machine case, however, is not quite as difficult and can be solved by a pseudopolynomial algorithm.) Therefore, the determination of optimal schedules for the makespan requires such general-purpose methods as branch-and-bound or dynamic programming. In the case of branch and bound, it is not easy to obtain tight lower bounds; in the case of dynamic programming, the number of states tends to be extremely large for $m \geq 3$. Thus, general-purpose techniques have not had much success except on relatively small problems.

Although optimal solutions to the makespan problem are difficult to obtain, some heuristic procedures perform quite well. A plausible way to build a schedule in practice is as follows. First, construct a list of the jobs, in some order. Then, remove the first job from the list, and place it in the schedule as early as possible. Next, repeat this step without changing the existing partial schedule, each time removing the first job on the list and placing it in the schedule to start at the earliest feasible time. We can think of this procedure, called *list scheduling*, as a dispatching mechanism for real-time decisions. That is, the list could represent a queue of waiting jobs. As some job finishes and its machine becomes free, the first job in the queue gets assigned to the free machine.

For deterministic processing times, the optimal schedule can always be produced by *some* list-scheduling procedure. In other words, given any schedule, some list could have produced it. Unfortunately, there is no obvious way to order the list so that it produces the optimal makespan. However, we at least know that to search for an optimal schedule, we can limit attention to list sche-dules – that is, to $n!$ possibilities. The number of dominant schedules is thus no larger with parallel machines than it would be for a complicated single-machine problem. As a consequence, we can use neighborhood searches to sequence the list, or many of the other heuristic procedures covered in Chapter 4. The same idea applies to heuristic solutions of the stochastic counterpart.

No known ordering of the list can reliably produce optimal makespans. Thus, any simple ordering rule will sometimes produce suboptimal results. This raises the question of how poor the performance of a list-scheduling procedure might be. A *performance guarantee* is a bound on the performance of a particular solu-tion method. In the case of makespan problems, it is an upper bound on the suboptimality of the makespan produced by a given heuristic procedure.

More formally, let M denote the makespan produced by the heuristic proce-dure (in this case, list scheduling), and let M^* denote the optimal makespan. A typical performance guarantee might take the form

$$M \leq rM^*$$

In this case, $r > 1$ (sometimes called an *error bound*) represents an upper bound on the ratio of the heuristic solution to the optimal solution. Thus, the performance of the heuristic procedure, as measured by this ratio, is guar-anteed to be no worse than r for any instance of the problem. For list scheduling, the following result provides a performance guarantee.

■ **Theorem 9.1** List scheduling for unrelated, nonpreemptable jobs yields a makespan satisfying $M/M^* \leq 2 - 1/m$.

Proof. Consider a schedule produced by a list-scheduling procedure that achieves a makespan of M. Let k denote a job that finishes at time M, so that job k starts at time $M - p_k$. At this point, all m machines must have been occu-pied continuously since time zero, and the amount of completed work must have been at most all the work in the set of jobs, exclusive of job k. Hence,

$$m(M - p_k) \leq \sum_{j=1}^{n} p_j - p_k$$

Algebraic rearrangement yields

$$M \leq \sum_{j=1}^{n} \frac{p_j}{m} + \frac{p_k(m-1)}{m} \tag{9.2}$$

From Eq. (9.1), we know that M^* is at least as large as $\sum_{j=1}^{n} p_j/m$ and at least as large as p_k. It follows that

$$M \leq M^* + M^*(m-1)/m$$

or, more simply, $M/M^* \leq 2 - 1/m$. □

Theorem 9.1 gives us an error bound on the result produced by an arbitrary list-scheduling procedure: The makespan cannot be as poor as twice the optimal value. However, this is merely an upper bound. By constructing schedules in a few examples, we could discover that the actual makespan produced by a list-scheduling procedure will often be much closer to the optimum than this bound suggests, and we might wonder whether Theorem 9.1 is too pessimistic. As it happens, there are cases in which the performance of a list-scheduling procedure is as poor as the bound in Theorem 9.1.

■ **Example 9.2** Consider a makespan problem with $m = 4$ machines in which we wish to schedule the following seven jobs.

Job j	1	2	3	4	5	6	7
p_j	3	3	3	1	1	1	4

When the list is ordered numerically, the list-scheduling procedure produces the schedule shown in Figure 9.2, with a makespan of $M = 7$. It should not be difficult to see that the optimal solution has a makespan of $M = 4$. The performance ratio is exactly $2 - 1/m$, and similar examples can be constructed for other values of m.

As this example demonstrates, not only does Theorem 9.1 provide an upper bound on the performance ratio, but no tighter upper bound is possible. For this reason, we refer to the formula in Theorem 9.1 as a *worst-case* performance ratio or, more simply, as a worst-case bound. Furthermore, under a mild condition on the processing times, worst-case performance is likely only when (n/m) is small, as we show next.

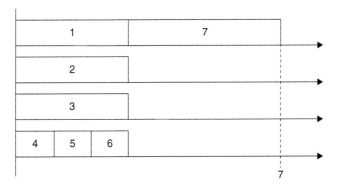

Figure 9.2 A list schedule for the seven-job example.

Let p_{max} denote the largest processing time in the set, so that Eq. (9.2) implies

$$M - M^* \le \frac{p_{max}(m-1)}{m} \tag{9.3}$$

Suppose that we generate the processing times so that in the limit as $n \to \infty$, $p_{max}/\sum p_j \to 0$ (in words, no job by itself dominates the total processing time). We then say that the processing times satisfy the *regularity condition*. For instance, if jobs are sampled independently from some distribution with a finite variance, the regularity condition is satisfied. Recall from Chapter 7 that a heuristic is asymptotically optimal if, in the limit as $n \to \infty$, the difference between the heuristic solution and the optimum becomes relatively negligible (i.e. $r \to 1$).

■ **Theorem 9.2** List scheduling is asymptotically optimal for the parallel-machine makespan problem with unrelated, nonpreemptable jobs that satisfy the regularity condition.

Proof. We must show that in the limit as $n \to \infty$, $(M - M^*)/M^* \to 0$. From Eq. (9.3), we have $p_{max}(m-1)/m \ge (M - M^*)$, and from Eq. (9.1) we have $\sum p_j/m \le M^*$. The ratio of these inequalities implies that $(M - M^*)/M^* \le p_{max}(m-1)/\sum p_j$. But $p_{max}/\sum p_j \to 0$ by the regularity condition, so $(M - M^*)/M^* \to 0$. □

When processing times are independent with finite variances, the asymptotic optimality result in Theorem 9.2 also holds for the stochastic counterpart. This is true because as $n \to \infty$, the coefficient of variation of the total processing time on each machine tends to zero. Even if processing times are not independent, any list is asymptotically optimal if we use it for dispatching decisions. Asymptotic optimality is important because it is increasingly used as an indicator of heuristic quality. Typically, sequencing problems are easy for small n and difficult for large n. However, when we discover a heuristic procedure that is computationally easy to implement and yet asymptotically optimal, we have a valuable result. In practical terms, we can solve the problem as follows:

- For small n, use some form of implicit or even explicit enumeration.
- For medium n, start with an asymptotically optimal heuristic, and use it as a seed for a neighborhood search.
- For large n, skip the neighborhood search or limit it to the first few jobs on the list.

When we introduced asymptotic optimality in Chapter 7, we linked it to a specific heuristic procedure. In that case, asymptotic optimality was also instrumental in selecting the heuristic. In contrast, Theorems 9.1 and 9.2 apply to a list schedule with any ordering. Thus, asymptotic optimality does not discriminate among list-scheduling heuristics for the parallel-machine makespan problem.

However, some orderings tend to perform better than others. From the proofs of Theorems 9.1 and 9.2, we can infer that it is desirable to make the last job ("job k") relatively short. To this end, an effective heuristic procedure is list scheduling according to the longest processing time (LPT). In Example 9.2, LPT list scheduling produces an optimal makespan. For LPT list scheduling, an improved performance guarantee exists.

■ **Theorem 9.3**   In the parallel-machine makespan problem with unrelated, nonpreemptive jobs, LPT list scheduling yields a makespan satisfying $M/M^* \leq 4/3 - 1/3m$.

Proof. If $n \leq 2m$, then it is not hard to see that LPT yields the optimal sequence. Therefore, the theorem must be true in that case. Henceforth, we assume that $n > 2m$, and for convenience, we assume that the jobs are indexed by LPT, so job n starts last and p_n is the shortest processing time. Consider two cases.

Case 1 (job n finishes last): Our task is equivalent to showing that

$$\frac{M - M^*}{M^*} \leq \frac{m-1}{3m}$$

If we replace $M - M^*$ by an upper bound and M^* by a lower bound and still show that the inequality holds, the theorem must be true because such bounds can only increase the left-hand side. In Eq. (9.2), we can substitute p_n for p_k and obtain

$$M \leq \frac{\sum_{j=1}^{n} p_j}{m} + p_n \frac{m-1}{m}$$

However, $\sum p_j/m$ is a valid lower bound on M^*, so $M \leq M^* + p_n(m-1)/m$. Rearranging terms, we obtain our upper bound on $M - M^*$:

$$M - M^* \leq p_n \frac{m-1}{m}$$

Because $n > 2m$, at least one machine must process three or more jobs, each requiring at least p_n. Thus, we can use $3p_n$ as our lower bound on M^*. Therefore, an upper bound on $(M - M^*)/M^*$ is given by $(m-1)/3m$, thus completing the proof for Case 1.

Case 2 (some other job finishes last): Let k be the index of the job that finishes last, and denote the makespan of the first k jobs in the LPT schedule by $M(k)$. For optimal values, $M^*(n) \geq M^*(k)$, and, in general, for a given list, $M(n) \geq M(k)$, although in this case $M(n) = M(k)$.

Case 2a: If $k \leq 2m$, then (as mentioned earlier) LPT is optimal. Therefore, $M(k) = M^*(k)$, so we have $M(n) = M(k) = M^*(k) \leq M^*(n)$. Therefore, $M(n)$ is optimal, and the theorem holds.

Case 2b: If $k > 2m$, then Case 1 holds for the first k jobs, so $M(k)/M^*(k) \leq 4/3 - 1/3m$. Because $M(n) = M(k)$, we have $M(n)/M^*(n) = M(k)/M^*(n)$. Because $M^*(n) \geq M^*(k)$, we have $M(k)/M^*(n) \leq M(k)/M^*(k)$. Combining these results we finally obtain $M(n)/M^*(n) = M(k)/M^*(n) \leq M(k)/M^*(k) \leq 4/3 - 1/3m$. □

The following brief table compares the error bounds for list scheduling (Theorem 9.1) and LPT list scheduling (Theorem 9.3), for different numbers of machines.

Machines m	2	3	4	5	10	20
List scheduling	1.50	1.67	1.75	1.80	1.90	1.95
LPT scheduling	1.17	1.22	1.25	1.27	1.30	1.32

Obviously, the specification of LPT ordering improves the worst-case performance of list scheduling dramatically.

An even more effective heuristic than LPT is available, but it requires somewhat more computational effort. Suppose we are given a possible value M of the makespan, and we wish to determine whether we can construct a schedule that is consistent with this value. We might use a heuristic procedure known as *first-fit decreasing* (FFD). The first step in FFD is to order the jobs according to LPT. At each stage, we attempt to assign the first job on the list to the first machine on which the job will fit. Specifically, we add the job to the existing partial schedule so that it completes on or before M. If no such machine exists, the procedure fails. If such a machine does exist, we remove the job from the LPT list and add it to the existing partial schedule. Then, we repeat this process until all jobs have been scheduled or until a failure occurs.

The FFD routine is an intuitively appealing procedure for determining whether a makespan of M is valid for a given set of jobs. It is only a heuristic procedure because it may sometimes fail when a feasible schedule actually exists. (In computational terms, determining whether M is valid is no easier than solving the makespan problem itself.) However, FFD serves our heuristic purposes as an efficient device for testing the validity of a particular trial value.

In the *multifit algorithm*, we search for the smallest feasible value of M, using FFD to test each trial value. This search can be conducted in an interval between the lower bound on M, which is given by Eq. (9.1), and an upper bound on M, which could be as simple as $\max[2\sum_{j=1}^{n} p_j/m, \max_j\{p_j\}]$, although any feasible solution is likely to provide a better upper bound. It can be shown that the multifit algorithm yields a makespan satisfying $M/M^* \leq 72/61$, or about 1.18. This bound is tighter than that of LPT for $m > 2$ and almost as tight for $m = 2$. However, it does not follow that multifit will always produce a better makespan than LPT.

■ **Example 9.3**   Consider a makespan problem with $m = 3$ machines in which we wish to schedule the following nine jobs.

Job j	1	2	3	4	5	6	7	8	9
p_j	3	3	3	2	2	2	2	2	2

The makespan generated by LPT is $M = 7$, which turns out to be optimal. The multifit algorithm, by contrast, fails to build a feasible schedule for any trial makespan less than $M = 8$ (yielding $M/M^* = 1.14$). Therefore, in this instance, the multifit algorithm does not perform as well as LPT. However, it makes sense to use LPT first, to at least find an upper bound, and then use the multifit algorithm to see whether a better makespan can be achieved. This combined procedure is asymptotically optimal and also performs relatively well for small n.

Theorems 9.1 and 9.3 provide performance guarantees for increasingly more detailed heuristic procedures for identical parallel machines and unrelated jobs. Additional results have been developed for *uniform* machines, a case in which job j has a processing time of p_j on the first machine and a processing time of p_j/s_i on the ith machine. In other words, we can think of s_i as the relative speed of machine i. For uniform machines (without preemption), it makes more sense to schedule according to the time a job will be completed than the time it can start; otherwise, we may schedule a long job on a slow machine and increase the makespan unnecessarily. With this interpretation, a list schedule assigns the next job on the list to the machine that could finish it first. Identifying the corresponding machine, however, requires looking ahead to determine when a faster machine will be available. With this look-ahead refinement in place, the performance ratio for LPT list scheduling on uniform machines is 19/12 or about 1.58. Even naive dispatching (assigning the next job on the list to the first available machine, regardless of speed) is still asymptotically optimal, as long as processing times are finite on all machines. The proof of Theorem 9.2 fails only for the more general case of *unrelated* machines, where each machine processes each job at a different speed.

9.2.2   Nonpreemptable Related Jobs

If there are precedence relations among the jobs, we say the problem involves *related* jobs, as explained in Section 8.3. When we add precedence relations to the makespan problem with parallel machines, we do not make the problem any easier – it remains NP-hard. It comes as no surprise, then, that we have results only for special cases. In this section, we focus on results that provide additional perspective on the makespan problem without precedence relations.

The first special case requires that the precedence relations take the form of an assembly tree. In an *assembly tree* (sometimes called an *intree*), no job has more than one direct successor. Furthermore, in such a tree, the final job – the job without any successors – is called a *terminal job*. In addition, let $p_j =$ 1 for all jobs, so that we have *unit-length* tasks. For this special case, we can solve the makespan problem with an algorithm consisting of a labeling phase followed by a scheduling phase.

Algorithm 9.2 *Minimizing M with an Assembly Tree and Unit-length Jobs (Labeling Phase)*

Step 1. Assign the label zero to the terminal job.

Step 2. Suppose labels 1, 2,..., j – 1 have been assigned. Assign the label j to all jobs with no unlabeled successors.

Step 3. Repeat Step 2 until labels have been assigned to all jobs.

The scheduling phase is essentially a list-scheduling procedure, with jobs in nonincreasing label order to the extent the precedence constraints allow. The labeling phase assigns to each job j a label equal to the length of time required to process the jobs that follow job j on the (unique) path connecting job j and the terminal job. Then, when the scheduling phase places the jobs with the largest labels into the schedule, it essentially gives priority to the jobs that initiate the longest paths in the remaining tree. See Figure 9.3 for an illustration. In the figure, job 1 receives the label 0, jobs 2-4 are labeled 1, 5–7 are labeled 2, 8–11 are labeled 3, 12–16 are labeled 4, and job 17 receives the highest label, 5. In the scheduling phase, job 17 is processed on one of the machines in the first period, and we can select any two additional jobs with label 4, except job 13 (which is not yet feasible), and so on. The longest path is often called the *critical path*. This interpretation echoes the result for the case without precedence relations. Although that problem was NP-hard, the LPT heuristic proved to be very effective. We can interpret the LPT heuristic as giving priority to the job that initiates the longest path in the remaining network of jobs. Thus, the two solution algorithms are structurally similar.

Algorithm 9.2 provides an optimal schedule when the problem contains unit-length jobs and a tree structure. Although a tree has just one terminal job, we can apply the algorithm to the scheduling of several trees by creating a dummy terminal job to serve as successor to the terminal jobs of each of the trees. If we assign the label zero to the dummy job, then each label represents the work remaining on the direct path from the node until completion (including the node itself).

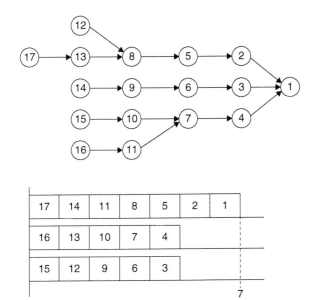

Figure 9.3 An example of implementing Algorithm 9.2.

We can also solve the makespan problem in the case of arbitrary precedence structure and two machines. Again, the algorithm is a list-scheduling procedure, with jobs ordered by label number. The labeling procedure also exhibits a longest-path flavor, but its precise tie-breaking mechanism accounts for its optimizing properties. The key to the algorithm is the notion of lexicographic ordering of two sequences. By *lexicographic* we essentially mean the order in which two sequences, interpreted as words, would appear in a dictionary. More formally, suppose we have sequences $L = (L_1, L_2, ..., L_r)$ and $H = (H_1, H_2, ..., H_s)$. Then we say that L is lexicographically smaller than H if either

1) $L_j = H_j$ for $j \leq i - 1$ and $L_i < H_i$, or
2) $L_j = H_j$ for $1 \leq j \leq r$ and $r < s$.

In other words, L is lexicographically smaller than H if their elements agree up to the $(j - 1)$st element, but the jth element of L is smaller than the jth element of H. Alternatively, L is lexicographically smaller than H if L is shorter than H, and the two sequences agree up to the length of L. The labeling phase of the procedure is shown below as Algorithm 9.3. We assume a single terminal job.

Algorithm 9.3 *Minimizing M with Two Machines, Related Jobs, and Unit-length Jobs (Labeling Phase)*

Step 1. Assign the label zero to the terminal job.

Step 2. Suppose the first (j − 1) labels have been assigned. Consider each job whose successors all have labels. For job k, let $L(k)$ denote the sequence of labels, in nonincreasing order, belonging to its direct successors. Choose the job with the lexicographically smallest $L(k)$, and assign it label j.

Step 3. Repeat Step 2 until labels have been assigned to all jobs.

Figure 9.4 provides an illustration. In this case each job has a unique label, so it is convenient to refer to jobs by their labels. After allocating the label zero to the terminal job, only job 1 can be labeled. Next, both jobs 2 and 3 could be labeled. For job 2 the list of immediate successors is (1) and for job 3 it is (1, 0); (1, 0) is lexicographically larger than (1), so job 2 is selected. When comparing jobs 3 and 4 – which are both ready to be labeled after 2 – the lists are (1, 0) and (2), thus dictating the order, and so on.

Although Algorithm 9.3 generalizes the longest-path notion of Algorithm 9.2 to arbitrary precedence relations, this generalization provides optimal schedules only for two machines and only for unit-length jobs. Beyond two machines, no further generalization seems possible, even with unit-length jobs. With regard to the number of machines, the makespan problem is NP-hard for $m \geq 3$, even

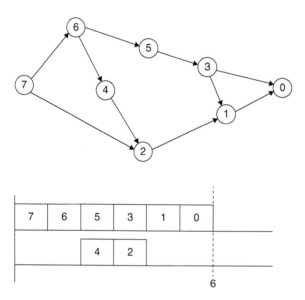

Figure 9.4 An example of implementing Algorithm 9.3.

for sets of unit-length jobs, but we can still use the algorithm as a heuristic. If so, the corresponding worst-case bound is given by Theorem 9.4 (which we present without proof).

■ **Theorem 9.4**   For the m-machine makespan problem with nonpreemptable jobs, arbitrary precedence relations, and m machines, Algorithm 9.3 yields a makespan satisfying $M/M^* \leq 2 - 2/m$.

9.2.3   Preemptable Jobs

We can apply some of the results for nonpreemptable jobs in problems containing preemptable jobs. The key is to think of each job as a chain of unit-length jobs. (Recall from Chapter 8 that each job in a chain has at most one direct predecessor and one direct successor.) Figure 9.5a shows an example containing a set of related jobs with different processing times to be scheduled on two machines. Each job corresponds to a node in the figure, and next to each node is the job's processing time. Figure 9.5b represents the same job set incorporating the chain structure. Specifically, jobs 5, 6, and 7 are represented by chains, and in this case the chains are of length two.

If there were no preemption, then we could construct a schedule from Figure 9.5a. In this case, it would not be hard to see that an optimal makespan on two machines has length $M = 7$. In order to build a schedule from Figure 9.5b, we use Algorithm 9.3, which we know is optimal for unit-length jobs on two machines. The resulting schedule appears in Figure 9.6, with a makespan of $M = 6$.

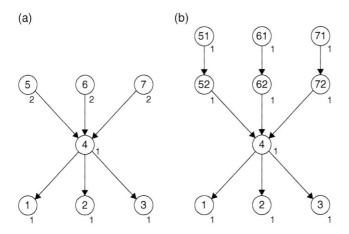

Figure 9.5 A seven-job example in (a) and its preemptable representation in (b).

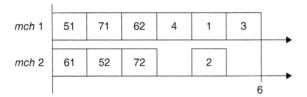

Figure 9.6 A schedule for the job set in Figure 9.5b.

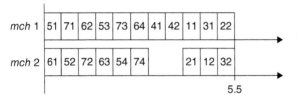

Figure 9.7 An optimal schedule for the example with preemptable jobs.

Clearly, the opportunity to preempt jobs creates some useful flexibility, and we should generally expect that the optimal makespan will be no worse if jobs are preemptable than if the jobs are nonpreemptable. The question that remains is whether schedules like the one shown in Figure 9.6 are in fact optimal when jobs are preemptable. The answer is that a shorter schedule than the one in Figure 9.6 is possible.

In order to find this schedule, we return to Figure 9.5b and replace each node with a chain of half-unit-length jobs. We then use Algorithm 9.3 to construct a schedule. The resulting makespan is $M = 5.5$, as shown in Figure 9.7.

For a two-machine problem, assume that we are given related jobs with integer processing times. Then, to find the optimal makespan for the preemptable version of the problem, we can apply Algorithm 9.3 to the set of related jobs formed when the jobs in the original job set are represented by chains of half-unit length.

9.3 Minimizing Total Flowtime

Whereas the makespan problem is essentially a problem in the optimal allocation of jobs to machines, the minimization of F and F_w requires that we recognize sequencing as well as allocation decisions. The generalization to parallel machines of optimal sequencing properties for the basic single-machine model is fairly straightforward for the F-problem but surprisingly difficult for the F_w-problem.

Consider first the problem of minimizing F. Adopt the following notation:

$p_{i[j]}$ = processing time of the jth job in sequence on the ith machine
$F_{i[j]}$ = flowtime of the jth job in sequence on the ith machine
n_i = number of jobs processed by the ith machine

Then the objective function is

$$F = \sum_{i=1}^{m} \sum_{j=1}^{n_i} F_{i[j]} = \sum_{i=1}^{m} \sum_{j=1}^{n_i} (n_i - j + 1) p_{i[j]}$$

As in the basic single-machine F-problem (see Chapter 2), we can determine a schedule by matching the integer coefficients $(n_i - j + 1)$ with the processing times $(p_{i[j]})$. The objective function corresponds to the scalar product of the coefficients vector and the processing times vector. The coefficients are

$$1, 2, \ldots, n_1, 1, 2, \ldots, n_2, \ldots, 1, 2, \ldots, n_m$$

Unlike the single-machine case, the parallel-machine case allows some discretion in the choice of the coefficients, because the n_i are arbitrary, subject to $n_1 + n_2 + \cdots + n_m = n$. Nevertheless, it should be clear that the scalar product cannot be minimized unless the n_i differ by at most one; that is, their values must satisfy the following inequality:

$$| n_i - n_k | \leq 1, \quad \text{for all pairs } (i, k)$$

In particular, if n is an even multiple of m, it is optimal to assign the same number of jobs to each machine: That is, $n_1 = n_2 = \cdots = n_m$. Once we determine the n_i values, we construct an optimal schedule by matching the processing times in nonincreasing order with the coefficients in nondecreasing order. Thus, we assign the m longest jobs to m different machines, the next m longest jobs to m different machines, and so on, until all jobs are assigned. We can think of this procedure as an assignment of m jobs at a time, which means that several optimal schedules exist, because the individual job-to-machine assignments are not specified at any stage of the algorithm. There is also no need to consider scheduled preemptions.

■ **Example 9.4**   Consider the F-problem with $m = 2$ machines in which we wish to schedule the following six jobs.

Job j	1	2	3	4	5	6
p_j	1	2	3	4	5	6

For two parallel machines the coefficients vector is $(1, 1, 2, 2, 3, 3)$. Therefore, jobs 5 and 6 are assigned to be last on different machines, then jobs 3 and 4 are assigned to different machines, and finally jobs 1 and 2 are assigned to be first on different machines. The algorithm might construct the schedule shown in Figure 9.8, or it might alternatively construct a different schedule, but one with the same optimal value of F.

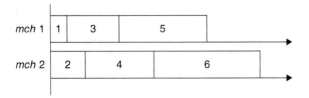

Figure 9.8 An optimal solution to the six-job F-problem.

We can also construct an optimal schedule using a list-scheduling algorithm with the jobs ordered by SPT. Except for ties in processing times, the list-scheduling algorithm produces a unique schedule, which matches one of the schedules produced by the m-jobs-at-a-time approach. The list-scheduling algorithm has two special virtues. First, the algorithm is a dispatching procedure, with scheduling decisions implemented in the order that they are made. Second, the algorithm can be extended in an obvious way to problems with dynamic arrivals, which is not the case for the m-jobs-at-a-time procedure. Thus, the F-problem on parallel machines is easy to solve by a highly intuitive approach.

A slight adaptation of the same approach can solve the F-problem when the machines are uniform. A dispatching algorithm for this case can be based on a list in SPT sequence, but it requires looking ahead. The first unscheduled job on the list should be assigned to the machine on which it would finish first. It is possible that a slow machine may not be used at all or used only for a short time relative to the makespan, but inserted idleness is not needed. The F-problem remains efficiently solvable even in case of unrelated machines, where each machine processes each job at a different speed. The known polynomial-time solution formulates the problem as a network flow model, but for this reason it does not lead to intuitive scheduling insights.

By contrast, the F_w-problem is NP-hard even for identical machines. Dynamic programming formulations are possible, but the "curse of dimensionality" renders a dynamic programming procedure impractical for problems of even moderate size. Two theoretical properties apply to this problem. First, any optimal solution must have SWPT job orderings at each machine. (If this were not true, a simple pairwise interchange on one machine could improve the schedule.) Second, we can calculate a simple lower bound on the optimum value of F_w. Let

$B(1)$ = the minimal value of F_w for the given job set if there were only one machine (obtained via SWPT)

$B(n)$ = the minimal value of F_w for the given job set if there were n machines (obtained by assigning each job to a different machine)

Then a lower bound for m machines ($1 \leq m \leq n$) is

$$B(m) = \frac{1}{2m}[(m-1)B(n) + 2B(1)] \tag{9.4}$$

Clearly, $B = \max\{B(m), B(n)\}$ is also a valid lower bound and may be better because of the rare occasions in which $B(m) < B(n)$.

We can easily imagine two heuristic strategies for solving the F_w-problem. One approach incorporates the m-jobs-at-a-time mechanism into a heuristic procedure denoted by H_m, which works as follows:

Step 1. Form a priority list of all unscheduled jobs according to some rule, R.
Step 2. Assign the first m jobs on the list to different machines. Repeat Step 2 until all jobs are scheduled.
Step 3. Apply SWPT sequencing to each machine.

The complementary heuristic procedure, called H_1, is a list-scheduling algorithm, which assigns one job at a time.

Step 1. Form a priority list of all unscheduled jobs according to some rule, R.
Step 2. Assign the first job on the list to the machine with the least amount of processing. Repeat until all jobs have been assigned.
Step 3. Apply SWPT sequencing to each machine.

■ **Example 9.5** Consider the F_w-problem with $m = 5$ machines in which we wish to schedule the following 10 jobs.

Job j	1	2	3	4	5	6	7	8	9	10
p_j	5	21	16	6	26	19	50	41	32	22
w_j	4	5	3	1	4	2	5	4	3	2
p_j/w_j	1.2	4.2	5.3	6.0	6.5	9.5	10.0	10.2	10.7	11.0

Under H_m an initial ordering must be specified in Step 1. If we choose longest weighted processing time (LWPT), then the jobs are initially in reverse numerical order. At the first stage, jobs 10 through 6 are assigned to different machines, and at the second stage, the remaining jobs are assigned to different machines. Clearly, Step 2 of the procedure does not specify exactly how this second assignment should be made. If the first five assignments were actually fixed, we could show that the optimal assignment of the remaining jobs would be to match the largest weighting factor with the machine having the smallest amount of processing already assigned. Pursuing this rule of thumb, and subsequently applying Step 3 of the procedure, we construct the schedule displayed in Figure 9.9a, with $F_w = 1078$. (The procedure is summarized in Table 9.1.)

Under H_1, with the jobs ordered by LWPT, the procedure simply assigns the jobs one at a time to the least loaded machine, as described in Table 9.2, and finally reorders all jobs so that SWPT prevails on each machine. The schedule that results is slightly better (with $F_w = 1070$) than the one produced above by H_m, as shown in Figure 9.9b.

(a)   (b)

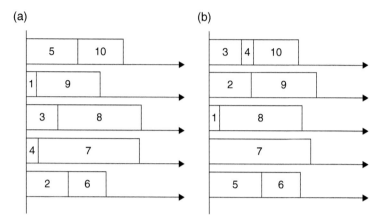

Figure 9.9 Schedules for the example problem from (a) H_m and (b) H_1.

Table 9.1

1. Initial job list	{10, 9, 8, 7, 6, 5, 4, 3, 2, 1}		
2. Assignment phase			
Stage	Processing commitments	Job (w_j)	Machine assigned
1	(0, 0, 0, 0, 0)	10(2)	1
		9(3)	2
		8(4)	3
		7(5)	4
		6(2)	5
2	(22, 32, 41, 50, 19)	5(4)	1
		4(1)	4
		3(3)	3
		2(5)	5
		1(4)	2

3. SWPT at each machine

Machine	Sequence
1	5-10
2	1-9
3	3-8
4	4-7
5	2-6

(See Figure 9.9a)

Table 9.2

1. Initial job list	{10, 9, 8, 7, 6, 5, 4, 3, 2, 1}	
2. Assignment phase		
Processing commitments	Job	Machine assigned
(0, 0, 0, 0, 0)	10	1
(22, 0, 0, 0, 0)	9	2
(22, 32, 0, 0, 0)	8	3
(22, 32, 41, 0, 0)	7	4
(22, 32, 41, 50, 0)	6	5
(22, 32, 41, 50, 19)	5	5
(22, 32, 41, 50, 45)	4	1
(28, 32, 41, 50, 45)	3	1
(44, 32, 41, 50, 45)	2	2
(44, 53, 41, 50, 45)	1	3
3. SWPT at each machine		
Machine	Sequence	
1	3-4-10	
2	2-9	
3	1-8	
4	7	
5	5-6	
(See Figure 9.9b)		

Some experimental research has studied several variations of these heuristic procedures and concluded that their relative behavior is extremely difficult to characterize. The study found that:

- H_1 and H_m may produce different schedules, and either method may produce different schedules when the initial ordering R is varied.
- There is no "best rule" R for H_1 or for H_m.

Those general conclusions aside, however, the most effective variation of the 15 procedures considered in the study was definitely H_1 used with R = SWPT. Not only did this combination produce the best schedule in most of the test problems, but it also has the virtues of list scheduling. In particular, it is a dispatching procedure (Step 3 of H_1 can be omitted), and it can easily be adapted to dynamic problems. The test problems used in these comparisons contained $n = 100$ jobs and up to $m = 6$ machines. The number of jobs was thus relatively large compared with the number of machines. A comparison when the number of jobs is only two or three times the number of machines has not been reported.

The effectiveness of H_1 with R = SWPT observed for a large number of jobs suggests that it may be an asymptotically optimal heuristic. Indeed, if job processing times and weights are obtained by independent sampling from distributions with finite variances, asymptotic optimality is virtually certain. Formally, we say it holds with probability one (*w.p.*1), alternatively described as *almost surely*.

■ **Theorem 9.5**   When processing times and weights are sampled from distributions with finite variances, Algorithm H_1 with R = SWPT is asymptotically optimal *w.p.*1; that is, if the algorithm yields Z and the optimal value is Z^*, then as n grows large, $(Z - Z^*)/Z^*$ tends to zero *w.p.*1.

We provide the proof in our Research Notes.

9.4   Stochastic Models

As we have seen, the parallel-machine makespan problem with nonpreemptable jobs is generally difficult to solve in the deterministic case. Logically, we would expect that the stochastic counterpart is even more difficult to solve. However, one special case exists in which the solution is surprisingly accessible. That is the case of exponentially distributed processing times with dispatching.

Judging by the number of research papers devoted to exponential processing times, we might think they are common in practice, but that is not the case. The exponential distribution is often an appropriate model for arrival processes and sometimes for waiting times, but it rarely fits physical processing times. Nevertheless, the exponential distribution is interesting to study because it possesses special characteristics that make it an important boundary case and because its special characteristics are conducive to elegant theoretical models. As discussed in Appendix A, the exponential distribution lies on the boundary between distributions with increasing and decreasing completion rates, whereas our intuition and much of the empirical data – especially in the context of machine scheduling (as contrasted with complex projects) – suggest that increasing completion rates (ICRs) are more typical.

9.4.1   The Makespan Problem with Exponential Processing Times

As a rule, the analysis of stochastic models tends to be more complex than the analysis of their deterministic counterparts. Sometimes, however, the stochastic aspects of a problem make heuristics more robust than in the deterministic case.

One such instance is the m-machine makespan problem with nonpreemptable jobs. In the special case of exponentially distributed and independent processing times, longest expected processing time (LEPT) dispatching minimizes the expected makespan.

By itself, the optimality of a specific dispatching rule for a highly specialized distribution such as the exponential may not be of crucial importance. Nevertheless, this special case helps us understand the general case, in two ways. First, the result confirms the usefulness of adapting the LPT rule for stochastic processing times. Second, the result highlights a broader question: Should we allocate jobs to machines in advance or use a dispatching rule?

This model illustrates a positive Jensen gap. Suppose we have a two-machine problem in which the machines are loaded equally according to mean processing times. Then the deterministic counterpart yields a makespan equal to half the total processing time. However, in the stochastic case, the probability that both machines finish simultaneously is negligible. On average, one machine finishes earlier than half the total processing time, while the other machine finishes later than half the total processing time. The makespan is always the later of the two finish times; therefore, the expected makespan extends beyond the deterministic makespan by a positive amount equal to the Jensen gap.

In the optimal schedule for the deterministic two-machine problem, the time between the last two job completions must not exceed the processing time of the last job to finish. Moreover, this time difference reveals how close the schedule is to splitting the work equally between the two machines. Thus, it makes sense to have the shortest job finish last, suggesting that LEPT has merit in the stochastic case, at least to the same extent that LPT is a good heuristic for the deterministic case. (These arguments apply to $m > 2$ and for other distributions as well.)

■ **Example 9.6**   Consider the M-problem with $m = 2$ machines in which we wish to schedule $n = 2$ jobs with exponential processing times.

Job j	1	2
μ_j	1	1

To find the expected makespan, we utilize a fundamental algebraic identity: $\max\{A, B\} = A + B - \min\{A, B\}$. Taking the expectation we get $E[\max\{A, B\}] = E[A + B] - E[\min\{A, B\}]$. In general, the minimum of two exponential random variables with means a and b (i.e. with completion rates $1/a$ and $1/b$) is an exponential random variable with a completion rate of $1/a + 1/b$ and thus a mean of $1/(1/a + 1/b)$. In our example, $E[\min\{p_1, p_2\}] = 1/(1/1 + 1/1) = 1/2$. Hence, $E[\max\{p_1, p_2\}] = 2 - 1/2 = 3/2$. This involves a Jensen gap of $1/2$ or 50% of the deterministic counterpart makespan.

In Example 9.6 there is no opportunity to benefit from dispatching because the optimal schedule allocates one job to each machine. To appreciate the more general case, we consider an example with more than two jobs.

■ **Example 9.7**   Consider the M-problem with $m = 2$ machines in which we wish to schedule $n = 4$ jobs with exponential processing times, as shown in the following table.

Job j	1	2	3	4
μ_j	1	2	3	4

The minimal makespan for the deterministic counterpart is $M = 5$ and can be found by the LPT heuristic: Jobs 4 and 3 are allocated to machines 1 and 2 first; then at time 3, job 2 is allocated to machine 2; and at time 4, job 1 is allocated to machine 1. In the stochastic counterpart, LEPT dispatching is optimal, as noted earlier, and a tedious calculation reveals that the expected makespan is 6.271. Without dispatching – that is, if we assign jobs to machines at the outset – the expected makespan would be even greater. Specifically, if we use the optimal deterministic counterpart assignment instead of dispatching, the expected value increases to 7.004.

Knowledge of the optimal dispatching rule should not be considered a full solution. We may also want to know the mean of the resulting makespan or its cdf. However, in deriving the makespan distribution for the LEPT dispatching rule, we must explicitly account for $2^{(n-2)}$ distinct possible allocations of jobs to machines. Thus, we can "solve" the stochastic counterpart in terms of specifying the optimal dispatching rule for minimizing the expected makespan, but we cannot calculate the value of that expectation in polynomial time. In practice, we can resolve this calculation problem by using simulation, but the logic required is more complicated than in the sample-based methodology we introduced in Chapter 6. In this case, each scenario requires its own sequencing decisions. In other words, after generating a set of processing times in a given scenario, we must simulate the job-to-machine assignments that LEPT dispatching would generate. Only then can we compute the makespan for that scenario.

9.4.2   Safe Scheduling with Parallel Machines

We continue with the m-machine makespan problem with nonpreemptable jobs and independent exponential processing time distributions. The LEPT dispatching rule then maximizes the likelihood that the last job will be the shortest one. Thus, LEPT dispatching is not only optimal but also yields the stochastically minimal makespan. To understand why this property is important for safe scheduling, consider two parallel-machine, safe-scheduling problems in which due dates are decisions. In meeting a service-level target, we minimize a due date d subject to a service-level constraint on the makespan, $SL = \Pr\{C_{max} \leq d\} \geq b$. In trading off tightness and tardiness, we optimize $d + \gamma E[T]$ $= d + \gamma E[\max\{0, C_{max} - d\}]$ and determine the optimal due date as a by-product of the optimization. For these two objectives, there is no reason to believe that the same sequence (or dispatching rule) is necessarily optimal for both. However, when a stochastically minimal sequence (or dispatching rule) exists, it must be the optimal sequence for both objectives.

■ **Theorem 9.6** Suppose a sequence exists that yields a stochastically minimal makespan distribution. Then this sequence is optimal for minimizing d subject to a service-level constraint $SL \geq b$ and for minimizing $d + \gamma E[T]$.

■ **Example 9.8** Revisit Example 9.7 with the objective of minimizing $d + \gamma E[T]$ with $\gamma = 10$.

Job j	1	2	3	4
μ_j	1	2	3	4

Recall from Chapter 7 that the optimal service level is given by $(\gamma - 1)/\gamma = 0.9$. Here, knowledge of the optimal dispatching rule is not sufficient because we cannot calculate the correct safety time without a distribution for the makespan. As we mentioned earlier, deriving this distribution is a challenging analytic problem, which would be exponentially more complicated for larger n. However, we can estimate the desired value using simulation. Building a simulation model with Analytic Solver Platform, as described in Chapter 6, we estimate the optimal due date at 11.125.

9.5 Summary

As noted at the outset of this chapter, problems of scheduling single-stage jobs with parallel processors contain both allocation and sequencing dimensions. The determination of optimal schedules is often rendered difficult by the need to make both kinds of decisions, and the thrust of analytic results has been aimed primarily at makespan problems for good reason: Makespan problems involve only allocation. Indeed, in single-machine models, the makespan criterion is seldom an important consideration unless sequence-dependent setup times are involved.

From a practical viewpoint, the emphasis on makespan in the parallel-machine case is quite reasonable, because a generic heuristic procedure for nonpreemptable jobs would be to solve the allocation problem first and then the sequencing problem. In other words, we should distribute the processing load among machines as evenly as possible and then determine an optimal sequence on each machine separately. Although an even distribution of the load (i.e. a minimal makespan) is not necessarily optimal for measures other than the makespan, it tends to provide good schedules. Moreover, this two-phase method of determining a schedule is a more practicable way of managing the large combinatorial problem represented by scheduling with parallel machines. The main exception to this approach is the *F*-problem, for which a straightforward optimization procedure exists.

In stochastic instances, the separation of allocation and sequencing is less effective. A simple four-job example demonstrated that significant differences in makespan may occur with and without dispatching, and using dispatching for the makespan objective implies that we cannot first allocate and then sequence. Furthermore, there is an inherent conflict between the two most important performance measures, namely, makespan and flowtime.

The important makespan results are the construction of an optimal schedule using Algorithm 9.1 for unrelated, preemptable jobs, the longest-first or "critical path" priorities contained in Algorithms 9.2 and 9.3, and the LPT list-scheduling procedure. Other specialized algorithms and heuristic procedures are largely based on the concepts underlying these fundamental results. Optimization in the stochastic model requires us, in practice, to use simulation. Finally, although different list-scheduling policies do lead to pronounced differences in the makespan, we showed that they are all asymptotically optimal, which means that they all converge to the optimal value as *n* grows large.

The minimization of total flowtime with parallel processors involves a generalization of single-machine analysis, but the minimization of total weighted flowtime or total tardiness is not easily accomplished. For the total weighted flowtime problem, it is possible to find an optimal schedule using an *m*-dimensional dynamic programming approach, but its computational requirements are severe. Fortunately, experimental evidence has indicated that, at least for large problems, simple heuristic approaches consistently produce schedules within 1% or 2% of optimum. The simplest heuristic of them all – SWPT dispatching – is asymptotically optimal, which explains its superior performance for large problems.

Asymptotic optimality of list scheduling applies to stochastic problems if processing times are independent and have finite variances. This is true even if we allocate jobs to machines in advance. If we use any list as the basis for dispatching, the result is asymptotically optimal even if processing times are correlated (as long as they do not depend on the sequence itself). Therefore, we can expect to obtain good performance from simple heuristics, such as list scheduling based on LEPT for makespan. For the total flowtime problem, SEPT is known to be optimal, even for preemptable jobs, provided that the processing time distributions exhibit ICRs. In the weighted version, we would expect that SWEPT is an effective heuristic.

Exercises

9.1 Consider a makespan problem involving three identical machines and the following set of eight jobs. Assume that no preemption is permitted.

Job j	1	2	3	4	5	6	7	8
p_j	1	2	3	4	5	6	7	8

   a) What is the makespan generated by an SPT list schedule?
   b) What is the makespan generated by an LPT list schedule?
   c) What is the minimum makespan?

9.2 The following 11 operations are to be scheduled on four parallel machines.

Job j	A	B	C	D	E	F	G	H	I	J	K
p_j	12	6	7	8	2	3	15	17	20	14	19

Management's goals are:
- Minimize F, the overall time in the shop.
- Reduce M, the maximum time in the shop.
     a) What sequence do you suggest? Justify your choice.
     b) Present your result in a Gantt chart, and calculate the F and M values.
     c) Is this result optimal for one of these measures? For both? Explain.

9.3 The following 12 operations are to be scheduled on three parallel machines.

Job j	A	B	C	D	E	F	G	H	I	J	K	L
p_j	12	6	7	8	2	3	15	17	20	14	19	10

Solve the problem using a list schedule and test the following variations:
   a) Use random order, and compare results with the bound in Theorem 9.1.
   b) Use SPT order, and compare results with (a) and the bound in Theorem 9.1.

c) Use LPT order, and compare results with (b) and the bound in Theorem 9.3.

9.4 Consider the scheduling of n nonpreemptable jobs on m identical parallel machines using an SPT list schedule. Show that this procedure assigns the jobs to machines in rotation. That is, if the jth job on the list is assigned to machine i ($1 \le i \le m - 1$), then the $(j + 1)$st job will be assigned to machine $(i + 1)$; and if the jth job on the list is assigned to machine m, then the $(j + 1)$st job will be assigned to machine 1.

9.5 Consider the makespan minimization problem on m machines with machine release dates. Show that Theorem 9.2 still applies.

9.6 Construct a two-machine example to show that SWPT list scheduling does not guarantee minimum F_w.

9.7 In the following example, there are eight jobs and three parallel, identical machines. The table gives the processing times for each job and the (unique) direct successor, S_j, for each job.

Job j	1	2	3	4	5	6	7	8
p_j	1	3	4	2	1	2	2	2
S_j	–	1	1	1	2	2	4	4

a) Find a schedule that minimizes the makespan, assuming that no preemption of the jobs is permitted.
b) Find a schedule that minimizes the makespan, assuming that preemption is permitted.

Bibliography

Baker, K.R. and Merten, A.G. (1973). Scheduling with parallel processors and linear delay costs. *Naval Research Logistics Quarterly* 20: 793–804.

Cheng, T.C.E. and Sin, C.C.S. (1990). A state-of-the-art review of parallel-machine scheduling research. *European Journal of Operational Research* 47: 271–292.

Coffman, E.G. and Graham, R.L. (1972). Optimal scheduling for two processor systems. *Acta Informatica* 1: 200–213.

Coffman, E.G., Garey, M.R., and Johnson, D.S. (1978). An application of bin packing to multiprocessor scheduling. *SIAM Journal of Computing* 7: 1–17.

Conway, R.W., Maxwell, W.L., and Miller, L.W. (1967). *Theory of Scheduling*. Reading, MA: Addison-Wesley.

Dobson, G. (1984). Scheduling independent tasks on uniform processors. *SIAM Journal of Computing* 13: 705–716.

Eastman, W.L., Even, S., and Isaacs, I.M. (1964). Bounds for the optimal scheduling of *n* jobs on *m* processors. *Management Science* 11: 268–279.

Friesen, D.K. and Langston, M.A. (1986). Evaluation of a multifit-based scheduling algorithm. *Journal of Algorithms* 7: 35–59.

Graham, R.L. (1969). Bounds on multiprocessor timing anomalies. *SIAM Journal of Applied Mathematics* 17: 416–425.

Hu, T.C. (1961). Parallel sequencing and assembly line problems. *Operations Research* 9: 841–848.

Kao, T.Y. and Elsayed, E.A. (1990). Performance of the LPT algorithm in multiprocessor scheduling. *Computers and Operations Research* 17: 365–373.

Lam, S. and Sethi, R. (1977). Worst case analysis of two scheduling algorithms. *SIAM Journal of Computing* 6: 518–536.

Lee, C.-Y. (1991). Parallel machines scheduling with nonsimultaneous machine available time. *Discrete Applied Mathematics* 30: 53–61.

Lee, C.-Y. and Massey, J.D. (1988). Multiprocessor scheduling: combining LPT and multifit. *Discrete Applied Mathematics* 20: 233–242.

McNaughton, R. (1959). Scheduling with deadlines and loss functions. *Management Science* 6: 1–12.

Portougal, V. (1993). Asymptotic behavior of some scheduling algorithms. *Asia-Pacific Journal of Operational Research* 10: 71–91.

Root, J.G. (1965). Scheduling with deadlines and loss functions on *k* parallel machines. *Management Science* 11: 460–475.

Rothkopf, M.H. (1966). Scheduling independent tasks on parallel processors. *Management Science* 12: 437–447.

10

Flow Shop Scheduling

10.1 Introduction

This chapter deals with a model based on the design in which machines are arranged in series. In this design, jobs flow from an initial machine, through several intermediate machines, and ultimately to a final machine before completing. Traditionally, we refer to this design as a *flow shop*, even though an actual shop may contain much more than a single serial configuration.

In a flow shop, the work in a job is broken down into separate tasks called *operations*, and each operation is performed at a different machine. In this context, a *job* is a collection of operations with a special precedence structure. In particular, each operation after the first has exactly one direct predecessor, and each operation before the last has exactly one direct successor, as shown in Figure 10.1. Thus, each job requires a specific sequence of operations to be carried out for the job to be complete.

The shop contains m different machines, and in the "pure" flow shop model, each job consists of m operations, each of which requires a different machine. The machines in a flow shop can thus be numbered 1, 2, ..., m; and the operations of job j are numbered $(1, j)$, $(2, j)$, ..., (m, j), so that they correspond to the machine required. For example, p_{53} denotes the operation time on machine 5 for job 3. Figure 10.2 represents the flow of work in a "pure" flow shop, in which all jobs require one operation on each machine.

Figure 10.3 represents the flow of work in a more general flow shop. In the general case, jobs may require fewer than m operations, their operations may not always require adjacent machines, and the initial and final operations may not always occur at machines 1 and m. Nevertheless, the flow of work is still unidirectional, and we can represent the general case as a pure flow shop in which some of the operation times are zero.

Principles of Sequencing and Scheduling, Second Edition. Kenneth R. Baker and Dan Trietsch.
© 2019 John Wiley & Sons, Inc. Published 2019 by John Wiley & Sons, Inc.

Figure 10.1 The precedence structure of a job in a flow shop.

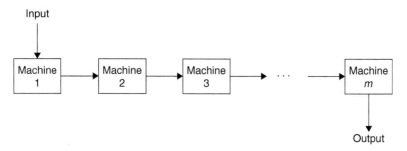

Figure 10.2 Workflow in a pure flow shop.

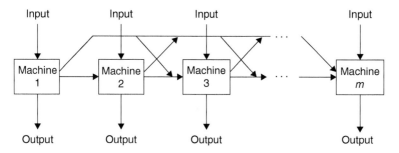

Figure 10.3 Workflow in a general flow shop.

With machines in series, the conditions that characterize the flow shop model are similar to the conditions of the basic single-machine model:

C1.   A set of n unrelated, multiple-operation jobs is available for processing at time zero. (Each job requires m operations, and each operation requires a different machine.)

C2.   Setup times for the operations are sequence independent and included in processing times.

C3.   Job descriptors are known in advance.

C4.   All machines are continuously available.

C5.   Once an operation begins, it proceeds without interruption.

One difference from the basic single-machine case is that inserted idle time may be advantageous. In the single-machine model with simultaneous arrivals, we can assume that the machine need never be kept idle when work is waiting. In the flow shop case, however, we may need inserted idle time to achieve optimality.

■ **Example 10.1**   Consider a problem containing $n = 2$ jobs in a four-machine flow shop.

Job j	1	2
p_{1j}	1	4
p_{2j}	4	1
p_{3j}	4	1
p_{4j}	1	4

Suppose that F is the measure of performance. The two schedules shown in Figure 10.4a, b are the only schedules with no inserted idle time, and in either schedule, $F = 24$. The schedule in Figure 10.4c is an optimal schedule, with $F = 23$. Note that in this third schedule, machine 3 is kept idle at time $t = 5$, when

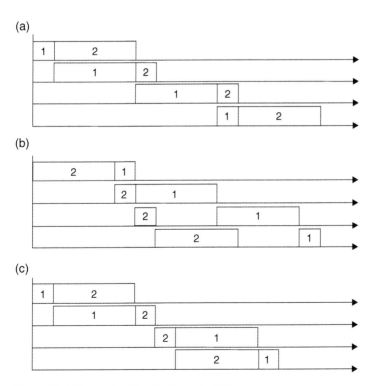

Figure 10.4 Three schedules for Example 10.1.

operation (3, 1) could be started, in order to await the completion of operation (2, 2). For minimizing the makespan, the advantage of the schedule in Figure 10.4c is even larger, a makespan of 12 instead of 14.

In the single-machine model, there is a one-to-one relation between a job sequence and a permutation of the numbers 1, 2, ..., n. To find an optimal sequence, it is necessary to examine (at least implicitly) each of the sequences corresponding to the $n!$ different permutations. Similarly, in the flow shop problem, there are $n!$ different job sequences possible for each machine and potentially as many as $(n!)^m$ different schedules. As we search for an optimum, it would obviously be helpful if we could ignore many of these possibilities. In the next section we discuss the extent to which the search for an optimum can be reduced. Then, we examine the case $m = 2$, which is an interesting problem in its own right and a building block for solving larger problems. We then look at optimization methods and heuristic approaches, and we introduce some variations of the basic model.

10.2 Permutation Schedules

Example 10.1 illustrates that it may not be sufficient to consider only schedules in which the same job sequence occurs on each machine. On the other hand, it is not always necessary to consider $(n!)^m$ schedules in determining an optimum. The two dominance properties given below indicate how much of a reduction is possible in flow shop problems.

■ **Theorem 10.1** With respect to any regular measure of performance in the flow shop model, it is sufficient to consider only schedules in which the same job sequence occurs on the first two machines.

Proof. Consider a schedule in which the sequences on machines 1 and 2 are different. Somewhere in such a schedule we can find a pair of jobs, i and j, with operation (1, i) preceding an adjacent operation (1, j) but operation (2, j) preceding (2, i), as in Figure 10.5a. For this pair, we can impose on machine 1 the order of the jobs on machine 2 (j before i), without adversely affecting the performance measure. If we interchange operations (1, i) and (1, j), resulting in the schedule shown in Figure 10.5b, then

- with the exception of (1, i), no operation is delayed,
- operation (2, i) is not delayed, and
- earlier processing of (2, j), and other operations as well, may result.

Therefore, the interchange would not increase the completion time of any operation on machine 2 or on any subsequent machine. This means that no increase in any job completion time could result from the interchange and hence no increase in any regular measure of performance. The same argument

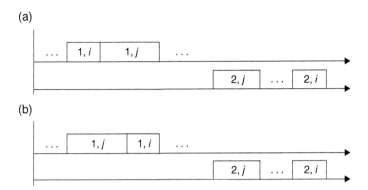

Figure 10.5 A pairwise interchange of two adjacent operations on machine 1.

applies to any schedule in which job sequences differ on machines 1 and 2, so the property must hold in general. □

■ **Theorem 10.2** With respect to the makespan of the flow shop model, it is sufficient to consider only schedules in which the same job sequence occurs on the last two machines.

Proof. Consider a schedule in which the sequences on machines $(m - 1)$ and m are different. Somewhere in such a schedule we can find a pair of jobs, i and j, with operation (m, j) preceding an adjacent operation (m, i) but operation $(m - 1, i)$ preceding $(m - 1, j)$. As a result of interchanging operations (m, i) and (m, j),

- with the exception of (m, j), no operation is delayed,
- operation (m, j) completes no later than (m, i) in the original schedule, and
- earlier processing of operations (m, i) and (m, j) may result.

Therefore, the interchange would not lead to an increase in the makespan of the schedule. Again, this type of argument applies to any schedule in which job sequences differ on machines $(m - 1)$ and m. Therefore, the property must hold. □

The implication of these two theorems is that in searching for an optimal schedule, it is necessary to consider different job sequences on different machines with these two general exceptions:

1) For any regular measure, it is sufficient for the same job order to occur on the first two machines, so that $(n!)^{m-1}$ schedules constitute a dominant set.
2) For makespan problems, it is also sufficient for the same job order to occur on the last two machines, so that $(n!)^{m-2}$ schedules constitute a dominant set for $m > 2$.

A *permutation schedule* is simply a schedule with the same job order on all machines – a schedule that is completely characterized by a single permutation of the job indices 1, 2, ..., n. As a consequence of Theorems 10.1 and 10.2, we may consider only permutation schedules in the following cases:

- Optimizing a regular measure of performance when $m = 2$.
- Optimizing makespan when $m = 2$ or 3.

In addition, the makespan problem is symmetric: If we can solve the problem with the machine order reversed, then we can reverse the optimal permutation, and we will have an optimal solution to the original problem. Even when it is sufficient to deal only with permutation schedules, and even when we can exploit symmetry, it may still be difficult to locate optima efficiently. The next section deals with one flow shop problem that is relatively easy to solve.

10.3 The Two-machine Problem

10.3.1 Johnson's Rule

The objective of minimizing makespan in the two-machine flow shop model is also known as Johnson's problem. The results originally obtained by Johnson (1954) are among the very first formal results in the theory of scheduling. In the formulation of this problem, job j is characterized by processing time p_{1j}, required on machine 1, and p_{2j}, required on machine 2 after the operation on machine 1 is complete. For convenience in the exposition, however, we use a_j in place of p_{1j} and b_j in place of p_{2j}. (We return to the use of double sub-scripts when there are several machines.) There exists some optimal sequence satisfying the following rule for ordering pairs of jobs.

■ **Theorem 10.3** (*Johnson's Rule*). Job i precedes job j in an optimal sequence if $\min\{a_i, b_j\} \leq \min\{a_j, b_i\}$.

In practice, an optimal sequence is directly constructed with an adaptation of Theorem 10.3. The positions in sequence are filled by a one-pass mechanism that, at each stage, identifies a job that should fill either the first or last available position.

Algorithm 10.1 *Implementing Johnson's Rule*

Step 1. Find the minimum processing time among unscheduled jobs.

Step 2. If the minimum time in Step 1 occurs on machine 1, place the associated job in the first available position in sequence and go to Step 4; otherwise, go to Step 3. (Ties for the minimum time on machine 1 may be broken arbitrarily.)

Step 3. The minimum in Step 1 occurs on machine 2, so place the associated job in the last available position in sequence. (Ties for the minimum time on machine 2 may be broken arbitrarily.) Go to Step 4.

Step 4. Remove the assigned job from consideration, and return to Step 1 until all sequence positions are filled.

We illustrate the algorithm with an example.

■ **Example 10.2** Consider a problem containing $n = 5$ jobs in a two-machine flow shop.

Job j	1	2	3	4	5
a_j	3	5	1	6	7
b_j	6	2	2	6	5

Table 10.1 shows how an optimal sequence is constructed in five stages using Algorithm 10.1. At each stage, Step 1 identifies $\min_j\{a_j, b_j\}$. Then Step 2 fills one position in sequence, and the process is repeated. The sequence that emerges is 3-1-4-5-2. The schedule produced by the algorithm, shown in Figure 10.6, has a makespan of 24.

Table 10.1

Stage	Unscheduled jobs	$\min_j\{a_j, b_j\}$	Assignment	Partial schedule
1	1,2,3,4,5	a_3	$[1] = 3$	3-x-x-x-x
2	1,2,4,5	b_2	$[5] = 2$	3-x-x-x-2
3	1,4,5	a_1	$[2] = 1$	3-1-x-x-2
4	4,5	b_5	$[4] = 5$	3-1-x-5-2
5	4	$a_4 = b_4$	$[3] = 4$	3-1-4-5-2

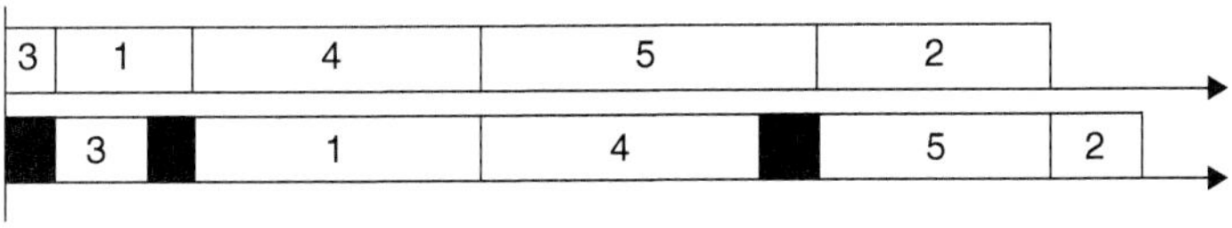

Figure 10.6 The schedule produced by Algorithm 10.1 for Example 10.2.

An alternative exists for implementing Johnson's rule that provides a different perspective on the structure of optimal schedules. In this implementation, shown as Algorithm 10.2, we first partition the jobs into two sets, according to whether the first operation is shorter or longer than the second operation. Then, we sequence the jobs with shorter first operations by applying SPT to their a_j values, and we sequence the jobs with longer first operations by applying LPT to their b_j values. Finally, we arrange the two sequences in tandem to produce a full sequence for the solution.

Algorithm 10.2 *Implementing Johnson's Rule*

Step 1. Let $U = \{j | a_j \leq b_j\}$ and $V = \{j | a_j > b_j\}$.
Step 2. Arrange the members of set U in nondecreasing order of a_j, and arrange the members of set V in nonincreasing order of b_j.
Step 3. An optimal sequence is the ordered set U followed by the ordered set V.

In Step 1 of the algorithm, including jobs with $a_j = b_j$ in U rather than in V is arbitrary. Such jobs may be assigned to set U or to set V. However, Algorithm 10.2 reduces the total flowtime relative to the alternative implementations. For the same reason, we may choose to break ties in Step 2 by placing the shortest b_j in U and the shortest a_j in V, but in principle we can break such ties arbitrarily.

10.3.2   A Proof of Johnson's Rule

This section provides two perspectives on Johnson's Rule. First, we justify Algorithm 10.1. Second, we address Theorem 10.3 and exploit the potential for using an adjacent pairwise interchange argument. For convenience, we number the jobs according to their position in sequence.

In the two-machine model, the completion time for operation k of job j can be calculated recursively as follows:

$$C_{1j} = C_{1,j-1} + a_j$$

$$C_{2j} = \max\{C_{1j}, C_{2,j-1}\} + b_j$$

where $C_{10} = C_{20} = 0$, and we assume that jobs are processed as early as possible (as in Figure 10.6). If we add a constant p to all operation times, then we simply increase the completion time of job j by jp on machine 1 and by $(j + 1)p$ on machine 2. In particular, the makespan increases by $(n + 1)p$, but the optimality of a sequence will not be affected by the transformation.

If $a_j = 0$, then there exists an optimal sequence in which job j comes first. (To show this property, suppose no such optimal sequence exists. Then interchange job *j* with the first job in the optimal sequence, and confirm that the makespan does not get worse.) From symmetry, if $b_j = 0$, then there exists an optimal sequence in which job *j* comes last.

These two properties – adding a constant to processing times and sequencing a zero processing time – justify Algorithm 10.1. Given a set of jobs, we can calculate the constant $p = -\min_i[\min\{a_i, b_i\}]$ and add it to all processing times. This creates at least one processing time of zero. If $a_j = 0$, then we can assign job *j* to the first position in sequence. This corresponds to Step 2 of Algorithm 10.1. Similarly, if $b_j = 0$, then we can assign job *j* to the last position in sequence. This corresponds to Step 3 of Algorithm 10.1. Thus, Algorithm 10.1 is optimal by construction.

We turn now to Johnson's rule itself and interpret it as a sorting rule, one that can be justified with an adjacent pairwise interchange argument. Suppose that there exists a schedule *S* containing a pair of adjacent jobs *i* and *j*, with *j* following *i*, satisfying $\min\{a_i, b_j\} > \min\{a_j, b_i\}$, thus violating Johnson's rule. We construct schedule S' by interchanging jobs *i* and *j*. We want to show that this interchange cannot increase the makespan and may reduce it. For this purpose, we use the notion of total idle time on machine 2, denoted i_2. We can express the makespan as follows:

$$M = i_2 + \sum_{j=1}^{n} b_j$$

In other words, our objective is to minimize i_2 because the sum of processing times on machine 2 is constant.

Let $b_0 = 0$ and define

$$y_j = \sum_{k=1}^{j} (a_k - b_{k-1})$$

Assuming that jobs are processed on machine 1 without inserted idle time, y_j represents the difference between two times: the time required to process the first *j* jobs on machine 1 and the time required to process the first $(j-1)$ jobs on machine 2. Before job *j* starts on machine 2, there must have been at least this much idle time on machine 2, so $i_2 \geq y_j$. Thus, we obtain $i_2 = \max\{y_j\}$, allowing us to express the makespan as

$$M = i_2 + \sum_{j=1}^{n} b_j = \max_j\{y_j\} + \sum_{j=1}^{n} b_j$$

Thus, we are interested in minimizing $\max_j\{y_j\}$. We rewrite the given condition $\min\{a_i, b_j\} > \min\{a_j, b_i\}$ as follows:

$$\max\{-a_i, -b_j\} < \max\{-a_j, -b_i\} \tag{10.1}$$

To both sides we add the constant P, where

$$P = \sum_{k \in B} a_k + a_i + a_j - \sum_{k \in B} b_k$$

and B denotes the set of jobs preceding i and j. Adding P to Eq. (10.1) yields

$$\max\{P - a_i, P - b_j\} < \max\{P - b_i, P - a_j\} \tag{10.2}$$

Now observe that

$$P - a_i = \sum_{k \in B} a_k + a_j - \sum_{k \in B} b_k = y_j(S')$$

$$P - b_j = \sum_{k \in B} a_k + a_i + a_j - \sum_{k \in B} b_k - b_j = y_i(S')$$

$$P - b_i = \sum_{k \in B} a_k + a_i + a_j - \sum_{k \in B} b_k - b_i = y_j(S)$$

$$P - a_j = \sum_{k \in B} a_k + a_i - \sum_{k \in B} b_k = y_i(S)$$

Hence Eq. (10.2) becomes

$$\max\{y_j(S'), y_i(S')\} < \max\{y_i(S), y_j(S)\}$$

so that the interchange leaves the objective function no worse off and may actually improve it. The remaining step in the proof is to show that Johnson's rule is transitive.

In a rigorous sense, transitivity may not hold if there are ties. Here lies an insight that did not arise in our single-machine cases. When we implement sorting rules such as SPT for a single machine, we are indifferent to tie-breaking mechanisms, and moreover, each different way of breaking a tie leads to an alternative optimum. Thus, SPT is necessary and sufficient for optimality. However, in the two-machine flow shop problem, Johnson's rule is sufficient but not necessary, and we may not be indifferent when ties occur. We provide an example to illustrate this point.

∎ **Example 10.3** Consider a problem containing $n = 3$ jobs in a two-machine flow shop.

Job j	1	2	3
a_j	4	2	4
b_j	3	2	5

The sequence 1-2-3 has the property that $\min\{a_i, b_j\} \leq \min\{a_j, b_i\}$ for consecutive pairs 1-2 and 2-3. However, its makespan of 15 is not optimal. The problem lies in the fact that $\min\{a_i, b_j\} \leq \min\{a_j, b_i\}$ does not hold for the pair 1-3. In other words, it is possible in this example to construct a sequence with the property that adjacent pairs satisfy Johnson's inequality, but nonadjacent pairs do not. This feature can occur only when there are ties, and it reflects the fact that Johnson's rule is not rigorously transitive. Thus, we could state the rule as a strict inequality. Then it would be transitive, but it might not order a given job set completely. On the other hand, when we state the rule as in Theorem 10.3, it orders a set of jobs completely; but only when we break ties correctly does it permit us to construct optimal sequences in $O(n \log n)$ time. Fortunately, Algorithms 10.1 and 10.2 always break ties correctly. In the example, Algorithms 10.1 and 10.2 both yield the sequence 2-3-1 (although 3-1-2 is also an optimal sequence).

10.3.3 The Model with Time Lags

Time lags (start lags and stop lags) allow for splitting and overlapping of jobs. That is, processing can begin at machine 2 on an early portion of a job, while the later portion is still at machine 1. We define a start lag u_j as the required delay between the start of a job's first operation and the start of its second operation. Analogously, a stop lag v_j is the required delay between the completion of a job's first operation and the completion of its second. A typical application would be a situation where each job is a batch consisting of several discrete and identical units. Once the first unit completes at machine 1, it can immediately begin processing at machine 2. In that case, the start lag represents the time to process one unit on machine 1, and the stop lag represents the time to process one unit on machine 2. In other words, we would be using a "transfer batch" of size 1. Obviously, we can also model larger transfer batches with the use of time lags. In the case of start lags and stop lags, the optimal permutation schedule is characterized by a rule analogous to Johnson's rule: Specifically, job i precedes job j in an optimal sequence if

$$\min\{a_i + d_i, b_j + d_j\} \leq \min\{a_j + d_j, b_i + d_i\} \tag{10.3}$$

where

$$d_j = \max\{u_j - a_j, v_j - b_j\} \tag{10.4}$$

The form of Eq. (10.4), in which d_j is usually negative, reflects the fact that one of the two time lags will always guarantee the other. If we have $d_j = u_j - a_j \geq v_j - b_j$, then a schedule that meets the start-lag constraint will automatically satisfy the stop-lag constraint. On the other hand, if we have $d_j = v_j - b_j \geq u_j - a_j$, then a schedule that meets the stop-lag constraint will automatically satisfy the start-lag constraint. In either case, d_j represents the time required between the completion of the first operation and the start of the second operation. Some expositions refer to d_j as the *transfer lag*.

10.3.4 The Model with Setups

In light of condition C2 for the basic two-machine model, setup times are assumed to be not only sequence independent but also contained in processing times. For certain applications, however, it is useful to treat the setup times explicitly. For this purpose we define s_{1j} as the setup time for job j on machine 1 and s_{2j} as the setup time on machine 2.

In the basic model, under C2, the first operation of a job must complete on machine 1 before setup of machine 2 can begin. This feature is sometimes called an *attached* setup time, meaning that the setup is "attached" to the job and cannot be done while the job is somewhere else. Stated another way, the setup cannot be scheduled in anticipation of arriving work. We can analyze this version of the two-machine flow shop problem in the original manner. Specifically, let $A_j = s_{1j} + a_j$ and $B_j = s_{2j} + b_j$, and then adapt Johnson's rule to construct the optimal sequence: job i precedes job j in an optimal sequence if $\min\{A_i, B_j\} \leq \min\{A_j, B_i\}$. The uppercase notation denotes a compound processing time, with "processing" taken to mean both setup time and run time.

As a variation, suppose that the setup times are *separable*. In other words, the setups at machine 2 can be detached and scheduled in anticipation of arriving work. Assume, nevertheless, that each job must be completed at machine 1 before it can begin work at machine 2. Under these assumptions, we can develop a schedule by using the time-lag model. Specifically, the start lag is $u_j = s_{1j} + a_j - s_{2j}$ and the stop lag is $v_j = b_j$. It follows that the transfer lag is $d_j = \max\{s_{1j} - s_{2j}, 0\}$, from which Eq. (10.3) can be used to construct an optimal sequence.

10.4   Special Cases of the Three-machine Problem

For the makespan criterion and $m = 3$ machines, it is sufficient to consider only permutation schedules in the search for an optimum, yet it is difficult to generalize the two-machine result. Indeed, the general three-machine problem is NP-hard. However, there are several special cases in which the three-machine problem can be solved efficiently, with procedures that resemble Johnson's rule for the two-machine problem. In the cases listed below, it is possible to find an optimum without resorting to enumerative search.

Case 1. Machine 1 dominates machine 2: $\min\{p_{1j}\} \geq \max\{p_{2j}\}$.
Solution: Apply Johnson's rule to the pseudo-two-machine problem formed by $a'_j = p_{1j} + p_{2j}$ and $b'_j = p_{2j} + p_{3j}$. The optimal sequence in the pseudoproblem is optimal for the original. (This procedure is sometimes called *Johnson's approximate method.*)

Case 2. Machine 3 dominates machine 2: $\min\{p_{3j}\} \geq \max\{p_{2j}\}$.
Solution: Johnson's approximate method.

Case 3. Regressive second stage: $p_{2j} \leq \min\{p_{1j}, p_{3j}\}$ for all j.
Solution: Johnson's approximate method.

Case 4. Machine 2 dominates machine 1: $\min\{p_{2j}) \geq \max\{p_{1j}\}$.
Solution: Solve the two-machine problem corresponding to machines 2 and 3. Let job k denote the first job in this sequence. Generate additional sequences by inserting in first position jobs with $p_{1j} \leq p_{1k}$. Among these sequences (the two-machine solution sequence and the additional sequences), the one with the smallest makespan in the three-machine problem is optimal.

Case 5. Machine 2 dominates machine 3: $\min\{p_{2j}\} \geq \max\{p_{3j}\}$.
Solution: A symmetric version of the procedure in Case 4.

Case 6. Johnson's extended rule: If job i is preferred to job j under Johnson's rule for each of the two-machine subproblems represented by machine pairs 1-2, 2-3, and 1-3, and if these (i, j) preference orderings form a complete sequence, then such a sequence is optimal for the three-machine problem.

Case 7. Constant second stage: If p_{2j} is a constant, and if shortest processing time (SPT) priority applied to machine 1 yields the same sequence as longest processing time (LPT) priority applied to machine 3, then this sequence is optimal.

Case 8. Lower bound condition: Let M denote the makespan corresponding to an optimal sequence to the pseudoproblem of Johnson's approximate method, and let M' denote the actual makespan in the three-machine problem for the same sequence. That sequence is optimal if

$$M = M' + \sum_{j=1}^{n} p_{2j}$$

Some experimental studies have explored the likelihood of these conditions in sample problems. In test problems, processing times were first drawn at random from a uniform distribution. This procedure gives rise to what might be called a "random shop" problem structure. However, the existing flow shop literature suggests a number of other interesting structures as well. Below we list six different structures that formed the basis of the test data:

S1. *Random shop:* Processing times are independent samples drawn from a uniform distribution.

S2. *Ordered shop:* Two relationships apply: (i) If job i has a smaller processing time than job j on machine k, then job i also has a processing time no larger than that of job j on each other machine; and (ii) if job i has its rth smallest processing time on machine k, then so does every other job.

S3. *Constant second stage:* Processing times for machines 1 and 3 are independent samples drawn from a uniform distribution; processing times on machine 2 are constant.

S4. *Correlated shop:* If the processing time of a job is large on one particular machine, then the job's processing times on other machines also tend to be large.

S5. *Trend shop:* Processing times are positively correlated with machine number.

S6. Correlation-trend shop: A combination of *S4* and *S5*.

Structures *S4* and *S6* were included because they seem to represent relatively difficult flow shop problems to solve by enumerative techniques.

For each of the six shop structures, test problems were created with 5, 20, and 50 jobs. For each combination of shop structure and problem size, 50 job sets were created, for a combined total of 900 test problems. Overall, at least one of the eight conditions held in approximately half the test problems, and in the vast majority of problems where at least one of the conditions held, the lower bound condition (*Case 8*) was successful. Correlation in the test data (*S4* and *S6*) led to fewer successes as problem size increased, while the opposite was true for trend alone (*S5*). In addition, *Case 8* accounted for most of the successes. In fact, for structures *S1*, *S4*, *S5*, and *S6*, it was, with one exception, the only condition that applied in any of the 600 test problems. For *S2* and *S3*, *Case 6* provided some degree of success, as well as *Case 8*.

We conclude that the three-machine special cases, in which the optimal solution can be found by a polynomial algorithm, are likely to occur reasonably often in sample problems. Moreover, among the various procedures that have been designed to detect special cases, the lower bound condition is by far the most powerful. The results also indicate that unless special shop structure is involved, the other conditions are virtually ineffective at detecting special cases.

10.5 Minimizing the Makespan

Except for the very special cases mentioned in the previous section, we need general-purpose procedures to solve the makespan problem with $m = 3$. For this purpose, branch-and-bound methods have been reasonably successful. For flow shop problems with more than three machines, the same branch-and-bound approaches have also been used to find optimal permutation schedules. Although permutation schedules are not a dominant set for makespan problems when $m \geq 4$, it seems plausible that the best permutation schedule should be close to the optimum. However, it has been shown that the worst-case behavior of permutation schedules is not even bounded by a constant but may be roughly as large as $0.5m^{1/2}$. Nevertheless, permutation schedules are asymptotically optimal for large n (i.e. $n \gg m$), for minimizing the makespan and for minimizing maximum tardiness.

Asymptotic optimality does not necessarily reveal what might happen in practice with flow shop problems of moderate size. However, the focus on permutation schedules brings to mind the various solution techniques discussed in Chapters 3 and 4 for finding the optimal job sequence in the single-machine model. In this section we build on that similarity and describe optimizing approaches and heuristic approaches for permutation schedules in the m-machine makespan problem.

10.5.1 Branch-and-Bound Solutions

The branching tree for the flow shop problem has the same structure as the permutation tree for single-machine schedules shown in Figure 7.4, where π represents a partial permutation occurring at the beginning of the sequence. In other words, the job sequence is constructed in a forward direction as we proceed down the tree. For each node on the tree, corresponding to a partially solved problem $P(\pi)$, we require a lower bound on the makespan associated with any completion of the corresponding partial sequence π. Again, we denote by π' the set of jobs not contained in π.

For a given partial sequence π, let $C_i(\pi)$ denote the completion time on machine i for the last job in π. This completion may also determine the earliest time at which some unscheduled job could begin processing at machine i. However, there may be other conditions that delay the start of the next job at machine i. Suppose that a particular job j is a candidate to be added to the partial sequence π. Then the earliest time that job j could begin processing on machine i may instead be determined by the work required on job j before it reaches machine i. This amount of work is $p_{1j} + p_{2j} + \cdots + p_{i-1,j}$. Since we do not yet know which unscheduled job will be next, we can take the most favorable case and conclude that the earliest time at which the next job will start on machine i is at least

$$\min_{j \in \pi'} \left\{ p_{1j} + p_{2j} + \cdots + p_{i-1,j} \right\}$$

We can use a similar logic, starting from machine $k < i$, and conclude that the earliest time at which the next job will start on machine i is at least

$$C_k(\pi) + \min_{j \in \pi'} \left\{ p_{kj} + p_{k+1,j} + \cdots + p_{i-1,j} \right\}$$

Thus, as the first component of the lower bound, we define the earliest time at which some unscheduled job could begin processing on machine i as follows:

$$r_i(\pi) = \max_{k \leq i} \left[C_k(\pi) + \min_{j \in \pi'} \left\{ \sum_{u=k}^{i-1} p_{uj} \right\} \right]$$

Once processing does begin on machine i, the amount of processing yet required on that machine is $\sum_{j \in \pi'} p_{ij}$. This is the second component of the lower bound. As a third component, observe that after the last job finishes on machine i, it must still be processed by subsequent machines. In the most favorable case, that amount of time is

$$q_i(\pi) = \min_{j \in \pi'} \left\{ \sum_{u=i+1}^{m} p_{uj} \right\}$$

where $q_m = 0$. Putting together the three components, we obtain the following lower bound on the makespan, from the perspective of machine i:

$$b_i(\pi) = r_i(\pi) + \sum_{j \in \pi'} p_{ij} + q_i(\pi)$$

This bound assumes that machine i will be the bottleneck. This premise accounts for the second component in the bound: When machine i is truly a bottleneck, there will be no inserted idle time in its remaining operations. Obviously, at the time we make the calculation, we do not know whether any particular machine will be the bottleneck; therefore, we take as a lower bound the maximum of the b_i values:

$$LB_1(\pi) = \max_i \left\{ r_i(\pi) + \sum_{i \in \pi'} p_{ij} + q_i(\pi) \right\}$$

In the literature on branch-and-bound procedures, LB_1, or minor variations of it, are called *machine-based bounds*. For our purposes, we can think of LB_1 as a lower bound based on the premise of a single bottleneck machine.

We can extend the notion of a machine-based bound and recognize two bottleneck machines instead of just one. The rationale for doing so is that the two-machine makespan problem can be solved efficiently by Algorithm 10.1 as part of the lower bound calculation. Also, by treating $(m - 2)$ of the machines as non-bottlenecks, we are assuming that work on those machines can be performed in parallel. In this context, we find it convenient to use a shorthand notation for partial sums of processing times over several adjacent machines. Let

$$P_j(i,h) = \sum_{u=i}^{h} p_{uj}$$

where $P_j(i, h) = 0$ if $h < i$.

If we assume that machines i and h are bottlenecks, then machines prior to i and machines following h are treated as simple nonbottlenecks. Thus, we have the first and third components of the lower bound as before:

$$r_i(\pi) = \max_{k \le i} \left[C_k(\pi) + \min_{j \in \pi'} \{ P_j(k, i - 1) \} \right]$$

$$q_i(\pi) = \min_{j \in \pi'} \{ P_j(h + 1, m) \}$$

For the second component, machines i and h are treated as bottlenecks, and processing on machines between i and h is treated as if it occurs on a dominated machine, as in *Case 1* of Section 10.4. Thus, the second component corresponds to the makespan of a three-machine pseudoproblem in which the processing times are p_{ij}, $P_j(i + 1, h - 1)$, and p_{hj}, for each unscheduled job j in π'. Denote this solution by M_{ih}. Then the lower bound can be written as follows:

$$LB_2(\pi) = \max_{(i,h)} \{ r_i(\pi) + M_{ih} + q_h(\pi) \}$$

where the maximum is taken over all pairs of machines (i, h). Experimental studies have shown that LB_2 is a very effective lower bound, but its computational requirement is $O(n^3 \log n)$, which is substantial. One way to limit the amount of computation done at each node is to use only $i = h$. This amounts to using just one bottleneck machine, which corresponds to using LB_1. Another simplification is to use only $h = m$. This simplification reduces the computational burden by a factor of n at each node by considering only bottleneck pairs that include the last machine. Either simplification reduces the effort required to compute a bound at each node, but since the resulting bounds may be less tight, the optimization procedure requires more effort in its tree search. In large problems, it makes sense to utilize the strongest possible bound because the tree search is quite extensive. We illustrate the calculations with an example.

■ **Example 10.4** Consider a problem containing $n = 4$ jobs in a four-machine flow shop.

Job j	1	2	3	4
p_{1j}	4	2	3	5
p_{2j}	3	8	2	4
p_{3j}	7	2	4	3
p_{4j}	3	5	1	5

The first node generated by the branch-and-bound algorithm corresponds to the subproblem $P(1)$, for which job 1 is assigned the first position in sequence and $\pi' = \{2, 3, 4\}$. For this partial sequence the values of $C_i(\pi)$ are 4, 7, 14, and 17. The lower bound calculations for LB_1 are shown below.

i	$\left\{r_i(\pi) + \sum_{j \in \pi'} p_{ij} + q_i(\pi)\right\}$	Max
1	$4 + 10 + 7 = 21$	
2	$7 + 14 + 5 = 26$	
3	$14 + 9 + 1 = 24$	
4	$17 + 11 + 0 = 28$	28

For the other partial solutions at the first level of the branching tree, similar calculations yield bounds of 27 for $P(2)$, 28 for $P(3)$, and 27 for $P(4)$.

The use of LB_2 can improve the lower bound for $P(2)$ and $P(4)$. To illustrate, consider the calculation of LB_2 for $P(2)$ when the two bottleneck machines are $i = 2$ and $h = 4$. The subproblem for these two machines uses the data shown below.

Job j	1	3	4
Machine $i = 2$	3	2	4
Nonbottleneck	7	4	3
Machine $h = 4$	3	1	5

The optimal sequence for this subproblem is 4-1-3, with a makespan of 18. Because we also have $r_2 = 10$ and $q_4 = 0$, it follows that $LB_2 = 10 + 18 + 0 = 28$. A similar set of calculations for $P(4)$ shows that $LB_2 = 28$ as well.

Computational results indicate that 3-machine problems containing as many as 1000 jobs can be solved in less than an hour of computer time. Problems with 4–10 machines and a total of up to 1000 operations can often be solved in a matter of minutes. However, some problems of this size require very extensive searching.

10.5.2 Integer Programming Solutions

An integer programming (IP) formulation can be built for the flow shop model and the makespan objective. The formulation uses sequence-position variables x_{ik} and corresponding assignment constraints, as in the single-machine model (Section 3.6.2). In addition, two other types of variables are useful:

I_{kj} = idle interval on machine k prior to the start of the job in sequence position j.
H_{kj} = idle time of the job in sequence position j after finishing on machine k.

Starting at the completion of the job in position j on machine k, we can measure the time until the start of the job in position $(j + 1)$ on machine $(k + 1)$ in two ways. First, we can add the idle interval on machine k prior to the start of the job in sequence position $(j + 1)$, the processing time on machine k of the job in sequence position $(j + 1)$, and the idle time for the job in sequence position $(j + 1)$ after finishing on machine k. This is the sum of three terms:

$$I_{k,j+1} + \sum_{i=1}^{n} p_{ki} x_{i,j+1} + H_{k,j+1}$$

As an alternative, we can add the idle time for the job in sequence position j after finishing on machine k, the processing time on machine $(k + 1)$ of the job in sequence position j, and the idle interval on machine $(k + 1)$ prior to the start of the job in sequence position $(j + 1)$. This is also the sum of three terms:

$$H_{k,j} + \sum_{i=1}^{n} p_{k+1,i} x_{i,j} + I_{k+1,j+1}$$

Thus, one set of compatibility constraints in the model must ensure that these two sums are identical or

$$I_{k,j+1} + \sum_{i=1}^{n} p_{ki} x_{i,j+1} + H_{k,j+1} - H_{k,j} - \sum_{i=1}^{n} p_{k+1,i} x_{i,j} - I_{k+1,j+1} = 0$$

which applies for all sequence positions $1 \leq j \leq n - 1$ and all machines $1 \leq k \leq m - 1$. A special version of this equation applies for the first job:

$$I_{k1} + \sum_{i=1}^{n} p_{ki} x_{i1} + H_{k1} - I_{k+1,1} = 0, \quad \text{for all machines } 1 \leq k \leq m - 1$$

To minimize the makespan, we can write the objective as follows:

$$\text{Minimize } M = \sum_{i=1}^{n} p_{mi} + \sum_{j=1}^{n} I_{mj}$$

The first sum in this expression, representing the total processing time required on the last machine, is simply a constant, so to minimize the makespan, we must minimize the sum of idle times on the last machine, $\sum_{j=1}^{n} I_{mj}$. The model contains $n^2 + 2mn$ variables and $n(m + 1)$ constraints.

■ **Example 10.5**   Consider the following six-job, three-machine problem, with the criterion of minimizing the makespan.

Job	1	2	3	4	5	6
Operation 1	75	36	62	8	25	32
Operation 2	43	48	26	10	12	83
Operation 3	67	50	18	37	18	57

A spreadsheet formulation of the integer program is displayed in Figure 10.7. The I-variables and H-variables appear in rows 8–13, and the assignment variables appear in rows 14–19. The given array of processing times appears in rows 4–6, and these are re-sorted, in rows 22–24, after a job sequence is determined

	A	B	C	D	E	F	G	H	I
1	Flow Shop								
2									
3	Job	1	2	3	4	5	6		
4		75	36	62	8	25	32		
5	Times	43	48	26	10	12	83		
6		67	50	18	37	18	57	247	
7									
8		0	0	0	0	0	47		
9	I-variables	34	0	0	0	14	41	Idle	Makespan
10		44	11	27	0	0	0	82	329
11		26	0	23	3	25	0		
12	H-variables	0	0	65	0	0	0		
13		0	0	0	0	0	0		
14		0	0	0	0	1	0	1	
15		0	1	0	0	0	0	1	
16	Assignment	0	0	0	0	0	1	1	
17	Variables	1	0	0	0	0	0	1	
18		0	0	1	0	0	0	1	
19		0	0	0	1	0	0	1	
20		1	1	1	1	1	1		
21	Sequence	4	2	5	6	1	3		
22		8	36	25	32	75	62		
23	Times	10	48	12	83	43	26		
24		37	50	18	57	67	18		
25	RHS2	0	0	0	0	0	0		
26	RHS3	0	0	0	0	0	0		
27									

Figure 10.7 Spreadsheet layout for the IP model of Example 10.5.

by the assignment variables. This layout is convenient for computing the expressions in the constraints. To specify the model for Solver, we provide the following information:

- Minimize the objective function, H10 corresponding to the sum.
- Take B8:G19 as the decision variables with B14:G19 as binary variables.
- Satisfy the row sum constraints H14:H19 = 1.
- Satisfy the column sum constraints B20:G20 = 1.
- Satisfy the compatibility constraints B25:G26 = 0.

The model contains 72 decision variables and 23 constraints, and the optimal solution shown in Figure 10.7 corresponds to the sequence 4-2-5-6-1-3. This sequence contains 82 units of idle time on machine 3. Together with total processing time of 247 on machine 3, the result is a makespan of 329.

Experiments reported in the literature indicate that three-machine problems with as many as 100 jobs can be solved in a few seconds. Also, 10-machine problems with 10 jobs can also be solved in a few seconds. However, the most sophisticated branch-and-bound algorithms are still more powerful than IP models.

A different IP approach is illustrated in a model for a three-machine flow shop with synchronous transfers. In this application, a machining center contains three stations around a rotary table. One station is a loading/unloading (L/U) station, where parts are placed into the production line and later removed from the line. The two other stations each house a multipurpose machine. A job moves from the L/U station to the first machine, then to the second machine, and finally back to the L/U station, where it leaves the center. We can think of the parts as traveling along a clock face from loading at 12 o'clock to a first operation at 4 o'clock to a second operation at 8 o'clock and then back to 12 o'clock to unload. The parts move around the machining center on a rotary table that transfers all resident parts simultaneously. (See Figure 10.8.)

Figure 10.8 Flow shop layout for synchronous transfers.

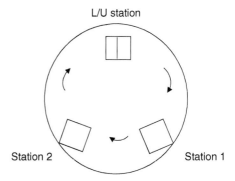

For the purposes of notation, let L_j be the loading time for job j and let U_j be the unloading time. In addition let A_j be the processing time for job j on the first machine and let B_j be the processing time for job j on the second machine. The schedule consists of a series of time intervals, or *cycles*, within which each job experiences one operation before the rotary table transfers it to the next station. If we let $[j]$ represent the job in sequence position j, then the cycle times y_j become

$$y_1 = L_{[1]}$$
$$y_2 = \max\left\{L_{[2]}, A_{[1]}\right\}$$
$$y_3 = \max\left\{L_{[3]}, B_{[1]}, A_{[2]}\right\}$$
$$\vdots$$
$$y_k = \max\left\{U_{[k-3]} + L_{[k]}, B_{[k-2]}, A_{[k-1]}\right\}, \quad \text{for } 4 \le k \le n$$
$$\vdots$$
$$y_{n+1} = \max\left\{U_{[n-2]}, B_{[n-1]}, A_{[n]}\right\}$$
$$y_{n+2} = \max\left\{U_{[n-1]}, B_{[n]}\right\}$$
$$y_{n+3} = U_{[n]}$$

The objective then becomes

$$M = \sum_{j=1}^{n+3} y_j. \tag{10.5}$$

To formulate the problem of minimizing the makespan, we use sequence-position variables, ($x_{ij} = 1$ if job i occupies sequence position j). Thus, a set of assignment constraints is necessary to ensure that a full sequence exists or

$$\sum_{j=1}^{n} x_{ij} = 1, \quad i = 1, 2, \ldots, n \tag{10.6}$$

and

$$\sum_{i=1}^{n} x_{ij} = 1, \quad j = 1, 2, \ldots, n \tag{10.7}$$

In addition let y_k denote the kth cycle time, as above, so that we require

$$y_k \ge \sum_{i=1}^{n} U_i x_{i,k-3} + \sum_{i=1}^{n} L_i x_{ik}, \quad k = 1, 2, \ldots, n+3 \tag{10.8}$$

$$y_k \ge \sum_{i=1}^{n} A_i x_{i,k-1}, \quad k = 2, 3, \ldots, n+1 \tag{10.9}$$

$$y_k \geq \sum_{i=1}^{n} B_i x_{i,k-2}, \quad k = 3, 4, \ldots, n+2 \tag{10.10}$$

Here we define $x_{ij} = 0$ for $j < 0$ or $j > n$. The problem can thus be posed as minimizing Eq. (10.5) subject to Eqs. (10.6)–(10.10), with the x_{ij} variables as binary variables. This formulation contains $(n^2 + n + 3)$ variables and $(5n + 3)$ constraints.

■ **Example 10.6** Consider the following five-job problem, with the criterion of minimizing the makespan.

Job	1	2	3	4	5
Loading	2	7	6	4	1
Machine 1	3	11	3	6	7
Machine 2	2	3	5	7	7
Unloading	3	2	3	2	2

A spreadsheet formulation of the integer program is displayed in Figure 10.9. The assignment variables appear in the range F4:J8, and the cycle times appear in cells F3:M3. For instance, we see that H5 = 1: Column H is associated with the third job in the sequence, and row 5 is associated with job 2, so we know that job 2 is scheduled in the third position. The sum of the cycle times, computed in cell

	A	B	C	D	E	F	G	H	I	J	K	L	M	N	O
1															
2					Cycle	1	2	3	4	5	6	7	8	Z	
3	Job	L	P1	P2	U	1	7	7	11	4	5	3	3	41	
4	1	2	3	2	3	0	0	0	0	1				1	
5	2	7	11	3	2	0	0	1	0	0				1	
6	3	6	3	5	3	0	0	0	1	0				1	
7	4	4	6	7	2	0	1	0	0	0				1	
8	5	1	7	7	2	1	0	0	0	0				1	
9						1	1	1	1	1					
10				L		1	4	7	6	2					
11				P1		7	6	11	3	3					
12				P2		7	7	3	5	2					
13				U		2	2	2	3	3					
14						1	4	7	8	4	2	3	3		
15							7	6	11	3	3				
16							7	7	3	5	2				

Figure 10.9 Spreadsheet layout for the IP model of Example 10.6.

N3, serves as the objective function. The given array of L/U times and machine times appears in the columns of B4:E8, and these are re-sorted after a job sequence is determined by the assignment variables, in the rows of F10:J13. This layout is convenient for computing the components of cycle time in rows 14–16: Row 14 provides $U_{[k+3]} + L_{[k]}$ values, whereas rows 15 and 16 are appropriately shifted operation times; for instance, H16 shows the processing time of the first job (job 5) on machine 2, which is 7 time units. We can now see that cells F3–M3 are the maxima of those three rows; for instance, H3 = 7 is associated with H14 (loading job 2) or with H16 (processing job 5 on machine 2), whereas job 4 takes only 6 on machine 1 during the same cycle. To specify the model for Solver, we provide the following information:

- Minimize the objective function, N3.
- Take F4:J8 and F3:M3 as the decision variables with F4:J8 as binary variables.
- Satisfy the row sum constraints N4:N8 = 1.
- Satisfy the column sum constraints F9:J9 = 1.
- Require feasible cycle times: for example, H14:H16 ≤ H3.

The model contains 33 decision variables and 28 constraints, and the optimal solution shown in Figure 10.9 corresponds to the sequence 5-4-2-3-1, for which the schedule length is 41.

Research studies indicate that 10-job problems can be solved in less than a second of CPU time, but 20-job problems may take as much as an hour. Nevertheless, the IP approach is competitive with specialized algorithms that have been designed for the scheduling of synchronous flow shops.

The two types of flow shop problems discussed here show how the flow shop structure can lend itself to IP modeling. The use of IP, however, is not limited to the makespan objective and can be adapted to several other objective functions.

10.5.3 Heuristic Solutions

The branch-and-bound approach has two inevitable disadvantages typical of combinatorial optimization methods. First, the computational requirements can be severe for large problems. Second, even for moderate-sized problems, there is no guarantee that the solution can be obtained quickly because the search effort depends on the data in the problem. Heuristic algorithms avoid these two drawbacks: They can obtain solutions to large problems with limited computational effort, and their computational requirements are predictable for problems of a given size. The drawback of heuristic approaches, of course, is that they do not guarantee optimality; and in some instances it may even be difficult to judge their effectiveness. The heuristic methods described in this section are representative of the many such techniques for the makespan problem.

A useful guideline for sequencing jobs in the flow shop can be stated qualitatively as follows: give priority to jobs having the strongest tendency to progress from short times to long times in the sequence of operations. Although there might be other ways of implementing this principle, the *slope index* makes the following calculation for each job:

$$SI_j = \sum_{i=1}^{m} (m - 2i + 1)p_{ij}$$

Then a permutation schedule is constructed by sequencing the jobs in nondecreasing order of their slope indices, SI_j.

For $m = 2$, the slope index sequences the jobs in nonincreasing order of $(p_{2j} - p_{1j})$. This method is slightly different from Johnson's rule and does not guarantee an optimum. In Example 10.2, however, the heuristic yields the sequence 1-3-4-5-2. Although this is different from the sequence constructed by Johnson's rule, it still has an optimal makespan. In the job set of Example 10.4, the slope index values are -1 for job 1, -3 for job 2, 4 for job 3, and 1 for job 4. The slope index thus generates the sequence 2-1-4-3, for which the makespan is $M = 29$ (as compared with the lower bound of 28).

Another heuristic method for makespan problems is the Campbell, Dudek, and Smith (CDS) algorithm. This algorithm uses Johnson's rule in a heuristic fashion and creates several schedules from which a "best" schedule can be chosen. The algorithm corresponds to a multistage use of Johnson's rule applied to a pseudoproblem, derived from the original, with processing times a_j and b_j. At stage 1, $a_j = p_{1j}$ and $b_j = p_{mj}$. In other words, the first and last processing times for each job comprise the pseudoproblem. At stage 2, $a_j = p_{1j} + p_{2j}$ and $b_j = p_{m-1,j} + p_{mj}$. Here, the first two and last two processing times, aggregated for each job, comprise the pseudoproblem. In general, at stage i,

$$a_j = \sum_{k=1}^{i} p_{kj} \text{ and } b_j = \sum_{k=m-i+1}^{m} p_{kj}$$

For each stage i, the job sequence obtained from the pseudoproblem is used to calculate a makespan for the original problem. The procedure consists of $(m - 1)$ stages, some of which may generate the same sequence, after which the algorithm selects the best makespan calculated. Ties can be broken arbitrarily, although it is not difficult to incorporate tie-breaking rules. For instance, we can break ties by using the job ordering that occurred in the previous stage. The computational effort for the CDS algorithm is greater than that of the slope index method, but the CDS algorithm has tended to produce better solutions in computational tests.

When we apply the CDS algorithm to Example 10.4, there are three stages. At stage 1, the pseudoproblem to be solved by Johnson's rule is the following.

Job *j*	1	2	3	4
a_j	4	2	3	5
b_j	3	5	1	5

The optimal sequence for this problem is 2-4-1-3. At stage 2, the pseudoproblem is

Job *j*	1	2	3	4
a_j	7	10	5	9
b_j	10	7	5	8

The optimal sequence for this problem is 3-1-4-2, using an arbitrary means of breaking ties. At stage 3, the pseudoproblem is

Job *j*	1	2	3	4
a_j	14	12	9	12
b_j	13	15	7	12

The optimal sequence for this problem is 4-2-1-3. Thus, the CDS algorithm selects three sequences to be evaluated. The best makespan among the three (from the original processing time data) is $M = 29$.

In addition to the slope index method and the CDS method, which are both specialized to the flow shop model, we can use general-purpose heuristic techniques. For instance, we can apply the insertion heuristic to the permutation sequences that define flow shop schedules. Computational experiments suggest that although the insertion heuristic requires more effort than the CDS algorithm, the additional effort produces slightly better solutions. Similarly, neighborhood search, simulated annealing, and tabu search procedures have also been tested in flow shop problems. The experimental results indicate that heuristic procedures can generate solutions that are on average within about 1% of optimum.

10.6 Variations of the *m*-Machine Model

10.6.1 Ordered Flow Shops

A special case of the flow shop problem is the *ordered flow shop*. The special case is defined by two conditions: (1) If job *j* has a smaller processing time than job *k* on machine *i*, then job *j* also has a processing time no larger than that of job *k* on each other machine; and (2) if job j has its rth smallest processing time on machine i, then so does every other job. These conditions tend to occur when the jobs being scheduled represent orders and the items comprising the orders have similar unit processing times on all machines. In this situation, the operation processing times reflect the order sizes.

Condition (1) of the ordered flow shop makes it possible to refer to the size of a job. That is, we can identify a longest job or a shortest job, since the ordering of jobs by their operation times for one machine will be identical to the ordering for any other machine. In particular, we can use SPT to refer to a shortest-first ordering of the jobs and LPT to refer to a longest-first ordering.

For the ordered flow shop, a dominant set of schedules exists for the makespan problem. Dominant schedules are determined by *pyramid sequences*, which are orderings of the jobs in which the first k jobs ($1 \le k \le n$) are in SPT order and the remaining jobs are in LPT order. Another way to think of a pyramid sequence is in terms of the position assigned to the longest job. In a pyramid sequence, if the longest job appears in position j, then the jobs in positions 1 to j are in SPT order, while the jobs in positions j to n are in LPT order.

The dominance of pyramid sequences does not dictate an optimal sequence; it simply reduces the number of sequences among which we have to search. The number of pyramid sequences is 2^{n-1}, which is much smaller than the number of feasible sequences. For example, if $n = 15$, the number of pyramid sequences is 32 768, whereas the number of permutations is over 1.3 trillion.

For the ordered flow shop, the optimal schedule for the F-problem is given by the SPT sequence. This result may not seem surprising given the optimality of SPT in the single-machine model, but the F-problem is NP-hard for the general flow shop model, even when $m = 2$.

10.6.2 Flow Shops with Blocking

In certain production settings, limited waiting space exists between adjacent machines. Equivalently, a policy constraint may limit the number of jobs between machines, as we often see, for example, in the kanban system of just-in-time production. When this waiting space is full, any job completed by the upstream machine must remain in place until space becomes available, so that machine is *blocked*. An extreme blocking case occurs when there is no waiting space between machines at all, so a job can be in the system only if it occupies a machine. If we limit ourselves to permutation schedules, however, then the model without waiting space is equivalent to the more general case. For example, if we want to allow space for k jobs to wait between two adjacent machines, we can insert k dummy machines between them with processing times of zero, and these dummy machines can then hold up to k jobs in queue as required. In light of this equivalence, we assume that flow shops with blocking allow no queues between machines.

Consider the case $m = 2$ with the makespan objective. For the first $(n - 1)$ jobs, there is no advantage in allowing a job to depart from machine 2 before machine 1 is ready to deliver the next job. Therefore, we can think of a schedule as a sequence of $n + 1$ (unequal) intervals such that during period 1, machine 1 processes job [1], in interval $(n + 1)$ machine 2 processes job [n], and otherwise at interval j, machine 1 processes job [j] and machine 2 processes job [$j - 1$]. This structure occurs because if job j follows job i, then there exists an interval during which machine 1 is occupied by job j and machine 2 by job i. If we define dummy jobs – job 0 and job $(n + 1)$ – at the beginning and the end of the schedule with processing times of zero, then the duration of interval j is $\max\{a_{[j]}, b_{[j-1]}\}$. The shortest path from job 0 to job $(n + 1)$ through all other jobs is an instance of the traveling salesperson problem (TSP) with distance elements D_{ij} given by $\max\{a_j, b_i\}$. This TSP has a special structure that allows for solution in polynomial time using a procedure known as the Gilmore and Gomory algorithm. In contrast, however, when $m \geq 3$, the problem cannot be formulated as a TSP, and in a practical sense, it is even more complex than the TSP. Example 10.6 is a three-machine flow shop with blocking, in which only permutation schedules are allowed.

10.6.3 No-Wait Flow Shops

In certain production settings, once the processing of a job begins, subsequent processing must be carried out with no delays in the operation sequence. In other words, no waiting is allowed before or during any operation. Such a requirement is frequently encountered in some process industries, particularly where material is formed while it is hot. Delays between operations result in cooling that makes the forming operation prohibitively difficult.

Consider the problem of minimizing makespan when no waiting is permitted. For simplicity, assume we are seeking an optimal permutation schedule. (In the general case, some jobs may have no operations on certain machines, so the set of permutation schedules is not dominant.) Suppose that jobs i and j are adjacent in sequence and that job i precedes job j. A certain delay would be incurred in the processing of job j if the two jobs were released to a shop at the same time and job i were processed first. Let I_{hj} denote the idle time incurred by job j prior to its operation on machine h. To process job j without any delays so that it will be completed at the same moment, the idle time must be incurred before the start of job j on machine 1. Now suppose that job j is followed in sequence by job k. The delays incurred in the processing of job k do not depend on what happened before job j in sequence, but only on the operation times of job j itself when it is processed without delay. Let D_{ij} denote the total delay (measured from the start of job i) incurred by job j when it follows job i in sequence. Recall the notation $P_j(g, h)$ for the sum of processing times of job j on machines g through h (inclusive), but let $P_j(g, 0) = 0$ (for any g and j). Because the structure of this problem is the same for any number of machines, we can assume that operation $(1, i)$ starts at time zero, and we can write

$$D_{ij} = I_{1j} + I_{2j} + \cdots + I_{mj} = \max_{1 \le h \le m} \left[P_i(1, h) - P_j(1, h-1) \right]$$

The right-hand side reflects the fact that if there is no waiting, then operation (h, j) is ready to start $P_j(1, h - 1)$ time units after the start of operation $(1, j)$, but machine h is not free until time $P_i(1, h)$. Thus, the machine for which the expression $P_i(1, h) - P_j(1, h - 1)$ is maximized dictates D_{ij}. By the same token, D_{jk} is the total delay (measured from the start of job j) incurred by job k when it follows job j in sequence. If the schedule consisted of only these three jobs, then an expression for the makespan of the schedule associated with the sequence i–j–k would be

$$M = D_{ij} + D_{jk} + p_{1k} + p_{2k} + \cdots + p_{mk}$$

In general, an expression for the makespan is

$$M = \sum_{j=1}^{n-1} D_{[j],[j+1]} + \sum_{h=1}^{m} p_{h,[n]}$$

Thus, the makespan is the sum of two quantities: (i) a sum of sequence-dependent delay terms and (ii) the total processing time of the last job in sequence. The structure of this expression closely resembles the criterion in the TSP (see Chapter 8), and, with some modification, this makespan problem can be recast as a TSP.

In the TSP, each city corresponds to a job, and the intercity distances correspond to the delay pairs D_{ij}. In addition, one dummy city must be added to the problem (corresponding to an idle state) to which the distance from city i is the sum of the operation times for job i and from which the distance to all other cities is zero, as shown in Table 10.2.

Table 10.2

—	D_{12}	D_{13}	...	D_{1n}	$\sum_{h=1}^{m} p_{h,1}$
D_{21}	—	D_{23}	...	D_{2n}	$\sum_{h=1}^{m} p_{h,2}$
...					
D_{n1}	D_{n2}	D_{n3}	...	—	$\sum_{h=1}^{m} p_{h,n}$
0	0	0	...	0	—

■ **Example 10.7** Consider a problem containing $n = 4$ jobs in a five-machine flow shop.

Job j	1	2	3	4
p_{1j}	4	2	5	3
p_{2j}	5	4	3	9
p_{3j}	7	6	2	9
p_{4j}	9	8	1	8
p_{5j}	3	7	6	4

We can verify that the corresponding TSP has the following distance matrix.

$$
\begin{array}{ccccc}
- & 13 & 17 & 6 & 28 \\
4 & - & 16 & 3 & 27 \\
5 & 6 & - & 5 & 17 \\
13 & 17 & 22 & - & 33 \\
0 & 0 & 0 & 0 & -
\end{array}
$$

For instance, if job 2 follows job 1, then $P_1(1, h) - P_2(1, h - 1)$ is maximized for $h = 4$ with $D_{12} = 4 + 5 + 7 + 9 - 2 - 4 - 6 = 13$. Thus, if job 2 is selected to follow job 1, then to avoid waiting, it should start 13 time units after the start of job 1. Suppose the closest unvisited city algorithm (see Chapter 8) is used to find a solution to this problem. If city 1 is chosen as an origin, then the procedure constructs the sequence 1-4-2-3, with a makespan of 56.

An instance where no wait and blocking merge is the two-machine case with a makespan objective: The same sequence is optimal for both the blocking case and the no-wait case. Given an optimal blocking solution, it is always possible to schedule starting times on machine 1 so that no waiting is required on machine 2, and yet the makespan does not exceed the blocking case. Given an optimal no-wait solution, queueing is not needed between machines. But for more than two machines, the no wait requirement is stronger: Any no-wait sequence ensures no blocking (without increasing the makespan), but a blocking solution may not satisfy the no-wait requirement because it may involve waiting on some machines. Indeed, for the no-wait case, we can model the problem as a TSP for any number of machines, whereas for the blocking case, only a two-machine model leads to the TSP formulation. One conceptual difference between the two models, even with just two machines, is that once we determine the sequence in the blocking case, we can simply release jobs into the system by dispatching, whereas in the no-wait case we must devise an explicit schedule and compute the release dates in advance.

10.7   Summary

In the development of scheduling models more general than single-machine models, the flow shop represents the most direct extension to jobs with multiple operations requiring distinct multiple resources. In the analysis of flow shop problems, scheduling theory has been strongly influenced by Johnson's two-machine result, very possibly because it is the only optimal scheduling rule applicable to a large class of flow shop problems. One disadvantage of this influence might be the disproportionate attention paid to the makespan criterion, because that is the focus of Johnson's rule. In view of the many intriguing and practical variations of the single-machine model, it is remarkable that no similar progress has been made with the flow shop using other performance measures.

On the other hand, the pivotal influence of Johnson's rule has had some definite advantages. First, by emphasizing the properties of permutation schedules, the original result focused flow shop research on problems of manageable size. Multiple-resource problems are certainly more difficult than single-resource problems. In a sense, the multiple-resource structure potentially represents a situation in which each resource is itself associated with a combinatorial problem and in which these several problems are closely interrelated. In such a case, it is an acceptable simplification to deal with only a limited set of alternatives. In the flow shop model, the problem of finding a best permutation schedule is no larger than related single-machine problems, and it seems plausible that the best permutation schedule should be close to optimal, even if permutation schedules do not constitute a dominant set.

A second advantage of the Johnson influence is that the two-machine analysis seems to capture the essence of larger makespan problems. As we have seen, Johnson's rule is an element in solving special cases of the three-machine model, in calculating tight lower bounds for an optimization procedure, and in implementing the CDS heuristic algorithm. This feature suggests that the two-machine case may be the key to resolving larger problems with other criteria. For example, if we were faced with a flow shop problem with several machines and setups, a reasonable solution strategy would be to adapt the CDS heuristic procedure using a pseudoproblem based on the form of the two-machine model with setup times.

Exercises

10.1   Consider the following three-job two-machine flow shop makespan problem.

Job j	1	2	3
aj	4	2	4
bj	3	2	5

a) Show that there is an optimal schedule in which job 1 precedes job 2.
b) Show that there is an optimal schedule in which job 2 precedes job 3.
c) Show that there is an optimal schedule in which job 3 precedes job 1.

10.2 The times required to complete eight jobs on two machines are shown in the table that follows. Each job must follow the same sequence, beginning with machine A and moving to machine B.

Job j	1	2	3	4	5	6	7	8
Machine A (a_j)	16	3	9	8	2	12	18	20
Machine B (b_j)	5	13	6	7	14	4	14	11

a) Determine a sequence that will minimize throughput time.
b) Construct a chart of the resulting sequence, showing B's idle times.
c) For the sequence in (a), how much could B's idle time be reduced by splitting the last two jobs (7 and 8) in half?

10.3 Consider the following three-job flow shop example.

Job j	1	2	3
a_j	4	4	3
b_j	7	1	2

Show that Johnson's condition is not necessary for optimality in the two-machine makespan problem.

10.4 Show that the jobs in the sequence produced by Algorithm 10.2 will satisfy Johnson's rule; that is, if job i precedes job j in that sequence, then $\min\{a_i, b_j\} \le \min\{a_j, b_i\}$.

10.5 Consider the two-machine problem with makespan objective and setup times. Suppose that the setup times are *separable* – that is, setups may be scheduled in anticipation of arriving jobs. Show that the rule for constructing an optimal sequence takes the following form:

Job i precedes job j in an optimal sequence if $\min\{e_{1i}, e_{2j}\} \le \min\{e_{1j}, e_{2i}\}$

where e_{1i} (e_{2i}) denotes the initial (final) idle time on machine 2 (machine 1) when job i is scheduled by itself.

10.6 Consider a flow shop with three proportional machines. In other words, the processing times satisfy $p_{ij} = c_i p_j$. For a problem that involves minimizing some regular measure of performance, is the proportional-machine structure any easier than the general three-machine problem? Is there an optimal permutation schedule?

10.7 How many different schedules are candidates for the optimal makespan in the four-job, four-machine flow shop problem?

10.8 For a flow shop problem containing n jobs and m machines, what is the order of magnitude of the computational effort required by:
a) The slope index method?
b) The CDS algorithm?
c) The insertion heuristic?

10.9 Find the optimal makespan for the following flow shop problem. If there is an additional constraint of no wait in process, does the optimal makespan change? Does the optimal sequence change?

Job j	1	2	3	4
p_{1j}	9	13	15	20
p_{2j}	11	17	18	24
p_{3j}	8	12	14	18
p_{4j}	6	10	12	15

Bibliography

Akkan, C. and Karabati, S. (2004). The two-machine flowshop total completion time problem: improved lower bounds and a branch-and-bound algorithm. *European Journal of Operational Research* 159: 420–429.

Baker, K.R. (2014). Spreadsheet-based computations for the flowshop problem with synchronous transfers. *International Journal of Planning and Scheduling* 2: 77–86.

Burns, F. and Rooker, J. (1976). Johnson's three-machine flow shop conjecture. *Operations Research* 24: 578–580.

Burns, F. and Rooker, J. (1978). Three stage flow shops with regressive second stage. *Operations Research* 26: 207–208.

Campbell, H.G., Dudek, R.A., and Smith, M.L. (1970). A heuristic algorithm for the *n*-job, *m*-machine sequencing problem. *Management Science* 16: 630–637.

Dannenbring, D. (1977). An evaluation of flow shop sequencing heuristics. *Management Science* 23: 1174–1182.

Emmons, H. and Vairaktarakis, G. (2013). *Flow Shop Scheduling: Theoretical Results, Algorithms, and Applications*. New York: Springer.

Gilmore, P.C. and Gomory, R.E. (1964). Sequencing a one state-variable machine: a solvable case of the traveling salesman problem. *Operations Research* 12: 655–679.

Ignall, E. and Schrage, L.E. (1965). Application of the branch and bound technique to some flow shop scheduling problems. *Operations Research* 13: 400–412.

Johnson, S.M. (1954). Optimal two-and three-stage production schedules with setup times included. *Naval Research Logistics Quarterly* 1: 61–68.

Ladhari, T. and Haouari, M. (2005). A computational study of the permutation flow shop problem based on a tight lower bound. *Computers & Operations Research* 32: 1831–1847.

Lageweg, B.J., Lenstra, J.K., and Rinnooy Kan, A.H.G. (1978). A general bounding scheme for the permutation flow shop. *Operations Research* 26: 53–67.

Lai, T.-C. (1996). A note on heuristics of flow shop scheduling. *Operations Research* 44: 648–652.

Mitten, L.G. (1959). Sequencing *n* jobs on two machines with arbitrary time lags. *Management Science* 5: 293–298.

Monma, C. and Rinnooy Kan, A.H.G. (1983). A concise survey of efficiently solvable special cases of the permutation flow-shop problem. *RAIRO Recherche Operationelle* 17: 105–119.

Nawaz, M., Enscore, E., and Ham, I. (1983). A heuristic algorithm for the *m*-machine *n*-job flow-shop sequencing problem. *Omega* 11: 91–95.

Osman, I.H. and Potts, C.N. (1989). Simulated annealing for permutation flow-shop scheduling. *Omega* 17: 551–557.

Palmer, D.S. (1965). Sequencing jobs through a multi-stage process in the minimum total time—a quick method of obtaining a near optimum. *Operational Research Quarterly* 16: 101–106.

Panwalkar, S.S. and Woolam, C.R. (1980). Ordered flow shop problems with no in-process waiting: further results. *Journal of the Operational Research Society* 30: 1039–1043.

Panwalkar, S.S., Smith, M.L., and Koulamas, C. (2013). Review of ordered and proportionate flow shop scheduling research. *Naval Research Logistics* 60: 46–55.

Portougal, V. and Scott, J.L. (2001). The asymptotic convergence of some flow-shop scheduling heuristics. *Asia-Pacific Journal of Operational Research* 18: 243–256.

Potts, C.N., Shmoys, D.B., and Williamson, D.P. (1991). Permutation vs non-permutation flow shop schedules. *Operations Research Letters* 10: 281–284.

Reeves, C.R. (1993). Improving the efficiency of tabu search for machine sequencing problems. *Journal of the Operational Research Society* 44: 375–382.

Smith, M.L., Panwalkar, S.S., and Dudek, R.A. (1976). Flow shop sequencing problems with ordered processing time matrices: a general case. *Naval Research Logistics Quarterly* 23: 481–486.

Smits, A.J.M. and Baker, K.R. (1981). An experimental investigation of the occurrence of special cases in the three-machine flowshop problem. *International Journal of Production Research* 19: 737–741.

Stafford, E., Tseng, F., and Gupta, J. (2005). Comparative evaluation of MILP flowshop models. *Journal of the Operational Research Society* 56: 88–101.

Szwarc, W. (1977). Optimal two machine orderings in the 3 × *n* flow shop problem. *Operations Research* 25: 70–77.

Szwarc, W. (1983). Flow shop problems with time lags. *Management Science* 29: 477–481.

Taillard, E. (1990). Some efficient heuristic methods for the flow shop sequencing problem. *European Journal of Operational Research* 47: 65–74.

Wismer, D.A. (1972). Solution of the flow shop scheduling problem with no intermediate queues. *Operations Research* 20: 689–697.

11

Stochastic Flow Shop Scheduling

11.1 Introduction

The analysis of stochastic flow shop problems has not proceeded very far and remains challenging. With few exceptions, research on the stochastic flow shop has been limited to the makespan as a performance measure, and much of the work addresses only the two-machine problem. In the stochastic flow shop model, the makespan typically exhibits a positive Jensen gap even with two machines, so the problem is inherently more complex than its deterministic counterpart. Nevertheless, the deterministic counterpart provides an effective heuristic for large n. For small and medium numbers of jobs, we can use neighborhood search heuristics to improve upon the performance of the deterministic counterpart. With more than two machines, we can at least adapt some of the heuristic procedures developed for the deterministic counterpart, which often depend on the two-machine solution in one way or another. Some special cases of the stochastic, two-machine makespan problem exist – not necessarily practical ones – in which optimal sequences can be found readily. In the context of safe scheduling for the stochastic flow shop, however, we must also recognize the need for safety time.

We begin our coverage in Section 11.2 with stochastic counterparts of models covered in the previous chapter, under the assumption of stochastic independence. In Section 11.3, we introduce safe scheduling models, again subject to stochastic independence. In Section 11.4, we study the implications of introducing linear association into both stochastic counterpart and safe scheduling models. In all these cases, we limit ourselves to permutation flow shops with a makespan objective.

Principles of Sequencing and Scheduling, Second Edition. Kenneth R. Baker and Dan Trietsch.
© 2019 John Wiley & Sons, Inc. Published 2019 by John Wiley & Sons, Inc.

11.2   Stochastic Counterpart Models

Few analytic results exist for the stochastic m-machine case. Those that are available rely on very restrictive assumptions. Therefore, we focus on the two-machine case. We use A_j and B_j to denote stochastic processing times on the two machines, but we retain a_j and b_j for the expected values. For general distributions without special conditions on processing times, the only full solution known for a stochastic counterpart applies to the two-job problem.

■ **Theorem 11.1**   In the two-job stochastic flow shop problem, job 1 precedes job 2 in an optimal sequence if $E[\min\{A_1, B_2\}] \leq E[\min\{A_2, B_1\}]$.

Proof. When job 1 precedes job 2, the makespan is given by $A_1 + \max\{A_2, B_1\} + B_2$. Furthermore, $A_1 + \max\{A_2, B_1\} + B_2 = A_1 + A_2 + B_1 + B_2 - \min\{A_2, B_1\}$. In words, the makespan is the total processing time of all operations minus the time during which the two machines operate in parallel. By symmetry, $A_1 + A_2 + B_1 + B_2 - \min\{A_1, B_2\}$ is the makespan of the same shop when job 2 is first. The condition then follows by comparing the expected values of the two makespan expressions.   □

Theorem 11.1 generalizes Johnson's rule for two jobs in the deterministic case, which calls for job 1 to be first if $\min\{a_1, b_2\} \leq \min\{a_2, b_1\}$. The theorem holds for any processing time distributions, but the calculations become more tractable if we assume independent processing time distributions because we can calculate the cdf of the minimum using the formula

$$F_{\min}(t) = 1 - [1 - F_X(t)][1 - F_Y(t)]$$

where $F_X(t)$, $F_Y(t)$, and $F_{\min}(t)$ denote the cdfs of X, Y, and their minimum. The expected value of the minimum can then be calculated as the area above the cdf and below 1 to the right of the origin. However, the formula does not lead to a closed-form calculation of the minimum for all distributions. Alternatively, we can use sample-based analysis to estimate the information we need. Such an approach would likely be needed as well when processing times are not independent.

To pursue the analysis beyond the two-job problem, we must make a more specific assumption about the distribution of processing times. To start, we consider exponential processing times. (As we mentioned in Chapter 9, the exponential is not necessarily very practical, but it is significant as a boundary case, and it sometimes provides us with general insights.) Suppose we have two exponential random variables, one with a mean of x and the other with a mean of y. Equivalently, we say that one has a completion rate (or processing rate) of $1/x$ and the other has a completion rate of $1/y$. The minimum of the two exponential random variables is an exponential random variable with processing rate $(1/x + 1/y)$. Therefore, the condition in Theorem 11.1 can be rewritten for the exponential case. The condition for job 1 to precede job 2,

$$E(\min\{A_1, B_2\}) \le E(\min\{A_2, B_1\}) \tag{11.1}$$

implies the reverse ordering of processing rates, or

$$\frac{1}{a_1} + \frac{1}{b_2} \ge \frac{1}{a_2} + \frac{1}{b_1} \tag{11.2}$$

Algebraic rearrangement yields

$$\frac{1}{a_1} - \frac{1}{b_1} \ge \frac{1}{a_2} - \frac{1}{b_2} \tag{11.3}$$

In words, the job with the larger difference in processing rates should come first.

■ **Example 11.1** Consider the scheduling of two jobs with independent exponentially distributed processing times. The mean of each processing time is given in the following table.

Machine	Job 1	Job 2
1	4	5
2	5	8

The processing rates associated with these means are 0.25 and 0.2 for job 1 and 0.2 and 0.125 for job 2. Since the difference for job 2 (0.0875) exceeds the difference for job 1 (0.05), job 2 should be scheduled first. This sequence reverses the solution of the deterministic counterpart and demonstrates that applying Johnson's rule to the mean values in a stochastic problem does not necessarily produce an optimal sequence. For this example, the expected makespan is 19.333 for the sequence 2-1 and 19.5 for sequence 1-2. The standard deviations are 10.424 and 10.548, respectively. The difference in both measures is on the order of 1%, and the optimal sequence is advantageous on both counts.

■ **Example 11.2** Consider the scheduling of two jobs with independent exponentially distributed processing times. The mean of each processing time is given in the following table.

Machine	Job 1	Job 2
1	1	1
2	1	$1 + \sqrt{7}$

In Example 11.2, the calculations yield an expected makespan of 5.861 for the sequence 2-1 and 6.146 for sequence 1-2. The standard deviations are 3.801 and 3.942, respectively. For the optimal sequence, the advantage in the mean is about 4.8%, and the advantage in the standard deviation is about 3.7%. The parameters of this example illustrate the maximum percentage improvement of the correct sorting rule for a two-job problem with exponential processing times. Johnson's rule, when applied to the means, results in a tie, but if we reduce a_1 infinitesimally, the sequence 1-2 becomes the deterministic optimum, whereas the sequence 2-1 remains the optimal solution for exponential processing times.

Sorting by the difference in mean processing rates $(1/a_j - 1/b_j)$ involves a transitive sequencing relation and can be extended to n jobs. Thus, at the very least, it provides a reasonable heuristic procedure for the n-job problem. In the exponential case, this sorting rule, which we refer to as *Talwar's rule*, turns out to be optimal.

■ **Theorem 11.2** (*Talwar's rule*). In the stochastic two-machine flow shop problem with exponential processing times, the expected makespan is minimized by sequencing the jobs so that $(1/a_{[1]} - 1/b_{[1]}) \geq (1/a_{[2]} - 1/b_{[2]}) \geq \cdots \geq (1/a_{[n]} - 1/b_{[n]})$.

(We omit the proof.)

In the n-job case, the condition for job j to precede job $(j + 1)$ can be written as

$$\frac{1}{a_j} - \frac{1}{b_{(j+1)}} \geq \frac{1}{a_{(j+1)}} - \frac{1}{b_j}$$

This condition involves a comparison between two means. Because they are means of exponential distributions, the cdf for $\min\{A_j, B_{(j+1)}\}$ lies entirely above the cdf for $\min\{A_{(j+1)}, B_j\}$. In other words, stochastic dominance holds in the comparison for each pair of successive jobs. This feature also holds when there are n jobs; that is, Talwar's rule yields not only a minimal expected makespan but also a stochastically minimal makespan.

When the problem involves distributions other than the exponential, we have to rely on heuristic procedures. One plausible heuristic sorts the jobs by $(1/a_{[1]} - 1/b_{[1]}) \geq (1/a_{[2]} - 1/b_{[2]}) \geq \cdots \geq (1/a_{[n]} - 1/b_{[n]})$, as in Theorem 11.2. We refer to this procedure as *Talwar's heuristic*. Another possibility, of course, is solving the deterministic counterpart – that is, applying Johnson's rule to the means – and using the sequence in the stochastic problem. We refer to that procedure as *Johnson's heuristic*. Johnson's heuristic may require a tie-breaking rule: When comparing processing times with the same mean, the one with the lower variance is considered smaller. Yet another heuristic procedure, which we refer to as the *adjacent pairwise interchange (API) heuristic*, starts with any sequence, such as the deterministic counterpart sequence, and tries to improve on it with an API neighborhood search. We call a pair of adjacent jobs *stable* if they satisfy Theorem 11.1. We call a sequence stable if every pair of adjacent jobs is stable. The API heuristic checks all adjacent job pairs in the initial sequence starting with the first two jobs, and if an unstable pair is found, the two jobs are interchanged. After each such interchange, the job that was moved downstream is stable with respect to its upstream neighbor, but the one that moved upstream may have to be interchanged repeatedly until it reaches a stable position, possibly as the first job. Then, the heuristic repeats its check of all pairs and stops when all adjacent pairs are stable.

Computational experiments with lognormal distributions for processing times indicate that none of these three heuristic methods dominate the others:

- Johnson's heuristic is best when little or no overlap exists among the job processing time distributions. When overlap exists, Johnson's heuristic deteriorates compared with the other heuristics.
- Talwar's heuristic performs relatively well when the processing time distributions exhibit substantial amounts of variation.
- The API heuristic seems to have robust performance in many situations. It performs nearly as well as Johnson's heuristic when little or no overlap exists, but it does not deteriorate as much when overlap is present.

The API heuristic requires $O(n^2)$ tests and always results in a stable sequence. The procedure is not guaranteed to find an optimal sequence. In fact, more than one stable sequence can exist. The heuristic is guaranteed only to converge to *some* stable sequence, but that does not mean it will locate the best one or that the optimal sequence is stable. However, if any transitive sorting rule is optimal, then the API heuristic will converge to it. For example, when all distributions are exponential, the API heuristic yields the optimal (Talwar) sequence.

Although the API heuristic cannot verify whether a sequence is optimal, we can theoretically determine whether the stable sequence it yields is unique by simply checking all pairwise relationships. If the stable sequence is not unique, even for a single instance, then no transitive optimality condition exists for that family of distributions in general. However, as we pointed out earlier, the formulas in the pairwise evaluation might be intractable for many types of probability distributions. Therefore, we can approximate the desired evaluation either by using sample-based analysis or by assuming a particular family of distributions for all processing times. For the latter approach, if we were to assume an exponential distribution for each processing time, we would generate the sequence of Talwar's heuristic. A more flexible approach is to evaluate Theorem 11.1 by assuming the normal distribution applies. The normal distribution has two parameters, unlike the exponential, so we can try to match its mean and standard deviation with those of the distributions in the problem data. In other words, we use the normal distribution as an approximation to the actual processing time distribution. The formulas for the normal case are tractable, as we show next.

In general, for any random variables X and Y,

$$\min\{X, Y\} = X - \max\{X - Y, 0\}$$

and therefore,

$$E(\min\{X, Y\}) = E(X) - E(\max\{X - Y, 0\})$$

Define $W = X - Y$ so that

$$E(\min\{X, Y\}) = E(X) - E(W^+)$$

Suppose that X and Y are independent normal random variables. Then, W is normal with mean $\mu_w = \mu_x - \mu_y$ and variance $\sigma_w^2 = \sigma_x^2 + \sigma_y^2$. In addition – as shown in Appendix B – $E[W^+] = \sigma_w[\phi(z) + z\Phi(z)]$, where ϕ and Φ denote the density function and cdf of the standard normal and $z = \mu_w/\sigma_w$. The expected minimum is then given by

$$E[\min\{X, Y\}] = \mu_x - \sigma_w[\phi(z) + z\Phi(z)] \tag{11.4}$$

■ **Example 11.3** Consider the following five-job, two-machine flow shop problem in which the jobs have normally distributed processing times on the two machines, A and B.

Job j	1	2	3	4	5
Mean A	9.94	10.14	10.15	10.30	10.45
Standard deviation A	0.32	0.02	0.73	0.91	0.27
Mean B	10.16	10.16	10.26	10.45	10.46
Standard deviation B	0.74	0.11	0.76	0.20	0.05

The application of Johnson's rule to the deterministic counterpart leads to the sequence 1-2-3-4-5. Using Eq. (11.4), Table 11.1 records the differences

Table 11.1

Job index	2	3	4	5
1	0.033	0.006	0.166	−0.037
2		0.032	0.275	0.005
3			0.168	−0.037
4				−0.305

between $E[\min\{A_i, B_j\}]$ and $E[\min\{A_j, B_i\}]$ for these jobs, with job i corresponding to a row and j to a column. For instance, the calculations for $E[\min\{A_1, B_2\}]$ yield $\mu_w = \mu_x - \mu_y = 9.94 - 10.16 = -0.22$, $\sigma_w^2 = 0.32^2 + 0.11^2 = 0.3384^2$, so $z = -0.22/0.3384 = -0.6502$, leading to $E[\min\{A_1, B_2\}] = 9.94 - 0.3384(0.3229 - 0.6502 \times 0.2578) = 9.8874$. Similarly, $E[\min\{A_2, B_1\}] = 9.8546$. The first entry in the table (recorded to three decimal places) is the difference $9.8874 - 9.8546 = 0.033$.

When the entry in row i and column j is negative, then placing job i directly ahead of j is stable. Here, no pair in the Johnson sequence is stable except the last. In the API heuristic, we work from left to right, so the first interchange occurs between jobs 1 and 2. As a result, jobs 1 and 3 become adjacent and unstable, so we interchange job 3 with job 1, obtaining 2-3-1-4-5. With the first pair now unstable, we interchange jobs 2 and 3, obtaining 3-2-1-4-5. Job 4 then migrates to the first position in a similar manner, giving us a stable API sequence, 4-3-2-1-5. However, it is not the only stable sequence. For example, the sequence 4-3-5-2-1 is also stable. Thus, no transitive optimality condition can hold for the normal distribution.

Although more than one stable solution exists in Example 11.3, the API heuristic yields a sequence that is slightly superior to the deterministic counterpart sequence in terms of the mean but with a higher standard deviation. Using Analytic Solver Platform with a sample size of 10 000, we estimated the mean for the API sequence at 62.07 and the mean for the deterministic counterpart sequence at 62.11, with standard deviations of 1.24 and 0.96, respectively. However, in some instances, the deterministic counterpart sequence could yield a lower expected makespan than the API sequence. Thus, even when the deterministic counterpart sequence is not stable, the API heuristic is not guaranteed to improve on it.

The existence of more than one stable sequence proves that there can be no transitive sorting rule for normal processing times. Suppose, however, that all processing times are distributed normally with equal means μ but different variances, $V(A_j)$, $V(B_j)$, and so on. Then, by Eq. (11.4),

$$E[\min\{A_1, B_2\}] = \mu - \phi(0)[V(A_1) + V(B_2)]^{1/2}$$

and similarly,

$$E[\min\{A_2, B_1\}] = \mu - \phi(0)[V(A_2) + V(B_1)]^{1/2}$$

Therefore, $E[\min\{A_1, B_2\}] \le E[\min\{A_2, B_1\}]$ if and only if $V(A_1) + V(B_2) \ge V(A_2) + V(B_1)]$, or equivalently,

$$V(A_1) - V(B_1) \ge V(A_2) - V(B_2)$$

In this special case, then, the API Heuristic does lead to a transitive sorting rule. This rule tends to place operations with high variance at the beginning or end of the schedule, whereas for operations performed in parallel, it favors low variances. Such placement aims to reduce the Jensen gap, which tends to be large when two high variance activities are performed in parallel. The following example elaborates on this point.

■ **Example 11.4**   Consider a two-job, two-machine flow shop problem with independent processing times. Let $A_1 = B_2 = 1 - \varepsilon$ (where $0 \le \varepsilon \le 1$), with certainty, and let A_2 and B_1 be independent exponential random variables with mean 1.

Initially, assume $\varepsilon = 0$, creating a tie when we solve the deterministic counterpart. For both sequences, the makespan in the deterministic counterpart is exactly 3. If we make ε slightly positive, however, the sequence 1-2 becomes the unique solution to the deterministic counterpart, with a makespan of $3 - 2\varepsilon$. The makespan of sequence 2-1 is longer, at $3 - \varepsilon$, and this is also the expected value of the makespan in the stochastic counterpart. If we use the sequence 1-2 in the stochastic counterpart, the two exponentials are processed in parallel. The expected value of the larger of the two is 1.5. Therefore, the expected value of the makespan under the sequence 1-2 is $3.5 - 2\varepsilon$. In other words, the optimal sequence for the deterministic counterpart is suboptimal in the stochastic problem.

In addition, the variance of the makespan for sequence 2-1 is 2, whereas the variance of the makespan for sequence 1-2 is 1.25. The example thus also shows that when the makespan is the objective for the stochastic problem, the sequence that minimizes the mean may not minimize the variance.

The deterministic counterpart is a good starting sequence for the API Heuristic because Johnson's rule is asymptotically optimal for any independent processing time distributions. For this result to hold, we require all jobs to satisfy two regularity conditions:

$$R1. (1/u)\Sigma_{j=1,\dots,u} \left(E\left[A_j\right] + E\left[B_j\right] \right) \ge 2\delta \text{ where } \delta > 0; \quad u = 1, 2, \dots$$

$$R2. (1/u)_{j=1,\dots,u} \left(V\left(A_j\right) + V\left(B_j\right) \right) \le \gamma^2 \text{ where } \gamma \text{ is finite; } \quad u = 1, 2, \dots$$

If, for example, processing times tend to decrease according to a geometric progression, then asymptotic optimality is not guaranteed. Condition R1 rules that out. Similarly, condition R2 requires that the *average variance* in the system, defined by $(1/n) \Sigma_{j=1,\dots,n}(V(A_j) + V(B_j))$, should not be an unbounded increasing function of n. The conditions are met, for instance, if jobs are selected at random from some pool of potential jobs, all with finite variances.

■ **Theorem 11.3**   Consider a stochastic, two-machine flow shop with independent processing time distributions subject to regularity conditions R1 and R2. Let s_j denote the deterministic counterpart sequence (from Johnson's rule), s^* the optimal sequence, and $M(s)$ the makespan associated with the sequence s. Then, as $n \to \infty$, $E[M(s_j) - M(s^*)]/E[M(s^*)] \to 0$ with probability 1.

The formal proof is beyond our scope. Essentially, it shows that the Jensen gap is bounded from below by 0 and from above by a function that is proportional to the square root of the total variance in the system, $\Sigma_{i=1,\ldots,n}(V(A_i) + V(B_i))$. Because the Jensen gap is nonnegative, $E[M(s^*)]$ cannot be lower than the makespan of the deterministic counterpart, which in turn cannot be lower than the deterministic counterpart makespan of s_J. Moreover, because the total variance grows in proportion to the number of jobs and the average variance of each, the square root becomes relatively negligible for large n.

As a consequence of Theorem 11.3, the advantage of Talwar's rule over the deterministic counterpart solution becomes negligible for large n, even in the case of exponential processing times. It is therefore plausible that this advantage tends to decrease with n.

11.3 Safe Scheduling Models with Stochastic Independence

In the safe scheduling problem with due dates as decisions, we start by considering two basic problems that also apply in the case of the flow shop model: (i) minimizing d subject to a service-level constraint and (ii) minimizing $d + \gamma E[T]$. The same sequence is not guaranteed to solve both versions even for the same optimal service level.

The analysis of makespan behavior in the stochastic flow shop is mathematically challenging. One of the few cases in which algebraic derivations are possible is the two-job, two-machine case with simplified processing time distributions.

■ **Example 11.5** Consider a two-job, two-machine flow shop problem with the following processing time specifications.

Machine	Job 1	Job 2
1	1	U
2	U	1

The processing times denoted 1 are deterministic. The processing times denoted U follow a uniform distribution with a range of (0, 3).

In Example 11.5, we might first compare the deterministic counterparts for the two sequences. Sequence 1-2 leads to a makespan of 3.5, whereas sequence 2-1 leads to a makespan of 4. Thus, in the deterministic counterpart, the sequence has an effect on the makespan.

The stochastic analysis of the makespan requires expressions for the sum of two random variables and for the maximum of two random variables. We omit the details but show the results graphically in Figure 11.1. We can show algebraically that both sequences have an expected makespan of 4, and their cdfs intersect at 13/3, corresponding to a service level of SL = 0.605.

First, consider the problem of minimizing d subject to the service-level target SL = 0.6. The sequence 2-1 attains SL = 0.6 for d = 4.317, just to the left of the intersection depicted in Figure 11.1. At that value, the cdf for sequence 2-1 lies above the cdf for sequence 1-2. Therefore, the sequence 1-2 attains SL = 0.6 for a slightly larger value of d. Because the objective is to minimize the due date, sequence 2-1 provides the better solution.

Now consider the problem of minimizing $d + \gamma E[T]$ with γ = 2.5, which requires an optimal service level of SL = 0.6. Recalling that $E[T]$ can be depicted as an area above the cdf to the right of the due date (see Figure 6.2), it can be shown that $d + \gamma E[T]$ is minimized by the sequence 1-2 with d = 4.324. This relatively simple example demonstrates that even with a common service-level target, the two safe scheduling formulations do not necessarily lead to the same optimal sequence.

Examples of this type rely on the property that the cdfs of the two makespan distributions intersect each other shortly after the due dates that achieve the prescribed service levels. For any SL ≥ 0.605, the sequence 1-2 is optimal for both objectives. If a stochastically minimal sequence exists (as in the case of two machines and exponential processing times), then its cdf does not intersect

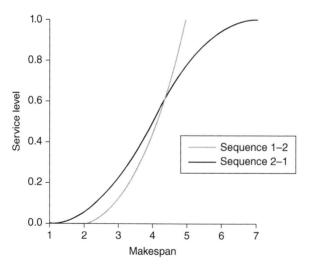

Figure 11.1 Comparison of the cdfs for two sequences in Example 11.5.

the cdf of any other sequence. A stochastically minimal sequence would be optimal for both objectives.

For the objective of minimizing $d + \gamma E[T]$, our general analysis parallels that of previous chapters, as summarized in the steps below.

1) The optimal due date is given by the critical fractile formula

$$SL = \Pr\{M \le d^*\} = \frac{\gamma - 1}{\gamma}$$

2) Assuming – as an approximation – that the makespan M follows a normal distribution with mean μ and standard deviation σ, we can also write

$$d^* = \mu + z^* \sigma$$

so that z^* represents the optimal standard normal variate corresponding to d^*.

3) The optimal value of the objective function can then be calculated as $H(d^*)$, where

$$H(d^*) = d^* + \gamma E[T] = \mu + \gamma \phi(z^*) \sigma$$

We simulated sequences for a seven-job, five-machine flow shop with independent normally distributed processing times with a sample-based analysis using 1000 realizations. For a particular sequence, the estimated mean makespan was 126.12, and the estimated standard deviation was 5.35. A chi-square goodness-of-fit test did not reject the hypothesis that the makespan distribution was normal. For $\gamma = 10$, corresponding to a service level of 90%, we would therefore set $z^* = 1.282$ and obtain $H(d^*) = 135.50$.

The formula for $H(d^*)$ also highlights the marginal economic trade-off between mean and standard deviation. Specifically, we should be willing to increase μ by up to $\gamma \phi(z^*)$ units for every unit decrease in σ or 1.75 in our instance. This is formally true only when the optimal service level is used, but otherwise it is even more important to decrease σ.

Two extensions of Theorem 11.3 apply to safe scheduling. Specifically, Johnson's rule is asymptotically optimal for any independent processing time distributions, not only for the stochastic counterpart model in Theorem 11.3 but also for safe scheduling. We consider a stochastic n-job, two-machine flow shop model with independent processing time distributions subject to regularity conditions R1 and R2 given earlier. Again, we use s_J to denote the deterministic counterpart sequence (given by Johnson's rule) and s^* to denote the (unknown) optimal sequence.

■ **Theorem 11.4** Consider the objective of minimizing d subject to a service-level constraint $SL \ge b$. Let $d^*(s)$ denote the optimal value associated with the sequence s. Then, as $n \to \infty$, $[d^*(s_J) - d^*(s^*)]/d^*(s^*) \to 0$ with probability 1.

■ **Theorem 11.5** Consider the objective of minimizing $Z(s) = d + \gamma E[T]$. Let $Z^*(s)$ denote the optimal value of the objective function associated with the sequence s. Then, as $n \to \infty$, $[Z^*(s_j) - Z^*(s^*)]/Z^*(s^*) \to 0$ with probability 1.

These last two theorems portray the state of the art in safe scheduling for the flow shop model. Thus far, the only safe scheduling results apply to the makespan problem. However, the state of the art resembles the traditional analysis of flow shop models, where little progress has been made beyond analyzing the makespan, except for special cases.

11.4   Flow Shops with Linear Association

We next remove the stochastic independence assumption and replace it by linear association, building on the results of Appendix A.4. As usual, we focus on the makespan objective. Theorems A.4, A.5, and A.6 assume a job shop environment, but a flow shop is a special case, so those theorems apply. Propositions A.1 and A.2 are also valid, suggesting that with safe scheduling models, we cannot rely on the initial solution to remain correct after the adjustment. Instead, it is necessary to calculate due dates and compare sequences *after* the adjustment. With this background, we address some flow shop models specifically.

The two-machine, two-job model is solved by comparing two minima, and we prefer to run job 1 first if $E[\min\{A_1, B_2\}] \leq E[\min\{A_2, B_1\}]$. By Theorem A.3 and Corollary A.1, our preference to schedule job 1 first does not change after adjustment. That is, we can sequence by the initial processing times, and the result is optimal for the linearly associated times. By serially implementing Theorem A.2 (according to which the sum of adjusted random variables is equal to the adjusted sum of their initial values) and Theorem A.3, we can see that the cdf of the makespan of a flow shop subject to linear association is given by the initial cdf of the same shop adjusted afterward. By applying Theorem A.1, we obtain the following result.

■ **Theorem 11.6** For a shop with linearly associated processing times with a common factor Q, let s_1 and s_2 be two sequences, let $M(s_j)$ be the adjusted makespan of sequence s_j, and let $M'(s_j)$ be the initial makespan of the same shop. If $M'(s_1) \geq_{ex} M'(s_2)$, then $M(s_1) \geq_{ex} M(s_2)$, and if $M'(s_1) \geq_{st} M'(s_2)$, then $M(s_1) \geq_{st} M(s_2)$.

Thus, for the stochastic counterpart m-machine flow shop, the optimal sequence subject to an independent processing time assumption remains optimal if we introduce a common factor and obtain linearly associated processing times. Furthermore, if a stochastically dominant sequence exists, it remains stochastically dominant. As an example, suppose that we have independent exponentially distributed raw processing times subject to a common factor element that need not be exponential. Then Talwar's rule can be applied to the raw processing times, and the result remains stochastically minimal after introducing the factor even though the adjusted distributions are not exponential.

By Theorem A.3, the optimal initial solution of the no-wait two-machine model remains optimal under linear association. In fact, practically all the results we presented for deterministic counterpart models remain valid for the linearly associated case. To cover safe scheduling flow shop models, we make use of Theorems A.5 and A.6 that provide the variance and coefficient of variation of adjusted variables. Theorem A.6 indicates that the squared coefficient of variation (scv) of the product exceeds the sum of the scv's of the components, and therefore the coefficient of variation of the product exceeds that of either component. In our context, the more important aspect of this observation is that the coefficient of variation of the makespan cannot be less than that of Q. Recall Example A.1 and Propositions A.1 and A.2: They could be recast for this chapter without any substantial change. In particular, empirical results and the lognormal central limit theorem (Appendix A) suggest that approximating the makespan by a lognormal approximation of a normal random variable would be appropriate.

11.5 Empirical Observations

Finding the minimum expected makespan for the stochastic flow shop is a challenging problem, and our main practical tools are likely to be heuristic procedures. For the two-machine case, we have only heuristic methods available unless we know that the processing time distributions are exponential. (Even in that special case, we can calculate the optimal sequence, but finding the distribution of the makespan, or even its mean, remains a formidable computational task.) For more than two machines, we might try to adapt heuristic procedures that perform well in the deterministic counterpart, but it would also be desirable to develop some general insights into this complicated problem.

In Example 11.3, we found that the API heuristic generated a better sequence for the stochastic problem than Johnson's rule as applied to the deterministic counterpart. Thus, compared with Johnson's sequence, the optimal stochastic sequence can have a higher makespan in the deterministic counterpart but a lower mean in the stochastic counterpart. This relationship implies that the Jensen gap must be smaller for the optimal sequence than for the sequence obtained from the deterministic counterpart. Similar observations could be made in Examples 11.1 and 11.2. In the former, the optimal makespan of 19.33 is associated with a deterministic counterpart makespan of 18 – a Jensen gap of 1.33, whereas the deterministic makespan of 17 leads to 19.50 – a Jensen gap of 2.50. Based on such examples, we might guess that the best sequence is one with a small Jensen gap. Similarly, we might guess that the best sequence for safe scheduling is also one with a small Jensen gap.

We call a schedule *dense* if its deterministic counterpart makespan is small – that is, if it exhibits relatively little idle time. Otherwise, the schedule is called *loose*. In a deterministic context, we would say that dense is "good," and loose is "bad." We might hypothesize that dense and loose schedules should perform roughly equally when stochastic processing times are involved. The intuitive reasoning would be that loose schedules provide protection with the very idleness built into them, so they should exhibit lower variance.

To elaborate on this argument, dense schedules are vulnerable to the Jensen gap because they are finely tuned and have little margin for stochastic variation. Stochastic processing times should therefore inflate the mean makespan of the deterministic counterpart. On the other hand, loose schedules contain more idle time and should be better able to absorb stochastic variations. The idle time should provide protection from a similar kind of inflation. Given the limits of our current theoretical knowledge, however, such hypotheses can only be tested empirically. To that end, we turn to empirical results obtained by simulation.

We explored the properties of dense and loose schedules in a seven-job, five-machine flow shop example. Using a sample-based approach with 1000 realizations, we compared all 5040 permutation schedules. We then tested each schedule to estimate the mean and the standard deviation of its makespan. The results allowed us to develop some quantitative perspective on the nature of the Jensen gap and the relationship between means and standard deviations. (The approximately normal makespan distribution that we discussed earlier belongs to one of those 5040 sequences.)

Figure 11.2 shows the Jensen gap as a function of the deterministic counterpart makespan for each permutation (called the *nominal* makespan). As expected, the Jensen gap is decreasing in the nominal makespan. Although the Jensen gap indicates the extent of the bias that occurs when the deterministic counterpart is used as a predictor of the stochastic outcome, it does not follow that schedules with large Jensen gaps are necessarily poor. In fact, the experiment showed just the opposite. Figure 11.3 plots the mean makespan

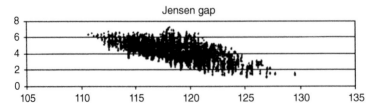

Figure 11.2 The Jensen gap as a function of the nominal makespan.

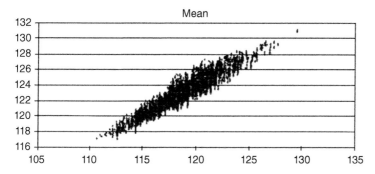

Figure 11.3 The mean makespan as a function of the nominal makespan.

of each sequence as a function of the nominal makespan, showing that dense schedules produce the smaller expected makespans. (The data points in this figure can be obtained from Figure 11.2 by adding the nominal makespan to the Jensen gap.) The mean makespan is increasing in the nominal makespan. Thus, our intuitive hypothesis is not supported. The implication is that solving the deterministic counterpart produces a good sequence for the stochastic problem. At the same time, however, predicting the value of the expected makespan requires that we adjust for the Jensen gap. Given the state of the art, simulation is still the best way to estimate the bias.

As discussed earlier, we might expect that looser schedules would exhibit larger means and smaller variances than dense schedules. In Figure 11.4, we show the relationship between mean and standard deviation of the makespan for the 5040 sequences. Contrary to our intuition, the smaller makespan values tend to be associated with smaller standard deviations.

In these experiments, the best schedules exhibited the largest Jensen gaps. In an empirical sense, the observation that large Jensen gaps were associated with low variance suggests that Jensen gaps somehow decrease variance. Nevertheless, when it comes to predicting schedule length, dense schedules may lead to prediction errors unless we allow for the Jensen gap. A dense schedule with a

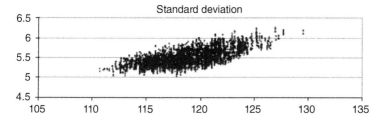

Figure 11.4 The standard deviation as a function of the expected makespan.

Jensen gap correction (as well as a buffer for safety time) should therefore perform very well in practice because it tends to have low variance *and* low mean. However, if we do not take the Jensen gap into account, we may be better off with a loose schedule and a makespan that is more likely to be achieved.

Figure 11.5 depicts a ranking of options for predicting schedule length. At the top, the most desirable option is to use a dense schedule but correct for the Jensen gap and add a buffer for safety time. We denote this combination by D + J + B (for dense + Jensen + buffer). Next come either dense schedules with a Jensen correction but no safety time (D + J) or loose schedules with a Jensen correction and a safety time buffer (L + J + B). We cannot order these options because both are suboptimal in different ways, so they are depicted in parallel. These two options dominate loose schedules with a Jensen correction but no safety time (L + J), which in turn dominates loose schedules without any correction or buffer (L). At the very bottom comes the raw dense schedule (D), because its inaccurate prediction is likely to lead to disappointment.

In spite of these results, it would be a mistake to conclude that high Jensen gaps are always associated with low variance. For instance, in Examples 11.1 and 11.2, we saw that Talwar's rule produced makespans with low Jensen gaps and low variances when compared with Johnson's rule. Along similar lines, an exploratory simulation study identified a case where sequences tended to yield very similar Jensen gaps but quite different variances. The particular simulation tested the hypothesis that the API heuristic yields superior results for the case of normal distributions with equal means, for which the pairwise-improvement condition is transitive. An experiment was devised to study different allocations of variance to jobs with equal means, subject to the same total variance in the system. When Johnson's rule compares two operations with the same mean, a

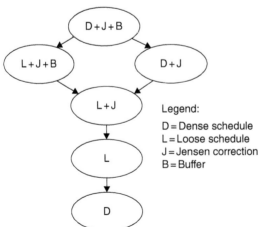

Figure 11.5 Some dominance relationships among schedules.

Legend:
D = Dense schedule
L = Loose schedule
J = Jensen correction
B = Buffer

tie occurs. We break such ties in favor of the smaller variance. With this tie-breaker in place, it is possible to allocate the variances so that the API heuristic reverses the Johnson sequence. Figures 11.6 and 11.7 portray the results of such a simulation, in which mean operation times are 10 and the total variance of each job is 2. The variance is allocated to operations starting with 0 on machine A and 2 on machine B for job 1, finishing with 2 on machine A and 0 on machine B for job n. Across the set of n jobs, the variance is monotone increasing on the first machine and monotone decreasing on the second. Using the tiebreaker, the Johnson sequence is $1 - 2 - \cdots - n$, and the API sequence is the reverse ($n, n - 1,$ ..., 1). The results fail to confirm the hypothesis that API is the superior sequence in this case: No discernible difference in the mean is observed (essentially the same Jensen gap occurs in both cases), as depicted in Figure 11.6, where the horizontal axis denotes the nominal makespan and the two graphs practically overlap. However, the API heuristic yielded a significantly higher standard deviation, as depicted in Figure 11.7.

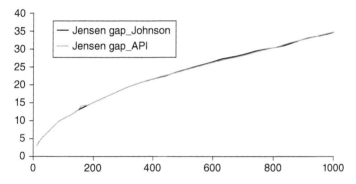

Figure 11.6 The Jensen gap of the two sequences as a function of the number of jobs.

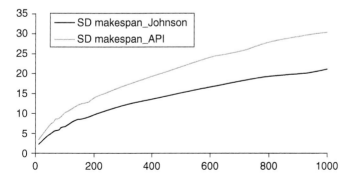

Figure 11.7 The standard deviation of the two makespans.

Whereas the disappointing results for the API heuristic in the transitive normal case are somewhat surprising, they support another hypothesis called the *variance effect*. It states that if we ignore the mean job processing times and schedule by variances – as if the variance were the processing time – then Johnson's rule tends to yield sequences with low variance. The converse was also observed empirically: Scheduling by $-\sigma_j^2$ tends to yield sequences with high variance.

Now consider the case where the mean and the variance are agreeable. We expect that Johnson's sequence might often be optimal in such a case because our empirical evidence suggests that the two criteria (reducing the mean and the standard deviation) would be satisfied at the same time. When all means are equal, then means and variances are agreeable, but in Figures 11.6 and 11.7, we saw that API reverses the Johnson sequence. Thus, we might expect the API heuristic to be inferior when agreeability holds because it may lead the API heuristic away from the Johnson sequence. Indeed, the empirical results for the Johnson sequence in such cases were good, but not perfect. Consider the case of exponential processing times, where Talwar's sequence is optimal but not identical to Johnson's sequence. This is a case where means and variances are agreeable. Furthermore, the API heuristic, when based on the true distributional values in Theorem 11.1 rather than a normal approximation, converges to Talwar's sequence in this case. Thus, there must be instances where the API heuristic is superior to Johnson's rule.

11.6 Summary

Although the two-job, two-machine stochastic flow shop model is easy to solve, this result does not lead to significant inroads even for the two-machine case with n jobs. One heuristic based on the two-job result combined with API is useful sometimes, but it also has a tendency to produce unnecessarily high variance. Thus, with one notable exception – Talwar's rule – all stochastic flow shop models are difficult to solve even for medium-sized instances and even for $m = 2$. Even Talwar's rule – on top of the fact that it requires the strong assumption that processing times are exponential – is not sufficient for safe scheduling purposes. If we wish to determine optimal safety time, then as a practical matter, we must use simulation to estimate the cdf of the makespan. (For this case, calculating the makespan distribution analytically requires exponential complexity.) This situation suggests that we should use heuristics and rely on sample-based analysis.

For two machines, we saw that using the deterministic counterpart (Johnson's rule) is asymptotically optimal. Furthermore, the deterministic counterpart is also asymptotically optimal for safe scheduling. Empirical experience suggests that this result extends to m machines, but formal proofs have not yet been developed.

When processing times are exponential, Talwar's rule yields sequences with low mean *and* low variance. Nonetheless, empirical results suggest that pursuing a low Jensen gap by using schedules that aren't dense can actually lead to makespan distributions with a higher mean *and* a higher variance than those of the deterministic counterpart sequence. This is surprising, especially when we consider that Johnson's rule tends to yield a large Jensen gap. Nevertheless, this observation reinforces the usefulness of Johnson's heuristic. But there is an important caveat: Because the Jensen gap tends to be large for the deterministic counterpart, it is imperative to recognize it for scheduling purposes and allow enough time for it. Otherwise, the schedule is practically guaranteed to be misleading, and practitioners would be justified if they were to conclude that the best deterministic counterpart sequence is not desirable in practice. Thus, using the deterministic counterpart may not be successful unless safe scheduling principles are pursued to account for the true mean, including the Jensen gap.

We also saw that when linear association is involved, the Jensen gap is not necessarily the most important issue for effective safe scheduling. The dominating issue may well be that the standard deviation of the makespan is likely to grow almost linearly with the mean, so we must not use safety times that tend to zero for large n. Again, the problem is easy to resolve once we understand the issue. Also, if the Jensen gap is expressed as a fraction of the makespan, it remains constant under linear association. Furthermore, Johnson's heuristic can safely be applied to the initial processing times, ignoring the adjustment for linear association, because it is sufficient to apply the adjustment to the final results.

The conclusions we obtained for the flow shop can be considered special cases of job shops, and thus they are also useful as a heuristic guide for more complex shops and for project scheduling.

Exercises

11.1 The following array records the differences $E[\min\{A_i, B_j\}] - E[\min\{A_j, B_i\}]$ for a set of five jobs, with job i corresponding to a row and j to a column. When the entry in row i and column j is negative, then placing job i directly ahead of j is stable.

	Job 2	Job 3	Job 4	Job 5
Job 1	−6.00	2.91	6.09	0.71
Job 2		6.01	−2.50	1.00
Job 3			3.66	0.77
Job 4				0.99

a) Using the API heuristic, find a stable job sequence, starting with the sequence 1-2-3-4-5.
b) Is the sequence in (a) the only stable sequence?

11.2 Consider the following five-job, two-machine flow shop problem with expected makespan objective. Each processing time follows a normal distribution, with the parameters for mean and standard deviation given in the table.

Job j	1	2	3	4	5
μ_{A_j}	8	12	15	10	14
μ_{B_j}	12	15	14	8	10
σ_{A_j}	1	2	3	1	2
σ_{B_j}	2	2	3	2	1

Find a solution using Talwar's heuristic, Johnson's heuristic, and the API heuristic. Initialize the API heuristic with the solution generated by Johnson's heuristic.

11.3 Find the solution to the problem in the previous exercise using the Evolutionary Solver.

11.4 Consider a two-machine, three-job example with independent normally distributed processing times.

Job j	1	2	3
μ_{A_j}	20	19	20
μ_{B_j}	20	19	20
σ_{A_j}	5	1	5
σ_{B_j}	5	2	5

a) Find the Johnson sequence (with ties broken by the smaller variance).
b) Find a stable sequence. Is it the only stable sequence?
c) Using simulation, compare the two sequences found above with the sequence 1-2-3, and determine which is optimal for the stochastic counterpart. Based on the results, is it true that an optimal sequence must be stable?

11.5 Consider the following five-job, two-machine flow shop problem. Each processing time follows a normal distribution, with the parameters for mean and standard deviation given in the table.

Job j	1	2	3	4	5
μ_{A_j}	8	12	15	10	14
μ_{B_j}	12	15	14	8	10
σ_{A_j}	1	2	3	1	2
σ_{B_j}	2	2	3	2	1

a) Estimate the mean and the standard deviation of the makespan for the job sequence 1-2-3-4-5, by simulation. Using these estimates, compute the due date for which the sequence provides a service level of 75%.

b) Using the simulation results from part (a), compute the optimal due date for minimizing the function $H(d) = d + \gamma E[T]$, with $\gamma = 5$.

c) Find the job sequence that minimizes the value of $H(d) = d + \gamma E[T]$, with $\gamma = 5$.

11.6 Show that the complexity of the API heuristic is $O(n^2)$. Does your proof extend to the complexity of finding all stable sequences?

11.7 Prove that if a transitive rule can generate an optimal sequence for the stochastic counterpart two-machine flow shop problem, then API is guaranteed to converge to that optimal solution. Does your proof suffice to show that if there is only one stable sequence, then the sequence is optimal?

Bibliography

Baker, K.R. and Trietsch, D. (2011). Three heuristic procedures for the stochastic, two-machine flow shop problem. *Journal of Scheduling* 14: 445–454.

Clark, C.E. (1961). The greatest of a finite set of random variables. *Operations Research* 9: 145–162.

Cunningham, A.A. and Dutta, S.K. (1973). Scheduling jobs with exponentially distributed processing times on two machines of a flow shop. *Naval Research Logistics Quarterly* 16: 69–81.

Dodin, B. (1996). Determining the optimal sequences and the distributional properties of their completion times in stochastic flow shops. *Computers & Operations Research* 23: 829–843.

Emmons, H. and Vairaktarakis, G. (2013). *Flow Shop Scheduling: Theoretical Results, Algorithms, and Applications.* New York: Springer.

Johnson, S.M. (1954). Optimal two- and three-stage production schedules with setup times included. *Naval Research Logistics Quarterly* 1: 61–68.

Kamburowski, J. (1999). Stochastically minimizing the makespan in two-machine flow shops without blocking. *European Journal of Operational Research* 112: 304–309.

Kamburowski, J. (2000). Non-bottleneck machines in three-machine flow shops. *Journal of Scheduling* 3: 209–223.

Ku, P.-S. and Niu, S.-C. (1986). On Johnson's two-machine flow shop with random processing times. *Operations Research* 34: 130–136.

Makino, T. (1965). On a scheduling problem. *Journal of the Operations Research Society Japan* 8: 32–44.

Pinedo, M. (1982). Minimizing the expected makespan in stochastic flow shops. *Operations Research* 30: 148–162.

Portougal, V. and Trietsch, D. (1998). Makespan-related criteria for comparing schedules in stochastic environments. *Journal of the Operational Research Society* 49: 1188–1195.

Portougal, V. and Trietsch, D. (2001). Stochastic scheduling with optimal customer service. *Journal of the Operational Research Society* 52: 226–233.

Portougal, V. and Trietsch, D. (2006). Johnson's problem with stochastic processing times and optimal service level. *European Journal of Operational Research* 169: 751–760.

Talwar, P.P. (1967). A note on sequencing problems with uncertain job times. *Journal of the Operations Research Society Japan* 9: 93–97.

12

Lot Streaming Procedures for the Flow Shop

12.1 Introduction

Lot streaming is the process of splitting a job into sublots so that its operations can be overlapped. We can think of lot streaming as a special type of lot splitting. The term lot splitting refers to breaking a given lot size into smaller sublots during production. The lot size itself is a predetermined quantity, typically set by the customer or by planning processes that precede scheduling. The opportunity to split lots arises in the short term – in the implementation of a detailed schedule – and two cases are worth distinguishing. The more common case involves interrupting a job, performing other kinds of work, and later returning to finish the interrupted job. We refer to this phenomenon as *preemption*, which is motivated by a desire to implement appropriate priorities in a situation where two or more jobs compete for limited resources.

The second case involves overlapping operations for a given job. Before an entire job is complete on a particular machine, some portion of the job is moved ahead to a downstream operation. We refer to this case as *lot streaming*, which is motivated by a desire to move a job through several work stations as quickly as possible. Lot streaming is distinct from preemption because it deals with a particular job: Rather than give priority to another job, the objective is to expedite the current job. Expediting by preemption can cause cascading instability, so it is often considered bad practice. By contrast, expediting a job by lot streaming tends to smooth the flow of materials. For this reason, even in environments that discourage preemption, expediting by lot streaming may be advantageous.

The concept of lot streaming appears in various places in the literature on production. For example, one motivation for group technology is the potential benefit for lead time and work-in-process inventory levels when operations are overlapped in a manufacturing cell. In addition, the concepts of synchronous manufacturing include the distinction between process batch and transfer

Principles of Sequencing and Scheduling, Second Edition. Kenneth R. Baker and Dan Trietsch.
© 2019 John Wiley & Sons, Inc. Published 2019 by John Wiley & Sons, Inc.

batch. The *process batch* is essentially the predetermined lot size, whereas the *transfer batch* is the size of a sublot moved from one operation to the next, permitting operations to overlap and throughput to be increased. In highly repetitive JIT production, the aim is to reduce setups enough to make the process batch very small. In those circumstances, we need not distinguish between the process batch and the transfer batch. However, when setup times remain large, the use of a small transfer batch is attractive.

The basic lot streaming model is a one-job flow shop model in which the lot size is known. To accelerate the job as much as possible, we look for a minimum makespan. Even when the overall criterion is something other than the makespan, minimizing the makespan of individual jobs improves performance. One example concerns utilization: As we saw in Chapter 10, reducing the makespan reduces total idleness of the machines, so this objective is associated with increased throughput. As another example, if we were solving an instance of the *T*-problem for *n* jobs in a flow shop (which is quite a difficult problem), a reasonable strategy would be to build a good schedule without lot streaming and then apply lot streaming procedures locally for each job to reduce job completion times (and hence total tardiness) even further. Contemporary research addresses more complex environments such as job shops, parallel machines, and assembly systems, as well as other objectives. Models may involve explicit consideration of several jobs, which gives rise to a sequencing problem as well as a lot streaming problem. In this chapter, however, we focus on the basic model. In addition to serving as a building block for more complex models, it has dominated research for a long time. Studying the basic model serves as a good introduction to more general lot streaming models.

■ **Example 12.1**   Consider a lot streaming problem consisting of 100 units to be processed sequentially by five machines with unit processing times of 5, 9, 4, 7, and 6.

Without lot streaming, the job is in process for a time of 3100. When we invoke lot streaming and split the job into two equal sublots, this time drops to 2000, as shown in Figure 12.1.

12.2   The Basic Two-machine Model

12.2.1   Preliminaries

The production model is a flow shop made up of m machines. A job lot, consisting of U identical items, must proceed in sequence through m operations, one at each machine. The processing time per unit at machine i is denoted by p_i. Thus, without lot streaming, the makespan for the lot becomes

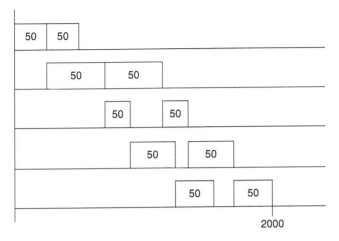

Figure 12.1 A solution to Example 12.1 with two equal sublots.

$$M = U \sum_{i=1}^{m} p_i$$

If the lot can be split, then lot streaming may allow M to be reduced. To describe a schedule containing sublots, we let L_{ij} represent the size of the jth sublot on machine i. (It may be useful to think about L_{ij} as the number of items contained in the jth transfer lot emanating from machine i.) As a convenient alternative, it is sometimes helpful to use decision variables x_{ij}, denoting the relative size of the jth sublot on machine i. That is,

$$x_{ij} = \frac{L_{ij}}{U}$$

where, for each machine i,

$$\sum_j L_{ij} = U$$

or equivalently,

$$\sum_j x_{ij} = 1$$

As in the flow shop model, we can work with the reversed problem, in which the machines and sublots are reversed in sequence. More formally, the processing time on the ith machine in the reversed problem is p_{m-i+1}. The optimal solution can always be obtained by solving the reversed problem and reversing the schedule.

We are ultimately interested in solving a form of the problem in which the variables L_{ij} are integers, corresponding to the discrete number of units in each sublot. Typically, this *discrete version* of the problem can be formulated as an integer linear program. Anticipating that this may be a difficult problem to solve, however, we may at least gain some insight from solving a *continuous version* of the problem, in which we relax the integer restrictions. We might actually be able to implement the continuous solution directly if it happens to be integer, or if we are willing to round off fractions in the continuous solution. (Such rounding may be acceptable if U is large and the number of sublots is small.) In addition, the optimal makespan in the continuous version serves as a lower bound on the optimal makespan in the discrete version, and the makespan produced by rounding the continuous solution serves as an upper bound. In some models, it is even possible to find the optimal integer solution by a polynomial search in the neighborhood of the optimal continuous solution.

In the discrete version, we can minimize the makespan by assigning just one item to each sublot – that is, by setting $L_{ij} = 1$. Nevertheless, practical considerations may make it undesirable to have a large number of unit-sized sublots. For example, material handling equipment may be limited, or difficulties may arise in tracking a large number of small sublots. Therefore, we formulate the basic lot streaming problem with a constraint on the number of sublots.

In general, the transfer lots between machines i and $(i + 1)$ may differ from the transfer lots between machines $(i + 1)$ and $(i + 2)$. Thus, the general form of the model allows for *variable* sublots. However, there may be technological constraints that affect the formation and movement of sublots; and in some applications, we may want to preserve the integrity of sublots throughout the schedule. If the sublot size is the same at each machine ($L_{ij} = L_j$), we call the sublots *consistent*. Any set of consistent sublots satisfies the conditions of an ordered flow shop (see Chapter 10), if we think of the sublots as jobs. Thus, if a set of consistent sublots is determined, we should want to sequence them in a pyramid sequence (an SPT/LPT sequence).

In some applications, a requirement may be imposed that each machine, once started, must process the entire lot continuously, with *no idling*. Such a restriction, when imposed on the first machine, does not affect the optimal makespan, and by symmetry, the same is true for the last machine. Thus, in the two-machine problem, the no-idling restriction does not affect the optimal makespan. When imposed on intermediate machines in larger problems, however, this restriction may increase the optimal makespan.

The least restrictive model allows variable sublots and intermittent idling. By comparison, the assumption of no idling is a special case, and the assumption of consistent sublots is also a special case. Thus, the model with variable sublots and intermittent idling *dominates* the others. From a scheduling point of view, it is unwise to impose additional restrictions, such as consistent sublots or no idling, unless a technological reason requires it. The only exception is the two-machine model, where performance is not sacrificed by assuming consistent sublots or no idling.

No dominance exists between a model prescribing variable sublots with no idling and a model prescribing consistent sublots with intermittent idling, but either model dominates the case of consistent sublots with no idling.

12.2.2 The Continuous Version

We begin the analysis with the two-machine case, which is the simplest lot streaming model. The concept of variable sublots does not really apply to the two-machine problem because only one set of transfers occurs. Therefore, we can assume the use of consistent sublots. Specifically, let s denote the number of sublots. For convenience, we can rescale the problem so that $p_1 = 1$ and $p_2 = q$, and we can take $U = 1$. Sublot k must be preceded by $(k - 1)$ sublots on machine 1 and followed by $(s - k)$ sublots on machine 2. Thus, the makespan must satisfy

$$M \geq \sum_{j=1}^{k} x_j + q \sum_{j=k}^{s} x_j \tag{12.1}$$

When $k = s$, the inequality simplifies to $M \geq 1 + qx_s > 1$, and when $k = 1$, it simplifies to $M \geq q + x_1 > q$. Thus, we have

$$M > \max\{1, q\} \tag{12.2}$$

In addition, the inequality in Eq. (12.1) must be satisfied as an equation for at least one index k. Let c denote such an index. We refer to sublot c as *critical*, and we have

$$M = \sum_{j=1}^{c} x_j + q \sum_{j=c}^{s} x_j \tag{12.3}$$

The following property characterizes the solution that minimizes makespan.

■ **Theorem 12.1**   In the optimal solution for a two-machine lot streaming problem, all sublots are critical.

Proof. Assume there is a schedule S that attains the optimal makespan M, but in which sublot k is noncritical. We will show how to increase the size of sublot k and reduce the sizes of all other sublots in order to improve the makespan. By definition of a noncritical sublot, we have

$$M - \sum_{j=1}^{k} x_j - q \sum_{j=k}^{s} x_j = \Delta > 0 \tag{12.4}$$

Now construct schedule S' (with primes denoting its sublot sizes) by setting

$$x'_k = x_k(1-\delta) + \delta \quad \text{and} \quad x'_j = x_j(1-\delta) \quad \text{for all } j \neq k$$

where $0 < \delta < \Delta/(\Delta + 1 + q - M)$. We know this fraction is no larger than one, because any form of lot streaming yields $M \leq 1 + q$. If M' is the makespan for schedule S', then

$$M' = \sum_{j=1}^{c'} x'_j + q \sum_{j=c'}^{s} x'_j \tag{12.5}$$

for some index c'. If $c' = k$, then substitution in Eq. (12.5) for x'_j yields

$$M' = (1-\delta) \left(\sum_{j=1}^{k} x_j + q \sum_{j=k}^{s} x_j \right) + \delta(1+q) \tag{12.6}$$

From Eq. (12.4) we have $\left(\sum_{j=1}^{k} x_j + q \sum_{j=k}^{s} x_j \right) = M - \Delta$. Substituting this relation into Eq. (12.6) yields

$$M' = (1-\delta)(M-\Delta) + \delta(1+q) = M + \delta(\Delta + 1 + q - M) - \Delta < M \tag{12.7}$$

where the inequality is obtained from the definition of δ. In other words, if we have $c' = k$, then we can improve on the optimal makespan. On the other hand, if $c' \neq k$, then substitution in Eq. (12.5) for x'_j allows us to write

$$M' \leq (1-\delta) \left(\sum_{j=1}^{c'} x_j + q \sum_{j=c'}^{s} x_j \right) + \delta \max\{1, q\} \tag{12.8}$$

which, in view of Eq. (12.1), gives us

$$M' \leq (1-\delta)M + \delta \max\{1, q\} \tag{12.9}$$

We know from Eq. (12.2) that $M > \max\{1, q\}$. Thus, it follows that $M' < M$, so again, we can improve on the optimal makespan. Thus, in either case, we can improve on the optimum, which contradicts the assumption that S is an optimal schedule. Hence, all sublots must be critical in an optimal solution. □

From Theorem 12.1 it follows that the optimal schedule contains no idling, so successive sublots satisfy the relation $x_{j+1} = qx_j$. From this relation we obtain

$$x_j = q^{j-1}x_1$$

and because the proportions must sum to 1, we have

$$\sum_{j=1}^{s} x_j = x_1 \sum_{j=1}^{s} q^{j-1} = 1$$

Therefore, the optimal set of sublot sizes is described by the proportions

$$x_j = \frac{q^{j-1}}{1+q+q^2+\cdots+q^{s-1}} = \frac{q^{j-1}(1-q)}{1-q^s} \tag{12.10}$$

Equivalently, successive sublots satisfy the relation $L_j = qL_{j-1} = q^{j-1}L_1$, or, in the original item scale,

$$L_j = \frac{Uq^{j-1}(1-q)}{1-q^s} \tag{12.11}$$

Both Eqs. (12.10) and (12.11) describe a geometric pattern of sublot sizes.

The optimal makespan must be equal to the time required by the first sublot on machine 1 plus the time required for the entire lot on machine 2. In the rescaled model, this sum is $x_1 + q$. In the original time scale, we obtain

$$M = Up_1\frac{1-q^{s+1}}{1-q^s} \tag{12.12}$$

All of these results assume that $p_1 \neq p_2$, so that $q \neq 1$. In the special case $q = 1$, we obtain equal sublots $L_j = U/s$, and $M = Up_1(1 + s)/s$.

■ **Example 12.2** Consider a two-machine lot streaming problem containing $U = 40$ units. The processing times are $p_1 = 5$ and $p_2 = 4$, and we seek a schedule with $s = 4$ sublots.

We have $q = 0.8$, so it follows from Eq. (12.11) that the optimal sublot sizes are approximately $L_j = (13.55, 10.84, 8.67, 6.94)$. From Eq. (12.12), the corresponding makespan is $M = 227.75$. Without lot streaming the makespan would be $M = 360$, so lot streaming improves the makespan by nearly 37%. The four-sublot schedule is shown in Figure 12.2.

When the number of sublots becomes quite large, the makespan approaches

$$M = U \max\{p_1, p_2\} \tag{12.13}$$

Figure 12.2 The continuous solution for Example 12.2.

In Example 12.2, this limit is 200. Therefore, we can compare the reduction of 37% in the makespan achieved with four sublots to a reduction of 44.4%, which represents a bound on the reduction that any amount of lot streaming could achieve. In other words, the use of four sublots achieves about 83% of the benefit that could be obtained using 40 sublots.

The determination of optimal sublot sizes for the continuous version of the model can be generalized to m machines with a no-idling constraint and a prescribed number of transfers between each pair of machines. In that case, we apply the two-machine solution of Eq. (12.11) to adjacent machine pairs and thereby construct the optimal schedule and the optimal makespan for m machines. In that m-machine solution, sublots are variable rather than consistent because for each pair of consecutive machines, we may have different q values.

12.2.3 The Discrete Version

Now we require that the sublots correspond to an integer number of items. Looking back at Example 12.2, we can see that a naive roundoff rule will not be satisfactory, because such a rule could lead us to round all the fractional sublot sizes in the same direction. We thus need a more sophisticated procedure for finding integer sublot sizes.

Let S_j denote the cumulative number of items in the first j sublots, that is,

$$S_j = L_1 + L_2 + \cdots + L_j$$

Suppose we have a trial value M of the makespan. Define the *late start time*, LS_j, for the jth sublot on machine 2 as the latest time at which the jth sublot could begin on machine 2 and still allow for all remaining work to be done on machine 2 by time M:

$$LS_j = M - p_2\left(U - S_{j-1}\right)$$

For feasibility, we must complete the jth sublot on machine 1 no later than LS_j, so that

$$p_1 S_j \le M - p_2\left(U - S_{j-1}\right) \tag{12.14}$$

or

$$S_j \le \frac{M - p_2\left(U - S_{j-1}\right)}{p_1} \tag{12.15}$$

This is a recursive formula for calculating S_j in terms of S_{j-1}. Equivalently, it calculates the values of L_j in sequence, starting with L_1. To initialize the process, we use $S_0 = 0$, and we terminate the process if S_j should reach U.

Observing that S_j is increasing in S_{j-1}, we choose each S_j in turn to be as large an integer as Eq. (12.15) will permit, but not larger than U. If $S_s < U$, then our trial value of M must have been infeasible, and the next trial value for the makespan should be slightly larger. If so, in order to find the appropriate increment in the trial makespan, let

$$f_j = \min\left\{\frac{M - p_2(U - S_{j-1})}{p_1}, U\right\} - S_j$$

An interpretation of f_j is as follows. If we operated machine 1 continuously and transferred the jth sublot as late as possible (just in time for it to start at machine 2), then f_j would be the fraction of the next item that machine 1 would have processed when the jth sublot arrived. In the actual schedule, we need not transfer the jth sublot as late as possible.

Next, let $e_j = 1 - f_j$. Then the appropriate increment to M is given by

$$\Delta M = p_1\left(\min_j\{e_j\}\right)$$

The search procedure begins with the optimal makespan in Eq. (12.12) because it is a lower bound on the discrete optimum. If the trial value proves to be infeasible, then we increase it by ΔM and test the new trial value. We repeat these steps until the trial value is feasible, which signals optimality. The optimal schedule is not always unique, and we can sometimes find an alternative optimum by solving the reversed problem.

The above procedure requires at most s iterations, so it is polynomial in s. This is a significant result, because the alternative is solving an integer program. It can also be shown that the problem is fully polynomial, even though being polynomial in s is only sufficient to show that it is pseudopolynomial.

As an illustration, we return to Example 12.2. The continuous optimum was 227.75, but because we have integer p_i in this example, we know that the optimal makespan must be integer. Thus, we start with a trial makespan of $M = 228$. Using Eq. (12.15), we obtain

$$S_1 \le \min\{[228 - 4(40)]/5, 40\} = 13.6; \quad S_1 = 13; \quad e_1 = 0.4$$

$$S_2 \le \min\{[228 - 4(27)]/5, 40\} = 24.0; \quad S_2 = 24; \quad e_2 = 1.0$$

$$S_3 \le \min\{[228 - 4(16)]/5, 40\} = 32.8; \quad S_3 = 32; \quad e_3 = 0.2$$

$$S_4 \le \min\{[228 - 4(8)]/5, 40\} = 39.2; \quad S_4 = 39; \quad e_4 = 0.8$$

We have $S_4 < U$, so the trial makespan is infeasible. We increment by $\Delta M = p_1(\min_j\{e_j\}) = 5e_3 = 1.0$ and obtain a new trial makespan of $M = 229$. Repeating the procedure, we obtain

$$S_1 \le \min\{[229 - 4(40)]/5, 40\} = 13.8; \quad S_1 = 13$$

$$S_2 \le \min\{[229 - 4(27)]/5, 40\} = 24.2; \quad S_2 = 24$$

$$S_3 \le \min\{[229 - 4(16)]/5, 40\} = 33.0; \quad S_3 = 33$$

$$S_4 \le \min\{[229 - 4(7)]/5, 40\} = 40.0; \quad S_4 = 40$$

Now, $S_4 = U$, so the trial makespan is optimal. We have $M = 229$ and optimal sublot sizes of $L_j = (13, 11, 9, 7)$. As shown in Figure 12.3, only the third sublot is critical, due to the integer constraints in the problem.

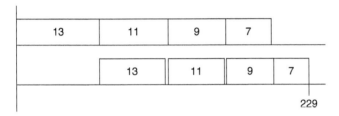

Figure 12.3 The discrete solution for Example 12.2.

12.2.4 Models with Setups

In general, setups may apply to the whole batch, to each sublot, or to each item. When setups occur for each item, setup time can be included in the item processing time, and our models require no change. For simplicity, we treat the other cases separately, starting with batch setups (although both could apply in practice). If a setup is required once on each machine before the batch can start, two possibilities exist. A setup is called *attached* if it cannot start until the arrival of the first sublot; otherwise, the setup is *separable* and can be performed in advance, before the first item arrives.

Let SU_k denote the setup time on machine k. In the case of a separable setup, consider two possibilities: (i) If $SU_1 \geq SU_2$, then for the purpose of optimizing the sublots, we can ignore both setups and just add SU_1 to the makespan; (ii) otherwise, we can subtract $\min\{SU_1, SU_2\}$ from both setups and add it to the makespan without changing the fundamental problem. Therefore, without loss of generality, we can ignore SU_1 and redefine SU_2 as $\max\{0, SU_2 - SU_1\}$. Next, let $h_1 = SU_2/p_1$ denote the number of items that can be processed on machine 1 while machine 2 is being set up. No incentive exists to send any items to machine 2 before it is ready for them, so $L_1 \geq h_1$. More precisely, the continuous version is solved by setting L_1 to $\max\{L_1', h_1\}$, where L_1' is the value obtained for the basic model without setups. Subsequent sublots should be geometric (because the no-idling principle remains intact), but the final sublot may be reduced to avoid exceeding U items in total. If $h_1 > L_1'$, it may happen that not all of the s sublots planned will actually be needed.

When the setup is attached, we can ignore SU_1 because it just adds a constant to the makespan, and we should still follow the no-idling principle. However, SU_2 should not be reduced because the setups cannot be performed in parallel. In this case, the first sublot should be smaller than it would be without setups.

When L_1 reaches machine 2, it takes $SU_2 + L_1 p_2$ to finish processing it. During this time, machine 1 can process $h_1 + L_1 q$ items, and we can always adjust L_1 to a high enough value to justify sending these items to machine 2 immediately without further delay. Thus, we obtain $L_2 = h_1 + L_1 q > L_1 q$ (which demonstrates that L_1 is indeed smaller than L_1'). Thereafter, we use geometric lots and obtain

$$L_j = L_{j-1}q = h_1 q^{j-2} + L_1 q^{j-1} = (h_1 + L_1 q)q^{j-2}$$

To determine L_1, we start by setting $L_1 = 1$, and if we can finish all the other items without requiring more than s sublots in total, then this is the optimal solution. Otherwise, we should increase L_1 to ensure that s sublots will suffice. We define

$$Q = \frac{1 - q^{s-1}}{1 - q}, \quad \text{if } q \neq 1$$
$$= s - 1, \quad \text{if } q = 1$$

Then, based on the no-idling requirement, we can show that

$$L_1 = \frac{U - Qh_1}{Q + q^{s-1}}$$

We next consider the case of sublot setups. By nature, such setups are attached. For example, we may need to stop the machine to mount the items that need to be processed. The general solution follows similar analysis to that of the attached setup, but the details are beyond our scope. Instead, we address the special case of $q = 1$ (i.e. $p_1 = p_2 = p$), because it provides insight as to the general trade-off involved in this model. We must balance the number of sublots: Too few, and we lose the benefit of lot streaming; too many, and we waste too much time on setups, increasing the makespan.

Again, the key idea is the requirement of no idling. This implies that L_j should be set up and processed on machine 2 during the same period that L_{j+1} is set up and processed on machine 1. Define $h_2 = \{(SU_2 - SU_1)/p\}$ as the number of items that can be processed on machine 1 while machine 2 is being set up but after machine 1 has completed its own setup (with a symmetric interpretation if $h_2 < 0$). Therefore, $L_{j+1} = L_j + h_2$, so that the sublots form an arithmetic series with a sum of $L_1 s + h_2 s(s-1)/2$. Thus, $U = [L_1 + h_2(s-1)/2]s$, and $L_1 = U/s - h_2(s-1)/2$. The makespan includes the time to set up and process the first sublot on machine 1, the time to process all items on machine 2, and the time for s setups on it. We thus obtain $M = SU_1 + (L_1 + U)p + SU_2 s$. Substituting for L_1 and h_2, and after some algebra, we obtain

$$M = pU/s + (s + 1)(SU_1 + SU_2)/2$$

This expression could also be derived by studying the reversed problem, so it should not be surprising that the effect of the two setups is symmetric. Setting the derivative with respect to s equal to 0, we obtain

$$s = \sqrt{\frac{2pU}{SU_1 + SU_2}}$$

To ensure an integer number, it is optimal to round down if $\lfloor s \rfloor / s > s / \lceil s \rceil$ and round up otherwise. Finally, solutions with discrete sublots for all the models discussed in this subsection can be obtained by the same approach that we outlined earlier for the case without setups.

12.3 The Three-machine Model with Consistent Sublots

12.3.1 The Continuous Version

For the three-machine problem, we first consider the case in which consistent sublots are required. Recall from our preliminary comments that this requirement may increase the makespan beyond what might otherwise be attainable. However, our approach to the three-machine problem can also be used for the m-machine case.

For the special case of two sublots ($s = 2$), we can specify the solution with a simple decision rule as follows.

Algorithm 12.1   *Solving the 3 × 2 Lot Streaming Problem*

Case 1. For $(p_2)^2 - p_1 p_3 > 0$ and $p_1 \geq p_3$,

$$\text{set } x_1 = \frac{p_1}{p_1 + p_2} \quad \text{and} \quad x_2 = \frac{p_2}{p_1 + p_2}$$

Sublots are in the ratio $p_1 : p_2$.

Case 2. For $(p_2)^2 - p_1 p_3 > 0$ and $p_1 < p_3$,

$$\text{set } x_1 = \frac{p_2}{p_2 + p_3} \quad \text{and} \quad x_2 = \frac{p_3}{p_2 + p_3}$$

Sublots are in the ratio $p_2 : p_3$.

Case 3. For $(p_2)^2 - p_1 p_3 \leq 0$,

$$\text{set } x_1 = \frac{p_1 + p_2}{p_1 + 2p_2 + p_3} \quad \text{and} \quad x_2 = \frac{p_2 + p_3}{p_1 + 2p_2 + p_3}$$

Sublots are in the ratio $(p_1 + p_2) : (p_2 + p_3)$.

In particular, the inequality $(p_2)^2 \leq p_1 p_3$ appears to define the case of a "short" operation time on machine 2, analogous to a dominated machine in the standard flow shop model. Obviously, the solution depends on whether machine 2 is dominated.

When more than two sublots exist, we might guess that the optimum is of the geometric form $L_j = qL_{j-1} = q^{j-1}L_1$, but that is not always the solution.

■ **Example 12.3** Consider a three-machine lot streaming problem with $U = 90$ units and processing times $p_1 = 2, p_2 = 4,$ and $p_3 = 3$. The job is to be processed in three sublots.

This case provides a counterexample to the optimality of geometric lots. The optimal makespan of 490 is achieved with sublot sizes of $L_j = (20, 40, 30)$, as shown in Figure 12.4. (We might call this solution a *pyramid sequence*.) Geometric sublots based on $q = 2, q = 0.75,$ or $q = 1.167$ lead to larger makespans. However, geometric sublots would be optimal when machine 2 is dominated, in which case they should maintain the ratio $(p_1 + p_2) : (p_2 + p_3)$.

In general, the optimal choice of consistent sublots can be found by linear programming (LP). Two LP formulations are of interest, and both generalize to more than three machines. We present the models with the number of machines denoted by m. The natural formulation uses sublot completion times as variables.

Variables

$\quad t_{ij}$ = completion time for sublot j on machine i

$\quad L_j$ = size of sublot j

Objective function

$\quad$ minimize t_{ms}

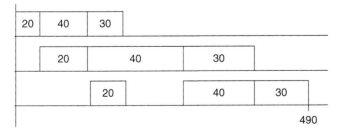

Figure 12.4 A counterexample to the optimality of geometric sublots.

Constraints

$$L_1 + L_2 + \cdots + L_s = U$$

$$t_{11} \geq p_1 L_1$$

$$t_{ij} \geq t_{i-1,j} + p_i L_j \qquad 2 \leq i \leq m,\ 1 \leq j \leq s$$

$$t_{ij} \geq t_{i,j-1} + p_i L_j \qquad 1 \leq i \leq m,\ 2 \leq j \leq s$$

This LP formulation contains $(2ms - s - m + 2)$ constraints and $s(m + 1)$ variables. If we replace the constraints $t_{ij} \geq t_{i-1,j} + p_i L_j$ with the corresponding equations, we obtain a no-idling version of the model.

An alternative structure focuses on the idle periods that occur in the schedule. Let z_{ij} denote the idle period immediately preceding the jth sublot on machine i. (These variables would be zero for $j > 1$ in a no-idling version of the model.) As a first step, we express z_{ij} in terms of the sublot completion times:

$$z_{ij} = \max\left\{0, t_{i-1,j} - t_{i,j-1}\right\}$$

The first machine can be scheduled without any idle time; therefore, $z_{1j} = 0$. In addition, the first sublot need not encounter any delay. Thus, for $i \geq 2$,

$$t_{i1} = L_1(p_1 + p_2 + \cdots + p_{i-1})$$

For the remaining combinations of (i, j), we can substitute for t_{ij} in terms of idle periods. That is,

$$t_{ij} = (z_{i1} + p_i L_1) + (z_{i2} + p_i L_2) + \cdots + (z_{ij} + p_i L_j)$$

Hence, the generic equation for z_{ij} becomes

$$z_{ij} = \max\left\{0, (z_{i-1,1} + p_{i-1}L_1) + (z_{i-1,2} + p_{i-1}L_2) + \cdots + (z_{i-1,j} + p_{i-1}L_j) \right.$$
$$\left. - (z_{i1} + p_i L_1) - (z_{i2} + p_i L_2) - \cdots - (z_{i,j-1} + p_i L_{j-1})\right\}$$

In an LP framework, this relationship can be represented by a single inequality:

$$z_{ij} \geq \left\{(z_{i-1,1} + p_{i-1}L_1) + (z_{i-1,2} + p_{i-1}L_2) + \cdots + (z_{i-1,j} + p_{i-1}L_j) \right.$$
$$\left. - (z_{i1} + p_i L_1) - (z_{i2} + p_i L_2) - \cdots - (z_{i,j-1} + p_i L_{j-1})\right\}$$

If the right-hand side is negative, then the variable z_{ij} will appear as zero in the LP solution, and the constraint will be a strict inequality. Equivalently, we can rewrite this constraint as follows:

$$z_{i1} + \cdots + z_{ij} - (z_{i-1,1} + \cdots + z_{i-1,j}) + (p_i - p_{i-1})(L_1 + \cdots + L_{j-1}) - p_{i-1}L_j \geq 0$$

With this type of constraint at its heart, the formulation can be posed in terms of the variables L_j and z_{ij}. Furthermore, the makespan is equal to total idle time on the last machine plus the total processing time on the last machine. The latter is a constant and can be left out of the optimization, so the objective function is simply the sum of idle periods on machine m.

Variables

z_{ij} = length of idle period preceding sublot j on machine i

L_j = size of sublot j

Objective function

minimize $z_{m1} + z_{m2} + \cdots + z_{ms}$

Constraints

$L_1 + L_2 + \cdots + L_s = U$

$$\sum_{k=1}^{j} z_{ik} - \sum_{k=1}^{j} z_{i-1,k} + (p_i - p_{i-1}) \sum_{k=1}^{j-1} L_k - p_{i-1} L_j \geq 0$$

where the range for the last constraint is $2 \leq i \leq m$, $1 \leq j \leq s$.

The fact that no idle time need occur on the first machine allows us to avoid constraints defining z_{1j} and also to avoid using those variables explicitly in the model. The formulation thus contains $(ms - s + 1)$ constraints and ms variables. For example, a problem containing 5 machines and 6 sublots requires a linear program with dimensions 25×30, as compared with 51×36 with the first formulation.

12.3.2 The Discrete Version

For the discrete version, we seek a solution to the linear programs described previously, but with the added requirement that the L_j values must be integers. Thus, we can find a solution by solving an integer LP model, based on the formulations given earlier.

12.4 The Three-machine Model with Variable Sublots

12.4.1 Item and Batch Availability

We turn our attention to the general version of the problem, in which the sublot sizes are allowed to vary. By way of background, however, we must first discuss the way in which items can be moved between machines. Problems involving batching and lot splitting require an assumption about the timing of movement, although in the two-machine problem, it is not usually necessary to make such an assumption explicit. Under *item availability* (or *item flow*), each item can be delivered immediately after its processing is complete. Under *batch availability* (or *batch flow*), the completion of a sublot determines when each of its items is available for the next operation. For example, when each sublot requires a setup and a teardown, batch availability is implied. In a particular application, the technology for moving items between machines may dictate which assumption is appropriate.

Item availability is the more general case: Any schedule that can be achieved under batch availability can also be achieved under item availability, but the reverse is not true. On the other hand, item availability cannot achieve improvements over batch availability when the problem requires consistent sublots. Thus, we can assume batch availability whenever the problem requires consistent sublots. To put it another way, when we examined the problem with consistent lots in the previous section, there was no reason to distinguish item availability from batch availability. We can also assume consistent sublots when we have batch availability. Therefore, in what follows, we assume item availability.

In the three-machine problem with item availability, an optimal schedule need not have consistent sublots. To illustrate this point, let $U = 24$ and $s = 2$ for processing times $p_1 = 1$, $p_2 = 2$, and $p_3 = 1$. According to Case 1 of Algorithm 12.1, an optimal solution for consistent sublots is given by the proportions $x_1 = \frac{1}{3}$ and $x_2 = \frac{2}{3}$. For $L_j = (8, 16)$ we obtain $M = 72$. An optimal solution for item availability is given by

$$x_{11} = \frac{1}{3}, \; x_{12} = \frac{2}{3}; \; \text{and} \; x_{21} = \frac{2}{3}, \; x_{22} = \frac{1}{3},$$

with a makespan of 64. The two schedules are compared in Figure 12.5. In the schedule with variable sublots, the shaded area represents items transferred

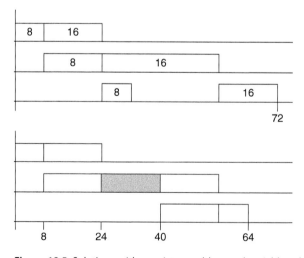

Figure 12.5 Solutions with consistent sublots and variable sublots.

from machine 1 to machine 2 as part of the second sublot, at time 24, but from machine 2 to machine 3 as part of the first sublot, at time 40.

In the previous section, we addressed the three-machine problem with consistent sublots, which implies batch availability. In the most general case, which we address next, we assume only item availability and allow variable sublots. We can then solve the no-idling case by applying the two-machine solution, first to machines 1 and 2, then to machines 2 and 3. (It is straightforward to extend that approach for $m > 3$.) For this purpose we assume we know how many transfer lots are required between each pair of adjacent machines. In summary, we assume item availability, variable sublots, and a given number of transfer lots for every pair of adjacent machines. Under these assumptions, we know how to solve the no-idling case (for any m). In what follows, we examine the case where idling is permitted.

12.4.2 The Continuous Version

In the three-machine model, any feasible makespan can be achieved while scheduling the first and third machines to operate continuously. On the first machine, we start each operation as soon as the machine becomes available. On the third machine, we start each operation as late as possible without delaying subsequent operations beyond the makespan. In general, we define the machines that operate continuously as the *partition set* or simply the partition. Therefore, machines 1 and 3 are always in the partition for the three-machine problem.

We define a *no-wait* schedule as one in which no queueing of sublots occurs. There must be an optimal schedule that is a no-wait schedule. If this were not true, then there would be some sublot that waits between its completion on one machine and its start on the next machine. It would then be possible to enlarge this sublot and shrink some earlier sublot, so that no wait would occur and the makespan would be no larger.

Suppose the partition is {1, 3}. Then one condition for a no-wait schedule is the following:

$$L_{j+1}(p_1 + p_2) = L_j(p_2 + p_3) \tag{12.16}$$

In words, Eq. (12.16) states that the time it takes to process a sublot on the first two machines is equal to the time to process the previous sublot on the last two machines. This condition is necessary for machines 1 and 3 to run continuously. Now, let

$$q = \frac{p_2 + p_3}{p_1 + p_2}$$

Consistent with Eq. (12.16), we construct a set of geometric sublots with the relation

$$L_j = qL_{j-1} = q^{j-1}L_1$$

As in Eq. (12.11), it follows that

$$L_j = \frac{Uq^{j-1}(1-q)}{1-q^s}$$

for $q \neq 1$, and $L_j = U/s$ for the special case $q = 1$. This solution will be a no-wait schedule at machine 2 if machine 2 can process each sublot as soon as it becomes available from machine 1. We write this requirement as

$$p_1\left(L_1 + L_2 + \cdots + L_{j+1}\right) \geq p_1 L_1 + p_2\left(L_1 + L_2 + \cdots + L_j\right)$$

It follows that

$$p_1\left(L_2 + \cdots + L_{j+1}\right) \geq p_2\left(L_1 + L_2 + \cdots + L_j\right)$$

$$p_1 L_1\left(q + q^2 + \cdots + q^j\right) \geq p_2 L_1\left(1 + q + \cdots + q_{j-1}\right)$$

$$q p_1 L_1\left(1 + q + \cdots + q^{j-1}\right) \geq p_2 L_1\left(1 + q + \cdots + q_{j-1}\right)$$

$$q p_1 \geq p_2$$

which we can equivalently express as

$$(p_2)^2 \leq p_1 p_3 \tag{12.17}$$

If Eq. (12.17) holds, we obtain consistent sublots, and the case above duplicates Case 3 in Algorithm 12.1. If Eq. (12.17) does not hold, then {1, 3} cannot be the optimal partition; instead, the optimal partition must be {1, 2, 3}. In this case, we decompose the problem into a two-machine subproblem for machines 1 and 2, which determines the transfers from machine 1 to 2, and a separate two-machine subproblem for machines 2 and 3, which determines the transfers from machine 2 to 3. We can then solve each of the two-machine subproblems using the analysis of Section 12.2. That case, then, duplicates the variable sublot model with no idling.

As an illustration, we revisit Example 12.3, for which the optimal solution for consistent sublots is shown in Figure 12.4. Because Eq. (12.17) fails, the problem decomposes into a pair of two-machine subproblems. Between machines 1 and 2, the transfer lots are determined by solving the two-machine problem with processing times of 2 and 4. The transfer lots are therefore in the ratios 1 : 2 : 4. Between machines 2 and 3, the transfer lots are determined by solving the two-machine problem with processing times of 4 and 3. These transfer lots are in the ratios 16 : 12 : 9. The resulting makespan is 451.39, as shown in Figure 12.6. (The two shaded areas in the figure show the first two sublots transferred from machine 2 to 3.) The makespan represents an improvement of about 8% compared with the optimum for consistent sublots shown in Figure 12.4.

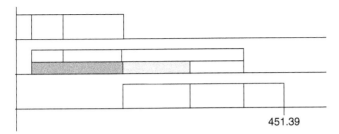

Figure 12.6 The continuous solution to the Example 12.3 with variable sublots.

12.4.3   The Discrete Version

We can extend the notion of decomposition to the discrete case in an analogous fashion. Again, the key condition is whether machine 2 is dominated. If condition (12.17) holds, then {1, 3} is the optimal partition, and no decomposition is needed. In that case, we invoke a three-machine extension of the solution procedure for two machines (details below). On the other hand, if Eq. (12.17) fails, then the optimal partition must be {1, 2, 3}. In this case, we decompose the problem into a subproblem for machines 1 and 2, and a separate subproblem for machines 2 and 3. Each subproblem is solved by the two-machine procedure for the discrete version, described in Section 12.2.

To complete the exposition, we extend the two-machine procedure for discrete sublots to three machines when machine 2 is dominated. As before, let S_j denote the cumulative number of items in the first j sublots, that is,

$$S_j = L_1 + L_2 + \cdots + L_j$$

Suppose we have a trial value M of the optimal makespan. Then, the late start time for the jth sublot on machine 3 is

$$LS_j = M - p_3(U - S_{j-1})$$

For feasibility, we must complete the jth sublot on machine 2 no later than LS_j; therefore,

$$p_1 S_j + p_2 L_j \le M - p_3(U - S_{j-1}) \tag{12.18}$$

where machine 2 processes L_j without delay after it completes on machine 1. Since $L_j = S_j - S_{j-1}$, we may write Eq. (12.18) as

$$p_1 S_j + p_2(S_j - S_{j-1}) \le M - p_3(U - S_{j-1}) \tag{12.19}$$

or

$$S_j \le \frac{M + p_2 S_{j-1} - p_3(U - S_{j-1})}{p_1 + p_2} \tag{12.20}$$

This is a recursive formula for calculating S_j in terms of S_{j-1}. Equivalently, it calculates the values of L_j in sequence, starting with L_1. To initialize the process, we use $S_0 = 0$, and we terminate the process if S_j should reach U.

Observing that S_j is increasing in S_{j-1}, we choose each S_j in turn to be as large an integer as Eq. (12.20) will permit, but not larger than U. If $S_s < U$, then our trial value of M must have been infeasible. Our next trial value for the makespan will be slightly larger. If so, the appropriate increment in the trial makespan is $(p_1 + p_2)(\min_j\{e_j\})$, where $e_j = 1 - f_j$ and

$$f_j = \min\left\{\frac{M + p_2 S_{j-1} - p_3\left(U - S_{j-1}\right)}{p_1 + p_2}, U\right\} - S_j$$

The search procedure begins with the optimal makespan of the continuous version as a trial makespan. If the trial value proves to be infeasible, then we increase it appropriately and test the new trial value. We repeat these steps until the trial value is feasible.

Again, we revisit Example 12.3. As in the continuous version, Eq. (12.17) fails, and the problem decomposes. Between machines 1 and 2, the transfer lots are determined by solving the two-machine problem with processing times of 2 and 4. The transfer lots are therefore 13, 26, and 51. Between machines 2 and 3, the transfer lots are determined by solving the two-machine problem with processing times of 4 and 3. The transfer lots are therefore 39, 29, and 22. The resulting makespan is 452. (As it happens, this figure is equal to the makespan in the continuous case, rounded up.)

■ **Example 12.4** Consider a lot streaming problem on three machines, with $U = 90$ units, as in Example 12.3, but with processing times $p_1 = 3$, $p_2 = 2$, and $p_3 = 4$. The job is to be processed in three sublots.

In this case, the condition in Eq. (12.17) holds, so {1, 3} is the optimal partition, and no decomposition is needed. The continuous solution therefore takes the geometric form $L_j = qL_{j-1} = q^{j-1}L_1$, with $q = 1.2$, yielding sublot sizes of 24.73, 29.67, and 35.60, and a makespan of 483.65. Using Eq. (12.20) for this trial makespan, we obtain transfer lots of 24, 29, and 35. When we compute $S_3 = 88 < U$, we must iterate, using the values of $e_j = \{0.27, 0.47, 0.67\}$. The next trial makespan is $483.6 + 5 \times 0.27 = 485$, which turns out to be feasible. The maximal values of S_j are 25, 55, and 91, implying transfer lots of 25, 30, and 35, as shown in Figure 12.7.

12.4.4 Computational Experiments

A computational comparison of alternative solutions with the continuous version of the three-machine problem is revealing. For this purpose, 6000 test problems were randomly generated, and the makespan was obtained by each of five

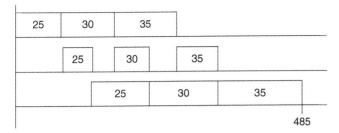

Figure 12.7 Optimal solution to Example 12.4 (with machine 2 dominated).

methods. The study tracked the relative error (suboptimality) in the solution, where the optimal makespan is given by the variable-sublot solution. Alternatively, we can constrain the solution to have no idling, consistent sublots, equal sublots, or equal sublots and no idling. Such constraints may increase the makespan substantially over what is optimally possible, or they may have no impact at all. The virtue of such constraints is that they render the problem readily solvable. In fact, formulas exist for the optimal makespan in three of the cases: equal sublots, no idling, and equal sublots with no idling. Simple algorithms are available for consistent sublots and, as discussed in Section 12.4.2, for the optimal solution. The study distinguished the subset of problems in which machine 2 was dominant from the subset in which it was dominated. Statistics were compiled on the average and maximum values of the relative error. The average values appear in Table 12.1.

The table confirms some important structural results. For example, the consistent sublots procedure yields optimal solutions when machine 2 is dominated, and the no-idling procedure yields optimal solutions when machine 2 is dominant. For that matter, equal sublot solutions also have no idling in the latter case, as the table indicates.

Table 12.1

Procedure	Sublots	Machine 2 dominant			Machine 2 dominated		
		3	5	8	3	5	8
Equal sublots, no idling		0.10	0.094	0.076	0.20	0.24	0.24
No idling		0.0	0.0	0.0	0.12	0.17	0.19
Equal sublots		0.10	0.094	0.076	0.074	0.072	0.059
Consistent sublots		0.044	0.028	0.014	0.0	0.0	0.0

On average, the suboptimality in the consistent-sublot solution is small, averaging about 4 or 5% in the problems with three sublots and machine 2 dominant, declining to about 1% with eight sublots. Considering that the consistent-sublot solution will in fact be optimal when machine 2 is dominated, this means that the amount of suboptimality tends to be quite small in problems with random processing times.

The largest amount of suboptimality observed for consistent-sublot solutions was 9.7%. This figure, along with maximum values for the other cases, is shown in Table 12.2.

Table 12.2 emphasizes the role of machine dominance. For example, the no-idling solution is optimal when machine 2 is dominant, but it may be suboptimal by 50% or more when machine 2 is dominated. The equal sublot solution may be suboptimal by as much as 10–20%, but this figure is not too sensitive to whether machine 2 is dominant.

An additional study examined the improvement in the makespan that results from increasing the number of sublots. Intuitively, we should expect the improvement to show diminishing returns to the number of sublots. This pattern has been demonstrated analytically in the two-machine case with consistent sublots and in the m-machine case with variable sublots. Moreover, by using just two sublots, we can realize at least half the gain associated with any number of sublots. To demonstrate that the same result applies with consistent sublots with more than two machines, Tables 12.3 and 12.4 summarize computational results for three-machine cases. Again, the metric is the percentage improvement, but here the base case is the makespan for one sublot – that is, without lot streaming. The computations are based on an additional set of 1000 test problems.

Both tables describe a clear pattern of diminishing returns, as anticipated. For every solution procedure, more than half of the potential benefit from 10 sublots is obtained with just two sublots, and roughly 80% of the benefit is obtained with 3 sublots. The relative performance of the various procedures remains consistent with the outcomes discussed earlier in connection with Table 12.1.

Table 12.2

Procedure	Sublots	Machine 2 dominant			Machine 2 dominated		
		3	5	8	3	5	8
Equal sublots, no idling		0.17	0.16	0.14	0.49	0.66	0.77
No idling		0.0	0.0	0.0	0.48	0.65	0.76
Equal sublots		0.17	0.16	0.14	0.13	0.13	0.11
Consistent sublots		0.097	0.077	0.056	0.0	0.0	0.0

Table 12.3

Procedure	Sublots	Machine 2 dominant				
		2	3	5	8	10
Equal sublots, no idling		0.246	0.328	0.394	0.430	0.443
No idling		0.300	0.388	0.446	0.472	0.478
Equal sublots		0.246	0.328	0.394	0.430	0.443
Consistent sublots		0.268	0.360	0.429	0.463	0.472
Variable sublots		0.300	0.388	0.446	0.472	0.478

Table 12.4

Procedure	Sublots	Machine 2 dominated				
		2	3	5	8	10
Equal sublots, no idling		0.177	0.236	0.283	0.310	0.318
No idling		0.227	0.289	0.328	0.343	0.347
Equal sublots		0.237	0.316	0.379	0.415	0.427
Consistent sublots		0.275	0.360	0.421	0.449	0.457
Variable sublots		0.275	0.360	0.421	0.449	0.457

Furthermore, when machine 2 is dominated, consistent sublots and variable sublots perform equivalently, whereas when machine 2 dominates, the advantage of variable sublots diminishes as s grows.

12.5 The Fundamental Partition

Earlier, we introduced partitions for the three-machine model to address the case of variable sublots. In the m-machine case, we can also identify partitions, and a particular one can lead to a solution of the m-machine problem with variable sublots. This partition has a role in the optimal solution of the consistent-sublot case as well, thus providing a connection between the two cases. To illustrate this role, we revisit the three-sublot Example 12.3. The optimal variable-sublot solution involves ratios of 4 : 2 for the sublots in the first transfer (between machines 1 and 2) and ratios of 3 : 4 for the second transfer (between machines 2 and 3). In the consistent-sublot solution, the ratio of the first two sublots is $4:2$, and the ratio of the last two sublots is $3:4$. In general, the ratio of any two successive sublots in the consistent-sublot case must match the optimal ratio that applies to some set of adjacent machines. For more downstream sublots, the ratio of successive sublots must either follow the same ratio or match the ratio of a subsequent set of adjacent machines.

12.5.1 Defining the Fundamental Partition

A machine can belong to a partition only if it operates continuously from the beginning of the first sublot until the end of the last sublot. Pairs of machines that appear consecutively in a partition set, along with all machines that may reside between them, form the sections of the partition. We are not obligated to include all machines that operate continuously in a partition, but, as in the special case of three machines, we always include machine 1 and machine m. The *fundamental partition* is then defined as the partition with the minimal number of machines such that the machines in the partition can operate continuously with no waiting and no change in sublots within each section of the partition. Let

$$P(i,k) = p_i + p_{i+1} + \cdots + p_k$$

In words, $P(i, k)$ represents the aggregate processing time per unit on machines i through k. Define $q_{uv} = P(u + 1, v)/P(u, v - 1)$ and suppose that two successive lots satisfy $L_j = q_{uv}L_{j-1}$. If no waiting occurs at the intermediate machines, then the first $(v - u)$ machines can complete the second sublot precisely when the last $(v - u)$ machines complete the first sublot. Thus, no waiting occurs at machine v if no waiting occurs at the $(v - u - 1)$ intermediate machines. This result is assured if $q_{uv} \geq q_{uw}$ for all $u < w < v$. The following algorithm uses these observations to generate the fundamental partition.

Algorithm 12.2 *Generating the Fundamental Partition*

Step 1. Initialize: Set $u = 1$ and place machine 1 in the partition.
Step 2. Find $\max_{v>u}\{q_{uv}\}$. Break ties in favor of the largest v.
Step 3. Add machine v to the partition immediately after machine u. If $v = m$, stop. Otherwise, let $u = v$ and return to Step 2.

To illustrate Algorithm 12.2, consider Example 12.1. After inserting machine 1 in the partition, we compare the values $9/5$ (for $v = 2$), $(9 + 4)/(5 + 9) = 13/14$, $(9 + 4 + 7)/(5 + 9 + 4) = 20/18$, and $(9 + 4 + 7 + 6)/(5 + 9 + 4 + 7) = 26/25$ (for $v = 5$). The maximum, $9/5$, is obtained for $v = 2$, so we add machine 2 to the partition. Returning to Step 2 with $u = 2$, we now compare the values $4/9$ (for $v = 3$), $(4 + 7)/(9 + 4)$

= 11/13, and $(4 + 7 + 6)/(9 + 4 + 7) = 17/20$ (for $v = 5$). The maximum is obtained for $v = 5 = m$, so we add machine 5 to the partition and stop with the final partition $\{1, 2, 5\}$. We denote the kth machine in the partition as machine $[k]$. It is also useful to record the ratios, namely, $q_{[1][2]} = q_{1,2} = 9/5 = 1.8$ and $q_{[2][3]} = q_{2,5} = 17/20 = 0.85$. Assume there are K sections (i.e. $K + 1$ machines) in the partition. Then, by construction, $q_{[1][2]} > q_{[2][3]} > \cdots > q_{[K][K+1]}$. In our example the final partition becomes $\{1, 2, 5\}$, corresponding to $K = 2$ sections, with $q_{[1][2]} = q_{1,2} = 1.8 > q_{[2][3]} = q_{2,5} = 0.85$.

We can use the fundamental partition to solve the m-machine variable-sublot problem by specifying geometric sublots for each part. Therefore, when only machines 1 and m are in the fundamental partition, the solution of the variable-sublot case yields consistent sublots, and the optimal solution features geometric sublots with ratios q_{1m}. It is also straightforward to apply the solution approach of the discrete version to each partition. Limiting our attention to other consistent-sublot cases, we assume that at least three machines (two sections) make up the fundamental partition. For the case $s = 2$, the following algorithm provides an optimal solution.

Algorithm 12.3 *Solution for Consistent Sublots and $s = 2$*

Step 1. Find the fundamental partition and let $u = 2$.
Step 2. If $[u] = m$ (machine $[u]$ is the last machine in the partition), go to Step 4.
Step 3. If $P(1, [u] - 1) \leq P([u] + 1, m)$, let $u = u + 1$ and return to Step 2.
Step 4. Let $L_1 = U/(1 + q_{[u-1][u]})$ and $L_2 = U - L_1$ (i.e. $L_2/L_1 = q_{[u-1][u]}$).

To illustrate, consider Example 12.1 again. Starting with $u = 2$ (in this case, machine 2), we find $P(1, [u] - 1) = P(1, 1) = p_1 = 5 \leq P([u] + 1, m) = P(3, 5) = 4 + 7 + 6 = 17$. Hence, we increment u to 3 and return to Step 3. This time $[3] = 5 = m$, so we go to Step 4, where we set $L_1 = U/(1 + q_{[u-1][u]}) = 100/(1 + 0.85) = 54.05$ and $L_2 = U - L_1 = 45.95$. Figure 12.8 displays the Gantt chart for this solution. Here, the two sublots are both critical on machines 2 and 5, which are the two machines that bound section 2 of the fundamental partition. (A small idle interval occurs on machine 4.) In section 1, however, the second sublot has to wait for the first sublot to complete on machine 2 before it can be processed, whereas it arrives to machine 5 exactly when machine 5 becomes free.

The proof that Algorithm 12.3 provides the optimal solution for the two-sublot case is based on the observation that it selects as u the first value for which $P(1, [u] - 1) > P([u] + 1, m)$. As a result, we have $P([u - 1], m) > P(1, [u])$, because $[u - 1] \leq [u] - 1$. If we increase L_2 by $\Delta > 0$, we add $\Delta P([u - 1],$

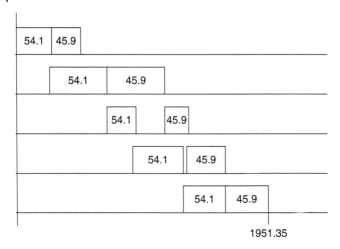

Figure 12.8 Optimal solution to Example 12.1.

m) to the completion time of the second sublot on machines $[u-1]$ to m and save $\Delta P(1, [u])$ on machines 1 through $[u]$, but the savings are not sufficient to compensate for the increase. To justify not decreasing L_2 either, we invoke the same observation for the symmetric problem, where decreasing L_2 implies increasing L_1. This is a special case of our general result, which we now state formally.

■ **Theorem 12.2** Optimal consistent sublots exist such that $L_{j+1} = q_{[u-1][u]}L_j$ for some u and for all $1 \le j < s - 1$. Furthermore, for any $1 \le k \le s - j - 1$, $L_{j+k+1} = q_{[v-1][v]}L_{j+k}$, where $v \ge u$ denote machines in the fundamental partition.

The formal proof of the theorem is complicated and beyond the scope of our coverage. Essentially, the theorem holds because if we partition the sublots and allocate the resulting subsets to the sections of the fundamental partition, then the makespan includes the sum of the partial makespans obtained by each subset of sublots on the section of machines with which it is associated. For this purpose, if the ratio between sublot $j - 1$ and sublot j corresponds to one section in the fundamental partition and the ratio between sublot j and sublot $j + 1$ corresponds to another, subsequent section, then sublot j is the last sublot associated with the former section and sublot $j + 1$ is the first sublot associated with the latter. In particular, because progressive sublots are associated with progressive sections of the fundamental partition, the theorem mandates sublots with a pyramid structure, as befits the ordered flow shop that is obtained if we treat each sublot as a job.

12.5.2 A Heuristic Procedure for *s* Sublots

The more general $m \times n$ problem with consistent sublots can be solved by LP, as discussed earlier. No procedure as efficient as Algorithm 12.3 is available. However, we can build a good heuristic procedure for the $m \times n$ problem using the solution to the $m \times 2$ problem.

Recall that the two-sublot solution involves a single ratio that specifies the allocation of work between the two sublots. To utilize this solution as a heuristic for the *s*-sublot problem, we simply set the ratio of successive sublots equal to this value and construct the corresponding geometric sublots.

In Example 12.1, we found that the critical machines are $u = 2$ and $v = 5$, and the optimal allocation of work is 0.5405 to the first sublot and 0.4595 to the second, for a ratio $L_2/L_1 = 0.85$. Using this ratio in a four-sublot solution, we obtain sublot sizes approximately as follows: 31.4, 26.7, 22.7, and 19.3. When this allocation is employed on the 5×4 problem, the makespan is 1384.5, which is about 0.2% above the optimum. In this case, it is also easy to find the optimum. If we assume the optimum is *not* given by the allocation presented above, then by Theorem 12.2 we should base at least one sublot ratio on the first section of the fundamental partition (because there are only two sections in the fundamental partition). If we set $L_1 = 1$ (tentatively), it follows that $L_2 = 1.8$, $L_3 = 1.8 \times 0.85$, and $L_4 = 1.8 \times 0.85^2$. Together, the sum is $1 + 1.8 + 1.8 \times 0.85 + 1.8 \times 0.85^2 = 5.63$, and hence we should multiply all tentative values by $100/5.63 = 17.8$, yielding 17.8, 32.0, 27.2, and 23.1, with a makespan of 1381.5. Thus, we have sublots 1 and 2 with a ratio that is dictated by the first section of the fundamental partition, whereas sublots 2, 3, and 4 have ratios based on the second section (sublot 2 belongs to both subsets of the sublots, and similarly machine 2 belongs to both sections of the fundamental partition). Indeed, the makespan of 1381.5 improves upon the previous result, but if we were to set another sublot with the ratio of section 1, the makespan would increase to 1489.2. The model is convex (it can be formulated as an LP), so we need not check the option of setting even more sublots per section 1: That would yield a yet worse result.

A brief computational study has investigated the two-sublot heuristic procedure on randomly generated problems. In the test problems, the procedure yielded an average relative error of only 1.2%, as compared with 4.6% for the equal sublot heuristic. In addition, it produced an optimal makespan in a majority of the test problems.

12.6 Summary

The lot streaming model extends our ability to produce good schedules, even though we limited our coverage to the analysis of the flow shop lot streaming problem with a single process batch. More general models in more general environments, such as multiple jobs in a job shop, are based on this foundation and many of the insights are similar. Lot streaming analysis raises important issues in modeling, such as the use of consistent sublots, the appropriateness of item availability, and the need for integer solutions.

Two features of simple models seem to capture key aspects of lot streaming analysis. Obviously, equal sublots are seldom optimal; but the two-sublot solution of Algorithm 12.2, together with the notion of geometric sublot sizes, seems to provide a useful construct for larger problems. The usefulness of a two-sublot solution recalls a similar finding in Chapter 10, where solving the two-machine case provided a key to solving larger flow shop problems.

A second important feature is the condition for a dominated machine 2 in three-machine models, as expressed by the condition $(p_2)^2 \le p_1 p_3$. Much of our analysis of the three-machine case hinged on the outcome of this condition, which suggests that dominance may be a key to solving larger problems. We also discussed partitioning of a larger set of machines and found that partitions are defined such that any intermediate set of machines within a partition are dominated. Again, this result recalls an analogous finding for the flow shop model, where three-machine problems can be solved by two-machine procedures when dominance occurs.

With respect to several jobs, a disquieting example illustrates the difficulties posed by the n-job model. A reasonable approach might be to sequence the jobs without lot streaming and then simply to split each job independently into optimal sublots. Although this hierarchical solution scheme is appealing, it may not be optimal.

■ **Example 12.5** Consider a two-job, two-machine problem in which two sublots are required for each job, as described in the following table.

	Job 1	Job 2
p_1	7	14
p_2	14	42

Example 12.5 shows that hierarchical solutions may not be optimal. The optimal flow shop sequence without lot streaming is 1-2. When lot streaming is applied to the individual jobs of this sequence, the resulting schedule is described in Table 12.5, with a makespan of 58.33. The optimal schedule is shown in Table 12.6, with a makespan of 57. In the optimal schedule, the sublots of jobs 1 and 2 alternate, indicating that the schedule cannot be produced by the hierarchical scheme.

If we restrict attention to equal sublots, the result for the two-machine case is different. When we apply lot streaming with equal sublots to a given flow shop sequence, Johnson's rule implies that no incentive exists to resequence those sublots.

Table 12.5

	Machine	Job 1_1	Job 1_2	Job 2_1	Job 2_2
Sublot times	1	2.33	4.67	3.50	10.50
	2	4.67	9.33	10.50	31.50
	Machine	Job 1_1	Job 1_2	Job 2_1	Job 2_2
Completion times	1	2.33	7.00	10.50	21.00
	2	7.00	16.33	26.83	58.33

Table 12.6

	Machine	Job 1_1	Job 1_2	Job 2_1	Job 2_2
Sublot times	1	1	6	2	12
	2	2	12	6	36
	Machine	Job 1_1	Job 2_1	Job 1_2	Job 2_2
Completion times	1	1	3	9	21
	2	3	9	21	57

If we allow a different number of sublots on each job, this implication remains true, although the optimal job sequence may change. The solution to an *n*-job problem using equal sublots is therefore straightforward to construct, although it is suboptimal on two counts. First, it is not as good as the hierarchical schedule based on optimal sublots (yielding 58.33 in our example), and second, that schedule is potentially inferior to a schedule in which sublots are resequenced and work reallocated (57 in our example). In Example 12.5, equal sublots yield a makespan of 59.5 or about 4.4% above the optimum.

In this chapter, we have addressed a number of lot streaming problems, all of which are characterized by deterministic conditions and the makespan criterion. In general, stochastic conditions and different criteria lead to rather difficult problems. A brief guide to some of the existing results can be found in our Research Notes.

Exercises

12.1 A special case of the model with consistent sublots is generated by the requirement that all sublot sizes be equal. Suppose there are *m* machines and *s* sublots. Construct a formula for the makespan in the case of equal sublots.

12.2 Consider the two-machine model with s sublots. Let M_1 represent the makespan when there is one sublot and no lot streaming. Let M_0 represent the limit of the makespan as the number of sublots approaches infinity. Thus, $M_1 - M_0$ denotes the potential improvement from lot streaming.

a) Show that when there are two sublots in the schedule, the makespan is improved by at least half of the potential improvement.

b) Generalize the result in (a), and show that when there are s sublots in the schedule, the makespan is improved by at least $(s-1)/s$ of the potential improvement. (*Hint*: The improvement analysis can be based on the makespan for equal sublot sizes; the optimal schedule is known to be at least as good.)

12.3 Consider lot streaming for a job lot consisting of 1200 items requiring three operations. The operation times (in order) are 2, 3, and 6 minutes.

a) What is the makespan of the schedule when the job is scheduled in one large lot at each operation?

b) What is the makespan of the schedule when lot streaming is used and $s = 2$?

c) What is the makespan of the schedule when lot streaming is used and $s = 3$?

d) What is the makespan of the schedule when lot streaming is used and the sublots are size 1?

e) What percentage of the improvement between the schedule in (d) and the schedule in (a) is achieved by the schedule in (c)?

12.4 In the three-machine problem with consistent sublots, geometric sublots are optimal if machine 2 is dominated – that is, if $(p_2)^2 \le p_1 p_3$. Assume that processing times are all randomly drawn from the same distribution.

a) Suppose that processing times are all randomly drawn from a uniform distribution on the interval (1, 2). Using simulation, estimate the probability that machine 2 will be dominated.

b) Find the probability in (a) when the processing times are all randomly drawn from a normal distribution with mean 10 and standard deviation 1.

c) Find the probability in (a) when the processing times are all randomly drawn from a lognormal distribution with mean 10 and standard deviation 1.

12.5 Construct a two-machine, two-job example with a different number of equal sublots on each job, demonstrating that the optimal job sequence may change when the number of sublots of one job increases.

12.6   Construct a three-machine, two-job, two-sublot example, demonstrating that even with equal sublots interleaving may be optimal when $m \geq 2$.

12.7   Consider lot streaming for a job lot consisting of a large number of items requiring three operations. The operation times per item are (in order) 2, 1, and 3.
a) What is the makespan of the schedule when the job is scheduled in one large lot at each operation?
b) What is the makespan using equal sublots and $s = 2$?
c) What is the makespan using no idling and $s = 2$?
d) What is the makespan using equal sublots, no idling, and $s = 2$?
e) What is the makespan without restrictions and $s = 2$?

12.8   Consider lot streaming for a job lot consisting of 1000 items requiring five operations. The operation times per item are (in order) 5, 9, 4, 7, and 6 minutes.
a) What is the makespan of the schedule when the job is scheduled in one large lot at each operation?
b) What is the makespan using equal sublots and $s = 3$?
c) What is the makespan using no idling and $s = 3$?
d) What is the makespan using equal sublots, no idling, and $s = 3$?
e) What is the makespan using consistent sublots and $s = 3$?
f) What is the makespan using variable sublots and $s = 3$?

Bibliography

Alfieri, A., Glass, C., and van de Velde, S. (2012). Two-machine lot streaming with attached setup times. *IIE Transactions* 44: 695–710.

Baker, K.R. (1995). Lot streaming in the two-machine flow shop with setup times. *Annals of Operations Research* 57: 1–11.

Baker, K.R. and Jia, D.F. (1993). A comparative study of lot streaming procedures. *Omega* 21: 561–566.

Baker, K.R. and Pyke, D.F. (1990). Solution procedures for the lot streaming problem. *Decision Sciences* 21: 475–491.

Chang, J.H. and Chiu, H.N. (2005). A comprehensive review of lot streaming. *International Journal of Production Research* 43: 1515–1536.

Chen, J. and Steiner, G. (1996). Lot streaming with detached setups in three-machine flow shops. *European Journal of Operational Research* 96: 591–611.

Chen, J. and Steiner, G. (1998). Lot streaming with attached setups in three-machine flow shops. *IIE Transactions* 30: 1075–1084.

Cheng, M., Mukherjee, N.J., and Sarin, S.C. (2013). A review of lot streaming. *International Journal of Production Research* 51: 7023–7046.

Glass, C.A. and Potts, C.N. (1998). Structural properties of lot streaming in a flow shop. *Mathematics of Operations Research* 23: 624–639.

Glass, C.A., Gupta, J.N.D., and Potts, C.N. (1994). Lot streaming in three-stage production processes. *European Journal of Operational Research* 75: 378–394.

Goyal, S.K. (1976). Manufacturing cycle time determination for a multi-stage economic production quantity model. *Management Science* 23: 332–333. and the rejoinder, 334–338.

Kulonda, D.J. (1984). Overlapping operations—a step toward just-in-time production. *Readings in Zero Inventory, APICS 27th Annual International Conference*, Falls Church, VA (9–12 October 1984), pp. 78–80.

Mukherjee, N.J., Sarin, S.C., and Singh, S. (2017). Lot streaming in the presence of learning in sublot-attached setup times and processing times. *International Journal of Production Research* 55: 1623–1639.

Potts, C.N. and Baker, K.R. (1989). Flow shop scheduling with lot streaming. *Operations Research Letters* 8: 297–303.

Sarin, S.C. and Jaiprakash, P. (2006). *Flow Shop Lot Streaming*. New York: Springer Science + Business Media.

Sarin, S.C., Yao, L., and Trietsch, D. (2011). Single-batch lot streaming in a two-stage assembly system. *International Journal of Planning and Scheduling* 1: 90–108.

Sen, A., Topaloglu, E., and Benli, O.S. (1998). Optimal streaming of a single job in a two-stage flow shop. *European Journal of Operational Research* 110: 42–62.

Smunt, T.L., Buss, A.H., and Kropp, D.H. (1996). Lot splitting in stochastic flow shop and job shop environments. *Decision Sciences* 27: 215–238.

Szendrovits, A.Z. (1975). Manufacturing cycle time determination for a multi-stage economic production quantity model. *Management Science* 22: 298–308.

Trietsch, D. (1987). Optimal Transfer Lots for Batch Manufacturing: A Basic Case and Extensions. *Technical Report NPS-54-87-010*. Naval Postgraduate School, Monterey, CA.

Trietsch, D. (1989). Polynomial Transfer Lot Sizing Techniques for Batch Processing on Consecutive Machines. *Technical Report NPS-54-89-011*. Naval Postgraduate School, Monterey, CA.

Trietsch, D. and Baker, K.R. (1993). Basic techniques for lot streaming. *Operations Research* 41: 1065–1076.

Truscott, W.G. (1985). Scheduling production activities in multi-stage batch manufacturing systems. *International Journal of Production Research* 23: 315–328.

Yao, L. and Sarin, S.C. (2013). Multiple-lot lot streaming in a two-stage assembly system. In: *Essays in Production, Project Planning and Scheduling: A Festschrift in Honor of Salah Elmaghraby* (ed. P.S. Pulat, S.C. Sarin and R. Uzsoy). New York: Springer.

13

Scheduling Groups of Jobs

13.1 Introduction

In some settings, the grouping of jobs is a desirable or necessary tactic, usually because of some technological feature of the processing capability. By exploiting this feature, we can find optimal schedules easily, or we can at least identify a relatively small set of dominant schedules and thereby avoid searching a very large number of alternatives.

The motivation for grouping often relates to the existence of changeover times, or setup times, on a machine. For example, jobs might belong to a particular family due to similarities in their required tooling or their container size. As a result of this similarity, a job does not need a setup when following another job from the same family, but a known "family setup time" is required when a job follows a member of a different family. We call this a *family scheduling model*. Typically, the family scheduling model contains a large number of jobs but a relatively small number of families.

We can almost think of the family scheduling model as one in which the elements to be scheduled are the families. Because the jobs are given, we know the processing time for each family, and we know that some changeover time will be required. Thus, we might be tempted to recast the problem as one of scheduling families, except that our measures of performance relate to the individual completion times of the jobs rather than to the completion times of families.

The motivation for grouping may instead be the capability of the machine to process several jobs at once. For example, jobs might be placed in an oven for a heat treat operation. The oven has a finite capacity, so several jobs can be processed simultaneously. As in baking cookies, a group of jobs processed together is called a *batch*, and we call this a *batch processing model*. Typically, the

Principles of Sequencing and Scheduling, Second Edition. Kenneth R. Baker and Dan Trietsch.
© 2019 John Wiley & Sons, Inc. Published 2019 by John Wiley & Sons, Inc.

capacity of the processor is related to the weight, size, or simply the number of jobs in a batch.

We can almost think of a batch processing model as one in which the elements to be scheduled are the batches. Here, again, however, the batch completion times would not tell the whole story. Instead, we have the flexibility to allocate jobs to batches in different ways, and it is the completion times of the individual jobs that determine the measure of performance.

In Section 13.2 we elaborate on the family scheduling model, relating the analysis to known results from the basic single-machine model and highlighting the more prominent generalizations. In Section 13.3, we examine a simple form of batching, where the jobs are not available until their batch completes, and we introduce the analysis of batch availability. Section 13.4 deals with problems involving a batch processor. We emphasize two criteria, namely, total flowtime and maximum lateness. However, we address other performance measures where results are available.

13.2 Scheduling Job Families

In the family scheduling model, we use the pair (i, j) to refer to job j of family i. We let f denote the number of families, n the number of jobs, and n_i the number of jobs belonging to family i. Thus, $n_1 + n_2 + \cdots + n_f = n$. In addition, p_{ij} denotes the processing time of job (i, j), and s_i denotes the setup time required in order to process a job in family i following a job in some other family. When $f = 1$, the problem reduces to the single-machine model, where, for example, SPT minimizes total flowtime and EDD minimizes maximum lateness. Therefore, we assume that $f > 1$.

In principle, any family scheduling model can be viewed as a single-machine model with sequence-dependent setup times. If a job follows a member of the same family, then its setup time is zero; otherwise, its setup time is the family setup time. We know that sequence-dependent setup times tend to make solutions difficult to find. (Recall the traveling salesperson problem presented in Chapter 8.) However, by exploiting the special structure of family scheduling, we can sometimes avoid the enumerative techniques that would ordinarily be required when setups are sequence dependent.

A simplifying assumption for family scheduling is the requirement of precisely f setups in the schedule, one for each family. Such a requirement may reflect long setups, or it may result from a desire to minimize the time spent on setup in situations where capacity is scarce. This condition may also be imposed simply to make the problem more tractable. We refer to this assumption as the *group technology* (*GT*) *assumption*. (In current parlance, the GT principle calls for the grouping of similar elements.) We refer to an optimal solution subject to the GT assumption as a *GT solution*.

The makespan is minimal in a GT solution, because additional setups would only make the makespan greater. Let p_i denote the total processing time for family i, or

$$p_i = \sum_{j=1}^{n_i} p_{ij}$$

Then the makespan for a GT solution is given by

$$M = \sum_{i=1}^{f} (s_i + p_i)$$

Because the elements of this sum are given, the makespan in a GT solution is a fixed quantity and cannot be influenced by sequencing.

13.2.1 Minimizing Total Weighted Flowtime

The next simplest problem in family scheduling is the F-problem under the GT assumption. A two-level approach works well in this case. Within families, we know that jobs should be sequenced according to SPT. (If this were not the case, an adjacent pairwise interchange would improve total flowtime.) We can then treat the family as a job string and exploit the sequencing rule for strings. (See Chapter 8.) In other words, we treat the family as if it were a single entity or *composite job*. In this case, there is a setup time for the string, along with its processing times, but the essential result is unchanged: The optimal sequence exhibits nondecreasing ratios $(s_i + p_i)/n_i$. We state this result formally below, omitting the proof.

■ **Theorem 13.1**   In the F-problem under the GT assumption, the jobs within a family should be scheduled according to SPT, and the families should be scheduled in nondecreasing order of $(s_i + p_i)/n_i$.

The same two-level reasoning applies to the F_w-problem. Let w_{ij} denote the weighting factor of job (i, j), and let

$$w_i = \sum_{j=1}^{n_i} w_{ij}$$

Within families, the jobs should be ordered by SWPT. Again, we can treat the families as composite jobs. In this case the composite jobs have processing times equal to $(s_i + p_i)$ and weighting factors equal to w_i. The optimal schedule applies the SWPT rule to the composite jobs as follows.

■ **Theorem 13.2**   In the F_w-problem under the GT assumption, jobs within a family should be scheduled according to SWPT, and families should be scheduled in nondecreasing order of $(s_i + p_i)/w_i$.

The proof of Theorem 13.2 follows from straightforward arguments based on adjacent pairwise interchanges, first for jobs within families and then for families. Thus, with respect to the F_w criterion, we use the SWPT rule at both levels. First, the rule determines the sequencing of jobs within families. Then, with the families treated as composite jobs, the SWPT rule determines the optimal sequence of the families.

Without the GT assumption, families may be split and processed in separate batches. In this case, we do not know in advance how many setups will occur, and the optimization of total flowtime is more difficult.

■ **Example 13.1**   Consider the F-problem for three jobs representing two families, with a setup time of 1 for either family.

Job (i, j)	(1, 1)	(1, 2)	(2, 1)
p_{ij}	2	7	4

Suppose family 1 comes first. The flowtimes of the three jobs are then 3, 10, and 15, for a total of 28. If the family sequence is reversed, then the total flowtime is still 28. But suppose we sequence the jobs (1, 1), (2, 1), and (1, 2), with a setup for each one. In this schedule, the flowtimes are 3, 8, and 16, for a total of only 27. This very small example illustrates the fact that the optimal solution of the F-problem (and therefore, also the F_w-problem) may be attained only by splitting the families.

For the general case, it is possible to use a dynamic programming solution procedure that exploits the fact that, for each family, the jobs appear in SWPT order in the optimal schedule, although not necessarily as a block of adjacent jobs. The multidimensional structure of this dynamic programming algorithm makes it computationally demanding even for small problems, and its significance is mainly conceptual. Because the GT solution is relatively straightforward to construct, it is of interest to study conditions under which we can limit ourselves to schedules in which each family is processed in a single batch.

■ **Theorem 13.3**   In the F_w-problem for the family scheduling model, suppose all jobs in each family have identical processing times and weights. Then there exists an optimal solution that is a GT solution.

Proof. We consider a schedule S in which there are at least two separate batches of family i. In particular, suppose that the first batch of family i contains a jobs and the second batch of family i contains b jobs. Assume temporarily that $a > 1$ and $b > 1$. Suppose also that the two batches are separated by k jobs of other families with a total weight of w_k taking up an interval of length t. We also use p_{ii} and w_{ii} to denote the processing time and weight of all individual jobs in family i.

Now consider the effects of inserting the last job from the first batch of family i into the second batch, thereby creating schedule S'. As a result, k jobs are accelerated by an amount p_{ii}, and the job that was moved is delayed by an amount $t + s_i$. Hence, the effect on total weighted flowtime is $(t + s_i)w_{ii} - p_{ii}w_k$. If this quantity is negative, schedule S' is better than schedule S. If it is positive, construct schedule S'' by inserting the first job from the second batch into the first batch. In this case, k jobs are delayed by p_{ii}, and the job that was moved is accelerated by $t + s_i$. The effect on total weighted flowtime becomes $p_{ii}w_k - (t + s_i)w_{ii}$, which is negative, so schedule S'' is better than S. Now relax the assumption that $a, b > 1$. If we insert from a one-job batch to another batch, we also save a setup, which improves the flowtime of any subsequent jobs even further.

One of the two insertions, resulting in either S' or S'', will improve F_w, or at least leave it no worse. As long as the batch from which we removed a job for that insertion is not empty, we can repeat the process until one of the two batches disappears and its jobs are consolidated into the other batch (at which stage we also save a setup). Thus, given any solution that does not represent a GT schedule, we can construct a better GT schedule. □

Theorem 13.3 identifies a special case in which we can limit attention to GT solutions and avoid dynamic programming. Qualitatively, Theorem 13.3 states that we should not split a family when its jobs are identical, suggesting that the reason for splitting a family is to exploit differences among its jobs.

13.2.2 Minimizing Maximum Lateness

Suppose that each job has its own due date, d_{ij}. Under the GT assumption, it is possible to attack the $L_{\max}$-problem using the EDD rule in a two-level approach, although a slight adjustment is necessary at the family level. At the job level, the result is straightforward: Jobs in each family should be sequenced according to EDD. Within a family, however, any one of the jobs could produce the maximum lateness.

Suppose that jobs in family i are indexed by EDD and that the family begins its setup at time t. Then, the lateness of job (i, j) becomes

$$L_{ij} = t + s_i + p_{i1} + p_{i2} + \cdots + p_{ij} - d_{ij}$$
$$= t + s_i + p_i - \left(d_{ij} + q_{ij}\right)$$

where q_{ij} denotes the processing time in the family beyond job (i, j), or

$$q_{ij} = p_i - \left(p_{i1} + p_{i2} + \cdots + p_{ij}\right)$$

The maximum lateness among jobs in family i becomes

$$\max_j\{L_{ij}\} = t + s_i + p_i - \min_j\{d_{ij} + q_{ij}\}$$

From this expression, we can see how to adapt the EDD rule for families. Define the *family due date*, d_i, as follows:

$$d_i = \min_j\{d_{ij} + q_{ij}\}$$

This quantity, which is independent of the time at which family i begins processing, can easily be determined once the family is ordered by EDD. This definition of a family due date allows us to use the two-level approach.

■ **Theorem 13.4** In the L_{max}-problem under the GT assumption, the jobs within a family should be scheduled according to EDD. Then the families should be ordered by EDD, using family due dates.

Proof. The first part of the theorem, regarding the sequence of jobs within families, follows Theorem 2.6. Therefore, we examine the sequencing of families. Consider a sequence S that is not the EDD sequence. That is, somewhere in S there must exist a pair of adjacent families, i and k, with k following i starting at time t in the schedule, such that $d_i > d_k$. Now construct a new sequence, S', in which families i and k are interchanged and all other families complete at the same time as in S. Let ix denote the job in family i that achieves the maximum lateness in the family, and let ky denote the analogous job in family k. Then, denoting by $L_i(S)$ the maximum lateness in S for family i, we have

$$L_i(S) = t + s_i + p_{i1} + p_{i2} + \cdots + p_{ix} - d_{ix} = t + s_i + p_i - d_i$$

$$L_k(S') = t + s_k + p_{k1} + p_{k2} + \cdots + p_{ky} - d_{ky} = t + s_k + p_k - d_k$$

$$L_k(S) = t + s_k + s_i + p_i + p_k - d_k$$

$$L_i(S') = t + s_i + s_k + p_k + p_i - d_i$$

It follows that $L_k(S) > L_i(S')$ and $L_k(S) > L_k(S')$. Hence,

$$L_k(S) > \max\{L_i(S'), L_k(S')\}$$

As a consequence,

$$L_{max}(S) \geq L_{max}(S')$$

In other words, the interchange of families i and k does not increase the value of L_{max} and may actually reduce it. The validity of the theorem follows from this result.   □

This theorem, like Theorem 13.2 earlier, shows how to extend an elementary result for the basic single-machine model to the GT scheduling model.

In the case of the L_{max}-problem, it may be desirable to split families when the GT assumption does not apply. Without the GT assumption, this problem is known to be NP-hard. It is possible to use a dynamic programming approach to find an optimal schedule, but it is even more computationally demanding than the one cited earlier for the F_w-problem. Therefore, we are interested in conditions for the optimality of a GT solution, such as the following.

■ **Theorem 13.5** In the L_{max}-problem for the family scheduling model, suppose all jobs within a family have identical due dates. Then there exists an optimal solution that is a GT solution.

Proof. Recall that our notation takes job ix as the job within family i for which the maximum lateness occurs. We first show that there is no incentive to split family i prior to job ix. In other words, job ix should appear in the first batch of family i. To see why, imagine a schedule S in which job ix does not appear in the first batch. Thus, somewhere in the schedule, there is a batch of family i jobs, followed by jobs from other families and then followed by another batch of family i jobs, and this second batch contains job ix. Construct schedule S' by shifting the first batch of family i jobs later, so that it is immediately followed by the second batch of family i jobs. Although some jobs in family i are thereby delayed, none will have a lateness larger than that of job ix because they are scheduled in a single batch with job ix, and by definition job ix attains the maximum lateness among these jobs when they are scheduled together. Because this shift saves the setup that preceded the first batch of family i jobs, the maximum lateness in family i is decreased by this shift. Meanwhile, no job in any other family completes later in schedule S' than in schedule S. Therefore, schedule S' is at least as good as schedule S, and there is no incentive to split family i prior to job ix.

Under the hypothesis of the theorem, all jobs in the family have the same due date and so job ix must be the last job in the family. Therefore, there is no incentive to split family i at all. □

Theorem 13.5 echoes the result of Theorem 13.3, showing that the GT solution occurs when jobs within a given family have identical urgencies. This result reinforces the notion that, in the minimization of L_{max} and F_w, it is not desirable to split a family into multiple batches unless the jobs differ in the value of a key parameter.

13.2.3 Minimizing Makespan in the Two-Machine Flow Shop

We can also address the scheduling of job families in the flow shop setting, at least under the GT assumption. The makespan problem for the two-machine case is of particular interest because, like the problems discussed above, its solution would reduce to ordering the jobs if there were only one family and no need for setups. (In the flow shop case, that ordering would be given by Johnson's rule, as discussed in Chapter 10.) Our notation is a_{ij} for the processing time of the jth job in family i on the first machine and b_{ij} on the second machine. Additionally, s_{1i} and s_{2i} denote the family setup times on machines 1 and 2, respectively. The setup on machine 1 merely adds a constant delay to any schedule, so for the purposes of scheduling jobs in a family, we can safely assume $s_{1i} = 0$. Initially, we assume that family setup times are *attached* (see Section 10.3), which means that they can begin only when a job from the corresponding family is available at the machine.

The problem can be decomposed into two levels. In the lower-level problem, we determine an optimal sequence for the jobs within each family. In the higher-level problem, we then schedule the families, treating the jobs in each family as a string. (It can be shown that there exists an optimal solution where the jobs within families are sequenced by their lower-level optima.)

First, we solve the lower-level problem when there are family setup times. Although it would be convenient to ignore setups and rely on Johnson's rule to schedule jobs within families, that procedure is not always optimal.

■ **Example 13.2**   Consider a two-machine family scheduling problem consisting of one three-job family, with no family setup on machine 1 and a family setup of length $s_2 = 5$ on machine 2.

Job j	1	2	3
a_j	10	8	2
b_j	12	5	1

The sequence 1-2-3, which is prescribed by Johnson's rule, yields a makespan of 33, but the sequence 3-1-2 yields a makespan of only 29.

Suppose we ignore setup times and construct a job sequence for family i using Johnson's rule, renumbering the jobs in the order obtained. As the example demonstrates, this sequence does not guarantee optimality within the family. Nevertheless, an optimal sequence exists in which Johnson's rule applies to all the jobs after the first. Although we can often narrow the set of possibilities, we may have to test all jobs in the family at the first sequence position to determine the solution to the lower-level problem.

Next, we examine the effects of the lower-level solution on the higher-level problem. Each family will appear in the schedule with its individual jobs sequenced by the lower-level rule. Also, a setup time will initiate the processing of the jobs comprising the family, as shown in Figure 13.1.

As reflected in the figure, we postpone the start of s_{2i} just long enough to avoid any intermittent idling on that machine thereafter. This can be done without increasing the family makespan M_i. Similarly, we forbid intermittent idling

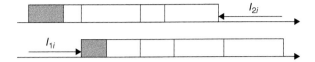

Figure 13.1 A two-machine schedule for a family containing four jobs.

on machine 1. Let I_{1i} denote the *run-in* time (for family i), and let I_{2i} denote the *run-out* time, as shown in the figure. The run-in time represents the period during which only machine 1 can process the family, so machine 2 remains idle unless an operation from the previous family is in process. The run-out time is defined symmetrically as the period when only machine 2 can process the family. Let

$$A_i = s_{1i} + \sum_{j=1}^{n_i} a_{ij}$$

and

$$B_i = s_{2i} + \sum_{j=1}^{n_i} b_{ij}$$

Then, because there is no intermittent idling,

$$I_{1i} = M_i - B_i \tag{13.1}$$

and

$$I_{2i} = M_i - A_i \tag{13.2}$$

Equations (13.1) and (13.2) show that by minimizing M_i, we also minimize I_{1i} and I_{2i}. The run-in and run-out times are important for optimizing the higher-level problem: They are the parameters of an equivalent problem that we can solve by Johnson's rule. Define the *body* of family i, C_i, as the period during which the two machines can operate in parallel, so that $M_i = I_{1i} + C_i + I_{2i}$. Hence, $C_i = A_i + B_i - M_i$. It follows that $I_{1i} = A_i - C_i$ and $I_{2i} = B_i - C_i$. By minimizing M_i, we maximize C_i, which can only help our objective. Conceptually, each family can now be replaced by a single *representative* job such that the representative operation on machine 1 takes A_i and the representative operation on machine 2 takes B_i. Because the body can be processed in parallel, the representative job has a start lag of I_{1i} and a stop lag of I_{2i} (as analyzed in Section 10.3.3). When we apply Eq. (10.4), we obtain $d_i = -C_i$, so the higher-level problem is solved by Johnson's algorithm with job processing times given by $A_i - C_i = I_{1i}$ and $B_i - C_i = I_{2i}$. That is, in the higher-level problem, family i precedes family k in an optimal sequence if $\min\{I_{1i}, I_{2k}\} \le \min\{I_{1k}, I_{2i}\}$.

We can also analyze *separable* setups (see Section 10.3.4), for which the family setup on machine 2 may take place before any job from the family completes its work at machine 1. In this case, the solution is simplified because Johnson's rule holds within families and a two-level approach finds the optimal schedule under the GT assumption.

Once again, as in the problems discussed earlier, we can relax the GT assumption by permitting families to be split.

■ **Example 13.3** Consider a two-machine family scheduling problem consisting of a two-job family and a one-job family, as described in the table. Suppose that setups are attached and all setups require one time unit.

Job (i, j)	$(1, 1)$	$(1, 2)$	$(2, 1)$
a_{ij}	1	5	3
b_{ij}	3	1	5

The example demonstrates that splitting families can be advantageous in the two-machine flow shop. There are two GT solutions, but neither is optimal, as shown in Figure 13.2.

We can expect that problems containing more than two machines will usually be much more difficult than the two-machine case, and heuristic methods will often be appropriate.

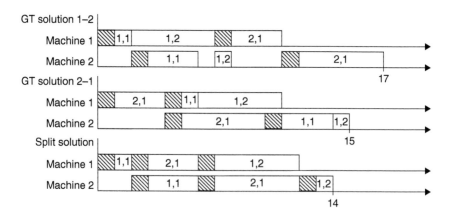

Figure 13.2 Three schedules for Example 13.3.

13.3 Scheduling with Batch Availability

In the models considered thus far, grouping permits the adjacent processing of several jobs in order to reduce the total number of setups. In these models, jobs complete individually and become available for delivery one at a time. This mode is sometimes called *item availability*. In contrast, under *batch availability*, all the jobs in a batch become available at the same moment. Batch availability is characteristic of systems in which jobs are transported and delivered in containers such as boxes, pallets, or trucks. For example, a key step in the manufacture of printed circuit boards is often the insertion operation. Each board has several components inserted into it (or mounted onto it) and is then placed in a rack. When the number of boards in the rack reaches a certain level, the operator stops production and transfers the rack to a subsequent operation. The number of boards in the rack constitutes the batch size, in which transfers occur, and the time required by the operator to check and move the rack between stations plays the role of the setup time between batches.

Sequencing problems involving batch availability tend to be more difficult than their analogs with item availability, and relatively few results exist. We look first at the minimization of total flowtime when there is only one family. (The F_w-problem, which is a generalization, is known to be NP-hard.)

■ **Example 13.4** Consider the F-problem for one family containing the six jobs shown in the table below, with a setup time of $s = 2$. We omit the subscript for family index because the problem contains only one family.

Job j	1	2	3	4	5	6
p_j	1	2	4	5	6	10

If we schedule the jobs in this sequence and in batches of size 2, we can describe the schedule in symbols as $s12s34s56$. The batches are described next.

Batch	Jobs	Completion
1	{1, 2}	5
2	{3, 4}	16
3	{5, 6}	34

In other words, two jobs complete at time 5, two more complete at 16, and the last two complete at 34. The total flowtime is $F = 2(5) + 2(16) + 2(34) = 110$.

For later reference, we provide an alternative expression for total flowtime. In any schedule, batch i contains n_i jobs, each of which completes at C_i, the completion time of batch i. Thus, at one level, we can think of total flowtime in the form

$$F = \sum_i n_i C_i \qquad (13.3)$$

The batch completion time C_i, in turn, is the sum of the processing times (including setup time) for each of the first i batches, or

$$C_i = \sum_{k=1}^{i} (s + P_k) \qquad (13.4)$$

where P_k denotes the total processing time in the kth batch and where the batches are indexed in the order of their appearance in sequence. The first batch contributes to all of these C_i values, the second batch contributes to all but the first, and so on. We can thus write total flowtime as follows:

$$F = \sum_i (s + P_i)[n - (n_1 + n_2 + \cdots + n_{i-1})]$$

Now suppose that $e(i)$ denotes the index of the first job in batch i. Then, we may rewrite this expression:

$$F = \sum_i (s + P_i)[n - e(i) + 1] \qquad (13.5)$$

In our example, we have

$$F = (2 + 3)[6] + (2 + 9)[4] + (2 + 16)[2]$$

$$= 30 + 44 + 36$$

$$= 110$$

In the F-problem, some simplifications are possible. Most importantly, we can limit consideration to SPT sequences.

■ **Theorem 13.6** In the F-problem with batch availability and one family, there is an optimal schedule in which the jobs appear in nondecreasing order of their processing times.

This property, which should not be surprising, is demonstrated by means of a pairwise interchange: For any allocation of jobs to batches, we can retain the number of setups and interchange a non-SPT pair without increasing F.

In light of Theorem 13.6, we can assume (as in our example above) that the jobs are numbered according to SPT and that they appear in numbered sequence in the optimal schedule. The problem becomes one of partitioning the n jobs and forming batches.

Table 13.1

	$j = 2$	$j = 3$	$j = 4$	$j = 5$	$j = 6$	$j = 7$	$G(k)$
$k = 6$	—	—	—	—	—	12	12
$k = 5$	—	—	—	—	28	36	28
$k = 4$	—	—	—	49	51	69	49
$k = 3$	—	—	73	72	80	108	72
$k = 2$	—	92	89	93	107	145	89
$k = 1$	107	102	103	112	132	180	102

The search for an optimal schedule can be accomplished using a dynamic programming approach that locates optimal partitions in the sequence of the n jobs. Suppose that the schedule for the first $(k-1)$ jobs has been determined and that it ends with the completion of a batch. Let $G(k)$ denote the minimum contribution to total flowtime from jobs k through n. This minimum value can be found, in turn, by considering all possible sizes for the first batch in this set. Thus,

$$G(k) = \min_j \{ g(k,j) : k < j \le n + 1 \}$$

where $g(k, j)$ represents the minimum contribution to total flowtime from jobs k through n when the first batch contains jobs k through $(j - 1)$. In light of Eq. (13.5), we have

$$g(k,j) = (n - k + 1)\left[s + p_k + p_{k+1} + \cdots + p_{j-1} \right] + G(j) \tag{13.6}$$

The recursion in Eq. (13.6) produces the optimal value of total flowtime as $G(1)$, starting the calculations with $G(n + 1) = 0$.

To illustrate the solution algorithm, we return to Example 13.4 and start with $G(7) = 0$. The calculated values of $g(k, j)$ are shown in Table 13.1. For instance, we obtain the optimal size of the first batch from $g(1, 3)$ as follows:

$$g(1,3) = (6 - 1 + 1)[2 + 1 + 2] + G(3) = (6)(5) + 72 = 102$$

where $G(3) = 72$ had previously been calculated.

Retracing the steps leading to the optimal value will reveal that the optimal schedule is $s12s34s5s6$.

A second property helps anticipate the structure of the solution and will be of interest later on.

■ **Theorem 13.7** In the F-problem with batch availability and one family, the batch sizes form a nonincreasing sequence.

Proof. Suppose that the optimal schedule S does not satisfy the theorem. Then there must be a pair of adjacent batches i and k, with k following i, such that a, the size of batch i, and b, the size of k, satisfy $a \leq (b-1)$. Form schedule S' by moving the first job from batch k into batch i. Jobs not contained in these two batches complete at the same time in S' as in S, so their contributions to total flowtime can be ignored. The one job moved between batches is accelerated by the construction of S'. Its flowtime is improved by the time required to set up and process the other jobs of batch k in schedule S, which we may write as

$$\Delta_1 = s + p_{k2} + \cdots + p_{kb}$$

Meanwhile, the reallocation delays the completion of batch i and hence each job remaining in it, by an amount equal to the processing time, p_{k1}, of the job that was moved. We can write the resulting increase in the total flowtime as

$$\Delta_2 = a p_{k1} \leq (b-1)p_{k1} \leq p_{k2} + \cdots + p_{kb} = \Delta_1 - s$$

The last inequality holds because the jobs are in SPT order. Thus, $\Delta_2 < \Delta_1$, so that the total flowtime of S' is smaller than the total flowtime of S. At the outset, we assumed that S was optimal, so this is a contradiction. Therefore, we must have $a \geq b$ as provided in the theorem. □

We did not make use of Theorem 13.7 in the solution of our example problem, although it would allow us to skip some of the calculations tabulated earlier. In particular, the calculations leading to $g(2, 3) = 92$ and $g(1, 2) = 107$ can be skipped. In both cases, the leading batch of size 1 would be followed by a batch of size 2, thus violating the nonincreasing property prescribed by the theorem.

When the jobs are all identical, some analytic simplifications are possible. First, ignoring the integer requirement, the optimal number of batches is given by the following expression:

$$k = \sqrt{\frac{1}{4} + \frac{2np}{s}} - \frac{1}{2}$$

where p denotes the common processing time. Then, the size of batch i is given by

$$b_i = \frac{n}{k} + \frac{(k+1)s}{2p} - \frac{is}{p}$$

This formula reinforces the notion that the batch sizes are generally unequal and (in the spirit of Theorem 13.7) nonincreasing in size.

Problems with multiple families and batch availability are somewhat more complicated, and no general results have been developed. However, when the GT assumption applies, two-level solutions exist.

13.4   Scheduling with a Batch Processor

A *batch processor* can accommodate several jobs simultaneously, and all jobs require the same amount of processing capacity. Batch availability is implicit in its mode of operation. In a batch processing scenario, we usually let B denote the capacity of the processor: This is the maximum number of jobs that can be processed at any one time. We let p denote the time required to process the jobs in any batch. This time is fixed and independent of the number of the jobs in the batch, and we sometimes refer to a *fixed* batch processor. Once processing is initiated on a batch processor, the batch cannot be interrupted, nor can other jobs be started. Batch processors can be found in various settings. For example, several layers of fabric are cut simultaneously on a cutting machine, several printed circuit boards are tested simultaneously, and several gears are heat treated simultaneously. Transportation of items between workstations can also occur in batches. We can view the cutter, tester, oven, or transporter as a batch processor. By contrast, we call the processor in the single-machine model a *discrete* processor, although we can also think of a discrete processor as a batch processor with $B = 1$.

We briefly consider the case of n jobs simultaneously available for scheduling on a batch processor. For any regular performance measure, it is desirable to start processing at time zero and to use batches of the maximum possible size for as long as possible. Such a schedule is called a *full-batch* schedule. The composition of the batches is irrelevant if the performance measure is M or F, and all full-batch schedules are optimal in these two cases. If the performance measure is L_{max}, a full-batch schedule is optimal if the jobs are initially sequenced by EDD, and if the performance measure is F_w, a full-batch schedule is optimal if the jobs are initially sequenced in nonincreasing order of their weighting factors (sometimes called the VIP sequence). In what follows, we turn to scheduling problems for which the solutions may not be so obvious.

13.4.1   Minimizing the Makespan with Dynamic Arrivals

Makespan minimization is obvious when all jobs are simultaneously available, but a more interesting problem arises when dynamic arrivals occur. In the dynamic single-machine problem, the optimal makespan is obtained by sequencing the jobs according to earliest release date (ERD). In the case of a batch processor, we first sequence the jobs by ERD and then assign jobs to batches. An optimal assignment has the property that only the first batch may need to be partially empty. This procedure is called the *first-only-empty* (FOE) algorithm. Here, $\lceil x \rceil$ denotes the smallest integer greater than or equal to x.

Algorithm 13.1   *FOE Algorithm*

Step 1. Let $m = \lceil n/B \rceil$ and let $k = n - B(m - 1)$.

Step 2. Assign jobs 1, 2, ..., k to the first batch.

Step 3. Assign the remaining jobs, one at a time and in ERD order, to the first batch with available capacity.

Step 4. Construct a detailed schedule by starting each batch at either the time its last job arrives or the time the previous batch finishes.

The FOE algorithm produces an optimal makespan.

■ **Example 13.5**   Consider the following set of $n = 11$ jobs, and suppose that the capacity of the batch processor is $B = 3$, with $p = 4$.

Job j	1	2	3	4	5	6	7	8	9	10	11
r_j	0	2	5	7	8	8	10	11	13	14	15

From Step 1 of the FOE algorithm, we calculate the number of batches as $m = 4$ and the size of the first batch as $k = 2$. Thus, the first two jobs make up the first batch, and the remaining jobs are assigned to batches as follows, with starting times shown:

Batch	Jobs	Start
2	{3, 4, 5}	8
3	{6, 7, 8}	12
4	{9, 10, 11}	16

The final batch starts at time 16, so the makespan must be $M = 20$. The optimality of the FOE algorithm is proved next.

■ **Theorem 13.8**   In the batch processor scheduling model, the FOE algorithm produces the minimum makespan.

Proof. For the purposes of this proof, let s_i denote the start time of the ith batch in the schedule, and let m denote the number of batches. Obviously, if $s_m = r_n$, then the theorem holds. This leaves us to consider the case of $s_m > r_n$, for which we know that the last two batches are consecutive (by construction). Suppose that the number of consecutive batches at the end of the schedule is denoted h, where $h \geq 2$. Then we know that the first batch in this set is the only member of the set that may not contain B jobs and it starts at the release date of its last job, or $s_{m-h+1} = r_{n-hB}$, so that job $(n - hB)$ completes as early as possible. We also know that job $(n - hB)$ must appear in a different batch than job $(n - hB + B)$, which must appear in a different batch than job $(n - hB + 2B)$. Thus, the set of jobs from job $(n - hB)$ to job n also completes as early as possible. Prior to the last h batches, the problem decomposes, and we can apply a similar argument to show that the set of remaining jobs completes as early as possible. $\square$

13.4.2 Minimizing Makespan in the Two-Machine Flow Shop

The two-machine flow shop problem with batch processors also has a relatively straightforward solution. In this model, the two batch processors may differ, so we use subscripts 1 and 2 to distinguish their respective capacities and processing times. From the perspective of the first machine, where all jobs are simultaneously available, it is desirable to use a full-batch policy. When we do so, the completion time of the jth full batch on machine 1 is simply jp_1. This is the completion time as well for jobs $(j - 1)B_1 + 1$ to jB_1.

From the perspective of the second machine, jobs arrive dynamically and are assigned to the second batch processor with the objective of minimizing $C_{\max}$ on the second machine. From our discussion of the FOE algorithm, we know that all batches on machine 2, except possibly the first, should be full batches. For trial makespan M to be feasible, the start time on machine 2 of the kth batch from the end must be no later than $s = M - kp_2$. This is also the start time for jobs $n - kB_2 + 1$ through $n - (k - 1)B_2$. The last of these jobs appears on machine 1 in batch number $\lceil [n - (k - 1)B_2]/B_1 \rceil$, which finishes at time $f = \lceil [n - (k - 1) B_2]/B_1 \rceil p_1$. Thus, for M to be feasible, we require that times s and f be compatible; that is, $s \geq f$, or

$$M - kp_2 \geq \lceil [n - (k - 1)B_2]/B_1 \rceil p_1$$
$$M \geq kp_2 + \lceil [n - (k - 1)B_2]/B_1 \rceil p_1$$

Thus, the makespan will be determined by the tightest of these inequalities, so that

$$M = \max_k \{ kp_2 + \lceil [n - (k - 1)B_2]/B_1 \rceil p_1 \} \tag{13.7}$$

where $k = 1, 2, \ldots, \lceil n/B_2 \rceil$.

■ **Example 13.6** Consider the problem of scheduling $n = 18$ jobs on two machines. The jobs have the following characteristics.

Machine i	1	2
B_i	5	3
p_i	5	4

From Eq. (13.7), and considering $k = 1, 2, \ldots, 6$, we have

$$M = \max\{24, 23, 27, 26, 30, 29\} = 30$$

Thus the optimal makespan is 30, and the constraining batch is $k = 5$. The fifth batch from the end on machine 2 contains jobs 4-6. Job 6 appears in the second batch on machine 1 and therefore completes on machine 1 at time 10. The last five batches on machine 2 then require total processing time of 20 even when done consecutively, so the schedule cannot complete before time 30. Figure 13.3 displays the schedule and the number of jobs assigned to each batch, along with selected batch completion times.

13.4.3 Minimizing Total Flowtime with Dynamic Arrivals

If all jobs are simultaneously available, as in the basic single-machine model, then, as mentioned earlier, many of the single-machine results carry over to the scheduling of a single-batch processor. In fact, the batch processor version tends to be easier, because any full-batch schedule is optimal for several measures of performance. When we turn to the dynamic version of the model with nonpreemptable jobs, we might expect that solutions are not as easy to find. In the single-machine model, the dynamic versions of the F-problem, the L_{max}-problem, and the U-problem are all NP-hard. For the batch processor model, there is some hope that solutions for these criteria can be found with limited computational requirements.

A dynamic programming approach is available for the F-problem. For convenience, we address the problem of minimizing the sum of completion times,

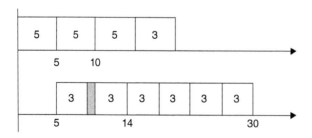

Figure 13.3 Optimal schedule for Example 13.6.

which is equivalent to the F-problem in the sense that the performance measures differ by a constant. To simplify the decisions, it is sufficient to consider initiating a batch either when a job arrives and the processor has been idle or when a batch completes and at least one job is waiting. If we were given a schedule in which a batch started at some other time, then we could shift that batch to an earlier time and improve the schedule. As a consequence, we need only consider schedules in which each batch starts either immediately after the previous batch or at a job release date.

These observations permit us to think of scheduling as deciding whether to initiate a batch when the processor has been idle and, if so, how many consecutive batches to run. Viewed in this light, scheduling decisions need be contemplated only at release dates. Thus, if there are n jobs, then there are at most n times (corresponding to the values of the release dates r_j) at which scheduling decisions need to be made.

Let $a(t)$ denote the number of available jobs waiting to be processed at time t, and as before, let B and p denote the capacity of the processor and its processing time, respectively. Suppose that we schedule h batches consecutively, starting at time r_j. In that case, the start time of the kth batch in that sequence is

$$t_k = r_j + (k-1)p$$

and its size is

$$b_k = \min\{B, a(t_k)\}$$

The value $a(t_k)$ must equal the sum of the number of jobs left behind by the $(k - 1)$st batch and the number of jobs arriving between t_{k-1} and t_k. Using this recursive relation, we can write

$$a(t_k) = [a(t_{k-1}) - B]^+ + |\{i : t_{k-1} < r_i \le t_k\}|$$

where $[x]^+ = \max\{x, 0\}$ and $|X|$ denotes the number of elements in set X.

In order to implement the dynamic programming algorithm, take the pair (r_j, a_j) as a state, where a_j is shorthand for $a(r_j)$. Define the function $G(r_j, a_j)$ as the minimum sum of completion times for the state (r_j, a_j). Then, the dynamic programming recursion takes the following form:

$$G(r_j, a_j) = \min\left\{ G(r_{j+1}, a_j + 1), \min_h \left\{ S(j,h) + G\left(r_j', a_j'\right) \right\} \right\}$$

where $S(j, h)$ denotes the sum of completion times for the jobs contained in the next h consecutive batches, r_j' denotes the first release date after the h consecutive batches complete, and a_j' denotes the number of available jobs waiting to be processed at time r_j'. Expressed in symbols, we have

$$S(j,h) = \sum_{k=1}^{h} (r_j + kp) b_k$$

$$r_j' = \min\{r_i : r_i > r_j + hp\}$$
$$d_j' = a(r_j + hp) + 1$$

The solution is found by calculating $G(r_1, 1)$, starting with the ending condition that $G(r_{n+1}, x) = 0$ for any x. The computational effort for each state is at worst linear in the number of jobs, n, and the total number of states cannot exceed n^2. Thus, the algorithm requires an effort of $O(n^3)$.

13.4.4 Batch-Dependent Processing Times

In the batch processor model, the processing times are typically a fixed constant, which we have denoted p. A slightly more complicated model allows the batch processing time to depend on the jobs assigned to the batch. Suppose that job j has a distinct processing time, p_j. When several jobs are assigned to a batch, the batch processing time is the maximum processing time among its assigned jobs. This generalization of the fixed batch model is motivated by the problem of scheduling burn-in operations for electronic components, and we refer to it as the *burn-in model*. Each component must be tested under high-temperature conditions for a given length of time, called the burn-in time. Different component types can have different burn-in times. The number of components that can be tested simultaneously is often larger than the number of any one type that is available for testing, so there is an incentive to mix component types in any test batch. The temperature is common to different types, and no significant harm is done by testing a component for longer than its required burn-in time. Therefore, the length of the batch run is determined by the longest required burn-in time in the batch.

For the burn-in model, we can develop a solution algorithm for the F-problem based on some dominance properties. First, suppose we have determined an assignment of jobs to batches and numbered the batches from 1 to b. Batch k has processing time P_k, which denotes the maximum processing time among the jobs assigned to the batch. Also, let n_k denote the number of jobs assigned to batch k. With this notation we can write the performance criterion as

$$F = \sum_{k=1}^{b} n_k \sum_{i=1}^{k} P_i \tag{13.8}$$

An alternative expression for the total flowtime follows from interchanging the order of summation:

$$F = \sum_{i=1}^{b} P_i \left(n - \sum_{j=1}^{i-1} n_j \right) \tag{13.9}$$

An adjacent batch interchange argument shows that in an optimal schedule, the batches should be sequenced in nondecreasing order of P_k/n_k.

A second dominance property assumes that the jobs are numbered in SPT order. Then it is possible to show that there is an optimal schedule in which all batches contain consecutively numbered jobs. This property simplifies the search for an optimum considerably. We can imagine the jobs listed in sequence, and we can view the scheduling problem as deciding where the batch boundaries should be placed among the $(n-1)$ possible locations.

■ **Example 13.7**   Consider a burn-in problem containing the following set of $n = 8$ jobs, and suppose that the capacity of the batch processor is $B = 3$.

Job j	1	2	3	4	5	6	7	8
p_j	4	6	7	9	12	18	20	24

With eight jobs, we know that any schedule will necessarily have at least three batches and as many as eight. The three-batch solutions, along with their F-values, are listed below.

Batches	Processing times	Completion times	F
{1, 2, 3}{4, 5, 6}{7, 8}	7, 18, 24	7, 25, 49	194
{1, 2, 3}{4, 5} {6, 7, 8}	7, 12, 24	7, 19, 43	188
{1, 2} {3, 4, 5} {6, 7, 8}	6, 12, 24	6, 18, 42	192

Similarly, we could enumerate the list of four-batch schedules, five-batch schedules, and so on, up to a single eight-batch schedule. Any schedule added to the list could be eliminated before evaluating its total flowtime if we encountered an adjacent pair of batches in conflict with the desired ordering of the ratio P_k/n_k. For example, consider the schedule made up of the batches {1} {2} {3, 4, 5} {6, 7, 8}. The second batch has a ratio of 6, but the third batch has a ratio of 4. Therefore, this schedule does not belong to the dominant set unless we interchange the second and third batches.

Although these two dominance properties limit the number of dominant schedules, the set of undominated candidates may still be quite large. We can take a branch-and-bound approach, based on the enumeration of partial schedules. A partial schedule consists of a set of batches at the start of the schedule. To this partial schedule, we append all possible batches. Admissible candidates for the appended batch must (a) contain a set of consecutive jobs, (b) contain at most B jobs, and (c) exhibit a P_k/n_k ratio no smaller than that of the last batch in the existing partial schedule. In our example, suppose we had the partial schedule {1, 2} on hand and were considering admissible candidates for the second batch. Batch {3} is admissible, but {3, 4} and {3, 4, 5} are not admissible because their P_k/n_k ratios are smaller than the ratio of 5 for the batch in the existing partial schedule. Conditions (a) and (b) prohibit any other batch containing job 3, although batches without job 3 are admissible.

For any partial schedule, there is a contribution to the performance measure from the jobs already scheduled. In addition, to pursue a branch-and-bound approach, we need a lower bound on the contribution from the remaining jobs. A straightforward way to obtain such a bound is to schedule the remaining jobs on B parallel, discrete processors in SPT order. A batch processor with capacity B is less flexible than B separate processors each with unit capacity, so the parallel-machine solution will always be at least as good as any potential batch processor solution for the same job set.

13.5 Summary

We have examined two types of scheduling models involving groups of jobs. In the family scheduling model, jobs belonging to the same family tend to be scheduled together in order to avoid nonproductive setup time. In various batching models, the several jobs assigned to the same batch are processed together and share the same completion time.

Scheduling job families is evidently more complicated than scheduling individual jobs, and only a few results for the basic single-machine model carry over to scheduling families. Optimal schedules for the L_{max}-problem and the F_w-problem are direct generalizations in the case of the GT model. However, the two-level approach at the heart of these generalizations has distinct limits.

In order for the two-level approach to work, there must be an efficient way of sequencing jobs within families. (This would not be the case, for example, in the T-problem.) In addition, the optimal sequencing within families must be independent of the time at which the family begins processing. (This would not be the case, for example, in the U-problem.) Without these properties, the two-level approach will not lead to an efficient algorithm for optimization, although it may provide a reasonable heuristic procedure. Little is known, however, about the effectiveness of such two-level heuristic procedures.

In the general case, where the GT scheduling model does not apply, few avenues seem to be available. While a dynamic programming formulation is possible for the L_{max}- and F_w-problems, even this approach is computationally demanding. For the special case of total flowtime, Mason and Anderson (1991) develop dominance conditions that are useful in enumerative search procedures and in branch-and-bound procedures. Their computational experience suggests that problems containing up to 30 jobs can be optimized with such methods, although they point out that solution times are noticeably affected by the size of setup times relative to processing times and by the number of families relative to the number of jobs. For the flow shop problem, general methods such as tabu search and simulated annealing appear to offer the best prospects for effective performance with reasonable computational requirements.

Batch availability introduces the simplest form of job dependence in that all jobs in the same batch complete at the same time. Few results have been obtained for sequencing models with batch availability, and we highlighted the *F*-problem as the one case that has received significant attention.

The more prevalent form of grouping into batches occurs in conjunction with the scheduling of a batch processor. For static problems involving a single-batch processor, solutions are often not difficult to find. Dynamic models, where jobs are released intermittently, call for more sophisticated solution techniques, but dynamic programming methods appear to work well. The burn-in model, which introduces the feature of batch-dependent processing times, gives rise to a difficult class of problems in the batch processing category. Uzsoy (1994) addressed a version of this model in which the jobs have different capacity requirements and showed that the makespan and total flowtime problems are both NP-hard.

Exercises

13.1 Consider the problem of scheduling twelve jobs that belong to three families, assuming that the GT assumption applies. In the following table, the family is denoted f_j, the setup time is denoted s_j, the processing time is denoted p_j, and the due date is denoted d_j.

Job *j*	1	2	3	4	5	6	7	8	9	10	11	12
f_j	1	1	1	1	2	2	2	3	3	3	3	3
s_j	5	5	5	5	8	8	8	2	2	2	2	2
p_j	6	16	80	61	97	12	55	23	32	46	55	67
d_j	26	33	137	157	75	52	162	65	136	81	30	121

a) Find the optimal GT schedule for the *F*-problem.

b) Find the optimal GT schedule for the $L_{\max}$-problem.

13.2 Consider the problem of scheduling four families with item availability, where family *i* requires a setup time. Each family contains three jobs. The objective for scheduling is to minimize total job completion time.

		Processing times		
	Setup time	Job 1	Job 2	Job 3
Family 1	5	5	11	8
Family 2	10	6	5	3
Family 3	8	3	5	7
Family 4	2	12	15	4

a) If no setup times existed, what would be the optimal value of the objective?

b) What is the optimal GT schedule and the corresponding value of the objective?

c) Suppose the GT assumption in (b) is relaxed. What is the optimal schedule and the corresponding value of the objective?

13.3 Consider the problem of scheduling n families with batch availability, where family i requires setup time s_i. Suppose that the GT assumption holds.

a) Describe how to construct an optimal schedule for the F-problem.

b) Describe how to construct an optimal schedule for the L_{max}-problem.

13.4 Consider the GT scheduling model with the criterion of minimizing the maximum cost, where each job's cost function is a nondecreasing function of completion time.

a) Devise an algorithm that will find an optimal schedule.

b) Determine the computational effort required to execute the algorithm in (a).

13.5 Consider the problem of scheduling n simultaneously available jobs on a single machine with a fixed batch processor. For each of the following performance measures, describe and justify a full-batch schedule that will provide an optimal solution.

a) Total flowtime.

b) Total weighted flowtime.

c) Maximum lateness.

d) Maximum weighted lateness.

e) Number of tardy jobs.

13.6 Consider a burn-in problem containing the following set of $n = 10$ jobs, and suppose that the capacity of the batch processor is $B = 3$.

Job j	1	2	3	4	5	6	7	8	9	10
p_j	2	5	7	8	8	10	11	13	14	15

a) Find the optimal schedule for the F-problem and the corresponding total flowtime.

b) Repeat (a) for a capacity of $B = 4$.

13.7 Consider the lower-level sequencing problem in the two-machine flow shop model with groups of jobs and attached setups.

a) Show that, without loss of generality, we can take the group setup time on machine 1 to be $s_1 = 0$ (for convenience, we omit the family index and index the jobs by Johnson's rule).

b) Prove that Johnson's rule applies to all jobs after the first.

c) Suppose we consider shifting job s ($s \neq 1$) to the first position. Show that there is no incentive to do so if $a_1 \leq a_s$.

d) Show that there is no incentive to shift job s unless it belongs to V as defined in Algorithm 10.2 (that is, unless $a_s > b_s$).

e) Show that there is no incentive to shift job s if $s_2 + b_s \leq a_s$.

f) Show that adding a job can reduce the optimal makespan.

13.8 Consider the problem of scheduling families of jobs in a two-machine flow shop with a GT policy. Prove that an optimal solution exists where the sequence within each family is given by the lower-level optimum. (*Hint:* Recall from the discussion in this chapter that this solution maximizes the body of each family and thus minimizes the run-in and the run-out times.)

Bibliography

Ahmadi, J.H., Ahmadi, R.H., Dasu, S., and Tang, C.S. (1992). Batching and scheduling jobs on batch and discrete processors. *Operations Research* 39: 750–763.

Albers, S. and Brucker, P. (1993). The complexity of one-machine batching problems. *Discrete Applied Mathematics* 47: 87–107.

Bruno, J. and Downey, P. (1978). Complexity of task sequencing with deadlines, setup times and changeover costs. *SIAM Journal of Computing* 7: 393–404.

Bruno, J. and Sethi, R. (1978). Task sequencing in a batch environment with setup times. *Foundations of Control Engineering* 3: 105–117.

Chandru, V., Lee, C.Y., and Uzsoy, R. (1993). Minimizing total completion time on batch processing machines. *International Journal of Production Research* 31: 2097–2122.

Coffman, E.G., Yannakakis, M., Magazine, M.J., and Santos, C. (1990). Batch sizing and job sequencing on a single machine. *Annals of Operations Research* 26: 135–147.

Dobson, G., Karmarkar, U.S., and Rummel, J.L. (1987). Batching to minimize flow times on one machine. *Management Science* 33: 784–799.

Gupta, J.N.D. (1988). Single facility scheduling with multiple job classes. *European Journal of Operational Research* 33: 42–45.

Ikura, Y. and Gimple, M. (1986). Efficient scheduling algorithms for a single batch processing machine. *Operations Research Letters* 5: 61–65.

Lee, C.Y., Uzsoy, R., and Martin-Vega, L.A. (1992). Efficient algorithms for scheduling semiconductor burn-in operations. *Operations Research* 40: 764–775.

Mason, A.J. and Anderson, E.J. (1991). Minimizing flow time on a single machine with job classes and setup times. *Naval Research Logistics* 38: 333–350.

Monma, C.L. and Potts, C.N. (1989). On the complexity of scheduling with batch setup times. *Operations Research* 37: 798–804.

Potts, C.N. and Van Wassenhove, L.W. (1992). Integrating scheduling with batching and lot-sizing: a review of algorithms and complexity. *Journal of the Operational Research Society* 43: 395–406.

Santos, C. and Magazine, M. (1985). Batching in single operation manufacturing systems. *Operations Research Letters* 4: 99–103.

Uzsoy, R. (1994). Scheduling a single batch processing machine with non-identical job sizes. *International Journal of Production Research* 32: 1615–1635.

Webster, S. and Baker, K.R. (1995). Scheduling groups of jobs on a single machine. *Operations Research* 43: 692–703.

14

The Job Shop Problem

14.1 Introduction

The classical job shop scheduling problem differs from the flow shop problem in one important respect: The flow of work is not unidirectional. The elements of the problem are a set of m machines and a collection of n jobs to be scheduled. Each job consists of several operations with the same linear precedence structure as in the flow shop model. Although a job can have any number of operations, the most common formulation of the job shop problem specifies that each job has exactly m operations, one on each machine. It is not difficult, however, to adapt the main ideas to general cases in which a job visits the same machine more than once or skips some machines. Because the workflow in a job shop is not unidirectional, we can think of each machine in the shop as having the input and output flows of work shown in Figure 14.1. Unlike the flow shop model, there is no initial machine that performs only the first operation of a job, nor is there a terminal machine that performs only the last operation of a job.

In the flow shop, machine k performs the kth operation of any job, and there is no need to distinguish between operation number and machine number. In the job shop, by contrast, it is appropriate to describe an operation with a triplet (i, j, k) to denote that for job i, operation j requires machine k. A problem setting can then be described by listing the processing times of all operations identified by such triplets.

Principles of Sequencing and Scheduling, Second Edition. Kenneth R. Baker and Dan Trietsch.
© 2019 John Wiley & Sons, Inc. Published 2019 by John Wiley & Sons, Inc.

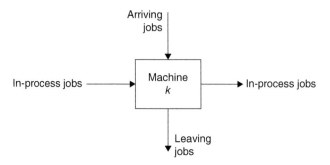

Figure 14.1 Workflow in a job shop.

■ **Example 14.1**   Consider a four-job, three-machine job shop problem with the following processing times.

	Job 1		Job 2		Job 3		Job 4	
	Operation	p_{ijk}	Operation	p_{ijk}	Operation	p_{ijk}	Operation	p_{ijk}
Machine 1	(1, 1, 1)	4	(2, 2, 1)	4	(3, 3, 1)	3	(4, 3, 1)	1
Machine 2	(1, 2, 2)	3	(2, 1, 2)	1	(3, 2, 2)	2	(4, 1, 2)	3
Machine 3	(1, 3, 3)	2	(2, 3, 3)	4	(3, 1, 3)	3	(4, 2, 3)	3

Alternatively, we may use the pair (i, j) to denote the jth operation of job i and a separate *routing* matrix $k(i, j)$ to represent the machine required by operation (i, j). Table 14.1 provides the data for Example 14.1 in the alternative format: (a) operation processing times and (b) operation machine assignments. The set of machine assignments for a given job constitutes its routing. For example, job 2 has a machine routing of 2-1-3.

Table 14.1

	(a) Processing times				(b) Routings		
	Operation				Operation		
	1	2	3		1	2	3
Job 1	4	3	2	Job 1	1	2	3
Job 2	1	4	4	Job 2	2	1	3
Job 3	3	2	3	Job 3	3	2	1
Job 4	3	3	1	Job 4	2	3	1

Aside from routings, the job shop model reflects the same assumptions that apply in the flow shop model. To complete a problem statement, we must specify a performance measure. The problem is then one of constructing a feasible schedule that optimizes the performance measure.

A graphical description of the job shop problem contains the jobs and a Gantt chart to be filled in. The graphical job description of Example 14.1 is given in Figures 14.2 and 14.3. Figure 14.2a consists of a collection of rectangles, each with a job–operation–machine triplet. The length of the rectangle is equal to the processing time of the corresponding operation, using the scale of the Gantt chart. The sequential numbering of operations for a given job indicates the operation sequence.

If we place the operation rectangles as compactly as possible on the Gantt chart in some arbitrary fashion, as in Figure 14.2b, the chart describes the workload for each machine but is unlikely to represent a valid schedule. A feasible schedule is shown in Figure 14.3a. A schedule is a feasible resolution of the resource constraints when no two operations ever occupy the same machine simultaneously. Another requirement is feasible resolution of the logical constraints, which means that all operations of each given job can be placed on a time axis in precedence order without overlapping. A graphical display of this property is shown in Figure 14.3b.

When we examined the flow shop problem in Chapter 10, it appeared at first glance that we might need to examine $(n!)^m$ schedules in the search for an optimum. Subsequently, we found that, for large problems, the subset of permutation schedules was likely to contain very good solutions even if it could not be guaranteed to contain an optimum. In a sense, the first step in analyzing the job

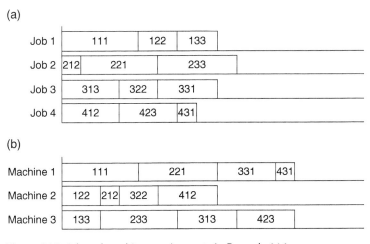

Figure 14.2 Job and machine requirements in Example 14.1.

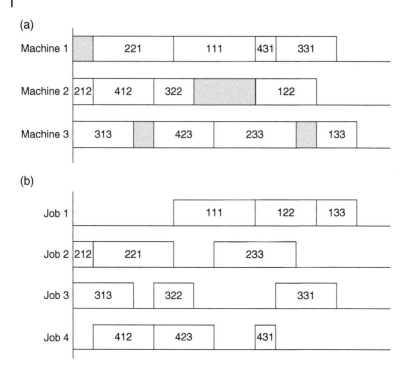

Figure 14.3 Two views of a feasible schedule for Example 14.1.

shop model is to locate a similar "very good" subset for more detailed exploration. This subset should be straightforward to construct and as small as possible. Section 14.2 discusses such a subset of schedules, and Section 14.3 describes how to generate the schedules of this subset systematically. Section 14.4 describes a procedure for solving the job shop problem with the makespan criterion. Section 14.5 addresses neighborhood search techniques.

14.2 Types of Schedules

In principle, the number of feasible schedules for any job shop problem is infinite, because we can insert an arbitrary amount of idle time between adjacent pairs of operations. Once we specify the operation sequence for each machine, however, this kind of idle time cannot be helpful for any regular measure of performance. Rather, it is desirable to schedule the operations as compactly as possible. Superfluous idle time exists in a schedule if we can begin some operation earlier in time without altering the sequence on any machine. Adjusting the start time of some operation in this way is equivalent to moving an operation rectangle to the left on the Gantt chart while preserving the rest of the schedule. This type of adjustment is thus called a *local left-shift*. Given an operation sequence for each machine, there is only one schedule in which no local left-shift is possible – a schedule in which every operation starts as early as possible for the given sequence. The set of all schedules in which no local left-shift is possible is called the set of *semiactive schedules* and is equivalent to the set of all schedules containing no superfluous idle time. This set dominates the set of all schedules, which means that it is sufficient to consider only semiactive schedules when we want to optimize any regular measure of performance.

The number of semiactive schedules is at least finite, although it may well be quite large. The exact number is usually difficult to determine. For the classical job shop problem, in which each job has exactly one operation on each machine, each machine must process n operations. The number of possible sequences is therefore $n!$ for each machine. If the sequences on each machine were entirely independent, there would be $(n!)^m$ semiactive schedules. However, the precedence structure and machine routing for each job usually render some of the potential combinations infeasible.

∎ **Example 14.2**   Consider a two-job, two-machine job shop problem with the following routings.

	Operation	
	1	2
Job 1	1	2
Job 2	2	1

Although $(n!)^m = 4$ in this case, there are only three semiactive schedules that are feasible. It is sometimes helpful to use a network model to represent the feasibility conditions in a job shop problem. Figure 14.4a displays the four operations of Example 14.2, with arcs denoting the precedence structures within each job's sequence of operations. We label each node with the pair

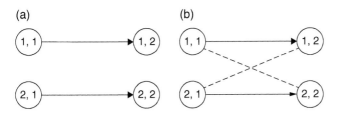

Figure 14.4 Network representation of Example 14.2.

(i, j) to denote the jth operation of job i. Using the routing matrix of the example, we draw a dotted arc between pairs of nodes corresponding to the same machine. Thus, in Figure 14.4b, operations $(1, 1)$ and $(2, 2)$ are connected this way, as are operations $(2, 1)$ and $(1, 2)$. We call these *disjunctive arcs*, whose direction remains undetermined. The construction of a schedule ultimately sequences the operations that require a given machine. This construction determines the direction of the disjunctive arc, in effect by choosing a precedence relation consistent with the sequence.

Figure 14.5 shows all four ways of resolving the directions of the disjunctive arcs in Example 14.2. Three of these are feasible, but the fourth, shown in Figure 14.5d, is infeasible. One way to identify infeasibility is to locate a cycle in the network. In this instance, no operation in the network of Figure 14.5d is initially schedulable because each operation has a predecessor.

Once we have chosen directions for the disjunctive arcs and obtained a feasible schedule, we can schedule the operations from left to right (in time sequence). An unscheduled operation is *schedulable* if all of its predecessors are already scheduled. At each stage we identify the schedulable operations and place one of them into the schedule as early as possible, without violating any precedence relations. Then we repeat the process until all operations have been scheduled. The resulting schedule is semiactive.

When makespan is the criterion of interest, computing its value is equivalent to finding the longest path in the precedence network after all disjunctive arcs have been resolved. This path is known as the *critical path*, and the operations on it are called *critical*. In Example 14.2, if all the operations are of length 1, then the schedule corresponding to Figure 14.5a will have length 2, while the other two feasible schedules will have length 4. In this instance, all operations are

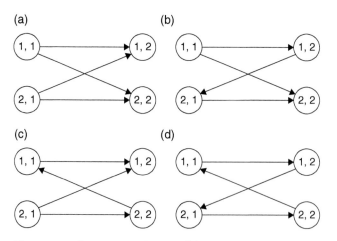

Figure 14.5 Alternative resolutions of disjunctive arcs in Example 14.2.

critical in all three schedules. This particular schedule also demonstrates that there may be two or more critical paths in parallel. Each such critical path consists of a chain of operations with precedence constraints between them and no idling between successive operations. If the longest path did not involve precedence constraints between consecutive operations, we could shorten it by processing these operations in parallel. A critical path must start on some machine where one or more critical operations are performed consecutively. Then, unless the critical path is defined by a single machine, the critical path shifts to another machine, where again one or more operations are critical. Similar shifts of the critical path may occur downstream (including shifts back to a machine that was already on the critical path). Consecutive operations on the critical path that are processed on the same machine constitute *blocks*. Each block has one or more operations and each operation belongs to one block. If all blocks have a single operation, the makespan must equal the time to finish one job, and therefore it must also be optimal. Otherwise, there must be at least one block of consecutive operations on the critical path that are processed on the same machine. If the critical path is defined by a single machine, there is exactly one such block, and the makespan is again optimal. Accordingly, we generally assume that the critical path has more than one block and at least one of these blocks has more than one operation.

Larger versions of the job shop problem also have the feature that $(n!)^m$ tends to overstate the number of feasible schedules. For instance, in terms of precedence relationships, our two-job Example 14.2 is contained in the four-job, three-machine problem of Example 14.1, so the number of semiactive schedules in that problem must certainly be smaller than $(4!)^3$. Again, the main point is simply that the number of semiactive schedules is finite, albeit quite large. Fortunately, it is possible to find a dominant subset among the semiactive schedules.

In a semiactive schedule, the start time of a particular operation is constrained either by the processing of a different job on the same machine or by the processing of the directly preceding operation on a different machine. In the former case, when the completion of an earlier operation on the same machine is constraining, it may still be possible to find obvious means of improvement. Suppose, in Example 14.1, that the job sequence 4-3-2-1 is used at each machine. The associated semiactive schedule is displayed in Figure 14.6a. Although no local left-shifts are possible in this schedule, we can easily make an improvement. For instance, we can start operation (1, 1) earlier than at time 18 without delaying any other operation. In fact, we can start operation (1, 1) at time 0, and the remaining operations of job 1 can also be started earlier without delaying any of the other operations. On the Gantt chart, such an alteration would correspond to shifting operation (1, 1) to the left and beyond other operations already scheduled on machine 1. This type of adjustment – in which we alter the sequence and begin some operation earlier, without delaying any other

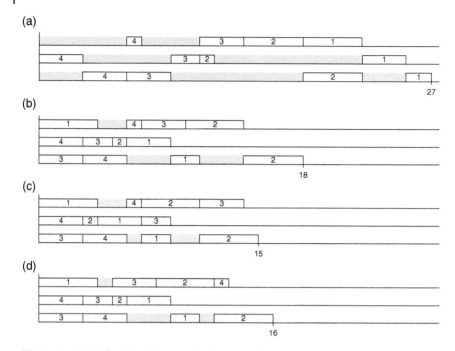

Figure 14.6 Four feasible schedules for Example 14.1.

operation – is called a *global left-shift*. The set of all schedules in which no global left-shift is possible is called the set of *active* schedules. It is clearly a subset of the set of semiactive schedules.

Just as the set of semiactive schedules dominates the set of all schedules, so the set of active schedules dominates the set of semiactive schedules. In other words, when optimizing any regular measure of performance, we need to consider only active schedules. The number of active schedules is a function of both the routings and the processing times in a given problem, but the number of semiactive schedules is a function of only the routings. Whereas one semiactive schedule corresponds to each feasible combination of machine sequences, as discussed previously, we can often transform several semiactive schedules into the same active schedule through a series of global left-shifts.

In addition, we can often transform a given semiactive schedule into several different active schedules by a series of global left-shifts. For example, suppose we left-shift the operations in Figure 14.6a as far as possible, in the job order 3-2-1. (We cannot left-shift the operations of job 4 at all.) The active schedule that emerges is shown in Figure 14.6b and has a makespan of 18. Alternatively, suppose we left-shift the operations in the job order 1-2-3. The active schedule that results is shown in Figure 14.6c and has a makespan of 15.

The number of active schedules tends to be large, and it is sometimes convenient to focus on a smaller subset called the *nondelay schedules*. In a nondelay schedule, no machine is kept idle at a time when it could begin processing some operation. For example, in Figure 14.6b, machine 1 remains idle at time 5 when it could start on operation (3, 3). Therefore, the schedule in Figure 14.6b is not a nondelay schedule. If the job sequence on machine 1 were changed to 1-3-2-4, then we would obtain a nondelay schedule (see Figure 14.6d). By examining the idle intervals in Figure 14.6c, we can determine that the schedule shown there is also not a nondelay schedule. This particular schedule shows that there may be alternatives in constructing a nondelay schedule from a given active schedule.

All nondelay schedules are active schedules because they allow no left-shifting. On the other hand, many active schedules are not nondelay schedules. Therefore, the number of nondelay schedules can be significantly less than the number of active schedules. Our dilemma is that there is no guarantee that the nondelay subset will contain an optimum.

In summary, active schedules are generally the smallest dominant set in the job shop problem. Nondelay schedules are smaller in number but not dominant. Nevertheless, we can usually expect the best nondelay schedule to provide a very good solution, if not an optimum. In a sense, the role of the nondelay schedules is similar to the role of permutation schedules in large flow shop problems: Although the set is not always dominant, it tends to produce a solution close to the optimum.

14.3 Schedule Generation

Procedures for generating schedules are fundamental to both optimal and heuristic solution techniques for job shop problems. Depending on how we determine operation start times, we can classify a generating procedure as a *single-pass* mechanism or an *adjusting* mechanism. In a single-pass procedure, we fix the start time of an operation permanently the first time it is assigned. Thus, a single pass through the list of operations generates a full schedule. In an adjusting procedure, we may reassign some start times as we add subsequent operations to the schedule. On the one hand, adjusting procedures seem to resemble the way schedulers develop manual solutions to a job shop problem – that is, revising the information on a Gantt chart. On the other hand, such revisions are essentially neighborhood search techniques. As such, they tend to work best when they are based on good initial schedules. Single-pass mechanisms can be used to create such initial schedules and are useful even if we intend to revise the schedule later. Furthermore, restricting attention to single-pass procedures is not a severe limitation in theory because for any given schedule (even an optimal one), some single-pass procedure is capable of producing it.

An important class of single-pass procedures for generating schedules is the class of *dispatching procedures*. As discussed in earlier chapters, dispatching has the property that we can execute the actual decisions affecting a given machine in the same order that they are made. This means that we do not have to determine scheduling decisions all at once, but only as they are needed. In the job shop problem, a scheduling decision is usually needed whenever a machine becomes idle. The decision is either to leave the machine idle or else to begin processing one of the operations waiting for it. With a dispatching procedure, we can postpone making this type of decision as long as possible, in order to take into account the latest shop data. For this reason, dispatching procedures are rather common in practice, where they can easily adapt to dynamic job arrivals, machine breakdowns, and other factors that affect shop status over time.

Dispatching procedures are single-pass procedures in two respects. Not only do they make one pass through the list of operations, assigning an irrevocable starting time to each, but they also make one pass in time from the beginning of the schedule to the end. They construct the schedule left to right on the Gantt chart. A different kind of single-pass approach, for example, would be a job-at-a-time procedure. This type of mechanism makes a single pass through the operations, job by job. It schedules all the operations of a given job before proceeding to schedule the operations of other jobs. Such an approach makes one pass through the list of operations, but several passes in the time dimension.

Schedule generation procedures treat operations in an order that is consistent with the precedence relations of the problem. In other words, no operation is considered until all of its predecessors have been scheduled. Once we schedule all the predecessors of an operation, that operation becomes schedulable, regardless of the time at which the next decision is required. Generation procedures operate with a set of schedulable operations at each stage, determined simply from precedence structure. The number of stages for a one-pass dispatching procedure is equal to the number of operations, or nm. At each stage, the operations that have already been assigned starting times make up a *partial schedule*. Given a partial schedule for any job shop problem, we can construct a unique set of schedulable operations. Let

$PS(k)$ = a partial schedule containing k scheduled operations
$SO(k)$ = the set of schedulable operations at stage k, corresponding to a given $PS(k)$
s_j = the earliest time at which operation $j \in SO(k)$ could be started
f_j = the earliest time at which operation $j \in SO(k)$ could be finished

For convenience, we use the single subscript j as an operation index.

For a given active partial schedule, the potential start time for schedulable operation j, denoted s_j, is determined by the completion time of the direct predecessor of operation j and the latest completion time on the machine required by operation j. The larger of these two quantities is s_j. The potential finish time f_j is simply $s_j + p_j$, where p_j is the processing time of operation j.

A systematic approach to generating active schedules works as follows.

Algorithm 14.1 *Active Schedule Generation*

Step 1. Let $k = 0$ and begin with PS(k) as the null partial schedule. Initially, SO(k) includes all operations with no predecessors.

Step 2. Determine $f^* = \min_{j \in SO(k)}\{f_j\}$ and the machine m^* on which f^* could be realized.

Step 3. For each operation $j \in$ SO(k) that requires machine m^* and for which $s_j < f^*$, create a new partial schedule in which operation j is added to PS(k) and started at time s_j.

Step 4. For each new partial schedule created in Step 3, update the data set as follows:

  a) Remove operation j from SO(k).
  b) Form SO($k + 1$) by adding the direct successor of j to SO(k).
  c) Increment k by one.

Step 5. Return to Step 2 for each partial schedule created in Step 3 and updated in Step 4, and continue in this manner until all active schedules have been generated.

The key condition that yields active schedules is the inequality $s_j < f^*$, employed in Step 3. By definition of f^*, it is impossible to add to PS(k) any operation that completes prior to f^*. In addition, any schedule that contained PS(k) and left machine m^* idle through time f^* would not be an active schedule, because some schedulable operation could be left-shifted into that idle interval. For the next scheduling decision, then, machine m^* must be assigned some processing prior to f^*. The possibilities to be explored are operations j requiring machine m^* and for which $s_j < f^*$ (including the job by which f^* was defined). If m^* is not unique, then we must extend Step 3 to every operation that requires the use of one of the machines associated with f^*.

To illustrate how Algorithm 14.1 generates partial schedules, consider Example 14.1. Suppose that we reach stage $k = 6$ with PS(6) as the partial schedule shown in Figure 14.7. It follows that

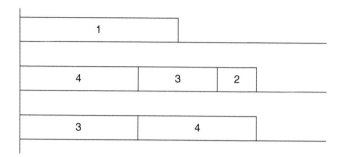

Figure 14.7 A partial schedule for Example 14.1.

$$SO(6) = \{(1,2),(2,2),(3,3),(4,3)\}$$

$$f^* = \min\{f_{12},f_{22},f_{33},f_{43}\} = \min\{9, 10, 8, 7\} = 7$$

$$m^* = 1$$

Thus, we must assign some operation to machine 1 and start work on it prior to time $f^* = 7$.

For machine 1, $s_{22} = 6$, $s_{33} = 5$, and $s_{43} = 6$. Since each of these three potential start times is less than f^*, we can form three active partial schedules for stage $k = 7$. These correspond to the following:

1) Start $(2, 2)$ at time 6; $SO(7) = \{(1, 2), (2, 3), (3, 3), (4, 3)\}$.
2) Start $(3, 3)$ at time 5; $SO(7) = \{(1, 2), (2, 2), (4, 3)\}$.
3) Start $(4, 3)$ at time 6; $SO(7) = \{(1, 2), (2, 2), (3, 3)\}$.

The third partial schedule on this list is contained in the full schedule shown in Figure 14.6b.

We can modify the structure of Algorithm 14.1 in Steps 2 and 3 so that it generates only nondelay schedules. Instead of identifying the earliest potential finish time in Step 2, we identify the earliest possible start time. Then, in Step 3, we consider only those alternatives in which an operation begins at this time. In our example, we generate only one nondelay schedule for stage $k = 7$:

$$\text{Start } (3, 3) \text{ at time 5; } SO(7) = \{(1, 2),(2, 2),(4, 3)\}.$$

That is one of the alternatives among the active schedules, but the other alternatives involve delaying machine 1 while work is available.

Algorithm 14.1 illustrates a tree-structured approach to schedule generation. The nodes in the tree correspond to partial schedules, and each time a new operation is added to a partial schedule, the algorithm proceeds from one level of the tree to the next. If we construct the tree in its entirety, then it enumerates all active schedules (or all nondelay schedules if we modify the algorithm accordingly). The enumeration tree could be the basis for an optimum-seeking approach using branch and bound. Unfortunately, in moderate-sized job shop problems, the computational effort of typical branch-and-bound applications based on this enumeration tree is quite demanding.

In contrast to an optimizing procedure, a suboptimal approach that generates only one complete schedule might entail a light computational effort even in very large problems. In Step 3 of the generation procedure, we create several branches in the tree of partial schedules, identifying all conflicts at a given machine. An enumeration procedure must resolve these conflicts in all possible ways at each stage. By contrast, a heuristic procedure that is designed to generate only one schedule can resolve a conflict in just one way. This means that the procedure must specify a rule for selecting one operation from among the conflicting operations. For a given priority rule R, Algorithm 14.1 can be adapted as a heuristic procedure by altering Step 3 as follows.

Step 3. For each operation $j \in$ SO(k) that requires machine m^* and for which $s_j <$ f^*, calculate a priority index according to a specific priority rule. Find the operation with the smallest index and add this operation to PS(k) as early as possible, thus creating only one partial schedule, PS($k + 1$), for the next stage.

The remaining problem is to identify an effective priority rule. To suggest the kinds of information that can be used effectively, the following list contains some common priority rules:

SPT (shortest processing time): Select the operation with the minimum processing time.

FCFS (first come first served): Select the operation that arrived at the machine earliest.

MWKR (most work remaining): Select the operation associated with the job having the most work remaining to be processed.

LWKR (least work remaining): Select the operation associated with the job having the least work remaining to be processed.

In makespan problems, research studies tend to find that no single priority rule dominates all others, although the most successful rules are often those favoring jobs with much processing remaining. The MWKR rule and similar priority schemes often produce a good makespan. (In Example 14.1, MWKR produces a makespan of only 14.) The SPT rule sometimes produces good schedules, too. When relatively simple priority rules such as these are in effect, nondelay dispatching tends to be better than active dispatching for generating heuristic schedules. In stochastic cases, nondelay scheduling is even more attractive because we prefer to process an available job rather than leave a machine idle and wait for the arrival of another job that is subject to random delays.

When the criterion is total flowtime, SPT and LWKR are usually more effective than other rules, and, again, nondelay dispatching tends to perform better than active dispatching.

Research experiments have demonstrated that schedule generation based on priority dispatching rules is a practicable method of finding good solutions to job shop problems, although, of course, optimal solutions cannot be guaranteed. This line of research supports the use of nondelay schedules as a basis for schedule generation, rather than the set of active schedules. For makespan problems, the most suitable priority assignments seem to favor jobs with a heavy unprocessed workload, while for total flowtime problems, the most suitable assignments seem to favor jobs with a light unprocessed workload. These tendencies are in line with our observations for parallel machines, where SPT minimizes total flowtime but LPT is effective in reducing the makespan.

For criteria other than makespan and total flowtime, the study of priority rules for the static job shop model has been limited. Most of our knowledge about priority rules has come from studies of the dynamic job shop model, which we examine in the next chapter.

14.4   The Shifting Bottleneck Procedure

Perhaps the most effective optimization algorithm for minimizing the makespan in the job shop problem is the *shifting bottleneck procedure*. (We shall see where its name comes from as we examine its detailed structure.) Essentially, this procedure is a branch-and-bound solution that employs especially powerful bounds by focusing on the machines that are most likely to dictate the minimal solution. Furthermore, these bounds are relatively easy to compute.

The algorithm has also been adapted as a heuristic procedure, which calls for scheduling one machine at a time. At any stage of the procedure, we have a set X of machines already scheduled, along with its complement, X'. We select a machine from the set X' and schedule all of its operations, allowing it to be moved to set X. This step allows us to revise the information pertaining to the other machines in X', and then, based on this information, we select the next machine to schedule. We then repeat the process iteratively until all machines are scheduled. Selecting the machine to schedule next is obviously a key feature of the procedure.

14.4.1   Bottleneck Machines

For background, we draw on the solution of the "head–body–tail" (*HBT*) problem for a single machine. The HBT model occurs as a subproblem when we implement the shifting bottleneck approach. As presented in Chapter 8, the HBT model involves n jobs, with each job characterized by a release date (r_i), a processing time (p_i), and a delivery time (q_i). The problem requires sequencing the jobs on one machine to minimize the latest delivery time. In Chapter 8, we also outlined a multimachine interpretation of the same model, in which r_i represents time spent at earlier operations in the shop and q_i represents time spent at later operations.

Although the HBT problem is NP-hard, it is possible to solve relatively large versions of the problem by using an algorithm due to Carlier (1982). Moreover, an effective heuristic procedure, known as the largest tail (LT) procedure, is available for this problem. The LT procedure was introduced in Algorithm 8.1.

We use the HBT model in two ways. First, when we select a machine from set X, we schedule its operations by solving the HBT problem corresponding to the selected machine. (Strictly speaking, we sequence the operations on that machine by resolving its disjunctive arcs in a feasible manner.) Second, for each machine remaining in set X', we solve a derived HBT problem in order to determine which machine is most critical. A machine is critical if the solution to its HBT problem is maximal among the machines in X'. This machine is called the *bottleneck* machine because it tends to constrain the overall length of the job shop schedule, given the scheduling commitments already made.

Consider a particular machine k in the job shop problem. Suppose that (i, j) denotes an operation that takes place on that machine. All n jobs will ultimately be processed on machine k, even though the jobs require processing elsewhere. We can think of the information about the n jobs, with respect to machine k, as comparable with the three job parameters in the HBT model, and we use this information to construct a derived HBT problem. First, for each job i, there is an earliest possible time at which it could be released for processing on machine k. Before any scheduling has been done, this time is simply the sum of all the operation times for job i, over all the predecessors of operation j, as if all such operations were on nonbottleneck machines. This time interval plays the role of the release date in the derived HBT problem. Second, the processing time for operation (i, j) plays the role of the processing time in the derived HBT problem. Third, after operation (i, j) completes, there is a minimum amount of time still required to finish the job. This time is simply the sum of all the operation times for job i, over all the successors of operation j, as if all such operations were on nonbottleneck machines. In symbols, the derived problem will have the following parameters for operation (i, j):

$$r_i = \sum_{u < j} p_{iu}$$

$$p_i = p_{ij}$$

$$q_i = \sum_{u > j} p_{iu}$$

Next, suppose we solve the derived problem and obtain a value for the latest delivery time, denoted M_k. If M_k is the optimal solution to the derived HBT problem, then M_k is a lower bound on the optimal makespan of the job shop problem because the HBT formulation assumed optimistic conditions about the predecessors and successors of operation (i, j). In particular, those operations were all assumed to be processed on nonbottlenecks. Among all m machines, the largest of the HBT solution values provides an even stronger bound. Let b denote the machine k on which the largest M_k occurs. In symbols, our lower bound becomes $M_b = \max_k\{M_k\}$. Machine b is called the *bottleneck* machine.

14.4.2 Heuristic and Optimal Solutions

To the extent that we are simply trying to identify a bottleneck machine, we may want to save time and solve the various derived HBT problems by using some heuristic method, such as the LT procedure. Only if we wish to compute lower bounds in the process would we need to use an optimizing method for the derived HBT problems.

Having identified a bottleneck machine, we next want to schedule its operations. More specifically, we want to resolve the disjunctive arcs corresponding to all the operations that require the bottleneck machine. In other words, we want to specify the sequence of operations on the bottleneck machine. This sequence is provided by the solution of the derived HBT problem that gave rise to M_b.

After we remove the bottleneck machine from set X' and sequence its operations, we can update the parameters of the derived HBT model for machines remaining in X'. First, consider how the derived parameter r_i might be affected. Initially, we set r_i equal to the sum of the operation times for job i prior to the given machine, a sum that we can think of as the longest path from the start of the network to node (i, j), with disjunctive arcs ignored. After some disjunctive arcs have been resolved, we can still think of r_i as longest such path, but its value may have increased by the resolution of certain disjunctive arcs in the sequencing of the bottleneck machine.

We treat the derived parameter q_i in an analogous fashion. Initially, we set q_i equal to the length of the longest path to the end of the network from node (i, j), again with disjunctive arcs ignored. The sequencing of the bottleneck machine resolves certain disjunctive arcs that may increase the length of this path.

Therefore, each time we identify a bottleneck machine and sequence its operations, we update the longest path calculations that give rise to the r_i and q_i parameters of HBT problems for machines remaining in X'. Once this updating process is complete, we can proceed to the next iteration and find a new bottleneck machine. Repeating this procedure m times will resolve all disjunctive arcs and allow us to build a complete schedule.

When used as a heuristic method, the shifting bottleneck procedure requires a subroutine for solving derived HBT problems and a criterion for designating a bottleneck machine. The subroutine could be as simple as the LT procedure, or it could be a full-fledged optimization algorithm. Similarly, the bottleneck criterion could be largest makespan value, M_b, or it could be something simpler to compute, such as the largest workload, or the largest makespan value if preemption were allowed, either of which is straightforward to calculate. Computational comparisons suggest that these choices do not lead to very substantial differences in overall performance.

To illustrate the shifting bottleneck approach, we apply it in heuristic fashion to Example 14.1. Figure 14.2 depicts the jobs involved and provides us with a convenient basis for constructing the HBT problems. Initially, the three derived problems take the forms shown below, along with their solutions from the LT heuristic procedure:

Machine 1	Job i	1	2	3	4	
	r_i	0	1	5	6	Solution
	p_i	4	4	3	1	1-2-3-4(12)
	q_i	5	4	0	0	
Machine 2	Job i	1	2	3	4	
	r_i	4	0	3	0	Solution
	p_i	3	1	2	3	2-4-3-1(11)
	q_i	2	8	3	4	
Machine 3	Job i	1	2	3	4	
	r_i	7	5	0	3	Solution
	p_i	2	4	3	3	3-4-2-1(12)
	q_i	0	0	5	1	

At this stage, we choose a bottleneck machine by breaking the tie between machines 1 and 3. Suppose we choose the latter. This fixes the operation sequence on machine 3 and, as a result, may alter the derived HBT problems on the other two machines. For example, when we reconstruct the derived problem for machine 1, we find that $q_2 = 6$. This follows from the fact that operation (2, 2) on machine 1 must be followed by operation (2, 3), which in turn must be followed by operation (1, 3) according to the fixed sequence on machine 3. The new derived problems are shown below:

Machine 1	Job i	1	2	3	4	
	r_i	0	1	5	6	Solution
	p_i	4	4	3	1	1-2-3-4(14)
	q_i	5	6	0	0	
Machine 2	Job i	1	2	3	4	
	r_i	4	0	3	0	Solution
	p_i	3	1	2	3	2-4-3-1(13)
	q_i	2	10	3	9	

This time, machine 1 is the unique bottleneck, so we fix its sequence and reconstruct the derived problem for machine 2, obtaining the following:

Machine 2	Job i	1	2	3	4	
	r_i	4	0	3	0	Solution
	p_i	3	1	2	3	2-4-3-1(13)
	q_i	2	10	4	9	

At this stage, we have determined the sequence at each of the machines as follows:

Machine 1	1-2-3-4
Machine 2	2-4-3-1
Machine 3	3-4-2-1

We can now construct a schedule for the entire job shop problem by following the rules for active schedule construction and breaking ties arbitrarily. (The ties may change the order in which we place operations into the schedule, but in this case, they do not affect the final schedule.) Figure 14.8 shows the resulting schedule, with a makespan of $M = 14$.

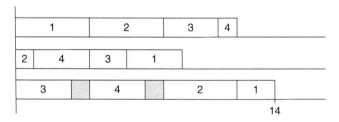

Figure 14.8 Heuristic solution for Example 14.1.

We built this schedule with a heuristic procedure using the LT algorithm to solve the derived problem. When we wish to find an optimal solution using the shifting bottleneck approach, the algorithmic requirements are more demanding. First, we must find optimal solutions to the derived HBT problem, so that we always have a lower bound on hand. Second, instead of constructing a solution by scheduling one machine at a time (and moving it from X' to X), we must be more patient. In the optimization approach, we enhance the schedule simply by resolving one disjunctive arc at a time and then updating the search for the bottleneck machine. In the branch-and-bound tree, each resolution of a disjunctive arc gives rise to a node at the next lower level of the tree. Paired with it is another node corresponding to the reverse resolution of the same disjunctive arc. For each of these nodes, the newly calculated value of M_b, based on optimization of the derived HBT problems, provides a lower bound on the eventual solution.

In this branch-and-bound algorithm, each time we resolve a disjunctive arc, we may change which machine represents the bottleneck. This shifting designation of the bottleneck as we proceed through the construction of a schedule gives the algorithm its name. Among optimization algorithms, the shifting bottleneck approach appears to represent the best computational procedure for finding optimal solutions. It is also effective when implemented as a heuristic procedure, although, in the next section, we describe an alternative approach that relies on neighborhood search concepts.

14.5 Neighborhood Search Heuristics

We continue to assume that the objective is to minimize the makespan. As we have seen, a job shop schedule can be expressed by a set of m job permutations that designate the sequence of operations on each machine. For instance, the set in Figure 14.8 is {1-2-3-4, 2-4-3-1, 3-4-2-1}. Equivalently, the schedule is determined by $n(n-1)/2$ disjunctive arcs at each machine. For instance, considering machine 1 in Figure 14.8, we can identify disjunctive arcs from $(1, 1)$ to $(2, 2)$, $(3, 3)$, and $(4, 3)$, from $(2, 2)$ to $(3, 3)$ and $(4, 3)$, and from $(3, 3)$ to $(4, 3)$. Similar sets of arcs apply in the other machine sequences. Every feasible semiactive schedule can be represented by a unique set of permutations.

Given a feasible schedule, we may try to improve on it using a neighborhood search, which we illustrate using adjacent pairwise interchange (API) neighborhoods. For convenience in ensuring feasibility, we limit our attention to APIs within blocks – that is, involving pairs of critical operations on a common machine. This is permissible because, given any feasible but suboptimal solution, a succession of APIs on the evolving critical paths can lead to optimality. This property is called *connectivity*. In more detail, starting with any suboptimal schedule, we perform selected APIs on the critical path. The critical path changes, but at each stage, at least one API opportunity within some block on the current critical path can bring us closer to an optimal sequence. Thus, although individual APIs in the succession may lengthen the makespan, an optimal schedule will eventually be reached. Our next theorem establishes this result formally, and the proof shows how such a series of APIs can be identified when an optimal sequence is known.

■ **Theorem 14.1** Any suboptimal feasible schedule S can be transformed to an optimal schedule by a finite succession of adjacent pairwise interchanges on evolving critical paths, starting with the critical path of S and ending with an optimal critical path.

Proof. Let S^* be an optimal schedule and suppose (i_1, j_1, k) precedes (i_2, j_2, k) in S^*. That is, there is a disjunctive arc oriented from (i_1, j_1, k) to (i_2, j_2, k) in this optimal solution. If the same orientation applies in S, we say that the order of these operations in S *agrees* with S^*. If the opposite orientation applies, the order is *in conflict*. Two operations (i_1, j_1, k_1) and (i_2, j_2, k_2) are *contiguous* if the starting time of (i_2, j_2, k_2) coincides with the completion time of (i_1, j_1, k_1) in a semi-active schedule. Contiguous operations in a critical path involve either the same job (such that $i_1 = i_2, j_1 = j_2 - 1$ and $k_1 \neq k_2$) or the same block (such that $i_1 \neq i_2$ and $k_1 = k_2$). By definition, all operations on a critical path are contiguous. Consider the contiguous operations within the blocks of any critical path of S. If the ordering of all pairs agrees with S^*, then the length of this path cannot exceed the longest path in S^*, thus contradicting the assumption that S is suboptimal. Therefore, the order of at least one pair of these operations is in conflict with S^*. Select any such pair and reverse its order by an API on that machine. If the result is not optimal, repeat the process. Each such API removes the conflict between the orientations of one disjunctive arc in the two sequences. Because the number of the disjunctive arcs is finite, the number of necessary APIs must also be finite, which completes the proof. □

In particular, connectivity implies that any randomized search using this neighborhood will eventually reach an optimal solution. To illustrate, Figure 14.9a traces the critical path of the solution in Figure 14.8 by shading the critical activities. The critical path includes operations (1, 1), (2, 2), (2, 3), and (1, 3). Therefore, there are only two APIs to consider: interchanging (1, 1) with (2, 2), as depicted in Figure 14.9b, and interchanging (2, 3) with (1, 3), as depicted in Figure 14.9c. Interchanging (1, 1) with (2, 2) does not change the makespan but leads to a dead end because the only API available on the critical path is to reverse that interchange. Interchanging (2, 3) with (1, 3) increases the makespan to 15. At this stage, we know that the starting solution was locally optimal in the API neighborhood. Suppose, however, that we perform the latter interchange – in the spirit of tabu search (TS) or simulated annealing (SA) – and study the new critical path, (2, 1), (4, 1), (3, 2), (1, 2), (1, 3), and (2, 3). We then can

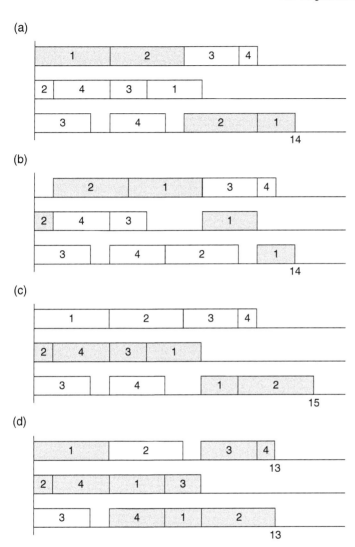

Figure 14.9 Performing API on the heuristic result.

exchange (3, 2) and (1, 2), reducing the makespan to 13, as in Figure 14.9d. It can be shown that this solution is optimal, illustrating connectivity in the example. The solution is neither active nor unique: Machine 1 can process job 4 before job 3 – an API step – without delaying job 3, thus obtaining another optimal solution. An additional optimal solution is associated with yet another API step.

We mentioned TS and SA because both allow consideration of inferior neighbors in the hope of discovering a better sequence later. That same notion lies behind the search illustrated in Figure 14.9. Alternatively, we could identify the necessary second interchange by observing that after the first API, job 1 is in process on machine 2 when machine 3 becomes ready for it. That conflict accounts for the increase in makespan. In other words, after the first API, the critical path changes, and another operation of a job that we interchanged becomes critical on an upstream machine. Thus, the second API on machine 2 was directly indicated by the first change to promote the progress of job 1. Similarly, after an interchange, the makespan may increase because the job that was delayed causes delays on downstream machines. Such delays may be handled by APIs on those machines to postpone the same job that was postponed by the initial API and therefore promote other jobs that may be ready earlier. Thus, any proposed interchange may induce a cascading sequence of APIs on other machines, all on the evolving critical path. If the objective is improved after two APIs, we can accept both even though the first alone was detrimental. Effectively, this neighborhood – which we call the *enhanced neighborhood* – checks neighbors defined by a succession of induced APIs. An option in the heuristic procedure is to restrict the number of induced APIs tested without improvement.

An operation that is neither first nor last in its block is called *internal*. Interchanging two adjacent internal operations cannot advance the start time of the block or its completion time, so it cannot immediately reduce the makespan. Thus, we may restrict our neighborhood by excluding APIs between internal operations. Similarly, we can also exclude APIs between the first two operations on a critical path if their block has three or more operations and, symmetrically, between the last two. In other words, for immediate benefit, only interchanges near the boundary between two successive blocks of the critical path need be considered. Unfortunately, this *restricted neighborhood* does not guarantee connectivity. This problem can be ameliorated by employing multiple seeds. Computational experience involving multiple seeds suggests that on balance the restricted neighborhood is significantly more efficient. Incidentally, in an enhanced neighborhood, when an initial interchange induces other APIs on upstream or downstream machines, the induced APIs automatically occur near the boundary between two successive blocks of the evolving critical path. In other words, induced APIs are legitimate for the evolving restricted neighborhood. Therefore, it is sufficient to enforce the restriction for the first API only. For instance, in Figure 14.9a, both API candidates were near a boundary and belonged to the restricted neighborhood. The second interchange, initiated in Figure 14.9c, occurred between operations (3, 2) and (1, 2), which were the last two jobs in the first block.

The two neighborhoods that we introduced – both with and without enhancement – can be used in a variety of search algorithms. More complicated neighborhoods have also been proposed with good results reported. In particular, a study of advanced TS methods produced the best heuristic solutions for most open benchmark problems in the literature and found several new optimal solutions as well. The neighborhood structure in that experiment includes a feature akin to genetic algorithms (GAs): A set of *elite solutions* – defined by their relatively small makespan – is used to generate new seeds for the search. Under GAs, such starting points are the offspring that we consider as candidate solutions, but in that experiment they were just starting points for TS in the restricted API neighborhood. These starting points were rarely elite solutions by themselves, so additional search was warranted. The experiment thus combined the strengths of GA and TS.

Earlier results had suggested that SA can achieve good results efficiently, so the question arises whether TS is better than SA. A definitive answer is not yet in. The superiority of TS performance may be due to the clever neighborhood structure and to highly efficient makespan-updating calculations. But the same neighborhood structure and updating calculations could be applied to other search approaches. Furthermore, a search technique tested earlier relied on a shifting bottleneck structure and that technique could also be revisited. At the moment, however, neighborhood search algorithms represent the most effective approach to solving large versions of the job shop problem.

14.6 Summary

The job shop model has been a central paradigm for scheduling since the early days of scheduling theory. This chapter introduced the static version of the job shop problem and showed that, for regular measures of performance, the set of active schedules is the relevant dominant set. However, the job shop problem is challenging to solve, even when we limit attention to active schedules. The computational demands of solving even moderately sized problems (such as 15-job, 15-machine problems) often become prohibitive. Although systematic optimization techniques are available for job shop problems, their computational limitations have drawn attention to heuristic procedures. In particular, priority dispatching rules are very useful in practice. Most of our knowledge about priority dispatching, however, derives from experimental studies of the dynamic version of the job shop model, which is our focus in the next chapter.

The shifting bottleneck approach constituted a major breakthrough and is currently the leading optimization technique for the job shop problem. The technique has been refined, and it has also been tested as a heuristic procedure, with promising results. Because of the equivalence between the HBT problem and the L_{max} problem, the shifting bottleneck procedure can also be used directly in solving the job shop problem with L_{max} criterion. At present, it appears possible to adapt the procedure to such other criteria as total flowtime or total tardiness, although such extensions have not yet been studied in depth. Nevertheless, problems with more than about 200 operations remain out of reach of current optimization approaches.

For any benchmark problem whose optimal solution is not known, the best available solution is the tightest upper bound on the optimal solution. Many existing upper bounds have been found by a highly tailored TS application (Nowicki and Smutnicki 2005). Exploiting the structure of the job shop problem, we can define efficient neighborhoods that either reduce the number of irrelevant neighbors that need to be examined or increase the chance that we examine only neighbors that are likely to provide improvement. Currently, such search heuristics are the most effective approach to all but small-scale versions of the static problem. In particular, the TS we mentioned searches the restricted API neighborhood and generates new search seeds by reference to an evolving set of stored superior (or elite) solutions, which require the use of long-term memory. It also utilizes a particularly efficient way to calculate makespans. With that in mind, subsequent research suggests that the success of that approach is not specific to the TS framework but to the other ingredients (Watson et al. 2006).

To date, stochastic job shops have only been addressed by heuristics. A practical heuristic approach to stochastic job shop scheduling is to use dispatching at the machine level, which typically implies nondelay scheduling. In Chapter 17, in a similar context, we discuss the notion of a scheduling *policy*. A policy determines in advance how to make dispatching decisions when two or more operations are available. A simple example of a policy is a priority list, but a policy can also incorporate more complex decision rules, such as added precedence constraints, that can prevent some inferior nondelay schedules and yet utilize dispatching. To compare different policies, it is possible to use sample-based analysis; and for a given sample, search methods (such as GA) can seek the best policy.

Exercises

14.1   Consider the following four-job, three-machine job shop problem.

	Processing times				Machines		
	Operation				Operation		
	1	**2**	**3**		**1**	**2**	**3**
Job 1	4	2	3	Job 1	1	2	3
Job 2	2	4	4	Job 2	1	3	2
Job 3	3	5	3	Job 3	3	2	1
Job 4	4	3	5	Job 4	2	1	3

a) Draw charts (see Figure 14.2) that show the job processing requirements and the machine requirements in this problem, thus identifying a lower bound for the makespan.

b) Draw a network diagram for the operations in this problem, showing all precedence requirements and all disjunctive arcs.

14.2 Revisit the problem in Exercise 14.1. Consider the partial schedule that contains the following assignments. At machine 1, jobs 1, 2, and 4 are sequenced in that order without idle time. At machine 2, jobs 4, 1, and 3 are sequenced in that order without idle time. At machine 3, job 3 is sequenced first, and the next time that a scheduling decision must be made occurs at time 6. At time 6 on machine 3, what scheduling alternatives are available? Which would be appropriate for a nondelay schedule? Which would be appropriate for an active schedule?

14.3 Revisit the problem in Exercise 14.1 and construct a full schedule using a priority dispatching rule.

a) Use FCFS and break ties with SPT and LWKR if needed. Calculate the makespan.

b) Use SPT and break ties with LWKR and FCFS if needed. Calculate the makespan.

c) Use LWKR and break ties with SPT and FCFS if needed. Calculate the makespan.

d) Use MWKR and break ties with LPT and FCFS if needed. Calculate the makespan.

14.4 Consider a series–parallel job shop in which jobs require three operations. The initial operation can be performed either at machine 1A or machine 1B, which are identical. The jobs then proceed to machines 2 and 3 in sequence. The operation times are shown below:

Machine	1	2	3
Job A	10	4	1
Job B	12	2	1
Job C	9	4	3
Job D	8	2	3
Job E	7	4	2
Job F	13	1	1

a) Find a schedule that minimizes the makespan.
b) Show a Gantt chart for your schedule.

14.5 Revisit the problem in Exercise 14.1. Construct a schedule using a neighborhood search algorithm based on adjacent pairwise interchanges and calculate the resulting makespan.

14.6 Revisit the problem in Exercise 14.1. Construct a schedule using the shifting bottleneck heuristic algorithm and calculate the resulting makespan.

14.7 Show that in an enhanced neighborhood, when an initial API induces other APIs on upstream or downstream machines, they automatically apply within the evolving restricted neighborhood.

14.8 Consider Figure 14.9. Show that the critical path has parallel operations. Show that the API between (4, 1, 2) and (2, 1, 2) makes no difference to the makespan but reduces the number of critical activities. Suggest an additional API that will reduce total flowtime without increasing the makespan.

Bibliography

Adams, J., Balas, E., and Zawack, D. (1988). The shifting bottleneck algorithm for job-shop scheduling. *Management Science* 34: 391–401.

Blackstone, J.H., Phillips, D.T., and Hogg, G.L. (1982). A state-of-the-art survey of dispatching rules for job shop operations. *International Journal of Production Research* 20: 27–45.

Blazewicz, J., Domschke, W., and Pesch, E. (1996). The job shop scheduling problem: conventional and new solution techniques. *European Journal of Operational Research* 93: 1–33.

Carlier, J. (1982). The one machine sequencing problem. *European Journal of Operational Research* 11: 42–47.

Carlier, J. and Pinson, E. (1989). An algorithm for solving the job-shop problem. *Management Science* 35: 164–176.

Carlier, J. and Pinson, E. (1994). Adjustment of heads and tails for the job-shop problem. *European Journal of Operational Research* 87: 146–161.

Conway, R.W., Maxwell, W.L., and Miller, L.W. (1967). *Theory of Scheduling.* Reading, MA: Addison Wesley.

Dauzere-Peres, S. and Lasserre, J. (1993). A modified shifting bottleneck procedure for job-shop scheduling. *International Journal of Production Research* 31: 923–932.

Giffler, B. and Thompson, G.L. (1960). Algorithms for solving production scheduling problems. *Operations Research* 8: 487–503.

Golenko-Ginzburg, D., Kesler, S., and Landsman, Z. (1995). Industrial job-shop scheduling with random operations and different priorities. *International Journal of Production Economics* 40: 185–195.

Laslo, Z., Golenko-Ginzburg, D., and Keren, B. (2007). Optimal booking of machines in a virtual job shop with stochastic processing times to minimize total machine rental and job tardiness costs. *International Journal of Production Economics* 111 (2): 812–821.

Mason, S.J., Fowler, J.W., and Carlyle, W.M. (2002). A modified shifting bottleneck heuristic for minimizing total weighted tardiness in complex job shops. *Journal of Scheduling* 5: 247–262.

Nowicki, E. and Smutnicki, C. (1996). A fast taboo search algorithm for the job shop problem. *Management Science* 42: 797–813.

Nowicki, E. and Smutnicki, C. (2005). An advanced tabu search algorithm for the job shop problem. *Journal of Scheduling* 8: 145–159.

Panwalkar, S.S. and Iskander, W. (1977). A survey of scheduling rules. *Operations Research* 25: 45–61.

Sarin, S.C., Sherali, H.D., Varadarajan, A., and Liao, L. (2015). Stochastic scheduling for a network of flexible job shops. In: *Heuristics, Meta-Heuristics and Approximation Methods in Planning and Scheduling* (ed. G. Rabadi). New York: Springer.

Vaessens, R.J.M., Aarts, E.H.L., and Lenstra, J.K. (1996). Job shop scheduling by local search. *INFORMS Journal on Computing* 8 (3): 302–317.

Van Laarhoven, P.J.M., Aarts, E.H.L., and Lenstra, J.K. (1992). Job shop scheduling by simulated annealing. *Operations Research* 40: 113–126.

Watson, J.-P., Howe, A.E., and Whitley, L.D. (2006). Deconstructing Nowicki and Smutnicki's *i*-TSAB tabu search algorithm for the job-shop scheduling problem. *Computers and Operations Research* 33: 2623–2644.

15

Simulation Models for the Dynamic Job Shop

15.1 Introduction

One of the most thoroughly studied and widely applied areas of scheduling research involves the dynamic version of the job shop model. When we refer to the "dynamic" version, we mean that jobs are released and arrive at the shop over time. In the dynamic version of simpler models, we have assumed that information about all arrivals is known in advance and that the list of arrivals is finite – no larger than, say, 100 jobs. The dynamic job shop model usually connotes a different setting: Information about arriving jobs is not known in advance – even the timing of arrivals is unknown – and the arrivals are ongoing. Some studies involve performance measures for thousands of jobs. Because different studies involve different numbers of jobs, it is common to use mean values (of flowtime, tardiness, etc.) instead of totals as performance measures.

Because the timing of arrivals is uncertain, we assume that jobs arrive randomly, so that the shop itself behaves like a network of queues. In this context, scheduling is typically carried out by means of dispatching decisions: Each time a machine becomes free, we must decide what it should do next. These scheduling decisions are unavoidable in the operation of such a system. Furthermore, research has demonstrated substantial differences among dispatching procedures, so it makes sense to seek out the decision rules that promote good performance.

The effects of dispatching procedures in queueing networks are very difficult to describe by means of analytic techniques. Nevertheless, the study of scheduling in dynamic job shops has made considerable progress with the use of computer simulation models. The rationale for using simulation methods in job shop studies is the same as the rationale for simulation in any other complex system: Short of testing alternative policies in the actual system, we cannot fully

Principles of Sequencing and Scheduling, Second Edition. Kenneth R. Baker and Dan Trietsch.
© 2019 John Wiley & Sons, Inc. Published 2019 by John Wiley & Sons, Inc.

anticipate how different operating procedures will affect performance. Experimentation with a computer simulation model has made it possible to compare alternative dispatching rules, test broad conjectures about scheduling procedures, and develop greater insight into job shop operation. The purpose of this discussion is to convey the flavor of job shop simulation experiments. After examining the typical features of simulation models, we highlight some of the major insights that have emerged from years of research on this topic.

15.2   Model Elements

The literature on the dynamic job shop model includes simulations of both actual and hypothetical systems. The hypothetical shops, in particular, typically consist of a small number of machines, usually less than 10. Models of actual shops sometimes contain dozens of machines, but no evidence has been found that the number of machines has a crucial influence on the relative performance of scheduling rules. Aside from the question of scale, several issues arise in the building of a model. It is desirable for the model to be somewhat simplified in order to isolate the effects of scheduling and to permit generalization of the experimental results. On the other hand, if the model is too simple, the conclusions may not apply under other, more realistic conditions. The successful work in this area exemplifies a blend of simple structure and elaborate detail, and the following list of model assumptions is typical:

1) Jobs consist of strictly ordered operation sequences.
2) A given operation can be performed by only one type of machine.
3) There is only one machine of each type in the shop.
4) Processing times as well as due dates are known at the time of arrival.
5) Setup times are sequence independent.
6) Once an operation starts, it cannot be interrupted.
7) An operation may not begin until its predecessors are complete.
8) Each machine can process only one operation at a time.
9) Each machine is continuously available for production.

The first five of these assumptions have sometimes been relaxed in simulation experiments, either to achieve a better representation of reality in the simulation of an actual shop or to examine the sensitivity of basic findings to alternative assumptions about the environment. The remaining assumptions are virtually standard in job shop studies.

The input to the simulation model is a job file that describes the entire set of jobs. The arrivals occur randomly over time, and the operation times are samples from a given probability distribution. (There has been little indication that the nature of the arrival process or the service process is critical in comparing scheduling rules, although greater variability in arrivals or operation times tends to magnify differences between rules.) The description of an arriving job also includes the number of its operations, which may vary among jobs or remain fixed, and its machine routing. In the *closed* job shop, each job must have one of a number of specified routings, representing a fixed line of products. By contrast, the *pure* job shop accommodates virtually any possible machine routing, as might be found with custom-ordered products. Finally, an aggregate description of workflow is contained in a routing matrix, R, in which element r_{ij} represents the proportion of jobs that proceed to machine j after completion of an operation on machine i. Values of r_{0j} indicate the destinations of jobs upon arrival to the shop, and $r_{i,m+1}$ indicates the proportion of jobs that leave the shop after an operation on machine i. Thus, if there are m machines, the R matrix has $(m + 1)$ rows and columns. The two extreme cases are the pure job shop, in which these proportions are equally distributed, and the pure flow shop, in which only one routing exists. Routing matrices for these two cases are displayed in Tables 15.1 and 15.2, respectively, for a four-machine shop.

Table 15.1

	A	1	2	3	4	L
Arrive	—	1/4	1/4	1/4	1/4	—
1	—	—	1/4	1/4	1/4	1/4
2	—	1/4	—	1/4	1/4	1/4
3	—	1/4	1/4	—	1/4	1/4
4	—	1/4	1/4	1/4	—	1/4
Leave	—	—	—	—	—	—

Table 15.2

	A	1	2	3	4	L
Arrive	—	1	0	0	0	—
1	—	—	1	0	0	0
2	—	0	—	1	0	0
3	—	0	0	—	1	0
4	—	0	0	0	—	1
Leave	—	—	—	—	—	—

The output of the simulation is a set of statistics that describes the behavior of the model over a simulated interval of operation. The statistical analysis of simulation outcomes is a topic beyond the scope of this coverage, but many articles on job shop experiments discuss statistical interpretations. Usually, the experiments are aimed at characterizing system performance in the long run, after the system reaches statistical equilibrium. Therefore, the first portion of the experiment is a warm-up period, after which performance data is gathered. To the extent that the experiments are aimed at obtaining qualitative insights and understanding, it may not be critical to invoke sophisticated statistical tests. However, an important feature of the experimentation is typically the maintenance of a stored or reproducible job file. (In the past, high-speed memory was at a premium, and good simulation models relied on the ability to reproduce the same set of random variables. Today, it is not difficult to store large samples in high-speed memory. For this reason, we have assumed that samples are stored. Most of the seminal results reported in this chapter, however, were obtained with reproducible files.) With a consistent set of input data, we can repeat a simulation several times, using the same input each time and varying only the scheduling rules. This approach helps focus on performance differences among scheduling rules and to remove those differences that could occur simply due to random factors.

15.3 Types of Dispatching Rules

Detailed scheduling decisions in a job shop are usually determined by dispatching rules. At the completion of any operation, a machine becomes free, and the dispatching rule specifies what the machine should do next. One of the options, of course, is to keep the machine idle for a certain period, but, in the spirit of nondelay schedules, most dispatching rules immediately assign work to the machine as long as work is available. This assignment is based on priorities determined for each of the waiting jobs.

Two types of classifications are important in describing priority rules. First, a rule is *local* if we base priority assignment only on information about the jobs represented in the individual machine queue. The SPT and LWKR rules, introduced in the previous chapter, are two examples of local rules. By contrast, a rule is *global* if it uses information from machines other than the one at which the decision is pending. Examples of global rules include the following:

AWINQ (anticipated work in next queue): Select the waiting operation whose direct successor operation will encounter the queue with the least work waiting. This includes work that has not yet arrived there but that is anticipated to arrive before the direct successor operation can begin.

FOFO (first off first on): Select the operation that will complete earliest. If this operation is not yet in the queue, the machine remains idle until it arrives.

Intuitively, global rules ought to be more effective than local rules, but there is no strong evidence to that effect, and it is not easy to determine which global rules are good. Moreover, the information base required for global rules may be so extensive as to preclude implementation in many shops. Simulation studies have mainly examined local rules.

A second classification of dispatching rules involves the dynamics of the information base. A rule is *static* if its relative assignment of priorities does not change over time and *dynamic* otherwise. A little elaboration on this distinction might be helpful. The simplest set of static rules provides that each operation of a given job has the same priority. For example:

ERD (earliest release date): Select the operation associated with the job that arrived at the shop (i.e. was released) earliest.

EDD (earliest due date): Select the operation associated with the job that has the earliest due date.

Certain rules, including SPT and LWKR, are static with respect to a particular operation, but dynamic with respect to a particular job, in the sense that individual operations of the same job acquire different relative priorities. Here are other examples:

MST (minimum slack time): Select the waiting operation associated with the job that has minimum slack time. Slack time is equal to the difference between the due date and the earliest possible finish time of the job.

ODD (operation due date): Select the operation that has the earliest operation due date. We determine an operation due date by dividing the interval between the job due date and its release date into as many subintervals as there are operations. The end of each subinterval represents a due date for the corresponding operation.

A dynamic version of ODD results if we replace the release date by the current (dispatching) time. Furthermore, slack-oriented versions can be developed by incorporating remaining work into the priority calculation. Some other dynamic rules are listed below:

S/OPN (slack per operation): Select the operation associated with the job that has the minimum ratio of slack time to remaining operations.

TSPT (truncated SPT): Select the operation with the shortest operation time (as under SPT), except when an operation has waited in the queue more than W time units. Operations with queue times larger than W receive overriding priority and are dispatched by first-come, first-served (FCFS) priority.

MDD (modified due date): Select the operation associated with the job that has the earliest modified due date. The modified due date is either the original due date or the earliest possible finish time, whichever is larger.

It is not difficult to devise a plausible dispatching rule, as the foregoing examples should demonstrate. In some situations, the rationale for using a particular rule may be that it helps produce rapid turnaround, but in other instances the motivating factor may be the need to meet due dates. Simulation research has examined a wide variety of alternative rules and identified a few simple but effective rules for each situation. The following sections suggest the tenor of these findings.

15.4   Reducing Mean Flowtime

The most commonly used measure of turnaround in a job shop has been mean job flowtime. An equivalent measure is mean number of jobs in the system, because the flowtime–inventory relationship described in Chapter 2 also pertains to the dynamic job shop. In light of the fact that SPT minimizes F in single-machine problems, it is natural to expect that shortest-first strategies should perform well in the job shop setting. Therefore, it is not surprising to find that the major comparative studies have found that SPT minimizes mean flowtime when compared with the dozen or so simple dispatching rules that are frequently considered as alternatives.

Conway (1965a) performed an elaborate study, using mean number of jobs in the system, J, as the performance measure. Conway simulated a pure job shop containing nine machines and operating under the assumptions listed in the previous section. The experiments gathered statistics on about 9000 jobs and reported results for over 30 priority rules. Table 15.3 reproduces some of those results, dramatizing the effectiveness of the SPT rule. Even the global rule AWINQ did not match the performance of SPT, although both performed substantially better than ERD, which essentially ignores both job traits and shop status in determining priorities. In search of a rule that performs better than SPT, Conway investigated the performance of several combination rules, two of which appear in Table 15.3. A combination of SPT and LWKR computes job priorities under each rule separately and then takes a weighted sum of the two values, weighting the SPT priority value by α and the LWKR priority value by $(1 - \alpha)$. Different values of the weighting parameter α generate a parametric set of combination rules. Conway's experiments showed that the proper choice of α could improve slightly over SPT, but a poor choice of α could lead to worse performance. There were also tests of combination rules using SPT and AWINQ, and in Conway's study one of these produced the smallest value of J.

Table 15.3

Dispatching rule	J
Simple rules	
ERD	57.51
FCFS	58.87
SPT	23.25
LWKR	47.52
AWINQ	34.03
Combination rules	
SPT, LWKR (α = 0.985)	22.98
SPT, AWINQ (α = 0.96)	22.67

The effectiveness of combination rules has limited practical value, for several reasons. First, any combination rule requires the specification of a weighting parameter, and it takes considerable effort to find an "optimal" value of α for a given situation. The range of desirable α values might well be sensitive to shop utilization and certain job parameters. Moreover, the added benefits of using a combination rule – and a global rule as well, if AWINQ is involved – seem marginal at best compared with the performance under SPT. Because the pure SPT rule is so much easier to implement, and because it accounts for nearly all of the good performance of the combination rules, it is, for all practical purposes, considered the best rule where the objective is to minimize mean flowtime. Conway's findings are representative of similar results in several other investigations.

Conway also studied whether the SPT rule was sensitive to the precision of processing time information in situations where priority assignments must employ estimates. His experimentation was motivated by the fact that in practice it is not always possible to have completely reliable information in advance about operation times. Instead, an estimate of each processing time is available, but the actual time is often subject to some uncertainty. Therefore, Conway described the quality of the estimates in terms of their precision. In the model, actual times were uniformly distributed random variables ranging from a specified proportion β below the estimate to the same proportion above the estimate. For example, if a particular operation had an estimated time of 10 hours and the quality parameter β was set at 0.2, then the actual time was equally likely to be any value between 8 and 12 hours. Of course, the case β = 0 corresponds to the implementation of SPT with perfect information. As shown in Table 15.4, the SPT rule is remarkably insensitive to imperfect information. Even when the estimate is allowed to be off by 100% from the true value

Table 15.4

Dispatching rule	J
SPT ($\beta = 0$)	23.25
SPT ($\beta = 0.1$)	22.23
SPT ($\beta = 1.0$)	27.13
2CLASS	35.29
FCFS	58.87

($\beta = 1.0$), the deterioration in performance is very slight, suggesting that SPT can still be effective when available information is unreliable. (When viewed in light of our current knowledge about the applicability of SEPT in a stochastic environment, this result should not be surprising.)

Table 15.4 also displays the result of simulating the performance of a two-class rule, which places "short" jobs in a high priority class and "long" jobs in a low priority class. The dispatching rule selects jobs in the queue from the high priority class whenever they are available and from the low priority class only when no high priority jobs are present. Within classes, however, dispatching uses FCFS priority. The dividing line between short and long in the study was arbitrarily taken as the mean of the processing time distribution. The significance of this rule is that it requires only a two-way classification of jobs, which is a coarse method of discrimination compared with SPT. Even though the performance of the two-class rule does not approach that of SPT, the use of a short–long distinction accounts for a significant improvement over a rule such as FCFS, which is completely blind to job characteristics. It is possible to envision a family of similar rules with three classes, four classes, and so on. In this family, a larger number of classes represent a finer discrimination among tasks until, in the limiting case, SPT represents perfect short–long discrimination. The two-class rule is the simplest rule in this family. Although it is the least demanding in terms of the quality of information required, it nevertheless accounts for about two-thirds of the benefit that SPT itself achieves over FCFS.

The mechanism by which SPT reduces mean flowtime should not be difficult to understand. By giving priority to short tasks, it accelerates the progress of several short jobs at the expense of a few long jobs. The SPT rule reduces mean flowtime, but long jobs tend to encounter very long delays. In other words, the turnaround is good for most of the jobs but extremely poor for the few long jobs assigned low priorities. Several suggestions for ameliorating this aspect of performance have been proposed, but all involve sacrificing some of the benefits of SPT. Conway first investigated TSPT, under which SPT is the normal

Table 15.5

Dispatching rule	J
Truncated SPT	
TSPT ($W = \infty$)	23.25 (SPT)
TSPT ($W = 32$)	32.85
TSPT ($W = 16$)	44.20
TSPT ($W = 8$)	53.50
TSPT ($W = 4$)	55.67
TSPT ($W = 0$)	58.87 (FCFS)
Relief SPT	
RSPT ($Q = 1$)	23.25 (SPT)
RSPT ($Q = 5$)	29.49
RSPT ($Q = 9$)	38.67
RSPT ($Q = \infty$)	58.87 (FCFS)

dispatching mode, but operations receive special priority once their waiting time in a given queue exceeds a certain value, W. The parametric performance of this rule is described in Table 15.5.

In Conway's study, the average waiting time per operation observed under FCFS was 7.27 and under SPT was only 2.78. Therefore, truncation at $W = 32$ still allows individual waiting times to be far above average, yet any earlier truncation appears to sacrifice most of the benefits of SPT. A second suggestion involves the use of SPT in a relief role (RSPT). Under this rule the normal dispatching mode is FCFS, but when the length of an individual queue grows too long, the local dispatching mechanism switches over to SPT. In particular, when the length of any queue reaches a certain number Q, then priorities within that queue are reassigned according to SPT. However, once the queue length drops below Q, the dispatching rule reverts to FCFS. Since FCFS is the normal dispatching mode, long jobs do not typically encounter excessive delays. Long jobs sometimes encounter temporary delays, however, while SPT provides relief to individual machines facing severe congestion. The mean queue length under pure FCFS was 6.54 and under SPT was 2.58. Therefore, a queue length parameter of $Q = 9$ allows machine queues to grow beyond their mean length before the dispatching rule suspends FCFS. At the same time, the parameter $Q = 9$ retains over half the benefit of SPT sequencing.

Compromise mechanisms such as TSPT and RSPT are necessary in systems that will not tolerate the long flowtimes associated with long jobs under SPT. Nevertheless, it is important to recognize that different mechanisms will exhibit different performance trade-offs, and any departure from a desirable pure rule should be explored thoroughly in order to avoid losing the advantages the pure rule achieves. In the case of TSPT and RSPT, the data in Table 15.5 suggest that RSPT is more effective at preserving the turnaround performance of pure SPT while meeting the objections raised about long jobs.

15.5 Meeting Due Dates

15.5.1 Background

When the scheduling objective involves meeting job due dates, the most significant performance measures are likely to be tardiness-based criteria, such as the proportion of jobs tardy or mean job tardiness. In such instances, it becomes relevant to consider dispatching strategies that employ due date information, as exemplified by many of the rules described earlier. In addition, the tardiness criterion appears to present a much more complex problem than the minimization of mean flowtime, because several factors can affect performance.

To begin with, consider the distribution of job latenesses. Since lateness is just the algebraic difference between the completion time and a (given) due date, we can expect that the mean of this distribution will be minimized by SPT. Nevertheless, it is not only the lateness mean that accounts for good tardiness performance but also the lateness variance. Figure 15.1 shows four hypothetical distributions of job lateness, with the due date (zero lateness) represented by the vertical axis. The distribution in Figure 15.1a represents the performance of a dispatching procedure that ignores both processing time and due date information. Figure 15.1b represents the performance of SPT, which tends to minimize mean lateness while allowing some jobs to become quite late. Figure 15.1c represents the performance of a low variance type of rule that attempts to schedule jobs for completion as close to their due dates as possible. While the low variance is achieved at the expense of an increased mean, the trade-off may still be desirable unless the mean increases so much that a large proportion of the jobs becomes tardy, as in Figure 15.1d.

Experts have advocated three main types of approaches in determining priorities using due date information:

- Allowance-based priorities
- Slack-based priorities
- Ratio-based priorities

A job's *flow allowance* is the time between its release date and its due date. As time passes, a job's remaining allowance shrinks. Under allowance-based priority rules, the urgency of a job is related to its remaining allowance. If we are dispatching at time t, the remaining allowance of job j may be expressed as

Figure 15.1 Hypothetical distributions of job lateness for four priority rules.

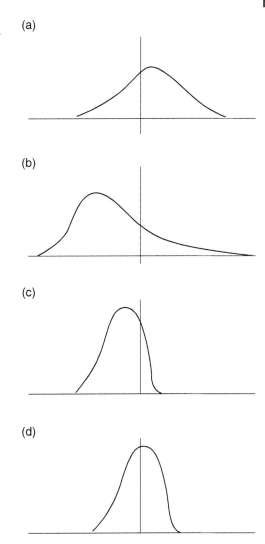

(a)

(b)

(c)

(d)

$a_j(t) = d_j - t$, where $a_j(t)$ is the remaining allowance and d_j is the due date. A basic allowance-based priority system gives priority to the smallest $a_j(t)$. Since t is the same for all jobs when we are making a dispatching decision, the job with the smallest $a_j(t)$ will also have the smallest d_j. Thus, the simplest allowance-based rule is just the earliest due date (EDD) rule.

A job's *slack time* is its remaining allowance adjusted for remaining work. The slack for job j is $s_j = a_j(t) - P_j$, where s_j is the slack time and P_j is the time required by the remaining operations of job j. The simplest slack-based priority rule is the minimum slack time (MST) rule, which gives priority to the smallest s_j. Slack-based priorities enjoy considerable popularity, but there is reason to be cautious about them. The intuitive justification for MST rules is that when two jobs have the same allowance, the longer job is more urgent because its due date allows less delay. However, SPT sequencing is often effective at meeting due dates, even though it does not explicitly use due date information. One structural problem with slack-based priorities is that by "netting out" remaining work against the remaining allowance, MST priorities incorporate some anti-SPT scheduling compared with EDD priorities, at least among jobs with similar due dates. At the margin, this effect may well be undesirable. (One way to ameliorate the problems with slack-based rules is to use $\max\{s_j, 0\}$ instead, but if so we need another rule when comparing jobs that are already doomed to be late.)

The third approach resembles slack-based priorities but uses ratio arithmetic instead. For instance, the simplest form of the *critical ratio* is $a_j(t)/P_j$ or the remaining allowance divided by the remaining work. In other words, critical ratio priorities measure urgency by the ratio of remaining allowance and remaining work rather than their difference, as in MST. Sometimes, remaining work is augmented by standard queue allowances in the critical ratio. Priorities based on smallest critical ratio (SCR) have some practical appeal in that the ratio value of 1 provides a standard for whether a job is running late. However, negative ratios are difficult to interpret, and SCR is open to the criticism that, like MST, it induces some anti-SPT performance at the margin. (Consider a case where two jobs have the same due date and just one operation remaining. The longer job will have a smaller slack, and when we divide the slack by its processing time, we exacerbate the effect of MST.)

Another factor in measuring urgency is the number of operations remaining on a job. When two jobs have the same remaining allowance and remaining work, the job with the larger number of operations is intuitively more urgent because it will encounter more opportunities for queueing delay, other things being equal. This reasoning leads to priority indices based on remaining allowance per operation (A/OPN) or slack per operation (S/OPN). Although these rules have performed well in some research experiments, they, along with SCR, have some practical drawbacks. First, ratio priorities may work in the wrong direction when their numerators are negative. Among jobs with negative slack, the job with minimum S/OPN might not be the logical dispatching choice. Second, ratio priorities are dynamic: As two jobs wait in queue, their relative priorities may change. This feature could be perplexing to people carrying out the schedule, although dynamic priorities may actually be effective.

An alternative way to recognize the number of remaining operations is to use operation milestones. After a job's due date is assigned, we can set milestones in place to show when each operation should complete if the job is to progress smoothly toward on-time completion. These milestones are called *operation due dates*, and they essentially break up a job's flow allowance into as many segments as the number of operations in the job. These segments then play the role of flow allowances for each operation, and they pace the job through the shop. Once operation due dates have been established, we can dispatch jobs by priority rules that use only the operation processing time and the operation due date in one of the three types of approaches. The allowance-based approach thus leads to earliest operation due date (ODD) priorities; the slack-based approach leads to minimum operation slack time (OST); and the ratio-based approach leads to smallest operation critical ratio (OCR).

Table 15.6 presents selected results reported by various investigators whose research involved some of these rules. Three measures of performance are considered in the table: mean tardiness (*MT*), proportion of jobs tardy (*PT*), and conditional mean tardiness (*CMT*). Algebraically, we have

Table 15.6

Performance measure	Best rule(s)	Other rules compared	Author(s)
MT	MST	S/OPN, SPT	Gere (1966)
	SPT	S/OPN, EDD	Conway et al. (1967) and Carroll (1965)
	S/OPN	SPT	Weeks (1979)
	SPT, ODD	MST, OST, SCR, OCR	Kanet and Hayya (1982)
	A/OPN	SCR, S/OPN	Miyazaki (1981)
	SPT, EDD	MST, SCR	Baker and Bertrand (1981)
	MST, SPT, EDD	OST, S/OPN, ODD, SCR	Muhlemann et al. (1982)
PT	S/OPN, SPT	EDD, MST	Conway et al. (1967)
	SPT	MST, EDD, S/OPN	Elvers (1973)
	SPT	EDD, ODD, MST, SCR, OST, S/OPN	Muhlemann et al. (1982)
	SCR, A/OPN	S/OPN	Miyazaki (1981)
	SPT	MST, OST, EDD, ODD, SCR, OCR	Kanet and Hayya (1982)
	SPT, S/OPN, MST	EDD	Elvers and Taube (1983)
CMT	S/OPN	SPT, EDD	Conway et al. (1967)
	SCR	SPT, EDD, ODD, MST, S/OPN, OST	Muhlemann et al. (1982)
	OCR	SPT, EDD, ODD, MST, OST, SCR	Kanet and Hayya (1982)

$$\text{CMT} = \frac{MT}{PT}$$

or, in other words, CMT represents the MT computed for the set of tardy jobs. The information in Table 15.6 must be interpreted in light of some qualifications. First, different researchers used different experimental conditions, which may account for their apparently conflicting conclusions, as discussed later. Second, the table reflects only the simpler rules discussed earlier and ignores rules that involve an additional parameter, such as TSPT. The table has been slightly simplified in other ways, but it conveys some distinct impressions:

- For PT, the SPT rule is consistently very effective.
- For CMT, critical ratio priorities are effective.
- For MT, the results are quite mixed.

In order to understand why the picture is mixed for the MT criterion, we need to examine some additional factors.

Absolute performance at meeting due dates is affected by how tight the due dates are. For example, tighter due dates tend to produce larger values of MT and PT, if other conditions remain unchanged. Beyond that, evidence exists that the *relative* performance of priority rules is also affected by due date tightness, at least for PT and for MT. The research evidence suggests the presence of crossover points, with one rule performing best for tighter due dates and another performing best for looser due dates. To some extent, the conflicting evidence in Table 15.6 may reflect the fact that different research experiments happen to have been conducted on opposite sides of a crossover point. This possibility has led to a search for rules that are robust with respect to due date tightness. One candidate is the MDD rule.

A variety of decision rules can be used to set due dates. If r_j denotes the release date for job j, then we set the job's due date equal to $d_j = r_j + a_j$, where $a_j = a_j(r_j)$ represents the original flow allowance. The following list describes a number of ways to set the original flow allowances. (Here, m_j denotes the number of operations for job j.)

CON: $a_j = k$ (constant flow allowances)

SLK: $a_j = P_j + k$ (equal slack)

NOP: $a_j = km_j$ (proportional to number of operations)

PPW: $a_j = P_j + km_j$ (processing plus waiting time)

TWK: $a_j = kP_j$ (proportional to total work)

The parameter k would be chosen differently for each rule in order to achieve a given average flow allowance. Some evidence exists that the due date assignment rule can influence the performance of certain priority rules, so another possible explanation for the conflicting results in Table 15.6 might be that different due date rules were used in different research studies.

Not only are there alternative rules for setting job due dates, but similar choices also arise for setting operation due dates. Once a job's due date is set, we divide its original flow allowance into as many segments as there are operations. These segments, which determine operation due dates, can be constant for all operations of the given job. Alternatively, they can reflect equal slack, or they can be proportional to total work. Thus, if we use the subscripts (i, j) to denote the ith operation of job j and adopt the convention $d_{0j} = r_j$, then we have

$$\text{CON}: \quad d_{ij} = d_{i-1,j} + a_j/m_j$$

$$\text{SLK}: \quad d_{ij} = d_{i-1,j} + p_{ij} + \left(a_j - P_j\right)/m_j$$

$$\text{TWK}: \quad d_{ij} = d_{i-1,j} + a_j p_{ij}/P_j$$

Kanet and Hayya (1982) compared CON and TWK as alternatives for setting operation due dates and found TWK to be superior. Using the TWK method, they observed that operation-based versions of EDD, MST, and SCR produced better tardiness performance than the job-based versions. Thus, in terms of Table 15.6, we might hypothesize that some of the conflicting evidence about such rules as ODD and OST may reflect differences in the choice of a decision rule for setting milestones.

In summary, the existing results comprise a mixed and apparently inconsistent set of results on priority rules for minimizing mean tardiness. At the same time, there are certain aspects of the experimental conditions, often overlooked, that might account for the inconsistencies in these studies.

15.5.2 Some Clarifying Experiments

Our brief review of simulation results leads directly to certain interesting questions. First, a question remains about how to set operation due dates for operation-based priority rules. The work of Kanet and Hayya indicates that TWK is a better rule than CON for setting milestones, but the SLK rule was not included in their comparisons. In addition, they did not investigate whether their results held for different ways of setting job due dates.

Once we gain insight into how to set milestones, we can compare the two approaches for recognizing the remaining number of operations, by comparing S/OPN with OST and A/OPN with ODD. We can also design an effective operation-based version of the MDD rule. Define an operation's modified due date as its original ODD or its early finish time, whichever is larger. The rule then gives priority to the job with minimum modified operation due date (MOD).

A second question involves setting job due dates. Some authors have simply assumed TWK to be desirable, but some single-machine experiments have suggested that there may be a crossover effect. The performance of due date rules still requires some additional study.

Once we gain insight into the setting of job due dates, we can make a meaningful comparison of priority rules, in which we incorporate considerations of due date tightness and recognize that the priority rule must be considered in conjunction with the due date rule. This comparison should reconcile many of the conflicting implications surrounding MT as a criterion.

Below, we summarize the experimental investigation in Baker (1984), which was aimed at answering these questions. The simulation model represented a four-machine job shop. Jobs arrived randomly and had four operations on average, and no successive pair of operations required the same machine. The specific number of operations was equally distributed among the integers from 2 to 6, and the routings were those of a pure job shop. The operation times were random samples from an exponential distribution with a mean of 1. Thus, the average operation time was taken as the unit of time, so that the mean amount of work per job was 4 time units. In such a system, the mean arrival rate determines shop utilization, defined as the ratio of work required to capacity available. In this model, the mean operation time was 1, and the mean number of operations per job was equal to the number of machines in the shop; therefore, utilization was equal to arrival rate.

The primary experiments were conducted with a utilization level of about 90%. A second job set was created, with a utilization of about 80%. This second data set allowed the experiments to be repeated, in order to verify the results observed in the primary data set. As it turned out, the utilization level – although it has a large effect on mean flowtime – was not a major factor in terms of which rule is best, and qualitatively similar results were observed in both data sets.

To provide some perspective on the numerical values observed in the experiments, the theoretical value of mean flowtime is 40 for a utilization of 90%. This value represents the long-run or equilibrium value of mean flowtime, based on the assumption that FCFS priorities apply at each machine. In other words, if we could get perfect information under FCFS about all future events in the shop, and thereby know at the time of a job's arrival the precise time of its ultimate completion, we could then set due dates so that each job would complete exactly on time. In that case, the average flow allowance would be 40. Without full information about the future, some tardiness inevitably occurs when the average flow allowance is 40, but this level anchors the tardiness scale. Table 15.7 shows the flow allowances that were included in the experiments. Also shown are the values of MT and PT observed in the simulation when FCFS priorities were imposed and constant flow allowances were assigned. We can see, for example, that allowances of 40 (or 20 in the 80% data set) represent moderately tight due dates for FCFS, in that roughly 40% of the jobs are late. Improved performance can result from a better choice of priority rule and a more effective way of setting due dates.

Table 15.7

		Flow allowance			
Utilization	Value	15	20	25	30
80%	*MT*	6.48	4.10	2.48	1.46
	PT	0.56	0.40	0.27	0.15

		Flow allowance			
Utilization	Value	30	40	50	60
90%	*MT*	14.82	9.86	6.28	3.87
	PT	0.58	0.42	0.30	0.20

As the parameters in Table 15.7 indicate, the experiments were designed with reference to theoretical mean flowtime. Thus, if a mean allowance of 40 represents "moderately tight" due dates for the case of 90% utilization, then a mean allowance of 20 represents "moderately tight" for the case of 80% utilization because the underlying theory tells us that the mean flowtimes are half as large. Suppose we want to test the effect of utilization. This experimental design involves changing the utilization but maintaining the ratio of mean flow allowance to mean flowtime derived from theory. In this framework, flow allowances with a mean of 50 in the case of 90% utilization are considered comparable with flow allowances of 25 in the case of 80% utilization. It is important to interpret flow allowances in terms of the system's utilization. If we increased the workload by raising the arrival rate, while keeping the flow allowances the same, then a higher proportion of jobs would be tardy. In other words, the frequency of tardiness does not reflect the size of the flow allowances alone, but only in the context of the average level of congestion in the system.

We could adopt a different convention. For example, some experiments have held mean flow allowance constant while raising utilization. Under our framework, that experimental design is viewed as tightening the due dates because mean flowtime was allowed to increase while the mean flow allowance was maintained. The crossover phenomena observed in those experiments can be interpreted as crossovers in tightness.

15.5.3 Experimental Results

Operation Milestones. Table 15.8 shows the *MT* outcomes in an experiment that compared the three methods of setting milestones (CON, SLK, and TWK). These methods correspond to the rows of the table, while the columns

Table 15.8

		Job due date rule		
		SLK	PPW	TWK
Operation	CON	2.28	2.92	1.49
Due date	SLK	2.11	2.08	1.47
Rule	TWK	1.45	1.18	0.87

represent three ways of setting job due dates. The priority rule in these experiments was ODD, the utilization was 80%, and the average flow allowance was 20. The table shows that for each choice of due date rule, TWK milestones led to the best tardiness performance. Furthermore, the combination of TWK for job due dates with TWK for milestones produced the lowest values of MT.

The robustness of this result was tested several ways. First, the tightness of the job due dates was varied by changing the average allowance to 15 and to 25. Then the priority rule was changed to OST and to MOD. Then the utilization was raised to 90%. In every comparison, TWK milestones produced the lowest value of MT. In addition, the combination of TWK for job due dates with TWK for milestones consistently produced the lowest MT.

Earlier research had concluded that milestones assigned on the basis of work content were more effective than those assigned by equal spacing. The results in Table 15.8 reinforce that notion, demonstrating that the dominance of TWK milestones is robust to certain changes in tightness, utilization, and priority rule. Therefore, in subsequent experiments, the TWK rule was used to set all milestones.

Due Date Assignment Rules. The five methods of setting job due dates (CON, SLK, NOP, PPW, and TWK) were compared for 10 of the priority rules at different tightness levels. The tightness levels were those implied by the four flow allowances given for each data set in Table 15.7. In every comparison except under FCFS, the TWK method produced the lowest values of MT and PT. This set of results provides strong evidence that the TWK rule is a reliable and effective method for setting due dates, at least in this tardiness range.

A few additional experiments were conducted in search of a crossover for the due date rule at larger flow allowances. This idea was motivated by the single-machine results in earlier studies, which indicate that the crossover occurs only when the due dates are quite loose. In fact, a similar crossover was eventually discovered for the job shop model, but it occurred only when tardiness levels were already extremely low. Although TWK was not superior in these cases, its performance was still very close to the best. (Some details are presented later.) For all practical purposes, the TWK rule provided superior tardiness performance.

Figure 15.2 Mean tardiness performance for allowance-based rules.

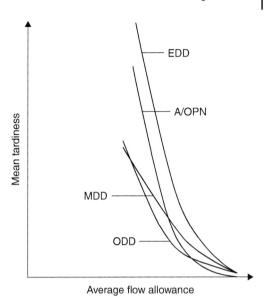

Allowance-based Rules. Figure 15.2 shows the graph of MT as a function of the average allowance for the priority rules EDD, ODD, A/OPN, and MDD. The graph emphasizes the fact that MT is a function of due date tightness. By smoothing the points produced by the simulation runs, the graph suggests the shape of these functions and shows the existence of crossover points. For example, the MDD rule produced the lowest MT at an average allowance of 30; ODD produced the lowest value at 40; and A/OPN produced the lowest at 50. All of the rules produced very little tardiness ($MT \le 0.01$) at 60.

In the region of the graph, the operation-based rules performed quite well. The rule A/OPN nearly avoided tardiness for average allowances of 50 and above, but its tardiness performance deteriorated quickly when the allowances were tightened.

Slack-based Rules. Figure 15.3 shows a similar graph for the priority rules MST, OST, and S/OPN. Two features of the figure resemble Figure 15.2: The slack-based rules performed well under tight due dates, and there was a visible crossover in the graphs of the two operation-based rules. If we superimposed Figures 15.2 and 15.3, the comparison would show A/OPN and S/OPN to be quite similar, while ODD would be slightly better than OST.

This pair of comparisons (which was reinforced by similar results for the case of 80% utilization) suggests that no significant advantage lies in using slack-based rules. Although the anti-SPT effect might be minor, S/OPN and OST appear to produce performance comparable with A/OPN and ODD, respectively, but the allowance-based rules are slightly simpler.

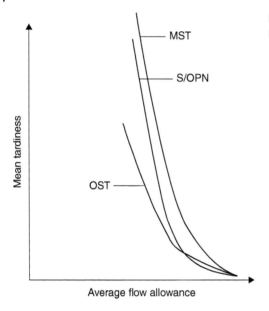

Figure 15.3 Mean tardiness performance for slack-based rules.

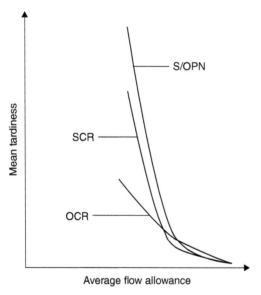

Figure 15.4 Mean tardiness performance for critical ratio rules and S/OPN.

Critical Ratio Rules. Figure 15.4 shows a graph of the critical ratio rules SCR and OCR, along with S/OPN. Comparing the two critical ratio rules, we observe that the operation-based version achieved smaller MT values when flow allowances were small, but the job-based version was preferable when allowances were large. This same type of crossover occurred for MST and OST in

Figure 15.3. These results suggest that the pacing induced by operation milestones improves performance when due dates are relatively tight but provides little benefit when due dates are relatively loose.

The comparison between the critical ratio rules and S/OPN in Figure 15.4 is also instructive. As in the case of A/OPN discussed earlier, the S/OPN rule achieved very small levels of MT for relatively long flow allowances, but performance deteriorated rapidly when allowances were shortened. By contrast, the critical ratio rules yielded more tardiness for loose due dates, but they were less sensitive to shortening the flow allowances.

This comparison is interesting in light of an earlier claim that SCR and S/OPN are equivalent. Although this equivalence does not hold for our definition of SCR (time remaining divided by work remaining), one variation is to replace the numerator in the critical ratio by job slack. If, in addition, we interpret "work remaining" as the allowance for remaining operations, and if those allowances are set by the CON rule for determining milestones, then SCR does become identical to S/OPN. However, the MT performance of SCR seems better without out the changes.

Modified Operation Due Dates. MDD did not always produce extremely low MT values, as Figure 15.2 indicates. However, the foregoing discussion suggests that an operation-based form can be more effective. The simulation runs certainly confirmed this point, as shown in Figure 15.5. The graph reproduces the results for A/OPN and ODD along with the results for MOD and SPT. Not only did MOD produce very small tardiness levels, but also its performance deteriorated far less quickly than the performance of other rules as due dates were

Figure 15.5 Mean tardiness performance for selected rules.

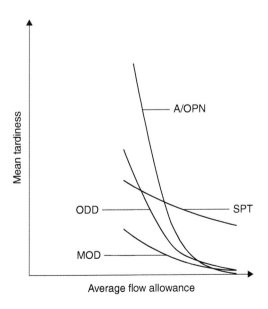

Table 15.9

	Allowance factor			
Priority rule	30	40	50	60
ODD	3.90	1.13	0.28	0.0061
S/OPN	7.54	1.60	0.0024	0.0043
A/OPN	6.94	2.09	0.0024	0.0029
MOD	1.43	0.48	0.14	0.0092
SPT	3.00	2.22	1.84	1.48

tightened. Additional studies have confirmed the robustness of modified due date priorities.

The results in Figure 15.5 are reproduced in Table 15.9. As the data indicate, MOD did not dominate the other rules, for at an average allowance of 60, its tardiness level was slightly higher than that of A/OPN, ODD, and S/OPN. However, the absolute value of MT was very small under those conditions.

As Figure 15.5 shows, the SPT rule exhibited its own kind of robustness, with a tardiness "curve" that was relatively flat. As a result, SPT produced less tardiness than all of the other rules except MOD when due dates were very tight, and SPT produced more tardiness than all of the other rules (except FCFS) when due dates were very loose. The flatness of the SPT curve created crossovers with most other priority rules, which may account for much of the conflicting evidence in the literature.

The performance of the MOD priority rule against the MT criterion was remarkable in these experiments. In addition, its performance on the PT criterion was also quite good. As stated earlier, in reference to Table 15.6, the SPT rule appears to be the benchmark for comparisons involving PT. Table 15.10,

Table 15.10

	Allowance factor			
Priority rule	30	40	50	60
ODD	0.40	0.15	0.05	0.006
S/OPN	0.56	0.24	0.01	0.002
A/OPN	0.54	0.30	0.009	0.003
MOD	0.14	0.06	0.03	0.01
SPT	0.08	0.04	0.03	0.02

which shows *PT* values, demonstrates that MOD generated *PT* performance that was almost as robust as the performance of SPT.

Crossovers in Due Date Rules. As mentioned earlier, some exploratory runs with very loose due dates revealed a crossover effect in the choice of the due date rule. In particular, the priority rules A/OPN and MOD were investigated in a region of due dates more loose than the region in Figures 15.2–15.5. Under TWK due dates, a small amount of tardiness persisted for average allowances up to 100. On the other hand, under NOP due dates, there was no tardiness at all for allowances of 80 and above with the A/OPN priority rule, and there was no tardiness at 90 and above with the MOD rule. In graphical terms, these results suggest that tardiness curves for NOP due dates exhibit smaller *x*-intercepts in graphs such as Figures 15.2–15.5, compared with curves for TWK. Nevertheless, this effect may be of little practical significance because even the TWK rule yields very little tardiness in the region where NOP yields none.

15.6 Summary

After looking at the main results relating to mean flowtime, we gave an overview of a simulation study on tardiness-oriented dispatching in a job shop. For minimizing the proportion tardy (*PT*), the evidence is quite strong that SPT is effective. For minimizing the *CMT*, the evidence is more limited, but it consistently suggests that the use of critical ratio priorities is effective. For the criterion of *MT*, there appears to be conflicting evidence in the research literature. It may be possible to explain such conflicts by recognizing that *MT* performance varies with due date tightness, and we can think of a graph in which *MT* performance is represented by a curve. Not surprisingly, if we increase flow allowances (and thereby loosen due dates), then *MT* drops. This relation gives rise to downward-sloping *MT* curves. More importantly, the shape of the *MT* curve depends critically on the priority rule in effect, as indicated in Figures 15.2–15.5.

The SPT rule exhibits a very flat *MT* curve, which gives rise to performance crossovers with nearly all of the other priority rules tested. In particular, SPT is relatively effective when due dates are very tight but not when due dates are loose. Thus, a particular experimental comparison might find SPT performance to be good or bad, depending on how tight the due dates are set.

The MOD rule also exhibits a relatively flat *MT* curve. It provides superior *MT* performance when due dates are tight, and it is close to the best rules when due dates are loose. This robustness appears to make MOD a desirable choice under conditions where we cannot guarantee loose due dates.

As a general guideline, operation-oriented priority rules perform better on the MT criterion than job-oriented rules. One such approach, embodied in MOD, is to set operation milestones and use them in priority calculations. In these cases, the evidence indicates that milestones should not be equally spaced; rather, they should reflect the work content in individual operations, as in the TWK rule.

A second operation-oriented approach, embodied in the A/OPN rule, is to use the number of remaining operations as a denominator in the priority calculation. In particular, the A/OPN rule exhibits a relatively steep MT curve, which makes it undesirable when due dates are tight. Nevertheless, the A/OPN rule appears superior when due dates are loose. This result suggests that A/OPN may be a desirable choice in situations where we can systematically keep tardiness very small.

In general, slack-based rules offer no great advantage over simpler allowance-based rules. For example, S/OPN produces MT performance very similar to that of A/OPN. Where S/OPN achieves better MT performance than A/OPN, the ODD and MOD rules seem even better.

Finally, the evidence is quite strong that due dates should reflect work content, in light of the fact that TWK was usually the best of the due date assignment rules studied. Some evidence, however, indicates that the NOP rule could yield efficient due dates for avoiding tardiness completely. However, we might wonder what information besides work content can be helpful in setting due dates.

The simulation approach is inherently suited to the study of stochastic job shops. However, in a true stochastic system, we don't know the processing time in advance. In most of the studies we reported, by contrast, the jobs are generated randomly but are assumed known when it comes time to actually apply the various rules. We noted one exception – Conway's finding that SEPT is as effective as SPT for minimizing average flowtime. One consequence of treating job parameters as known is that no Jensen gap occurs. Thus, we may still want to study the effect of using dispatching rules that are based on known distributions rather than known realizations. On the one hand, adapting rules such as MDD or its derivatives (such as MOD) to stochastic times is conceptually easy: We can calculate the expected modified due date, $E[\max\{d_j, t + p_j\}]$, and use it instead of MDD. On the other hand, we need research to determine whether this refinement is important.

When we consider more complex job shops, we may have to deal with additional heterogeneity in jobs and machines. The economics associated with performing different jobs may justify the use of weights in measures of performance and in priority rules. The economics of acquiring different machines may lead to a shop configuration in which some machines are busier than others. In such a setting, throughput as well as due date performance becomes important. When throughput is at stake, it is important to focus on bottlenecks, and we may find it helpful to treat heavily loaded machines and lightly loaded machines differently.

For example, operation due dates are especially useful on heavily loaded machines, but lightly loaded machines may function well with only flowtime-oriented priority rules such as SWPT. We discuss these issues in more detail in our Research Notes.

Bibliography

Anderson, E.J. and Nyirenda, J.C. (1990). Two new rules to minimize tardiness in a job shop. *International Journal of Production Research* 28: 2277–2292.

Baker, K.R. (1968). Priority dispatching in the single channel queue with sequence-dependent setups. *Journal of Industrial Engineering* 19: 203–206.

Baker, K.R. (1984). Sequencing rules and due date assignments in a job shop. *Management Science* 30: 1093–1104.

Baker, K.R. and Bertrand, J.W.M. (1981). An investigation of due date assignment rules with constrained tightness. *Journal of Operations Management* 1: 109–120.

Baker, K.R. and Kanet, J.J. (1983). Job shop scheduling with modified due dates. *Journal of Operations Management* 4: 11–22.

Berry, W.L. and Rao, V. (1975). Critical ratio scheduling: experimental analysis. *Management Science* 22: 192–201.

Bertrand, J.W.M. (1983). The effect of workload dependent due-dates on job shop performance. *Management Science* 29: 799–816.

Blackstone, J.H., Phillips, D.T., and Hogg, G.L. (1982). A state-of-the-art survey of dispatching rules for job shop operations. *International Journal of Production Research* 20: 27–45.

Buzacott, J.A. and Shantikumar, J.G. (1993). *Stochastic Models of Manufacturing Systems*. Englewood Cliffs, NJ: Prentice Hall.

Carroll, D.C. (1965). Heuristic sequencing of single and multiple component jobs. PhD dissertation. MIT.

Conway, R.W. (1965a). Priority dispatching and work-in-process inventory in a job shop. *Journal of Industrial Engineering* 16: 123–130.

Conway, R.W. (1965b). Priority dispatching and job lateness in a job shop. *Journal of Industrial Engineering* 16: 228–237.

Conway, R.W., Maxwell, W.L., and Miller, L.W. (1967). *Theory of Scheduling*. Reading, MA: Addison-Wesley.

Eilon, S. and Chowdhury, I.G. (1976). Due dates in job shop scheduling. *International Journal of Production Research* 14: 223–237.

Elvers, D.A. (1973). Job shop dispatching using various due date setting criteria. *Production and Inventory Management* 14: 62–69.

Elvers, D.A. and Taube, L. (1983). Time completion for various dispatching rules in a job shop. *Omega* 11: 81–89.

Fry, T.D., Philipoom, P.R., and Markland, R.E. (1989). Due date assignment in a multistage job shop. *IIE Transactions* 21: 153–161.

Gere, W.S. (1966). Heuristics in job shop scheduling. *Management Science* 13: 167–190.

Kanet, J.J. (1981). A critical look at critical ratio. *Proceedings of the APICS 24th Annual Conference*, Falls Church, VA, (October 1981), pp. 182–183.

Kanet, J.J. and Hayya, J.C. (1982). Priority dispatching with operation due-dates in a job shop. *Journal of Operations Management* 2: 155–163.

Kanet, J.J. and Li, X. (2004). A weighted modified due date rule for sequencing to minimize weighted tardiness. *Journal of Scheduling* 7: 261–276.

Miyazaki, S. (1981). Combined scheduling system for reducing job tardiness in a job shop. *International Journal of Production Research* 19: 201–211.

Muhlemann, A.P., Lockett, A.G., and Farn, C.I. (1982). Job shop scheduling heuristics and frequency of scheduling. *International Journal of Production Research* 20: 227–241.

Pai, A.R. and McRoberts, K.L. (1971). Simulation research in interchangeable part manufacturing. *Management Science* 17: B732–B743.

Panwalkar, S.S. and Iskander, W. (1977). A survey of scheduling rules. *Operations Research* 25: 45–61.

Vepsalainen, A.P.J. and Morton, T.E. (1987). Priority rules for job shops with weighted tardiness costs. *Management Science* 33: 1035–1047.

Vig, M.M. and Dooley, K.J. (1991). Dynamic rules for due-date assignment. *International Journal of Production Research* 29: 1361–1377.

Weeks, J.K. (1979). A simulation study of predictable due dates. *Management Science* 25: 363–373.

Wein, L.M. (1991). Due-date setting and priority sequencing in a multiclass *M/G/1* queue. *Management Science* 37: 834–850.

16

Network Methods for Project Scheduling

16.1 Introduction

This is the first in a module of four chapters covering classical and emerging project scheduling techniques. Here, we introduce the quintessential network methods for project scheduling, namely, critical path method (CPM) and program evaluation and review technique (PERT). Although we mention some modern insights, essentially this chapter could have been written in the early 1960s. However, several of the historical assumptions it is based on can no longer be considered tenable or necessary. It is not that these weaknesses were not known – most of them were already covered in the textbooks of the 1970s – but that they have been allowed to stand due either to inertia or to a lack of better models. The next chapter focuses on sequencing and briefly touches developments spanning half a century. The third chapter is about project analytics and introduces recent results that make it possible to generate valid simulated samples for a new project, based on historical information regarding other projects. The last chapter completes the module by adding safe scheduling analysis, based on such simulated samples. The chapter also shows how to implement safe scheduling hierarchically. Altogether, but especially in Chapters 18 and 19, the module presents a contemporary version of the PERT/CPM combination, which we also call PERT 21 (or PERT for the twenty-first century).

Network models are widely used in the formulation of resource allocation problems and sequencing problems, so it is appropriate to think of network models as fundamental in scheduling. The purpose of this chapter's introductory treatment of network models is twofold. The first objective is to describe the elements of network models: many of the scheduling problems discussed later can be visualized more clearly and analyzed more effectively with the use of network concepts. The second objective is to discuss the basic elements of CPM and PERT, which are well-known approaches to network scheduling.

CPM and PERT emerged independently in the late 1950s and are regarded as tools for planning and scheduling large, nonrepetitive projects. However, their

Principles of Sequencing and Scheduling, Second Edition. Kenneth R. Baker and Dan Trietsch.
© 2019 John Wiley & Sons, Inc. Published 2019 by John Wiley & Sons, Inc.

potential usefulness has a much broader scope. They have won rapid acceptance as practical techniques and have been employed successfully in a variety of areas, including research and development, construction, maintenance, marketing, and production.

For the purpose of using network methods in project scheduling, a *project* represents a collection of well-defined tasks called *activities*. When all of these activities are carried out, the project is completed. (In job shop terminology, a project is called a job and an activity is called an operation.) The activities of a project are subject to logical constraints, which restrict activity scheduling to feasible sequences. Within a feasible sequence, however, activities may be started and stopped independently of each other, as long as the logical constraints are not violated. The graphical representation of logical relationships among project activities is more precisely called an *activity network model*, but, for simplicity, we refer to network models. As we shall see, the network model not only depicts logical constraints, but it also provides a structure for analysis.

Section 16.2 describes the construction of network models to display logical information. Section 16.3 discusses the fundamentals of analyzing simple, deterministic networks. Section 16.4 discusses a classic trade-off involving cost and time. Section 16.5 describes the stochastic approach of PERT along with a critical look at some of its assumptions.

16.2 Logical Constraints And Network Construction

Network representations of logical constraints were introduced in Chapter 8 for describing sets of related jobs. In the same way, a network model can be used to describe the precedence relationships among activities in a project. The particular network model employed in previous chapters represented activities as nodes in the network and represented direct precedence relations as directed arcs. This type of network is called an *activity-on-node* (AON) network because of its structure. An alternative model, the *activity-on-arc* (AOA) network, is frequently employed in project scheduling.

Networks are made up of nodes and directed arcs. In an AOA network, the arcs represent activities and nodes represent events. The distinction between activities and events in AOA networks is subtle but important. Activities are processes and are associated with intervals of time over which they are performed; events are stages of accomplishment and are associated with points in time. For example, in the development of a prototype of an automobile emission control device, "testing cold weather performance" might be an activity, whereas "test completed" would be an event.

In a network, the direction of an arc indicates the direction of a precedence relation. For instance, if A directly precedes B, an appropriate AOA network representation is given in Figure 16.1. Here, event 1 (node 1) represents the start of activity A, and event 3 represents the completion of activity B. Event 2 has two interpretations: it can be considered the completion of activity A or the start of activity B. The network structure indicates that these two events are not logically distinct. In other words, whereas they may occur *temporally* at different points, they occur *logically* at the same point.

If two activities, C and D, are allowed to be concurrent, but C directly precedes E and D directly precedes E, the network representation is shown in Figure 16.2. Here, the interpretation of node 6 in logical terms is the completion of both activities C and D (or equivalently, the start of activity E, which requires that both C and D be complete). Similarly, if F directly precedes G and F directly precedes H, where G and H can be concurrent, then the network representation is shown in Figure 16.3. Here, the interpretation of node 9 in logical terms is the completion of activity F or, equivalently, the potential start of either activity G or activity H, or both.

Several conventions are usually prescribed for the construction of AOA networks. Here are the principal rules:

1) The network should have a unique starting event (a single *origin* node).
2) The network should have a unique completion event (a single *terminal* node).

Figure 16.1 Activity A directly precedes B, in an AOA representation.

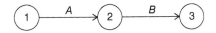

Figure 16.2 Activities C and D directly precede E, in an AOA representation.

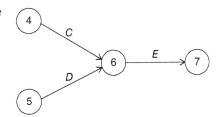

Figure 16.3 Activity F directly precedes G and H, in an AOA representation.

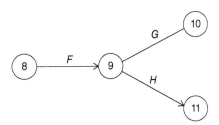

3) The nodes should be numbered so that for any activity, the completion event has a larger number than the starting event. (Such a numbering can always be found unless the network contains logical inconsistencies that would lead to circular precedence relationships.)
4) No activity should be represented by more than one arc in the network.
5) No two activities should share both a starting event and a completion event. In particular, we want to be able to identify activities by the node numbers of their starting and ending events and to do so uniquely.

Rule 5 may create a problem for the basic AOA network, as in the following example:

■ **Example 16.1** Consider the following simple project (planning and holding a fund-raising concert).

Activity	ID	Predecessors
Plan concert	A	—
Advertise	B	A
Sell tickets	C	A
Hold concert	D	B, C

Figure 16.4 shows a simple AOA network representation for the example. However, a reference to activity (2, 3) would be ambiguous: it could refer to either activity *B* or activity *C*.

For informal purposes or hand calculations, this network diagram is suffi-cient. To avoid violating Rule 5, however, we must include a dummy activity (dotted arc), as shown in Figure 16.5. The dummy activity allows the same

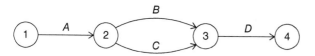

Figure 16.4 An AOA network for Example 16.1.

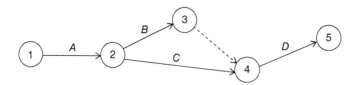

Figure 16.5 Revision of Figure 16.4, using a dummy arc.

logical relationships to be accommodated without violating Rule 5 or some other rule. No physical process corresponds to the dummy activity, but it is often necessary to use dummy activities to exhibit correct logical relationships under the standard conventions. Also, computer programs for project scheduling techniques often rely on the ability to use dummy activities.

Given these conventions, the task of constructing a suitable network requires two types of input: a detailed list of the individual activities and a specification of their precedence relations. To help provide the latter information, we answer the following questions for each activity:

Which activities precede it? (What controls its start?)
Which activities follow it? (What are its consequences?)
Which activities may be concurrent with it?

With this information available, the next step is to draw an intelligible network diagram. Often, this will be a trial-and-error process. It is desirable, but not always possible, to adhere to the following guidelines:

Avoid drawing arcs (arrows) that cross.
Draw arcs as straight lines.
Avoid too wide variation in arc lengths.
Keep the angles between arcs as large as possible.
Maintain a left-to-right component in each arc.

The use of AON networks leads to a different approach to constructing network diagrams for project scheduling. Recall that in an AON network, the nodes represent activities and the arcs represent the logical constraints. Because each arc corresponds to a direct precedence relation between two activities, we need not introduce dummy activities. For example, Figure 16.6 is the AON network for the fund-raising concert of Example 16.1.

The direct correspondence of arcs with precedence information and the observation that dummy activities appear to be unnecessary for expressing logical constraints make AON networks somewhat easier to construct than AOA networks. For this reason, when network models are used in formulating scheduling problems that contain logical constraints, we often prefer the AON type of network. Nevertheless, in practical applications of CPM and PERT, good reasons exist for using AOA networks. First, when computer programs perform the

Figure 16.6 AON network for the activities in Example 16.1.

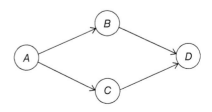

requisite calculations for large projects, the computational task can be carried out more efficiently with AOA formulations. Second, the event orientation of AOA networks can be advantageous from a project management point of view. In particular, events in the network represent milestones – points in time when project status can be conveniently updated, prospects can be reevaluated, and plans can be revised. Because of the particular usefulness of event-oriented networks in project scheduling, our coverage of CPM and PERT in the following sections emphasizes AOA networks.

16.3 Temporal Analysis of Networks

The underlying motivation of temporal analysis involves the question, "When will the project be complete?" A closely related question is, "Which activities will contribute directly to the duration of the project?" To help answer both questions, the network is first analyzed under the simplifying assumption that all activity durations are known constants, p_j.

In the standard terminology, "time" refers to a point in time and is associated with the occurrence of an event, whereas "duration" refers to an interval in time and is associated with an activity. Corresponding to each event in the network are two time values: an *early event time* (ET), which is the earliest point in time at which the event could possibly occur; and a *late event time* (LT), which is the latest point in time at which the event could possibly occur without delaying the completion of the project. These are complementary definitions, and they suggest complementary methods of calculation.

Algorithm 16.1 *Calculation of Early Event Times*

Step 1. Assign an ET of zero to the origin event.

Step 2. Using the node numbering convention of Rule 3, consider the events in numerical order. For each event, make the following calculations: (a) to the ET of each directly preceding event, add the duration of the connecting activity; (b) select the maximum of the sums calculated in (a).

Algorithm 16.2 *Calculation of Late Event Times*

Step 1. Assign an LT equal to the project due date to the terminal event. (As a default project due date, use the ET of the project completion event.)

Step 2. Consider the events in reverse numerical order. For each event, make the following calculations: (a) from the LT of each directly succeeding event, subtract the duration of the connecting activity; (b) select the minimum of the differences found in (a).

A forward pass calculates ET values, and a backward pass calculates LT values. If the project does not have an explicit due date, the backward pass is initialized by using the ET for the terminal event as the due date. Once all ET and LT values are computed, attention shifts to activity information. In particular, four quantities are calculated for each activity.

Early start time (ES): The earliest time at which the activity could possibly be started (equal to the ET of the activity's starting event).

Early finish time (EF): The earliest time at which the activity could possibly be completed (equal to the sum of the ES and the activity duration).

Late finish time (LF): The latest time at which the activity could be completed without delaying the project beyond its due date (equal to the LT of the activity's completion event).

Late start time (LS): The latest time at which the activity could be started without delaying the project beyond its due date (equal to the difference between LF and the activity duration).

■ **Example 16.2**   Consider the following project.

Activity ID	Direct predecessors	Duration
A	—	5
B	—	4
C	—	3
D	A	1
E	C	2
F	C	9
G	C	5
H	B, D, E	4
I	G	2

The network diagram corresponding to this example is shown in Figure 16.7, where each arc is labeled with both activity ID and duration. The forward and backward passes produce the ET and LT values displayed in Figure 16.8. The ET values of nodes 2 and 3 are 5 and 3, respectively, because the only predecessor of activities A and C is the start node. Node 4 then receives an ET of max$\{5 + 1, 4, 3 + 2\} = 6$. Node 5 receives an ET of $3 + 5 = 8$, and the terminal node has ET = max$\{3 + 9, 6 + 4, 8 + 2\} = 12$. Implementing Algorithm 16.2, we calculate LT for nodes 5 and 4 as $12 - 2 = 10$ and $12 - 4 = 8$, respectively. Node 3 then receives LT = min$\{8 - 2, 12 - 9, 10 - 5\} = 3$. Node 2 is addressed next with LT = $8 - 1 = 7$, and finally node 1 receives LT = min$\{8 - 4, 3 - 3, 7 - 5\} = 0$. (Because no project due date was given, the LT for event 6 is taken to be 12, its ET. For this reason, we can anticipate that the LT of node 1 should be 0.)

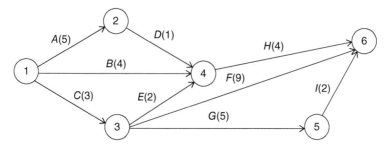

Figure 16.7 Network model for the example project.

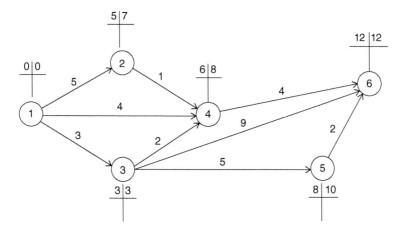

Figure 16.8 Network for the example project with ET and LT shown for each event.

One of the motivating questions has now been answered. Assuming that activity durations are deterministic, the ET of the terminal event represents the minimum project length. The project can be completed by this time provided sufficient resources are available. To address the second question, it is necessary to understand what accounts for the project length.

Activities that contribute directly to the duration of the project are called *critical*. Any delay in a critical activity will ultimately cause a delay in the completion of the project. The chain of arcs formed by the critical activities is called the *critical path*; it is the longest path from the origin event to the terminal event and may not be unique. In Example 16.2 the critical path is *C–F*. Because the logical constraints require that the activities on the critical path be carried out sequentially, event 6 cannot be realized prior to time 12. In general, if the project is to be completed by the ET of the terminal event, we cannot tolerate any delay along the critical path.

For noncritical activities, however, some scheduling flexibility exists. Consider the scheduling of activities G and I in Example 16.2. Activity G can start no earlier than time 3, and to avoid delaying the project, activity I must be completed by time 12. Because seven units of time are required to carry out activities G and I in sequence, and because an interval of length nine is available, some flexibility remains. The two extra units of time can be absorbed before or after either activity, or perhaps in some combination, as shown in Figure 16.9. This kind of flexibility is called *float* or *slack*. Along the critical path (or critical paths, if there are several), no float exists, whereas along other paths, some amount of float occurs. To quantify the scheduling flexibility, we can use various measures of float.

To describe the various measures of float concisely, consider activity j and let

p_j = duration of activity j

i = start node of activity j

k = end node of activity j

ET_i = early event time corresponding to node i, etc.

Then the four measures of float are

$$\text{Total float (TF)} = LT_k - ET_i - p_j$$

$$\text{Safety float (SF)} = LT_k - LT_i - p_j$$

$$\text{Free float (FF)} = ET_k - ET_i - p_j$$

$$\text{Independent float (IF)} = \max\{0, ET_k - LT_i - p_j\}$$

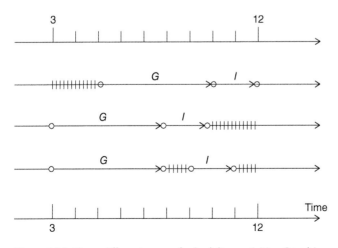

Figure 16.9 Three different ways of scheduling activities G and I.

Of the four measures, the most frequently used is total float, which – as observed above – actually measures float along a path. The total float represents the delay in start time that could be absorbed by an activity without delaying the project, assuming no other activity on the path is delayed further. The safety float is similar but assumes that the direct predecessors of an activity have already been delayed as much as possible. Free float measures the delay in start time that could be absorbed by an activity without preventing any other activity from being started at its own ES. Finally, independent float represents the delay in start time that can be absorbed by an activity unconditionally – that is, independent of any scheduling decisions made elsewhere in the network. The calculations of the four types of float for Example 16.2 are summarized in Table 16.1. The critical activities are identified by the condition TF = 0.

Returning to the two questions posed at the outset of this section, we can see how the temporal analysis of a network provides answers. If we assume that activity durations are known constants, then the duration of a project is equal to the length of the longest path in the network. The critical activities, those that lie along this longest path, are the activities that contribute directly to project length. Any delay in a critical activity will lead to a delay in the project. Furthermore, for noncritical activities, the amount of scheduling flexibility available and the nature of that flexibility can be represented by the various measures of activity float.

The assumption of constant, deterministic activity durations on which temporal analysis is based certainly has some shortcomings. To address these limitations, and to develop more practical forms of network analysis, the basic project model has historically been extended in two important ways. One (associated with CPM) treats each activity duration as a function of the resources

Table 16.1

Activity	TF	SF	FF	IF
A	2	2	0	0
B	4	4	2	2
C	0	0	0	0
D	2	0	0	0
E	3	3	1	1
F	0	0	0	0
G	2	2	0	0
H	2	0	2	0
I	2	0	2	0

applied, leading to a resource allocation problem in which resource levels (and therefore activity durations) are decisions. The other extension (associated with PERT) allows activity durations to be probabilistic and answers the motivating questions in probabilistic terms. These extensions are discussed in the next two sections.

16.4 The Time/Cost Trade-off

The first generalization of the basic model treats activity durations as decision variables. The premise is that activity durations can be shortened by the application of greater amounts of labor, capital, or both. More simply, this means that the expenditure of more money can reduce the duration of an activity. A time/cost trade-off therefore exists for each activity in the project, and an aggregate trade-off exists between project duration and project expense. Decreasing the project duration by spending more money is also known as *crashing*.

To illustrate the structure of a time/cost model, suppose that the relationship between activity duration and cost satisfies the following properties:

1) Each activity duration is a linear function of the costs incurred in carrying out the activity.
2) Each activity has a minimum feasible duration and a maximum feasible duration.

Under these conditions, the time/cost trade-off for a given activity can be represented by the graph shown in Figure 16.10, using the following notation:

a = minimum feasible duration

b = maximum feasible duration

p = activity duration

c = cost per unit time of expediting the activity

K = total cost incurred in carrying out the activity

c_0 = vertical intercept

Within this framework, it is possible to formulate several problems in finding minimum-cost project schedules.

Suppose that, in addition to the activity-related costs described in Figure 16.10, there is also a fixed overhead cost, c_f, incurred on a daily basis until the project is completed. Example 16.3 illustrates the decision procedure involved in finding a minimum-cost schedule.

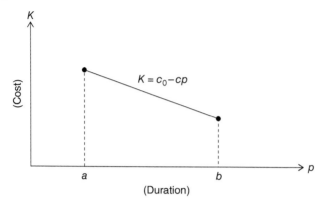

Figure 16.10 The time/cost function for an individual activity.

■ **Example 16.3**   Consider the following project, where the fixed cost $c_f =$ $450 per day.

Activity ID	Predecessors	a_j	b_j	c_j	c_{0j}
A	—	1 day	3	$400	$1400
B	A	3	7	100	1100
C	A	2	4	400	1800
D	C	2	5	200	1300

First, suppose that all activities are scheduled at their maximum durations, with a total cost of $6500 (activity A costs $1400 − 3 × $400 = $200, and similarly, we obtain 400, 200, 300, and $5400 for B, C, D, and the fixed costs). The corresponding network diagram, displayed on a time scale, is shown in Figure 16.11a. To reduce fixed costs, a reduction must be made in the length of the project. In other words, the length of the critical path (A–C–D) must be shortened in a manner that reduces costs. Among the critical activities, D is the least expensive to expedite. A two-day reduction in its duration (costing $400) achieves a reduction in overhead costs of $900. The net reduction is $500, reducing the total cost from 6500 to $6000. At this stage, activity B is also critical (see Figure 16.11b) and the alternatives for reducing the length of the project are

1) Expedite activity A at $400 per day.
2) Expedite activities B and C at $500 per day.
3) Expedite activities B and D at $300 per day.

Clearly, the third alternative is most desirable, but a reduction of only one day is possible, because activity D must be at least two days in length (Figure 16.11c).

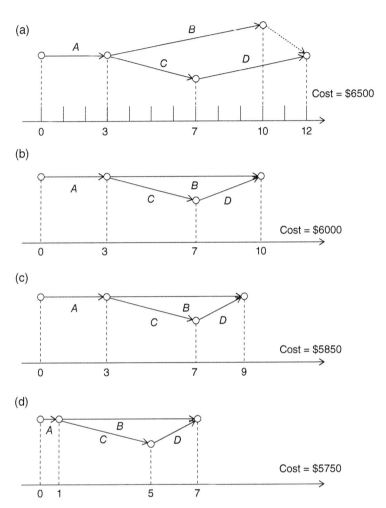

Figure 16.11 A sequence of schedule modifications in Example 16.3.

This change costs $300 but saves $450, leading to a total cost of $5850. A further improvement requires alternative 1 in the above list. Activity *A* can be scheduled at its minimal duration, and the resulting total cost is lowered to $5750 (Figure 16.11d). The cost of a further one-day reduction in the project length, achieved by crashing activities *B* and *C*, would more than offset the savings in overhead cost; therefore, the cost of $5750 is optimal.

As this simple example illustrates, when variable activity costs and fixed project costs are of concern, it can be expected that total cost will exhibit a U shape, resembling the function sketched in Figure 16.12. In such a case, finding an

Project cost

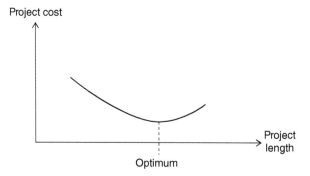

Figure 16.12 The total cost curve.

optimal project length – and an associated project schedule – is a meaningful optimization problem.

For larger projects, the heuristic solution method illustrated above will seldom be practicable. With a great many more activities present, there will be more stages at which several paths are critical. The identification of all alternatives for reducing project length in such cases can be a formidable task, not to mention the large number of stages that might also occur. Furthermore, as we progress through a process of greedily collecting the best crashing opportunities, as described above, we may find it necessary to reverse an early crashing decision. Therefore, solutions to large-scale time/cost problems rely heavily on more sophisticated techniques.

When the cost functions are linear, as in Figure 16.10, the problem can be solved by linear programming. Let activity j be characterized by start node i and completion node k. In other words, activity j can also be referred to as activity (i, k). The basic decision variables are the activity durations or, equivalently, the times at which the nodes in the network are realized. Let

N = number of nodes in the network
x_i = early event time of node i (ET_i)
p_{ik} = duration of activity (i, k)

Then the length of the project is $(x_N - x_1)$ or simply x_N if x_1 is taken to be zero. The two feasibility constraints on activity durations may be expressed as

$p_{ik} \leq b_{ik}$ for each activity (i,k)

$p_{ik} \geq a_{ik}$ for each activity (i,k)

and the relationship between ETs and activity durations may be written

$x_k - p_{ik} - x_i \geq 0$, for each activity (i,k)

The objective function is simply the sum of project costs and activity costs, or

$$c_f x_N + \sum_j \left(c_{0j} - c_j p_j\right)$$

Because the sum of the c_{0j} values is a constant, the objective is essentially to minimize $c_f x_N - \sum_j c_j p_j$. The full linear program, with activities represented by double subscripts (i, k) is shown below:

Minimize $\quad c_f x_N - \sum_{(i,k)} c_{ik} p_{ik}$

Subject to

$$x_k - p_{ik} - x_i \ge 0, \quad \text{for all } (i,k)$$
$$p_{ik} \le b_{ik}, \quad\quad\quad \text{for all } (i,k)$$
$$p_{ik} \ge a_{ik}, \quad\quad\quad \text{for all } (i,k)$$
$$x_i \ge 0, \quad\quad\quad\quad \text{for all } i$$
$$p_{ik} \ge 0, \quad\quad\quad\quad \text{for all } (i,k)$$

16.5 Traditional Probabilistic Network Analysis

Historically, PERT included the earliest practical modeling of stochastic processing times in scheduling applications, including rudimentary safe scheduling. PERT was devised for the US Navy, and its first application was an R&D project related to the development of the Polaris missile. By nature, development projects involve highly uncertain activity times. In the original application, many activities were subcontracted to external contractors, so the activity durations were perceived to be stochastically independent and not subject to simple crashing. Completion times, however, were known to be dependent because a delay in one completion time can cause delays downstream. The challenge was to model this type of stochastic behavior. However, to keep the framework simple, the analysis essentially (and intentionally) ignored the dependencies created by the precedence relations. This simplification has been universally adopted and practiced for many years, although it has also been increasingly criticized. In this section, we describe the simplified framework and some of the criticisms.

16.5.1 The PERT Method

Once again, the motivating question is, "When will the project be complete?" The objective of probabilistic analysis is to answer this question with explicit recognition that activity durations are uncertain. Let

p_j = duration of activity j (treated as a random variable)
μ_j = mean of p_j, or $E[p_j]$
σ_j^2 = variance of p_j

The analysis therefore recognizes that p_j is a random variable and begins with the assumption that μ_j and σ_j^2 are known. The PERT model requires two basic assumptions:

A1. The activities in the network are statistically independent.
A2. The critical path in the network (as defined below) contains a large enough number of activities so that the central limit theorem applies when analyzing its length.

The mean of a sum of random variables is equal to the sum of the means. For independent random variables, the variance of a sum also equals the sum of the variances. Furthermore, the central limit theorem states that (under mild regularity conditions) the distribution of the sum of a large number of independent random variables is approximately normal, and the approximation improves as the number of components in the sum grows. Therefore, if L_π denotes the duration along path π in the network and if there are many activities on the path, then L_π can be treated as a normal random variable with mean

$$\mu_\pi = \sum_{j \in \pi} \mu_j \tag{16.1}$$

and variance

$$\sigma_\pi^2 = \sum_{j \in \pi} \sigma_j^2 \tag{16.2}$$

This analysis ignores the possibility that some activities along the path will be delayed by activities outside the path. Starting with a deterministic counterpart approach, PERT identifies the critical path by taking μ_j to be the duration of activity j and performing the deterministic temporal analysis described in Section 16.3. However, depending on the realizations of the stochastic elements, this path is not certain to be critical. Therefore, we also refer to it as the *nominal* critical path.

Let λ denote the nominal critical path, and let L_λ denote its length – that is, L_λ is the nominal project makespan. PERT treats L_λ as having an approximately normal distribution with parameters μ_λ and σ_λ^2, calculated by Eqs. (16.1) and (16.2) with $\pi = \lambda$. Accordingly, the distribution of the project length is taken to be normal with parameters μ_λ and σ_λ^2. The motivating question posed earlier can then be answered in probabilistic terms. If we use the PERT approximation, the probability that the project will be completed by a due date d is

$$\Pr\{L_\lambda \le d\} = \Phi\left[\frac{d - \mu_\lambda}{\sigma_\lambda}\right]$$

where $\Phi(z)$ denotes the cumulative distribution for a standard normal random variable.

To support this analysis, the method relies on knowledge of μ_λ and σ_j^2. PERT was developed under the assumption that no data will be available to estimate these parameters, and it may be difficult for even knowledgeable personnel to provide good estimates. For such situations, PERT provides a mechanism for obtaining μ_j and σ_j^2 from subjective estimates that were considered easier to obtain in practice. For a given activity, let

a = an optimistic duration; that is, an estimate of the activity duration under the most favorable conditions
b = a pessimistic duration; that is, an estimate of the activity duration under the least favorable conditions
m = the most likely duration

These three parameters are incorporated in a beta distribution as a probabilistic model for the duration of the activity. (The original choice of the beta distribution was arbitrary but never used explicitly in the model except for estimation purposes. Nonetheless, it unduly influenced subsequent research and development for a very long time.) Parameters a and b are the minimum and maximum values of the distribution, and m is the mode. Depending on the choice of those parameters, the beta distribution can be symmetric or else skewed in either direction, as depicted in Figure 16.13. Based on its professional judgment, the original PERT team recommended the following calculations to approximate μ_j and σ_j^2:

$$\mu_j = \frac{a + 4m + b}{6} \tag{16.3}$$

$$\sigma_j = \frac{b - a}{6} \tag{16.4}$$

Both of these formulas are merely convenient rules of thumb. Suppose that we consider the range between a and b as 100%, with $a = 0\%$ and $b = 100\%$. If the mode is between 5 and 95%, then a beta distribution exists that approximately satisfies Eqs. (16.3) and (16.4). On this scale, a mode of 50% yields a symmetric beta distribution, and any other value gives rise to a skewed distribution. Even when μ_j and σ_j^2 are not known at the outset, PERT offers simple calculations for the two parameters from estimates of a, m, and b. In addition, perhaps because PERT was originally developed for a project where activities were assigned to independent contractors, an important assumption was that activity durations were statistically independent. (Historical evidence indicates that this assumption has often caused major problems. More typically, activity durations are positively correlated.)

(a)

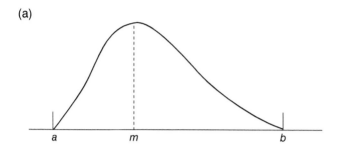

(b)

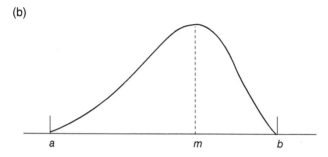

Figure 16.13 The density functions of two beta distributions, (a) skewed to the right and (b) skewed to the left.

■ Example 16.4 Consider the following project, and suppose that we wish to estimate the probability that the project will be completed by time 15.

Activity	Predecessors	a_j	m_j	b_j	μ_j	σ_j^2
A	—	2	4	12	5	2.78
B	—	3	6	9	6	1.00
C	A	1	2	9	3	1.78
D	A	1	4	7	4	1.00
E	B	1	2	3	2	0.11
F	B	4	7	10	7	1.00
G	C	1	2	9	3	1.78
H	D, E	4	5	12	6	1.78
I	F	1	3	5	3	0.44

We illustrate the PERT calculations for Example 16.4, where the last two columns in the table follow Eqs. (16.3) and (16.4) using the given values of a, m, and *b.* The next step is to construct the network diagram and label activity *j* with its mean duration, μ_j, as shown in Figure 16.14. Then, by using these mean values, we can identify the nominal critical path as *B–F–I*. From Eqs. (16.1) and (16.2), we find that the length of the path *B–F–I* has a mean of 6 + 7 + 3 = 16 and a variance of 1.00 + 1.00 + 0.44 = 2.44. If we use the probabilistic characteristics of this path as a model for the project duration, then under the independence assumption, the probability that the project will be completed by time 15 becomes

$$\Pr\{L_\lambda \le 15\} = \Phi\left[\frac{15-16}{2.44^{0.5}}\right] \approx 0.26$$

In summary, PERT recognizes that the duration of the project is a random variable and that questions about the completion of the project can be answered only in probabilistic terms. The PERT approach utilizes mean values and deterministic analysis to identify the critical path, λ. Then, assumptions A1 and A2 are invoked to characterize the length of this path, L_λ. The properties of the random variable L_λ are then substituted for the duration of the project to make statements about project completion. Finally, where information about the duration of individual activities is scarce, PERT uses a model that is loosely associated with the beta distribution to generate means and variances for activity durations. Although many theoretical objections can be raised to PERT, in contemporary terms, its practical value has proven to be very real. In many cases, the advent of PERT made available a powerful planning tool when no comparable tool had formerly existed. Furthermore, the roots of safe scheduling can be traced back to the original PERT model. Also, in the years since PERT was introduced, several refinements have been developed to compensate for some of its theoretical shortcomings.

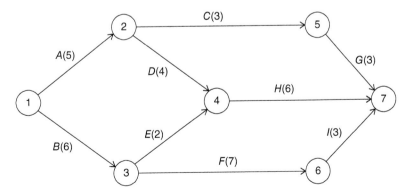

Figure 16.14 Deterministic analysis using mean values, for Example 16.4.

16.5.2 Theoretical Limitations of PERT

The objections that are most often raised about PERT fall into two categories: problems arising at the project level and problems arising at the individual activity level. Perhaps the most popular indictment of PERT is that its estimate of mean project duration is biased downward. Whereas the true mean project duration takes the form $E[\max_\pi\{L_\pi\}]$, PERT substitutes $\max_\pi\{E[L_\pi]\}$. Because the maximum function is convex, a positive Jensen gap is likely to exist.

The extent of the error that is involved in this calculation depends on the structure of the network and the properties of activity distributions. For example, suppose that a project consists of four different path lengths that are independent and have normal distributions. (This structure occurs only if the project is composed of four independent chains of activities that share start and finish events.) Figure 16.15a depicts a case where the length of the nominal critical path is likely to be exceeded by another path length. In that case, a large Jensen gap may be expected. By contrast, Figure 16.15b depicts a case where the nominal critical path is very likely to be the longest, as all other paths are practically certain to complete earlier. In this case, the Jensen gap is negligible.

Under the independence assumption, the distribution of project completion time in a series–parallel network structure can be calculated by a decomposition procedure akin to the one illustrated in Section 8.3. However, most project networks include activities that cross from one path to another and are therefore difficult to analyze. The most basic network structure that resists analysis is the

(a)

(b)

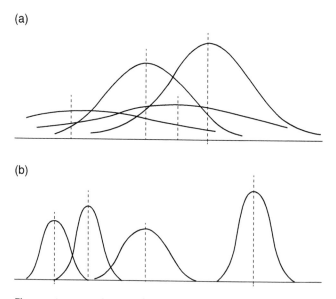

Figure 16.15 Distribution of individual paths in a network for two hypothetical projects.

interdictive graph, shown in Figure 16.16. Any project network that has the interdictive graph embedded in it cannot be decomposed. In such cases, only bounds or approximations can be obtained analytically, and simulation remains the best approach to estimating completion times. Simulation was proposed for this purpose as early as 1963, but at the time it had not become an effective tool. Today, with much more powerful and ubiquitous computers, simulation provides a practical resolution of the Jensen gap issue. Serendipitously, simulation is also an excellent way to deal with dependent processing times.

A second shortcoming in PERT concerns its identification of critical activities. By using a deterministic counterpart to identify the critical path, PERT necessarily partitions the activities into two distinct subsets: the critical activities and the noncritical activities. Because the network is probabilistic, however, it is possible that an activity that lies on the nominal critical path may not lie on the longest path in a particular realization of the project. In fact, that is precisely why the Jensen gap arises. Furthermore, the two-way partition in PERT may not reflect the likelihood that the various activities will be critical. For instance, in Example 16.4, PERT identifies activities *B*, *F*, and *I* as critical. Nevertheless, an intuitive argument can be made that *B* is somehow "more critical" than *F* because *B* is critical whenever *F* is critical and *B* is also critical when *B–E–H* turns out to be the longest path. Define the *criticality* (or *criticality index*) of an activity as the probability that it will lie on the longest path. (For example, when we use sample-based analysis, the criticality of an activity is estimated by the proportion of times in which it is on the longest path.) The problem with the deterministic counterpart analysis of PERT is that it leads to criticalities of

Figure 16.16 The interdictive graph.

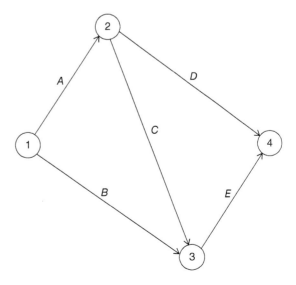

either 0 or 1, whereas criticalities should ideally be probabilities. Moreover, the PERT substitute is not even an effective rounding approach, as we demonstrate with an example.

■ **Example 16.5**   Consider the following project.

Activity	Predecessors	a_j	m_j	b_j
A	—	7	9	11
B	—	7	8	10
C	A	1	3	5
D	A	1	3	7
E	B	1	3	7
F	B	1	3	5
G	C	1	1	1
H	F	1	1	1

The network depiction of this project is given in Figure 16.17. We assume that a_j, m_j, and b_j are each realized with probability 1/3. (We are not using the beta approximation, opting for a discrete distribution instead. We can retain the names a_j, m_j, and b_j, however, because the likelihood of m_j is still maximal.) One feature in this example is that parallel critical paths exist under some realizations. For instance, there is a probability of $1/27^2 = 1/729$ that the project duration will be 9, which requires all the realizations to be a_j. In such a case, both A and B are critical, but they clearly cannot belong to the same path. We then allocate the criticality to the two paths (and to the activities along

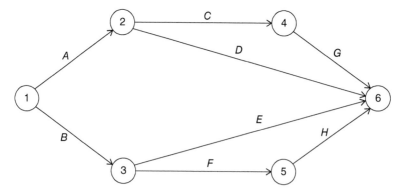

Figure 16.17 Network representation for Example 16.5.

Table 16.2

Activity	Criticality
A	0.58
B	0.42
C	0.27
D	0.30
E	0.24
F	0.19
G	0.27
H	0.19

the paths) equally. This allocation would not be necessary when continuous distributions are involved, in which case the probability of two paths attaining the same length is zero. Using this allocation rule, Table 16.2 lists the criticalities of Example 16.5 obtained by enumerating all 729 possible realizations.

The following properties emerge.

1) Although the nominal critical path is A–C–G, the analysis reveals that A–C–G will be the longest path with a probability of 0.27, which is less than the probability that A–D will be the longest path (0.30).
2) Although the PERT method identifies activity C as critical, it is on the longest path with a probability of only 0.27.
3) Although the PERT method identifies activity B as noncritical, it is on the actual longest path with a probability of 0.42.

The example demonstrates that we cannot compute the true criticality indices using PERT. Furthermore, the activities along a single path may be critical to different degrees, suggesting that criticality is more a trait of individual activities than of entire paths. Unfortunately, the difficulties inherent in a mathematical analysis of the problem are substantial, and simulation is often more suitable.

A third problem with the PERT calculations involves its assumption A1 that the activity durations are independent. A comprehensive analytical treatment of more general situations requires a model for dependence among activities, and it may be quite difficult to formulate (much less analyze) such a model. However, linear association provides a first approximation for practical dependence. Field data shows that ignoring dependence is more likely to cause disappointment with project performance than the Jensen gap (even though the latter has received more attention in the literature). The same data suggests most projects can be modeled well by using linear association or, in some cases, by a mixture of two linearly associated processing time distributions. (One advantage of simulation is that it can accommodate dependence, including models based on linear association or mixtures.)

At the level of individual activities in the network, another set of PERT assumptions can be challenged.

1) There is no reason to assume that the true form of the distribution of an activity duration follows a beta distribution. (Empirical evidence supports the assumption that it is lognormal instead.)
2) Regardless of the true distribution, its mean and variance may not be those prescribed in Eqs. (16.3) and (16.4). (Indeed, the empirical evidence suggests that variance is often higher than can be modeled by the beta approximation used in PERT.)
3) The estimates on which the entire procedure is based (i.e. estimates of a, m, and b) may be inaccurate. (Again, empirical evidence shows that such estimates are highly unreliable.)

These issues reflect a deeper problem: PERT is based on an implicit assumption that projects are completely unique, and therefore all activities are unique. As such, historical experience with other projects is assumed irrelevant. That assumption led to the use of subjective estimates. But whereas projects are sometimes unique, they are rarely unique when we drill down to the activity level. For instance, architecturally designed buildings are unique, but they typically comprise standard components. Therefore, activity distributions may often be estimated from historical data or historical experience in a reliable manner. Subjective estimates are justified only when such history does not exist, and even then there is no particular reason to use the PERT method: it has dominated merely because it was the first approach proposed for this purpose, and no better way was known. In reality, the estimates of a, m, and b could be subject to political and psychological biases, and even though the original PERT paper suggested a program of calibration – which would have resolved some of these issues – that recommendation had been virtually ignored for decades.

16.6 Summary

Network models are building blocks for scheduling and are especially popular for project planning. Because logical constraints often appear as basic elements in scheduling problems, the ability to visualize and describe logical relationships with network structures is a fundamental aspect of scheduling. We encountered AON networks earlier in the book, but in this chapter we relied on the AOA network as a model for precedence relationships.

As suggested earlier, the significance of CPM and PERT lies primarily in their role as useful tools for project planning and project management. The historical success of these network-based techniques in finding rapid acceptance among practitioners can be attributed to several factors. First, the basic model provides information in a useful form. It analyzes the project in a way that makes pertinent information explicit and that can be used as a basis for communication throughout the administrative organization. In addition, the model accommodates sufficient detail so that important aspects of the project will not be overlooked, and it provides a framework for testing and evaluating alternative project management strategies. The methodology also helps managers focus on what's important (the critical path) and delegate other issues.

A focus on the critical path should include questioning the assumptions behind the model. Specifically, the precedence relationships that dictate the critical path should be examined. One anecdote involves the construction of a skyscraper, where installing windows was the last activity on the critical path. When asked why windows could not be installed on lower floors, while the upper floors were completed, the answer was that experience revealed that windows might be broken due to mishaps during construction. However, the expected savings by avoiding such breakage did not even nearly justify the delay in project completion.

The basic aim of CPM and PERT is to answer two questions: (1) When will the project be complete? and (2) Which activities will be critical? The answers are straightforward using a deterministic perspective and CPM, but the PERT approach to the stochastic problem is open to criticism. Regarding question (1), the main criticism is that the PERT answer is biased due to the inherent Jensen gap. Regarding question (2), the main criticism is that the PERT answer is oversimplified, and in some cases could be misleading. Of course, the fact that CPM assumes deterministic times is even more open to criticism.

Additional criticisms have been offered regarding the PERT model for activity durations. According to Woolsey (1992), estimates of the mode are relatively easy to elicit (although this does not imply that they are necessarily accurate and precise), but when asking for estimates of a and b, we often get highly unreliable answers based on political calculations of the acceptability of the answer. Woolsey's evidence may be anecdotal, but similarly troubling criticism comes from generic research by Tversky and Kahneman (1974). They discovered that people, even experts, tend to greatly underestimate the necessary range between a and b: when asked to provide a confidence interval of 98%, respondents come up with intervals that miss the mark in about 30% of the cases. In our context, that error is roughly equivalent to estimating a confidence interval of about two standard deviations rather than six. Tversky and Kahneman speak to honest mistakes, whereas Woolsey questions the sincerity of the estimates. In combination, these two causes could inject serious error into the picture. The observation (made earlier) that the independence assumption is not reliable only exacerbates the problem.

The basic versions of CPM and PERT address two central aspects of project planning by supplying information about the length of the project and by identifying the particular activities on which the project duration depends. The simplest approach to these topics is through temporal analysis of deterministic networks with constant activity durations. The analysis is enriched by the two extensions introduced in this chapter: the time/cost trade-off and stochastic analysis of project timing.

More advanced models allow different kinds of precedence constraints, which make it possible to model start lags and stop lags between activities (see Chapter 10). Even more complex networks have a stochastic structure, allowing activities to be repeated due to quality problems or skipped until more information becomes available. We recommend approaching such network models by simulation.

Exercises

16.1 The following is a list of logical relations among a set of project tasks.

Predecessor	Successor
A	D
A	E
A	F
B	D
B	F
C	E
C	F

a) Draw an AON representation of the project network.
b) Draw an AOA representation of the project network.

16.2 The table below describes the elements of a project.

Task	Predecessors	Duration
A	—	5
B	—	9
C	—	8
D	A	6

(Continued)

Task	Predecessors	Duration
E	A	10
F	C	7
G	C	3
H	D,E	9
I	G	8
J	B,F	10

a) Draw an AON representation of the project network.
b) Draw an AOA representation of the project network.
c) Calculate the length of the critical path.
d) List the critical activities.

16.3 Revisit the project of the previous exercise. For each activity in the project:
a) Calculate the total float.
b) Calculate the safety float.
c) Calculate the free float.
d) Calculate the independent float.

16.4 The table below describes the elements of a project.

Task	Predecessors	Duration
A	—	5
B	—	9
C	—	8
D	A	6
E	A	10
F	C	7
G	B,C,D	3
H	C,D,E	12
I	E,G	8
J	B,D,F	10

a) Draw an AON representation of the project network.
b) Draw an AOA representation of the project network.

    c) Calculate the length of the critical path.
    d) List the critical activities.

16.5 Revisit the project of the previous exercise. For each activity in the project:
    a) Calculate the total float.
    b) Calculate the safety float.
    c) Calculate the free float.
    d) Calculate the independent float.

16.6 For the project of Example 16.4, identify all the embedded interdictive graphs.

16.7 Show that $TF \geq SF \geq IF$ and $TF \geq FF \geq IF$, but SF and FF are not ordered.

16.8 The table below describes the elements of a project.

Task	Predecessors	a	m	b
A	—	1	4	7
B	—	1	5	9
C	A	3	6	9
D	B	1	2	3
E	A	1	2	9
F	C,D	2	4	6
G	C,D,E	2	9	10
H	F	2	2	2

    a) Draw an AOA representation of the project network.
    b) Using PERT, calculate the mean length of the critical path.
    c) Identify which activities are critical.
    d) Find the probability that the project will be completed by time 20.

16.9 The table below describes the elements of a project. The project contains six activities, each represented by its start node and finish node in the network diagram. Each activity duration follows a normal duration, and each can be shortened to its minimum duration, both measured in days. The daily cost of shortening each activity is listed in the last column.

Start node	Finish node	Normal	Minimum	Cost
1	2	9	6	20
1	3	8	5	25
1	4	15	10	30
2	4	5	3	10
3	4	10	6	15
4	5	2	1	40

a) Draw an AOA representation of the project network.
b) What is the normal project length and the minimum project length?
c) Find the minimum cost of completing the project at each possible length in the interval represented by the answers in (b).
d) Suppose that overhead costs amount to 60 per day and that total project costs are the sum of overhead costs and crashing costs. For each of the project lengths in (c), find the total project cost.

16.10 Build a simulation model for the project in Example 16.4, but replace each beta distribution by a normal distribution with the same mean and variance.
a) Estimate the mean and variance of the project duration.
b) Estimate the probability that the project will be completed by time 15.
c) Estimate the criticality of each activity.

Bibliography

Baker, K.R. (1974). *Introduction to Sequencing and Scheduling*. Hoboken, NJ: Wiley.

Clark, C.E. (1961). The greatest of a finite set of random variables. *Operations Research* 9: 145–162.

Clark, C.E. (1962). The PERT model for the distribution of an activity time. *Operations Research* 10: 405–406.

Elmaghraby, S.E. (1977). *Activity Networks: Project Planning and Control by Network Models*. Hoboken, NJ: Wiley.

Fulkerson, D.R. (1961). A network flow computation for project cost curves. *Management Science* 7 (2): 167–178.

Kelley, J.E. (1961). Critical-path planning and scheduling: mathematical basis. *Operations Research* 9 (3): 296–320.

Levy, F.K. and Wiest, J.D. (1969). *A Management Guide to PERT/CPM*. Englewood Cliffs, NJ: Prentice Hall.

MacCrimmon, K.R. and Ryavec, C.A. (1964). An analytical study of the PERT assumptions. *Operations Research* 12 (1): 16–37.

Malcolm, D.G., Roseboom, J.H., Clark, C.E., and Fazar, W. (1959). Application of a technique for a research and development program evaluation. *Operations Research* 7: 646–669.

Pritsker, A.A.B. (1966). *GERT: Graphical Evaluation and Review Technique, Memorandum RM-4973-NASA*. Santa Monica, CA: The Rand Corporation.

Tversky, A. and Kahneman, D. (1974). Judgment under uncertainty: heuristics and biases. *Science* 185: 1124–1131.

Van Slyke, R.M. (1963). Monte Carlo methods and the PERT problem. *Operations Research* 11 (5): 839–860.

Woolsey, R.E. (1992). The fifth column: the PERT that never was or data collection as an optimizer. *Interfaces* 22 (3): 112–114.

17

Resource-Constrained Project Scheduling

17.1 Introduction

In this chapter, we synthesize much of the previous material to address the deterministic resource-constrained project scheduling model. Later we discuss stochastic counterpart models, briefly. Recall from Chapter 1 that scheduling decisions are generally subject to both precedence constraints and resource constraints. The resource-constrained project scheduling model contains both types of constraints. The preceding chapters have dealt with a variety of situations in which one or both of these types of constraints are relaxed or at least simplified. In a sense, the difficulties in those simpler problems are superimposed in resource-constrained project scheduling.

A general precedence structure accommodates arbitrary precedence constraints, such as those found in the network models of Chapter 16. In that analysis, however, the critical path calculations assume that resources of the appropriate type and amount are sufficiently available, so resource capacities are never binding on scheduling decisions. Chapter 8 covered some problems involving precedence constraints, but with only one resource (machine). In flow shop and job shop problems, where more general resource models apply, precedence relations are restricted to special structures.

A general resource structure contains multiple units of each of several different resources. Chapter 9 introduced models with resource parallelism but only for one resource type, and the multiple-resource models of the flow shop and the job shop contain only one unit of each resource. The extension to parallel resource structure involves combinatorial problems in a whole new dimension.

The relation of this topic to the material in earlier chapters can therefore be interpreted in two ways. First, the resource-constrained project scheduling problem can be formulated by adding explicit resource requirements and resource capacities to the basic network model of CPM and PERT. Alternatively, the problem can be formulated by allowing general precedence structures in the job shop model and replacing machines by machine groups, for parallelism. In essence, a project is a single but complex job, and project activities are analogous to job shop operations. We cover the job shop perspective first, to stress that the philosophy of solving job shop problems carries over to project scheduling.

Project scheduling has important applications, and in practice, such problems are almost always analyzed using heuristic procedures. For that reason, we ultimately emphasize simple heuristics rather than optimization approaches.

17.2 Extending the Job Shop Model

In the terminology of network models, we can state the problem as scheduling a project consisting of several activities in the presence of limited resources. The purpose of this section is to show how the job shop approach of Chapter 14 can be adapted to the resource-constrained project scheduling problem, in which general precedence structures and general resource structures apply.

To begin, suppose that each activity requires a specific resource and a single unit of each resource is available. In other words, two activities that require the same resource cannot be scheduled in parallel. Let

$$P(j) = \text{the set of all direct predecessors of activity } j$$

$$S(j) = \text{the set of all direct successors of activity } j$$

$$|P(j)| = \text{the number of elements in } P(j)$$

$$R_j = \text{the resource type required by activity } j$$

Also, let n denote the total number of activities to be scheduled, and let m denote the number of resource types.

The concepts of schedule classification carry over directly from the job shop discussion. Therefore, where regular measures of performance are concerned, it is sufficient to examine active schedules in the search for an optimum. In this context, an active partial schedule is a feasible schedule for a subset of the activities with the property that no scheduled activity can start earlier without delaying some other activity in the partial schedule. As in Chapter 14, PS(k) refers to a partial schedule containing k activities. For a given partial schedule, let u_j denote the number of activities in $P(j)$ that is contained in the partial schedule. Then the set SA(k) of schedulable activities corresponding to a given PS(k) is defined by

$$SA(k) = \{j \mid u_j = |P(j)| \text{ for } j \notin PS(k)\}$$

In words, after completing the scheduled activities in PS(k), any unscheduled activity for which all direct predecessors are scheduled is a *schedulable activity*.

Given an active partial schedule PS(k) and an activity j in the corresponding set SA(k), the conditional early start and early finish times associated with activity j are defined, respectively, by

$$ES_j = \max\left\{\left\{\max\{\{C_i | i\epsilon P(j)\}\}, \max\{C_i | i\epsilon PS(k) \text{ and } R_i = R_j\}\right\}\right.$$
$$EF_j = ES_j + p_j$$

The formula for ES_j reflects the fact that an activity's start time is dictated by both precedence and resource constraints. When resource constraints apply, ES_j and EF_j are defined with respect to a given partial schedule. As a result, activity j may appear in several of the schedulable sets SA(k) that occur successively in the construction of a complete schedule, and the associated ES_j (and EF_j) can change as those schedulable sets expand. Specifically, ES_j may change whenever the resource that activity j requires is engaged by another activity that has been appended to the partial schedule.

When arbitrary precedence structures are introduced into the job shop model, the procedure for generating all active schedules is a straightforward extension of Algorithm 14.1, as given below.

Algorithm 17.1 *Active Schedule Generation*

Step 1. Let $k = 0$ and begin with PS(k) as the null partial schedule. Initially, SA(k) includes all operations with no predecessors.

Step 2. Determine $EF^* = \min_{j\epsilon SA(k)}\{EF_j\}$ and the resource type R^* on which EF^* could be realized.

Step 3. For each activity $j \epsilon$ SA(k) that requires resource type R^* and for which $ES_j < EF^*$, create a new partial schedule in which activity j is added to PS(k) and started at time ES_j.

Step 4. For each new partial schedule PS($k + 1$) created in Step 3, update the data set as follows:

    a) Remove activity j from SA(k).
    b) For each activity $i \epsilon S(j)$, increment u_i by one.
    c) Form SA($k + 1$) by adding to SA(k) those activities $i \epsilon S(j)$ for which $u_i = |P(i)|$.
    d) Increment k by one.

Step 5. Return to Step 2 for each partial schedule created in Step 3 and updated in Step 4, and continue in this manner until all active schedules have been generated.

One way to structure a heuristic procedure is to choose just one partial schedule (one of the schedulable activities) among the alternatives created at Step 3.

The next step in extending the job shop model is to incorporate resource parallelism. The simplest such model contains only one resource type but allows activities to require more than one unit of the resource. (This kind of single-resource model is particularly relevant to certain construction and maintenance problems in which labor is the key resource.) The crucial difference occurs in Step 3, where it is necessary to examine not just single activities but groups of activities as well. Basically, a new partial schedule can be generated at Step 3 for any *subset* of schedulable activities that can be accommodated by available resources. The task is then to eliminate the subsets that do not result in active partial schedules and keep all the rest for Step 4. The partial schedules are denoted PS($k + a$) in Step 4 because several activities might have been added to PS(k). Although a complete schedule for n activities may be generated in fewer than n stages, the implementation of Step 3 involves an additional combinatorial effort. Conceptually, the approach can be extended to problems containing several resource types. Further generalizations of Algorithm 17.1 could also be pursued for problems in which resource substitutability is possible or in which activities require several different resources simultaneously. Finally, once the generation scheme is designed, we can embed it in a branch-and-bound procedure for determining an optimal schedule.

Lower bounds in the resource-constrained project scheduling problem can be developed using the concepts introduced in Chapter 14 in connection with the job shop problem. For example, an activity-based bound can be obtained by ignoring all resource constraints, and a resource-based bound can be obtained by ignoring all precedence constraints. To illustrate the calculation of an activity-based bound, consider a problem containing general precedence structure and unit resource availabilities (so that Algorithm 17.1 applies), and assume that makespan is the criterion. For each activity j let π_j denote the length of the longest path in the project network from the completion of activity j to the end of the project. (In other words, π_j is the critical path length for the subproject containing all the successors of activity j.) Then, by ignoring the resource constraints, we can construct the following lower bound on the makespan for a given partial schedule PS(k):

$$b_1 = \max_{j \in SA(k)} \left\{ ES_j + p_j + \pi_j \right\}$$

In this type of calculation, ES_j depends on the commitments in the partial schedule, but π_j has to be calculated only once for each activity.

To illustrate the derivation of a resource-based bound, let U_R denote the set of unscheduled jobs that require resource R. Then, by ignoring the precedence constraints, we can construct the following lower bound on the makespan:

$$b_2 = \max_R \left\{ \max\{C_j | j \in PS(k) \text{ and } R_j = R\} + \sum_{i \in U_R} p_i \right\}$$

These two simple bounds can be strengthened somewhat by accommodating some resource constraints in the activity-based bound or some precedence information in the resource-based bound. A combination activity-based bound explicitly considers the resource availabilities, one at a time. Temporarily, number the activities in set U_R in nondecreasing order of their critical path length, π_j. (In this way, activities near the end of the project will appear relatively early in the numbered list.) Then, taking the activities in numbered order, calculate

$$v_j = \max\{v_{j-1}, \pi_j\} + p_j$$

where $v_0 = 0$. Let the last (and largest) of these v_j be denoted V_R. Then

$$b_3 = \max_R\{V_R + \max\{C_j | j \in PS(k) \text{ and } R_j = R\}\}$$

A combination resource-based bound explicitly considers precedence relations among all activities that require a given resource. This time, number the activities in set U_R in nondecreasing order of their early start times, ES_j. (In this way, activities near the beginning of the project will appear relatively early in the numbered list.) Then, taking the activities in numbered order, calculate

$$w_j = \max\{w_{j-1}, ES_j\} + p_j$$

where $w_0 = 0$. Let the last of these w_j be denoted W_R. Then

$$b_4 = \max_R\{W_R\}$$

Obviously, the bounds b_3 and b_4 are at least as tight as b_1 and b_2 and generally tighter, although they require some additional calculations. A composite bound is therefore $B = \max\{b_3, b_4\}$.

■ **Example 17.1** Consider a project containing 10 activities and two resource types, as described in the following table. The last column is calculated from the information in the previous columns.

Activity	p_j	R_j	$P(j)$	π_j
A	4	1	—	2
B	3	2	—	5
C	2	1	—	5
D	4	2	—	8
E	4	2	D	4
F	2	1	B	3
G	2	2	C	3
H	1	1	E	3
I	2	2	A	0
J	3	1	F,G,H	0

As an instance of the calculations of π_j in Example 17.1, take activity D. It is followed directly by E and later by H and J, with processing times of 4, 1, and 3, so $\pi_D = 4 + 1 + 3 = 8$. To illustrate the bound calculations, suppose that at an intermediate stage in the generation of active schedules, we have the partial schedule shown in Figure 17.1. In this partial schedule, activity A occupies resource 1 beginning at time 0, and activity D occupies resource 2 beginning at time 0. With these two activities constituting PS(2), the set of schedulable activities is SA(2) = {B, C, E, I}. The sets U_1 and U_2 are {C, F, H, J} and {B, E, G, I} with total processing times of $2 + 2 + 1 + 3 = 8$ and $3 + 4 + 2 + 2 = 11$, respectively. Given this partial schedule, the conditional project network is depicted in Figure 17.2. In this figure, the constraints imposed by the partial schedule are accounted for, but any additional resource constraints are not. Figure 17.2 shows that the early start times of the schedulable activities are

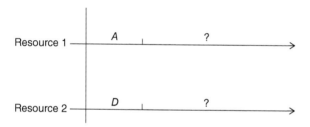

Figure 17.1 A partial schedule for Example 17.1.

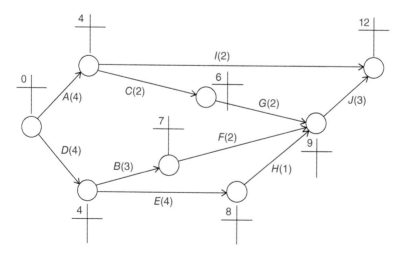

Figure 17.2 The conditional project network given PS(2).

$$ES_B = ES_C = ES_E = ES_I = 4$$

We now can calculate b_1 for B, C, E, and I:

$$b_1 = \max\{4 + 3 + 5, 4 + 2 + 5, 4 + 4 + 4, 4 + 2 + 0\} = 12$$

Next, we have

$$\max\{C_j | j \in PS(2) \text{ and } R_j = 1\} = 4 = \max\{C_j | j \in PS(2) \text{ and } R_j = 2\}$$

so

$$b_2 = \max\{4 + 8, 4 + 11\} = 15$$

In calculating b_3, the activities requiring resource 1 are considered in the order J–H–F–C (because in this order, their π_j values – 0, 3, 3, 5 – are nondecreasing) and $V_1 = 8$. The activities requiring resource 2 are considered in the order I–G–E–B, and we list the V_2 calculations in detail:

$$v_I = \max\{v_0, \pi_1\} + p_1 = \max\{0, 0\} + 2 = 2$$

$$v_G = \max\{2, 3\} + 2 = 5$$

$$v_E = \max\{5, 4\} + 4 = 9$$

$$v_B = \max\{9, 5\} + 3 = 12 = V_2$$

Thus,

$$b_3 = \max\{4 + 8, 4 + 12\} = 16$$

Finally, $W_1 = 13$ and $W_2 = 15$, so $b_4 = 15$. We trace the calculation of W_1. Figure 17.2 shows that the early start times for $U_1 = \{C, F, H, J\}$ are 4, 7, 8, and 9. These values lead to the following calculations:

$$w_C = \max\{w_0, ES_C\} + p_C = \max\{0, 4\} + 2 = 6$$

$$w_F = \max\{6, 7\} + 2 = 9$$

$$w_H = \max\{9, 8\} + 1 = 10$$

$$w_J = \max\{10, 9\} + 3 = 13 = W_1$$

As a result, b_3 is the tightest bound for this PS(2), indicating that the makespan must be at least 16 for this partial schedule.

For resource-constrained project scheduling problems with criteria other than makespan, the basic approach is similar. First, a tree-structured schedule generation scheme, such as Algorithm 17.1, forms the basis for constructing schedules. An activity-based bound is obtained by ignoring resource constraints and evaluating the resulting CPM network. A resource-based bound is obtained by ignoring precedence constraints and evaluating the resulting single- or parallel-machine sequencing problem. The success of such an approach depends on tightness of these bounds and on the computational effort they require.

17.3 Extending the Project Model

To illustrate how the temporal analysis of CPM can be useful in resource-constrained problems, consider the project model in which all activities require only one resource type. Let

a_j = resource units required to perform activity j

A = total resource units available

An *early start schedule* is constructed by starting each activity at its own early start time, as calculated by CPM. If the resources required in this schedule never exceed availabilities, then this schedule achieves the minimum possible duration. Similarly, a *late start schedule* is constructed by starting each activity at its late start time, and if this schedule is resource feasible, then it achieves the minimum possible duration. If neither schedule is feasible, it is still possible to extract some information for the calculation of a lower bound on project duration.

Let G_t denote the set of activities in process at time t in some given schedule with duration D. In addition, let

$$r_E(t) = \sum_{j \in G_t} a_j \quad \text{for the early start schedule}$$

$$r_L(t) = \sum_{j \in G_t} a_j \quad \text{for the late start schedule}$$

$$r_S(t) = \sum_{j \in G_t} a_j \quad \text{for some arbitrary schedule } S$$

In other words, $r_E(t)$ represents the resource consumption at time t under the early start schedule. If we examine cumulative resource consumptions, we find that

$$\sum_{u=1}^{t} r_E(u) \geq \sum_{u=1}^{t} r_S(u) \geq \sum_{u=1}^{t} r_L(u) \tag{17.1}$$

where we are treating time as discrete. The following properties address the question of whether a feasible schedule can be found to achieve the given duration D.

■ **Theorem 17.1** If $\sum_{u=1}^{t} r_L(u) > tA$ for any $1 \le t \le D$, then no feasible schedule of length D exists.

Proof. Under the hypothesis of the theorem, and the inequalities in Eq. (17.1), it follows that $\sum_{u=1}^{t} r_S(u) > tA$. In other words, there are insufficient resources available to carry out the activities in an arbitrary schedule of length D. □

An analogous argument for the reversed project establishes a symmetric result.

■ **Theorem 17.2** If $\sum_{u=D-t+1}^{D} r_E(u) > tA$ for any $1 \le t \le D$, then no feasible schedule of length D exists.

■ **Example 17.2** Consider a project containing 10 activities that require a single-resource type, as described in the following table.

Activity	p_j	$P(j)$	a_j	ES_j	LF_j
12	4	—	1	0	10
13	3	—	4	0	7
14	2	—	3	0	7
15	4	—	4	0	4
56	4	15	3	4	8
37	2	13	2	3	9
47	2	14	6	2	9
67	1	56	4	8	9
28	2	12	5	4	12
78	3	37,47,67	3	9	12

Suppose that $A = 7$, and consider whether it is possible to complete the project by time 12, which is the length of the critical path. First construct the resource profile of the late start schedule, shown in Table 17.1. For $t = 9$, we have $tA = 9 \times 7 = 63$, but $\sum_{u=1}^{9} r_L(u) = 69$, so the critical path length cannot possibly be

Table 17.1

Time, t	1	2	3	4	5	6	7	8	9	10	11	12
Resources, $r_L(t)$	4	4	4	4	7	10	11	12	13	4	8	8
Cumulative resources	4	8	12	16	23	33	44	56	69	73	81	89

achieved. (A similar conclusion can be reached by applying Theorem 17.2 to the early start schedule.) Suppose instead that $A = 8$. Then neither theorem will apply, yet we can't conclude that a schedule of length 12 can be found when 8 resource units are available.

It is also possible to develop a resource-based bound using the information in the early and late start schedules. Let the total resource requirement in the project be

$$Q = \sum_{u=1}^{D} r_E(u)$$

Then a feasible schedule of length D cannot exist unless

$$Q \le DA \qquad (17.2)$$

In effect, Eq. (17.2) yields a lower bound on project duration D, but this bound can be strengthened somewhat by examining the first part of the early start schedule and the last part of the late start schedule. Let τ represent the first period u at which $r_E(u) > A$. Then the resources that are not used in the beginning of the early start schedule sum to

$$\sum_{u=1}^{\tau-1} [A - r_E(u)]$$

These resources cannot be utilized by any feasible schedule. Analogously, let η represent the latest time u at which $r_L(u) > A$. Then an additional expression for resources that cannot be utilized by any feasible schedule of duration D is

$$\sum_{u=\eta+1}^{D} [A - r_L(u)]$$

Therefore, the inequality (17.2) can be amended to reflect usable resource capacity. A feasible schedule of length D cannot exist unless

$$Q \le DA - \sum_{u=1}^{\tau-1} [A - r_E(u)] - \sum_{u=\eta+1}^{D} [A - r_L(u)] \qquad (17.3)$$

This bound is sometimes called the *skyline bound* because it makes use of the profile of resource requirements in the schedule.

Theorems 17.1 and 17.2 and the bound in Eq. (17.3) are all based on conditions that can be examined before a schedule generation procedure begins. To adapt the bounds for use at intermediate stages of a branch-and-bound scheme, the inequalities must be generalized to accommodate fluctuating resource availabilities. In addition, the same type of analysis can be extended to problems in which several resource types exist and problems in which activities require different resources simultaneously.

As we saw in the last two sections, the problem is amenable to branch-and-bound solutions: Algorithm 17.1 is a viable approach for generating a branch-and-bound tree structure, and lower bounds can be obtained by extending both the job shop model and the project model. Indeed, there is a rich literature on branch-and-bound solutions to the resource-constrained project scheduling problem, including several other tree generation options and more elaborate bounds. At this time, however, none of these solutions are capable of solving anything but small problems.

17.4 Heuristic Construction and Search Algorithms

The resource-constrained project scheduling problem is NP-hard in the strong sense and may be intractable for $n > 50$. The majority of practical projects reportedly have 50–100 activities, whereas a "large" project might have as many as 300. Therefore, project scheduling software packages invariably rely on heuristics, usually keeping the details proprietary. Here, we consider heuristics that generalize those described in Chapter 4, and we limit our scope to the nonpreemptive case.

It is difficult to judge the performance of heuristics except by testing them against each other, but for tractable instances (of up to about 30–50 activities), such tests can also compare heuristics with the optimal solution. The best-performing commercial scheduling packages seem to achieve results similar to those obtained by a priority-based construction heuristic in which priority is determined on the basis of earliest late-finish time (LFT). There are two good reasons to favor this priority rule. First, the LFT acts as an activity due date, so the priorities reflect the properties of EDD and tend to reduce the maximum tardiness. But the maximum tardiness among the activities equals the tardiness of the whole project, so this priority list is likely to produce relatively short project lengths. (Recall from Chapter 8 that in the dynamic single-machine model, minimizing the makespan is equivalent to minimizing maximum tardiness.) Second, LFT priority is logically feasible automatically because an activity's predecessor must have an earlier LFT and so appears earlier in the priority list. Nevertheless, such a simple heuristic cannot guarantee optimality and should not be the only heuristic in use. An opportunity exists to improve on the performance of the typical commercial package by using more advanced heuristics such as we explore in this section. We usually start with some priority list and develop it into a schedule. Improvements can then be sought by changing the list by such mechanisms as a neighborhood search.

17.4.1 Construction Heuristics

The two major construction heuristic approaches for project scheduling are *parallel* and *serial*, and both are based on priority lists. These approaches can be used either in the forward direction or in reverse. We can even construct sequences from both ends toward the middle. For illustration, we describe the forward direction.

The parallel approach is based on dispatching logic. It can accept any priority list – logically feasible or not – and yields a nondelay sequence. We construct the sequence from beginning to end, and whenever resources are free, we schedule the highest-priority schedulable activity. (In Section 17.2, we defined an activity as schedulable once its predecessors have been completed, but here we must also consider the availability of resources.) The result is a nondelay schedule because we always schedule at least one schedulable activity when available. To illustrate, we revisit Example 17.2, and we schedule it by LFT priority with ties broken by LPT and any remaining ties broken in favor of the highest resource consumption. This ranking yields the list 15, 13, 14, 56, 47, 37, 67, 12, 78, and 28. (We need the tiebreaker to decide that 13 should precede 14, 78 should precede 28, and 67 should follow both 37 and 47. The latter two have the same duration and require the second tiebreaker to place 47 ahead of 37.) Recall that in this example, if we use $A = 8$, Theorems 17.1 and 17.2 do not indicate whether a schedule of length 12 is feasible. Therefore, it is interesting to examine the heuristic for $A = 8$. Figure 17.3 shows the results as a Gantt chart in which the vertical scale shows the resource consumption of an activity and the horizontal scale shows its duration. Shaded areas denote resource idleness between activities. Proceeding with the priority list, activity 15 is scheduled first at time zero, leaving enough free resources to schedule activity 13 in parallel. The next decision point is at time 3, when 4 resource units are released by activity 13, and activity 14 is now scheduled, leaving 1 resource unit unutilized. Only activity 12 fits in the single free resource slot, and it is scheduled in parallel to 14 and 15, even though activities with higher priorities remain unscheduled.

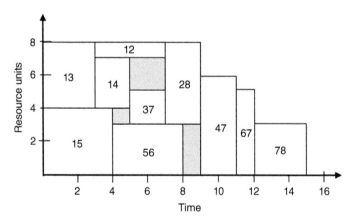

Figure 17.3 Scheduling Example 17.2 by the parallel approach.

Activity 56 becomes schedulable next, and 37 follows because it is schedulable right after 14, whereas 47 is not yet schedulable. Both 12 and 37 complete at time 7, and 28 becomes schedulable. At time 8, activity 56 completes, but no activity is schedulable until 28 completes at time 9. The remaining activities on the list (47, 67, and 78) are then scheduled consecutively. The makespan is 15.

One feature of the parallel approach is that increasing a processing time may make the schedule shorter. This can happen if the increased duration prevents a low-priority activity from starting too soon and subsequently delaying a high-priority one. For instance, in Example 17.2, if we increase the duration of 37 from 2 to 4 and use the same priority list, the makespan decreases to 14.

In the serial approach, only the highest-priority activity is considered schedulable, and resources may remain idle if they don't suffice for that activity, even if they could have accommodated other activities. When we schedule an activity, however, we use the earliest possible slot even if higher-priority activities have already been scheduled with later starting times. That is, during the procedure we may leave resources unused, but we may still allocate them in subsequent steps. As a result, the schedule is active but not necessarily nondelay, so this approach cannot be used for dispatching. Figure 17.4 illustrates the use of the serial approach in the same example with the same priority list as before. Activities 15, 13, 14, 56, and 47 are scheduled according to the list, with nondecreasing starting times. When activity 37 is then considered, it is possible to fit it before 47, in parallel to 56, yielding an active schedule. However, an idle slot of one time unit exists just ahead of activity 37 (utilized by 12 in the parallel approach). This outcome demonstrates that the serial approach may allow resources to remain idle even when an activity is available to start. As the process continues, activity 12 is also scheduled earlier than higher-priority activities,

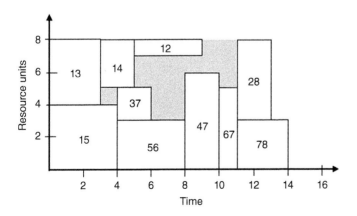

Figure 17.4 Scheduling Example 17.2 by the serial approach.

but it delays no activity with a higher priority because they have all been scheduled as early as possible in previous steps. For that reason, activity 37 starts earlier at the expense of 12, in accordance with the prescribed priority. The makespan is 14, which happens to be optimal.

As noted before, the LFT priority list is logically feasible. Other priority lists generated by CPM logic share this advantageous trait. In general, however, priority lists may not be logically feasible. For example, if we use LPT to prioritize, logical feasibility is not guaranteed. This is not a problem in the parallel approach, but it is crucial in the serial approach: During the process, the next activity on the list must be schedulable as soon as enough resources are released by earlier activities or the procedure cannot continue. However, if we wish to test only a small number of lists, we can make any list comply by preprocessing. One way to do that is to allow unlimited resources and record the order in which the parallel approach schedules activities; this order becomes the required preprocessed list. Alternatively, we can adapt the heuristic to allow skipping the highest-priority activity if it is logically infeasible and scheduling the first logically feasible activity as soon as resources are sufficient. This approach requires returning to the skipped activities and is identical to the preprocessing alternative. In effect, the same preprocessing steps are intermingled with scheduling activities. Although the parallel approach does not require preprocessing, it performs the equivalent function – skipping logically infeasible activities and returning to them later – during the scheduling process. Again, preprocessing is not always necessary.

Both approaches have advantages. The serial approach can produce all active schedules. If we were given the optimal priority list, then the serial approach would produce an optimal schedule. However, we don't know the optimal priority list, and we want to avoid evaluating many different lists. Therefore, we can't easily exploit the fact that the serial approach produces active schedules. In contrast, the parallel approach produces only nondelay schedules. In a given problem instance, the parallel approach may not be able to generate the optimal schedule. However, nondelay schedules are an appealing subset in practice, and the parallel approach is relatively easy to implement. It may also be desirable to try out both approaches. In Section 17.5, we also consider adding precedence constraints to a priority list so that we can enable dispatching while preventing selected low-priority activities from preceding high-priority ones.

17.4.2 Neighborhood Search Improvement Schemes

Once a schedule is constructed, we can improve on it by neighborhood searches (including genetic algorithms, tabu search, and simulated annealing) following the template of Chapter 4. We have already discussed such approaches in Chapter 14, for the job shop. But although project scheduling is a generalization of the job shop, we cannot describe a schedule with a sequence of permutations, so the approach of Chapter 14 is not directly applicable.

■ **Example 17.3** Consider the following project containing four resource types. Activity j requires a_{ij} units of resource type i. For each type, the availability is $A_i = 7$.

Activity	p_j	$P(j)$	a_{1j}	a_{2j}	a_{3j}	a_{4j}
12	1	—	6	3	4	5
13	4	—	5	4	3	2
14	2	—	1	1	2	3
16	3	—	2	4	2	4
17	4	—	2	2	4	3
18	2	—	2	3	3	4
25	2	12	1	1	3	3
58	4	25	5	3	2	3
68	3	12, 13, 16	2	3	4	2
78	4	14, 17	2	3	3	2

The project network is given in Figure 17.5.

Critical path analysis shows that the length of this project (without accounting for resource constraints) is 8, but the limit on resource 3 implies a makespan of at least 13 time units. (This resource has a load of 86, so 7 resource units would require more than 12 time units.) Suppose we take a serial approach using the logically feasible priority list obtained by sorting activities by their origin node first and destination node second. In this case, the list is {12, 13, 14, 16, 17, 18,

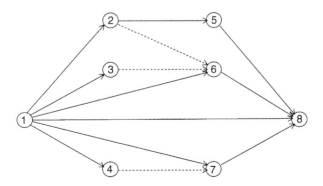

Figure 17.5 A project network for Example 17.3.

25, 58, 68, 78}. The serial approach yields a makespan of 17. Activity 17 is scheduled earlier than activity 16 because 13 and 16 cannot run in parallel due to resource constraints. However, after interchanging 68 and 78, the makespan improves to 16. The schedule is summarized in Table 17.2.

When we introduced neighborhood search in Chapter 4, we illustrated the procedure with unrelated jobs, but when precedence constraints apply, we may have to modify search procedures accordingly and work with blocks of jobs. Suppose we want to construct adjacent pairwise interchange (API) neighborhoods for a feasible four-job sequence *a-b-c-d*, but with precedence restrictions. If the two adjacent activities *b* and *c* are logically unrelated, then interchanging these two activities yields a logically feasible sequence. Suppose instead that *b* is an immediate predecessor of *c*, which makes the interchange infeasible. If we wish to start activity *c* earlier, we can exchange the block *b-c* with *a* to obtain the new sequence *b-c-a-d*. Similarly, if the intention is to start activity *b* later, we can switch to the partial sequence *a-d-b-c*. More generally, blocks may contain more than two activities, which are identified iteratively.

To illustrate a modified API, consider Example 17.2. Suppose we start with the sequence {12, 13, 14, 15, 28, 37, 47, 56, 67, 78}, which is logically feasible. If we wish to shift activity 67 to an earlier position, we must also shift activity 56 with it, obtaining the sequence {12, 13, 14, 15, 28, 37, 56, 67, 47, 78}. We can repeat this modified API two more times with the same block to obtain the sequence {12, 13, 14, 15, 56, 67, 28, 37, 47, 78}. If we next wish to shift activity 67 earlier, we must append activity 15 to the block. In the same example, if we try to shift activity 78 to an earlier position, activities {37, 47, 56, 67, 78} must be shifted as a block, and the resulting sequence is {12, 13, 14, 15, 37, 47, 56, 67, 78, 28}. To shift the activity earlier, the block must be expanded to include {13, 14, and 15}, and the modified API yields the feasible sequence {13, 14, 15, 37, 47, 56, 67, 78, 12, 28}. After that interchange, activity 78 cannot be shifted further. In general, all sequences generated by the modified API from any logically feasible initial sequence are logically feasible. Furthermore, all the logically feasible sequences that can be reached by a series of adjacent job interchanges can also be reached by adjacent block interchanges. In a similar way, we can define modified insertion steps and modified pairwise interchanges (consisting of two modified insertions). For insertion steps, feasibility forbids inserting an activity earlier than a predecessor.

Table 17.2

Activity	12	13	14	16	17	18	25	58	68	78
Start time	0	1	1	5	3	8	7	9	13	10
Finish time	1	5	3	8	7	10	9	13	16	14

An alternative approach is conceptually simpler, at least in the API case: Forbid any API that violates a precedence constraint. It can be shown that a series of permissible API steps exists that is equivalent to modified API. In our example above, the first modified API step changed our sequence from {12, 13, 14, 15, 28, 37, 47, 56, 67, 78} to {12, 13, 14, 15, 28, 37, 56, 67, 47, 78}, but the following two unmodified API steps lead to the same result: interchanging 56 and 47 followed by interchanging 67 and 47. The difference between the two approaches is that the former may demonstrate an immediate improvement, whereas the latter may increase the makespan temporarily in its partial steps. Therefore, the modified approach is recommended when we wish to decide whether to postpone or advance a particular activity. Incidentally, in the context of genetic algorithms, it is desirable that mutations avoid infeasibility. Modified perturbations can serve as feasible mutations. Implementations that allow infeasibility simply reject mutations that cause it, but the question is whether it is more effective to prevent infeasible mutations or to allow them tentatively.

Biased random sampling is a popular way to generate distinct sequences for a search. In Chapter 4, we saw that it is not necessarily a very effective approach in the single-machine tardiness problem. In project scheduling, however, it has the advantage that if we make the random choices at decision points of a dispatching procedure, only logically feasible sequences are selected. Therefore, random sampling is less wasteful in project scheduling than in the single-machine model. For project scheduling, simple priority rules such as LFT can be used to bias the random selection and improve its effectiveness.

17.4.3 Selecting Priority Lists

We now return to the selection of priority lists. Many priority lists have been recommended for project scheduling. Three prominent priority rules are the following.

1) (LST) Select activity j according to smallest LS_j (dynamically calculated).
2) (Delta) Select activity j according to smallest δ_{jk}, where

$$\delta_{jk} = \max_{j \neq k} \left\{ \max\left\{ 0, EF_j - LS_k \right\} \right\}$$

3) (LFT) Select activity j according to smallest LF_j.

The LST rule minimizes slack, so it is analogous to MST. However, because we update the latest start time as we proceed, based on the current project information, all LS_j values remain nonnegative. The LST priority list is logically feasible, which is convenient in constructing schedules, but the rationale for LST is not necessarily persuasive. In Chapter 2, for example, we saw that in the single-machine case, MST maximizes the minimum lateness. In Chapter 15, we saw that slack-related priority rules were sometimes effective but not necessarily for the criterion of maximum tardiness.

The Delta rule aims to reduce the potential incremental delay in the whole project caused by scheduling activity j before activity k. The pair of activities having maximal δ_{jk} is scheduled by LFT, but, in general, the sequences generated by LFT and by the Delta rule are not identical.

The LFT rule derives its effectiveness from emulating the EDD rule, which minimizes maximum tardiness in the single-machine case. But even in the single-machine case, EDD is not guaranteed to be optimal with nonzero release dates. That fact may explain why no single rule is always superior in the project scheduling context. It may also explain why a rule like MST, with properties of dubious value in the single-machine case, seems to perform well in project scheduling.

In general, running multiple heuristics, possibly in both directions and also from both ends to the middle, is often a good meta-heuristic. Dozens of priority rules have been proposed and tested for the project scheduling problem. However, some intuitively appealing rules do not seem to perform better than random dispatching. Therefore, at some point, adding more rules may become less effective than generating trial sequences by biased sampling. A similar argument also suggests that (at least for sequences that are logically feasible) we should run both serial and parallel list scheduling heuristics. There is clear empirical evidence, however, that parallel scheduling is likely to outperform serial scheduling for any single list. The serial approach becomes advantageous only when we perform multiple runs. For instance, it is known to perform better in the context of biased sampling. LFT seems to be the best list to use for biased sampling. (However, any of these considerations may change in the stochastic case.)

To illustrate, we return to Example 17.3 using the LFT priority list with ties broken by LPT. This tiebreaker is identical to LST because the slack is given by $LF_j - p_j$, and the tie implies that LF_j values are equal for all candidate activities. Any remaining ties can be broken in favor of the resource with the largest total load, given here by the order 3, 4, 1, 2. (These tie-breaking selections are motivated by the largest-fit heuristic covered in Chapter 9.) The resulting list is {12, 17, 25, 14, 13, 16, 78, 68, 58, 18}. For this list, both the parallel and serial approaches yield a makespan of 15, which happens to be optimal. The schedule is summarized in Table 17.3.

Table 17.3

Activity	12	13	14	16	17	18	25	58	68	78
Start time	0	5	3	9	1	13	1	9	12	5
Finish time	1	9	5	12	5	15	3	13	15	9

Once a priority list has been adopted, its implications can be influenced by adding precedence constraints, colloquially known as *soft constraints*, to the technological requirements of the original problem, to signal that they do not come from technological requirements. Soft constraints can even be reversed or removed during the course of building a schedule. We can account for resource limits by adding soft constraints between pairs of activities that compete for the same resources, but because we may have machine groups instead of single machines, we should allow for the possibility that activities can run in parallel. Hence, not every pair of competing activities requires a soft constraint.

For instance, we can enforce the sequencing decisions of Table 17.3 by adding a soft constraint between activity 12 and 17 (observing that 12 cannot run in parallel to any other activity due to its resource requirements) and similarly between the pairs of activities {17, 13}, {25, 14}, {14, 13}, {13, 16}, {16, 18}, {13, 58}, {78, 58}, and {58, 18}. In general, different sets of soft constraints might lead to the same final result. Finally, for stochastic sequencing, our subject in the next section, we introduce another type of soft constraint that may also be useful in deterministic sequencing.

17.5 Stochastic Sequencing with Limited Resources

Although deterministic models for project sequencing with limited resources have been researched intensively since the early 1960s, and although the original PERT model considered stochastic scheduling and included safe scheduling considerations, the optimal sequencing of stochastic project activities under resource constraints did not receive much attention until the twenty-first century. Some purely theoretical work is based on distributional assumptions (such as independent exponential activity durations), but more realistic models are based on simulated scenarios, so they essentially use sample-based techniques. These models address the problem of minimizing the expected makespan – that is, they are stochastic counterpart models. They also assume early start times; that is, activities start as soon as their predecessors are complete and sufficient resources have been allocated to them. Typically, they assume that activities whose predecessors have been completed can be started as soon as resources are allocated to them, ignoring the possible need for other preparations. Because of this last assumption – which is usually implicit – resources of a given type are considered completely interchangeable. (The deterministic models we covered make the same assumption, which is tantamount to assuming *all* necessary preparations are modeled as explicit project activities. But in practice, all but the smallest projects are scheduled hierarchically, with preparation and staging activities often ignored at higher levels of the hierarchy. In the deterministic case, it is very easy to schedule preparations for any given high-level schedule, but that is not necessarily the case in a stochastic environment.) Furthermore, randomness applies to activity durations but not to the logical structure of the project. A final assumption is that all activities will be completed eventually. In this section, we briefly discuss such models, limiting ourselves to tractable heuristic procedures even though branch-and-bound models have been proposed and may be useful for small projects.

If we treat resources of the same type as truly interchangeable, and if we ignore the need for preparations beyond the availability of resources, it becomes attractive to sequence activities dynamically, based on the actual durations once they are realized. That is, whenever we have enough resources to support at least one schedulable activity – which occurs upon activity completions – we select and dispatch the next activity (essentially, by the parallel approach), so the sequence cannot be predicted in advance. The sequencing problem then boils down to specifying a *policy* for the dispatching decisions. The simplest possible policy would be a priority list. More elaborate policies impose soft constraints that prevent some low-priority activities from being scheduled too early. When we apply a policy to each simulated scenario in our sample, we can easily estimate its expected makespan by taking the average of the results and then choose the best policy.

We saw in Section 17.4 that the serial approach cannot be used for dispatching but may lead to the best active schedule, which is not necessarily a nondelay schedule. The parallel approach uses a priority list to make dispatching decisions, and using it with such a list constitutes a dispatching policy. However, as we saw in our analysis of Example 17.2, the parallel approach may schedule a low-priority activity too early and thereby increase the makespan. Referring specifically to Example 17.2, suppose we have a second scenario in which activity 37 takes 4 time units instead of 2. As mentioned earlier, when we apply the parallel approach to that scenario – with the priority list {15, 13, 14, 56, 47, 37, 67, 12, 78, 28} – the makespan is reduced to 14, which is optimal for both scenarios. If both scenarios are equally likely, the expected value is 14.5. Now suppose we enhance the priority list by adding a soft *start–start* constraint requiring 28 not to start before 47. A start–start constraint allows one activity to start as early as another activity, but no earlier, allowing the two activities to run in parallel. In the example, such a constraint would allow 28 to run in parallel to 47 (if sufficient resources were available), but it would not allow 28 to delay 47.

In a stochastic environment, the price of using soft constraints is loss of flexibility, possibly leading to increased makespan. Start–start soft constraints provide more flexibility than finish–start soft constraints, but in principle we may use both to enhance a priority list and support dispatching. In our example, this soft constraint does not alter the makespan in the second scenario but reduces the makespan of the first scenario to 14, reducing the expected makespan from

14.5 to 14. As a rule, we want to specify only a subset of the possible soft constraints. In Example 17.2, adding a start–start constraint between each pair of successive activities in the priority list would lead to suboptimal makespan of 16 with a schedule that is neither active nor nondelay; unnecessary finish–start constraints would be even more deleterious.

As in the deterministic case, because we use a sample with a finite number of scenarios, we can find a good priority list (for the sample) by using a neighborhood search. However, if we want to also use soft constraints, we must avoid adding a constraint that conflicts with any existing (hard or soft) constraint. Recall that the parallel approach allows logically infeasible priority lists, but when we add a soft constraint, it restricts the selection of schedulable activities. When a soft constraint conflicts with an existing constraint (hard or soft), the process will abort because at some stage there will be no schedulable activity even though resources are available and not all activities are complete. The point is that the parallel process can change the sequence of activities that have no direct or indirect precedence between them, but it cannot resolve cycles. To avoid cycles, we can record all hard-and-soft precedence constraints in a matrix. Soft constraints can then be added only between unrelated activities, but the matrix must be updated for each such addition because a new soft constraint implies that the same type of constraint exists between all predecessors of the first activity and all successors of the second activity. A simpler way is to require the priority list to be logically feasible and then restrict the soft constraints to the direction of the activities in the list. For instance, requiring 28 not to start before 47 is in the order of the priority list. Because that is easier, we can try more priority lists without increasing the total computation time. Currently, the most effective approach is the use of a genetic algorithm that searches for a combination of a priority list and suitable soft constraints. Soft constraints may be generated by random mutations, and if they are restricted to the direction of a feasible list, they will be feasible too. Recall that except for mutations, a genetic algorithm creates new schedules by combining parts of two existing schedules. Furthermore, doing so for two feasible sequences yields a feasible sequence. In this context, it is useful to list soft constraints by their ordinal position in the priority list rather than by naming the activities they apply to explicitly. That way, when we change the priority list, as long as the new list is logically feasible, the soft constraints that become part of the offspring will not cause infeasibility.

17.6 Summary

The scheduling of a project in the presence of limited resources is a challenging decision-making problem. It is a full-blown scheduling problem in the sense that solutions must cope with both technological precedence constraints and resource availability constraints. In its general forms, it is a combinatorial problem of such magnitude that virtually all existing methods for finding optimal schedules are impractical for problems of realistic dimensions. The problem is especially frustrating because it initially appears simple. First, the problem is fairly easy to formulate and visualize. Second, the problem extends the CPM and PERT models, which themselves have been readily and widely adapted to practical network scheduling problems. Third, the substantial literature on the subject contains any number of sophisticated and clever optimum-seeking schemes, yet the barrier of computational practicality still exists.

For relatively small problems, optimal solutions have been achieved mostly by branch and bound and also by integer programming. An integer programming approach can harness the power of classical-constrained optimization techniques and accommodate fairly general criteria. A branch-and-bound approach, based on the implicit enumeration of all active schedules, is more flexible in its structure and may provide better insights into the nature of the solution. In addition, the tree structure embedded in the branching procedure provides a basis for implementing heuristic techniques.

Just as in the job shop problem, priority dispatching procedures and biased sampling schemes appear to be effective heuristic devices. On the one hand, such suboptimal approaches are quite rapid and are the most flexible in their ability to accommodate realistic criteria and decision constraints. On the other hand, they achieve their speed and flexibility at the expense of failing to guarantee optimality. As mentioned earlier, many heuristic programs are commercially available, although their details have often been withheld on proprietary grounds. Evidence suggests, however, that these commercially available heuristics could be significantly improved by utilizing state-of-art alternatives.

We also discussed stochastic sequencing models devised to minimize the expected duration; that is, they address the stochastic counterpart problem. Practicable approaches rely on sample-based analysis with dynamic dispatching guided by priority lists and soft precedence constraints, including start–start soft constraints. The state of the art utilizes a genetic algorithm to find good priority lists and soft constraints. It is also possible to address such problems by branch and bound, but that approach has proven to be impractical for anything but small projects. Last but not least, using the deterministic counterpart sequence but adding safety time where appropriate is a reasonable heuristic approach to project scheduling. In the next two chapters, we elaborate on such aspects; that is, we assume that the sequencing problem has been addressed and what remains is to schedule release dates and due dates.

Exercises

17.1 Consider Example 17.1, where we showed that if A and D are scheduled at time 0, a lower bound for the makespan is 16.
  a) Construct a full schedule with makespan 16 for this PS(2).
  b) Show that the schedule in part (a) is an optimal solution. (*Hint*: Given the feasible solution of part (a), it is sufficient to show the same lower bound for PS(0). One way to do so is by studying the reversed project, where there are only two PS(2) that satisfy Algorithm 17.1, one of which is nondelay. Calculate b_4 for the nondelay PS(2), and show that the other is inferior – for instance, by calculating b_4 for it too.)

17.2 Consider the project described in the following table. Each of the tasks A–H has a given duration p_j, a set of predecessors $P(j)$, and a resource requirement a_j. The total number of resource units available is 5.

Activity	p_j	$P(j)$	a_j
A	5	—	3
B	3	—	2
C	4	—	2
D	1	A	2
E	4	A	2
F	3	D, E	1
G	5	B, D	1
H	6	C	3

  a) Draw an AOA network for this project.
  b) If no resource limit existed, what would be the length of the critical path?
  c) Construct an early start schedule for the project.
  d) Construct a late start schedule for the project.
  e) Use the schedules in (c) and (d) to compute bounds on the project duration.

17.3 Revisit the project in the previous exercise. Find the minimum makespan by comparing three schedules constructed using heuristic procedures.
  a) Apply the LST priority rule and calculate the makespan.
  b) Apply the Delta priority rule and calculate the makespan.
  c) Apply the LFT priority rule and calculate the makespan.

17.4 Consider the project described in the following table. Each of the tasks $A-L$ has a given duration p_j, a set of predecessors $P(j)$, and a resource requirement a_j. The total number of resource units available is 5.

Activity	p_j	$P(j)$	a_j
A	6	—	2
B	8	—	3
C	4	—	3
D	4	A	4
E	4	A	2
F	12	B, E	3
G	14	B, E	1
H	6	B, C, E	4
I	8	D, F	2
J	16	D, F, G	1
K	2	D, F, G	1
L	12	H, K	3

a) Draw an AOA network for this project.
b) If no resource limit existed, what would be the length of the critical path?
c) Construct an early start schedule for the project.
d) Construct a late start schedule for the project.
e) Use the schedules in (c) and (d) to compute bounds on the project duration.

17.5 Revisit the project in the previous exercise. Find the minimum makespan by comparing three schedules constructed using heuristic procedures.
a) Apply the LST priority rule and calculate the makespan.
b) Apply the Delta priority rule and calculate the makespan.
c) Apply the LFT priority rule and calculate the makespan.

17.6 Consider the project described in the following table. Each of the tasks $A-J$ has a given duration p_j, a set of predecessors $P(j)$, and a resource requirement a_j. The total number of resource units available is 10.

Activity	p_j	$P(j)$	a_j
A	1	—	7
B	4	A	1
C	3	A	4
D	2	A	3
E	2	A	5
F	2	B	8
G	2	C	2
H	3	D	6
I	1	G, H	9
J	3	I	10

a) Draw an AOA network for this project.
b) If no resource limit existed, what would be the length of the critical path?
c) Construct an early start schedule for the project.
d) Construct a late start schedule for the project.
e) Use the schedules in (c) and (d) to compute bounds on the project duration.

17.7 Revisit the project in the previous exercise. Find the minimum makespan by using a parallel approach and LFT priority.

17.8 Consider Example 17.2, where the infinite resource critical path is 12 but for 8 capacity units and the list {15, 13, 14, 56, 47, 37, 67, 12, 78, 28}, the serial approach yielded a makespan of 14.
a) Prove the optimality of the serial list.
b) Suppose you can release resources early if they are not required downstream, to reduce idleness. Let the reduction of resource requirements by such release be our secondary objective, to be pursued without increasing the makespan. Show that the parallel list solution (Figure 17.3) involves 12 fewer idle resource time units then the optimal solution (Figure 17.4). (*Hint:* The total area of the white rectangular blocks is a constant, and a direct comparison of the gray areas in the two figures shows a difference of 10.)
c) Suppose now that 37 takes 4 time units instead of 2. Compare the results of the parallel and serial approaches.

d) Suppose we have nine capacity units. Compare the performance of the two approaches with the same list, in terms of makespan and idleness (assuming early release of resources is allowed as in part b).

e) Can the makespan be reduced relative to the better schedule found above by adding resource units?

17.9 Consider Example 17.3, where the initial list was {12, 13, 14, 16, 17, 18, 25, 58, 68, 78} and an optimal list for serial construction is {12, 17, 25, 14, 13, 16, 78, 68, 58, 18}.

a) Prove the optimality of the serial list.

b) List a series of modified API steps that leads from the initial list to the optimal list.

Bibliography

Davis, E.W. and Patterson, J.H. (1975). A comparison of heuristic and optimum solutions in resource constrained project scheduling. *Management Science* 21: 944–955.

Demeulemeester, E. and Herroelen, W. (1992). A branch and bound procedure for the multiple resource-constrained project scheduling problem. *Management Science* 38: 1803–1818.

Demeulemeester, E. and Herroelen, W. (2002). *Project Scheduling: A Research Handbook*. Norwell, MA: Kluwer Academic Publishers.

Fleszar, K. and Hindi, K. (2004). Solving the resource-constrained project scheduling problem by a variable neighbourhood search. *European Journal of Operational Research* 155: 402–413.

Herroelen, W. (2005). Project scheduling—theory and practice. *Production and Operations Management* 14 (4): 413–432.

Kelley, J.E. (1963). The critical path method: resources planning and scheduling. In: *Industrial Scheduling* (ed. J. Muth and G.L. Thompson), 347–365. Englewood Cliffs, NJ: Prentice Hall.

Kolisch, R. and Hartmann, S. (2006). Experimental investigation of heuristics for resource-constrained project scheduling: an update. *European Journal of Operational Research* 174: 23–37.

Morton, T.E. and Pentico, D.W. (1993). *Heuristic Scheduling Systems*. Hoboken, NJ: Wiley.

Pritsker, A.A.B., Watters, L.J., and Wolfe, P.M. (1969). Multi project scheduling with limited resources: a zero–one programming approach. *Management Science* 16: 93–108.

Rostami, S., Creemers, S., and Leus, R. (2018). New strategies for stochastic resource-constrained project scheduling. *Journal of Scheduling* 21: 349–365.

Schrage, L.E. (1970). Solving resource constrained network problems by implicit enumeration—nonpreemptive case. *Operations Research* 18: 263–278.

Stork, F. (2001). Stochastic resource-constrained project scheduling. PhD thesis. Technical University of Berlin.

Wiest, J.D. (1964). Some properties of schedules for large projects with limited resources. *Operations Research* 12: 395–418.

Wiest, J.D. (1967). A heuristic model for scheduling large projects with limited resources. *Management Science* 13: B359–B377.

18

Project Analytics

18.1 Introduction

The methods of analytics constitute the main bridge from theory to practice. Those methods analyze data to reveal facts that must be addressed by any practicable theory. If such facts are congruent with the theory, we say the theory is *valid*, and we expect valid theory to guide us toward successful implementation. In our context, a project scheduling framework that does not involve validation is simply not credible. Classical PERT assumptions, including statistical independence and reliance on the beta distribution, are examples of what we now recognize as invalid theory. *Project analytics* replace the flawed PERT assumptions and support project management in general. In this chapter, we argue that the beta distribution should be replaced by the lognormal, and the independence assumption should be replaced by a model of dependence such as linear association. To fully justify these claims, however, we must show how to resolve various implementation challenges.

Unfortunately, the bulk of stochastic scheduling research has focused on mathematically convenient distributions that have rarely been validated. That is, with few exceptions, no attempt has been made to prove that the stochastic models fit actual observations. Similarly, the vast majority of that research also relies on the assumption that processing times are statistically independent. We discuss evidence that the lognormal distribution is often valid but that estimates may be subject to distortion by hidden earliness and rounding errors. In addition, activity durations are likely to be positively correlated. We lay the groundwork for simulating reliable analytics-based samples of activity durations.

In Appendix A we discuss how to use a Q–Q chart to judge whether a given sample is likely to represent a normal distribution and, if so, how to estimate the parameters of that distribution. In this chapter, we show how to apply that method to a new project based on historical data from similar

Principles of Sequencing and Scheduling, Second Edition. Kenneth R. Baker and Dan Trietsch.
© 2019 John Wiley & Sons, Inc. Published 2019 by John Wiley & Sons, Inc.

projects and thus validate the assumption that project activity durations follow the lognormal distribution. We also show how to obtain estimates of the lognormal parameters m and s.

Suppose we have a sample of n independent and identically distributed observations that we believe are lognormal. We can test that belief with a normal Q–Q chart based on the logarithms of the observations. In practice, however, we often know that the observations are not identically distributed. In such cases, we can first try to convert them to identically distributed variables before proceeding with the analysis. In particular, a typical project has several activities, each with its own estimated duration, e_j. (Those estimates are known in advance and ideally rely on historical data rather than subjective judgment.) As the project unfolds, the activity time realizations, p_j, are observed. If we treat e_j as deterministic, or even as a lognormal variate, it follows that p_j/e_j is also lognormal, even though e_j and p_j are likely to be correlated. Furthermore, if the estimates are accurate (or unbiased), then p_j/e_j is basic (that is, has a mean of 1), so each ratio will have a lognormal distribution. However, there is no compelling reason to assume that all these distributions will have the same coefficient of variation (cv) and thus that their logarithms will have the same standard deviation (s). Therefore, the n activities may not be identically distributed even after conversion to ratios. When that is the case, there is no conceivable way to use the data to prove or disprove that the original distributions were lognormal. In practice, however, if we assume the same cv applies – at least to planned durations of the same order of magnitude – we obtain good Q–Q charts, thus validating not only the lognormal assumption but also the equal-cv assumption. In such a Q–Q chart, the intercept is our estimate of the mean (m) and the slope estimates s. (To use the results specifically for activity j, we should add $\ln(e_j)$ to the estimate of m and take the exponent.) Furthermore, even when the same cv assumption fails, we can often identify mixtures of very few cv levels that will serve our purposes.

Several issues remain to be addressed. First, as briefly mentioned above, there is usually a need to partition project activities into subsets of similar planned duration. Each of these subsets then acquires its own Q–Q chart. Indeed, typical projects involve activities whose planned durations are too dissimilar to be pulled together into a single Q–Q chart. Section 18.2 deals with basic partitioning by planned duration or other known differences. Second, historical activity durations are often provided in rounded terms, which may mask the true distribution. Section 18.3 concerns rounding of estimates. Third, the Parkinson effect often applies: The reported duration of an activity is heavily influenced by the time allotted to it, although it may take longer. Nevertheless, we must be able to obtain valid parameter estimates even when observations are distorted by the Parkinson effect, an approach we discuss in Section 18.4. In addition, there may be reasons why a project represents a mixture of distributions. For instance, in a construction project some activities may be sensitive to weather, while others are not. We cannot predict the behavior of the next project reliably without accounting for such mixtures and understanding their root causes, as discussed in Section 18.5. We also have to be aware of possible bias in our data, especially estimation bias. We address this concern in Section 18.6. In practice, some projects run faster than expected, whereas other projects are systemically slower. This behavior implies stochastic dependence among the durations within a project but would not occur if durations were independent. Specifically, after we encounter a few shorter-than-expected durations, it becomes more likely that they will be followed by short durations, whereas longer-than-expected durations early in a project will tend to be followed by other, longer ones. In Section 18.7, we discuss how to model that behavior by linear association, allowing us to generate random samples under the assumption that the durations of the next project will also be subject to dependence.

Our analysis implies that the PERT model is not credible because it is based on the independence assumption, does not correct for bias, and relies on subjective estimates. Furthermore, empirical evidence reveals that some activities have very high cv, whereas the beta approximation in PERT has a limited cv that is inadequate for $cv > 0.66$. For these reasons the PERT method cannot yield reliable samples for medium and high variation cases. Our modeling rests on much more solid ground when we rely on the lognormal distribution.

18.2   Basic Partitioning

Typical projects involve activities with a wide range of planned durations. They are also often composed of several distinct subprojects. For example, when the project network is a large assembly tree, each major branch of the tree is usually a subproject that may be performed with a large degree of autonomy. Subprojects may still be subject to common problems, such as funding, but they may be largely independent from each other. The first step in analyzing activities of historical projects is to partition them into subsets reflecting planned duration and any known subproject structure. Incidentally, project data available in the public domain today rarely include subproject structure, but planned durations are documented and can be used for partitioning.

A useful rule of thumb is that the ratio between the longest and shortest planned activity duration in each subset should not exceed four or five. Instances with much larger differences may behave well (thanks to the normalization we achieve by using ratios of actual to planned times), but we should at least check for possible systemic differences. More disparate activities often belong to different hierarchical levels. Longer ones are more likely to involve several subactivities and therefore may exhibit less variation on a proportional

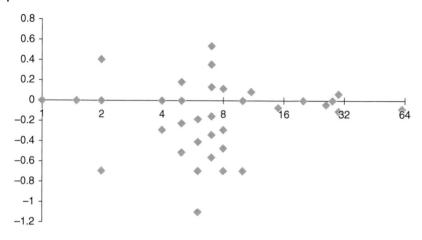

Figure 18.1 ln(*p_j/e_j*) as a function of planned duration.

basis. Very short activities often exhibit small variation for other reasons. Partitioning by planned duration is a reliable approach in either case.

We illustrate partitioning with field data from a construction project in Yerevan, Armenia. The project had 107 activities with planned durations between 1 and 62 days. In this case, both early and tardy activities were quite common, but all 12 activities planned for less than two days reportedly completed precisely on time and so did a very high proportion of activities planned for exactly two days. That, by itself, indicates that partitioning is helpful here, rather than analyzing all 107 activities together. Furthermore, even if we separate out all activities planned for two days or less, we still have a ratio of 15 for the maximum time in the remainder to the minimum time, so we should check further.

Consider Figure 18.1, where the horizontal axis measures the planned duration (on a logarithmic scale) and the vertical axis measures $\ln(p_j/e_j)$. We should clarify that in this figure, some points represent a single activity, whereas others represent a larger number. For instance, all 11 activities planned for a single day are represented by the leftmost single point on the planned duration axis, and the 3 points visible for 2-day activities represent 1, 11, and 6 activities (from top to bottom). We observe that the range of values for $\ln(p_j/e_j)$ is highest for medium-sized activities, and henceforth we focus on these activities, defined as having planned durations from 4 to 15. A full analysis includes separate treatment for long activities – which are important precisely because they are long – and for short activities. More formally, all activities with planned durations between 1 and 4, with 4 itself excluded, make up the first subset of the partition, denoted by [1, 4). The other two subsets are with planned durations of [4, 16) and [16, 64). All of them involve max-to-min ratios of no more than 4, and it is impossible to create fewer than 3 subsets that follow

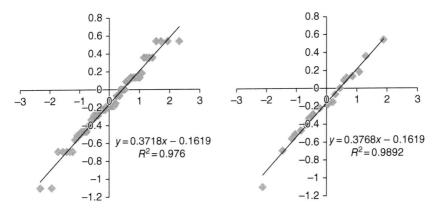

Figure 18.2 Q–Q charts before and after correcting for rounding.

the rule of thumb. Figure 18.1 supports this particular partition also by the clearly higher proportional variation that the middle group exhibits. A partition into, say, [1, 3), [3, 15), and [15, 75) would also be justified, with almost the same membership in each subset: Only the activity planned for 15 would shift. As this example demonstrates, there may be room for some flexibility, but partitioning by planned duration is generally useful. Henceforth, we assume this initial partition has been followed and our discussion will concern analysis of a single subset.

There are 61 activities with planned durations between 4 and 15. On the left side of Figure 18.2, we show the Q–Q chart of their $\ln(p_j/e_j)$ values. Although we observe several values with the same $\ln(p_j/e_j)$ but different scores, the regression line has $R^2 = 0.976$. Taking the square root, 0.988, we find that it passes the normality test with a probability of almost 0.25. That is, we cannot reject normality.

18.3 Correcting for Rounding

As we have seen for the planned durations [4, 15), we cannot reject the hypothesis that the $\ln(p_j/e_j)$ values follow a normal distribution. However, even if the underlying distribution is normal (after the logarithmic transformation), problems with the data may make it impossible to confirm normality without some remedy. One type of deviation from normality is due to rounding. Although processing times are continuous, *reported* processing times are usually rounded to integers, sometimes using excessively coarse units, such as reporting in weeks when some activities take less than a day. Planned durations are virtually always given in integers, so the computed ratios are rational numbers, such as 12/7 or 1/3. Thus, one problem is rounding error. A related problem occurs when two or more realizations are reported as equal, although it is virtually impossible for two realizations from a continuous distribution to be precisely equal. Because we associate each of these reportedly equal points with a different score, if many points are rounded to the same value, the Q–Q chart exhibits a flat horizontal segment for this value, causing a reduction in R^2. The left side of Figure 18.2 shows several such flat horizontal segments: At the top, we observe four points corresponding to the ratio 12/7 (for which $\ln(p_j/e_j) = 0.539$) and at the bottom, two points corresponding to the ratio 1/3 (for which $\ln(p_j/e_j) = -1.099$). In between, most $\ln(p_j/e_j)$ values appear more than once, and in particular, the ratios 8/7, 5/6, 4/5, and 1/2 each appear at least five times. Empirical evidence suggests that normality is often rejected due to this cause, but in our context that should not be a valid reason for rejection.

A common remedy is to assign all such points the same score. One way to do so is to use the average of all the relevant scores. That is, we replace each horizontal strip, say, with k observations, by k overlapping repetitions of a single observation at their horizontal average. For instance, if two activities, with scores of 1.16 and 1.22, have the same reported $\ln(p_j/e_j)$, we treat them as two repetitions of the same $\ln(p_j/e_j)$ value, each with a score of $(1.16 + 1.22)/2 = 1.19$. The right-hand side of Figure 18.2 shows the Q–Q chart after this treatment. The regression line has $R^2 = 0.9892$ (as compared with 0.976 on the left). The probability associated with the normality test rises to slightly above 0.5. The regression parameters on the two sides are quite close: The main difference is the increase in R^2. For medium-sized activities in this project, then, we cannot reject the hypothesis that they are all lognormal with the same cv. From Eq. (A.2), using 0.3718 (from the left-side chart) as our s estimate, we calculate $cv^2 = \exp(0.3718^2) - 1$ or $cv = 0.385$. If instead we use 0.3768 (from the right-side chart), we get $cv = 0.391$. Our estimates for μ_j are $0.911e_j$ and $0.913e_j$, so in this example, correcting for rounding does not make a big difference. However, in general, the correction for rounding can mean the difference between accepting and rejecting normality.

We can choose to remedy rounding as soon as we discover repetitions due to suspected rounding in the sample, or we can postpone it until it becomes clear that normality would be rejected without the correction.

18.4 Accounting for the Parkinson Effect

Another common deviation from normality (after log-transformation) is associated with the Parkinson effect. As discussed in Appendix A, the Parkinson effect describes a distribution of actual activity times when they are influenced by a predicted or targeted activity time. When random factors lead toward a faster-than-predicted outcome, the reported time gets matched to the target,

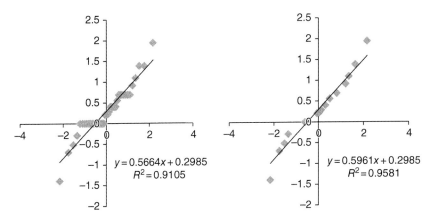

Figure 18.3 Normal Q–Q plot of $\ln(p_j/e_j)$ for a development project before (left) and after correcting for rounding (right).

but when similar factors lead toward a slower-than-predicted outcome, the actual time is reported faithfully. The left side of Figure 18.3 is the Q–Q chart of a development project from the Eurasia Foundation in Armenia. The project had 52 activities with planned durations between 4 and 48 weeks. Preliminary analysis suggests that we should analyze activities of up to 15 weeks separately, and here we focus on these (41) activities. A subset of 15 activities is reported exactly on time – that is, with $p_j/e_j = 1$ and $\ln(p_j/e_j) = 0$. Four activities are reported as strictly early, with $p_j/e_j < 1$ and $\ln(p_j/e_j) < 0$. Because of the large proportion of observations with ratios of unity, there is a wide flat segment in the chart for $\ln(p_j/e_j) = 0$. Largely due to that reason, the chart fails the normality test with a probability of about 0.005. Rounding helps, as the right-side chart demonstrates, but the test remains marginal (a low pass). Even after the rounding correction, the Q–Q chart still has an inverted S shape. Such a shape, specifically for observations with $\ln(p_j/e_j) = 0$, is likely when the number of ratios that is ostensibly rounded is excessive. In other words, we suspect that a sizable Parkinson effect exists. The question is how to demonstrate that and how to estimate the parameters so we can use them later for prediction in similar projects.

This task is a bit more challenging than dealing with rounding alone, in part, because the reported processing time can exactly match the plan for two reasons: possibly due to the Parkinson effect of a faster-than-predicted outcome (in which case we refer to the relevant observations colloquially as *Parkinsonian*) or else due to rounding (to which we refer colloquially as *on time*). For instance, in the Armenian construction project, four activities (out of 61) were deemed to be on time; that is, we treated them as rounded to unity and the result was deemed normal. In general, however, we may have a mixture of two types of activities with unity ratios, so we must somehow decide how many observations are on time and how many are Parkinsonian. For the time being, assume that we have made that decision, perhaps tentatively. On-time activities and strictly tardy activities are similar in the sense that all of them are reported correctly, at least approximately. All other activities are strictly early but possibly Parkinsonian. Hence, by the assumption, we know exactly how many activities are reported correctly because they are strictly tardy (denoted n_T), how many are on time but rounded to unity (denoted n_O), how many are early and reported correctly (denoted n_E), and how many are Parkinsonian (denoted n_P).

Our task now is to construct a Q–Q chart for which the regression line would be linear under the normality assumption, in spite of the Parkinson effect, and such that its intercept will still provide an estimate of m and its slope will provide an estimate of s. To that end, it is straightforward to estimate p_P by $n_P/(n_E + n_P)$. Because p_P is the fraction of early activities that cannot be used in the Q–Q chart (their true duration is unknown), we modify Blom's scores for the remaining early activities. Instead of $z_k = \Phi^{-1}((k - 0.375)/(n + 0.25))$, which applies to full samples and to correctly reported activities, we use $z_k = \Phi^{-1}((k - 0.375)/(n(1 - p_P) + 0.25))$. The adjustment reflects the effective reduction in sample size that applies to early activities. That is, we use the unadjusted $z_k = \Phi^{-1}((k - 0.375)/(n + 0.25))$ values for the n_T strictly tardy activities; the same applies to the n_O on-time activities, but we use adjusted scores of $z_k = \Phi^{-1}((k - 0.375)/(n(1 - p_P) + 0.25))$ for the n_E strictly early activities. That leaves out the n_P Parkinsonian observations, which are simply omitted from the chart.

Returning to the Eurasia project, assume now that six of the activities are on time, so nine are Parkinsonian. Because $n_E = 4$, our estimate of p_P is $9/(4 + 9) = 0.692$. The left side of Figure 18.4 is the Q–Q chart of $\ln(p_j/e_j)$ for the updated data, but excluding the nine Parkinsonian observations. After correcting for

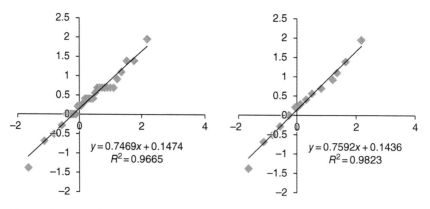

Figure 18.4 Normal Q–Q plot of $\ln(p_j/e_j)$ for a development project with partial Parkinson correction before (left) and after correcting for rounding (right).

rounding, we obtain the right side of the figure, which passes the normality test comfortably.

It is not our intention to prove that exactly nine out of the 15 points are Parkinsonian or that the estimated parameters ($m = 0.14$ and $s = 0.76$) are exact. Rather we show that *if* that were the case, then the sample would be plausible. Hence there is a way to fit the model to the data, which is essentially what validation is all about. With that in mind, we chose to assume that exactly six points are due to rounding by a heuristic designed to increase the likelihood the chart will pass the normality test. The key is that if the fit is good, then the regression standard error, denoted SE_Y and reported in standard software output, should be relatively small. In our particular case, we compared SE_Y (after rounding, as in the right side of Figure 18.4) for 0, 5, 6, 7, and 15 on-time activities (including the assumed rounding). Here, 0 corresponds to the assumption that all those points are Parkinsonian, and 15 corresponds to the assumption that none is Parkinsonian. Respectively, we obtain the following SE_Y values: 0.098 22, 0.085 72, 0.085 65, 0.086 86, and 0.120 34. The assumption we chose, six on-time but rounded activities, is associated with the minimum SE_Y value, 0.085 65. It is also interesting to compare the respective R^2 values, which are 0.9749, 0.9827, 0.9823, 0.9815, and 0.9581. Here, the maximum is associated with $n_O = 5$, that is, five on-time observations rather than $n_O = 6$, yet we focus on SE_Y, and for the purpose of the heuristic, we essentially ignore R^2 altogether. We don't recommend using R^2 for selection purposes because it applies to samples with different sizes. (A related statistic, R^2-adjusted, is often used to decide whether to add explaining variables to a regression with a given sample size. It can be shown that maximizing R^2-adjusted is then equivalent to minimizing SE_Y. Hence, for the purpose of deciding whether to add an explaining variable, our heuristic would be equivalent to maximizing R^2-adjusted.)

To conclude this section we discuss how to run normality tests when the Parkinson effect occurs. Unlike the case with complete samples, with or without rounding, unless $p_P = 1$, there are no standard tests available. Although relevant theoretical results exist for censored samples, they do not apply for $p_P < 1$, and they are not tabulated sufficiently to cover all pure Parkinson instances. The issue is important not only for testing Q–Q charts but also for analysis of variance (ANOVA), on which we rely later. For these statistical tests, it is required to have complete samples. If $n(1 - p_P)$ is sufficiently large – which implies $p_P < 1$ – it is possible to trim the sample by randomly removing a proportion p_P of the tardy and on-time activities. By assumption, the remaining *trimmed sample* retains a proportion of $(1 - p_P)$ of the strictly early activities, and the same proportion also applies to the on-time and tardy activities. Thus the trimmed sample is a random sample where all activities have the same probability of being retained, namely, $(1 - p_P)$. However, a random sample from a complete population or from a larger random sample is a complete sample, to which we can apply standard tests. Because the trimming is random, we may choose to repeat it several times and use average results. However, trimming is problematic when p_P is large, impossible when $p_P = 1$, and definitely requires throwing information away. For those reasons, we avoid trimming as much as possible in what follows.

Fortunately, when $p_P = 1$ the sample is censored (it retains only positive realizations), and tests for censored Q–Q charts are available. Furthermore, if p_P is too large, the implication is that very few early activities are reported correctly, and in such cases we can choose to ignore those early activities and perform the analysis as if the sample is fully censored. Nevertheless, it is still useful to be able to test for any p_P value. To that end, we adopt a better approach, also adopted by major statistical software packages even for complete samples: to compare the fit – as judged by R^2 – to a large simulated sample and reject normality if R^2 is lower than that of 5% of the simulated sample. (5% is the conventional threshold but we can use any other predetermined threshold.) Next, we discuss how to run this simulation.

During the Q–Q chart construction described above, *before* correcting for rounding, we obtain a list of n_T scores for the ratios of actual to planned durations of the activities originally reported as tardy, the average score of the n_O on-time activities (whose logarithm is zero), and n_E scores for the ratios of activities reported strictly early. Altogether, there are $(n - n_P)$ scores in the final chart. We also obtain the R^2 value associated with the Q–Q chart *after* correcting for rounding, if necessary. To construct a Q–Q chart for a random set of n simulated values obtained from a normal distribution subject to similar Parkinson effects, we need to allocate the same $(n - n_P)$ scores to a subset of the n simulated independent standard normal realizations. Equivalently, we need to select n_P simulated values to ignore and select which simulated values play the role of the on-time activities. We start by sorting the sample by descending size, and we allocate the highest n_T scores to the highest simulated values in the sample. Next we allocate the average score associated with the n_O observations to the average of the next n_O values in the sample, so we have n_O identical points (as was also the case originally). It is not necessary to make that average match any particular value because shifting the Q–Q chart vertically or horizontally does not change the R^2 value ultimately reached. Next, we select n_E simulated values randomly from the subset of the lowest $(n_E + n_P)$ simulated values and allocate to them the lowest scores. Finally, we fit a regression line and record the R^2 value. Repeating that process r times, we can then sort the R^2 results and estimate the probability that our original data is indeed normal subject to the Parkinson distribution with a normal core by its rank in the sampled list: The higher the original R^2 ranking, the higher the plausibility of the hypothesis.

The prevalence of the Parkinson effect probably depends on the industry and on culture, but it is noteworthy that in a large set of Belgian construction projects, on-time activities – Parkinsonian or otherwise – tended to be very short, one or two periods. Hence, at least in established industries with relatively small variation, such as construction, the Parkinson effect is not likely to apply to long (and thus important) activities. Furthermore, the Eurasia project is one of five projects by the same organization, but none of the other four exhibited clear evidence of the Parkinson effect. To determine how important it is in other industries and cultures requires more research. In conclusion, there is no doubt the Parkinson effect is sometimes real, but it is an open question how likely it is to occur in practice and how damaging it may be when it occurs. Theoretically, it is important because it enables us to show that the lognormal distribution applies, sometimes even when direct evidence seems to contradict it. Furthermore, performing analytics to identify the Parkinson effect where it prevails can help improve operations by changing the practice. Such change is not necessarily easy, but it can be facilitated by better addressing the real variation in the system that the same analytics reveal. Similarly, in instances with excessive rounding (that is, rounding to time units that are too crude), the analytics approach can motivate more precise reporting.

18.5 Identifying Mixtures

In the Parkinson case, the distribution we observe is not lognormal even if the core is lognormal. The lognormal distribution may also apply, in spite of contradictory observations, in a mixture of two or more lognormal distributions. For example, tests were carried out on 24 projects from the Belgian data set. After accounting for rounding and for the Parkinson effect, 16 of those projects passed lognormality tests. Further research focusing on the eight failing projects has shown that three of them pass the tests after removing one or two clear outliers. The five remaining projects can all be explained as mixtures of a few lognormal distributions. The existence of an outlier can also be interpreted as a mixture in which the outlier represents a distinct distribution. Therefore, analysis of mixtures is important to consider when performing the analysis.

In project applications, in addition to equipment failures that are directly analogous to machine breakdowns, the effects of bad weather on some activities may be similar to the same model: Good weather is akin to an up machine, and it can go up and down several times during an activity. We also know that some weather events are rare but more disruptive than others and thus increase the coefficient of variation sizably. When some activities are subject to weather disruptions but others are not, we may observe a mixture.

We illustrate mixtures by analyzing project C2014-03 from the Belgian data set, which is one of the eight projects that did not pass the first normality test. Focusing on activities planned for one week – the smallest time unit used in this case – the left side of Figure 18.5 shows the Q–Q plot of $\ln(p_j/e_j)$ for the 73 activities in this subset. Of those, no activity is early and 45 are reported precisely on time. It is quite unlikely that all 45 on-time points are due to rounding

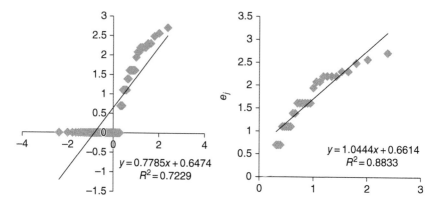

Figure 18.5 Normal Q–Q plot of ln(p_j) for project C2014-03 where $e_j = 1$, with the on-time activities included (left) and after correcting for the Parkinson effect (right).

and the right side of the figure supports the analysis under the assumption that the on-time points reflect hidden earliness – that is, we hypothesize that a strong pure Parkinson effect is present. Even if rounded, lognormality is rejected for the right-side chart, with a probability below 5%. Furthermore, based on the estimated parameters, there should not be so many points near and below zero. However, if we assume the tardy points and the on-time points reflect two distinct distributions, lognormality cannot be rejected. Figure 18.6 shows the Q–Q chart of the tail with the scores it would have if it were a complete sample, before and after rounding. Both sides pass the normality test with probabilities of about 0.25 and 0.75 (based on statistical tables for curtailed normal samples). In this project, activities planned for more than a week are also apparently lognormal, but with different parameters. Therefore, the project exhibits a mixture of three distributions, although we cannot estimate the parameters of the points that are planned for one week and finished early or on time.

In Figure 18.6, all values are strictly positive, and we might ask whether some on-time observations should be added to the subset. However, using the estimated parameters ($m = 1.69$ and $s = 0.61$), we find that the probability an observation might belong to this subset is associated with a very small z-value of -2.77. This value corresponds to a probability of about 0.003, so the chance that one on-time observation has been missed in a subset of $73 - 41 + 1 = 29$ observations is less than 8%.

In this case, the partition is based on observing how different the tail is from the other observations. In general, we need a way to partition sets of activities that do not pass normality tests. In principle, this is a cluster analysis problem, and it can be addressed with cluster analysis tools. As a rule, one should not expect a perfect resolution, but it helps when we can use related field information such as subproject structure. When dealing with published data sets,

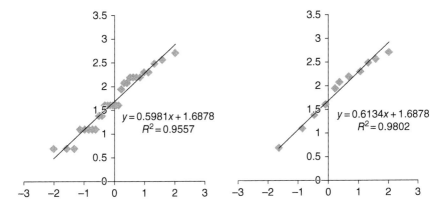

Figure 18.6 Normal Q–Q plot of ln(p_j) for project C2014-03 where $e_j = 1$ and $p_j > 1$ before (left) and after correcting for rounding (right).

however, only final results are provided, and the analysis must be based purely on those data. Success in this case is showing that a mixture of very few lognormal distributions fits the data. With the data we have, it is *always* possible to fit the data using *many* lognormal distributions: In the extreme case, each activity could have its own expected ratio. However, when very few (m_i and s_i) pairs can cover a full project, the evidence is more compelling.

Once planned durations and all project-specific information (such as subproject structure) have been utilized, we may still not be able to identify a mixture that passes the normality test. In that case, we can adopt the heuristic of minimizing the standard error, SE_Y. We start with the Q–Q chart that failed the normality test and remove from it the activity that will decrease SE_Y most. Then we continue to remove observations this way as long as SE_Y decreases (but with the caveat that once we drop below three activities, it is no longer possible to estimate a standard error). When SE_Y has been minimized, we are left with one subset that may (or may not) pass a normality test and a complementary subset of removed observations. We can now repeat the procedure on the removed observations. Ideally, there will be very few sub-subsets. Single points that do not fit well with larger subsets should be considered as outliers, and if we have too many that we can't explain, their presence suggests it may be difficult to make predictions for future projects.

Once a mixture is identified, we must find its cause if we want to use it for prediction in future projects. If the cause is analogous to machine breakdown (for instance, bad weather), then every future activity in similar projects may be subject to the same problem, and the mixture distribution applies to each activity separately. On the other hand, we may be able to identify subsets of activities that have different distributions for some other identifiable reason, and that information can be used in future projects to partition similar activities in advance, applying to each subset its own distribution.

18.6   Addressing Subjective Estimation Bias

The first step in understanding variation in our context is to realize that activity durations are always subject to random effects that make it impossible to predict them exactly. To describe those effects, we fit a distribution to historical data, with *estimated* parameters such as mean and variance. These estimates are subject to error. In general, estimation error often includes *estimation bias*, which is usually measured as an additive average deviation from the true expected value of the estimated distribution. In our context, however, we are applying that measurement to log-transformed data, so with respect to the original data, we consider multiplicative bias.

Estimation bias is due to such factors as the following:

- Mistakes caused by human error.
- Failure to anticipate possible problems.
- Optimism and pressure to produce attractive estimates from project champions who tend to emphasize opportunities.
- Pessimism and pressure to produce cautious estimates from skeptics who tend to emphasize risks.

Most of these factors involve subjective judgment or personal traits. Historically, when PERT was first developed, practitioners pointed out that different people exhibit different biases. In response, the authors of the seminal PERT paper suggested calibrating subjective estimates by studying the accuracy of estimates by each person who provides them, over time, so that the average bias can be corrected in future estimates. Field data suggests that some managers provide relatively accurate estimates, but, in general, that historical PERT recommendation has been observed in the breach. It certainly failed to enter standard PERT coverage in the literature. Therefore, in a practical sense, we can say that calibration is not part of PERT. Nevertheless, it is often possible to produce objective estimates using regression analysis of historical durations of similar activities. In one published instance, the analysis of historical data suggested that a good estimate of the duration, p_j, of one company's programming project was given by the regression model

$$\ln(p_j) = 0.249 + 1.034\ln(Subs) - 0.423Mgr5$$

where *Subs* denotes the number of subroutines and *Mgr5* is an indicator variable that takes the value 1 if a particular manager is responsible for the task, and 0 otherwise. The regression indicates that programming takes over 1/3 less time under Manager 5 on average (although the model does not tell us the cause). This regression had $SE_Y = 0.8259$, and all three factors were highly significant. An almost equally good result was obtained by the simpler single-variable regression model

$$\ln(p_j) = 0.201 + 1.035\ln(Subs)$$

for which $SE_Y = 0.836$.

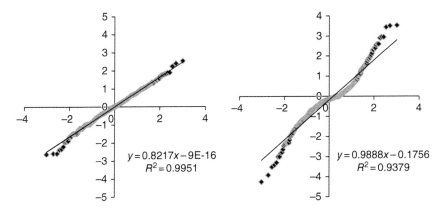

Figure 18.7 Normal Q–Q plot of the residuals of the Hill et al. (2000) estimates by regression (left) and subjective estimates (right), with log-transformed data.

Both models above are unbiased, because they were based on regression using objective data. That is, they produced accurate estimates. The original study also included estimated durations produced by the six managers. On average, the quality of those estimates proved to be lower than that of the regression-based ones. The left side of Figure 18.7 is a Q–Q chart of the residuals of the first model (with the two explaining variables), whereas the right side is a similar chart showing the residuals of the subjective estimates (subject to the same logarithmic transformation). In this case, $SE_Y = 1.018$. Clearly the chart on the right shows a non-normal distribution with a higher average standard deviation. Indeed, the maximal errors are larger, as can be seen by comparing the vertical scales. Incidentally, the slope on the left, 0.8246, matches the corresponding SE_Y value very closely (at 0.8259), whereas on the right, the slope 0.9888 is a less precise match of the corresponding value (1.018). A close match is an indication of normality, and it is clear that the distribution on the right, where the match is not as good, is not normal. In terms of personal bias, three of the managers had surprisingly small bias values, possibly indicating that they have learned to calibrate their estimates, but the three other managers exhibited logarithmic bias ranging from a pessimistic −0.90 (leading to largely conservative estimates) to optimistic biases of 0.15 and 0.77, tending to lead to tardiness. Interestingly enough, Manager 5 was one of those whose estimates were accurate. Therefore, his programmers took shorter than average time to complete tasks, and he was able to predict that effect accurately. (Regarding the right side of Figure 18.7, one might think that it is a mixture of normal distributions, given that it reflects a mix of estimates from six different individuals, but even when judged one by one, most of these managers did not produce normally distributed residuals.)

In the next section we consider another family of Armenian projects consisting of nine diverse projects run by the same manager employing various subcontractors. These projects involved a highly optimistic estimation bias as well as high variation and the Parkinson effect; that is, activities were never reported early and often very late. Among other results, the analysis demonstrates that the original PERT calibration recommendation was meritorious, but not sufficient: We must also account for the variance of the bias.

18.7 Linear Association

18.7.1 Systemic Bias

Alongside the subjective causes of bias, several activities are often affected by common factors and unpredictable events, including weather conditions, general economic conditions, accidents, and employee turnover. Such factors are random and, importantly, they may be different for different projects. In other words, bias can occur for various reasons, and all such causes may be different for different projects. For convenience, we treat the combination of all these causes as estimation bias. In general, estimation bias is not known in advance for any project, so it must be treated as random. Therefore, in addition to adjusting for the *average* bias, we must also account for the *variance* of the bias. To clarify this statement, assume that we have a set of K projects, with ratio data drawn independently from a single lognormal distribution. For convenience, assume also that the distribution is basic (that is, without bias), so $\mu = 1$ and $cv = \sigma$. Under these assumptions, the parameters of the lognormal distribution are $m = -s^2/2$ and $s = [\ln(1 + \sigma^2)]^{1/2}$. We can now think about the K lists of log-transformed ratios as independent samples of n_k draws each (for $k = 1, 2, ..., K$), drawn independently from a normal distribution. Therefore, if we run an ANOVA on those K lists, we should not be able to reject the hypothesis that the assumptions are valid. Furthermore, the same applies even if the original distribution is biased: ANOVA is not sensitive to adding or removing any constant to all the data (or to scaling), and calibration is achieved by adding a constant to all log-transformed ratios. Hence, calibration, or lack thereof, has no effect on the ANOVA test result. However, in several data sets obtained from organizations with more than one project, none passed the ANOVA test; that is, biases differed from each other sufficiently to trigger rejection of the hypothesis that the bias was constant for all projects. In other words, when predicting the results of a new project considered sufficiently similar to a set of historical projects with such random bias values, we should create a sample in which different runs are each subject to a random realization from the distribution of the bias (in addition to the randomness of individual activities). Accounting for the variance of the bias is important because when it is high, those individual runs will be more diverse than when it is low. In practical terms, we typically need more safety time.

The variance of the bias is the cause of statistical dependence among the deviations from predicted durations in a given project. If all estimates in all projects were equally biased, we could eventually learn to adjust for bias perfectly. However, because the deviations are random and cannot be predicted precisely, the estimation errors of single projects, measured relative to their original estimates, are positively correlated with each other even if the underlying distributions are independent. Specifically, optimistic estimates will lead to longer-than-expected activity durations throughout the project, whereas pessimistic estimates will lead to shorter-than-expected activity durations. A similar technical observation applies to other differences, such as the differences between managers in the Hill et al. (2000) case, where we did not distinguish among projects but among managers. In either case, the deviations from the estimates are positively correlated.

Bias applies not only to duration estimates but also to cost estimates. For instance, data provided by Lipke et al. (2009) suggest that the ratio of duration to estimate and the ratio of cost to budget both follow a lognormal distribution. Figure 18.8 provides the Q–Q charts for 12 projects, duration on the left and expenditure on the right. Both sides pass normality tests, suggesting that the biases that apply to the projects are distributed lognormally. Incidentally, almost all those projects were over budget and missed their due dates. Two of them were either Parkinsonian or almost on time, and we depict them as on time (on the axis) because that minimizes SE_Y. Although the charts may not appear very linear, they pass the normality tests with p-values of slightly above 0.5 and about 0.9. That is because, with only 12 points, large deviations are not unlikely.

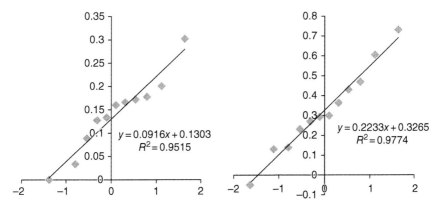

Figure 18.8 Normal Q–Q plot for durations (left) and expenditures (right) for 12 projects as reported by Lipke et al. (2009).

From Figure 18.8, we may hypothesize that the 12 projects were subject to significantly different average budget and schedule means. Furthermore, the figure suggests that the bias distribution itself is lognormal (before log-transformation). This is an important observation because ANOVA cannot be used to find the distribution of the bias: It only serves to indicate whether significant bias differences exist or not. As discussed earlier, in predicting the performance of a new project, we must take into account the variance of the random bias effect as well as the variance exhibited by single projects – that is, we must anticipate the effects of both the between-projects and within-projects variation. The linear association model can serve this purpose. It does that essentially by assuming that we will experience lognormally distributed ratios of durations to plan, multiplied by a single random bias. It is because that random bias is different between projects that ANOVA rejects the hypothesis that all duration distributions are independent. Furthermore, because field data suggests that the random bias tends to be lognormal, too, we obtain positively correlated lognormal ratios.

Consider again the case in which we have a history of K projects, each with its own bias. In general, we use the single index k to denote any particular project in that set. For instance, we denote the bias of project k by b_k, for $k = 1, 2, ..., K$. We use a double index, jk, for activity j of project k. For instance, p_{jk} is the duration of this activity (where $k = 1, 2, ..., K$ and $j = 1, 2, ..., n_k$). Let $y_{jk} = p_{jk}/e_{jk}$ and $x_{jk} = y_{jk}/b_k = p_{jk}/(b_k e_{jk})$. That is, y_{jk} is the ratio of the duration to the estimate, and x_{jk} is the same ratio adjusted for bias. Equivalently, $b_k x_{jk} = y_{jk}$. If we now think about x_{jk} and y_{jk} each as the jth realization of random variables X_k and Y_k, respectively, then $Y_k = BX_k$, and B – the random variable of which b_k is a realization – is independent of X_k. Therefore, by definition, the vector $y_{jk} = p_{jk}/e_{jk}$ consists of n_k linearly associated realizations (see Appendix A).

In previous sections, we mainly considered solitary projects, and by focusing on p_{jk}/e_{jk} ratios, we essentially analyzed realizations of Y. We found empirically that Y can be modeled as lognormal. In other words, after log-transformation, we established that Y is normal. Now we consider groups of related projects, and we model Y_k as a product of two independent random variables, B and X_k. After log-transformation, however, this product becomes a convolution (that is, a sum). It can be shown that no convolution of two independent random variables can have a normal distribution unless both of them are normal. In other words, the sum is normal if and only if the two components are normal. Therefore, by claiming that Y_k is lognormal, we imply that B and X are both lognormal too. Furthermore, following the analysis in Appendix A, the elements of Y are positively correlated.

To estimate the necessary parameters, recall that we have historical records for $K > 1$ projects. For project k, our historical data consist of n_k pairs (p_{jk}, e_{jk}), where p_{jk} is the realization and e_{jk} is the original estimate. We can estimate the logarithm of the bias for project k, $\ln(b_k)$, by the following estimator:

$$\text{l}\hat{\text{n}}(b_k) = \frac{\sum_{j=1}^{n_k} \ln(p_{jk}/e_{jk})}{n_k}$$

If we give each of these estimators a weight proportional to n_k, we obtain the following estimator of $\ln(\mu_B)$, where μ_B is the mean of B,

$$\text{l}\hat{\text{n}}(\mu_B) = \frac{\sum_{k=1}^{K} n_k \text{l}\hat{\text{n}}(b_k)}{\sum_{k=1}^{K} n_k}$$

and we obtain the following unbiased estimator of s_B^2, which is the variance of $\ln(\mu_B)$:

$$\hat{s}_B^2 = \frac{\sum_{k=1}^{K} n_k (\text{l}\hat{\text{n}}(b_k) - \text{l}\hat{\text{n}}(\mu_B))^2}{\sum_{k=1}^{K} n_k - K}$$

To estimate s_k, the standard deviation of $\ln(p_{jk}/e_{jk})$ for project k, we can use the standard deviation of the set $\{\ln(p_{jk}/b_k e_{jk})\}$ for $j = 1, \ldots, n_k$, where the bias element is neutralized by b_k and where b_k is estimated by the exponent of $\text{l}\hat{\text{n}}(b_k)$. When there is no significant difference between the K values of s_k, we can estimate a single s value for all projects by pooling their values of $\{\ln(p_{jk}/b_k e_{jk})\}$ together. For the time being, we assume that is the case. Therefore, we expect that any new project in the same family will possess a logarithmic bias drawn from a normal distribution with mean $\text{l}\hat{\text{n}}(\mu_B)$ and variance $\hat{s}_B^2$. Similarly, we expect that new project to have a basic lognormal estimate distribution with s drawn from the same distribution that generated the s_k values for the K projects in the history. The reason we assume basic distributions here is that average bias, if any, is now incorporated in μ_B.

Given those estimated parameters and a new set of activity estimates, it is straightforward to generate a sample for a future project with the same s where, for each run in the sample, we generate one bias realization that multiplies all the basic normal sampled values. In more detail, suppose we wish to generate a sample containing r replications (or runs). (Think of r rows for the replications and n columns for the activities.) First, we generate one bias element, b, per row and store it in an auxiliary column. Similarly, we generate n basic lognormal realizations with $cv = s$ and multiply them by the activity estimates, e_j, and by the single simulated bias value. Keep in mind that adding logarithms corresponds to multiplying their exponents. Thus, all elements in the row share the same bias element and the same variance, but no two rows have the same bias. We can extend the methodology to cases where we expect different projects to have different estimates of s by fitting a distribution to s as well. Another approach that does not require a single s value for all projects is by a nonparametric bootstrap resampling approach, which we discuss in Subsection 18.7.3.

18.7.2 Cross-Validation

Linear association has been validated for few families of projects by cross-validation. Cross-validation is an analytics technique whereby if we have full information about a family of K projects, we use $K - 1$ of them to "predict" the performance of the other project, and we repeat this process for all K projects. Each such "prediction" involves generating a random sample with parameters based on the analysis of the $K - 1$ remaining projects. Those provide us with estimates of m and s both for the within-project variation and the bias element (between-projects variation). We denote the latter by the subscript B, that is, m_B and s_B. To simulate a run we start by simulating n normal values for $\ln(p_j/e_j)$, all with mean m and standard deviation s, and one normal value with mean m_B and standard deviation s_B (the simulated bias value). We may place these values in the first $n + 1$ columns of a table with $2n + 1$ columns. In the remaining n columns, we can place either the sums of the first n columns with the bias value (thus recording logarithms) or the exponent of the same sum multiplied by e_j (if we wish to record simulated durations). Next, we use the last n columns to obtain a simulated project duration. Together, our r runs can then provide us with an empirical distribution of the project duration. For this purpose, we may assume that our projects are serial, so the project length is given by the sum of all activity durations. Serial projects have no Jensen gaps. Therefore, we can study the independence assumption without confounding it with the Jensen gap. (Real projects are seldom serial, however, so we may choose to find the simulated duration by simulating a project with network information incorporated. For cross-validation, however, that is not necessary.) Our true duration – which we know because we are "predicting" for a project we already performed – corresponds to a probability, $F(C)$, where F is the empirical (simulated) distribution and C is the project completion time. After repeating this process for all K projects, we obtain a set of K such probabilities. If linear association is valid for the K projects, these K probabilities should be a sample of K standard uniform random variables. We can test the hypothesis that they are indeed such a sample by P–P chart analysis. For our purpose, a P–P chart is a special case of a Q–Q chart designed specifically for the standard uniform distribution, and it assumes that the input is a sample from the uniform distribution. Under the assumption the points depicted should be close to the diagonal from the bottom left to the top right of the chart. When we say that linear association has been validated for field data, we mean that such analysis could not reject the hypothesis that such samples are indeed independent draws from a standard uniform distribution. In the two P–P charts of Figure 18.9, depicting the nine Armenian projects mentioned in Section 18.6, the one on the left shows the results of using original estimates with correct within-project variation but assuming independence, whereas the right side is based on linear association and thus incorporates the random bias element. Recall that the bias element induces dependence between project activity durations (because all of

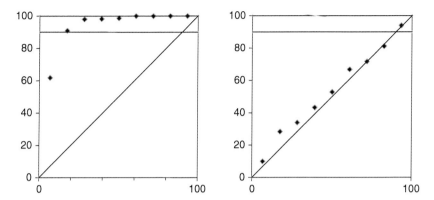

Figure 18.9 P–P charts for a family of nine projects based on the PERT independence assumption (left) and on cross-validation of linear association by nonparametric bootstrap (right) (Trietsch et al. 2012).

them tend to be lower or higher than planned, based on the bias). The left side of the figure shows that most projects took much longer than expected under the PERT assumptions. In general, poor performance is due to two PERT weaknesses. First, there is no calibration, and indeed, in the case of these nine projects, apparently, the project manager generated highly optimistic estimates. Second, the independence assumption tends to push realizations to either too high or too low $F(C)$ values (a point to which we return later). Here, the high bias pushes all but one of the projects above the 90% line. That implies that if we were to provide enough safety time to match SL = 90%, it would fail badly in seven out of the nine projects, fail slightly in one project, and suffice in only one project. In other words, the PERT safe-scheduling model would fail badly. On the right, however, exactly one project exceeds the 90% level, which is well within what we should expect; the probability that exactly one project out of nine fails at the 90% level is 39% (and the probability it will be one or less is 77%). Technically, in the case depicted, cross-validation for the right-hand side was performed by the nonparametric bootstrap resampling approach, as we discuss next.

18.7.3 Using Nonparametric Bootstrap Sampling

When historical data is scarce, *nonparametric bootstrap resampling* is a simple yet effective way to generate samples of a useful size. In brief, nonparametric bootstrap sampling uses historical data as an empirical distribution and creates samples of any desired size by sampling from that distribution. The sampling is conducted with replacement, which implies that the same value may be sampled more than once.

In more detail, we rely on the observation that the ratios p_j/e_j are lognormal, so the historical data we need for each past project is a list of such ratios. To generate a simulated scenario for an activity of a new project, we first sample a ratio from some historical project (with replacement) and then multiply this sampled ratio by the new estimate. In this procedure, it is crucial to keep the historical information separated by project and to use a single project for sampling each new ratio. (Sampling from a pooled list would essentially be assuming independence and would be appropriate if all bias elements were equal.) That is, for each run we should sample ratios from a single historical project and permit different runs to reflect different realizations of the historical common factor. Because the sampling is done with replacement, we can keep the projects separate even if some historical project has fewer activities than the new one, although large projects in the historical data set should attract sampling more often than small ones. Furthermore, we may also wish to discount old projects, by reducing the frequency at which they are sampled. In what follows, however, we do not use such discounting.

Given historical data sets of K projects, it is generally possible to "predict" the performance of any one of them by using the other $(K - 1)$ projects as our "history." In the following example, we illustrate the technique (as it might be implemented both under the PERT independence assumption and under the linear association assumption) and the methodology by which it can be validated when field data are available.

■ **Example 18.1** Suppose we have historical data for three projects, as given by the three parts of Table 18.1, where the double index (j, k) indicates activity j of project k.

If we were just starting Project 3, our combined history from Projects 1 and 2 would be a list of nine ratios ranging from 0.50 to 2.00. In that history, Project 1 has a higher weight because it has five activities compared with four for Project 2. To simulate one run of Project 3 under the PERT independence assumption, we first sample three ratios from the combined history, say, 1.25, 0.57, and 2.0. By multiplying these ratios by the estimates of Project 3, namely, $e_{1,3} = 4$, $e_{2,3} = 2$, and $e_{3,3} = 1$, and summing the products, we simulate the project duration as 5 + 8/7 + 2 = 8.14. We repeat the same process multiple times to obtain our bootstrapped sample. By sorting the results we obtain an empirical cdf, denoting the empirical cdf of project k by $F_k(t)$. In what follows, we assume for convenience that $F_k(t)$ is continuous. (It is actually a step function, but our assumption is mild if we use a large number of repetitions.) In a similar vein, $F_k(t)$ is based on sampling from a small set, so repetitions are quite likely. We can avoid repetitions by adding some white noise into the picture. Such white noise could represent rounding effects, for instance. We ran 100 repetitions for Project 3 (sampling from the data of Projects 1 and 2) and obtained a distribution ranging between

Table 18.1

Project 1					
Index	1, 1	2, 1	3, 1	4, 1	5, 1
Estimate	4	1	7	2	6
Actual	5	1	4	2	5
Ratio	1.25	1.00	0.57	1.00	0.83
Project 2					
Index	1, 2	2, 2	3, 2	4, 2	
Estimate	2	4	2	6	
Actual	2	2	4	4	
Ratio	1.00	0.50	2.00	0.67	
Project 3					
Index	1, 3	2, 3	3, 3		
Estimate	4	2	1		
Actual	1	4	1		
Ratio	0.25	2.00	1.00		

3.5 and 13. The run demonstrated above has a p-value of $F_3(8.14) = 0.69$ (because 68 of the 100 runs were strictly smaller than 8.14).

Next, let C_k denote the actual completion time of Project k, and suppose that each project has a serial precedence structure. Then, from Table 18.1, we obtain $C_1 = 5 + 1 + 4 + 2 + 5 = 17$, $C_2 = 12$, and $C_3 = 6$. Given the empirical distribution and the actual completion times, we calculate the value $F_k(C_k)$ for each project. In our example, $F_3(C_3) = F_3(6) = 0.29$ because 29 of the 100 runs were strictly smaller than 6. (By itself, this value is plausible. It might be considered suspicious if it were very close to 0 or to 1.)

To use the same data set under the assumption that projects are subject to linear association, we sample each scenario from either Project 1 or Project 2, with frequencies of 5/9 and 4/9, respectively. Suppose Project 2 is selected. Then we sample three ratios, with replacement, out of the set {1.00, 0.50, 2.00, 0.67}, and use them to calculate the run's duration as we did before. As a result, if there is indeed a systemic difference in the mean of each historical project, that difference will manifest as variation *between* runs. Thus, the variance we observe for the sum of all activity durations will be larger.

Figure 18.10 revisits the nine Armenian projects and demonstrates the difference between sampling from a pooled list (on the left) and sampling each run from a single historical project such that the frequency at which a historical project is resampled is proportional to its number of activities. The right side of the figure is the same as in Figure 18.8, and we repeat it to facilitate comparing

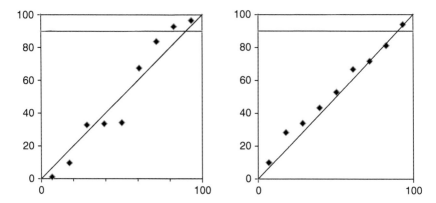

Figure 18.10 Cross-validation of nine Armenian projects by nonparametric bootstrap, with correction for average bias only (left) and accounting for the variance of the bias by linear association (right).

the two approaches. We observe that the left side is significantly better than in the previous figure, thus confirming that correcting for average bias – as historically recommended by the PERT team – is highly beneficial. But we also observe that there is a tendency for projects to have either very high or very low probabilities, which is an indication of underestimated variance. In this case, four out of nine projects are either below 10 or above 90%, an event with a probability of less than 2% if we believe the sample represents nine independent draws from a uniform distribution. In other words, we can reject the hypothesis that accounting for only average bias is sufficient.

18.8   Summary

Our basic premise is that in order to bridge the gap between theory and practice, we should consider stochastic models that take into account the need for safety time, that is, safe scheduling. Nevertheless, even the most elegant stochastic model is useless in practice if it is based on invalid assumptions. For instance, models based on the independence assumption may be useful for providing insights into the effects of stochastic activity durations but should not be used in practice without validating the assumption. Similarly, models based on the exponential distribution are almost invariably useful only for such insights, and models based on the normal distribution are inherently restricted to low variation environments. Our focus in this chapter was on validating the lognormal distribution and showing how to use it to generate reliable samples for projects.

The key insight behind our empirical observations is that typical deviations are not additive but multiplicative. For instance, if we planned on a duration of 12 and the realization was 15, we should not think about it as 12 + 3 but rather as 12 × 1.25. In other words, to obtain additive models, we should work with logarithms. Once we do that, the normal distribution appears to be ubiquitous, but it is still subject to various masking effects. Those include rounding errors, the Parkinson effect (hidden earliness), and mixtures. In response, we must correct for rounding and for the Parkinson effect, and we must be able to partition the data to reveal mixtures. In addition, we must be able to model stochastic dependence. Research on all these issues is fairly recent, and we still do not have fully adequate models for complex cases that combine several of the issues mentioned above. For instance, we presented linear association as a useful model for dependence, but we assumed it applied to comparable projects or parts of projects. Suppose we have several similar projects, each of which is partitioned to three subsets of activities. We should not expect the same common factor to apply for the subsets of a single project and between projects. This situation calls for a hierarchical model where one bias element applies to different projects and a second bias element applies between subsets of each project. In summary, to build a sample, we would start by generating a project bias, then generate subset biases, and finally generate runs. Therefore, each run will reflect a global bias element and subset bias elements relative to the global bias. At this stage, however, there are no published results on such hierarchical bias models. However, one advantage of nonparametric bootstrap sampling is that it is not necessary to be able to calculate all the necessary parameters. To predict a new project with three subsets of activities that are similar to a set of historical projects, each with similar subsets, each run of the simulation can use information from a single project as applied to all subsets. Thus, if there is a bias element between subsets of single projects, it will be reflected in each run.

Another important point is that to make predictions for future projects – that is, to construct reliable samples for them – we rely on historical information from similar projects. Ideally, that implies these historical projects are inherently similar (for instance, construction projects), come from the same organization, and run under the same management. One might think that if we do not have such ideal history, the methodology will not be implementable. However, some reflection reveals that without such history, we simply face more randomness. For instance, if we don't know anything about the performance of the particular manager assigned to the new project, we should anticipate a "between-managers" bias element. Likewise, if we don't even have history from our own organization, we are facing an additional "between-organizations" bias element. When that is the case, we can use industry-wide history but expect high variation. Again, this high variation is not because the model is inadequate but because our historical knowledge is scant. Indeed, such projects are inherently more risky.

The next chapter addresses safe scheduling for projects and builds on the basic project scheduling concepts of Chapters 16 and 17. In addition, it assumes we already have a reliable sample for all activities of a new project, generated as described in this chapter.

Bibliography

Batselier, J. and Vanhoucke, M. (2015). Construction and evaluation framework for real-life project database. *International Journal of Project Management* 33: 697–710.

Colin, J. and Vanhoucke, M. (2015). Empirical perspective on activity durations for project-management simulation studies. *Journal of Construction Engineering Management* 142 (1): 1–13.

Gevorgyan, L. (2008). Project duration estimation with corrections for systemic error. Master Thesis. American University of Armenia, Yerevan, Armenia.

Hill, J., Thomas, L.C., and Allen, D.E. (2000). Experts' estimates of task durations in software development projects. *International Journal of Project Management* 18: 13–21.

Johnston, J. and Dinardo, J. (1997). *Econometric Methods*, 4e. New York: McGraw-Hill/Irwin.

Lipke, W., Zwikael, O., Henderson, K., and Anbari, F. (2009). The application of statistical methods to earned value management and earned schedule performance indexes. *International Journal of Project Management* 27: 400–407.

Looney, S.W. and Gulledge, T.R. (1985). Use of the correlation coefficient with normal probability plots. *The American Statistician* 39 (1): 75–79.

Malcolm, D.G., Roseboom, J.H., Clark, C.E., and Fazar, W. (1959). Application of a technique for a research and development program evaluation. *Operations Research* 7: 646–669.

May, J.H., Strum, D.P., and Vargas, L.G. (2000). Fitting the lognormal distribution to surgical procedure times. *Decision Sciences* 31: 129–148.

Shapiro, S.S. and Wilk, M.B. (1965). An analysis of variance test for normality (complete samples). *Biometrika* 65: 591–611.

Strum, D.P., Sampson, A.R., May, J.H., and Vargas, L.G. (2000). Surgeon and type of anesthesia predict variability in surgical procedure times. *Anesthesiology* 92: 1454–1466.

Trietsch, D. (2005). The effect of systemic errors on optimal project buffers. *International Journal of Project Management* 23: 267–274.

Trietsch, D., Mazmanyan, L., Gevorgyan, L., and Baker, K.R. (2012). Modeling activity times by the Parkinson distribution with a lognormal core: theory and validation. *European Journal of Operational Research* 216: 386–396.

Trietsch, D. and Baker, K.R. (2012). PERT 21: fitting PERT/CPM for use in the 21st century. *International Journal of Project Management* 30: 490–502.

Verrill, S. and Johnson, A. (1988). Tables and large-sample distribution theory for censored-data correlation statistics for testing normality. *Journal of the American Statistical Association* 83: 1192–1197.

19

PERT 21

Analytics-Based Safe Project Scheduling

19.1 Introduction

Historically, CPM and PERT were not merely theoretical frameworks for project scheduling and resource allocation, but they were also marketed successfully as decision support systems (DSS). To this day they retain that function. Our coverage in the previous three chapters provides the theoretical underpinnings of project scheduling as reflected in most of those systems. In this chapter, we progress beyond the standard functionality. We do so mainly by introducing more advanced safe scheduling models. Furthermore, these models utilize reliable samples that reflect historical experience for simulation-based analysis as discussed in Chapter 18. We refer to the framework we describe as PERT 21, because it adapts PERT/CPM for use in the twenty-first century. The most important difference between PERT 21 and PERT/CPM as implemented in project management DSS today is that it is based on validated distributional assumptions. Those assumptions are justified by empirical evidence validating the use of lognormal processing times subject to linear association and possibly the Parkinson effect (see Chapter 18). Serendipitously, instead of triplets as in PERT, users need to input only estimates of mean durations. All other necessary parameters can then be estimated from the historical performance of similar single-point estimates. It is even possible to bypass the need to estimate parameters explicitly and still achieve reliable samples by using nonparametric bootstrap resampling, which treats historical samples as empirical distributions. Those distributions can then be used to generate new samples by drawing from them randomly with replacement. Because the sampling is done with replacement, it is possible to generate samples larger in size than the original data. As the name implies, we do not need to estimate distributional parameters to generate a new sample. Therefore, for stochastic analysis, it is easier to use PERT 21 than conventional PERT.

Principles of Sequencing and Scheduling, Second Edition. Kenneth R. Baker and Dan Trietsch.
© 2019 John Wiley & Sons, Inc. Published 2019 by John Wiley & Sons, Inc.

The main objective of safe scheduling is to set due dates and release dates in anticipation of stochastic variation. In some cases, it is also possible to characterize the optimal sequence as the basis for these decisions, but in complex environments (such as flow shops, job shops, and projects), the state of the art, at least in practice, relies on deterministic analysis for sequencing decisions followed by stochastic analysis for timing decisions. In this chapter, we assume that sequencing decisions have been made and enforced by soft precedence constraints or by a policy comprising a priority list as well as soft constraints, as discussed in Section 17.5. As a rule, activities that require complex and lengthy preparations should be sequenced in advance, whereas activities that can be started easily may be sequenced dynamically. We study how to set release dates for a given due date by addressing a stochastic earliness and tardiness (E/T) problem in which activity earliness is balanced against project tardiness. We also discuss the implications of stochastic variation for crashing. Our analysis departs from traditional PERT assumptions in two major ways: (i) We do not assume stochastic independence among activity durations, and (ii) we do not assume beta distributions. In Chapters 16 and 18, we discussed how the independence assumption may lead to implausible conclusions. We also discussed the difficulties associated with the triplet elicitation method and the beta assumption. Those problems are avoided by the simulation-based analysis in PERT 21.

In project scheduling, we often find that expenses are incurred during the project's execution but revenue is generated only when the project is complete. We therefore have an incentive to postpone activities as much as possible without violating the due date. When no due date is imposed, we want to postpone non-critical activities as much as possible without increasing the makespan. As in the single-machine case (see Section 7.6), we can enforce such a policy by imposing release dates (r_j) for activities. The imposition of release dates is important for a project because the default is usually to begin each activity at its early start time, thus incurring unnecessary earliness costs.

To create a framework for analysis, we begin with a deterministic environment in which a project consists of n activities and has a due date (d). Each activity incurs an earliness cost per unit time denoted α_j for activity j. This earliness cost reflects the economic value of postponing the activity and may also be viewed as a holding cost. The project incurs a tardiness cost per unit time denoted β. In practice, tardiness cost reflects the delay in obtaining revenue and often includes explicit compensation to customers when a due date is missed. Ideally, we would like to balance activities' earliness costs against the project's tardiness cost. The objective is thus to minimize total E/T cost, or

$$Z = \beta(C-d) + \sum_{i=1}^{n} \alpha_j\left(C - r_j\right)$$

where $C \geq d$ represents the project completion time. We assume that d is given, as if it had been negotiated with a customer. The customer provides no external incentive for early completion, so we proceed as if the output of the project is provided to the customer at the due date or as soon as possible thereafter. In other words, if the project completes prior to the due date, delivery to the customer still occurs on the due date, fulfilling the negotiated agreement. If the project completes later than the due date, then the tardiness cost applies. On the other hand, earliness cost reflects the length of time an activity is held in the system – that is, its flowtime. In the project setting, this length of time is given by $(C - r_j)$ for activity j because the activity incurs holding cost until the entire project is completed.

If no due date is imposed, we can set $d = 0$. This convention ensures that tardiness costs will be incurred, thus providing an incentive to achieve a short makespan. In this case, the tardiness cost reflects the makespan incentive, which must be traded off against the earliness costs in the project. Thus, whether we have a given due date or not, we can use Z as an objective function.

For convenience, we may sometimes write β as α_{n+1} and the project due date d as r_{n+1}. This substitution allows us to rewrite the objective as follows:

$$Z = \sum_{j=1}^{n+1} \alpha_j \left(C - r_j \right)$$

We define $\alpha = \alpha_1 + \alpha_2 + \cdots + \alpha_n$, obtaining

$$Z = (\alpha + \beta)C - \sum_{j=1}^{n+1} \alpha_j r_j$$

In the deterministic context, we minimize this objective by starting each activity as late as possible (at its late start time) and by finishing the project exactly at its due date.

19.2 Stochastic Balance Principles for Activity Networks

In our E/T model for a project, earliness cost reflects the difference between an activity's release date and the project due date, so we can reduce earliness cost by increasing the release date. However, in the stochastic case, postponing release dates may increase project completion time, exposing the project to greater risk of tardiness. Therefore, the interval between an activity's release date and the project due date should accommodate safety time as well as expected processing time. Our model calls for balancing E/T costs, including the effect of safety times. However, we need not calculate these safety times explicitly because they are determined implicitly by setting optimal release dates.

Mathematically, a release date has the same effect as a predecessor activity. We can think of a release date r_j as the time required by a preceding "activity" that starts at time zero and has a duration of r_j. Although we do not actually count release dates as activities, we may associate a criticality measure with each one. In Chapter 16, we defined the criticality of an activity as the probability that it lies on the critical path. Accordingly, the criticality, q_j, of a release date is the probability that the longest path includes the corresponding "activity." When the due date is sufficiently large, the optimal criticality of each release date, q_j^*, should satisfy a critical ratio that resembles the critical ratio that appeared in earlier chapters for similar problems. In particular, the optimal project service level, $\Pr\{C \le d\}$, should be set equal to $\beta/(\alpha + \beta)$, which we recognize as the critical ratio we saw in Chapter 7. By setting the release dates so that their criticalities are optimal, we essentially optimize the safety times for the project. We first derive this result for a case with special structure. Thereafter, we generalize the result and later discuss hierarchical implementation of the model (which also allows modeling progress payments).

19.2.1   The Assembly Coordination Model

In the *assembly coordination model* (ACM), n stochastically independent inputs must be coordinated to arrive on or before a given due date, in time for a planned assembly operation. Initially, we assume that procurement lead times for the inputs have continuous distributions. We also assume that the assembly operation is instantaneous (or at least that it takes a fixed amount of time) and that it starts on the due date or when the last input arrives, whichever is later. Figure 19.1 depicts the ACM as an AOA network. For convenience, we use the index 0 for the start node, so we can index the completion nodes of the release

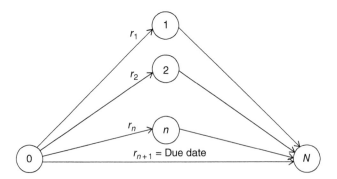

Figure 19.1 The ACM network structure.

date arcs from 1 to n. The due date is represented by the activity connecting node 0 to node N (the project completion node), and we represent its length as r_{n+1}.

The objective is to minimize

$$
\begin{aligned}
Z &= E\left[\sum_{j=1}^{n+1} \alpha_j (C - r_j)\right] \\
&= E\left[\sum_{j=1}^{n} \alpha_j (C - r_j) + \beta(C - d)\right] \\
&= E\left[\sum_{j=1}^{n} \alpha_j (C - d + d - r_j) + \beta(C - d)\right] \\
&= \sum_{j=1}^{n} \alpha_j (d - r_j) + (\alpha + \beta)E[(C - d)] \\
&= \sum_{j=1}^{n} \alpha_j (d - r_j) + (\alpha + \beta)\int_{d}^{\infty}\left[1 - \prod_{j=1}^{n} F_j (y - r_j)\right] dy
\end{aligned}
\tag{19.1}
$$

where $C \geq d \geq r_j$ for $j = 1, \ldots, n$. In this expression, $F_j(\cdot)$ denotes the cdf of the duration of activity j, so $F_j(y - r_j)$ represents the probability that input j will have arrived by time y. The product is the probability that all inputs will have arrived by time y. Therefore, this product is the cdf of the completion time. The integral (from d) of the complement of this probability yields the expected tardiness. The integral is multiplied by $(\alpha + \beta)$ because, during tardiness, all holding costs and the tardiness cost apply. Holding costs that occur with certainty while the project is in progress but before the due date are given by $\sum \alpha_j(d - r_j)$. Taking partial derivatives with respect to r_j, we obtain

$$
\frac{\partial Z}{\partial r_j} = -\alpha_j + (\alpha + \beta)\int_{d}^{\infty} f_j (y - r_j)\prod_{k \neq j} F_k(y - r_k)dy
$$

The criticality of r_j is given by the integral in this expression. First, $f_j(\cdot)$ denotes the probability density function (pdf) of a random variable representing the completion time of job j, provided it is critical. That will happen if input j arrives at time y (after the due date) and the other inputs have already arrived. In the expression, the product of the remaining cdf's represents the probability that the other inputs have already arrived. Integrating over all possible tardy completion times yields the criticality. The optimal criticality, q_j^*, is obtained when the release dates are selected so that the partial derivative is zero. This condition implies $q_j^* = \alpha_j/(\alpha + \beta)$, which we call *stochastic balance*. Although this analysis applies only to the release dates of the n activities, the same formula applies to the criticality of the due date as well, because the $(n + 1)$ criticalities must sum to 1. (With continuous distributions, the probability that more than one input is critical at the same time is zero.) Thus, the due date has a criticality of $\beta/(\alpha + \beta)$. The due date criticality is also the optimal service level of the project because the due date is critical when the project completes on time. Assuming that d is sufficiently large, we can adjust all n physical release dates to the required values.

If the distribution is discrete (or, equivalently, when using sample-based analysis), we modify the condition: An optimal release date is the smallest feasible value for which $q_j > \alpha_j/(\alpha + \beta)$. (See Appendix B.) If $q_j \leq \alpha_j/(\alpha + \beta)$, then it cannot harm us (and may help us) to increase the release date to the next level. In addition, we may obtain multiple critical paths, in which case the sum of criticalities exceeds unity.

We next remove the assumption that the due date is sufficiently large. Without this assumption, it may happen that even if we set release dates of zero, the criticality of some activities will already exceed $\alpha_j/(\alpha + \beta)$. For those activities, $r_j = 0$ is optimal. Other activities may be free to attain their optimal criticality. As a result, the project service level cannot reach its optimum. In effect, criticality is shifted from the due date to constrained resources, thus reducing the project service level. Therefore, the criticality of a constrained resource must be higher than $\alpha_j/(\alpha + \beta)$. To prove this, suppose that $q_j^* < \alpha_j/(\alpha + \beta)$ occurred at $r_j^* = 0$. Then we could increase the release date and by doing so increase the criticality and thus increase the partial derivative $\partial Z/\partial r_j$ toward zero – a contradiction. Thus, if r_j is set to zero due to a constraint, then we must have $q_j > \alpha_j/(\alpha + \beta)$. For constrained release dates, the true economic impact of postponing activity j is not α_j per time unit but some higher rate, v_j^*, such that $q_j^* = v_j^*/(\alpha + \beta)$.

Although the optimality conditions are analytical, it is seldom possible to compute optimal release dates from formulas, so we must resort to a numerical search. To facilitate this search, it is possible to calculate a bound on the optimal release dates. For example, we might set the release dates such that the probability an input arrives after the due date is at most $\alpha_j/(\alpha + \beta)$. Because an input that arrives on or before the due date cannot cause tardiness, these release dates (denoted r_j^L) constitute lower bounds on the optimal r_j.

Suppose that the due date is a decision variable and that our secondary objective is to minimize it. To minimize the objective function – our primary objective – we must drive n partial derivatives to zero, but we have $n + 1$ decision variables. Because there are too many variables, we can set one of them arbitrarily. However, our secondary objective dictates setting the earliest release date to zero. We can do so by starting with a large due date and then subtracting the minimal r_j from all $n + 1$ release dates.

Although the ACM can be solved numerically by minimizing Eq. (19.1) directly or by driving the partial derivatives to zero, that approach requires evaluating integrals and is computationally demanding. Sample-based analysis is more effective and can also be applied in more complex models.

■ **Example 19.1** Consider an ACM with 10 input activities and a due date of d = 94. The duration of each activity follows a lognormal distribution with mean (μ) and coefficient of variation (cv) given in the table. Also shown in the table are the earliness costs (α_j), which sum to α = 75. The tardiness cost is β = 225.

Input	1	2	3	4	5	6	7	8	9	10
μ	63	49	53	77	69	43	57	87	40	45
cv	0.20	0.35	0.30	0.10	0.15	0.45	0.25	0.05	0.50	0.40
α_j	3	4	5	6	7	8	9	10	11	12

We tackle this problem with a sample-based approach using a sample of 10 scenarios to demonstrate the calculations. (Such a small sample is not adequate to analyze this problem, and we comment later on the results of using a more appropriate sample size.) The 10 scenarios, along with some additional calculations, are shown in Table 19.1. All outcomes have been rounded to the first decimal place.

Below the table of scenarios, the first calculation is the maximum duration in the ten scenarios for each activity. The next row displays the given values of α_j. The next row shows the calculated values of the critical ratio, $\alpha_j/(\alpha + \beta)$. Ideally, we would like each activity to be critical with this probability, but because we have only 10 scenarios, the probability that an activity is critical must be either zero or some multiple of 0.1. Generalizing the insights of Chapter 7, the optimal criticality of each release date is obtained by $\lceil s\alpha_j/(\alpha + \beta) \rceil / s$, where s is the number of scenarios in the stored sample; that is, we use the smallest possible multiple of $1/s$ that is not smaller than the critical ratio. Note that $1 \le \lceil s\alpha_j/(\alpha + \beta) \rceil \le s$, so there must be a duration in the sample that provides this optimal criticality precisely. In our example, all $\alpha_j/(\alpha + \beta)$ values are below 0.1, so our target criticality is 0.1 for each of them.

The row of lower bounds shows the values of r_j^L. This value is the difference between the due date (94) and the maximum shown three rows above, or zero if that difference is negative. This value represents the latest time the activity could be released without violating the due date in any of the scenarios, or zero if necessary.

The formula is

$$r_j^L = \max\left(0, d - \max_s\{p_{sj}\}\right)$$

where p_{sj} denotes the duration of activity j in scenario s.

Table 19.1

Scenario					Input						
	1	2	3	4	5	6	7	8	9	10	Due date
1	62.9	51.5	44.2	66.2	54.5	35.7	88.6	85.3	23.2	46.9	94
2	41.6	46.8	61.5	80.5	75.3	35.1	81.1	80.2	21.8	31.7	Alpha
3	44.9	59.0	39.1	81.8	72.0	32.1	81.1	86.0	71.6	68.7	75
4	48.6	43.5	45.0	69.8	62.8	68.0	50.8	81.8	39.3	26.5	Beta
5	73.6	36.1	31.4	82.7	62.4	128.9	39.8	81.2	31.5	49.1	225
6	50.4	41.9	33.5	80.6	86.4	35.4	69.8	86.5	32.0	56.9	Total
7	50.9	68.8	57.6	84.1	80.4	31.3	63.3	93.2	67.3	70.1	300
8	56.6	28.1	74.5	76.5	82.7	107.2	63.6	87.6	44.9	17.3	
9	51.0	88.8	77.4	81.0	84.4	32.2	58.2	86.3	23.5	25.2	
10	53.7	36.0	80.2	80.3	63.9	46.2	71.3	84.1	34.8	56.7	
Max	73.6	88.8	80.2	84.1	86.4	128.9	88.6	93.2	71.6	70.1	
Alpha(j)	3	4	5	6	7	8	9	10	11	12	
Critical ratio	0.010	0.013	0.017	0.020	0.023	0.027	0.030	0.033	0.037	0.040	
Lower bound	20.4	5.2	13.8	9.9	7.6	0	5.4	0.8	22.4	23.9	

The first step is to set the release dates equal to these lower bounds and determine the criticality of each activity. The calculations are summarized in Table 19.2. In the body of the table, we calculate the completion time of each activity in each scenario, given the release dates shown in the row labeled Release. For each scenario, the project length is calculated in the column labeled Length, and the time for the assembly is shown on the right. Activity j is critical if its completion time matches the time at which assembly takes place. The frequency with which this event occurs for each activity is shown in the row labeled "Criticality." For example, if we scan the column for activity 10, we find only one scenario (the seventh) out of ten in which activity 10 completes at the assembly time. Thus, its criticality is 0.1. Activity 6, which postpones the assembly beyond the due date in two scenarios, has a criticality of 0.2. Similarly, activity 1 has a criticality of 0. Finally, the project has criticality of 0.8 because the due date is achieved in 8 of the 10 scenarios.

Comparing Table 19.2 with the critical ratios in Table 19.1, we find that the criticality is at least 0.1 for all activities except the first, so in those cases, the lower bound release date is optimal. When we explore larger release dates for activity 1, we find that at $r_1 = 31.1$, its criticality jumps to 0.1. At this stage, all inputs except input 6 have criticalities of 0.1, and input 6 has a criticality of 0.2. The optimality conditions are thus satisfied, so this solution is optimal for the sample. Based on the data in this sample, the estimated value of the optimal objective function is 7608. The due date has a criticality of 0.8, indicating that the optimal solution achieves a service level of 0.8. This value differs from the critical ratio target of $225/(75 + 225) = 0.75$ largely because the small sample size provides a discrete approximation to a problem involving continuous distributions.

Using a sample of 10 discrete scenarios to determine 10 release dates will obviously not yield precise results in a problem involving continuous distributions. As in other stochastic problems where we have used a sample-based approach, we need much larger sample sizes. To illustrate, we started with a sample containing 10 000 scenarios to provide us with precise estimates of "true" values. For this large sample, the optimal value of the objective function was 7453, and the optimal service level, 0.7312. The service level is less than the desired 0.75 due to constrained release dates. We then calculated that the optimal release dates obtained from the sample of size 10 actually yield an objective of 8798, or 18% higher than the more precise estimate. When we tested the performance of samples of 100 and 1000, we obtained much better results: The objective function values were 7519 (0.9% above the optimum) and 7471 (0.2%). As these results demonstrate, a reasonable sample size tends to yield a small optimality gap.

Our numerical search above exploited the structure of the problem, adjusting the release dates one by one until the correct criticality was achieved for each of them. One advantage of rounding the sample realizations (as we did to one

Table 19.2

	Input										Length	Assembly
Release	1 20.4	2 5.2	3 13.8	4 9.9	5 7.6	6 0.0	7 5.4	8 0.8	9 22.4	10 23.9		
1	83.3	56.7	58.0	76.1	62.1	35.7	94.0	86.1	45.6	70.8	94.0	94.0
2	62.0	52.0	75.3	90.4	82.9	35.1	86.5	81.0	44.2	55.6	90.4	94.0
3	65.3	64.2	52.9	91.7	79.6	32.1	86.5	86.8	94.0	92.6	94.0	94.0
4	69.0	48.7	58.8	79.7	70.4	68.0	56.2	82.6	61.7	50.4	82.6	94.0
5	94.0	41.3	45.2	92.6	70.0	128.9	45.2	82.0	53.9	73.0	128.9	128.9
6	70.8	47.1	47.3	90.5	94.0	35.4	75.2	87.3	54.4	80.8	94.0	94.0
7	71.3	74.0	71.4	94.0	88.0	31.3	68.7	94.0	89.7	94.0	94.0	94.0
8	77.0	33.3	88.3	86.4	90.3	107.2	69.0	88.4	67.3	41.2	107.2	107.2
9	71.4	94.0	91.2	90.9	92.0	32.2	63.6	87.1	45.9	49.1	94.0	94.0
10	74.1	41.2	94.0	90.2	71.5	46.2	76.7	84.9	57.2	80.6	94.0	94.0
Criticality	0.0	0.1	0.1	0.1	0.1	0.2	0.1	0.1	0.1	0.1		

decimal place) is that the numerical search is greatly facilitated by the coarse grid. For instance, consider the search for r_1. In this case $r_1^L = 20.4$ yields a criticality that is too low, and so does $r_1^L + 0.1 = 20.5$. Therefore, we can repeat our trials for the values 20.7, 21.1, 21.9, 23.5, 26.7, 33.1, doubling the step size every time. At $r_1 = 33.1$, the criticality exceeds the target value of 0.1. We now know that 26.7 is too low and 33.1 is probably too high (although it could be precisely right). We now try 29.9 (in the middle) and continue the search by halving the remaining search interval each time. If $r_j - r_j^L = K$, then it will take at most $O(\log K)$ trials to identify the optimal value (given the other release dates). If we search this way, starting with the lower bound solutions and increasing them one by one, then each iteration takes us closer to the optimal solution, and therefore the optimal solution can be found in polynomial time. In this particular example, when we used a sample of 10 000, we had to adjust two inputs twice: The rest required at most one adjustment, and three constrained inputs required no adjustment at all. This search approach can be generalized for any PERT network.

19.2.2 Balancing a General Project Network

In a general project network, we can show that the same stochastic balance result remains intact. Furthermore, we do not have to assume stochastic independence. Although Eq. (19.1) is no longer valid, our objective is still to minimize the expected total weighted flowtime, including delay. As in Chapter 17, we denote the set of direct physical predecessor activities of j by $P(j)$. If any of the incoming activities of j is a dummy, then for the purpose of defining $P(j)$, we replace it by its physical predecessors. Release dates are excluded. With this notation in place, we obtain the following *project stochastic balance* (PSB) model:

$$\text{Minimize } Z = E\left[\sum_{j=1}^{n+1} \alpha_j(C - r_j)\right] = (\alpha + \beta)E(C) - \sum_{j=1}^{n+1} \alpha_j r_j \tag{19.2}$$

subject to

$$C_j \geq r_j + p_j;\, j = 1,\ldots,n \tag{19.3}$$

$$C_j \geq C_k + p_j;\, \forall k \in P(j),\, j = 1,\ldots,n \tag{19.4}$$

$$C \geq d = r_{n+1} \tag{19.5}$$

$$C \geq C_k;\, \forall k \in P(N) \tag{19.6}$$

The decision variables are the release dates, excluding the due date. (The due date can be set to the minimal value as a secondary objective later, as in the ACM.) Equation (19.3) states that the completion time of an activity cannot be lower than the release date plus the processing time. Equation (19.4) states that completion times are also constrained by the latest completion time of any predecessor activity. The condition in Eq. (19.5) implies that the project is not considered finished before d, even if the physical activities are completed earlier. Equation (19.6) is analogous to Eq. (19.4) but applies to the project completion and not to a physical activity: The project is not complete until all predecessor activities of the terminal node, N, are complete.

We use the notation $r_j = \text{ES}_j$ to denote the early start time for activity j. By setting $r_j = \text{ES}_j$, we ensure that the activity will never be delayed by the release date. For processing times with a lower bound, define $p_j^{\min}$ as the minimal possible processing time. Specifically, if we use a sample-based approach, then $p_j^{\min}$ corresponds to the lowest realization of activity j in the sample. If activity j has no predecessors, then $\text{ES}_j = 0$; otherwise, $\text{ES}_j = \max\{r_k + p_k^{\min} | k \in P(j)\}$. In the latter case, ES_j is the largest possible release date that cannot delay activity j. We say that such a release date is *inactive*, whereas a release date that has a positive probability of delaying the activity is *active*. Any earlier release would not delay activity j either, but our objective function is improved if we postpone release dates as much as possible without increasing tardiness. If $P(j)$ is not empty, then setting $r_j = \text{ES}_j$ typically leads to $q_j = 0$. If $q_j > 0$ in this situation, another critical path exists, so reducing r_j cannot reduce the makespan. If $P(j)$ is empty, then even if we set $r_j = \text{ES}_j$, it may dictate the makespan (and $q_j > 0$). Thus, although the PSB problem does not include explicit constraints of the form $r_j \geq \text{ES}_j$, the optimal solution will still comply with these constraints.

Unlike the ACM case, we cannot compute partial derivatives in the PSB problem, so we cannot compute criticalities. Partial derivatives still exist and must vanish when the release dates are optimal, except when they are constrained by the release date. For continuous processing time distributions, the optimal solution is characterized by the following theorem, which generalizes the results we obtained for the ACM.

■ **Theorem 19.1** The following are necessary and sufficient optimality conditions for the PSB problem with probability 1:

1) $q_j^* = \dfrac{v_j^*}{\alpha + \beta} \geq \dfrac{\alpha_j}{\alpha + \beta}; \ j = 1, \ldots, n;$

2) if $v_j^* > \alpha_j$, then $r_j^* = \text{ES}_j;$

3) $q_{n+1}^* = 1 - \sum_{j=1}^{n} \dfrac{v_j^*}{\alpha + \beta} \leq \dfrac{\alpha_{n+1}}{\alpha + \beta};$

where v_j^* reflects the true marginal economic implication of postponing r_j per time unit.

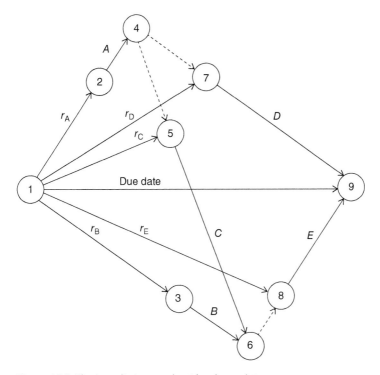

Figure 19.2 The interdictive graph with release dates.

The PSB problem is a convex model, so the global minimum is achieved if local optimality conditions are satisfied. The theorem lists such local optimality conditions.[1]

To illustrate, we refer to Figure 19.2, which is essentially an interdictive graph with release dates depicted as activities starting at node 1 and ending at nodes 2, 3, 5, 7, 8, and 9, where (1, 9) is the due date. (The figure uses r_A, r_B instead of r_1, r_2, etc.) If we set $r_E = ES_E = \max\{r_B + p_B^{min}, \max\{r_C, r_A + p_A^{min}\} + p_C^{min}\}$, then r_E cannot delay the project because activity E cannot be started earlier due to the precedence constraints. Similarly, there is no incentive to set $r_C < r_A + p_A^{min}$. In contrast, if we set r_A or r_B to their early start times (zero), then the longest path can still start at one of them. When *all* release dates (including the due date) are equal to the corresponding early start times, then one of these two *must* be critical ($q_A + q_B = 1$). Consequently, it is possible to postpone r_C, r_D, and r_E just enough to achieve any desired criticality for each of them, but release dates r_A and r_B may yield higher than desired criticalities, in which case their optimal value is their early start time.

---

1 A formal proof can be found in our Research Notes for Chapter 19.

Finally, the due date can be effectively removed by setting $r_{n+1} = ES_{n+1}$ or even $r_{n+1} = 0$. If we set $r_{n+1} < ES_{n+1}$, then we incur a tardiness penalty of $\beta(ES_{n+1} - r_{n+1})$ before we even start. This initial penalty is a constant, however, and does not change the structure of the optimal solution except in one way: It implies that the release date of at least one activity that has no predecessors must be zero, and the project service level is zero, as well. In effect, criticality must be transferred from the due date to a set of activities with $r_j = ES_j$.

19.2.3 Additional Examples

In this section, we discuss some additional examples to demonstrate the generality of our approach.

■ **Example 19.2**   Consider a project valued at $10 000 000, and suppose the annual holding cost is 18.25%. Assume we manage a hundred activities with the same holding cost and that the policy is to meet the due date with a service level of 90%. Assume further that the resulting project buffer is about six months.

The interest rate is about $5000 per day, and since there are 100 activities, it follows that $\alpha_j = \$50$ per day for $1 \le j \le 100$. To achieve a service level of 90%, we require $\beta = \$45\,000$ per day, so $(\alpha + \beta) = \$50\,000$. Stochastic balance will be achieved with criticalities of 0.1% for each release date and 90% for the due date. As this requires a project buffer of half a year, the approximate cost of the policy is $91 250. (Calculating the exact cost of such policies is best done by simulation, comparing the option of $\beta = 0$, in which no tardiness penalty exists and we focus only on holding cost.) The customer pays for this service level both as part of the price and by waiting, unless early deliveries are allowed.

To actually calculate the optimal release dates in such examples, we continue to rely on sample-based analysis. Formally, when a sample is available, the optimal release dates can be found by linear programming (LP) (which can also solve the ACM with a given sample). The model is essentially an elaboration of the generic PSB problem, but instead of using the expected value in the objective function, we use the average cost computed for the scenarios in the sample. For each scenario, we use its own processing time realizations, but the same release date decisions apply to all s scenarios. The project completion time of scenario i is denoted C_i. For other variables, we use a double index (i, j) to denote the jth activity of the ith scenario. We obtain

$$\text{Minimize } Z = \frac{(\alpha + \beta)}{s} \sum_{i=1}^{s} C_i - \sum_{j=1}^{n+1} \alpha_j r_j \tag{19.7}$$

subject to

$$C_{ij} \geq r_j + p_{ij}; \quad i = 1,\ldots,s, \;\; j = 1,\ldots,n$$

$$C_{ij} \geq C_{ik} + p_{ij}; \quad \forall k \in P(j), \;\; i = 1,\ldots,s, \;\; j = 1,\ldots,n$$

$$C_i \geq d = r_{n+1} \quad i = 1,\ldots,s$$

$$C_i \geq C_{ik}; \quad \forall k \in P(N), \;\; i = 1,\ldots,s$$

We can solve this model as a generic linear program. In practice, however, it is more efficient to find the optimal solution by a numerical search, as in Example 19.1. For a sample with an appropriate number of scenarios, the LP formulation is unwieldy even when the project is small. It is important mainly because it implies that the problem is convex, so once a local optimum is found by such a search, we know that it is globally optimal. The next example demonstrates that analysis of this type can also help schedule repetitive operations. Again, for the purpose of illustration, we utilize a sample that is not sufficiently large to be reliable.

■ **Example 19.3** Consider a bus route consisting of five segments. The travel time for each segment is random, and 10 recent observations have been compiled, as shown below:

Segment j	1	2	3	4	5
$E(p_j)$	13.51	24.27	8.15	21.53	10.27
σ_j	3.89	7.08	1.96	7.50	2.54

Scenario	Segment j	1	2	3	4	5
1	p_j	16.60	20.10	10.66	21.52	7.45
2	p_j	11.92	19.49	9.05	15.99	10.96
3	p_j	14.82	33.39	7.59	19.51	14.81
4	p_j	11.32	23.12	12.18	17.36	9.41
5	p_j	21.15	20.77	6.62	37.72	12.60
6	p_j	10.58	24.15	7.98	23.23	7.49
7	p_j	17.57	19.09	7.96	30.79	9.14
8	p_j	9.72	40.49	6.61	12.90	13.21
9	p_j	12.17	22.37	6.35	19.80	9.57
10	p_j	9.28	19.77	6.47	16.48	8.05

Travel time to a particular station does not depend on the departure times at the previous station. The number of passengers boarding the bus at each station is also random, and observations have produced the following expected values:

Segment j	1	2	3	4	5
Passengers	12.2	9.4	5.5	8.2	4.1

All passengers go to the same final destination at the end of segment 5. The due date at the final destination is 8:45 a.m.

Having decided that they wish to take this bus, the passengers consult the bus schedule, which publishes departure times from each station, and they arrange to arrive at their station before the corresponding departure time. The objective function includes the time value of these passengers from the scheduled departure time until the scheduled arrival at the final station, and any tardiness of the bus at the destination is also penalized for disrupting its next assignment. The bus costs $3 per minute, and each passenger-minute is evaluated at $0.20. The tardiness cost at the destination is $1 per minute, and the penalty per passenger is $0.30. Thus, the total cost of the bus during such tardiness is $4 per minute, and the cost of each passenger is assessed at $0.50 per minute.

Reasonable time units for such a schedule are minutes, but unlike the approach of Example 19.1, we postpone rounding until the last step. Mathematically, this example is equivalent to a serial project with release dates, as depicted in Figure 19.3. For convenience, we do not index the release date nodes, but instead we index the bus arrival events by station numbers. We adopt the convention that station j precedes segment j, and the destination is denoted station 6. The release date also controls the start time of segment j. That is, we model each segment (between stations) as an activity and the scheduled departure time as a release date. Conceptually, the release date decisions require a balance of two types of waiting costs. One waiting cost applies to the bus and the passengers on it. If the bus arrives at a station too early, then the bus and those passengers are delayed while the bus waits at the station. We

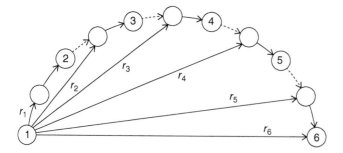

Figure 19.3 The bus scheduling problem as a project.

also assume that if the bus arrives at the final destination too early, a similar earliness cost applies. The other waiting cost applies to the boarding passengers: If the bus arrives at a station too late to meet its release date, then those passengers are delayed while they wait for the bus to arrive. In effect, if we knew in advance that the bus would be delayed, we could set a later release date and reduce the cost contribution of these passengers. We can capture all these costs by measuring the time value of the nominal trip durations of the bus and of the passengers from all stations plus the expected tardiness penalty. That is, once we compute the correct waiting costs, we can model this as a PSB problem. Our first task is to calculate the correct parameters. Then, because we are using a sample-based approach, we have the option of solving the problem as a linear program (which we do not recommend in practice) or using a generic search instead.

Let α_0 denote the unit time cost for the bus and α_p denote the unit time cost for each passenger, both during scheduled operation. When the bus is tardy, we add to these two costs the tardiness penalties of β_0 and β_p, respectively. Denote the expected number of passengers who board the bus at station j by w_j. To cast the problem as a PSB model, let α_j denote the unit time cost of those passengers who board the bus at station j. At the first station, α_1 also accounts for the value of the bus (because the bus "joins" at that station). Thus, $\alpha_1 = \alpha_0 + \alpha_p w_1 = 3 + 0.2 \times 12.2 = 5.44$, $\alpha_2 = \alpha_p w_2 = 0.2 \times 9.4 = 1.88$, and so on. Similarly, $\alpha_{n+1} = \beta = \beta_0 + \beta_p \sum_{k=1}^{n} w_k = 1 + 0.3 \times 39.4 = 12.82$. These rates are given in the second row of Table 19.3. We can also calculate $(\alpha + \beta) = 23.7$. The next row in the table is the ratio between the respective rate and 23.7 – this calculation yields the critical ratios. Given the cost rates and the sample, we can construct and solve the PSB problem. The optimal release dates are given in the next row. However, we still have to round the schedule to integer minutes, and it is not straightforward to characterize the optimal rounding: Theoretically, it transforms the linear program into an integer program, which is NP-hard. In this case, rounding up seems to work well. Such a rounded solution is given in the next to last row. After adjusting the release dates for a scheduled arrival at 8:45 a.m., we obtain

Table 19.3

Segment	1	2	3	4	5	d	
α_j	5.44	1.88	1.1	1.64	0.82	12.82	
q_j^* (%)	23	8	5	7	3	54	Objective
r_j^*	0.00	9.72	36.70	44.66	65.37	76.33	766.278
Rounded	0	10	37	45	66	77	766.754
Adjusted	7:28	7:38	8:05	8:13	8:34	8:45	

the schedule in the last row. For instance, the calculation shows that the departure should precede the due date by 76.33 minutes, which we round up to 77, yielding the listed departure of 7:28 a.m.

Figure 19.4 shows the associated stochastic Gantt chart (without rounding). The vertical segments in the figure correspond to the delay of the bus in a station due to a release date. A positive probability exists that the bus won't even reach the fifth station by the due date. (In general, specifying a very high delay penalty would reduce the incidence of such events, but the nominal trip lengths will be longer.)

Table 19.4 shows the solution in more detail (without rounding or adjusting the due date to 8:45), based on the sample. It lists the departure times in the example. The last row gives the release dates. The shaded elements in the table denote critical release dates. If we were to increase any release date, the project would take longer in every scenario for which the release date is shaded. By using a sample-based approach to optimize release dates, we essentially represent the processing time distribution by a discrete sample. As was the case in Example 19.1, this approach leads to more than one critical release date in some

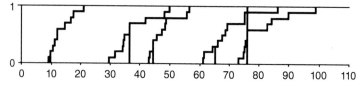

Figure 19.4 A stochastic Gantt chart for Example 19.3.

Table 19.4

Scenario	1	2	3	4	5	d
1	0.00	16.60	36.70	47.36	68.88	76.33
2	0.00	11.92	36.70	45.75	65.37	76.33
3	0.00	14.82	48.21	55.80	75.31	90.12
4	0.00	11.32	36.70	48.88	66.24	75.65
5	0.00	21.15	41.92	48.54	86.26	98.86
6	0.00	10.58	36.70	44.68	67.91	75.40
7	0.00	17.57	36.70	44.66	75.45	84.59
8	0.00	9.72	50.21	56.82	69.72	82.93
9	0.00	12.17	36.70	44.66	65.37	74.94
10	0.00	9.72	36.70	44.66	65.37	73.42
Release	0.00	9.72	36.70	44.66	65.37	76.33

scenarios. For instance, the first scenario contains three shaded release dates: r_1, r_3, and r_6 ($= d$). If we trace that scenario, we see that the bus arrives at station 2 almost seven minutes after r_2 (so r_2 cannot be critical), but it arrives at station 3 precisely at r_3 (hence, no waiting occurs). The bus then reaches stations 4 and 5 after their release dates but arrives at the destination precisely on time. Thus, both r_1 and r_3 satisfy the criterion of criticality (increasing either of them would make the trip longer), and the due date is critical, too. The table contains $s + n = 10 + 5 = 15$ shaded elements. In general, there may be up to $s + n$ such elements in the optimal solution. Therefore, if n is not negligible relative to s, the observed criticalities may seem out of order, as we also saw in Example 19.1. Denote the frequency at which r_j is critical (shaded) by q_j, and the question is how to verify that q_j is optimal. If we assume temporarily that $r_j > \mathrm{ES}_j$, then the criticality is optimal under two conditions: (i) $q_j > \alpha_j/(\alpha + \beta)$, and (ii) decreasing r_j infinitesimally reduces q_j sufficiently to obtain $q_j \leq \alpha_j/(\alpha + \beta)$. If $r_j = \mathrm{ES}_j$, the first condition is sufficient. In our instance, the first condition is satisfied because $q_1 = 0.4 > \alpha_1/(\alpha + \beta) = 0.23$. If we slightly decrease r_1 (which, in this case, is allowed to be negative), it remains critical in two scenarios. (Specifically, these are scenarios 3 and 5, under which only r_1 is critical.) Thus, we obtain $q_1 = 2/10 \leq 0.23$, so the second condition is also satisfied. (This test verifies local optimality, which is sufficient because our model is convex. We caution, however, that the test becomes invalid once we round to integer release dates. The integer model is not convex and therefore local optimality is not sufficient. One practical way to avoid this problem is to round the data in the sample to the desired units, in which case the final result will not require rounding and the optimality conditions are sufficient. That is the approach taken in Example 19.1.)

When travel times are stochastically dependent, a large sample is the best practical approach. One way to model dependence is by assuming linear association. Although we have been assuming the use of field data, it is often more convenient to use such data to estimate the parameters required to generate a simulated sample, as we now discuss in more detail. As reported in this example, travel times are approximately lognormal with $s = 0.25$, but also subject to linear association. Using rounded figures that match the given data, let $s_B = 0.15$ and $s_X = 0.2$, which leads to $s = 0.25$ as stated above (because $0.15^2 + 0.2^2 = 0.25^2$). Also, assume mean travel times are given by 13, 25, 8, 22, and 10. Accordingly, for segment j, we obtain $m_j = \ln(\mu_j) - 0.25^2/2$. Segment 1, for instance, yields $\ln(13) - 0.031\,25 = 2.5337$, and the full list is $\{2.5337, 3.1876, 2.0482, 3.0598, 2.2713\}$. Each simulated scenario requires sampling six independent standard normal variables. Five of them are multiplied by 0.2 and one by 0.15 (to represent the common element). Next, we add the common element result to each of the five values. Finally, simulated travel times for the scenario are obtained by taking the exponents of the five results plus their respective m_j values, as calculated above. This way, each scenario has the same bias, but different scenarios have different biases.

■ **Example 19.4**   Consider a project with the network of Figure 19.2, and let the earliness and tardiness costs be given by $\alpha_A = 10$, $\alpha_B = 20$, $\alpha_C = 30$, $\alpha_D = 15$, $\alpha_E = 5$, and $\beta = 120$. The due date is 60. Activity times are based on a sample of 1000 repetitions with expected durations of $\mu_A = 15$, $\mu_B = 36$, $\mu_C = 18$, $\mu_D = 25$, $\mu_E = 12$. The sample was generated by using lognormal and positively correlated distributions.

We solved this example with a spreadsheet model. Figure 19.5 depicts the optimal solution as a stochastic Gantt chart, with criticalities $q_A = 6\%$, $q_B = 14.9\%$, $q_C = 15\%$, $q_D = 7.5\%$, $q_E = 2.5\%$. The release dates of activities C, D, and E yield the required optimal criticalities dictated by $\alpha_j/(\alpha + \beta)$. For instance, $q_C = \alpha_C/(\alpha + \beta) = 30/200 = 15\%$. However, both A and B have release dates of zero, and their criticalities exceed their respective $\alpha_j/(\alpha + \beta)$ values. For instance, $q_B = 14.9\% > \alpha_B/(\alpha + \beta) = 10\%$. When combined, the criticalities of these two activities exceed their optimal unconstrained targets by $(6 - 5)\% + (14.9 - 10)\% = 5.9\%$. Accordingly, the project service level, 54.1%, is 5.9% lower than its unconstrained target of 60%. Thus, some criticality is shifted from the due date to the constrained release dates. Because we use a larger sample and continuous processing times, our criticalities match Theorem 19.1 precisely.

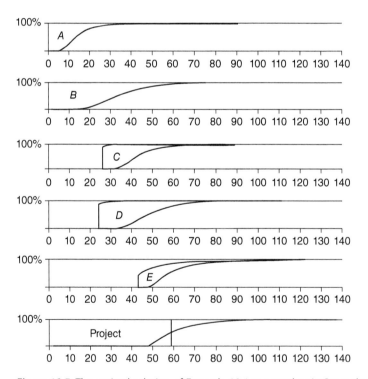

Figure 19.5 The optimal solution of Example 19.4 as a stochastic Gantt chart.

19.3   Hierarchical Balancing and Progress Payments

One interesting historical difference between the development of CPM and that of PERT is their fundamental approach to managing large projects. PERT set out to provide the full detail in one chart and was recommended for modeling thousands of activities. Although the need for hierarchical management was addressed briefly, the major thrust involved managing the whole project using one network. CPM, by contrast, explicitly assumed that each project activity could be a subproject. In addition, implicit staging activities might not be represented on the project network at all. For instance, in Example 19.3, the bus should be prepared for its scheduled departure at 7:28. The preparation activity must start earlier than that and may be considered a subproject. However, the project network does not include preparation, so it is an *implicit subproject*. Our topic in this section is scheduling hierarchical projects, regardless of whether they involve implicit or explicit subprojects. We take a hierarchical approach, first treating subprojects as independent projects and then showing how to coordinate them with all other subprojects and activities. With this coordination, we effectively schedule the full project at a higher hierarchical level. It turns out that both levels can be balanced by our single-subproject basic model.

When subprojects are explicit, projects typically involve *milestones*, which mark the completion of important subprojects. Furthermore, progress payments may be due when a milestone is reached and the subproject is deemed satisfactory by the customer. To avoid the risk of having to make a payment earlier than expected and to schedule their own milestone inspection activities, customers may prefer explicit milestone due dates, and we will assume that is the case. For that reason, milestones may also be regarded as release dates for the remainder of the project. Our previous model, however, allows only one payment at project completion. The solution is obtained by hierarchical scheduling, essentially treating each subproject with a milestone as a full project. Then those subprojects are treated as single activities in the full project. For instance, if we interpret Figure 19.5 as a stochastic Gantt chart of such a subproject, we would use the project distribution (as depicted in the bottom of the figure) to represent this subproject as a single activity at the next higher level. The due date depicted in the figure then serves as the anchor for the adjustments the high-level balancing requires. (For this purpose, we ignore the fact that two activities in the depicted subproject are constrained. In principle, this is an example where additional iterative adjustments may be required because high-level balancing can change the constraints used at the local level.) Even if customers are not entitled to a penalty payment when a milestone is missed, just delaying the receipt of progress payments constitutes a tardiness penalty for such milestones. Therefore, subprojects should have optimal service levels that guide the balancing at the low level.

From here on, we treat project completion as a special milestone, called the *completion milestone*. All other milestones can be described as *proper*. We say that an activity is a *proper predecessor* of a milestone if there is a directed path from it to the milestone *not* passing through another milestone. To begin, assume no activity is a proper predecessor of more than one milestone. (That condition is guaranteed if milestones signal the end of proper subprojects whose activity sets are independent of each other.) With this assumption, the milestones effectively partition all activities to mutually exclusive and exhaustive subsets, and each milestone is associated with one subset. For a while, we also ignore the possibility that milestones can be predecessors of other milestones. Let $m \geq 2$ denote the number of subsets, so at least one proper milestone exists in addition to the completion milestone. At the lower level, each milestone is treated as the due date of a single project (that is, each subproject is treated as a single project), balanced as per our basic model. It is then straightforward to find the completion time distribution of the subproject relative to its due date. For the higher-level balancing, define the holding cost of proper milestone i as the sum of all holding costs of the activities associated with it. The top-level balancing model is obtained by replacing all activities associated with the $m - 1$ proper milestones by their milestone due dates; that is, our task is reduced to finding release dates for $m - 1$ milestones – each of which now has a known distribution – and for any activity that is a proper predecessor of the completion milestone (and thus, by current assumption, not the proper predecessor of any other milestone). In other words, for the purpose of scheduling the upper level, we can ignore the partial payments associated with milestones; the delay penalty associated with partial payments only matters for the adjustment of local criticalities at the lower level. Finally, although we have illustrated how to handle exactly two hierarchical levels, the same mechanism allows as many levels as we may wish.

Now consider that a milestone can be a proper predecessor of another milestone. In such a case, it can be treated as a single activity among those that feed the subsequent milestone. As a result, the two milestones are coordinated and act as a single milestone for the purpose of high-level balancing; that is, the subsequent milestone represents both the set of its proper preceding activities and the proper preceding milestone (which represents its own set of proper preceding activities and, possibly, earlier milestones). The weight of the downstream milestone represents all the milestones incorporated in it (directly or indirectly) and all the proper predecessor activities associated with it directly. It is even conceivable that the network structure creates no need for a separate high-level balancing: Instead, in such a case, the high-level balancing is achieved by assembling milestones into subsequent milestones, locking their respective release dates as per the milestone balancing step, and moving on to the next milestone.

A more complex issue arises when we remove the assumption that each activity can be the proper predecessor of only one milestone. It is then not clear in advance how to allocate such activities to milestones in a mutually exclusive and exhaustive manner. One possible resolution is allocating each such activity to the earliest likely milestone that it precedes. A better but more elaborate resolution is seeking a fractional weight allocation that matches both the low-level criticalities and the high-level ones.

The key to understanding why this hierarchical approach works is that shifting the milestone as a whole (such that the release dates of all the feeding activities shift by the same amount) is sufficient to adjust the milestone's top-level criticality to any desired feasible level, whereas shifting the feeding activities relative to each other is sufficient to adjust local criticalities. The approach works because the two adjustments are independent of each other. This may be confusing because the criticalities in question are *not* independent. For instance, an activity that is early for a milestone cannot be critical at the project level because there is a delay between its completion and the milestone due date. But that dependence does not change the fact that the two adjustments are independent of each other.

We now turn our attention to implicit subprojects, which may not terminate in a milestone with an explicit due date. In such cases, it is often necessary to book unique resources that may be necessary for performing an activity but are released once the activity is complete. The next example illustrates why the booking of such resources requires special attention.

■ **Example 19.5** Consider the construction of a floor in a new low-rise building. This subproject requires, among other things, staging reinforced concrete slabs and using a mobile crane and a truck. Furthermore, it cannot start before the retaining walls of the lower floor are complete. Let the desired criticality of the retaining wall activity be 10%, and assume that the booking lead time is too long to allow waiting for the completion of the wall before booking the truck and the crane. Because there is no space for storing the slabs, they are lifted directly from the truck by the crane. For simplicity, assume the truck and the slabs are inducted together, as one combination unit (called "the truck"). Suppose the rental cost for the truck is $300 per hour and for the crane, $500 per hour. Once complete, the floor is assessed a holding cost of $\alpha = \$10$ per hour. Suppose further that the holding cost of the full project is $1900 per hour. Our task is to determine the optimal criticalities of the truck and the crane and how to use the release date of the slab-laying operation to schedule their booking.

In this example, expensive equipment performs an activity whose holding cost is a fraction of the value of the equipment. However, the equipment is released at the end of the activity, whereas the holding cost is charged until the project is complete. If the equipment is staged before it can start, its rental cost is wasted. For this reason, the activity does not require a release date. We assume, however, that the retaining wall activity does have a release date, and we will use that to anchor the booking time of the resources. It would make no sense to idle the expensive equipment just to satisfy an arbitrary constraint. Furthermore, the low holding cost of the floor says nothing about how sensitive the project is to delays in this activity. The activity itself can have a much higher criticality than that of its release date because it may be on the critical path even if the critical path starts at an earlier release date. The most important information about the project comes from the criticality of the wall, from which we can deduce that the expected time value of the activity is $1900 \times 10\% = \$190$ per hour. Adding the floor holding cost, we obtain $200 per hour. We now schedule the truck and the crane such that the probability the truck will be last is $300/(200 + 300 + 500) = 30\%$, the crane's criticality should be 50%, and that of the retaining wall, 20%. These are, in effect, optimal *local criticalities*.

Now consider how to actually achieve the desired balance. That is done in a hierarchical manner as described earlier, starting with the lower level. Without loss of generality, let 0 denote the start time of the retaining wall activity (so all other start times will be measured from that point). Now adjust the booking times of the truck (including slabs) and the crane such that their respective frequencies of being last among the three will be 0.3 and 0.5 (and thus the wall will complete last with a probability of 0.2). Suppose that the starting times that achieve these probabilities are b and c. This completes the lower-level balancing. At the higher level, because there is no real due date, the floor construction will start upon the arrival of the last input, but our task now is to set the release date of the retaining wall, r_w, without changing the relative start times of the other lower-level activities, so that the criticality of the retaining wall will match the required 0.1. Therefore, the truck and crane booking times will be at $r_w + b$ and $r_w + c$, respectively; that is, we use r_w as an anchor to make sure the lower-level local criticalities remain constant as we adjust the higher-level criticality of the retaining wall. Technically, this anchoring implies that we can use a single distribution for that purpose: the distribution of the maximum of the three inputs for the initial $r_w = 0$ setting with starting times of b and c for the truck and the crane. (That distribution is analogous to the project distribution in Figure 19.5 that we interpreted as a subproject distribution earlier.) If we had a release date for the floor construction, we could have used it as our anchor for the high-level balancing instead, as described above. But that makes no fundamental difference to the basic idea that we first schedule the lower level and then treat it as a single activity at the higher level. Incidentally, this solution is quite likely to delay the floor construction by delaying the truck or the crane, but in effect, we are balancing 10% of the project against quite expensive rental charges.

19.4 Crashing Stochastic Activities

Setting active release dates is a form of continuous crashing. We can treat the release dates as project activities and control the length of these activities at a cost, exactly as in the CPM crashing model of Chapter 16. If we assume that crashing reduces only the mean and does not change the variance or the shape of the distribution, we can solve for the optimal crashing policy and the optimal safety time by adapting Theorem 19.1. The activity with the lowest c_j/q_j (where c_j is the marginal cost of crashing the activity by one time unit) is the first candidate to be crashed. If c_j/q_j is higher than the time value of the project, c_f (where $c_f = \alpha + \beta$), then crashing should stop. As in the deterministic case, it may become necessary to reduce the planned crashing of an activity that was originally a good candidate for crashing if its criticality is sufficiently reduced due to other crashing decisions.

The following example demonstrates the risk of a sizable error from assuming that only the mean is subject to crashing. (In this and the following example, we use independent exponential processing times to achieve mathematical tractability, but the principle applies in general.)

■ **Example 19.6** Consider a project consisting of one activity with an exponential activity time distribution. Assume that the mean time is $\mu = 5$, the due date is $d = 5$, the cost of crashing is $c_1 = 10$, $\alpha_1 = 1$, and the tardiness penalty is $\beta = 19$, so $(\alpha + \beta) = 20$. Assume the distribution remains exponential after crashing.

In this case, the due date is fixed, and because the holding cost is small, we have no incentive to set an active release date. Assume temporarily that crashing does not change the distribution but just shifts it to the left. That assumption would imply starting at a negative time. Crashing would cost $c_1 = 10$ per time unit and save $(\alpha + \beta) = 20$ per time unit *if* tardiness occurs. But the probability of tardiness is $\exp(-1) = 0.368$ (yielding a service level of 63.2%), so the savings is $20 \times 0.368 = 7.36 < 10 = c_1$ per time unit. Thus, such crashing cannot be justified economically. Viewed from a different perspective, the optimal service level would be $c_1/(\alpha + \beta) = 0.5$, whereas we already achieve 0.632 without crashing, so crashing cannot be justified. Furthermore, if we could save money by negative crashing (i.e. increasing μ), then we might be tempted to examine this option instead. However, the true optimal μ in this case is 2.98, leading to a total cost of 31.33 and a service level of 0.813. This high service level is justified because the gain from crashing is higher than with simple shifting. To follow the necessary calculations formally, the objective function is given by

$$Z = c_1(d - \mu) + (\alpha + \beta)q_1\mu$$

$$= c_1(d - \mu) + (\alpha + \beta)\mu \exp\left(\frac{-d}{\mu}\right)$$

where q_1 is the criticality of the activity, and therefore, for the exponential distribution, $q_1 = \exp(-d/\mu)$. From the memoryless property, the conditional tardiness is μ, *given* that tardiness occurs. Taking the derivative with respect to μ and setting it to zero, we obtain

$$c_1 = (\alpha + \beta)\left(1 + \frac{d}{\mu}\right) \exp\left(-\frac{d}{\mu}\right) = (\alpha + \beta)\left(1 + \frac{d}{\mu}\right) q_1$$

$$q_1 = \frac{c_1}{(\alpha + \beta)\left(1 + \frac{d}{\mu}\right)}$$

That is, we must set μ to the value that adjusts the criticality of activity 1 to the right-hand side. If we compare this equilibrium condition to the result when crashing is limited to reducing the mean, $q_1 = c_1/(\alpha + \beta)$, we may say that the division by $(1 + d/\mu)$ *modifies* c_1. We refer to $(1 + d/\mu)$ as the cost *modifier*, and because the modification involves division, a high modifier effectively reduces the crashing cost and encourages more crashing than would otherwise be justified, leading to lower criticalities and higher service levels. In general, the cost modifier depends on (i) the rate at which σ_j is reduced by crashing; (ii) the effect of this reduction on the final project standard deviation, σ; and (iii) the effect of σ on the expected project tardiness. Let $E[T]$ denote the expected project tardiness. The cost modifier then has the form

$$1 + \frac{d\sigma_j}{d\mu_j}\frac{\partial\sigma}{\partial\sigma_j}\frac{\partial E[T]}{\partial\sigma} \tag{19.8}$$

To actually calculate the necessary derivatives for a general project structure requires simulation, but if we assume a serial project structure with many activities and independent processing time distributions, then we may invoke the normal approximation. We illustrate this analysis with another example involving exponential processing times, but this time there are many activities in series, so the effect on the project variance is lower.

■ **Example 19.7**   Consider a project involving 30 exponential activities in series, such that for the first 10 activities ($j = 1, ..., 10$), $\mu_j = 10$, and for the next 20 activities ($j = 11, ..., 30$), $\mu_j = 5$. Activities remain exponential after crashing and may be crashed by up to 50%. Let $c_j = 9.8 + (31 - j)/100$; for example, $c_1 = 10.1$, $c_{11} = 10$, and $c_{30} = 9.81$. Let $(\alpha + \beta) = 20$ and $d = 150$. Our task is to find the optimal crashing plan. Assume α is sufficiently small to preclude active release dates.

The project distribution is approximately normal by the central limit theorem. If we choose to crash the cheapest activities, namely, activities 30, 29, ..., 11 (in that order), and crash them maximally, we obtain a service level of 50% because after crashing 20 activities by 2.5 each, the project mean matches the due date and the normal distribution is symmetric. Consider the crashing costs that are available at this stage. Activities 30, 29, ..., 12 have an infinite crashing cost, having reached their crashing limit. The same applies for activity 11, but in this case, we might notice that at the moment we stopped crashing it, it still had a crashing cost of 10. If we ignore the need to modify the crashing costs, it would be optimal to stop crashing that activity at precisely the same value because the service level now matches $c_{11}/(\alpha + \beta) = 50\%$. The next available activity to crash costs 10.01, so it is justified only if we desire a service level higher than 50%. The total cost associated with the current solution is 762.9. This crashing plan reduces the variance from 1500 to 1125. If instead we crash the first 10 activities maximally, paying more for crashing but reducing the variance to 750, we obtain the same service level, and the objective function drops to 721.26. Therefore, selecting activities to crash based on c_j alone is not optimal. Furthermore, the optimal value is 717.11 and entails a higher service level. It involves crashing all activities to progressively smaller μ_i values, following an arithmetic series with $\mu_1 = 5.326$ and $\mu_{30} = 4.345$. (The maximal crashing constraints are not tight.) The optimal service level is 57.37%, instead of 50%. Thus, it is very important to consider the variance reduction effect, which in this case accounts for a savings of 5.5%, and it is also useful to optimize the service level, which accounts for an additional 0.5%.

If the influence of crashing on activity time distributions is linear, we can incorporate crashing decisions in the LP model we presented for optimizing release dates. When using LP, it is convenient to assume that the sample records values for maximally crashed activity times such that the mean of activity j is μ_j (which we may also write as $\mu_j(0)$) and its standard deviation is σ_j (or $\sigma_j(0)$). Denote the amount of crashing the mean by $-\Delta_j$. Because we assume that activities are maximally crashed, this implies increasing the mean by Δ_j. We may also denote the mean after negative crashing by $\mu_j(\Delta_j)$ and the standard deviation by $\sigma_j(\Delta_j)$ – that is, $\mu_j(\Delta_j) = \mu_j + \Delta_j$. Let λ_j be a given constant (which is likely to be between 0 and 1). One proposed model transforms the cdf of the processing time in such a manner that for any given probability of completion, the argument is multiplied by $(1 + \Delta_j/\mu_j)\lambda_j$, and then the cdf is shifted to the right by $\Delta_j(1 - \lambda_j)$. Two important special cases are $\lambda_j = 0$ and 1. In the former, the transformation consists of shifting the cdf to the right by Δ_j, and this is the simplest case. In the latter, the coefficient of variation is held constant (as in Examples 19.5 and 19.6). Selecting λ_j between 0 and 1 leads to a coefficient of variation that decreases with the mean (i.e. decreases with negative crashing), yet the standard deviation increases with the mean. After negative crashing, this transformation yields stochastically larger processing times. Denote the processing time after negative crashing by $p_{ij}(\Delta_j)$ – that is, the sample consists of $p_{ij}(0)$ data. The desired transformation is obtained by setting

$$p_{ij}\left(\Delta_j\right) = p_{ij}(0)\left(1 + \Delta_j\lambda_j/\mu_j(0)\right) + \Delta_j\left(1 - \lambda_j\right) \tag{19.9}$$

In this equation, $p_{ij}(\Delta_j)$ is a linear function of the decision variable Δ_j, so we can use it within a linear program. The model we obtain is then a simple generalization of the model we presented for setting release dates and can be used to make release date decisions alongside crashing decisions:

$$\text{Minimize } Z = \frac{(\alpha + \beta)}{S} \sum_{i=1}^{s} C_i - \sum_{j=1}^{n+1} \alpha_j r_j - \sum_{j=1}^{n+1} c_j \Delta_j \tag{19.10}$$

subject to

$$C_{ij} \geq r_j + p_{ij}(\Delta_j); \quad i = 1,\ldots,s, \quad j = 1,\ldots,n$$

$$C_{ij} \geq C_{ik} + p_{ij}(\Delta_j); \quad \forall k \in P(j), \quad i = 1,\ldots,s, \quad j = 1,\ldots,n$$

$$C_i \geq d = r_{n+1} \quad i = 1,\ldots,s$$

$$C_i \geq C_{ik} \quad \forall k \in P(N), \quad i = 1,\ldots,s$$

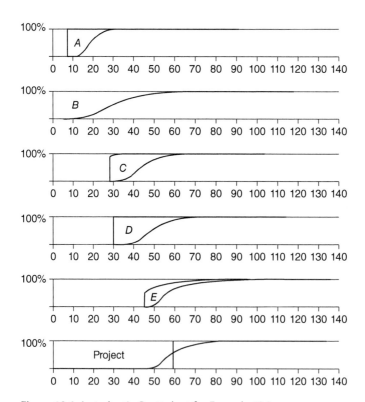

Figure 19.6 A stochastic Gantt chart for Example 19.8.

As in the special case, this LP formulation is not an efficient solution approach. It is significant mainly as a demonstration of convexity. A numerical search for the optimal solution is recommended. As an illustration, we add a crashing option to Example 19.4.

■ **Example 19.8** Consider a project with the network of Figure 19.2 with earliness and tardiness costs given by $\alpha_A = 10$, $\alpha_B = 20$, $\alpha_C = 30$, $\alpha_D = 15$, $\alpha_E = 5$, and $\beta = 120$ with expected durations of $\mu_A = 15$, $\mu_B = 36$, $\mu_C = 18$, $\mu_D = 25$, $\mu_E = 12$. Crashing is possible by up to $\Delta_A = 3$, $\Delta_B = 6$, $\Delta_C = 4$, $\Delta_D = 5$, $\Delta_E = 2$ at cost rates of $c_A = 20$, $c_B = 40$, $c_C = 60$, $c_D = 30$, and $c_E = 10$. Crashing maintains the coefficient of variation of the processing time distributions; that is, we use $\lambda_j = 1$ for all activities in Eq. (19.9).

Figure 19.6 depicts the optimal solution as a stochastic Gantt chart. Activities A, D, and E are crashed maximally, whereas activities B and C are crashed partly. The release dates are adjusted to yield criticalities $q_A = 5\%$, $q_B = 10.5\%$, $q_C = 15\%$, $q_D = 7.5\%$, and $q_E = 2.5\%$. Comparing the results to Figure 19.5, we see that activity A has been crashed sufficiently to reduce its criticality to the target value of $\alpha_A/(\alpha + \beta) = 10/200 = 5\%$, but activity B still has a release date of zero, and its criticality exceeds the target of 10% by 0.5%. The total costs of crashing are 7.8% of the total cost, followed by a savings of 12.4% to yield a net savings of 4.6%.

19.5 Summary

In this chapter, we introduced the stochastic balance approach to scheduling projects with optimal safety times, and we outlined how the approach can be extended to hierarchical scheduling problems. The underlying principle behind these applications is economic balance, but our system is stochastic, so we require *stochastic* economic balance, or stochastic balance, for short. Stochastic balance, in turn, is associated with achieving optimal criticalities. Specifically, balance is achieved when the marginal cost of providing protection is equal to the marginal benefit. In our particular case, the benefit is associated with controlling tardiness in the project completion time. This benefit is gained by reducing the sum of the marginal earliness costs of all activities plus the cost of tardiness $(\alpha + \beta)$. The criticality of an activity is the probability it will cause a tardy completion time. Stochastic balance is achieved when the criticality of each activity is given by its marginal cost (α_j) divided by $(\alpha + \beta)$. We saw, however, that if the completion time is constrained, an activity may acquire excessive criticality. In such cases, we should not delay that activity. We discussed examples showing how to apply stochastic balance in passenger transportation and in hierarchical systems. Next, we considered the issue of crashing stochastic activities, thus incorporating the historical CPM approach into PERT. We showed that stochastic balance principles can guide such decisions, and we formulated the problem as a linear program. In this case, however, our decision variables influence not only the criticality but also the distribution of a delay, given that a delay occurs. In response, we have to modify the marginal costs to reflect such effects.

At this stage, results have been reported only for single projects. We can view a job shop as a multiproject environment, but the projects (jobs) in a job shop all have a very simple structure. Although we showed how to balance projects with a hierarchical structure, including subprojects with individual milestones, models of stochastic balance in more general multiproject environments remain to be developed.

In our examples we implicitly assumed static sequencing and scheduling. That is, we did not consider the option to use data collected during the project for scheduling the remainder of the project. As part of our static approach, we also assumed that soft constraints force activities to be scheduled in a predetermined way. Furthermore, our convexity proofs (using LP formulations) implicitly relied on this static assumption. Our discussion of hierarchical scheduling supports the notion that dynamic scheduling is not as easy in practice as theory might suggest, so our static assumption is perhaps defensible. In Section 17.5, however, we discussed the dynamic use of policies for sequencing decisions. When the assumptions behind that usage are satisfied, it is possible to find balanced release dates by a process similar to the one we described, except that for any given set of release dates the simulated progress of the project should involve dynamic sequencing. That is, we can think of release dates as part of an enhanced policy and thus combine the setting of optimal release dates with stochastic sequencing heuristics. Such an application may involve iterations between searching for good sequencing policies based on given release dates and setting release dates given a sequencing policy. A similar iterative approach can also accommodate crashing decisions. However, the models are no longer necessarily convex, and the balanced release dates that we may achieve are not guaranteed to be globally optimal. It may make sense to develop scheduling systems that are static for the near future but dynamic beyond that. All that requires further research, however.

Perhaps the single most important advance made by PERT 21 is the use of validated distributional assumptions to generate practicable simulated samples that can be used reliably and provide safe scheduling. Whereas safe scheduling has roots in PERT, scheduling without validated distributional assumptions is not really safe at all. Our history-based approach ensures that the service levels we set will actually be achieved. Essentially, this methodology accounts for historical variation among projects, whereas PERT is almost universally associated with the independence assumption. The independence assumption leads to variance estimates that are much too small, and that is tantamount to indefensible optimism. But PERT 21 also provides calibration. The need for calibration has been recognized right from the start, but too often – practically always as far as the literature is concerned – it has been observed in the breach.

Exercises

19.1 The search procedure used in the chapter to optimize release dates starts with $r_j^L +$ `step size` (where `step size` is one unit of the desired time unit), tests the criticality, and, if the criticality is not yet excessive, increases the release date by increments of 2`step size`, 4`step size`, and so on. Once a release date with an excessive criticality is found, the procedure implements a bisection search within the last section identified:

   a) Show that if $r_j - r_j^L = K$, then it will take at most $O(\log K)$ trials (each requiring $O(s)$ steps) to identify the optimal value in the given `step_size` units (while holding the other release dates constant).

   b) By the text, the optimal release date for Activity 1 in Example 19.1 is 31.1. Now consider Table 19.2. Add a column for the difference between the assembly time and the completion of Activity 1. Show that the optimal release date can be found by adding the minimal value in the new column to the current release date (20.4).

19.2 Consider the ACM with a large enough due date to avoid constrained release dates. Suppose we use an algorithm that searches the optimal release dates by starting at the lower bounds r_j^L and adjusting inputs one by one to their optimal criticalities (possibly requiring several iterations).

   a) Show that release dates gradually increase toward their optimal values.

   b) Describe a similar approach for projects with a general PERT network structure. Show how to obtain lower bound values for this case and provide an argument showing that release dates are monotone increasing in this case, too. (*Hint:* The release dates of jobs that succeed activity *j* are *not* equivalent to due dates for activity *j*, but one of them can serve for the purpose of calculating reasonable lower bounds.)

19.3 Consider the ACM and the PERT model as in the previous problem, but now assume that the due date is not large enough to avoid constrained release dates. Update the previous algorithm. Will the search be easier or more difficult?

19.4 Consider Example 19.1 as analyzed by the small sample of Table 19.1. Suppose now that the due date can be adjusted and a secondary objective is to minimize it. Find the optimal release dates and due date. What is the total criticality of the solution?

19.5 Explain why it is impossible to obtain a high project service level without a sufficiently high due date. Alternatively, explain why, if we wish to have the project delivered as early as possible, we may have to accept a low service level. Which release dates tend to be critical in such a case? What is the correct criticality of other release dates relative to the case where the due date is delayed sufficiently to obtain the desired service level?

19.6 One way to model a multiproject environment is by generalizing the job shop model. Each job is a project, and those projects are considered together because they compete for resources. Beyond that, multiple projects often share activities or feed each other. One way to model such cases is by combining them to a single project. However, the essence of a multiproject environment is that each project has its own completion time. Therefore, each project should also have its own due date and tardiness penalty. For a given sequence of projects with known due dates and a given sequence of project activities, consider how the LP formulation can be used to set release dates for all activities.

a) Consider Example 19.5. Can a hierarchical model be presented as a multiproject case?

b) Consider Example 19.3, but assume that there are only two destination stations (so the last three columns in the segment times table are irrelevant) and that of the 12.2 expected number of passengers who board the bus for the first segment, 7.1 leave the bus at the first station, and 5.1 continue to the final station. Let d_1 denote the due date of the passengers who leave the bus at station 2, after one segment. Construct an LP model for optimizing the release dates and d_1. Can you optimize d_1 as a separate subproblem?

c) In principle, can such LP models include crashing considerations?

d) What is the theoretical significance of such LP formulations? (*Hint:* Would you actually use LP to solve such models?)

19.7 Consider Example 19.3 again. In that example, all passengers go to the final destination. But, in general, bus schedules should also accommodate passengers who board the bus at station i and depart at station k ($k > i$). Traditionally, such schedules (e.g. for trains or for connecting flights) involve just one timing decision per station: that is, the scheduled arrival time is also the scheduled departure time. A *service gap* sufficient to allow passengers to disembark and embark (and to service the equipment, if necessary) may also be specified.

a) Show that service gaps can be considered part of the next leg travel time without affecting the optimal solution.

b) Explain why, if we wish to provide a high service level to disembarking passengers, we must pay by often delaying the vehicle in the station.

c) Suppose that we specify a departure time and an arrival time separately. By way of notation, let r_k denote the scheduled departure time from station k, and let d_k denote the due date at that station. Also, let $T_k = (C_k - d_k)^+$, where C_k is the arrival time at station k. For convenience, assume that the bus departs from station 0 at time 0 (so $r_0 = d_0 = 0$). Any departure delays from that station can be considered part of the travel time of the first segment. Construct a model for this purpose where release dates *and* due dates are decisions.

d) Show that your model is convex. (*Hint:* Demonstrate convexity by recasting the model as an LP for any given sample.)

Bibliography

Britney, R.R. (1976). Bayesian point estimation and the PERT scheduling of stochastic activities. *Management Science* 22 (9): 938–948.

Elmaghraby, S.E., Ferreira, A.A., and Tavares, L.V. (2000). Optimal start times under stochastic activity durations. *International Journal of Production Economics* 64: 153–164.

Herroelen, W. and Leus, R. (2004). Robust and reactive project scheduling: a review and classification of procedures. *International Journal of Production Research* 42 (8): 1599–1620.

Herroelen, W., Leus, R., and Demeulemeester, E. (2002). Critical chain project scheduling: do not oversimplify. *Project Management Journal* 33 (4): 48–60.

Kumar, A. (1989). Component inventory costs in an assembly problem with uncertain supplier lead-times. *IIE Transactions* 21 (2): 112–121.

Mitchell, G. and Klastorin, T. (2007). An effective methodology for the stochastic project compression problem. *IIE Transactions* 39: 957–969.

Ronen, B. and Trietsch, D. (1988). A decision support system for planning large projects. *Operations Research* 36: 882–890.

Trietsch, D. (1993). Scheduling flights at hub airports. *Transportation Research Series B (Methodology)* 27B (2): 133–150.

Trietsch, D. (2005a). Why a critical path by any other name would smell less sweet: towards a holistic approach to PERT/CPM. *Project Management Journal* 36 (1): 27–36.

Trietsch, D. (2005b). The effect of systemic errors on optimal project buffers. *International Journal of Project Management* 23: 267–274.

Trietsch, D. (2006). Optimal feeding buffers for projects or batch supply chains by an exact generalization of the newsvendor model. *International Journal of Production Research* 44: 627–637.

Trietsch, D. and Baker, K.R. (2012). PERT 21: fitting PERT/CPM for use in the 21st century. *International Journal of Project Management* 30: 490–502.

Trietsch, D., L. Mazmanyan, L. Gevorgyan, and K.R. Baker (2010). A New Stochastic Engine for PERT, Working Paper. http://faculty.tuck.dartmouth.edu/images/uploads/faculty/principles-sequencing-scheduling/Engine.pdf (accessed 28 April 2018).

Trietsch, D., Mazmanyan, L., Gevorgyan, L., and Baker, K.R. (2012). Modeling activity times by the Parkinson distribution with a lognormal core: theory and validation. *European Journal of Operational Research* 216: 386–396.

Van Slyke, R.M. (1963). Monte Carlo methods and the PERT problem. *Operations Research* 11 (5): 839–860.

Wollmer, R.D. (1985). Critical path planning under uncertainty. *Mathematical Programming Study* 25: 164–171.

Appendix A

Practical Processing Time Distributions

A.1 Important Processing Time Distributions

Three distributions are prevalent in stochastic scheduling research – the *uniform*, *exponential*, and *normal* distributions. In addition to these three, we discuss two less prevalent distributions that may even be more important in practice: the *lognormal* distribution and the *Parkinson* distribution. Because the various properties of these two distributions are seldom covered among common probability distributions, we provide detailed coverage of each. In this section, we introduce all of these distributions and discuss how to simulate them. We also briefly discuss the Poisson distribution, which we need later. In Chapter 16 we introduce the beta distribution, but we omit it here because for our purposes it is not necessary to study its general properties or to simulate it. Some other distributions that we mention later are common in the literature but lack validation.

A.1.1 The Uniform Distribution

The uniform distribution describes a random outcome that is equally likely to occur anywhere between a minimum value a and a maximum value b. We denote the uniform distribution by U[a, b], where a is the minimum possible realization and b the maximum possible realization. This distribution has mean $\mu = (a + b)/2$ and variance $\sigma^2 = (b - a)^2/12$. An important special case, U[0, 1], can be simulated by computers very efficiently. For example, in Excel, this is done by the RAND function. If we wish instead to simulate a uniform random variable on the interval from a to b, we employ the transformation

$$u = a + (b - a)\,rand$$

where *rand* is the result of the U[0, 1] simulation.

Principles of Sequencing and Scheduling, Second Edition. Kenneth R. Baker and Dan Trietsch.
© 2019 John Wiley & Sons, Inc. Published 2019 by John Wiley & Sons, Inc.

For nonnegative random variables with strictly positive means, we have $cv = \sigma/\mu$, where cv is called the *coefficient of variation*. For the uniform distribution, cv is meaningful when $a \geq 0$ and is given by

$$cv = \frac{b-a}{(a+b)\sqrt{3}}$$

The result is maximized if $a/b = 0$, yielding $cv = 1/\sqrt{3} = 0.577$; but as a/b approaches 1, cv approaches zero.

A.1.2 The Exponential Distribution

The exponential distribution describes a random outcome (typically a waiting time) with the property that the event we are awaiting is no more likely to occur when we have been waiting a long time than when we have been waiting a short time. The exponential distribution with mean μ is defined by the cumulative distribution function (cdf)

$$F(t) = 1 - e^{-t/\mu}$$

where $t \geq 0$, and we use T to denote the random variable itself. (Some sources use the rate parameter, often also denoted by μ but defined as the reciprocal of the mean time – or $1/\mu$ in our notation – for which $F(t) = 1 - e^{-\mu t}$. There is no consensus in this case. Our choice is consistent with our general treatment of μ as a mean time.) The standard deviation of an exponential distribution is always the same as its mean. Thus, $\sigma = \mu$ and $cv = 1$, which we call medium variation. This distribution is often realistic for estimating the time between machine breakdowns or other randomly occurring events, but it is usually not realistic as a model for the duration of production operations. In this text, we use the exponential distribution for mathematical convenience and for developing useful insights, but doing so does not imply that we expect processing times to be exponential in practice.

For symmetric distributions, such as the uniform, the mean (that is, the expected value) and the median (the value for which the cdf is 0.5) coincide. (We denote the median by M; that is, $M = F^{-1}[0.5]$.) As a result, it is a well known but all too common error to assume that M and μ always coincide. For instance, one might allow enough time for the median, thinking that it should be sufficient on average. However, for right-skewed distributions, the probability of falling below the mean exceeds 0.5, and thus $M < \mu$. For the exponential, the probability of an outcome no larger than the mean is $\Pr\{T \leq \mu\} = 1 - e^{-1} = 0.632 > 0.5$, and $M = -\ln(0.5)\mu = 0.693\mu < \mu$.

The cdf of a continuous random variable transforms it into a U[0, 1] random variable. For instance, if the realization of an exponential random variable with mean μ is 2μ, then the cdf of this value is $F(2\mu) = 1 - e^{-2\mu/\mu} = 1 - e^{-2} = 0.8647$.

We can interpret this event as equivalent to a realization of 0.8647 for a U[0, 1] random variable. Therefore, it is always possible to simulate any continuous random variable by simulating a U[0, 1] outcome first, thereby obtaining a result (*rand*) between 0 and 1, and then finding the value of t for which $F(t) = rand$. A *basic* exponential random variable has $\mu = 1$, in which case $F^{-1}(rand) = -\ln(1 - rand)$. We can simulate a basic exponential random variable using the transformation

$$t = -\ln(1 - rand)$$

Because $1 - rand$ is also distributed U[0, 1], an equally valid simulated value is obtained from the transformation

$$t = -\ln(rand)$$

For the case of a general exponential random variable, we simply multiply by μ and use

$$t = -\mu \ln(rand)$$

If we add up several basic exponential distribution realizations and count the number of realizations that do not yet exceed a given deterministic limit, say, λ, we obtain a simulated realization of the (discrete) Poisson distribution. As an event counter, the Poisson random variable is a nonnegative integer: It is 0 if the first realization exceeds λ.

A.1.3 The Normal Distribution

The normal distribution describes a random outcome that follows the so-called bell curve. The normal distribution also represents the aggregate influence of a large number of independent, additive factors. We denote the normal distribution by $N(\mu, \sigma^2)$. The *probability density function* (pdf) of the normal random variable is given by

$$f(x) = \frac{1}{\sqrt{2\pi\sigma^2}} \exp\left(\frac{-(x-\mu)^2}{2\sigma^2}\right)$$

If we set $\mu = 0$ and $\sigma^2 = 1$, we obtain the *standard normal* distribution. We denote the pdf of the standard normal random variable by $\phi(z)$ and its cdf by $\Phi(z)$. That is,

$$\phi(z) = \frac{1}{\sqrt{2\pi}} \exp\left(\frac{-z^2}{2}\right)$$

If X is distributed $N(\mu, \sigma^2)$, then the transformation $z = (x - \mu)/\sigma$ yields a standard normal. Using this transformation and its inverse, $x = \mu + z\sigma$, it is straightforward to use standard normal tables or computerized equivalents to analyze any normal random variable.

Most stochastic models assume independent processing times. Subject to this assumption, the sum of many independent small random variables can be approximated by the normal distribution with mean equal to the sum of the individual means and variance equal to the sum of the variances. This well-known result is called the *central limit theorem*. The independence assumption is required both for normality and for making the variance equal to the sum of the variances. The normal distribution is considered practical because we often encounter such sums in practice. For example, the normal distribution has been validated in some low variation surgery instances (May et al. 2000). Nonetheless, we use it with the same caveats that apply to the exponential distribution.

It is not straightforward to simulate a normal random variable by the usual method because $\Phi(z)$ does not have an analytic inverse. However, Excel and similar platforms provide an approximate function (NORM.S.INV) for calculating the inverse. An alternative method, known as the *Box–Muller transformation*, draws two U[0, 1] samples ($U1$ and $U2$) and transforms them into an independent pair ($Z1$ and $Z2$) of standard normal samples using the following formulas:

$$Z1 = \sqrt{-2\ln(U1)}\left[\cos(2\pi U2)\right]$$
$$Z2 = \sqrt{-2\ln(U1)}\left[\sin(2\pi U2)\right]$$

When only one normal sample is needed, we can simply use $Z1$ and ignore $Z2$.

The first row of Table A.1 lists seven simulated values of a standard normal random variable, in the order in which they were generated. That is, $z_1 = 1.140$, $z_2 = 0.329$, and so on. The second row repeats the same values, but sorted from small to large. When sorted, we enclose the indices by brackets; that is, $z_{[1]} = -1.064$, $z_{[2]} = -0.667$, etc., and $z_{[k]}$ is known as the kth *order statistic*; hence the sorted sample comprises the order statistics.

Consider the following analytics task: Given a sample of n independent and identically distributed (iid) realizations that we suspect to be normal, we must judge whether it is indeed normal and estimate the parameters, μ and σ^2. For example, take the first row of Table A.1 but interpret the values as x_i. (We reserve z for the standard normal. Here, even though we know that we simulated a standard normal with parameters 0 and 1, we do not use this information directly.) Using hats to denote estimated parameters, the most straightforward estimation approach, for any distribution, is to use the mean of the sample as $\hat{\mu}$

Table A.1 A simulated normal random sample.

1.140	0.329	−0.124	−0.482	−0.667	0.174	−1.064
−1.064	−0.667	−0.482	−0.124	0.174	0.329	1.140

and then divide the sum of squares of deviations around $\hat{\mu}$ by $(n - 1)$ to yield an unbiased variance estimate. (In Excel, the functions AVERAGE and VAR.S perform these tasks.) Formally, we write,

$$\hat{\mu} = \frac{1}{n}\sum_{i=1}^{n} X_i$$

and

$$\hat{\sigma}^2 = \frac{1}{n-1}\sum_{i=1}^{n} (X_i - \hat{\mu})^2$$

In our example, $\hat{\mu} = -0.099$ and $\hat{\sigma}^2 = 0.532$ (that is, $\hat{\sigma} = 0.730$). These results may appear sizably different from 0 and 1, but a sample of seven may simply be too small when we want precise estimates. It is also common practice to use a histogram of the sample to judge visually whether it is plausibly normal. A chi-square test can then be used for more formal testing. In our case, however, the sample is too small to create a meaningful histogram. An alternative that can be used even with such a small sample is the *Q–Q chart* (see Figure A.1). Q–Q charts can also be adapted for incomplete samples (see Chapter 18), which are very common in practice.

To create a Q–Q chart (for any distribution), we match the order statistics to their scaled expected values or a good approximation of those, also known as *scores*. We then construct a regression line through the matched set. If the points appear to hug the regression line closely, it is plausible that the distributional assumption we used to obtain the scores is valid. For the normal case, very exact scores can be calculated, but that requires complex numerical integration. Empirical evidence suggests, however, that a much simpler set of scores, called Blom's scores, works very well (Looney and Gulledge 1985). Blom's score for $x_{[k]}$ is given by $z_k = \Phi^{-1}[(k - 0.375)/(n + 0.25)]$, that is, the z-value for which the standard normal distribution cdf, $\Phi(z)$, yields a probability of $(k - 0.375)/(n + 0.25)$. The values on the horizontal axis of the Q–Q chart in Figure A.1 are the scores, whereas the vertical axis measures the simulated order statistics. The regression line parameters can be used directly to estimate the mean and standard deviation of the sample: the intercept serves as $\hat{\mu}$ and the slope as $\hat{\sigma}$. Here we obtain $\hat{\mu} = -0.099$ and $\hat{\sigma} = 0.780$. (Compare to -0.099 and 0.730, as derived directly before.)

Visual inspection of Figure A.1 suggests a good fit, but that involves a subjective judgment. A more formal test compares the square root of the R^2 statistic (in our example, $\sqrt{0.975} = 0.987$) to tabulated cutoff values. If the square root is above the cutoff for a given significance level, we cannot reject the hypothesis that the distribution selected is valid. Looney and Gulledge provide such cutoff values for the normal distribution and several probability levels. In this instance, if we choose a significance level of 5%, the tabulated cutoff value for $n = 7$ is

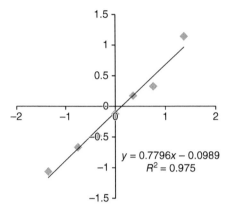

Figure A.1 A normal Q–Q chart for Table A.1.

0.898 (<0.987), so we cannot reject normality. Furthermore, the full table suggests that the fit is better than 90% of random sample fits. In such a case, we say that this sample *passes* with a probability of 0.9, a value calculated relative to other samples of seven normal variates. Intuitively, when this probability is high, our confidence in the normality of the sample increases. Indeed, it is remarkable that a sample too small to provide precise estimates or offer a meaningful histogram can still be used to test normality. However, we must be aware that when the sample is small, the test lacks power. In other words, it may fail to reject when it should; that is, only a large deviation from normality is likely to trigger rejection.

To avoid negative realizations when using the normal distribution for processing times, we usually require a low σ/μ value. For instance, if we set $\sigma/\mu = 0.324$ (or $1/3.09$), the probability of a negative realization is 0.001 and may be ignored for some purposes. Another resolution is to consider a truncated normal, such that any value below zero is removed from consideration and replaced by a newly simulated positive realization. Usually, such truncation occurs for negative z values; that is, the mean of the original distribution is assumed nonnegative. For normal distributions truncated at zero, the coefficient of variation is at most 0.756, and the maximum occurs for truncation at the original mean. If we allow truncation for positive z values, the coefficient of variation remains strictly below 1. Thus, the normal, truncated or not, is inappropriate as a model for random variables with high coefficients of variation.

A.1.4 The Lognormal Distribution

We know from experience that processing time distributions are typically skewed to the right and processing times are never negative. The normal distribution, however, is defined for negative realizations and is symmetric around the mean. Relative to these features, the exponential distribution may appear to be a more realistic model than the normal, but practical experience suggests that, for very low variation instances, the normal is a better approximation than the exponential. The exponential distribution has a constant coefficient of variation, which may be reasonable for medium variation – say, between 0.75 and 1.33 – but not for either low or high variation. By the same token, neither the normal nor the exponential works well for *cv* values between about 0.33 and 0.75. Therefore, ideally, we prefer a distribution that is always positive, skewed to the right, and accommodates any coefficient of variation. The lognormal distribution satisfies these conditions.

Consider a random variable that is obtained not as the sum of many independent positive small components but rather as their product. If we take the logarithm of each individual random variable in the product, the sum of these logarithms is approximately normal by the central limit theorem. The exponent of this sum – that is, the product itself – is strictly positive and skewed to the right, as desired. The random variable associated with this structure is known as the *lognormal* distribution.

Suppose we wish to simulate a lognormal random variable, say, X, with mean μ and standard deviation σ. Let Y be the natural logarithm of X, that is, $Y = \ln(X)$; conversely, $X = \exp(Y)$. By definition, Y is distributed normally, so if we know its mean and standard deviation (denoted here by m and s), we already know how to simulate it. If the result of simulating Y is y, then we obtain $x = \exp(y)$ as a simulated X value. Some software platforms (including Excel) also require the user to directly specify the mean and standard deviation of Y. So our task is to find m and s, and it is convenient to start by simulating X/μ and then multiply the result by μ. X/μ is a lognormal random variable with mean $\mu = 1$ and standard deviation $\sigma = cv$. We refer to any lognormal random variable with mean 1 as *basic*. Because $\ln(1) = 0$, it can be shown that, for the basic case,

$$s^2 = \ln\left(1 + cv^2\right) \quad m = -\frac{s^2}{2}$$

To multiply by μ, we can add $\ln(\mu)$ to y before taking the exponent. Therefore, we can evaluate m and s for X directly from the following relationships:

$$s^2 = \ln\left(1 + \sigma^2/\mu^2\right) \quad m = \ln(\mu) - s^2/2 \tag{A.1}$$

Using these values, the pdf of the lognormal distribution is given by

$$f(x) = \begin{cases} \dfrac{1}{x\sqrt{2\pi s^2}} \exp\left(\dfrac{-(\ln(x) - m)^2}{2s^2}\right), & \text{if } x > 0 \\ 0, & \text{otherwise} \end{cases}$$

and the mode is equal to $\exp(m - s^2)$. When a lognormal distribution is given directly by m and s^2, we can use Eq. (A.1) to solve for μ and σ^2. Specifically, we obtain

$$\mu = \exp\left(m + s^2/2\right) \quad \sigma^2 = \mu^2\left[\exp\left(s^2\right) - 1\right] \tag{A.2}$$

When s is high, the implication is that the ratio between realizations can be high. As a numerical example, McKay et al. (1988) observed in a particular shop that the difference between consecutive processing times of identical items can easily have a ratio of 2 (i.e. the slower item takes twice as long as the faster one). If we assume a lognormal processing time distribution and interpret this observation as implying that the two fractile values associated with probabilities of 0.1 and 0.9 demonstrate this ratio, then we have $cv \approx 0.27$. (For the standard normal distribution, 0.1 and 0.9 are associated with z values of -1.282 and 1.282. We require $\exp(1.282\sigma) = \sqrt{2}$, because that implies $\exp(-1.282\sigma) = \sqrt{1/2}$, and $\sqrt{2}/\sqrt{1/2} = 2$. Solving for σ we obtain 0.27.) By Eq. (A.1) we then obtain $s = 0.2653$ and $m = \ln(\mu) - 0.0352$. They also noted, however, that setup times are even less predictable, and by assumption C3 we include setup times in our processing times. Larger ranges have also been observed in machine shops. For instance, Buzacott and Shantikumar (1993) report a ratio of 10 for a particular precision machining operation. This would lead to $cv \approx 0.90$, with $s = 0.7703$ and $m = -0.2967$. (As we discuss later, some projects exhibit high cv values, well above 1.33.)

Figure A.2 depicts the pdf of basic lognormal distributions with $cv = 0.25$, 0.5, 1, and 2. As the figure demonstrates, a higher cv yields a more skewed pdf. The figure also includes the pdf of a basic exponential random variable, for comparison. As the figure demonstrates, when cv is low, the lognormal distribution is quite similar to the normal – and thus it can substitute for the normal when it is a better approximation than the exponential. But when the coefficient of variation is 1, the lognormal is more similar to the exponential (which has $cv = 1$).

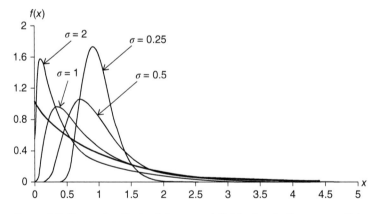

Figure A.2 Comparing the basic lognormal distribution to the exponential.

Table A.2 Comparing the mean and the median for the lognormal distribution.

cv	s	Pr{X < μ}	M/μ	Mode/μ	Φ(−s)
0.25	0.246	0.549	0.970	0.913	0.403
0.5	0.472	0.593	0.894	0.716	0.318
1	0.833	0.661	0.707	0.354	0.203
2	1.269	0.737	0.447	0.089	0.102

The probability that a lognormal random variable is below the mean, μ, is given by $\Phi(s/2)$, which always exceeds 0.5 because $s > 0$. The third column in Table A.2 lists some values for cv = 0.25, 0.5, 1, and 2. The median, M, is given by $\exp(m) = \exp(\ln\mu - s^2/2) = \mu\exp(-s^2/2)$, which is always smaller than μ, as the fourth column in Table A.2 illustrates. The mode is even smaller, $\mu\exp(-3s^2/2)$, as listed in the fifth column of the table, and the probability of falling at or below the mode is $\Phi(-s)$, as listed in the last column. When $cv = 1$, the relationship between the mean and the median (given in the third line of Table A.2) is comparable to the exponential case (where $\Pr\{T < \mu\} = 0.632$ and $M = 0.693\mu$). The approximation is within 5%. However, when $cv = 0.25$, the results are far from those of the exponential (namely, 0.549 and 0.970) but provide a better fit for the normal, for which we expect 0.5 and 1. The table demonstrates that it is especially risky to confuse the most likely time – the mode – with the average. As the table shows, when cv grows large, it becomes progressively unlikely to meet or beat the mode: For $cv = 1$, the probability of exceeding the mode is almost 80%, and for $cv = 2$, almost 90%.

Two special features of the lognormal distribution are relevant. First, the sum of many independent, strictly positive random variables, each with a finite coefficient of variation, is lognormal in the limit. We refer to this result colloquially as the *lognormal* central limit theorem (because, for nonnegative random variables, we can use it instead of the regular central limit theorem). Formally, however, it is not a proper central limit theorem so we also refer to it, more correctly, as the *lognormal sum approximation* (Paul and Trietsch 2012). In particular, when all the components are lognormal, the lognormal sum approximation is also known as the *Fenton–Wilkinson approximation* (Fenton 1960). Other approximations of the sum of lognormal components by a lognormal, including the case of correlated components, are also available (Mehta et al. 2007), but for tractability, we focus on the simpler version. In calculating the parameters of the lognormal sum approximation, we first add the independent means and variances to obtain the mean and the variance of the sum and then apply Eq. (A.1). (Compare this property to the regular central limit theorem, which uses the same mean and variance calculation but does not require positive random variables. In the limit, however, the lognormal and the normal approximations of the sum approximate each other.) Furthermore, if we apply the Fenton–Wilkinson approximation to the sum of few lognormal distributions, the result is a better approximation than the normal random variable with the same mean and standard deviation. To this end, if the lognormals are given in terms of m and s^2, we must first apply Eq. (A.2) to obtain their means and variances, add them, and finally apply Eq. (A.1) to the sums. Second, suppose that the processing time of an activity is the reciprocal of the capacity dedicated to the processing, and suppose further that the capacity is lognormal. The processing time that results is then also lognormal, with the same coefficient of variation. (This would not be true for any other distribution mentioned in this appendix. It holds because we are taking the exponent of a symmetric random variable.)

A.1.5 The Parkinson Distribution

Extensive research shows that the lognormal distribution is often valid, but even if every processing time follows a lognormal distribution, the processing time that we observe is not always lognormal. For instance, if there are really several processes operating in parallel, each taking lognormal time, but we can only observe the slowest one (the maximum), the distribution we observe will not be lognormal. A special case of such a maximum is the pure Parkinson distribution, which was originally introduced in our first edition. It combines a known threshold value and some core distribution that is visible only if it exceeds the threshold. Since then, the Parkinson distribution has been generalized by Trietsch et al. (2012) to better fit field data sets. We start with the original pure version.

Parkinson's law states that "work expands so as to fill the time available for its completion." There is no "law," however, to suggest that work compresses. Suppose then that work is allotted q units of time but it really requires Y, where q is deterministic but Y is a random variable. Then the time, X, that we can observe and measure is given by

$$X = \max\{q, Y\}$$

and we say that X has a pure Parkinson distribution. The value of q is often agreed upon by negotiation, while Y (called the *core*) reflects real randomness. For example, when processing times are monitored, workers may be concerned that if they report good performance today, it will be the basis of a more demanding norm tomorrow. In that situation they may hide their performance when it exceeds expectations. As a result, the Parkinson distribution arises: Delays are observable but earliness is hidden. In other words, we can observe X but not Y.

The pure Parkinson distribution can be described as "deterministic with a random tail." For example, if the probability of on-time completion is 0.9, then with probability 0.9 the reported (and thus observable) processing time will match the plan; otherwise, it will follow a tail such as the tail of a lognormal distribution. In such an environment, tight processing time estimates yield thick tails and vice versa.

Conceptually, specifying a high value of q can be viewed as a large hidden buffer against tardiness. Indeed, it can be shown that the mean of a Parkinson random variable is always higher than the mean of Y but the variance is always lower. In other words, we reduce variation by specifying a buffer of capacity. However, because we do not admit it, the buffer is hidden and thus not likely to be optimized. This phenomenon becomes pronounced when q is relatively large, and thus the tail is relatively small. Again, this direction increases the predictability of the system, but at the price of wasted capacity. When the predictability is high enough, one advantage is that deterministic sequencing models become more relevant. Our assumption in this text, however, is that the price of wasted capacity is too high. For that reason, we need stochastic scheduling models that can handle the real underlying variation of Y without resorting to excessive q estimates and allowing the system to waste earliness too recklessly. Although the use of buffers is necessary and rational, they should not be hidden, and they should not be determined by such a process.

In their study of field data from several project organizations, Trietsch et al. (2012) found several cases that fit the pure Parkinson pattern. Furthermore, the hypothesis that Y had a lognormal distribution could not be rejected (that is, they validated that Y was lognormal at the same time). However, they found even more instances where many realizations were at the q level but many others were reported early, sometimes even very early. For those instances they introduced a more general (and less pure) version of the Parkinson distribution. Let p_P denote the probability that an early activity is falsely recorded as precisely on time. Assume that this probability applies to each early activity independently. That is, early activities are recorded correctly with a probability of $(1 - p_P)$ and precisely on time otherwise; tardy activities are always recorded correctly. For $p_P = 1$ we obtain the pure Parkinson distribution, whereas for $p_P = 0$ we obtain a conventional distribution; that is, the Parkinson distribution generalizes all single variate distributions, with or without the Parkinson effect.

To simulate a Parkinson distribution with given q and p_P values and a given distribution for Y (estimated from historical data when applicable), we start by simulating Y. If $Y < q$, we generate a *rand* value and we use the value q if *rand* $\leq p_P$; otherwise, we use Y directly.

A.2 Mixtures of Distributions

In the Parkinson case, the distribution we observe is not lognormal even if the core is lognormal. Other instances occur for which the lognormal distribution may apply, but the evidence may seem to contradict it. An example is the mixture of two or more distributions.

As a conceptual model, suppose a job can be processed on one of m different machines, and the time distribution it takes depends on which machine is used. If each machine has a given probability, v_i, of being selected (with $\sum v_i = 1$), we obtain a *mixture distribution* for the processing time. Let the processing time associated with machine i be X_i, with density function $f_i(x)$. Then the density function, $f(x)$, of the processing time is given by

$$f(x) = \sum_{i=1}^{m} v_i f_i(x)$$

That is, the mixture's density function is a weighted average of the components' density functions. Similarly, if the cdf of machine i is $F_i(x)$, then

$$F(x) = \sum_{i=1}^{m} v_i F_i(x)$$

and

$$\mu = \sum_{i=1}^{m} v_i \mu_i$$

That is, the mixture's cdf and mean are also weighted averages with the same weights. The same applies to all the moments around the origin. However, this feature is not inherited by the moments around the mean. The variance, which is the second moment around the mean, can be calculated as follows:

$$\sigma^2 = \sum_{i=1}^{m} v_i \left(\sigma_i^2 + \mu_i^2 \right) - \mu^2 = \sum_{i=1}^{m} v_i \left(\sigma_i^2 + \mu_i^2 - \mu^2 \right)$$

$$= \sum_{i=1}^{m} v_i \left(\sigma_i^2 + \mu_i^2 - 2\mu^2 + \mu^2 \right) = \sum_{i=1}^{m} v_i \left(\sigma_i^2 + \mu_i^2 - 2\mu_i\mu + \mu^2 \right)$$

$$= \sum_{i=1}^{m} v_i \left[\sigma_i^2 + (\mu_i - \mu)^2 \right]$$

The last form demonstrates that the weighted average of the variances is a lower bound on the variance, realized as an equality if and only if all component means are equal. For the case $m = 2$, it can be shown that the variance expression can be expressed as follows:

$$\sigma^2 = v_1 \sigma_1^2 + v_2 \sigma_2^2 + v_1 v_2 (\mu_2 - \mu_1)^2$$

For convenience, we assume that the component distributions (of X_i) are each unimodal. The normal, lognormal, and exponential distributions are all unimodal (but the uniform is not). A mixture of unimodal components can have several modes, but that depends on the relative distance between means and on the distribution. For instance, a mixture of exponentials is always unimodal. Nonetheless, when a multimodal distribution is observed in practice, it is often a mixture. A particularly important example that is often bimodal or multimodal in the single-machine model arises when machines break down sometimes, in which case the reported processing time includes repair time; that is, it is the sum of the real processing time and the repair time, but we might choose to use the lognormal sum approximation to represent it as a single lognormal distribution. (In parallel machine models we should distinguish between processing time and repair time because we can switch the job to a different machine upon a breakdown.) If machines break down frequently and repairs are quick, the effect may be masked by the natural processing time variation, and the result can be unimodal. But if they break down infrequently and then take a long time to repair, we may obtain a bimodal distribution. In general, if we consider the possibility of more than one breakdown per job, there is no theoretical limit on the number of modes that can result. In the case of infrequent breakdowns, however, the third and higher modes are typically negligible for practical purposes. For example, suppose job processing time is a basic lognormal (with mean 1) and $cv = 0.4$. Suppose the probability the machine breaks down during a job is 5% and the time to repair is lognormal with $\mu = 10$ and $cv = \sqrt{0.192}$ (about 0.438). If we ignore the possibility of two or more breakdowns, we obtain a mixture where, with probability 0.95, the distribution is per the pure processing time (with $\mu_1 = 1$ and $cv_1 = 0.4$), and otherwise, we face the sum of repair time and pure processing time. Assuming processing time repair time are statistically independent, we can use the lognormal sum approximation to determine that if the machine breaks down then the total time distribution is approximately lognormal with $\mu_2 = 11$ and $cv_2 = 0.4$, and now we have a mixture of these two distributions (where the two components have the same cv). Calculating the mean and variance, we obtain $\mu = 1.5$ and $\sigma^2 = 5.87$, leading to $cv = 1.615$. The contribution of the weighted average of the component variances alone, namely, 1.12, would yield $cv = 0.706$, which is higher than that of either component (and higher than the cv of repair time alone). In general, it can be shown that when the components have the same cv, the weighted average variance element is always sufficiently high by itself to ensure that the cv of the mixture will be higher. On the other hand, suppose processing time and repair times are deterministic, so we obtain a mixture of 1 or 11, with probabilities 0.95 and 0.05. The variance will be 4.75, leading to $cv = 1.453$. So in this example, considering both effects, we observe a very sizable increase in cv. This is typical for mixtures where one component is rare but much larger than the other (as in the case of infrequent machine breakdowns). It is perhaps the most important feature of mixtures of this type.

To simulate such a mixture, we may first sample the pure processing time and then take a side lottery by generating a random number, *rand*. If *rand* ≤ 0.05, we generate a repair time and add them up. An alternative approach relies on the lognormal sum approximation. First generate *rand*, and then, depending on the result, generate either a pure processing time or a combined processing and repair time. In terms of μ and *cv*, the two approaches are equivalent. This equivalence is guaranteed because the lognormal sum approximation matches the mean and the variance of the sum.

If we remove the assumption that only the first repair event during a processing time counts, we can devise a more realistic model for frequent repairs. Whereas this model is difficult to analyze theoretically, it is straightforward to simulate, and we present it in simulation terms. Recall that time between random events such as breakdowns is the main practical case for which the exponential is often valid. Accordingly, suppose that the time between breakdowns follows an exponential distribution with a given rate, λ (equivalent to the reciprocal of the mean). Then, if the simulated pure job processing time is x, the number of breakdowns during the job follows a Poisson distribution with parameter λx. The next step is to simulate the number of repairs necessary as a Poisson realization with parameter λx. (A straightforward way to do that is by counting the number of basic exponential random variables required for their sum to exceed λx for the first time and subtracting 1. It is also possible to simulate a Poisson random variable based on a single *rand* realization. Both approaches require iterative computation.) Whereas the coefficient of variation increases in all cases, the effect is stronger with rare and large repairs, in which case the resulting mixture distribution is clearly far from lognormal. When repairs are very frequent but small, their effect on the mean can be comparable with that of infrequent large repairs, but their effect on *cv* is smaller and the mixture distribution can be approximately lognormal. Figure A.3 depicts the

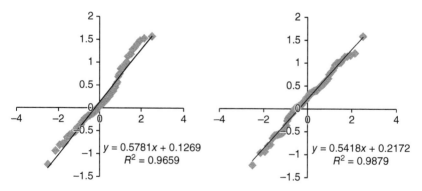

Figure A.3 Normal Q–Q plot of $\ln(p_j/e_j)$ for machine breakdown mixture models with large infrequent repairs (left) and small frequent repairs (right).

result of such a simulation for 100 jobs, in which the pure processing time is basic lognormal with $cv = 0.4$ and the repair time has the same cv. In the left-hand figure, a single repair occurs on average every four time units and takes an average of two time units. In the right-hand figure, the frequency of repairs is quadrupled, but their average duration is quartered. On both sides, the mean increases by 50%, but whereas the left side fails the normality test with a probability of about 1.5%, the right side passes with a probability of about 40%. (These probabilities fluctuate wildly among different simulation runs, but the qualitative difference between the two sides is consistent.) Note specifically the S wave shape of the left-side graph and that its slope exceeds that of the right-side graph. If we were to fit the regression line to only the negative points, it would reflect mostly instances without breakdowns, its slope would be lower than for the full set, and the most positive points would be strictly above the regression line. That becomes more pronounced as we reduce the breakdown probability further (while holding the mean total time constant). However, when the frequency of repair is very low, we may need a larger sample, with a sufficient likely number of repair events, to see this effect.

A.3 Increasing and Decreasing Completion Rates

Suppose that we start processing a job, and after x time units, it has not been completed. Consider the distribution of the time remaining to complete the job given that processing has lasted longer than x. To obtain the conditional density function, $f(t|t > x)$, we must divide $f(t)$ by $[1 - F(x)]$, the probability that processing did not finish by x. As a result the area under the conditional density function above x is 1. Therefore, if δ is an infinitesimal time interval, the probability the job will complete during the next δ time units is $\delta \times f(t)/[1 - F(t)]$. For this reason, the ratio $f(t)/[1 - F(t)]$ is known as the *completion rate*. In general, the completion rate is a function of t, and it may or may not be monotone. If it is monotone increasing, we refer to the processing time distribution as having an *increasing completion rate* (ICR), and if it is monotone decreasing, we refer to the processing time distribution as having a *decreasing completion rate* (DCR). If a processing time distribution is ICR, then its conditional remaining expectation, that is, $(E[t|t > x] - x)$, is monotone decreasing, which is the case we intuitively expect. (In reliability theory, completion rates are known as *failure rates,* so ICR is denoted IFR and DCR is denoted DFR.)

The uniform and normal distributions exhibit ICR. The exponential distribution is a boundary case, with constant completion rate. Thus, it lies between the cases of ICR and DCR. If an exponentially distributed processing time does not complete during the first x time units, we might want to know the distribution of the remaining time. Surprisingly, the distribution of the remaining time follows exactly the same distribution as it did initially. In other words, as long as the job is not yet complete, the probability it will complete in the next small time interval is constant for an interval of given length, no matter how much processing has taken place. This feature is sometimes referred to as the *memoryless property*.

For nonnegative random variables, constant completion rate and unit coefficient of variation are related: ICR random variables are associated with coefficients of variation below 1, and DCR random variables are associated with coefficients of variation above 1. More precisely, ICR implies low coefficient of variation, but the converse is only true in an approximate sense because the completion rate is not necessarily increasing everywhere. Similarly, DCR implies high coefficient of variation, whereas the converse is only true in an approximate sense.

Now consider the lognormal and the pure Parkinson distributions. The lognormal can be shown to exhibit an ICR initially, but if processing does not complete by some threshold (that depends on the parameters), it becomes DCR. Similarly, the pure Parkinson is ICR for any processing time below q, but once q is exceeded, there is an immediate increase in the expected remaining processing time. The behavior thereafter depends on the tail distribution of Y. Thus, these two distributions show that the completion rate need not be a monotone function. A similar observation holds for some mixtures, such as breakdown models with infrequent and long repair time.

A.4 Stochastic Dominance

When $E[p_1] \leq E[p_2]$, we say that p_1 is (weakly) smaller than p_2 *by expectation*. We also write $p_1 \leq_{ex} p_2$. Example 6.5 demonstrates that $p_1 \leq_{ex} p_2$ is not sufficient to generalize deterministic dominance rules requiring $p_1 \leq p_2$, because the worst-case realization of p_1 could be larger than that of p_2. However, stochastic ordering relationships exist that preclude a worst-case reversal. We say that one random variable, X, is *stochastically smaller* than another, Y (denoted $X \leq_{st} Y$), if $\Pr\{X \leq t\} \geq \Pr\{Y \leq t\}$ for any t. This implies that the cdf of X, $F_X(t)$, is at or above the cdf of Y, $F_Y(t)$. In other words, $F_X \geq F_Y$ everywhere. We also refer to this relationship as *stochastic dominance*, and if it applies to several random variables, we say that they are *stochastically ordered* (because the dominance relationship is transitive). Stochastic dominance is a strong relationship in the sense that $\leq_{st}$ implies $\leq_{ex}$. A useful way to see this relationship is by noting that the expected value of a nonnegative random variable is given by the area captured above its cdf below 1 and to the right of the origin (see Figure A.4). But if $F_X \geq F_Y$, then the area above F_X cannot exceed the area above F_Y.

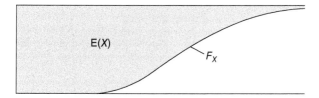

Figure A.4 Depicting the expected value as an area over the cdf.

The definition of $\leq_{st}$ does not require statistical independence. For example, let X and Y be two *iid* random variables, and let Z be any nonnegative random variable (including the degenerate case, in which $Z = 0$ with certainty). Then $X \leq_{st} Y + Z$ and $X \leq_{st} X + Z$. The first relation is between independent random variables. When $Z = 0$ with certainty, this relation implies that iid random variables are stochastically smaller than each other. However, in the second relation, X and $X + Z$ are statistically dependent because of a common element shared by the two random variables.

A.5 Linearly Associated Processing Times

When random variables are subject to common causes of variation affecting more than one of them in the same direction, they are said to be *associated* (Esary et al. 1967). More formally, random variables are associated if the correlation between any positive increasing functions of any two of them is nonnegative. Independent random variables are associated (weakly), but negatively correlated ones are not. We need to consider associated processing times because, in practical settings, there are often many common causes of variation that affect more than one job in the same direction. For example, if the quality of a particular tool deteriorates, then those jobs that require it may all take longer to process. Because this applies to several jobs, the processing times are positively correlated. In general, it is likely that various causes affect different subsets of jobs in such a way that positive correlation is introduced among them to various degrees. Furthermore, when processing times are associated random variables, the completion time variance is higher than for independent random variables, for all but the first job. For independent random variables, the variance of a sum equals the sum of the variances. However, two associated random variables have a nonnegative covariance by definition, and the variance of a sum of random variables with a positive covariance is higher than the sum of the variances. Therefore, the independence assumption is optimistic for the variance of a completion time. In a scheduling context, because our penalty functions are nondecreasing, when two processing times are associated, their penalties are associated. This, in turn, implies that the variance of performance measures that are based on processing times that are associated random variables is also higher than for independent processing times. Thus, it is optimistic to ignore positive dependence.

One way in which association may arise is by adding the same random variable to two or more independent random variables. Another way is if two or more positive random variables are multiplied by the same *common factor*. For example, if a regular worker may be sick tomorrow, and the replacement worker is 10% slower, then it would constitute a common factor of $1/0.9$ multiplying all processing times. Therefore, for today's scheduling purposes, we must consider tomorrow's job processing times as positively dependent. Limiting ourselves to linear causes of association, consider the case where two positive random variables, X_1 and X_2, are given by $X_1 = (R_1 + \alpha_1 S)B$ and $X_2 = (R_2 + \alpha_2 S)B$, where R_1, R_2, and S are independent nonnegative random variables; B is a positive independent random variable; and α_1 and α_2 are nonnegative scalars. (Because $X_1, X_2 > 0$, it follows that if S or $\alpha_1 = 0$ then $R_1 > 0$, and so on.) If we set $S = 0$ and $B = 1$, then $X_1 = R_1$, $X_2 = R_2$, and they are independent by assumption (and thus associated). At the other extreme, if R_1 and R_2 are 0, then X_1 and X_2 are proportional (and thus associated). Here B is a common factor shared by X_1 and X_2, whereas S represents any additive element they may share. Alternatively, we could have modeled S without subjecting it to the common factor. To construct general scheduling models with this type of association, we might assume that several common factors exist (generalizing B), such as workers, tools, weather, and so on. Similarly, we can model multiple common elements (generalizing S), and let each job incorporate a weighted subset of them. Then each job is subject to a subset of common factors and a subset of common elements. For each particular pair of jobs, the product of the common factors in the intersection of common factors acts as B, and the intersection of common elements acts as S. Common factors and elements that are not shared by the two jobs can be incorporated into R_j. Such models, however, would pose a very significant estimation challenge, and for this reason we often simplify by using just one common factor and up to one common element with $\alpha_j = \alpha = 1$.

Suppose that a set of random variables is defined by $X_j = R_j B > 0$ for a set of independent nonnegative R_j and an independent positive common factor B. Then we say that the members of the set $\{X_j\}$ are *linearly associated*. In a project management setting, Trietsch et al. (2012) show how to estimate the necessary distributions for this case. They also identified linear association in field data; that is, they validated the hypothesis that linear association can explain the positive dependence observable in field data (see our Research Notes for Chapter 18). An extended definition includes the common element; that is, $X_j = (R_j + S)B$, in which case we can say that the members of the set X_j are *linearly associated with a common factor and a common element.* The following theorem was also presented – without proof – as Theorem 6.7.

■ **Theorem A.1**   Given three positive independent random variables – R_1, R_2, and B – and one nonnegative random variable S, let $X_1 = (R_1 + S)B$ and $X_2 = (R_2 + S)B$. Then $X_1 \leq_{ex} X_2$ if and only if $R_1 \leq_{ex} R_2$ and $X_1 \leq_{st} X_2$ if and only if $R_1 \leq_{st} R_2$.

Proof. For $\leq_{ex}$ (i.e. to show that $E[X_1] \leq E[X_2]$ if and only if $E[R_1] \leq E[R_2]$), by independence, $E[X_j] = E[B]E[R_j + S]$, so the theorem holds. For $\leq_{st}$, let $W_1 = R_1 + S$ and $W_2 = R_2 + S$. By construction, $W_1 \leq_{st} W_2$ if and only if $R_1 \leq_{st} R_2$. Even if $S = 0$, W_1, $W_2 > 0$, so $\log(W_j)$ is well defined. By the definition of stochastic dominance and because the log function is monotone, $\log(W_1) \leq_{st} \log(W_2)$ if and only if $W_1 \leq_{st} W_2$. Therefore, $\log(W_1) + \log B \leq_{st} \log(W_2) + \log B$ (and thus $W_1 B \leq_{st} W_2 B$) if and only if $R_1 \leq_{st} R_2$.   □

In scheduling, we focus on completion times. Completion times are typically composed of sums of processing times and often involve maximum operators (when we must wait for more than one operation to complete before we can start a new operation). Furthermore, it may happen that we set release dates for some jobs, in which case the start time is given by the maximum of the previous completion time and the release date. For our basic results, however, we assume that no due dates or release dates exist. Therefore, all processing times are based on sums of random variables or on maxima of two or more random variables. We now study the effect of linear association on completion times. Some of our results could be extended to include a common element, but we omit such details.

To make our results easier to visualize and to simplify the proofs, we imagine a very large sample that represents reality precisely. In this sample space, we assume that n columns represent *initial* independent nonnegative values. One additional column gives realizations, b, of the positive common factor, B. We can then add n additional columns, each representing the product of b and one of the initial columns. We refer to these last n columns as the *adjusted* values. By construction, the adjusted values are linearly associated. In general, we should use the adjusted values for our scheduling decisions, but we might wonder to what extent we can make the decisions first and then apply the adjustment. Performing the analysis in this order is always more convenient because the initial values are independent.

■ **Theorem A.2**   Let X_j ($j = 1, 2, ..., n$) and B be ($n + 1$) independent random variables, where B is positive. Then $\sum_j BX_j = B\sum_j X_j$.

Proof. For every run with realizations x_j and b, it does not make a difference if we add the adjusted columns or adjust the sum of the initial columns.   □

Corollary A.1   Let X_j ($j = 1, 2, ..., n$) and B be ($n + 1$) independent random variables, where B is positive. Then $E[\sum_j BX_j] = E[B]E[\sum_j X_j]$.

It is difficult to work with convolutions of dependent random variables such as BX_j and BX_k. Fortunately, this result tells us that it is permissible to perform the convolution of X_j and X_k on the initial processing times and then adjust the result (multiply by B). Because the initial values are independent and processing times are positive, we can often use the lognormal (or even the regular) central limit theorem to obtain a reasonable convolution for the initial values. If B is lognormal and we use the lognormal central limit theorem for the convolutions, the product has a lognormal distribution (because the logarithms of the convolutions and of B are normal). In such a case we add up the parameters m and s^2 of the convolution and of B to obtain the corresponding parameters of the product.

■ **Theorem A.3**   Let X_j ($j = 1, 2, ..., n$) and B be ($n + 1$) independent random variables, where B is positive. Then $\min\{BX_j\} = B\min\{X_j\}$ and $\max\{BX_j\} = B\max\{X_j\}$.

Proof. Because B is positive, for every run with realizations x_j and b, $\min\{bx_j\}) = b\min\{x_j\}$ and $\max\{bx_j\}) = b \max\{x_j\}$. Hence, it does not matter if we adjust first or take the minimum (or the maximum) first.   □

Corollary A.2   Let X_j ($j = 1, 2, ..., n$) and B be ($n + 1$) independent random variables, where B is positive; then $E[\min\{BX_j\}] = E[B]E[\min\{X_j\}]$ and $E[\max\{BX_j\}] = E[B]E[\max\{X_j\}]$.

Thus, for any completion time that is obtained by a series of max and convolution operations, we can implement Theorems A.2 and A.3 serially. The cdf of the completion time subject to linear association is then given by the initial cdf of the same completion time adjusted afterward. Corollaries A.1 and A.2 yield the adjusted expected completion time. Similar analysis proves the following.

■ **Theorem A.4**   Consider a job shop where all jobs are available for their initial operation at time zero (i.e. without active release dates). Assume linearly associated processing times with a common factor element B. Let $C_j(s)$ be the adjusted completion time of job j under sequence s, and let $C_j'(s)$ be the initial completion time under the same sequence; then $C_j(s) = BC_j'(s)$.

For such a shop let s_1 and s_2 be two sequences in which $C_j(s_j)$ is the adjusted completion time under sequence s_j and $C_j'(s_j)$ is the respective initial completion time. By Theorem A.1, if $E\left[C_j'(s_1)\right] \geq_{ex} E\left[C_j'(s_2)\right]$, then $C_j(s_1) \geq_{ex} C_j(s_2)$, and if $C_j'(s_1) \geq_{st} C_j'(s_2)$, then $C_j(s_1) \geq_{st} C_j(s_2)$.

The symmetrical result also holds. For safe scheduling, we are especially interested in identifying stochastic dominance, because it often suffices to ensure the optimal sequence for safe scheduling as well as for the stochastic counterpart. But obtaining stochastic dominance for stochastic counterpart solutions is the exception and not the rule. More generally, typical results available for stochastic counterpart models remain valid for the linearly associated case. For such models, however, if we assume (without loss of generality) that $E[B] = \mu_b = 1$, then there is no real difference introduced by linear association. The consequences of linear association are more important for safe scheduling, however, where we may encounter some difficulties in generalizing all results based on the independence assumption. The reason is that due dates and release dates that are optimal for the initial processing times are not likely to remain optimal after adjustment. In other words, service levels are subject to change. This difficulty would apply even if a stochastically dominant sequence exists because we still need to adjust our due dates and release dates. Nevertheless, to study safe scheduling models with linear association, we must first consider the variance in more detail.

■ **Theorem A.5** Consider a job shop where all jobs are available for their initial operation at time zero (i.e. without active release dates). Assume linearly associated processing times with a common factor element B, such that $E[B] = \mu_q$. Let $C'_j(s)$ be the initial completion time of job j under sequence s, with mean μ_s and variance σ_s^2, and let $C_j(s)$ be the adjusted completion time of the job under the same sequence. Then

$$V\left(C_j(s)\right) = E\left[B^2\right]\sigma_s^2 + V(B)\mu_s^2 = E\left[C'_j(s)^2\right]V(B) + \mu_b^2\sigma_s^2$$

Proof. By a fundamental identity, $V(C_j(s)) = E[C_j(s)^2] - (E[C_j(s)])^2$ (which is nonnegative because by Jensen's inequality $E[C_j(s)^2] \geq (E[C_j(s)])^2$). Substituting $BC'_j(s)$ for $C_j(s)$, we obtain $V\left(C_j(s)\right) = E[B^2]C'_j(s)^2 - \left[\left(BC'_j(s)\right)\right]^2$. Because B and $C'_j(s)$ are independent, we can also write $V\left(C_j(s)\right) = E[B^2]E\left[C'_j(s)^2\right] - \mu_b^2\mu_s^2$. By the same identity we can substitute $\sigma_s^2 + \mu_s^2$ for $E\left[C'_j(s)^2\right]$ and $V(B) + \mu_b^2$ for $E[B^2]$ to obtain $V\left(C_j(s)\right) = \mu_b^2\sigma_s^2 + V(B)\sigma_s^2 + V(B)\mu_s^2$. The two (symmetrical) results follow by recombining either the first two elements to $E[B^2]\sigma_s^2$ or the last two elements to $E\left[C'_j(s)^2\right]V(B)$. □

By dividing the interim result obtained in this proof by $\mu_b^2\mu_s^2$, we obtain the following theorem.

■ **Theorem A.6** Consider a job shop where all jobs are available for their initial operation at time zero (i.e. without active release dates). Assume linearly associated processing times with a common factor element B, such that $E[B] = \mu_b$. Let $C'_j(s)$ be the initial completion time of job j under sequence s, with mean μ_s and variance σ_s^2, and let $C_j(s)$ be the adjusted completion time of the job under the same sequence. Then

$$\frac{V(C_j(s))}{(E[C_j(s)])^2} = \frac{V(B)}{\mu_b^2} + \frac{V(B)\,\sigma_s^2}{\mu_b^2\,\mu_s^2} + \frac{\sigma_s^2}{\mu_s^2}$$

Theorem A.6 indicates that the squared coefficient of variation (*scv*) of the product exceeds the sum of the *scv*s of the components (by their product), and therefore the coefficient of variation of the product exceeds that of either component. In our context, the more important aspect of this observation is that the coefficient of variation of the makespan cannot be less than that of B. Henceforth, we assume that B is normalized so that $\mu_b = 1$. We can do so without loss of generality because, for any positive μ_b, $BC'_j(s) = (B/\mu_b)$ $\left(C'_j(s)\mu_b\right)$. With $\mu_b = 1$, Theorem A.5 implies that the variance of the makespan cannot decrease by incorporating the common factor in the model. If the means and variances of two makespan distributions are agreeable, they remain agreeable after multiplication by B; otherwise, the one with the larger mean may also acquire a larger variance due to the element $V(B)\mu_s^2$. In more detail, $E[B^2] - 1 = V(B)$ (because $\mu_b^2 = 1$), so the variance of s increases by $V(B)\mu_s^2 + V(B)\sigma_s^2$ (where σ_s^2 denotes the variance of s before the multiplication).

■ **Example A.1** Suppose the initial makespans of two sequences have lognormal distributions with $\mu_1 = 95$, $\mu_2 = 97$, $\sigma_1 = 5$, and $\sigma_2 = 3$. Suppose further that the common factor, B, is lognormal with mean 1 and $cv = 0.5$. Let the objective be minimizing $d + \gamma E[T]$ with $\gamma = 3$. Compare the two sequences before and after adjustment, and repeat for $\gamma = 2.5$.

For details on calculating the optimal due date for the objective of minimizing $d + \gamma E[T]$ and for calculating the objective function value, see Appendix B. The makespan, C_{max}, is a completion time and thus subject to Theorems A.5 and A.6. Table A.3 summarizes the results for the example. The first four rows are for $\gamma = 2.5$, two before adjustment and two after. The last four rows are for $\gamma = 3$. Each row lists the calculated m and s parameters, the optimal due date, d^*, and the total cost, TC.

Table A.3 Calculated values for Example A.1.

	μ	σ	m	s	d^*	TC
2.5, unadjusted	95	5	4.552	0.0526	96.14	99.86
2.5, unadjusted	97	3	4.574	0.0309	97.72	99.91
2.5, adjusted	95	5	4.522	0.2518	98.10	118.60
2.5, adjusted	97	3	4.544	0.2482	100.16	120.75
3, unadjusted	95	5	4.552	0.0526	97.04	100.51
3, unadjusted	97	3	4.574	0.0309	98.25	100.29
3, adjusted	95	5	4.522	0.2518	102.58	122.26
3, adjusted	97	3	4.544	0.2482	104.67	124.42

By comparing TC for the first two rows we see that for $\gamma = 2.5$ the first sequence is best ($99.86 < 99.91$). Rows 5 and 6 indicate that sequence 2 is optimal for $\gamma = 3$. It can be shown that for $\gamma = 2.587$ we get the same objective function value, 99.98 (but the due dates are different, namely, $d_1 = 96.32$ and $d_2 = 97.82$). Therefore, before adjustment, sequence 1 is optimal for any $\gamma < 2.587$, whereas sequence 2 is optimal for $\gamma > 2.587$. The two initial distributions intersect each other at 100.0, which happens to be higher than both initial due dates and corresponds to SL = 0.842. Sequence 2 has the more attractive distribution beyond $x_0 = 100.0$ and above $SL_0 = 0.842$. To evaluate the situation after the adjustment, we utilize the observation that the product of two lognormal variables is lognormal, and the product's m and s parameters are the sums of the components. Rows 3 and 4 indicate that for $\gamma = 2.5$, sequence 1 remains optimal, but the objective function is increased substantially. For $\gamma = 3$, however, sequence 2 becomes inferior after adjustment in favor of sequence 1. The two adjusted distributions intersect at such a high value that sequence 1 has the more attractive cdf anywhere below SL = $\Phi(6.0) > 0.999\,999\,999$; that is, in a practical sense sequence 1 is stochastically dominant. Thus, for $\gamma > 2.587$, the initial optimal sequence should be rejected. After the adjustment, we prefer the sequence with the higher variance, which may be counterintuitive, but by comparing the s values before and after adjustment in Table A.3, we see that the variance of the initial sequence in this example is negligible relative to the variance induced by B. Therefore, the mean becomes the crucial issue. Various aspects of this example prove the next three propositions.

Proposition A.1   The initial optimal sequence for minimizing $d + \gamma\, E[T]$ is not identical to the optimal adjusted sequence.

Proposition A.2   The initial optimal sequence for minimizing d subject to a service-level constraint SL $\geq b$ is not identical to the optimal adjusted sequence.

Proposition A.3   Consider two intersecting cdfs of initial completion times and the cdfs of the same completion times after adjustment. The adjusted cdfs may intersect at a different service level than the initial cdfs.

For makespan minimization, safe scheduling models based on initial (independent) processing times, it often happens in the limit as $n \to \infty$ that the coefficient of variation of the makespan, cv, becomes negligible. If $cv \to 0$, however, then the optimal safety time becomes negligible relative to the expected makespan. This is a highly suspicious result that most practitioners would not and should not accept. Indeed, it is implausible that the true coefficient of variation tends to zero as $n \to \infty$, so including linear association in the model is one way to improve the practicality of a model. Thus, on the one hand, linear association makes the model more realistic and yet tractable. On the other hand, setting due dates and release dates must not be performed before the adjustment. A reasonable heuristic is to solve the stochastic counterpart on the initial values, apply the adjustment to the result, and only then set due dates and release dates.

Bibliography

Aitchison, J. and Brown, J.A.C. (1957). *The Lognormal Distribution*. Cambridge: Cambridge University Press.

Buzacott, J.A. and Shantikumar, J.G. (1993). *Stochastic Models of Manufacturing Systems*. Englewood Cliffs, NJ: Prentice Hall.

Esary, J.D., Proschan, F., and Walkup, D.W. (1967). Association of random variables, with applications. *Annals of Mathematical Statistics* 38: 1466–1474.

Fenton, L.F. (1960). The sum of log-normal probability distributions in scatter transmission systems. *IRE Transactions on Communications Systems* 8 (1): 57–67.

Looney, S.W. and Gulledge, T.R. Jr. (1985). Use of the correlation coefficient with normal probability plots. *The American Statistician* 39 (1): 75–79.

May, J.H., Strum, D.P., and Vargas, L.G. (2000). Fitting the lognormal distribution to surgical procedure times. *Decision Sciences* 31: 129–148.

McKay, K.N., Safayeni, F.R., and Buzacott, J.A. (1988). Job-shop scheduling theory: what is relevant. *Interfaces* 18: 84–90.

Mehta, N.B., Wu, J., Molisch, A.F., and Zhang, J. (2007). Approximating a sum of random variables with a lognormal. *IEEE Transactions on Wireless Communications* 6: 2690–2699.

Paul, A. and Trietsch, D. (2012). A note on activity correlation and performance metrics in stochastic project networks. Working Paper. http://faculty.tuck. dartmouth.edu/images/uploads/faculty/principles-sequencing-scheduling/ Correlation_sensitivity_analysis.pdf (Also available through ResearchGate.)

Robb, D.J. (1992). Scheduling in a management context: stochastic tasks and non-regular reward functions. Unpublished Doctoral Dissertation. University of Calgary, Calgary.

Ross, S.M. (1996). *Stochastic Processes*, 2e. Hoboken, NJ: Wiley.

Shapiro, S.S. and Wilk, M.B. (1965). An analysis of variance test for normality (complete samples). *Biometrika* 52: 591–611.

Trietsch, D., Mazmanyan, L., Gevorgyan, L., and Baker, K.R. (2012). Modeling activity times by the Parkinson distribution with a lognormal core: theory and validation. *European Journal of Operational Research* 216: 386–396.

Appendix B

The Critical Ratio Rule

B.1 A Basic Trade-off Problem

A common planning problem involves trading off surplus and shortage outcomes in an uncertain environment. Conceptually, we make a decision and then await the value of an uncertain outcome. However, due to uncontrollable factors, the outcome may turn out to be larger or smaller than what we decide. If the outcome is larger than the value we decide, we incur costs due to underestimation; if the outcome is smaller, we incur costs due to overestimation. Faced with these possibilities, we look for a decision that navigates optimally between the two kinds of risks.

In a scheduling environment, the uncertain outcome is often the completion time of a particular job (or a set of jobs). The job's due date, assuming that we can choose it, plays the role of our decision. If the job completes before the due date, then we incur earliness costs, and if the job completes after the due date, we incur tardiness costs. Unless our decisions are perfect, we can anticipate incurring one cost or the other, and our objective is to minimize the expected cost.

The use of expected cost as an objective function derives from the theory of decision making under risk and uncertainty. If we interpret the scheduling scenario literally, as a repeating operational problem, then an appropriate objective is the long-run cost, which is optimized by minimizing the expected cost corresponding to each decision.

To analyze the decision problem, we let d denote the due date (the decision variable), and we let C denote the completion time. (We use capital letters to represent random variables.) Then the difference between completion time and due date is $(C - d)$. If this quantity is negative, we incur an earliness cost equal to $\alpha(d - C)$; if this quantity is positive, we incur a tardiness cost equal to $\beta(C - d)$. We can write the total cost as follows:

$$G(C,d) = \alpha \max\{0, d - C\} + \beta \max\{0, C - d\} \tag{B.1}$$

The objective is to minimize expected cost. In light of Eq. (B.1), the criterion becomes

$$E[G(C,d)] = \alpha E[\max\{0, d - C\}] + \beta E[\max\{0, C - d\}]$$
$$= \alpha E[E] + \beta E[T] \tag{B.2}$$

In reference to Chapter 7, we should clarify that for a given distribution, and for $\gamma > 1$, minimizing the tightness/tardiness objective, $d + \gamma E[T]$ corresponds to minimizing a special case of the expected cost objective, $\alpha E[E] + \beta E[T]$. To justify this comment, we substitute β for $(\gamma - 1)$ and obtain

$$d + \gamma E[T] = d + E[T] + (\gamma - 1)E[T]$$
$$= d + E[T] + \beta E[T] \tag{B.3}$$

Also,

$$d = C + \max\{0, d - C\} - \max\{0, C - d\}$$

Because d is not random, $E[d] = d$, and after taking the expectation of both sides, we obtain

$$d = E[d] = E[C] + E[\max\{0, d - C\}] - E[\max\{0, C - d\}]$$

or,

$$d = E[C] + E[E] - E[T] \tag{B.4}$$

Rearranging Eq. (B.4) yields

$$d - E[C] = E[E] - E[T]$$

That is, the *safety time*, $d - E[C]$, is the difference between the expected earliness and the expected tardiness. Therefore, a positive safety time implies that the expected earliness exceeds the expected tardiness. Substituting Eq. (B.4) into Eq. (B.3), we obtain

$$d + \gamma E[T] = d + E[T] + \beta E[T]$$
$$= E[C] + E[E] + \beta E[T]$$

In this expression, $E[C]$ is constant, so in the tightness/tardiness trade-off, the optimal due date is the same value that minimizes $E[E] + \beta E[T]$, which corresponds to the expected E/T cost for the specific choice $\alpha = 1$ and $\beta = (\gamma - 1)$, although the objective function value is higher by $E[C]$.

The most general tightness/tardiness objective for the single-machine model contains job-dependent parameters:

$$\sum_{j=1}^{n} \alpha_j \left(d_j + \gamma_j E[T_j] \right) = \sum_{j=1}^{n} \left(\alpha_j E[C_j] + \alpha_j E[E_j] + \beta_j E[T_j] \right)$$

where $\beta_j = \alpha_j(\gamma_j - 1)$; equivalently, $\gamma_j = (\alpha_j + \beta_j)/\alpha_j$. Here, the contribution of job j to the objective function exceeds that of the weighted E/T model by $\alpha_j E[C_j]$. Therefore, minimizing the sum involves a combination of the weighted flowtime model with the weighted E/T model (Baker and Trietsch 2009).

In what follows, we first examine the implications of the expected E/T cost objective. Then, for convenience, and to provide a slightly different perspective, we obtain the main results again for the tightness/tardiness objective, $d + \gamma E[T]$.

B.2   Optimal Policy for Discrete Probability Models

The mechanics of optimizing expected cost differ slightly according to whether we use a discrete model or a continuous model to describe random outcomes. There is no essential difference in the conclusions drawn from these two cases, but treating them separately serves to illustrate how we might apply different mathematical assumptions in the analysis.

In the discrete case, we use p_t as the *probability distribution function* (pdf) for completion time. Specifically, we define p_t as the probability that the job will complete at time t. (For convenience, we assume that t is integer.)

$$p_t = \Pr\{C = t\}$$

Also, we define the *cumulative distribution function* (cdf) for completion time to be

$$F(t) = \Pr\{C \le t\}$$

Stated in words, $F(t)$ represents the probability that the job completes on or before time t.

Suppose that we choose a due date of d and then we observe a completion time of C. In retrospect, we can ask whether it would be desirable to have increased d by one initially. An increase in d would have been desirable if the job finished late, but not if it finished early or on time. Specifically, a unit increase in d would have reduced tardiness if the job finished late – that is, if $C > d$. The probability of this outcome can be written as $[1 - F(d)]$. On the other hand, a unit increase in d would have increased earliness if the job finished early or on time, the probability of which is $F(d)$.

Thus, there would be a unit increase in earliness with probability $F(d)$ and a unit reduction in tardiness with probability $[1 - F(d)]$. The expected incremental cost can be expressed as

$$\alpha F(d) - \beta[1 - F(d)]$$

It follows that we should increase the due date as long as this expected incremental cost drops, that is, while

$$\alpha F(d) - \beta[1 - F(d)] < 0$$

With terms rearranged, this condition states that we should increase the due date while

$$F(d) < \frac{\beta}{(\alpha + \beta)} \tag{B.5}$$

Because $F(d)$ is the probability that the job will finish by its due date, it is also called the *service level* (SL). The ratio $\beta/(\alpha + \beta)$ is often called the *critical ratio*. Our condition in Eq. (B.5) implies that we should continue to increase the due date as long as the critical ratio exceeds the SL. Or, to state it another way, we should increase d until we reach the first value for which SL $= F(d) \geq \beta/(\alpha + \beta)$. This value of d, denoted d^*, is known as the *critical fractile*. When viewed as a function of d, the total weighted E/T cost is a piecewise linear convex function. Usually, $F(d^*) > \beta/(\alpha + \beta)$, and that implies that d^* is the unique optimum. However, if $F(d^*) = \beta/(\alpha + \beta)$, then the objective function has a flat (horizontal) segment and any d in that range is optimal.

Conceptually, we can determine the optimal due date from a graph of the cdf. For a discrete probability model, the cdf is a step function that takes on values between 0 and 1 (see Figure B.1). The critical ratio $\beta/(\alpha + \beta)$ is a number between 0 and 1, and we can plot it on the vertical axis of the graph. Then the optimal due date, d^*, is simply the first d value for which the cdf equals or exceeds this height, as sketched in Figure B.1.

As an example, suppose we have a unit earliness cost of $\alpha = 20$ and a unit tardiness cost of $\beta = 80$. Suppose also that the completion time follows the discrete distribution shown below:

Time	t	12	13	14	15	16	17	18
Probability	p_t	0.05	0.10	0.30	0.25	0.15	0.10	0.05
CDF	$F(t)$	0.05	0.15	0.45	0.70	0.85	0.95	1.00

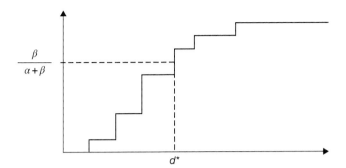

Figure B.1 Finding d^* for a discrete distribution.

In this case the ratio $\beta/(\alpha + \beta)$ equals $80/(20 + 80)$, or 0.8, and the optimal due date is the first level at which the cdf equals or exceeds this value. Therefore, the optimal due date is 16, because

$$F(15) < 0.8 \le F(16)$$

We can also calculate the expected cost for the optimal decision from Eq. (B.2). For the discrete case, this calculation typically involves multiplying each cost outcome by its probability and taking the sum of those products:

$$E[G(C,d)] = \alpha E[\max\{0, d - C\}] + \beta E[\max\{0, C - d\}]$$

$$= 20[4 \times 0.05 + 3 \times 0.1 + 2 \times 0.3 + 1 \times 0.25] + 80[1 \times 0.1 + 2 \times 0.05]$$

$$= 43$$

For an additional perspective, note that the area below the cdf to the left of the due date (16) is given by $4 \times 0.05 + 3 \times 0.1 + 2 \times 0.3 + 1 \times 0.25 = 1.35$, whereas the area above the cdf and below 1 to the right of the due date is given by $1 \times 0.1 + 2 \times 0.05 = 0.2$. These values are also the expected earliness and the expected tardiness. Indeed, it is always possible to depict $E[E]$ and $E[T]$ as such areas. This observation can also be used to justify the critical fractile result graphically as follows: Suppose we postpone the due date by a small amount, Δ, measured from the optimal value we calculated. This will increase the expected earliness area by at least $\Delta\beta/(\alpha + \beta)$ and decrease the expected tardiness area by at most $\Delta\alpha/(\alpha + \beta)$. The result is an expected loss (by increased earliness) of at least $\Delta\alpha\beta/(\alpha + \beta)$ and an expected gain (by decreased tardiness) of at most $\Delta\alpha\beta/(\alpha + \beta)$, so on balance, such a postponement should not be entertained. By a symmetric argument, the due date should not be reduced, either.

B.3   A Special Discrete Case: Equally Likely Outcomes

A special case arises when the probability distribution contains N equally likely outcomes. In other words, each outcome has probability $1/N$, so the kth smallest outcome corresponds to

$$F(k) = \frac{k}{N}$$

In this case, we can determine the optimal due date by choosing the kth smallest outcome, where k is the first value for which $k/N \geq \beta/(\alpha + \beta)$. We can denote this value by $k = \lceil N\beta/(\alpha + \beta) \rceil$, where $\lceil x \rceil$ is the smallest integer that is at least as large as x.

As an example, suppose we have a unit earliness cost of $\alpha = 20$ and a unit tardiness cost of $\beta = 80$. Suppose also that a simulation experiment produces the following completion times in nine independent runs:

Experiment	1	2	3	4	5	6	7	8	9
Outcome	27	41	38	33	45	48	35	39	36

Here, we have $\beta/(\alpha + \beta) = 0.8$. The first value of k for which $k/9 \geq 0.8$ is $k = 8$, so we choose the 8th smallest outcome, or 45, as the due date.

B.4   Optimal Policy for Continuous Probability Models

Sometimes it is convenient to treat the probability model as continuous rather than discrete. In the continuous case, we describe the processing time with a continuous probability model by specifying either its cdf, $F(x)$, or its probability density function, $f(x)$. The argument used earlier involving incremental costs and revenues still holds, but in this case, because the cdf is continuous, there will always be a value of d for which Eq. (B.5) can be satisfied as an equation. However, we can develop a more formal derivation.

We can think about the objective function in Eq. (B.2) as a function of the decision d. Thus, we define $H(d) = E[G(C, d)]$, so that

$$H(d) = \alpha E[\max\{0, d - C\}] + \beta E[\max\{0, C - d\}]$$

To find the optimal due date, we take the derivative with respect to d and set it equal to zero. This step is made easier if we swap the order of expectation and differentiation, as shown below, where we use the notation $\delta(x) = 1$ if $x > 0$ and $\delta(x) = 0$ otherwise:

$$\frac{\partial H(d)}{\partial d} = \alpha E[\partial/\partial d(\max\{0, d - C\})] + \beta E[\partial/\partial d(\max\{0, C - d\})]$$

$$= \alpha E[\delta(d - C)] + \beta E[\delta(C - d)](-1)$$

$$= \alpha \Pr\{C < d\} - \beta \Pr\{C > d\}$$

$$= \alpha F(d) - \beta[1 - F(d)]$$

Setting this expression equal to zero yields the continuous form of Eq. (B.5):

$$F(d^*) = \frac{\beta}{(\alpha + \beta)} \tag{B.6}$$

In graphical terms, we solve Eq. (B.6) by plotting the cdf and locating the point at which its height equals $\beta/(\alpha + \beta)$, as shown in Figure B.2. Again, $E[E]$ and $E[T]$ are depicted by the areas below F to the left of the due date (earliness) and above F (but below 1) to the right of the due date (tardiness).

The critical ratio, $\beta/(\alpha + \beta)$, has a general interpretation that arises in settings other than scheduling, as long as there are costs for overestimation and underestimation. A statement of the optimality condition that covers both the discrete and continuous cases is the following:

Set the due date equal to the smallest value x for which $F(x) \geq \beta/(\alpha + \beta)$.

As an example of the continuous case, suppose we have a unit earliness cost of $\alpha = 20$ and a unit tardiness cost of $\beta = 80$, and suppose that the completion time follows a uniform distribution from 100 to 300. In other words, mean completion time is 200, but completion is equally likely to occur anywhere between 100 and 300. More formally, the cdf takes the form

$$F(x) = 0.005(x - 100), \quad 100 \leq x \leq 300$$

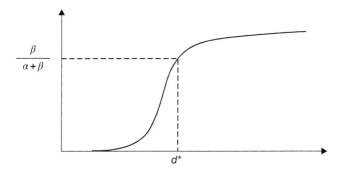

Figure B.2 Finding d^* for a continuous distribution.

Here the critical ratio is equal to $80/(80 + 20)$ or 0.8. The procedure illustrated in Figure B.2 calls for this ratio to be set equal to $F(d^*)$. We have

$$0.005(d^* - 100) = 0.8$$

which allows us to obtain $d^* = 260$.

The uniform distribution characterizes completion as occurring in the range 200 ± 100, with equally likely outcomes in this range. However, the optimal due date does not lie at the center of this interval. In this case, the relative values of unit earliness cost and unit tardiness cost dictate a due date above the mean of the distribution. If we think of the quantity 200 as a naïve forecast, and the tolerance of ±100 as representing possible forecast error, we can see that it is logical to make a decision different from the naïve forecast because of the cost structure that applies to forecast errors. Specifically, errors that create earliness penalties cost 20 per unit. On the other hand, errors that create tardiness penalties cost 80 per unit. Because the opportunity cost is greater for tardiness than for earliness, it makes sense to bias the decision toward protecting against the risk of tardiness. We achieve this result by choosing a due date that is greater than the naïve forecast.

The next step is to develop an expression for the expected cost function:

$$H(d) = \alpha E[\max\{0, d - C\}] + \beta E[\max\{0, C - d\}]$$

For $E[E]$ we can write

$$E[E] = \int_0^d (d - x) f(x) dx = dF(d) - \int_0^d x f(x) dx$$

$$= dF(d) + \int_d^\infty x f(x) dx - \mu \tag{B.7}$$

The definite integral in the last part of this expression, called the *partial expectation*, takes on a form that depends on the probability distribution for the completion time, C. For now, we simply use the general expression, but we elaborate important special cases later. From Eq. (B.4), we also have $E[T] = E[E] + \mu - d$, so

$$E[T] = dF(d) + \int_d^\infty x f(x) dx - d \tag{B.8}$$

Using these values, we can express the expected cost function as

$$H(d) = \alpha \left[dF(d) + \int_d^\infty x f(x) dx - \mu \right] + \beta \left[dF(d) + \int_d^\infty x f(x) dx - d \right]$$

$$= (\alpha + \beta) \left[dF(d) + \int_d^\infty x f(x) dx \right] - \alpha\mu - \beta d \tag{B.9}$$

This formula for $H(d)$ represents the expected cost for any choice of a due date d. We could set the derivative of $H(d)$ equal to zero to find the optimal due date, but we already know that Eq. (B.6) applies in general. Thus, the optimal due date d^* satisfies

$$F(d^*) = \frac{\beta}{(\alpha + \beta)}$$

Rearranging this condition yields $(\alpha + \beta)d^* F(d^*) - \beta d^* = 0$. When we substitute d^* for d in Eq. (B.9), we can use this condition to simplify Eq. (B.9), leaving us with

$$H(d^*) = (\alpha + \beta) \int_{d^*}^{\infty} x f(x) dx - \alpha \mu \tag{B.10}$$

Once the distribution is specified, we can substitute its partial expectation in Eq. (B.10) and calculate the optimal cost.

For completeness, we now consider minimizing $d + \gamma E[T]$. We can compute it directly by adding d to the product of γ and Eq. (B.8), that is,

$$H(d) = d + \gamma \left[dF(d) + \int_{d}^{\infty} x f(x) dx - d \right]$$

$$H(d) = d(1 - \gamma) + \gamma \left[dF(d) + \int_{d}^{\infty} x f(x) dx \right]$$

This formula applies to any due date d. When d is optimized, we have $F(d^*) = (\gamma - 1)/\gamma$, so the final result is

$$H(d^*) = d^* (1 - \gamma) + \gamma \left[d^* \left(\frac{\gamma - 1}{\gamma} \right) + \int_{d^*}^{\infty} x f(x) dx \right]$$

$$H(d^*) = \gamma \int_{d^*}^{\infty} x f(x) dx \tag{B.11}$$

If we set $\alpha = 1$ and $\beta = \gamma - 1$ in Eq. (B.10), the difference between Eqs. (B.11) and (B.10) is μ, in agreement with our observation in Section B.1. In Eq. (B.10), $H(d^*)$ is always positive, which implies that Eq. (B.11) exceeds μ.

B.5 A Special Continuous Case: The Normal Distribution

An important continuous case is that of the normal distribution, where we allow only a negligible probability that the random variable will be negative. That is, we assume both the mean completion time, μ, and the due date, d, are positive and σ/μ is sufficiently small that we can ignore the probability of a negative realization. It is also convenient to use the standard normal distribution (mean of zero and standard deviation of 1). For this purpose, we use the notation $\Phi(\cdot)$ for the cdf and $\phi(\cdot)$ for the density function of the standard normal, as introduced in Appendix A.

The expected E/T cost is obtained from Eq. (B.10). In the case of the normal distribution, the partial expectation in Eq. (B.10) can be written as

$$\int_d^\infty xf(x)dx = \frac{1}{\sigma\sqrt{2\pi}}\int_d^\infty x\exp\left[\frac{-1}{2}\left(\frac{x-\mu}{\sigma}\right)^2\right]dx$$

Next, we use the transformation $x = \mu + z\sigma$, so that $dx = \sigma dz$ and the transformed due date becomes $d' = (d - \mu)/\sigma$. In addition, the derivative of $\phi(z)$ is $-z\phi(z)$, allowing us to write the partial expectation follows:

$$\int_d^\infty xf(x)dx = \int_{d'}^\infty (\mu + z\sigma)\phi(z)dz = \mu\left[1 - \Phi\left(\frac{d-\mu}{\sigma}\right)\right] + \sigma\phi\left(\frac{d-\mu}{\sigma}\right)$$

Then Eq. (B.7) yields

$$E[E] = d\Phi\left(\frac{d-\mu}{\sigma}\right) + \mu\left[1 - \Phi\left(\frac{d-\mu}{\sigma}\right)\right] + \sigma\phi\left(\frac{d-\mu}{\sigma}\right) - \mu$$

$$= (d-\mu)\Phi\left(\frac{d-\mu}{\sigma}\right) + \sigma\phi\left(\frac{d-\mu}{\sigma}\right)$$

Similarly, Eq. (B.8) yields

$$E[T] = d\Phi\left(\frac{d-\mu}{\sigma}\right) + \mu\left[1 - \Phi\left(\frac{d-\mu}{\sigma}\right)\right] + \sigma\phi\left(\frac{d-\mu}{\sigma}\right) - d$$

$$= \sigma\phi\left(\frac{d-\mu}{\sigma}\right) - (d-\mu)\left[1 - \Phi\left(\frac{d-\mu}{\sigma}\right)\right]$$

From Eq. (B.9) the expected E/T cost becomes

$$H(d) = (\alpha + \beta)\left[d\Phi\left(\frac{d-\mu}{\sigma}\right) + \mu\left[1 - \Phi\left(\frac{d-\mu}{\sigma}\right)\right] + \sigma\phi\left(\frac{d-\mu}{\sigma}\right)\right] - \alpha\mu - \beta d$$

$$= (\alpha + \beta)\left[d\Phi\left(\frac{d-\mu}{\sigma}\right) - \mu\Phi\left(\frac{d-\mu}{\sigma}\right) + \sigma\phi\left(\frac{d-\mu}{\sigma}\right)\right] + \beta(\mu - d)$$

$$\tag{B.12}$$

Next, we substitute for the optimal due date, d^*, from Eq. (B.6), which, in the normal case, is given by

$$\Phi\left(\frac{d^* - \mu}{\sigma}\right) = \frac{\beta}{(\alpha + \beta)} \tag{B.13}$$

Thus, the optimal expected E/T cost is

$$H(d^*) = (\alpha + \beta)\left[d^* \frac{\beta}{(\alpha + \beta)} - \mu \frac{\beta}{(\alpha + \beta)} + \sigma\phi\left(\frac{d^* - \mu}{\sigma}\right)\right] + \beta(\mu - d^*)$$

$$H(d^*) = (\alpha + \beta)\sigma\phi\left(\frac{d^* - \mu}{\sigma}\right) \tag{B.14}$$

Operationally, we compute the critical ratio and use normal tables or the corresponding spreadsheet function to determine $d^* = \mu + \sigma\Phi^{-1}[\beta/(\alpha + \beta)]$. If we set $d = \mu$ in Eq. (B.12), we obtain

$$H(\mu) = (\alpha + \beta)\sigma\phi(0)$$

This result is very similar to Eq. (B.14), but this form holds for $H(d)$ only for the special values $d = \mu$ or $d = d^*$. Furthermore, as $\phi(0)$ is the maximum possible value of $\phi(\cdot)$, we can say that the benefit of using the optimal safety time relative to not using safety time is a relative reduction of $[\phi(0) - \phi((d - \mu)/\sigma)]/\phi(0)$ in the expected E/T penalty. This benefit is zero for $\alpha = \beta$ but exceeds 50% when max $\{\beta/\alpha, \alpha/\beta\} > 7.365$.

In Chapter 11, we use a variation on this type of analysis in the formula for $E[\min\{X, Y\}] = E[X - \max\{X - Y, 0\}] = E[X] - E[W^+]$, where $W = X - Y$. If X and Y are normally distributed, then W is normally distributed with mean equal to $\mu = \mu_x - \mu_y$ and variance equal to $\sigma^2 = \sigma_x^2 + \sigma_y^2$. Then $E[W^+]$ is given by the following definite integral:

$$\int_0^\infty wf(w)dw = \int_0^\infty w\frac{1}{\sigma}\phi\left(\frac{w - \mu}{\sigma}\right)dw$$

Let $v = (w - \mu)/\sigma$, so that $dv = dw/\sigma$, and let $z = \mu/\sigma$. Then the lower limit of integration corresponds to $v = -z$. The integral becomes

$$\sigma\int_{-z}^\infty (v + z)\phi(v)dv = \sigma\int_{-z}^\infty v\phi(v)dv + \sigma z\int_{-z}^\infty \phi(v)dv = \sigma\phi(z) + \sigma z\Phi(z)$$

Thus, we have $E[W^+] = \sigma\phi(z) + \sigma z\Phi(z)$, and we can write

$$E[\min\{X, Y\}] = E[X] - E[W^+] = \mu_x - \sigma[\phi(z) + \sigma z\Phi(z)] \tag{B.15}$$

B.6   Calculating $d + \gamma E(T)$ for the Normal Distribution

We return to a consideration of the specific objective function $H(d) = d + \gamma E(T)$ and derive the formula for its optimal value. As before, let μ represent the mean of the normal distribution that describes completion time and σ its standard deviation. The critical ratio in this case is given by Eq. (B.13):

$$\Phi\left(\frac{d^* - \mu}{\sigma}\right) = \frac{\gamma - 1}{\gamma}$$

which can also be written as $1 - \Phi\left(\frac{d^* - \mu}{\sigma}\right) = 1/\gamma$, or as $\gamma = 1/\Phi\left(\frac{\mu - d^*}{\sigma}\right)$. Using Eq. (B.8) for $E[T]$ and substituting the formula for the partial expectation of the normal, we obtain

$$H(d^*) = d^* + \gamma\left\{\mu - d^*\left[1 - \Phi\left(\frac{d^* - \mu}{\sigma}\right)\right] - \mu\Phi\left(\frac{d^* - \mu}{\sigma}\right) + \sigma\phi\left(\frac{d^* - \mu}{\sigma}\right)\right\}$$

$$= d^* + \gamma\left\{\mu - d^*\left[\frac{1}{\gamma}\right] - \mu\left(\frac{\gamma - 1}{\gamma}\right) + \sigma\phi\left(\frac{d^* - \mu}{\sigma}\right)\right\}$$

$$= \mu + \gamma\sigma\phi\left(\frac{d^* - \mu}{\sigma}\right)$$

$$\text{(B.16)}$$

If we set $\alpha = 1$ and $\beta = \gamma - 1$, Eq. (B.16) exceeds Eq. (B.14) by μ, a relationship related to our observation in Section B.1.

From Eq. (B.16) it is clear that for the objective $d + \gamma E(T)$, a makespan with both a lower mean and a lower variance is dominant. (This result holds for any convex increasing objective.) Nonetheless, for two normal distributions, if one has lower mean and lower variance than the other, it is still not stochastically dominant in the ordinary sense. The only case in which one normal variable is stochastically smaller than another, independent normal variable occurs when their variances are equal. Otherwise, the cdfs of two normal distributions with different means and standard deviations always intersect each other exactly once. It may happen, however, that this intersection yields stochastic dominance for all practical purposes. For example, when the intersection is for a negative argument, then by definition it occurs outside the range of our interest and may be ignored.

B.7   Calculations for the Lognormal Distribution

We adopt the notation introduced in Appendix A for a random variable X that follows a lognormal distribution with the corresponding random variable $Y = \ln(X)$ following a normal distribution. Our notation takes μ and σ as the mean and standard deviation of X, while m and s represent the mean and standard deviation of Y. Given the lognormal parameters (μ, σ), we evaluate m and s directly from the following relationships:

$$s^2 = \ln\left(1 + \sigma^2/\mu^2\right) \quad m = \ln(\mu) - s^2/2$$

Given (m, s), the reverse evaluation leads to

$$\mu = \exp\left(m + s^2/2\right) \quad \sigma^2 = \mu^2\left[\exp\left(s^2\right) - 1\right]$$

These formulas are sufficient for the calculations required in the problem of minimizing the sum of the due dates subject to SL requirements (Section 7.2). For the more complicated safe scheduling problems, we make use of the kth *raw partial moment*, denoted $M_k(d)$, defined for any nonnegative random variable and any nonnegative integer k by

$$M_k(d) = \int_d^\infty x^k f(x)\,dx$$

In particular, $M_0(d) = 1 - F(d)$ (so $M_0(0) = 1$) and $M_1(0) = \mu$. With this notation, we can alternatively express Eq. (B.8) as follows:

$$E[T] = dF(d) + \int_d^\infty xf(x)\,dx - d = M_1(d) - dM_0(d)$$

In addition, Eq. (B.10) can be expressed as follows:

$$H(d^*) = (\alpha + \beta)\int_{d^*}^\infty xf(x)\,dx - \alpha\mu = (\alpha + \beta)M_1(d^*) - \alpha\mu \tag{B.17}$$

When we turn to minimizing $d + \gamma E[T]$, the objective in Eq. (B.11) becomes

$$H(d^*) = \gamma\int_{d^*}^\infty xf(x)\,dx = \gamma M_1(d^*) \tag{B.18}$$

To specialize these formulas to the lognormal distribution, we first develop $M_k(d)$ for the lognormal. By definition

$$M_k(d) = \int_d^\infty x^k f(x)\,dx = \frac{1}{\sqrt{2\pi}s}\int_d^\infty x^{k-1}\exp\left(\frac{-(\ln(x) - m)^2}{2s^2}\right)dx$$

For justification, recall from Appendix A that the density function of the log-normal includes division by x. Now let $z = (\ln(x) - m)/s$ and $d' = (\ln(d) - m)/s$. It follows that $dx = sxdz$ and $x = \exp(sz + m)$. Therefore,

$$M_k(d) = \frac{1}{\sqrt{2\pi}} \int_{d'}^{\infty} x^k \exp\left(\frac{-z^2}{2}\right) dz = \frac{1}{\sqrt{2\pi}} \int_{d'}^{\infty} \exp\left(\frac{-z^2}{2} + k(sz + m)\right) dz$$

$$= \frac{\exp(km)}{\sqrt{2\pi}} \int_{d'}^{\infty} \exp\left(\frac{-z^2 + 2ksz}{2}\right) dz$$

$$= \frac{\exp(km)}{\sqrt{2\pi}} \int_{d'}^{\infty} \exp\left(\frac{-z^2 + 2ksz - (ks)^2}{2} + \frac{(ks)^2}{2}\right) dz$$

$$= \frac{\exp\left(km + \frac{(ks)^2}{2}\right)}{\sqrt{2\pi}} \int_{d'}^{\infty} \exp\left(\frac{-(z - ks)^2}{2}\right) dz$$

Let $w = z - ks$, leading to $dz = dw$. We now have

$$M_k(d) = \exp\left(km + \frac{(ks)^2}{2}\right) \int_{d' - ks}^{\infty} \phi(w) dw$$

In the limit, as $d \to 0^+$, $d' - ks \to -\infty$, so the kth moment, μ_k, is

$$\mu_k = E\left(X^k\right) = \exp\left(km + \frac{k^2 s^2}{2}\right) = \mu^k \left(1 + cv^2\right)^{k(k-1)/2}$$

Here, the right-hand side follows because $k^2/2 = k/2 + k(k - 1)/2$, $\exp(km + ks^2/2) = \exp(k(m + s^2/2)) = \mu^k$, and $\exp(s^2) = 1 + cv^2$. In particular, the first moment is μ, as should be expected, and the second moment is $\mu^2(1 + cv^2)$. Because $1 - \Phi(z) = \Phi(-z)$, for any positive d, we also have

$$M_k(d) = \mu^k \left(1 + cv^2\right)^{\frac{k(k-1)}{2}} \Phi\left(ks - \frac{\ln(d) - m}{s}\right) = \mu^k \left(1 + cv^2\right)^{\frac{k(k-1)}{2}} \Phi(ks - d')$$

$$(B.19)$$

To minimize $d + \gamma E(T)$, by Eq. (B.18), $H(d^*) = \gamma\mu\Phi(s - z^*)$, where $z^* = \Phi^{-1}[(\gamma - 1)/\gamma]$ and $d^* = \exp(z^*s + m)$. The minimal early/tardy objective function is given by $\mu[\alpha\Phi(z^* - s) + \beta\Phi(s - z^*)]$, for the same value of z^* (with $\alpha = 1$ and $\beta = \gamma - 1$). This result can be obtained by subtracting $\alpha\mu$ from the previous result.

When processing time is a nonnegative continuous random variable, such as the lognormal, tardiness relative to $d > 0$ is a nonnegative mixed random variable: With probability SL it is zero, and otherwise it is continuous. We have already seen that $E[T] = M_1(d) - d[1 - F(d)]$. By similar analysis, $E[T^2] = M_2(d) - 2dM_1(d) + d^2[1 - F(d)]$. Using these values, we can calculate the variance of the tardiness, $V(T) = E[T^2] - E^2[T]$. This is particularly useful for the purpose of using the lognormal sum approximation for jobs with release dates when a job's completion time may be increased due to tardiness of an earlier job. For instance, such an approximation could be useful for Example 19.3, where travel times between stations are assumed lognormal but the bus departure from interim stations may be delayed due to previous tardiness. The quality of the approximation depends on the parameters.

Bibliography

Baker, K.R. and Trietsch, D. (2009). Safe scheduling: setting due dates in single-machine problems. *European Journal of Operational Research* 196: 69–77.

Index

Principles of Sequencing and Scheduling, Second Edition. Kenneth R. Baker and Dan Trietsch.
© 2019 John Wiley & Sons, Inc. Published 2019 by John Wiley & Sons, Inc.